DONALD MILLER

GREATEST HITS

BLUE LIKE JAZZ

SEARCHING FOR GOD KNOWS WHAT

THROUGH PAINTED DESERTS

THOMAS NELSON
Since 1798

NASHVILLE   DALLAS   MEXICO CITY   RIO DE JANEIRO   BEIJING

Published in Nashville, Tennessee, by Thomas Nelson. Thomas Nelson is a trademark of Thomas Nelson, Inc.

Thomas Nelson, Inc. titles may be purchased in bulk for educational, business, fund-raising, or sales promotional use. For information, please e-mail SpecialMarkets@ThomasNelson.com.

Blue Like Jazz and *Searching for God Knows What* published in association with the literary agency of Alive Communications, 7680 Goddard Street, Suite 200, Colorado Springs, CO 80920.

Scripture quotations noted NKJV are from THE NEW KING JAMES VERSION. © 1979, 1980, 1982, Thomas Nelson, Inc., Publishers.

Scripture quotations noted NIV are from the HOLY BIBLE: NEW INTERNATIONAL VERSION®. © 1973, 1978, 1984 by International Bible Society. Used by permission of Zondervan Publishing House. All rights reserved.

Scripture quotations noted KJV are from the KING JAMES VERSION of the Bible.

Scripture quotations noted THE MESSAGE are from *THE MESSAGE.* © 1993, 1994, 1995, 1996, 2000, 2001, 2002. Used by permission of NavPress Publishing Group.

ISBN 978-1-4002-0211-9

Printed in the United States of America

07 08 09 10 11 QW 5 4 3 2 1

CONTENTS

BLUE LIKE JAZZ

SEARCHING FOR GOD KNOWS WHAT

THROUGH PAINTED DESERTS

495

Blue Like Jazz

Nonreligious Thoughts on Christian Spirituality

For David Gentiles

Contents

Author's Note   5

1. Beginnings: God on a Dirt Road Walking Toward Me   7

2. Problems: What I Learned on Television   19

3. Magic: The Problem with Romeo   31

4. Shifts: Find a Penny   43

5. Faith: Penguin Sex   57

6. Redemption: The Sexy Carrots   65

7. Grace: The Beggars' Kingdom   85

8. gods: Our Tiny Invisible Friends   93

9. Change: New Starts at Ancient Faith   101

10. Belief: The Birth of Cool   109

11. Confession: Coming Out of the Closet   119

12. Church: How I Go Without Getting Angry   135

13. Romance: Meeting Girls Is Easy   145

14. Alone: Fifty-three Years in Space   157

15. Community: Living with Freaks   181

16. Money: Thoughts on Paying Rent   193

17. Worship: The Mystical Wonder   207

18. Love: How to Really Love Other People   213

19. Love: How to Really Love Yourself   229

20. Jesus: The Lines on His Face   239

Acknowledgments   247

Author's Note

I NEVER LIKED JAZZ MUSIC BECAUSE JAZZ MUSIC doesn't resolve. But I was outside the Bagdad Theater in Portland one night when I saw a man playing the saxophone. I stood there for fifteen minutes, and he never opened his eyes.

After that I liked jazz music.

Sometimes you have to watch somebody love something before you can love it yourself. It is as if they are showing you the way.

I used to not like God because God didn't resolve. But that was before any of this happened.

Beginnings

God on a Dirt Road Walking Toward Me

I ONCE LISTENED TO AN INDIAN ON TELEVISION say that God was in the wind and the water, and I wondered at how beautiful that was because it meant you could swim in Him or have Him brush your face in a breeze. I am early in my story, but I believe I will stretch out into eternity, and in heaven I will reflect upon these early days, these days when it seemed God was down a dirt road, walking toward me. Years ago He was a swinging speck in the distance; now He is close enough I can hear His singing. Soon I will see the lines on His face.

My father left my home when I was young, so when I was introduced to the concept of God as Father I imagined Him as a stiff, oily man who wanted to move into our house and share a bed with my mother. I can only remember this as a frightful and threatening idea. We were a poor family who attended a wealthy church, so I imagined God as a man who had a lot of money and drove a big car. At church they told us we were children of God, but I knew God's family was better than mine, that He had a daughter who was a cheerleader and a son who played football. I was born with a small bladder so I wet the bed till I was ten and later developed a crush on the homecoming queen who was kind to me in a political sort of way, which is something she probably learned from her father, who was the president of a bank. And so from the beginning, the chasm that separated me from God was as deep as wealth and as wide as fashion.

In Houston, where I grew up, the only change in the weather came in late October when cold is sent down from Canada. Weathermen in Dallas would call weathermen in Houston so people knew to bring their plants in and watch after their dogs. The cold came down the interstate, tall and blue, and made reflections in the mirrored windows of large buildings, moving over the Gulf of Mexico as if to prove that sky holds magnitude over water. In Houston, in October, everybody walks around with a certain energy as if they are going to be elected president the next day, as if they are going to get married.

In the winter it was easier for me to believe in God, and I suppose it had to do with new weather, with the color of leaves clinging to trees, with the smoke in the fireplaces of big houses in opulent neighborhoods where I would ride my bike. I half believed that if God lived in one of those neighborhoods, He would invite me in, make me a hot chocolate, and talk to me while His kids played Nintendo and stabbed dirty looks over their shoulders. I would ride around those neighborhoods until my nose froze, then back home where I closed myself off in my room, put on an Al Green record, and threw open the windows to feel the cold. I would stretch across my bed for hours and imagine life in a big house, visited by important friends who rode new bikes, whose fathers had expensive haircuts and were interviewed on the news.

I have been with my own father only three times, each visit happening in my childhood, each visit happening in cold weather. He was a basketball coach, and I do not know why he left my mother. I only know he was tall and handsome and smelled like beer; his collar smelled like beer, his hands like beer, and his coarse, unshaven face smelled like beer. I do not drink much beer myself, but the depth of the scent has never left me. My friend Tony the Beat Poet will be drinking a beer at Horse Brass Pub and the smell will send me to a pleasant place that exists only in recollections of childhood.

My father was a big man, I think, bigger than most, stalky and strong like a river at flood. On my second visit to my father I saw him throw a football across a gym, drilling the spiral into the opposite hoop where it shook the backboard. There was no action my father committed that I did not study as a work of wonder. I watched as he shaved and brushed his teeth and put on his socks and shoes in motions that were more muscle than grace, and I would stand at his bedroom door hoping he wouldn't notice my awkward stare. I looked purposely as he opened a beer, the tiny can hiding itself in his big hand, the foam of it spilling over the can, his red lips slurping the excess, his tongue taking the taste from his mustache. He was a brilliant machine of a thing.

When my sister and I visited my father we would eat from the grill every night, which is something we never did with my mother. My father would crumble Ritz crackers into the meat and add salt and sauces, and I thought, perhaps, he was some sort of chef, some sort of person who ought to write books about cooking meat. Later he would take my sister and me to the grocery store and buy us a toy, any toy we wanted. We'd pace the long aisle of shiny prizes, the trucks and Barbies and pistols and games. In the checkout line I'd cling to the shiny, slick box in stillness and silence. On the drive home we'd take turns sitting on his lap so we could drive, and whoever wasn't steering would work the shifter, and whoever worked the steering wheel could drink from my father's can of beer.

It is not possible to admire a person more than I admired that man. I know, from the three visits I made to him, the blended composite of love and fear that exists only in a boy's notion of his father.

There were years between his calls. My mother would answer the phone, and I knew by the way she stood silently in the kitchen that it was him. A few days later he would come for a visit, always changed in the showing of his age—the new wrinkles, the grayed hair, and thick skin around his eyes—and within days we would go to his apartment for the weekend. About the time I entered middle school, he disappeared completely.

o   o   o

Today I wonder why it is God refers to Himself as "Father" at all. This, to me, in light of the earthly representation of the role, seems a marketing mistake. Why would God want to call Himself Father when so many fathers abandon their children?

As a child, the title *Father God* offered an ambiguous haze with which to interact. I understood what a father did as well as I understood the task of a shepherd. All the vocabulary about God seemed to come from ancient history, before video games, Palm Pilots, and the Internet.

If you would have asked me, I suppose I would have told you there was a God, but I could not have formulated a specific definition based on my personal experience. Perhaps it was because my Sunday school classes did much to help us memorize commandments and little to teach us who God was and how to relate to Him, or perhaps it was because they did and I wasn't listening. Nevertheless, my impersonal God served me fine as I had no need of the real thing. I needed no deity to reach out of heaven and wipe my nose, so none of it actually mattered. If God was on a dirt road walking toward me, He was on the other side of a hill, and I hadn't begun to look for Him anyway.

o   o   o

I started to sin about the time I turned ten. I believe it was ten, although it could have been earlier, but ten is about the age a boy starts to sin, so I am sure it was in there somewhere. Girls begin to sin when they are twenty-three or something, but they do life much softer by their very nature and so need less of a run at things.

I sinned only in bits at first—small lies, little inconsistencies to teachers about homework and that sort of thing. I learned the craft well, never looking my teacher in the eye, always speaking quickly, from the diaphragm, never feeble about the business of deception.

"Where is your homework?" my teacher would ask.

"I lost it."

"You lost it yesterday. You lost it last week."

"I am terrible about losing things. I need to learn." (Always be self-deprecating.)

"What am I going to do with you, Donald?"

"I am grateful for your patience." (Always be grateful.)

"I should call your mother."

"She's deaf. Boating accident. Piranha." (Always be dramatic. Use hand gestures.)

I also used a great deal of cusswords. Not those churchly cusswords—*dang* and *darnit, dagnabit* and *frickin'*—but big, robust cusswords like the ones they use in PG movies, the ones the guys would say only to each other. Cusswords are pure ecstasy when you are twelve, buzzing in the mouth like a battery on the tongue. My best friend at the time, Roy, and I would walk home from school, stopping at the playground by the Methodist church to cuss out Travis Massie and his big sister Patty. Travis always made fun of Roy because his last name was Niswanger. It took me two years to understand why the name Niswanger was so funny.

Words turned to fists by the end of the year, and I was thirteen when I took my first punch. Square in the face. It was Tim Mitchell, the little blond kid who went to my church, and the whole time we were circling each other he was saying he was going to give me a fat lip, and I was shouting cusswords in incomplete sentences; scary cusswords. He hit me in the face and I went down beneath a sky as bright and blue as jazz music, and there were children laughing, and Patty Massie was pointing her finger, and Roy was embarrassed. There was a lot of yelling after that, and Tim backed down when Roy said he was going to give Tim a fat lip. Travis was singing the whole time: "nice-wanger, nice-wanger, nice-wanger."

Before any of this happened, though, when I was in kindergarten, I got sent to the principal's office for looking up a girl's dress during nap time, which is something that I probably did, but not for the immediately considered motive. It's more likely that her open skirt was in the way of something I really wanted to look at, because I remember the age quite well and had no interest whatsoever in what might be up a girl's dress. I received a huge lecture on the importance of being a gentleman from Mr. Golden, who stood just taller than his desk and had a finger that wagged like the tail of a dog and a tie with a knot as big as a tumor, and he might as well have been talking to me about physics or politics because I wasn't interested in whatever it was that I wasn't supposed to be interested in. But everything changed in the summer of my twelfth year.

Across the street from Roy's house was a large, empty field divided by railroad tracks, and it was there that I first identified with the Adam spoken of at the beginning of the Bible, because it was there that I saw my first naked woman. We were playing with our bikes when Roy stumbled across a magazine whose pages were gaudily dressed in colorful type and the stuff of bad advertising. Roy approached the magazine with a stick, and I stood behind him as he flipped the pages from the distance of a twig. We had found a portal, it seemed, into a world of magic and wonder, where creatures exist in the purest form of beauty. I say we found a portal, but it was something more than that; it was as if we were being led *through* a portal because I sensed in my chest, in the pace of my heart, that I was having an adventure. I felt the way a robber might feel when he draws a gun inside a bank.

At last Roy confronted the magazine by hand, slowly devouring its pages, handing it to me after diving deeper into the woods, off the trail common to us and our bikes. We were not speaking, only turning the pages, addressing the miraculous forms, the beauty that has not been matched in all mountains and rivers. I felt that I was being shown a secret, a secret that everybody in the world had always known and had kept from me. We were there for hours until the sun set, at which time we hid our treasure beneath logs and branches, each swearing to the other that we would tell no one of our find.

That night in bed, my mind played the images over as a movie, and I felt the nervous energy of a river furling through my lower intestines, ebbing in tides against the gray matter of my mind, delivering me into a sort of ecstasy from which I felt I would never return. This new information seemed to give grass its green and sky its blue and now, before I had requested a reason to live, one had been delivered: naked women.

o   o   o

All this gave way to my first encounter with guilt, which is still something entirely inscrutable to me, as if aliens were sending transmissions from another planet, telling me there is a right and wrong in the universe. And it wasn't only sexual sin that brought about feelings of guilt, it was lies and mean thoughts and throwing rocks at cars with Roy. My life had become something to hide; there were secrets in it. My thoughts were private thoughts, my lies were barriers that protected my thoughts, my sharp tongue a weapon to protect the ugly me. I would lock myself in my room, isolating myself from my sister and my mother, not often to do any sort of sinning, but simply because I had become a creature of odd secrecy. This is where my early ideas about religion came into play.

The ideas I learned in Sunday school, the ideas about sin and how we shouldn't sin, kept bugging me. I felt as though I needed to redeem myself, the way a kid feels when he finally decides to clean his room. My carnal thinking had made a mess of my head, and I felt as though I were standing in the doorway of my mind, wondering where to begin, how to organize my thoughts so they weren't so out of control.

That's when I realized that religion might be able to hose things down, get me back to normal so I could have fun without feeling guilty or something. I just didn't want to have to think about this guilt crap anymore.

For me, however, there was a mental wall between religion and God. I could walk around inside religion and never, on any sort of emotional level, understand that God was a person, an actual Being with thoughts and feelings and that sort of thing. To me, God was more of an idea. It was something like a slot machine, a set of spinning images that doled out rewards based on behavior and, perhaps, chance.

The slot-machine God provided a relief for the pinging guilt and a sense of hope that my life would get organized toward a purpose. I was too dumb to test the merit of the slot machine idea. I simply began to pray for forgiveness, thinking the cherries might line up and the light atop the machine would flash, spilling shiny tokens of good fate. What I was doing was more in line with superstition than spirituality. But it worked. If something nice happened to me, I thought it was God, and if something nice didn't, I went back to the slot machine, knelt down in prayer, and pulled the lever a few more times. I liked this God very much because you hardly had to talk to it and it never talked back. But the fun never lasts.

My slot-machine God disintegrated on Christmas Eve when I was thirteen. I still think of that night as "the lifting of the haze," and it remains one of the few times I can categorically claim an interaction with God. Though I am half certain these interactions are routine, they simply don't feel as metaphysical as the happenings of that night. It was very simple, but it was one of those profound revelations that only God can induce. What happened was that I realized I was not alone in my own surroundings. I'm not talking about ghosts or angels or anything; I'm talking about other people. As silly as it sounds, I realized, late that night, that other people had feelings and fears and that my interactions with them actually meant something, that I could make them happy or sad in the way that I associated with them. Not only could I make them happy or sad, but I was responsible for the way I interacted with them. I suddenly felt responsible. I was supposed to make them happy. I was not supposed to make them sad. Like I said, it sounds simple, but when you really get it for the first time, it hits hard.

I was shell-shocked.

This is how the bomb fell: For my mother that year I had purchased a shabby Christmas gift—a book, the contents of which she would never be interested in. I had had a sum of money with which to buy presents, and the majority of it I used to buy fishing equipment, as Roy and I had started fishing in the creek behind Wal-Mart.

My extended family opens gifts on Christmas Eve, leaving the immediate family to open gifts the next morning, and so in my room that night were wonderful presents—toys, games, candy, and clothes—and as I lay in bed I counted and categorized them in the moonlight, the battery-operated toys of greatest importance, the underwear of no consequence at all.

So in the moonlight I drifted in and out of anxious sleep, and this is when it occurred to me that the gift I had purchased for my mother was bought with the petty change left after I had pleased myself. I realized I had set the happiness of my mother beyond my own material desires.

This was a different sort of guilt from anything I had previously experienced. It was a heavy guilt, not the sort of guilt that I could do anything about. It was a haunting feeling, the sort of sensation you get when you wonder whether you are two people, the other of which does things you can't explain, bad and terrible things.

The guilt was so heavy that I fell out of bed onto my knees and begged, not a slot-machine God, but a living, feeling God, to stop the pain. I crawled out of my room and into the hallway by my mother's door and lay on my elbows and face for an hour or so, going sometimes into sleep, before finally the burden lifted and I was able to return to my room.

We opened the rest of our gifts the next morning, and I was pleased to receive what I did, but when my mother opened her silly book, I asked her forgiveness, saying how much I wished I had done more. She, of course, pretended to enjoy the gift, saying how she wanted to know about the subject.

I was still feeling terrible that evening when the family gathered for dinner around a table so full of food a kingdom could feast. I sat low in my chair, eye-level with the bowls of potatoes and corn, having my hair straightened by ten talking women, all happy the holiday had come to a close.

And while they ate and talked and chatted away another Christmas, I felt ashamed and wondered silently whether they knew they were eating with Hitler.

2

Problems

What I Learned on Television

SOME PEOPLE SKIP THROUGH LIFE; SOME PEOPLE are dragged through it. I sometimes wonder whether we are moving through time or time is moving through us. My brilliant friend Mitch says that light, unlike anything else in the universe, is not affected by time. Light, he says, exists outside of time. He tells me it has something to do with how fast it travels and that it is eternal, but it is still a mystery to physicists.

I say this only because time kept traveling through me. When I was young I thought I had forever to figure things out. I am talking about feeling like Hitler. But I didn't. I didn't have long to figure things out. I believe that the greatest trick of the devil is not to get us into some sort of evil but rather have us wasting time. This is why the devil tries so hard to get Christians to be religious. If he can sink a man's mind into habit, he will prevent his heart from engaging God. I was into habit. I grew up going to church, so I got used to hearing about God. He was like Uncle Harry or Aunt Sally except we didn't have pictures.

God never sent presents either. We had this dumpy house and

dumpy car, and I had zits. Looking back, I suppose God sent sunsets and forests and flowers, but what is that to a kid? The only thing I heard from God was what I heard on Christmas Eve, that story I told you, when God made me feel so guilty, and I didn't like that at all. I didn't feel like I knew God, and yet He was making me experience this conviction. I felt that the least He could have done was to come down and introduce Himself and explain these feelings of conviction in person.

If you don't love somebody, it gets annoying when they tell you what to do or what to feel. When you love them you get pleasure from their pleasure, and it makes it easy to serve. I didn't love God because I didn't know God.

Still, I knew, because of my own feelings, there was something wrong with me, and I knew it wasn't only me. I knew it was everybody. It was like a bacteria or a cancer or a trance. It wasn't on the skin; it was in the soul. It showed itself in loneliness, lust, anger, jealousy, and depression. It had people screwed up bad everywhere you went—at the store, at home, at church; it was ugly and deep. Lots of singers on the radio were singing about it, and cops had jobs because of it. It was as if we were broken, I thought, as if we were never supposed to feel these sticky emotions. It was as if we were cracked, couldn't love right, couldn't feel good things for very long without screwing it all up. We were like gasoline engines running on diesel. I was just a kid so I couldn't put words to it, but every kid feels it. (I am talking about the broken quality of life.) A kid will think there are monsters under his bed, or he will close himself in his room when his parents fight. From a very early age our souls are taught there is a comfort and a discomfort in the world, a good and bad if you will, a lovely and a frightening. There seemed to me to be too much frightening, and I didn't know why it existed.

I was recently reminded about all of this.

○   ○   ○

It started while I was watching television. I live with four other guys, pretty cool guys in a pretty cool house in Laurelhurst. I have this killer room upstairs. It is tucked away from everybody, sort of hidden through a door in the back of the upstairs den. The walls in my room are cedar, like something you'd find in a wood cabin. There is a birch tree so big and dignified outside my window that I often feel I am in its limbs. In the evening when it rains, the birch sounds like an audience giving a standing ovation. Sometimes when the tree is clapping I stand at the window and say thank you, thank you, as if I am Napoleon.

Along my wood-paneled walls are small, wood-paneled doors that open into attic space. I stuck a television inside one of these doors, and in the evenings I lie in bed and watch television. When you are a writer and a speaker, you aren't supposed to watch television. It's shallow. I feel guilty because for a long time I didn't allow myself a television, and I used to drop that fact in conversation to impress people. I thought it made me sound dignified. A couple of years ago, however, I visited a church in the suburbs, and there was this blowhard preacher talking about how television rots your brain. He said that when we are watching television our minds are working no harder than when we are sleeping. I thought that sounded heavenly. I bought one that afternoon.

So I've been watching *Nightline* with Ted Koppel lately. He isn't as smart as Ray Suarez but he tries, and that counts. He's been in the Congo, in Africa, and it has been terrible. I mean the show is fine, but the Congo isn't doing so well. More than 2.5 million people have been killed in the last three years. Each of eight tribes is at war with the other seven. Genocide. As the images moved across the screen I would lie in bed feeling so American and safe, as if the Congo were something in a book or a movie. It is nearly impossible for me to process the idea that such a place exists in the same world as Portland. I met with Tony the Beat Poet the other day at Horse Brass and told him about the stuff on *Nightline*.

"I knew that was taking place over there," Tony said. "But I didn't know it was that bad." I call Tony a beat poet because he is always wearing loose European shirts, the ones that lace up the chest with shoestring. His head is shaved, and he has a long soul patch that stretches a good inch beneath his chin. He isn't actually a poet.

"It's terrible," I told him. "Two and a half million people, dead. In one village they interviewed about fifty or so women. All of them had been raped, most of them numerous times."

Tony shook his head. "That is amazing. It is so difficult to even process how things like that can happen."

"I know. I can't get my mind around it. I keep wondering how people could do things like that."

"Do you think you could do something like that, Don?" Tony looked at me pretty seriously. I honestly couldn't believe he was asking the question.

"What are you talking about?" I asked.

"Are you capable of murder or rape or any of the stuff that is taking place over there?"

"No."

"So you are not capable of any of those things?" he asked again. He packed his pipe and looked at me to confirm my answer.

"No, I couldn't," I told him. "What are you getting at?"

"I just want to know what makes those guys over there any different from you and me. They are human. We are human. Why are we any better than them, you know?"

Tony had me on this one. If I answered his question by saying yes, I could commit those atrocities, that would make me evil, but if I answered no, it would suggest I believed I am better evolved than some of the men in the Congo. And then I would have some explaining to do.

"You believe we are capable of those things, don't you, Tony?"

He lit his pipe and breathed in until the tobacco glowed orange and let out a cloud of smoke. "I think so, Don. I don't know how else to answer the question."

"What you are really saying is that we have a sin nature, like the fundamentalist Christians say."

Tony took the pipe from his lips. "Pretty much, Don. It just explains a lot, you know."

"Actually," I told him reluctantly, "I have always agreed with the idea that we have a sin nature. I don't think it looks exactly like the fundamentalists say it does, 'cause I know so many people who do great things, but I do buy the idea we are flawed, that there is something in us that is broken. I think it is easier to do bad things than good things. And there is something in that basic fact, some little clue to the meaning of the universe."

"It's funny how little we think about it, isn't it?" Tony shook his head.

"It really is everywhere, isn't it?" By this we were talking about the flawed nature of our existence.

"Yeah," Tony started in. "Some friends were over at the house, and they have a kid, about four or five years old or something, and they were telling me all about child training. They said their kid had this slight problem telling them the truth about whether or not he had broken something or whether or not he had put away his toys, you know, things like that. So later I started wondering why we have to train kids at all. I wondered, you know, if I ever had a couple of kids and I trained one of them, taught him right from wrong, and the other I didn't train at all, I wonder which would be the better kid."

"The kid you teach right from wrong, of course," I told him.

"Of course, but that really should tell us something about the human condition. We have to be taught to be good. It doesn't come completely natural. In my mind, that's a flaw in the human condition."

"Here's one," I said, agreeing with him. "Why do we need cops?"

"We would have chaos without cops," Tony said matter-of-factly. "Just look at the countries with corrupt police. It's anarchy."

"Anarchy," I repeated.

"Anarchy!" Tony confirmed in sort of a laugh.

"Sometimes I think, you know, if there were not cops, I would be fine, and I probably would. I was taught right from wrong when I was a kid. But the truth is, I drive completely different when there is a cop behind me than when there isn't."

And what Tony and I were talking about is true. It is hard for us to admit we have a sin nature because we live in this system of checks and balances. If we get caught, we will be punished. But that doesn't make us good people; it only makes us subdued. Just think about the Congress and Senate and even the president. The genius of the American system is not freedom; the genius of the American system is checks and balances. Nobody gets all the power. Everybody is watching everybody else. It is as if the founding fathers knew, intrinsically, that the soul of man, unwatched, is perverse.

o   o   o

Earlier that afternoon, the afternoon I got together with Tony, my friend Andrew the Protester and I went downtown to protest a visit by the president. I felt that Bush was blindly supporting the World Bank and, to some degree, felt the administration was responsible for what was happening in Argentina. Andrew and I made signs and showed up a few hours early. Thousands of people had already gathered, most of them protesting our policy toward Iraq. Andrew and I took pictures of ourselves in front of the cops, loads of cops, all in riot gear like storm troopers from *Star Wars*.

Andrew's sign said "Stop America's Terroism"—he spelled *terrorism* wrong. I felt empowered in the sea of people, most of whom were also carrying signs and chanting against corporations who were making slaves of Third World labor; and the Republican Party, who gives those corporations so much power and freedom. I felt so far from my upbringing, from my narrow former self, the me who was taught the Republicans give a crap about the cause of Christ. I felt a long way from the pre-me, the pawn-Christian who was a Republican because my family was Republican, not because I had prayed and asked God to enlighten me about issues concerning the entire world rather than just America.

When the president finally showed, things got heated. The police mounted horses and charged them into the crowd to push us back. We shouted, in unison, that a horse is not a weapon, but they didn't listen. The president's limo turned the corner so quickly I thought he might come tumbling out, and his car was followed by a caravan of shiny black vans and Suburbans. They shuttled him around to a back door where we watched through a chain-link fence as he stepped out of his limousine, shook hands with dignitaries, and entered the building amid a swarm of secret service agents. I was holding my sign very high in case he looked our way.

The president gave his speech inside the hotel and left through a side door, and they whisked him away before we could shake hands and explain our concerns. When we were done, I started wondering if we had accomplished anything. I started wondering whether we could actually change the world. I mean, of course we could—we could change our buying habits, elect socially conscious representatives and that sort of thing, but I honestly don't believe we will be solving the greater human conflict with our efforts. The problem is not a certain type of legislation or even a certain politician; the problem is the same that it has always been.

I am the problem.

I think every conscious person, every person who is awake to the functioning principles within his reality, has a moment where he stops blaming the problems in the world on group think, on humanity and authority, and starts to face himself. I hate this more than anything. This is the hardest principle within Christian spirituality for me to deal with. The problem is not out there; the problem is the needy beast of a thing that lives in my chest.

The thing I realized on the day we protested, on the day I had beers with Tony, was that it did me no good to protest America's responsibility in global poverty when I wasn't even giving money to my church, which has a terrific homeless ministry. I started feeling very much like a hypocrite.

More than my questions about the efficacy of social action were my questions about my own motives. Do I want social justice for the oppressed, or do I just want to be known as a socially active person? I spend 95 percent of my time thinking about myself anyway. I don't have to watch the evening news to see that the world is bad, I only have to look at myself. I am not browbeating myself here; I am only saying that true change, true life-giving, God-honoring change would have to start with the individual. I was the very problem I had been protesting. I wanted to make a sign that read "I AM THE PROBLEM!"

That night, after Tony and I talked, I rode my motorcycle up to Mount Tabor, this dormant volcano just east of the Hawthorne District. There is a place near the top where you can sit and look at the city at night, smoldering like coals and ashes beneath the evergreens, laid out like jewels under the moon. It is really something beautiful. I went there to try to get my head around this idea, this idea that the problem in the universe lives within me. I can't think of anything more progressive than the embrace of this fundamental idea.

○   ○   ○

There is a poem by the literary critic C. S. Lewis that is more or less a confession. The first time I read it I identified so strongly with his sentiments, I felt as though somebody were calling my name. I always come back to this poem when I think soberly about my faith, about the general precepts of Christian spirituality, the beautiful precepts that indicate we are flawed, all of us are flawed, the corrupt politician and the pious Sunday school teacher. In the poem C. S. Lewis faces himself. He addresses his own depravity with a soulful sort of bravery:

> All this is flashy rhetoric about loving you.
> I never had a selfless thought since I was born.
> I am mercenary and self-seeking through and through;
> I want God, you, all friends, merely to serve my turn.
>
> Peace, reassurance, pleasure, are the goals I seek,
> I cannot crawl one inch outside my proper skin;
> I talk of love—a scholar's parrot may talk Greek—
> But, self-imprisoned, always end where I begin.

I sat there above the city wondering if I was like the parrot in Lewis's poem, swinging in my cage, reciting Homer, all the while having no idea what I was saying. I talk about love, forgiveness, social justice; I rage against American materialism in the name of altruism, but have I even controlled my own heart? The overwhelming majority of time I spend thinking about myself, pleasing myself, reassuring myself, and when I am done there is nothing to spare for the needy. Six billion people live in this world, and I can only muster thoughts for one. Me.

I know someone who has twice cheated on his wife, whom I don't know. He told me this over coffee because I was telling him how I thought, perhaps, man was broken; how for man, doing good and moral things was like swimming upstream. He wondered if God had mysteriously told me about his infidelity. He squirmed a bit and then spoke to me as if I were a priest. He confessed everything. I told him I was sorry, that it sounded terrible. And it did sound terrible. His body was convulsed in guilt and self-hatred. He said he would lie down next to his wife at night feeling walls of concrete between their hearts. He had secrets. She tries to love him, but he knows he doesn't deserve it. He cannot accept her affection because she is loving a man who doesn't exist. He plays a role. He says he is an actor in his own home.

Designed for good, my friend was sputtering and throwing smoke. The soul was not designed for this, I thought. We were supposed to be good, all of us. We were supposed to be good.

For a moment, sitting there above the city, I imagined life outside narcissism. I wondered how beautiful it might be to think of others as more important than myself. I wondered at how peaceful it might be not to be pestered by that childish voice that wants for pleasure and attention. I wondered what it would be like not to live in a house of mirrors, everywhere I go being reminded of myself.

It began to rain that night on Mount Tabor. I rode my motorcycle home in the weather, which I hate doing because the streets are so slick. I got home white-knuckled and wet. My room was warm and inviting, as it always is with its wood panels and dignified birch outside the window.

I sat on my bed and looked out at my tree, which by this time was gathering rain in applause. I didn't feel much like Napoleon that night. I didn't like being reminded about how self-absorbed I was. I wanted to be over this, done with this. I didn't want to live in a broken world or a broken me. I wasn't trying to weasel out of anything, I just wasn't in the mood to be on earth that night. I get like that sometimes when it rains, or when I see certain sad movies. I put on the new Wilco album, turned it up and went into the bathroom to wash my hands and face.

I know now, from experience, that the path to joy winds through this dark valley. I think every well-adjusted human being has dealt squarely with his or her own depravity. I realize this sounds very Christian, very fundamentalist and browbeating, but I want to tell you this part of what the Christians are saying is true. I think Jesus feels strongly about communicating the idea of our brokenness, and I think it is worth reflection. Nothing is going to change in the Congo until you and I figure out what is wrong with the person in the mirror.

Magic

The Problem with Romeo

WHEN I WAS A CHILD MY MOTHER TOOK ME TO see David Copperfield the magician. I think she had a crush on him. It was the same year he made the Statue of Liberty disappear on national television. Later he made a plane disappear and later still he got engaged to Claudia Schiffer.

David Copperfield said, at the beginning of the show, that there is no such thing as magic. Everything he would do would be an illusion. He got into a box and his sexy assistants turned the box upside down. When they opened it again he wasn't there. He made a lady levitate. He turned a tiger into a parrot, then back to a tiger, only the wrong color for a tiger, then back to the right color. Everybody gasped. There was a man in front of me with a fat head, so I had to lean over to see.

Later I became a magician myself. My mother bought me a magic set, and I studied the book that came with it. I could make three pieces of string turn into one long piece and one long piece into three pieces. I made a nickel pass through a plate. I guessed whatever card you pulled out of a deck. I was amazing. I was going to get very good at it, hire a sexy assistant and move to

Vegas. After a few months, though, I got frustrated because everything that was magic was only a trick, meaning it wasn't really magic, it was an illusion. I decided to grow up and become an astronaut with a sexy assistant. I imagined myself in a fancy white astronaut outfit with a girl who looks like Katie Couric gazing sheeplike at me while I worked levers and buttons on our flying saucer. Every few minutes Katie would wipe my brow.

Everybody wants to be somebody fancy. Even if they're shy. I have one friend who is so shy she wets her pants if you look at her. She doesn't really wet her pants, but she practically does. She is very good-looking, too, but never goes out because she is so shy. If you didn't know her pretty well, you wouldn't think she wants to do anything but hide in a closet. You wouldn't think she wants to be anybody people look at, but she told me after I got to know her that she wanted to be an actress. After you get to know her you forget how shy she is, so I told her to go and be an actress; she certainly is good-looking enough to be an actress. But later I thought that might not be a good idea because she'd probably get up in front of people and start crying or something because she is so shy.

I never wanted to be an actor, but I always wanted to be a rock star. Even when I was a magician I wanted to be a rock star. When I was young I would listen to the radio and pretend I was the singer and thousands of people were in the audience, all the girls I knew in the front row. I would wave to them while I was singing, and they would scream like their heads were going to explode. I wanted to be a rock star, but I never wanted to be an actor.

o   o   o

I've been to a play. It was *Romeo and Juliet,* and I took a date. It was my first date ever. Even though I never wanted to act myself, taking a girl to a play was a good move. My date sat so close to me I could hear her nose breaths. She felt warm like sunlight and soft like she used special soap.

Even though it is a good move to take a girl to a play, I screwed it up.

There is a part in the play where Juliet, the main girl, is standing on a balcony and Romeo, the main guy, is hiding in the bushes below. It is pretty tense because Juliet is going on about how she likes Romeo, but she doesn't know Romeo is in the bushes. It was great at first. My date scrunched in so close I could feel the softness of her side, the smoothness of her arms wrapped around mine. I thought what the actors were saying was pretty mushy, but I would make noises every few minutes as if they had said something beautiful. When I did this my date would glance at me in wonder. It is a pretty good idea to make some noises when you are at a play.

My date was wrapped up in the whole love theme, but I wasn't buying it. I didn't let on, I just wasn't buying a lot of the crap they were saying. Juliet kept going on about how Romeo should deny his family, and Romeo was like, Duh, okay. Then Juliet told Romeo that he smelled like a rose. Duh, okay, he said.

And then the key lines, the lines on which I now know the play hinges:

Romeo: Call me but love, and I'll be new baptiz'd;
Henceforth I never will be Romeo.

Later in the play they accidentally kill themselves. It was not very believable but that is what happened. My date was crying. I was thinking they got what they deserved. It seemed stupid to me. I didn't understand everything they were talking about, but what I did understand I thought must have been written for girls. People really should put a limit on how much they give to emotion. When we were walking out my date clasped my hand, and even though I wasn't feeling very mushy I smiled at her. We ascended the aisle and made our way through the crowded lobby onto the steps of the playhouse. There were girls everywhere, all of them misty-eyed. Two girls in front of us were talking to each other. One of them threw her arms in the air and cried out, *I wish I could know love like Romeo and Juliet!*

I couldn't take it anymore. I whispered under my breath, *They're dead.*

I didn't think anybody heard me, but my date did. Two girls next to us heard me also, and they told the people next to them. One idiot guy repeated what I said and laughed, pointing at me. All the girls looked at me like I had just stepped on a cat. My date's body grew cold. She let go of my hand. She crossed her arms over her chest and walked a few feet in front of me all the way back to the truck. On the way home she hugged the far door so tightly I thought she was going to fall out. When we got to her house I asked her if she would like to go out again.

"I don't think so," she said.

"Why?"

"I don't think I could like you."

"Why?"

"I just don't."

"Can we kiss? I hear that helps a girl fall in love."

"You are evil," she said. "The Antichrist!"

She went into her house, shutting the door firmly on our relationship. I honestly never liked her in the first place. She was pretty and all, but I never liked her deeply. I was only a little sad about it.

My mother had given me her Texaco card for my date, so on the way home I stopped in for some Cheetos and donuts. I sat in the Texaco parking lot and thought about poor old Romeo, begging for love, running off with his woman, and then accidentally dying. Some dates go terrible, it's a fact. If you would have asked me then, I would have told you he was doomed from the beginning. I figured he was doomed because he believed in magic. He believed hooking up with Juliet would make him new, change his name, have him baptized and shiny.

Everybody wants to be fancy and new. Nobody wants to be themselves. I mean, maybe people want to be themselves, but they want to be different, with different clothes or shorter hair or less fat. It's a fact. If there was a guy who just liked being himself and didn't want to be anybody else, that guy would be the most different guy in the world and everybody would want to be him.

One night, when I was watching television, I saw an infomercial about a knife that could cut through a boot and remain sharp enough to slice a tomato. They called it the Miracle Blade. Another night I saw a cleanser made with orange juice that could get blood out of carpet. They said it worked like magic.

The whole idea of everybody wanting to be somebody new was an important insight in terms of liking God. God was selling something I wanted. Still, God was in the same boat as the guy selling the knives and Juliet promising to make Romeo new. Everybody exaggerates when they are selling something. Everybody says their product works like magic. At the time I understood God's offer as a magical proposition, which it is. But most magical propositions are just tricks. The older you get, the harder it is to believe in magic. The older you get, the more you understand there is no Wizard of Oz, just a schmuck behind a curtain. I pictured my pastor as a salesman or a magician, trying to trick the congregation into believing Jesus could make us new. And, honestly, I felt as though he was trying to convince himself, as though he only half believed what he was saying. It's not that Christian spirituality seemed like a complete con, it's just that it had some of those elements.

The message, however, was appealing to me. God said He would make me new. I can't pretend for a second I didn't want to be made new, that I didn't want to start again. I did.

○ ○ ○

There were aspects of Christian spirituality I liked and aspects I thought were humdrum. I wasn't sure what to do. I felt I needed to make a decision about what I believed. I wished I could have subscribed to aspects of Christianity but not the whole thing.

I'll explain.

I associated much of Christian doctrine with children's stories because I grew up in church. My Sunday school teachers had turned Bible narrative into children's fables. They talked about Noah and the ark because the story had animals in it. They failed to mention that this was when God massacred all of humanity.

It also confused me that some people would look at parts of the Bible but not the whole thing. They ignored a lot of obvious questions. I felt as if Christianity, as a religious system, was a product that kept falling apart, and whoever was selling it would hold the broken parts behind his back trying to divert everybody's attention.

The children's story stuff was the thing I felt Christians were holding behind their back. The Garden of Eden, the fall of man, was a pretty silly story, and Noah and the ark, all of that, that seemed pretty fairy-tale too.

It took me a while to realize that these stories, while often used with children, are not at all children's stories. I think the devil has tricked us into thinking so much of biblical theology is story fit for kids. How did we come to think the story of Noah's ark is appropriate for children? Can you imagine a children's book about Noah's ark complete with paintings of people gasping in gallons of water, mothers grasping their children while their bodies go flying down white-rapid rivers, the children's tiny heads being bashed against rocks or hung up in fallen trees? I don't think a children's book like that would sell many copies.

I couldn't give myself to Christianity because it was a religion for the intellectually naive. In order to believe Christianity, you either had to reduce enormous theological absurdities into children's stories or ignore them. The entire thing seemed very difficult for my intellect to embrace. Now none of this was quite defined; it was mostly taking place in my subconscious.

○   ○   ○

Help came from the most unlikely of sources. I was taking a literature course in college in which we were studying the elements of story: setting, conflict, climax, and resolution.

The odd thought occurred to me while I was studying that we didn't know where the elements of story come from. I mean, we might have a guy's name who thought of them, but we don't know why they exist. I started wondering why the heart and mind responded to this specific formula when it came to telling stories. So I broke it down. Setting: That was easy; every story has a setting. My setting is America, on earth. I understand setting because I experience setting. I am sitting in a room, in a house, I have other characters living in this house with me, that sort of thing. The reason my heart understood setting was because I experienced setting.

But then there was conflict. Every good story has conflict in it. Some conflict is internal, some is external, but if you want to write a novel that sells, you have to have conflict. We understand conflict because we experience conflict, right? But where does conflict come from? Why do we experience conflict in our lives? This helped me a great deal in accepting the idea of original sin and the birth of conflict. The rebellion against God explained why humans experienced conflict in their lives, and nobody knows of any explanation other than this. This last point was crucial. I felt like I was having an epiphany. Without the Christian explanation of original sin, the seemingly silly story about Adam and Eve and the tree of the knowledge of good and evil, there was no explanation of conflict. At all. Now some people process the account of original sin in the book of Genesis as metaphor, as symbolism for something else that happened; but whether you take it metaphorically or literally, this serves as an adequate explanation of the human struggle that every person experiences: loneliness, crying yourself to sleep at night, addiction, pride, war, and self-addiction. The heart responds to conflict within story, I began to think, because there is some great conflict in the universe with which we are interacting, even if it is only in the subconscious. If we were not experiencing some sort of conflict in our lives, our hearts would have no response to conflict in books or film. The idea of conflict, of having tension, suspense, or an enemy, would make no sense to us. But these things do make sense. We understand these elements because we experience them. As much as I did not want to admit it, Christian spirituality explained why.

And then the element of story known as climax. Every good story has a climax. Climax is where a point of decision determines the end of the story. Now this was starting to scare me a little bit. If the human heart uses the tools of reality to create elements of story, and the human heart responds to climax in the structure of story, this means that climax, or point of decision, could very well be something that exists in the universe. What I mean is that there is a decision the human heart needs to make. The elements of story began to parallel my understanding of Christian spirituality. Christianity offered a decision, a climax. It also offered a good and a bad resolution. In part, our decisions were instrumental to the way our story turned out.

Now this was spooky because for thousands of years big-haired preachers have talked about the idea that we need to make a decision, to follow or reject Christ. They would offer these ideas as a sort of magical solution to the dilemma of life. I had always hated hearing about it because it seemed so entirely unfashionable a thing to believe, but it did explain things. Maybe these unfashionable ideas were pointing at something mystical and true. And, perhaps, I was judging the idea, not by its merit, but by the fashionable or unfashionable delivery of the message.

○   ○   ○

A long time ago I went to a concert with my friend Rebecca. Rebecca can sing better than anybody I've ever heard sing. I heard this folksinger was coming to town, and I thought she might like to see him because she was a singer too. The tickets were twenty bucks, which is a lot to pay if you're not on a date. Between songs, though, he told a story that helped me resolve some things about God. The story was about his friend who is a Navy SEAL. He told it like it was true, so I guess it was true, although it could have been a lie.

The folksinger said his friend was performing a covert operation, freeing hostages from a building in some dark part of the world. His friend's team flew in by helicopter, made their way to the compound and stormed into the room where the hostages had been imprisoned for months. The room, the folksinger said, was filthy and dark. The hostages were curled up in a corner, terrified. When the SEALs entered the room, they heard the gasps of the hostages. They stood at the door and called to the prisoners, telling them they were Americans. The SEALs asked the hostages to follow them, but the hostages wouldn't. They sat there on the floor and hid their eyes in fear. They were not of healthy mind and didn't believe their rescuers were really Americans.

The SEALs stood there, not knowing what to do. They couldn't possibly carry everybody out. One of the SEALs, the folksinger's friend, got an idea. He put down his weapon, took off his helmet, and curled up tightly next to the other hostages, getting so close his body was touching some of theirs. He softened the look on his face and put his arms around them. He was trying to show them he was one of them. None of the prison guards would have done this. He stayed there for a little while until some of the hostages started to look at him, finally meeting his eyes. The Navy SEAL whispered that they were Americans and were there to rescue them. Will you follow us? he said. The hero stood to his feet and one of the hostages did the same, then another, until all of them were willing to go. The story ends with all the hostages safe on an American aircraft carrier.

I never liked it when the preachers said we had to follow Jesus. Sometimes they would make Him sound angry. But I liked the story the folksinger told. I liked the idea of Jesus becoming man, so that we would be able to trust Him, and I like that He healed people and loved them and cared deeply about how people were feeling.

When I understood that the decision to follow Jesus was very much like the decision the hostages had to make to follow their rescuer, I knew then that I needed to decide whether or not I would follow Him. The decision was simple once I asked myself, *Is Jesus the Son of God, are we being held captive in a world run by Satan, a world filled with brokenness, and do I believe Jesus can rescue me from this condition?*

If life had a climax, which it must in order for the element of climax to be mirrored in story, then Christian spirituality was offering a climax. It was offering a decision.

The last element of story is resolution. ~~Christian spirituality offered a resolution, the resolution of forgiveness and a home in the afterlife~~. Again, it all sounded so very witless to me, but by this time I wanted desperately to believe it. ~~It felt as though my soul were designed to live the story Christian spirituality was telling. I felt like my soul wanted to be forgiven. I wanted the resolution God was offering.~~

And there it was: ~~setting~~, ~~conflict~~, ~~climax~~, and ~~resolution~~. As silly as it seemed, it met the requirements of the heart and it matched the facts of reality. It felt more than true, it felt meaningful. I was starting to believe I was a character in a greater story, which is why the elements of story made sense in the first place.

The magical proposition of the gospel, once free from the clasps of fairy tale, was very adult to me, very gritty like something from Hemingway or Steinbeck, like something with copious amounts of sex and blood. ~~Christian spirituality was not a children's story. It wasn't cute or neat. It was mystical and odd and clean, and it was reaching into dirty. There was wonder in it and enchantment.~~

~~Perhaps, I thought, Christian spirituality really was the difference between illusion and magic.~~

Shifts

Find a Penny

SOME OF THE CHRISTIANS IN PORTLAND talk about Reed College as if it is hades. They say the students at Reed are pagans, heathens in heart. Reed was recently selected by the *Princeton Review* as the college where students are most likely to ignore God. It is true. It is a godless place, known for existential experimentation of all sorts. There are no rules at Reed, and many of the students there have issues with authority. Reed students, however, are also brilliant. Loren Pope, former education editor for the *New York Times,* calls Reed "the most intellectual college in the country." Reed receives more awards and fellowships, per capita, than any other American college and has entertained more than thirty Rhodes scholars.

For a time, my friend Ross and I got together once each week to talk about life and the Old Testament. Ross used to teach Old Testament at a local seminary. Sometimes Ross would talk about his son, Michael, who was a student at Reed. During the year Ross and I were getting together to talk about the Old Testament, I had heard Michael was not doing well. Ross told me Michael had gotten his girlfriend pregnant and the girl was not allowing him to see the child. His son was pretty heartbroken about it.

During his senior year at Reed, Ross's son died by suicide. He jumped from a cliff on the Oregon coast.

After it happened, Ross was in terrible pain. The next time I got together with him, about a month after the tragedy, Ross sat across from me with blue cheeks and moist eyes. It was as if everything sorrowful in the world was pressing on his chest. To this day, I cannot imagine any greater pain than losing a child.

I never knew Michael, but everybody who did loved him. The students at Reed flooded his e-mail box with good-bye letters and notes of disbelief. Through the years after Michael's death, even after Ross and I stopped meeting because I moved across town, Reed remained in the back of my mind. Not too many years went by before I started thinking about going back to school. I wasn't sure what to study, but I heard Reed had a terrific humanities program. I am a terrible student. I always have been. Deadlines and tests do me in. I can't take the pressure. Tony the Beat Poet, however, told me he was considering auditing a humanities class at Reed: ancient Greek literature. He asked me if I wanted to join him.

At the time I was attending this large church in the suburbs. It was like going to church at the Gap. I don't know why I went there. I didn't fit. I had a few friends, though, very nice people, and when I told them I wanted to audit classes at Reed they looked at me as if I wanted to date Satan. One friend sat me down and told me all about the place, how they have a three-day festival at the end of the year in which they run around naked. She said some of the students probably use drugs. She told me God did not want me to attend Reed College.

o   o   o

The first day of school was exhilarating. It was better than high school. Reed had ashtrays, and everybody said cusswords.

There were four hundred freshmen in my humanities class. Dr. Peter Steinberger, the acting president, delivered a lecture of which I understood about 10 percent. But the 10 percent I understood was brilliant. I loved it. I made noises while he was teaching, humming noises, noises in agreement with his passionate decrees.

After class I would usually go to Commons to get coffee and organize my notes. It was in Commons where I met Laura, who, although she was an atheist, would teach me a great deal about God. Her father, whom she loved and admired dearly, was a Methodist minister in Atlanta, and yet she was the only one in her family who could not embrace the idea of God. She explained that her family loved her all the same, that there was no tension because of her resistance to faith. Laura and I started meeting every day after lecture, rehashing the day's themes. I don't believe I had ever met anybody as brilliant as Laura. She seemed to drink in the complicated themes of Greek literature as though they were cartoons.

"What did you think of the lecture?" I once asked her.

"I thought it was okay."

"Just okay?" I asked.

"Yeah, I mean, this is supposed to be a pretty challenging school, and I wasn't that challenged. Not that good of an introduction if you ask me. I hope they don't put the cookies on a lower shelf all year."

"Cookies?" I asked. I thought she had cookies.

Laura would go on to explain the ideas I didn't understand. In time she figured out that I was a Christian, but we didn't talk much about it. We normally discussed literature or the day's lecture, but one day Laura brought up an odd topic: racism in the history of the church. She had moved to Portland from Georgia where, though she is an atheist, she told me she witnessed, within a church, the sort of racial discrimination most of us thought ended fifty years ago. She asked me very seriously what I thought about the problem of racism in America and whether the church had been a harbor for that sort of hatred. It had been a long time since I'd thought about it, to be honest. Just out of high school I got hooked on Martin Luther King and read most of his books, but since then the issue had faded in my mind. I am sure there are exceptions, but for the most part I think evangelical churches failed pretty badly during the civil rights movement, as did nearly every other social institution. Laura looked down into her coffee and didn't say anything. I knew, from previous conversations, she had dated a black student back in Atlanta who was now at Morehouse College where Dr. King himself earned a degree. Her question was not philosophical. It was personal.

I told her how frustrating it is to be a Christian in America, and how frustrated I am with not only the church's failures concerning human rights, but also my personal failure to contribute to the solution. I wondered out loud, though, if there was a bigger issue, and I mistakenly made the callous comment that racism might be a minor problem compared to bigger trouble we have to deal with.

"Racism, not an issue?!" she questioned very sternly.

"Well, not that it's not an issue, only that it is a minor issue."

"How can you say that?" She sat back restlessly in her chair. "Don, it is an enormous problem."

I was doing a lot of backpedaling at first, but then I began to explain what I meant. "Yeah, I understand it is a terrible and painful problem, but in light of the whole picture, racism is a signal of something greater. There is a larger problem here than tension between ethnic groups."

"Unpack that statement," Laura said.

"I'm talking about self-absorption. If you think about it, the human race is pretty self-absorbed. Racism might be the symptom of a greater disease. What I mean is, as a human, I am flawed in that it is difficult for me to consider others before myself. It feels like I have to fight against this force, this current within me that, more often than not, wants to avoid serious issues and please myself, buy things for myself, feed myself, entertain myself, and all of that. All I'm saying is that if we, as a species, could fix our self-absorption, we could end a lot of pain in the world."

Laura didn't say much more that afternoon, but we got together several weeks later, and she hinted she agreed about this problem of self-absorption. She called it sin.

"Wait," I began. "How can you believe in sin but not in God?"

"I just do," she said.

"But you can't."

"I can do what I want." She looked at me sternly.

"Okay," I said, knowing that if we got into an argument she would win.

Laura and I didn't talk much about religion after that. She had dreams of becoming a writer, so we talked about literature. She would give me articles or essays she had written. I ate them. They were terrific. It was very much an honor to even know her. I could sense very deeply that God wanted a relationship with Laura. Ultimately, I believe that God loves and wants a relationship with every human being, but with Laura I could feel God's urgency. Laura, however, wanted little to do with it. She never brought up the idea of God, so I didn't either.

o o o

I felt alive at Reed. Reed is one of the few places on earth where a person can do just about anything they want. On one of my first visits to campus, the American flag had been taken down and replaced with a flag bearing the symbol for anarchy. As odd as it sounds, having grown up in the church, I fell in love with the campus. The students were brilliant and engaged. I was fed there, stimulated, and impassioned. I felt connected to the raging current of thoughts and ideas. And what's more, I had more significant spiritual experiences at Reed College than I ever had at church.

One of the things I cherished about Reed was that any time I stepped on campus I would find a conversation going about issues that mattered to me. Reed students love to dialogue. There are always groups of students discussing global concerns, exchanging ideas and views that might solve some of the world's problems. I was challenged by the students at Reed because they were on the front lines of so many battles for human rights. Some of them were fighting just to fight, but most of them weren't; most of them cared deeply about peace. Interacting with these guys showed me how shallow and self-centered my Christian faith had become. Many of the students hated the very idea of God, and yet they cared about people more than I did.

There were only a few students on campus who claimed to be Christians. Though I was only auditing classes, I was accepted into this small group. We would meet in the chapel to pray each week or hold Bible studies in one of the dorm rooms. It was very underground. Secret. There has always been a resistance to Christianity on the campus at Reed. The previous year, a few Christians made a small meditation room on campus on Easter Sunday. They simply turned down the lights in a room in the library, lit some candles, and let students know the room was there if anybody wanted to pray. When Easter morning rolled around, students decided to protest. They purchased a keg of beer, got drunk, and slaughtered a stuffed lamb inside the meditation room.

The perspective the students in our group had about the event was Christlike. They were hurt, somewhat offended, but mostly brokenhearted. The event was tough on our group. We did not feel welcome on campus. But I learned so much from the Christians at Reed. I learned that ~~true love turns the other cheek, does not take a wrong into account, loves all people regardless of their indifference or hosti~~lity. The Christians at Reed seemed to me, well, revolutionary. I realize Christian beliefs are ancient, but I had never seen them applied so directly. The few Christians I met at Reed showed me that ~~Christian spirituality was a reliable faith, both to the intellect and the spirit~~.

I knew that Laura would fit in with this group. I knew that Laura, no matter how far she was from God, could come to know him.

The story of how my friend Penny came to know God gave me hope for Laura. I was first introduced to Penny at a party on the front lawn, but I thought she was too good looking to talk to, so I sort of slid off into the crowd. Later she showed up at a prayer meeting we had in my friend Iven's room, and I got to know her pretty well. We discovered that we were both ridiculously insecure, and so we became friends. Penny is living proof that Jesus still pursues people. Even Reedies.

Penny had a crazy experience with God while she was studying in France. She gives all the credit to Nadine, another of the very few Christians at Reed, and a member of our little rebel religious outfit.

When Penny and Nadine first met, Penny wasn't a Christian. They had both spent their freshman years at Reed but never knew each other. Individually they decided to study at the same school in France during their sophomore year.

Penny wanted nothing to do with religion. Her perception of Christians was that they were narrow-minded people, politically conservative and hypocritical. Penny disliked Christians because it seemed on every humanitarian issue, she found herself directly opposing the opinions held by many evangelicals. She also felt that if Christianity were a person, that is all Christians lumped into one human being, that human being probably wouldn't like her.

After arriving in France, Penny was scheduled to spend a few weeks in Paris on vacation before heading north to Sarah Lawrence College in Rennes. When she arrived, she contacted some of the girls she would be studying with. One of these girls happened to be Nadine. You have to know that Penny and Nadine are very different, opposites in fact. It is amazing that they hit it off at all. Not only did they have completely different religious ideas, but they also came from starkly contrasting backgrounds. Nadine, for instance, descended from Scottish royalty, still having a copious amount of pomp in her bloodline. Penny was born in a green army tent on a hippie commune in the Pacific Northwest.

I should paint the background for you a little bit so you can understand why I find it so interesting these girls became friends: Nadine's grandmother was born into the Stuart clan, a royal family in Scotland. Her grandmother married and moved to the Congo where the family was stationed as diplomats for the Belgian government. Nadine's mother was raised with a slew of servants including a driver, a cook, a butler, and a nanny. She was never allowed to speak to her parents unless spoken to first. Nadine's mother ran her home in similar fashion, passing down many of the traditions of aristocracy.

When Nadine and Penny met in France it was as if they were exchanging notes from different planets. No less interesting than Nadine's story is Penny's, whose parents originally named her Plenty. She changed her name shortly after she realized she could. At the hippie commune where Penny was born, her parents experimented with drugs in an effort to find truth. The experiment failed, and her mother and father left the commune and moved to Florida where her father got a job working on boats.

Penny has painful memories of her mother slipping into delusion, first believing John Kennedy was her lover, then claiming she was being hunted by the FBI. Her mother was diagnosed as a paranoid schizophrenic when Penny was a child. Today Penny's mother lives on the streets of Seattle where she adamantly refuses help from anyone, including Penny.

Penny once told me that no matter how gingerly she put the puzzle of her past together, she was always cut by the sharp edges: the fact that her mother was stoned while giving birth, the enticing but deceptive delusions presented to her as a child, and the breakup, not only of her mother from her father, but her mother from all reality. When I talk to Penny about driving up to Seattle to meet her mother, she tells me that I wouldn't enjoy the experience, that her mother will hate me.

"She hates everybody, Don. She thinks people are out to get her. If I call her on the phone in the shelter, she will come to the phone and hang it up. She doesn't answer my letters. She probably doesn't even open them."

"But she was normal at one time, right?" I once asked.

"Yes, she was beautiful and fun. I loved my mom, Don, and I still do. But I hate that her mind has been taken. I hate that I can't have normal interaction with her."

When Penny was eleven her parents divorced, and after the breakup she moved west with her father, spending a year sailing around the Pacific on her father's sailboat before eventually settling in a tiny mountain town in eastern Washington.

During those first three weeks in France, it was comforting for Penny that Nadine cared so much about her past and her story. This helped Penny listen to Nadine's story, and one night while walking on a beach in the south of France, Nadine explained to Penny why she was a Christian. She said that she believed Christ was a revolutionary, a humanitarian of sorts, sent from God to a world that had broken itself. Penny was frustrated that Nadine was a Christian. She couldn't believe that a girl this kind and accepting could subscribe to the same religion that generated the Crusades, funded the Republicans, or fathered religious television. But over the year at Sarah Lawrence, Nadine's flavor of Christianity became increasingly intriguing to Penny. Penny began to wonder if Christianity, were it a person, might in fact like her. She began to wonder if she and Christianity might get along, if they might have things in common.

The first time Penny told me the story of how she became a Christian we were walking through Laurelhurst Park, the beautiful park down the street from my house where lesbians go to walk their dogs.

"Nadine and I would sit for hours in her room," she began. "Mostly we would talk about boys or school, but always, by the end of it, we talked about God. The thing I loved about Nadine was that I never felt like she was selling anything. She would talk about God as if she knew Him, as if she had talked to Him on the phone that day. She was never ashamed, which is the thing with some Christians I had encountered. They felt like they had to sell God, as if He were soap or a vacuum cleaner, and it's like they really weren't listening to me; they didn't care, they just wanted me to buy their product. I came to realize that I had judged all Christians on the personalities of a few. That was frightening for me, too, because it had been so easy just to dismiss Christians as nuts, but here was Nadine. I didn't have a category for her. To Nadine, God was a being with which she interacted, and even more, Don, Nadine believed that God liked her. I thought that was beautiful. And more than that, her faith was a spiritual thing that produced a humanitarianism that was convicting. I was really freaked out, because I wanted to be good, but I wasn't good, I was selfish, and Nadine, well, she was pretty good. I mean she wasn't selfish. So she asked me if I wanted to read through the book of Matthew with her, and in fact I did. I wanted to see if this whole Jesus thing was real. I still had serious issues with Jesus, though, only because I associated Him with Christianity, and there was no way I would ever call myself a Christian. But I figured I should see for myself. So I told her yes."

"So then you started reading the Bible?" I asked.

"Yes. We would eat chocolates and smoke cigarettes and read the Bible, which is the only way to do it, if you ask me. Don, the Bible is so good with chocolate. I always thought the Bible was more of a salad thing, you know, but it isn't. It is a chocolate thing. We started reading through Matthew, and I thought it was all very interesting, you know. And I found Jesus very disturbing, very straightforward. He wasn't diplomatic, and yet I felt like if I met Him, He would really like me. Don, I can't explain how freeing that was, to realize that if I met Jesus, He would like me. I never felt like that about some of the Christians on the radio. I always thought if I met those people they would yell at me. But it wasn't like that with Jesus. There were people He loved and people He got really mad at, and I kept identifying with the people He loved, which was really good, because they were all the broken people, you know, the kind of people who are tired of life and want to be done with it, or they are desperate people, people who are outcasts or pagans. There were others, regular people, but He didn't play favorites at all, which is miraculous in itself. That fact alone may have been the most supernatural thing He did. He didn't show partiality, which every human does."

"I never thought of it that way," I told her.

"He didn't show partiality at all, Don, and neither should we. But listen, this is the best part. We got to the part of the book where Jesus started talking about soil."

"Soil?"

"Yeah. There is a part in Matthew where Jesus talks about soil, and He is going to throw some seed on the soil and some of the seed is going to grow because the soil is good, and some of the seed isn't because it fell on rock or the soil that wasn't as good. And when I heard that, Don, everything in me leaped up, and I wanted so bad to be the good soil. That is all I wanted, to be the good soil! I was like, Jesus, please let me be the good soil!"

"So that is when you became a Christian!"

"No. That was later."

"So what happened next?" I asked.

"Well, later that month, it was in December, there was a raging party going on downstairs in the dorm, and I was pretty drunk and high, you know, and I wasn't feeling too well, so I started up the stairs to see if my friend Naomi was in her room, and she wasn't, so I went down to my room and sort of crashed on the floor. I just sort of lay there for a little while and then it happened. Now you have to promise to believe me."

"Promise what?"

Penny stopped walking and put her hands in her coat pockets.

"Okay, but I'm not crazy." She took a deep breath. "I heard God speak to me."

"Speak to you?" I questioned.

"Yes."

"What did He say?"

"He said, 'Penny, I have a better life for you, not only now, but forever.'" When Penny said this she put her hand over her mouth, as if that would stop her from crying.

"Really," I said. "God said that to you."

"Yes." Penny talked through her hand. "Do you believe me?"

"I guess."

"It doesn't matter whether you believe me or not." Penny started walking again. "That is what happened, Don. It was crazy.

God said it. I got really freaked out about it, you know. I thought maybe it was the drugs, but I knew at the same time it wasn't the drugs." Penny put her hand on her forehead and smiled, shaking her head. "I should read you my journal from that night. It was like, oh my God, God talked to me. I am having this trippy God thing right now. God is talking to me. I kept asking Him to say it again, but He wouldn't. I guess it's because I heard Him the first time, you know."

"Yeah, probably. So is that when you became a Christian, the night God talked to you?"

"No."

"You didn't become a Christian, even after God talked to you."

"No."

"Why?"

"I was drunk and high, Don. You should be sober when you make important decisions."

"That's a good point," I agreed. But I still thought she was crazy. "So what happened next?"

"Well," Penny started. "A couple of nights later I got on my knees and said I didn't want to be like this anymore. I wanted to be good, you know. I wanted God to help me care about other people because that's all I wanted to do, but I wasn't any good at it. I had already come to believe that Jesus was who He said He was, that Jesus was God. I don't know how I came to that conclusion. It wasn't like doing math; it was something entirely different, but I knew it, I knew inside that He was God. But this time I just prayed and asked God to forgive me. And that is when I became a Christian. It was pretty simple." Penny put her hands back in her pockets and looked at me with her gorgeous blue eyes. "There," she said. "Are you happy?" And with that last comment she stuck her tongue out and laughed.

"Tell me the story again, Penny. Start with arriving in France."

"Why?"

"Because it's a good story. Tell it again," I told her.

"No. Once is enough. You will probably put it in one of your Christian books or something."

"Never," I said adamantly.

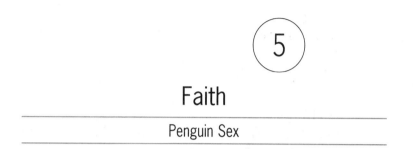

Faith

Penguin Sex

THE GOOFY THING ABOUT CHRISTIAN FAITH IS that you believe it and don't believe it at the same time. It isn't unlike having an imaginary friend. I believe in Jesus; I believe He is the Son of God, but every time I sit down to explain this to somebody I feel like a palm reader, like somebody who works at a circus or a kid who is always making things up or somebody at a Star Trek convention who hasn't figured out the show isn't real.

Until.

When one of my friends becomes a Christian, which happens about every ten years because I am such a sheep about sharing my faith, the experience is euphoric. I see in their eyes the trueness of the story.

Everybody at Reed was telling me something was wrong with Laura. They said she was depressed or something. I ran into her at a lecture in Vollum Lounge, which is beautiful like a museum with its tall white walls. Laura sat in front of me, and when the lecture was over she didn't leave. Neither did I. I didn't want to bother her, but I could tell she was sad about something.

"How are you?" I asked.

"I am not good." She turned to face me. I could see in her eyes she had spent the morning crying.

"What is wrong?"

"Everything."

"Boy stuff?" I asked.

"No."

"School stuff?" I asked.

"No."

"God stuff?"

Laura just looked at me. Her eyes were sore and moist. "I guess so, Don. I don't know."

"Can you explain any of it? The way you feel."

"I feel like my life is a mess. I can't explain it. It's just a mess."

"I see," I said.

"Don, I just want to confess. I have done terrible things. Can I confess to you?"

"I don't think confessing to me is going to do you any good." As I said it Laura wiped her eyes with her fingers.

"I feel like He is after me, Don."

"Who is after you?" I asked.

"God."

"I think that is very beautiful, Laura. And I believe you. I believe God wants you."

"I feel like He is after me," she repeated.

"What do you think He wants?"

"I don't know. I can't do this, Don. You don't understand. I can't do this."

"Can't do what, Laura?"

"Be a Christian."

"Why can't you be a Christian?"

Laura didn't say anything. She just looked at me and rolled her tired eyes. She dropped her hands into her lap with a sigh. "I wish I could read you my journal," she said, looking blankly at the wall. "There is this part of me that wants to believe. I wrote about it in my journal. My family believes, Don. I feel as though I need to believe. Like I am going to die if I don't believe. But it is all so stupid. So completely stupid."

"Laura, why is it that you hang out with the Christians on campus?"

"I don't know. I guess I am just curious." She wiped her eye again. "You're not dumb, I don't think. I just don't understand how you can believe this stuff."

"I don't either, really," I told her. "But I believe in God, Laura. There is something inside me that causes me to believe. And now I believe God is after you, that God wants you to believe too."

"What do you mean?" she asked, dropping her hands in her lap and sighing once again.

"I mean the idea that you want to confess. I think that God is wanting a relationship with you and that starts by confessing directly to Him. He is offering forgiveness."

"You are not making this easy, Don. I don't exactly believe I need a God to forgive me of anything."

"I know. But that is what I believe is happening. Perhaps you can see it as an act of social justice. The entire world is falling apart because nobody will admit they are wrong. But by asking God to forgive you, you are willing to own your own crap."

Laura sat silent for a while. She sort of mumbled under her breath. "I can't, Don. It isn't a decision. It isn't something you decide."

"What do you mean?"

"I can't get there. I can't just say it without meaning it." She was getting very frustrated. "I can't do it. It would be like, say, trying to fall in love with somebody, or trying to convince yourself that your favorite food is pancakes. You don't decide those things, they just happen to you. If God is real, He needs to happen to me."

"That is true. But don't panic. It's okay. God brought you this far, Laura; He will bring you the rest of the way. It may take time."

"But this hurts," she said. "I want to believe, but I can't. I hate this!"

Laura went back to her room. The next day I got an e-mail from Penny saying she, too, had talked with Laura. Penny asked me to pray for her as Laura felt trapped. Penny said she was going to spend a great deal of time with her, really walking through her emotions.

o   o   o

I had no explanation for Laura. I don't think there is an explanation. My belief in Jesus did not seem rational or scientific, and yet there was nothing I could do to separate myself from this belief. I think Laura was looking for something rational, because she believed that all things that were true were rational. But that isn't the case. Love, for example, is a true emotion, but it is not rational. What I mean is, people actually feel it. I have been in love, plenty of people have been in love, yet love cannot be proved scientifically. Neither can beauty. Light cannot be proved scientifically, and yet we all believe in light and by light see all things. There are plenty of things that are true that don't make any sense. I think one of the problems Laura was having was that she wanted God to make sense. He doesn't. He will make no more sense to me than I will make sense to an ant.

o   o   o

Tony and I were talking about Laura at the Horse Brass the other day; we were talking about belief, what it takes to believe, and he asked me how I believed in God.

I felt silly trying to explain it, even though Tony is a Christian. I felt as if I were saying I believed in Peter Pan or the Tooth Fairy, and yet I don't believe in Peter Pan or the Tooth Fairy. I believe in God, and as I said before it feels so much more like something is causing me to believe than that I am stirring up belief. In fact, I would even say that when I started in faith I didn't want to believe; my intellect wanted to disbelieve, but my soul, that deeper instinct, could no more stop believing in God than Tony could, on a dime, stop being in love with his wife. There are things you choose to believe, and beliefs that choose you. This was one of the ones that chose me.

"You know what really helped me understand why I believe in Jesus, Tony?"

"What's that?"

"Penguins," I told him.

"Penguins?"

"Penguins," I clarified. "Do you know very much about penguins?"

"Nope." Tony smiled. "Tell me about penguins."

"I watched a nature show on OPB the other night about penguins. They travel in enormous groups, perhaps five hundred of them, and they swim north in the coldest of winter, so far north they hit ice. They look like cartoons, like something out of that movie *Fantasia*. All five hundred of them swim till they hit ice then they jump out of the water, one by one, and start sliding on their bellies. They sort of create ruts as they slide, and they follow each other in a line. They do this for days, I think."

"They slide on their bellies for days?" Tony asked.

"Days," I told him.

"Why?"

"I don't know," I confessed. "But after a while they stop sliding, and they get around in a big circle and start making noises. And what they are doing is looking for a mate. It's crazy. It's like a penguin nightclub or something—like a disco. They waddle around on the dance floor till they find a mate."

"Then what?" Tony asked, sort of laughing.

"Penguin sex," I said.

"Penguin sex?"

"Yes. Penguin sex. Right there on television. I felt like I was watching animal porn."

"What was it like?" he asked.

"Less than exciting," I told him. "Sort of a letdown."

"So what does penguins having sex have to do with belief in God?" Tony asked.

"Well, I am getting to that. But let me tell you what else they do. First, the females lay eggs. They do that standing up. The eggs fall down between their legs, which are about an inch or something long, and the females rest the eggs on their feet. Then, the males go over to the females and the females give the males the eggs. Then, and this is the cool part, the females leave. They travel for days back to the ocean and jump in and go fishing."

"The females just take off and leave the men with the eggs?" Tony asked.

"Yes. The males take care of the eggs. They sit on them. They have this little pocket between their legs where the egg goes. They gather around in an enormous circle to keep each other warm. The penguins on the inside of the circle very slowly move to the outside, and then back to the inside. They do this to take turns on the outside of the circle because it is really cold. They do this for an entire month."

"A month!"

"Yes. The males sit out there on the eggs for a month. They don't even eat. They just watch the eggs. Then the females come back, and right when they do, almost to the day, the eggs are hatched. The females somehow know, even though they have never had babies before, the exact day to go back to the males. And that is how baby penguins are made."

"Very interesting." Tony clapped for me. "So what is the analogy here?"

"I don't know, really. It's just that I identified with them. I know it sounds crazy, but as I watched I felt like I was one of those penguins. They have this radar inside them that told them when and where to go and none of it made any sense, but they show up on the very day their babies are being born, and the radar always turns out to be right. I have a radar inside me that says to believe in Jesus. Somehow, penguin radar leads them perfectly well. Maybe it isn't so foolish that I follow the radar that is inside of me."

Tony smiled at my answer. He lifted his glass of beer. "Here's to penguins," he said.

o   o   o

In his book *Orthodoxy*, G. K. Chesterton says chess players go crazy, not poets. I think he is right. You'd go crazy trying to explain penguins. It's best just to watch them and be entertained. I don't think you can explain how Christian faith works either. It is a mystery. And I love this about Christian spirituality. It cannot be explained, and yet it is beautiful and true. It is something you feel, and it comes from the soul.

o   o   o

I crawled out of bed a few days later and cracked open the Bible on my desk. I didn't feel like reading, honestly, so I turned on my computer and fidgeted with a Sim City town I had been working on. I checked my e-mail and noticed one from Laura.

She had sent it in the early hours of the morning. The subject read: *So, anyway, about all of that stuff . . .*

Dearest Friend Don,

I read through the book of Matthew this evening. I was up all night. I couldn't stop reading so I read through Mark. This Jesus of yours is either a madman or the Son of God. Somewhere in the middle of Mark I realized He was the Son of God. I suppose this makes me a Christian. I feel much better now. Come to campus tonight and let's get coffee.

Much love,
Laura

Redemption

The Sexy Carrots

LONG BEFORE I LANDED IN PORTLAND BUT shortly after my own conversion to Christian spirituality, I experienced periods of affinity with God. I would lie on my bedroom floor, reading my Bible, going at the words for hours, all of them strong like arms wrapped tightly around my chest. It seemed as though the words were alive with minds and motions of their own, as though God were crawling thoughts inside my head for guidance, comfort, and strength.

For a while, I felt as though the world were a watch and God had lifted the lid so I could see the gears. The intricate rules of the sociospiritual landscape were something like a play to me, and I was delighted at every turn in the plot.

The truths of the Bible were magic, like messages from heaven, like codes, enchanting codes that offered power over life, a sort of power that turned sorrow to joy, hardship to challenge, and trial to opportunity. Nothing in my life was mundane. After I became a Christian, every aspect of human interaction had a fascinating appeal, and the intricate complexity of the natural landscape was remarkable in its perfection: the colors in the sky melding with the horizon, those south Texas sunsets burning distant clouds like flares, like fireworks, like angel wings starting flight.

God was no longer a slot machine but something of a Spirit that had the power to move men's souls. I seemed to have been provided answers to questions I had yet to ask, questions that God sensed or had even instilled in the lower reaches of my soul. The experience of becoming a Christian was delightful.

○   ○   ○

I don't think, however, there are many people who can stay happy for long periods of time. Joy is a temporal thing. Its brief capacity, as reference, gives it its pleasure. And so some of the magic I was feeling began to fade. It is like a man who gets a new saw for Christmas, on the first morning feeling its weight and wondering at its power, hardly thinking of it as a tool from which he will produce years of labor.

Early on, I made the mistake of wanting spiritual feelings to endure and remain romantic. Like a new couple expecting to always *feel* in love, I operated my faith thinking God and I were going to walk around smelling flowers. When this didn't happen, I became confused.

What was more frustrating than the loss of exhilaration was the return of my struggles with sin. I had become a Christian, so why did I still struggle with lust, greed, and envy? Why did I want to get drunk at parties or cheat on tests?

○   ○   ○

My best friends in high school were Dean Burkebile and Jason Holmes. Dean and Jason were both on the tennis team, and I was good enough as a practice partner, so we spent the majority of our hot Houston nights pounding the courts at the city park. We'd show up early in the afternoon and play till ten or eleven when the city shut down the lights, then we'd sit in the parking lot and drink beer, and Jason would smoke pot.

Dean's dad was a recovering alcoholic who had been sober for something like seven years. He was a handsome man, short, but he talked with a tongue swagger the way John Wayne talked in *True Grit*. Mr. Burkebile had amazing stories of his drinking days. He told us that he was driving drunk one night and blacked out at the wheel, steering his car directly into a parked police cruiser. I always looked up to Dean's dad, what with his drinking stories and tattoos and that sort of thing. He worked in a hospital now and drove a black Volvo. My family had a Buick. My mother never drove drunk. My father probably did, but I hadn't seen him in years.

When Dean and Jason and I would sit around in the parking lot, I felt earthy and real, like a guy out of a movie. They both came from wealthy families whose lives didn't revolve around church. I felt cool when I was with them, very sophisticated, as if I were going to play at Wimbledon the next week, sipping wine and signing autographs after the match.

Dean and I were serving as copresidents of the church youth group at the time. Dean never took any of it seriously. He took being president seriously but not the stuff about spirituality, not the stuff about metaphysical things taking place in your life. I'd try to get him to go to church camp, but he never wanted to. Camp was at the end of the summer, and it was too close to the school year, and if he went to camp, he'd feel convicted and it would take him a good two months to start drinking again, so he never went. One time, right after I got back from camp, Dean bought two cases of beer and had me stay over at his house. He said I had to get drunk to get over the initial guilt so I could have a good time at all the fall parties. I drank about a case all by myself. Dean and

I walked over to the city park and shot baskets under the moon, staggering and swearing because we could never hit the rim.

I didn't mind the drinking, mostly. Dean was about the best friend a guy could have. He really cared about people, I think, and so did Jason for that matter. They just liked to have a good time like anybody. With me, though, it was different. I really wanted to please God. I mean, I sort of wanted to please God. I felt like God had done something personal and real in my life. I also felt that I should probably try staying sober for a while, being copresident of the youth group and all.

One night while hanging out by the tennis courts, Jason pulled out a pretty-good-size bag of weed. Dean hardly smoked the stuff. He hated the taste and said it never got him high. I had never tried it, but that night Jason was pretty insistent on all of us giving it a go. I wasn't big on the idea. I had already had about five beers and was feeling pretty drunk. I had heard you shouldn't mix those things. Dean started packing Jason's pipe, and Jason got pretty excited, so I told him I'd take a hit.

To be honest, it didn't do anything for me. Anything good. Like I said, I was already pretty drunk, and the pot just put me over the edge. I got sick about five minutes into it. I felt like I was stuck in a suitcase at the bottom of a ship in the middle of a storm. Everything started sloshing around in my stomach. My hands and forehead began to sweat and my knees felt weak and yellow. I was poultry.

o   o   o

We walked back to Dean's house, and I lay down in his dog-smelling backyard. I slipped into seasick dreams of alligators and TBN talk show hosts. Jason came out and lay next to me and went on and on about what truth was, and did I think there was anybody out there. Jason had come to believe that truth was something imparted to you when you were high. Later he would go off to college. Friends of mine told me that he became known for waking up miles from campus, in his underwear, never knowing how he got there. On this night he was telling me about truth, about how it is something you know but you don't know you are knowing it. He was saying the key to the meaning of life is probably on other planets.

"Don. Don." He tried to get my attention.

"What, man?" I lay there, seasick.

"They could live on that one, man."

"Who, Jason?"

"Aliens, man."

As soon as one of the guys sobered up enough to drive, they took me home. I crawled through my bedroom window, stretched out on the floor, and waited for the ship to run aground.

I wondered, in that moment, about the conviction I had felt so many years before, the conviction about my mother's Christmas present. I figured all of this was God's fault. I thought that if God would make it so I felt convicted all the time, I would never sin. I would never get drunk or smoke pot.

I didn't feel worldly wise that night, rolling over on my stomach trying to hold down the vomit. I didn't feel like a guy after a tennis match at Wimbledon. I don't guess Mr. Burkebile was all that happy when he was drunk and wrecking police cars either. If he was happy he probably wouldn't have sobered up, and he probably wouldn't have to attend all those meetings. I think the things we want most in life, the things we think will set us free, are not the things we need. I wrote a children's story about this idea, but it's not really for children . . .

There once was a Rabbit
named Don Rabbit.

Don Rabbit went to
Stumptown Coffee every morning.

One Morning at Stumptown,
Don Rabbit saw Sexy Carrot.

And Don Rabbit decided
to chase Sexy Carrot.

But Sexy Carrot was very fast.

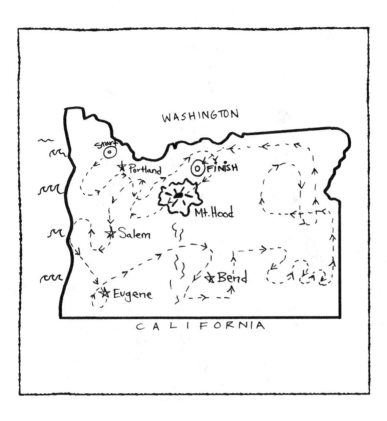

And Don Rabbit chased
Sexy Carrot all over Oregon.

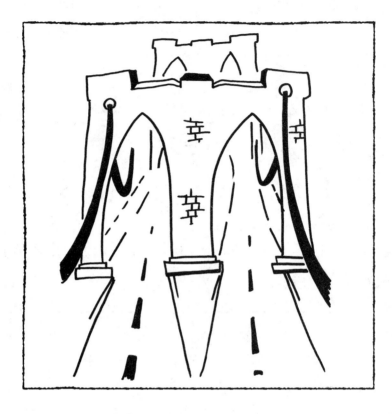

And all over America,
all the way to New York City.

And Don Rabbit chased Sexy Carrot
all the way to the Moon.

And Don Rabbit was very, very tired.

But with one last burst of strength,
Don Rabbit lunged at Sexy Carrot.

And Don Rabbit caught Sexy Carrot.

And the moral of the story is
that if you work hard, stay focused,
and never give up, you will eventually
get what you want in life.

Unfortunately, shortly after this story was told, Don Rabbit choked on the carrot and died. So the second moral of the story is:

Sometimes the things we want most in life are the things that will kill us.

And that's the tricky thing about life, really, that the things we want most will kill us. Tony the Beat Poet read me this ancient scripture recently that talked about loving either darkness or loving light, and how hard it is to love light and how easy it is to love darkness. I think that is true. Ultimately, we do what we love to do. I like to think that I do things for the right reasons, but I don't, I do things because I do or don't love doing them. Because of sin, because I am self-addicted, living in the wreckage of the fall, my body, my heart, and my affections are prone to love things that kill me. Tony says Jesus gives us the ability to love the things we should love, the things of Heaven. Tony says that when people who follow Jesus love the right things, they help create God's kingdom on earth, and that is something beautiful.

I found myself trying to love the right things without God's help, and it was impossible. I tried to go one week without thinking a negative thought about another human being, and I couldn't do it. Before I tried that experiment, I thought I was a nice person, but after trying it, I realized I thought bad things about people all day long, and that, like Tony says, my natural desire was to love darkness.

My answer to this dilemma was self-discipline. I figured I could just make myself do good things, think good thoughts about other people, but that was no easier than walking up to a complete stranger and falling in love with them. I could go through the motions for a while, but sooner or later my heart would testify to its true love: darkness. Then I would get up and try again. The cycle was dehumanizing.

7

Grace

The Beggars' Kingdom

I WAS A FUNDAMENTALIST CHRISTIAN ONCE. IT lasted a summer. I was in that same phase of trying to discipline myself to "behave" as if I loved light and not "behave" as if I loved darkness. I used to get really ticked about preachers who talked too much about grace, because they tempted me to not be disciplined. I figured what people needed was a kick in the butt, and if I failed at godliness it was because those around me weren't trying hard enough. I believed if word got out about grace, the whole church was going to turn into a brothel. I was a real jerk, I think.

I hit my self-righteous apex while working at a fundamentalist Christian camp in Colorado. I was living in a cabin in the Rockies with about seven other guys, and the whole lot of us fell into this militant Christianity that says you should live like a Navy SEAL for Jesus. I am absolutely ashamed to admit this now.

We would fast all the time, pray together twice each day, memorize Scripture, pat each other on the back and that sort of thing. Summer was coming to a close, and we were getting pretty proud of ourselves because we had read a great deal of

Scripture and hadn't gotten anybody pregnant. We were concerned, however, about what to do after we split up, thinking that if we didn't have each other we'd fall apart and start selling drugs to children. One of us, and it was probably me, decided to create a contract that listed things we wouldn't do for an entire year, like watch television or smoke pipes or listen to music. It was the constitution of our self-righteous individualism. The contract stated we would read the Bible every day, pray, and memorize certain long passages of Scripture. We sat around one night with pen and paper and offered sacrifices, each of us trying to outman the other with bigger and brighter lambs for the slaughter. We were the direct opposite of a frat house; instead of funneling our testosterone into binge drinking and rowdy parties, we were manning up to Jesus, bumping Him chest to chest as it were, like Bible salesmen on steroids.

I hitched a ride back to Oregon and got an apartment in the suburbs where I didn't know anybody and nobody knew me. I had this necklace on my neck, this string of beads, each bead representing one of the guys in the contract, and a cross in the center, a reminder that we had all gone in on this thing, that we were going to be monks for a year. At first it was easy, living in a new place and all, a new city, but after a while that necklace started to choke me.

The first of the exploits to go was the Bible. It wasn't that I didn't want to read it or didn't agree with it, I would just forget. It sat on the floor next to my bed beneath a pile of dirty clothes. Out of sight, out of mind. I'd forget about it for a month until I cleaned my room, and then I'd lift up a pile of dirty clothes and there would be my Bible, staring up at me like a dead pet.

One evening I was walking around Pioneer Square in downtown Portland when I noticed a pipe and tobacco store across the street. I decided I'd step inside and take a look-see. I came out with a new pipe that I swore I wouldn't smoke till the year was up.

It was a good deal, you know, about fifteen dollars or something. I couldn't pass up the sale on tobacco, either, even though it would go bad before the contract expired. I sat down in Pioneer Square with the skateboarders and musicians, chess players and coffee drinkers. I decided to pack my pipe, just to get a feel for it. I stuck it in my mouth to bring back that sensation, the feel of the stem between my teeth. Then I lit it. Then I smoked it.

After the Bible and the pipe thing fell apart, I decided to yield a bit on the television aspect of the contract. There was this indie pizza place down the street from my apartment, Escape from New York Pizza or something like that, and they had a big-screen television. I'd go down and watch Monday night football, which was a double sin because on Mondays we were supposed to be fasting. I figured none of the guys would mind if I switched the fasting day to Wednesday, just to shuffle things around. I shuffled so many fasting days around that after three months I was supposed to go twelve days without eating. I think I fasted twice that year. Maybe.

I hated the entire year. Hated it. I felt like a failure every morning. I hated looking in the mirror because I was a flop. I got ticked at all the people who were having fun with their lives.

I'd walk home from the pizza place feeling criminal for my mischief, feeling as though I were not cut out to be a Christian, wondering what my punishment would be for disobeying God. Everything was failing. I'd get letters from the other guys, too, some of them doing quite well. I wouldn't answer them. Not only was I failing God, I was failing my fundamentalist brothers!

o   o   o

My pastor, who is one of my best friends, experienced similar emotions early in his faith. Rick became a Christian when he was nineteen. Before he became a Christian he played football at Chico State, which, at the time, was the number one party school in the nation. And Rick did his share of partying. After months of drunken binges, though, he began to wonder whether there was anything more fulfilling in life than alcohol and sex. He began to long for God. So the next Sunday morning he made a point of being sober, and in fact walked to a local church to attend services. This was Rick's first time to step foot inside a church, and that morning the pastor happened to talk about sin, and how we are all sinners, and he talked about Jesus, and how Jesus died so that God could forgive us of our sin. At the end of the service, Rick prayed and became a Christian.

After a few weeks the pastors from Rick's new church came to visit, each in their suit and tie, and Rick entertained them and made them coffee, all of them sitting around sipping their coffee and talking nicely while the smell of marijuana lofted above their heads. Rick's friend was smoking pot in the next room. Rick laughs when he tells me he offered the pastors a hit, not being too offended when they turned him down.

The pastors talked to Rick about his conversion, explaining that he had been forgiven of his sins, and that it was important to try to live a righteous life. And Rick agreed with them, noting how much easier it would be to listen to the sermon on Sunday morning if he didn't have a hangover. So Rick began to choose purity over sin, and for a while he did well, but soon he found that he wanted to party with his friends, or he wanted to have sex with his girlfriend, and from time to time he would fail at his moral efforts. Rick tells me that those were the most depressing moments of his life, because he felt that he was failing the God who had saved him.

My pastor was anguished by an inability to control his desires. He felt that he had been given this new life, this key to heaven, and yet couldn't obey Jesus in return. So one evening he got on his knees and told God he was sorry. He told God how much he wished he could be good and obedient. He then sat on the edge of his bed and swallowed enough muscle relaxants and sleeping pills to kill three people. He lay down in a fetal position and waited to die.

o   o   o

Rick tells me, looking back, that he was too proud to receive free grace from God. He didn't know how to live within a system where nobody owes anybody else anything. And the harder it was for Rick to pay God back, the more he wanted to hide. God was his loan shark, so to speak. Though he understood that God wanted nothing in return, his mind could not communicate this fact to his heart, so his life was something like torture.

For a very long time, I could not understand why some people have no trouble accepting the grace of God while others experience immense difficulty. I counted myself as one of the ones who had trouble. I would hear about grace, read about grace, and even sing about grace, but accepting grace is an action I could not understand. It seemed wrong to me not to have to pay for my sin, not to feel guilty about it or kick myself around. More than that, grace did not seem like the thing I was looking for. It was too easy. I wanted to feel as though I earned my forgiveness, as though God and I were buddies doing favors for each other.

Enlightenment came in an unexpected place: a grocery store. I was on my way over Mount Hood to spend some time in the high desert with a few friends. I was driving alone and decided to stop in at Safeway to pick up some provisions for the weekend. While standing in line at the checkout counter, the lady in front of me pulled out food stamps to pay for her groceries. I had never seen food stamps before. They were more colorful than I

imagined and looked more like money than stamps. It was obvious as she unfolded the currency that she, I, and the checkout
girl were quite uncomfortable with the interaction. I wished
there was something I could do. I wished I could pay for her
groceries myself, but to do so would have been to cause a greater
scene. The checkout girl quickly performed her job, signing and
verifying a few documents, then filed the lady through the line.
The woman never lifted her head as she organized her bags of
groceries and set them into her cart. She walked away from the
checkout stand in the sort of stiff movements a person uses when
they know they are being watched.

On the drive over the mountain that afternoon, I realized that
it was not the woman who should be pitied, it was me. Somehow
I had come to believe that because a person is in need, they are
candidates for sympathy, not just charity. It was not that I wanted
to buy her groceries, the government was already doing that. I
wanted to buy her dignity. And yet, by judging her, I was the one
taking her dignity away.

I wonder what it would be like to use food stamps for a month.
I wonder how that would feel, standing in line at the grocery
store, pulling from my wallet the bright currency of poverty, feeling the probing eyes of the customers as they studied my clothes
and the items in my cart: frozen pizza, name-brand milk, coffee.
I would want to explain to them that I have a good job and make
good money.

I love to give charity, but I don't want to be charity. This is
why I have so much trouble with grace.

A few years ago I was listing prayer requests to a friend. As I
listed my requests, I mentioned many of my friends and family
but never spoke about my personal problems. My friend candidly
asked me to reveal my own struggles, but I told him no, that my
problems weren't that bad. My friend answered quickly, in the

voice of a confident teacher, "Don, you are not above the charity of God." In that instant he revealed my motives were not noble, they were prideful. It wasn't that I cared about my friends more than myself, it was that I believed I was above the grace of God.

Like Rick, I am too prideful to accept the grace of God. It isn't that I want to earn my own way to give something to God, it's that I want to earn my own way so I won't be charity.

As I drove over the mountain that afternoon, realizing I was too proud to receive God's grace, I was humbled. Who am I to think myself above God's charity? And why would I forsake the riches of God's righteousness for the dung of my own ego?

○   ○   ○

Rick tells me that as he lay there in his bed waiting to die, he heard God say to him, "Your life is not your own, but you have been bought with a price," and at this point he felt a certain peace. Rick told me he understood, cognitively as well as emotionally, that his role in his relationship with God was to humbly receive God's unconditional love.

My pastor, of course, is still alive, a miracle he cannot explain. Before he could save himself, he drifted into sleep, but he woke the next morning with ample energy, as if he had never swallowed the pills at all.

After surviving the suicide attempt, Rick went to Bible college, married a girl he met in school, and now they have four children. A little over a year ago he planted a church in downtown Portland, widely considered the most unchurched region in the United States. There were only about eight of us at our first meeting, and now the church has grown to more than five hundred people. On a given Sunday there are dozens of nonbelievers at our church, and each week Rick shares with them the patient love of God. He talks about Jesus as if he knows Him, as if he has talked to Him on the phone earlier that morning. Rick loves God because he accepts God's unconditional love first.

Rick says that I will love God because he first loved me. I will obey God because I love God. But if I cannot accept God's love, I cannot love Him in return, and I cannot obey Him. Self-discipline will never make us feel righteous or clean; accepting God's love will. The ability to accept God's unconditional grace and ferocious love is all the fuel we need to obey Him in return. Accepting God's kindness and free love is something the devil does not want us to do. If we hear, in our inner ear, a voice saying we are failures, we are losers, we will never amount to anything, this is the voice of Satan trying to convince the bride that the groom does not love her. This is not the voice of God. God woos us with kindness, He changes our character with the passion of His love.

o   o   o

We dream of Christ's love for His bride reading like *Romeo and Juliet;* two equals enflamed in liberal love. I think it is more like Lucentio's pursuit of Bianca in *The Taming of the Shrew.* That is, the groom endearing the belligerent bride with kindness, patience, and love.

Our "behavior" will not be changed long with self-discipline, but fall in love and a human will accomplish what he never thought possible. The laziest of men will swim the English channel to win his woman. I think what Rick said is worth repeating that by accepting God's love for us, we fall in love with Him, and only then do we have the fuel we need to obey.

In exchange for our humility and willingness to accept the charity of God, we are given a kingdom. And a beggars's kingdom is better than a proud man's delusion.

gods

Our Tiny Invisible Friends

EVERY YEAR OR SO I START PONDERING AT HOW silly the whole God thing is. Every Christian knows they will deal with doubt. And they will. But when it comes it seems so very real and frightening, as if your entire universe is going to fall apart. I remember a specific time when I was laying there in bed thinking about the absurdity of my belief. *God. Who believes in God? It all seems so very silly.*

I felt as if believing in God was no more rational than having an imaginary friend. They have names for people who have imaginary friends, you know. They keep them in special hospitals. Maybe my faith in God was a form of insanity. Maybe I was losing my marbles. I start out believing in Christ, and the next thing you know I am having tea with the Easter Bunny or waltzing with my toaster, shouting, "The redcoats are coming!"

And then I started thinking about other religions. I wasn't seriously cheating on God or anything, I was just thinking about them. I read through the Koran before it was even popular. It never occurred to me that if Christianity was not rational, neither were other religions. There were times I wished

I was a Buddhist, that is, I wished I could believe that stuff was true, even though I didn't know exactly what a Buddhist believed. I wondered what it would be like to rub some fat guy's belly and suddenly be overtaken with good thoughts and disciplined actions and a new car. I would go into real estate and marry a beautiful blond, and when the beautiful blond tilted her head to the side as I talked about socialized education, I could rub the Buddha, and she would have the intellect of Susan Faludi. Or Katie Couric.

○   ○   ○

About the time I was thinking through some of this stuff, really letting my imagination go into creative answers about the meaning of the universe, I took the bus to Powells because one of my favorite authors was scheduled to read from his new book. Powells, I should tell you, is the largest bookstore in the world. New and used books. Cheap food, one of my friends says about it. Powells is one of the reasons I love Portland. The old downtown building houses more than a half million books, all of them smelling like dust and ink, two terrible smells that blend mystically to make something beautiful. Powells is another church to me, a paperback sort of heaven.

When an author speaks at Powells, I go early to browse. I start in the literature section and move to religion before glancing through politics and social movements, then finally to art, which is where they house author events. The writer I went to see that night is a Christian guy, a fisherman and outdoorsman who writes stories about fly-fishing and Oregon waters. All of the chairs were taken when I got there, so I was leaning against a pole when he entered the room. He was taller than I imagined, skinnier, with languid legs and arms. He wore khaki pants and a plaid flannel shirt. He looked like somebody who watches PBS, or like a man who knew a lot about birds.

The author came in through the back of the crowd, appearing from the stairwell, escorted by a Powells employee around the short shelf that held autographed copies of his books. He had newspapers in his hands and a file folder, papers disheveled within. He had a weathered copy of his newest book. He was introduced as one of Oregon's treasures, a great writer who brings water to life, giving us in his words the beauty of the outdoors and a reminder that we are human, having a beautiful experience. The audience applauded, and I let out a little hoot. The author gathered himself at the podium with a smile, gentle enough, and started the evening by reading from national newspaper articles on foreign policy and religion, leisurely flipping through editorials. He read as if he were sharing old family recipes, as if we were all taking notes, which we weren't.

He was having a bad night I think, or a bad year or something, because he was a little sluggish and seemed to be reading from the articles as if to prove that other people agreed with his political ideas. We sat uncomfortably as he shared his opinion on one political idea after another, followed by a columnist who proved his idea. I really wanted him to read about fish. Fish are so safe, really. There is not a lot that is scandalous about fish. I began to turn on him to be honest. It was like watching Ernest Hemingway impersonate Ray Suarez.

The author I am talking about is a great writer. I want you to know that. I dearly love the man's work. And if he wants to read from the newspaper, who am I to tell him he can't? If he wanted to, he could have stood up there and colored in a coloring book. But I wanted to hear about fish. I wanted to close my eyes and see them swimming their silver sides along green rocks. I wanted to hear the river, feel it rush around my legs, flip the fly softly through the air, resting it on the tension of the river surface. Instead, I was up to my ears in foreign policy.

I wish I were the sort of person who liked everybody and everything. I feel so negative sometimes. I have friends who can listen to any song, watch any movie, or read any book, and they think everything is just great. I truly envy people who can do that. I say all of this because, as the author finally started reading from his new book, I didn't like it at all. I fought my critical nature but couldn't help but compare his new stuff to the genius of his previous work. His words were vaporous and cliché, trendy and full of sales pitches. They weren't his words, they were words that sell, words that tickle ears and reach a specified demographic.

In regard to spirituality, he surprised me by straying from his Christian convictions and bringing Muhammad into the light. He said that Muhammad was one of his heroes. I don't have so many problems with Muhammad, but I have problems with middle-aged white guys who grew up in America claiming Muhammad as a hero, not because Muhammad never did anything good (he did), but because calling Muhammad a hero is such an incredibly trendy thing to do. I know I am judging the guy's motives and all, but can you get any more trendy than subscribing to half-Christian, half-Islamic ideas? The guy was layering religious propositions like clothes in a J. Crew catalog.

The absolute most annoying thing about this guy's religious ideas was that they were so precisely where I was going with mine. It was like seeing my future pass before my eyes. I was on my way to becoming Captain Trendy Spiritual Writer. It was spooky.

Trendy Writer talked about how Khwaja Khandir is his fishing guide. He described Khwaja Khandir as the Islamic version of the Holy Spirit: Khwaja Khandir tells him where the fish are and teaches him things about life like how to manage his money or achieve inner peace or please his wife. It was all hokey and hoo-ha.

I felt as if I were being visited by the ghost of Christmas future, and the ghost was saying, "Hey, Don, you're going to end up like this guy: A yuppie Christian writer with no backbone!"

○   ○   ○

I think my desire to believe in a god other than Jesus had mostly to do with boredom. I wanted something new. I wanted something fresh to think about, to believe, to twiddle around in my mind. I understand the plight of the children of Israel, to be honest. Moses goes off to talk to God, he doesn't come back for a while, and so the people demand a god they can see and touch—a god they can worship with the absolute certainty it exists. So they build a golden cow (odd choice, but to each his own). Moses comes back from talking with God and finds the children of Israel worshiping a false god, so he goes postal. I imagined myself as the children of Israel when Moses comes down off of the mountain.

"What are you doing, Don?" Moses asks.

"Worshiping a golden cow."

"Why? Why would you reject the one true God?"

"Because I don't get to see Him or talk to Him. I am not even certain that He exists."

"Are you on crack, Don? Weren't you there when God parted the Red Sea? Weren't you there when God fed us from the ground, made water from a rock, led us with a cloud?" Moses screams.

"Calm down, Mosey. Listen, man, you always go up and talk to God and come back with a sunburn, and you have God hover around your tent in a cloud, and you have God turn your staff into a snake, and we get nothing. Nothing! It's not like we have this personal communication going with God, you know, Moses.

We are just sheep out here in the desert, and, honestly, we were better off as slaves to the Egyptians. That is where your God brought us. We need a god too. We need a god to worship. We need a god to touch and feel and interact with in a very personal way. So I made a cow. You can also wear it as a necklace."

"Don," Moses responds, "before I put you to death and send you home to the one true God, I want you to understand something. I want you to understand that God has never been nor ever will be invented. He is not a product of any sort of imagination. He does not obey trends. And God led us out of Egypt because you people cried out to Him. He was answering your prayers because He is a God of compassion. He could have left you to Satan. Don't complain about the way God answers your prayers. You are still living on an earth that is run by the devil. God has promised us a new land, and we will get there. Your problem is not that God is not fulfilling, your problem is that you are spoiled."

o   o   o

And Moses was right. God is not here to worship me, to mold Himself into something that will help me fulfill my level of comfort. I think part of my problem is that I want spirituality to be more close and more real. I understand why people wear crystals around their necks and why they perform chants and gaze at stars. They are lonely. I'm not talking about lonely for a lover or a friend. I mean lonely in the universal sense, lonely inside the understanding that we are tiny little people on a tiny little earth suspended in an endless void that echoes past stars and stars of stars. And it's not like God has a call-in radio show.

But as Trendy Writer read from his book that night at Powells, I thought about the Muslim babies dying in Afghanistan and

Pakistan. I thought about the economic crisis in Saudi Arabia and the children of Iraq who are being bombed because their ridiculous dictator won't cooperate with the United Nations. And then I thought about Khwaja Khandir, and I wondered what gave Trendy Writer the audacity to assume that Khwaja Khandir would have the time, or the desire, to take him fishing. Trendy Writer was trying to be hip and relevant, but in doing so he was cheapening the entire nation of Islam. And he was cheating on Jesus. He reminded me of Lot, who offered his daughters to the perverts because he wanted peace. Trendy Writer was sending out Muhammad and Jesus, asking them to hold hands so nobody would have to feel wrong or, rather, so he could have something fashionable to believe.

o   o   o

I talked to Tony about Trendy Writer. I told him how offensive it was that this guy was betraying Jesus and trampling all over Islam. When I told him the story of Trendy Writer, Tony closed his eyes and sighed. I asked him why he looked so troubled. He said it was because he felt convicted.

"Convicted about what, Tony?"

"I am convicted about what you are saying," he began. "Here is a guy using Islamic verbiage to make himself look spiritual, and yet he really hasn't researched or subscribed to the faith as it presents itself. He's just using it. Raping it for his own pleasure."

"Why are you convicted about that?" I asked him. "I've never heard you talk about Islamic ideas that way."

"I know," Tony said. "But I do the same thing with Jesus."

When Tony said that, it was as if truth came into the room and sat down with us. I felt as though Jesus were gently holding my head so He could work the plank out of my eye. Everything became clear. I realized in an instant that I desired false gods because Jesus wouldn't jump through my hoops, and I realized that, like Tony, my faith was about image and ego, not about practicing spirituality.

For me, Trendy Writer coming to town was the beginning of something. It was the beginning of my authentic Christianity. Trendy Writer, Khwaja Khandir, and Tony the Beat Poet were the seeds of change. I knew Christ, but I was not a practicing Christian. I had the image of a spiritual person, but I was bowing down to the golden cows of religiosity and philosophy. It was one of those enlightenments, one of those honest looks in the mirror in which there is no forgetting who you are. It was a moment without make-believe. After that moment, things started to get interesting.

Change

New Starts at Ancient Faith

THERE IS A TIME WHEN EVERY PERSON WHO encounters Jesus, who believes Jesus is the Son of God, decides that they will spend their life following Him. Some people, like the Apostle Paul, make this decision the minute they meet Him, the minute they become a Christian. Others, like the Apostle Peter, endure years of half-hearted commitment and spiritual confusion before leaping in with all their passion. Still others may enjoy some benefits of God's love and grace without entering into the true joy of a marriage with their maker.

Not long after I graduated from high school, I found myself leading a college group at a large church just outside Houston. I cherished the role, at first, because it was a place of honor. I studied the Bible for hours, putting talks together that students enjoyed. It started as a substitute teaching job. The college minister couldn't be there one week, so he asked me to fill in. When I was asked to speak again, I jumped at the chance like Homer Simpson at a donut. Pretty soon I was teaching all the time. I swam in the attention and the praise, I loved it, I lusted for it, I almost drowned in it.

The more attention I got, the stranger I became. I was on my way to having my own religious television show. Okay, that's a bit much, but you know what I mean. I was a smiler, a hand-shaker, a baby-kisser, a speech-giver. I said things like "God be with you," and "Lord bless you." I used clichés like a bad novelist.

I led the college group for a couple of years and enjoyed it at first, but it wasn't long before I felt like a phony. I got tired of myself. I didn't like to hear my own voice because I sounded like a talk-show host.

One afternoon I made an appointment with my pastor and told him I was leaving, that I was going into the world to get my thinking straight.

"How long will you be gone?" he asked.

"I don't know." I shrugged.

"Are you okay?"

"I think so. Maybe," I told him.

"Can you talk about it?" He looked concerned.

"No, not really."

"I understand you need a break. Why don't you take a couple weeks off."

"I was thinking longer," I told him.

"How long?"

"I don't know. Can you put a time limit on these things?"

"What things, Don?"

"I don't know," I told him, sort of staring out the window.

"Can you tell me how you feel?"

"No. I've tried to put words to it, you know, but I can't. I'm just really tired. Mentally drained. I feel like I am jumping through hoops or something. I don't feel like God is teaching through me. I feel like I am a fake person, you know. I say what I need to say, do what I need to do, but I don't really mean it."

"What does the real you want to say and do?" he asked me.

"I don't know. That is what the trip is about."

"Are you having a crisis of faith?" He looked concerned again.

"Maybe. What is a crisis of faith?" I asked him.

"Do you believe in God?"

"Yes. I want to go on a trip with Him."

"You aren't having any doubts at all?" he asked.

"No. I don't have any doubts about God or anything; it's just me. I feel like I am constantly saying things I don't mean. I tell people they should share their faith, but I don't feel like sharing my faith. I tell people they should be in the Word, but I am only in the Word because I have to teach the Word. I said to a guy the other day, 'God bless you.' What does that mean? I have been saying that stuff all my life, but what does that mean? Then I started thinking about all the crap I say. All the clichés, all the parroted slogans. I have become an infomercial for God, and I don't even use the product. I don't want to be who I am anymore."

"So you think you should go away," he clarified.

"Yes."

"Where will you go?"

"America."

"America?" He looked confused.

"America."

"We are in America right now, Don."

"Yeah, I know. But there are other parts to America. I'd like to see the other parts. I was looking at a map the other day, you know, and Texas was sort of brown with some green, a few hills, but then there were other places that were more green with big lumpy mountains. I'd like to go to those places."

"Do you think God is out there somewhere? Out there in the lumpy places?"

"I think God is everywhere."

"Then why do you have to leave?"

"Because I can't be here anymore. I don't feel whole here. I feel, well, partly whole. Incomplete. Tired. It has nothing to do with this church; it's all me. Something got crossed in the wires, and I became the person I should be and not the person I am. It feels like I should go back and get the person I am and bring him here to the person I should be. Are you following me at all? Do you know what I am talking about, about the green lumpy places?"

The conversation went on like this for about an hour. I went on and on about how the real me was out in the green lumpy places. I wasn't making any sense. I can't believe my pastor didn't call the guys with the white coats to take me away.

o   o   o

I suppose what I wanted back then is what every Christian wants, whether they understand themselves or not. What I wanted was God. I wanted tangible interaction. But even more than that, to be honest, I wanted to know who I was. I felt like a robot or an insect or a mysterious blob floating around in the universe. I believed if I could contact God, He would be able to explain who and why I was.

The days and weeks before a true commitment to Jesus can be terrible and lonely. I think I was feeling bitter about the human experience. I never asked to be human. Nobody came to the womb and explained the situation to me, asking for my permission to go into the world and live and breathe and eat and feel joy and pain. I started thinking about how odd it was to be human, how we are stuck inside this skin, forced to be attracted to the opposite sex, forced to eat food and use the rest room and then stuck to the earth by gravity. I think maybe I was going crazy or something. I spent an entire week feeling bitter because

I couldn't breathe underwater. I told God I wanted to be a fish. I also felt a little bitter about sleep. Why do we have to sleep? I wanted to be able to stay awake for as long as I wanted, but God had put me in this body that had to sleep. Life no longer seemed like an experience of freedom.

About twelve hours after I had the conversation with my pastor, a friend and I jumped into one of those Volkswagen camping vans and shoved off for the green lumpy places. A week into our American tour, we found ourselves at the bottom of the Grand Canyon, which is more lumpy than green, it turns out. It was a heck of a hike, let me tell you. I was in no shape to do it. So by the time I got to the bottom of that gargantuan hole in the ground, I was miserable. It was beautiful, don't get me wrong, but when your head is throbbing and you can't feel your lower half, you don't want to sit and reflect on how beautiful things are. Lumpy or not.

The canyon is more spectacular from the rim than from the river. Once in it, everything looks like Utah. As my friend and I fell asleep by the river, however, I had a cherished moment with God. I was in a lot of pain from the hike, so I was in no mood to mess around. There was no trying to impress Him, no speaking the right words. I simply began to pray and talk to God the way a child might talk to his father.

Beneath the billion stars and beside the river, I called out to God, softly.

"Hello?"

The stars were quiet. The river spoke in some other tongue, some vernacular for fish.

"I'm sorry, God. I'm sorry I got so confused about You, got so fake. I hope it's not too late anymore. I don't really know who I am, who You are, or what faith looks like. But if You want to talk, I'm here now. I could feel You convicting me when I was a kid, and I feel like You are trying to get through to me. But I feel like You are an alien or something, somebody far away."

Nothing from the stars. Fish language from the river. But as I lay there, talking to God, being real with Him, I began to feel a bit of serenity. It felt like I was apologizing to an old friend, someone with whom there had been a sort of bitterness, and the friend was saying it was okay, that he didn't think anything of it. It felt like I was starting over, or just getting started. That is the thing about giving yourself to God. Some people get really emotional about it, and some people don't feel much of anything except the peace they have after making an important decision. I felt a lot of peace.

There is something quite beautiful about the Grand Canyon at night. There is something beautiful about a billion stars held steady by a God who knows what He is doing. (They hang there, the stars, like notes on a page of music, free-form verse, silent mysteries swirling in the blue like jazz.) And as I lay there, it occurred to me that God is up there somewhere. Of course, I had always known He was, but this time I felt it, I realized it, the way a person realizes they are hungry or thirsty. The knowledge of God seeped out of my brain and into my heart. I imagined Him looking down on this earth, half angry because His beloved mankind had cheated on Him, had committed adultery, and yet hopelessly in love with her, drunk with love for her.

I know a little of why there is blood in my body, pumping life into my limbs and thought into my brain. I am wanted by God. He is wanting to preserve me, to guide me through the darkness of the shadow of death, up into the highlands of His presence and afterlife. I understand that I am temporary, in this shell of a thing on this dirt of an earth. I am being tempted by Satan, we are all being tempted by Satan, but I am preserved to tell those who do not know about our Savior and our Redeemer. This is why Paul had no questions. This is why he could be beaten one day, imprisoned the next, and released only to be beaten again and never ask God why. He understood the earth was fallen. He understood the rules of Rome could not save mankind, that mankind could not save itself; rather, it must be rescued, and he knew that he was not in the promised land, but still in the desert, and like Joshua and Caleb he was shouting, "Follow me and trust God!"

I see it now. I see that God was reaching out to Penny in the dorm room in France, and I see that the racism Laura and I talked about grows from the anarchy seed, the seed of the evil one. I could see Satan lashing out on the earth like a madman, setting tribes against each other in Rwanda, whispering in men's ears in the Congo so that they rape rather than defend their women. Satan is at work in the cults of the Third World, the economic chaos in Argentina, and the corporate-driven greed of American corporate executives.

I lay there under the stars and thought of what a great responsibility it is to be human. I am a human because God made me. I experience suffering and temptation because mankind chose to follow Satan. God is reaching out to me to rescue me. I am learning to trust Him, learning to live by His precepts that I might be preserved.

Belief

The Birth of Cool

MY MOST RECENT FAITH STRUGGLE IS NOT ONE of intellect. I don't really do that anymore. Sooner or later you just figure out there are some guys who don't believe in God and they can prove He doesn't exist, and some other guys who do believe in God and they can prove He does exist, and the argument stopped being about God a long time ago and now it's about who is smarter, and honestly I don't care. I don't believe I will ever walk away from God for intellectual reasons. Who knows anything anyway? If I walk away from Him, and please pray that I never do, I will walk away for social reasons, identity reasons, deep emotional reasons, the same reasons that any of us do anything.

My friend Julie Canlis from Seattle has this beautiful mother named Rachel who is small and petite and always remembers my name when I come for a visit. One morning I was sitting at the counter in the kitchen talking to Rachel about love and marriage, and she was gleaming about her husband a little, and I told her in one of those rare moments of vulnerability that I was scared to get married because I thought my wife might fall out of love with me, suddenly, after seeing a movie or reading a book or seeing me naked. You never know what might trigger these things. Rachael looked at me through the steam that was coming off her coffee and said, very wisely and comfortingly, that when a relationship is right, it is no more possible to wake up and want out of the marriage than it is to wake up and stop believing in God. What *is*, is what is, she said.

And that's when I realized that believing in God is as much like falling in love as it is like making a decision. Love is both something that happens to you *and* something you decide upon. And so I bring up that story about Julie's mom not because I want to talk about love, but because I want to talk some about belief. I have come to think that belief is something that happens to us too. Sure, there is some data involved, but mostly it is this deep, deep conviction, like what Julie's mom feels about her husband, this idea that life is about this thing, and it really isn't an option for it to be about something else.

I talked to a girl recently who said she liked Ethan Hawke, the actor and writer. He has a couple of novels out, and they are supposed to be really good, but I haven't read them. I know he is a fan of Douglas Coupland, which is a good thing if you ask me, so I'd probably like to read his stuff some day. But she was saying how much she liked him as a person, and I asked her why. She had to think quite a bit about it before she answered, but her answer was that he was an actor *and* a writer, not just an actor. He is an actor *and* a writer, and that is why you like him? I asked. Yes, she said. I thought that was profound. I was in a cranky mood so I asked her if she knew what he believed. What do you mean, she said. I mean do you know what he believes. I looked at her very squarely. Believes about what? she asked. Believes about anything, I said. Well, she told me as she sat back in her chair, I don't know. I don't know what he believes. Do you think he is cool? I asked her. Of course he is cool, she said.

And that is the thing that is so frustrating to me. I don't know if we really like pop-culture icons, follow them, buy into them because we resonate with what they believe or whether we buy into them because we think they are cool.

I was wondering the other day, why it is that we turn pop figures into idols? I have a theory, of course. I think we have this need to be cool, that there is this undercurrent in society that says some people are cool and some people aren't. And it is very, very important that we are cool. So, when we find somebody who is cool on television or on the radio, we associate ourselves with this person to feel valid ourselves. And the problem I have with this is that we rarely know what the person believes whom we are associating ourselves with. The problem with this is that it indicates there is less value in what people believe, what they stand for; it only matters that they are cool. In other words, who cares what I believe about life, I only care that I am cool. Because in the end, the undercurrent running through culture is not giving people value based upon what they believe and what they are doing to aid society, the undercurrent is deciding their value based upon whether or not they are cool.

I don't mean to pick on my friend who likes Ethan Hawke. She is very smart and has deep beliefs, but I just like the fact that I caught her being shallow. By shallow I mean she associated herself with somebody, thought somebody was "cool," and yet didn't know what he believed. I like that I caught her because she doesn't really live in that place, and I mostly do, and I hate that about myself and love that about her, so when she brought her head up to the surface, I wanted to point out the fact that she was in my neighborhood.

I had a crush on a girl who went to a rally in Chicago opposing

Bush's plan to attack Iraq. We were sitting around in my friend's living room and talking about it and she was in a huff and at one point raised her fist and said, "Down with Bush!" After that I didn't have a crush on her anymore. It wasn't because I like George W. Bush, it was because she had no idea why she didn't like George W. Bush. She only went to a rally and heard a good band and saw a lot of cool people with cool clothes and hippie haircuts. She decided what to believe based on whether other people who believed it were of a particular fashion that appealed to her. I saw myself in her quite a bit and that scared me. Girls like that make me want to marry Penny because Penny actually believes things. She lives them. I told Penny that I wanted to marry her, but she wasn't interested. I propose to Penny once a month now on the phone, but she just changes the subject.

The thing I have to work on in myself is this issue of belief. Gandhi believed Jesus when He said to turn the other cheek. Gandhi brought down the British Empire, deeply injured the caste system, and changed the world. Mother Teresa believed Jesus when He said everybody was priceless, even the ugly ones, the smelly ones, and Mother Teresa changed the world by showing them that a human being can be selfless. Peter finally believed the gospel after he got yelled at by Paul. Peter and Paul changed the world by starting small churches in godless towns.

Eminem believes he is a better rapper than other rappers. Profound. Let's all follow Eminem.

Here is the trick, and here is my point. Satan, who I believe exists as much as I believe Jesus exists, wants us to believe meaningless things for meaningless reasons. Can you imagine if Christians actually believed that God was trying to rescue us from the pit of our own self-addiction? Can you imagine? Can you imagine what Americans would do if they understood over half the world was living in poverty? Do you think they would change the way they live, the products they purchase, and the politicians they elect? ~~If we believed the right things, the true things, there wouldn't be very many problems on earth.~~

~~But the trouble with deep belief is that it costs something.~~ And ~~there is something inside me, some selfish beast of a subtle thing that doesn't like the truth at all because it carries responsibility, and if I actually believe these things I have to do something about them.~~ It is so, so cumbersome to believe anything. And it isn't cool. I mean it's cool in a *Reality Bites, Welcome to Sarajevo,* Amnesty International sense, but that is only as good as dreadlocks. Chicks dig it to a point, but you can't be all about it; you also have to want a big house and expensive clothes because in the end, our beliefs are about as enduring as seasonal fashion. In the end, we like Ethan Hawke even though we don't know what he believes. ~~Even our beliefs have become trend statements. We don't even believe things because we believe them anymore. We only believe things because they are cool things to believe.~~

The problem with Christian belief—I mean real Christian belief, the belief that there is a God and a devil and a heaven and a hell—is that it is not a fashionable thing to believe.

I had this idea once that if I could make Christianity cool, I could change the world, because if Christianity were cool then everybody would want to deal with their sin nature, and if everybody dealt with their sin nature then most of the world's problems would be solved. I decided that the best way to make Christianity cool was to use art. I attempted to write a short story about a fashionable Christian, so that everybody would want to be like him.

My fashionable Christian was deep. Deep water. A poet. He studied Thompson during his drug years, during the prostitute years. He had studied *The Hound of Heaven, In No Strange Land,* T. S. Eliot's *Four Quartets.* He smoked a pipe and read the

Romantics. And the Americans. Ginsberg's *"I watched the great-est minds of my generation descend into madness . . ."* was, to him, about sin nature. Part of him was about social justice. He could also skateboard and was in a rock band.

His name was Tom Toppins, and even though he had a goofy name, he overcame it because he rode an old Triumph motorcycle. In my story, Tom Toppins was casually dating a girl with blonde dreadlocks. She was a Buddhist; he was a Christian. He attended a Greek Orthodox church. She would go with him to church every once in a while, but he would not participate in her faith. He thought it was shallow, too much about fashion. He told her this over lunch at her loft apartment, and she exploded in anger. Then she cried, but he did not comfort her. He stood up and put on his jacket and lit up a cigarette and told her he was going to church. She screamed out, "How can you Christians maintain such an exclusive hold on truth!" He straightened his jacket while looking in a mirror and whispered to himself, *"'Cause that's the way it is, baby. That's the way it is."*

He walked out the door and left her weeping in agony, rubbing the belly of her little statue of Buddha. He didn't think of her again till the next day when he went by her apartment. Tom Toppins walked in and, though it was afternoon, found her sleeping, her face all red and wet with tears. He pulled a book of poems from his motorcycle jacket, Elizabeth Barrett Browning, and read to her from *Sonnets from the Portuguese* until she gently woke up. He lay down next to her and set her head on his free arm. She buried her head in his armpit and sobbed, but he didn't stop reading.

> My own beloved, who has lifted me
> From this drear flat of earth where I was thrown,
> And, in betwixt the languid ringlets, blown
> A life-breath, till the forehead hopefully

Shines out again, as all the angels see,
Before thy saving kiss! My own, my own,
Who camest to me when the world was gone,
And I who looked for only God, found *thee*.

I saw a movie the other day about all these people at this college back East, and it was a pretty grimy movie. There was a character in the movie, this guy who was a drug dealer and a jerk, and everybody else in the movie loved him and wanted to have sex with him. One of my housemates, Grant, was saying to me the other day that girls always like bad guys. My friend Amy is like that I think. And so was my friend Suzy, but Suzy said she got over it and now she likes guys who are relatively nice and stable.

The thing about Tom Toppins, though, is that he really believed things. He wasn't swayed. The same thing that was in the drug dealer in that grimy movie that I absolutely do not recommend is the same thing that was in Tom Toppins: belief. Drug Dealer Dude was not looking for somebody to pat him on the back and teach him things, he was moving, going, sure of something, even if it was all depravity, even if he was leading people into hell. If you believe something, passionately, people will follow you. People hardly care what you believe, as long as you believe something. If you are passionate about something, people will follow you because they think you know something they don't, some clue to the meaning of the universe. Passion is tricky, though, because it can point to nothing as easily as it points to something. If a rapper is passionately rapping about how great his rap is, his passion is pointing to nothing. He isn't helping anything. His beliefs are self-serving and shallow. If a rapper, however, is rapping about his community, about oppression and injustice, then he is passionate about a message, something outside himself. What people believe is important. What

115

people believe is more important than how they look, what their skills are, or their degree of passion. Passion about nothing is like pouring gasoline in a car without wheels. It isn't going to lead anybody anywhere.

My friend Andrew the Protester believes things. Andrew goes to protests where he gets pepper-sprayed, and he does it because he believes in being a voice of change. My Republican friends get frustrated when I paint Andrew as a hero, but I like Andrew because he actually believes things that cost him something. Even if I disagree with Andrew, I love that he is willing to sacrifice for what he believes. And I love that his beliefs are about social causes.

Andrew says it is not enough to be politically active. He says legislation will never save the world. On Saturday mornings Andrew feeds the homeless. He sets up a makeshift kitchen on a sidewalk and makes breakfast for people who live on the street. He serves coffee and sits with his homeless friends and talks and laughs, and if they want to pray he will pray with them. He's a flaming liberal, really. The thing about it is, though, Andrew believes this is what Jesus wants him to do. Andrew does not believe in empty passion.

All great Christian leaders are simple thinkers. Andrew doesn't cloak his altruism within a trickle-down economic theory that allows him to spend fifty dollars on a round of golf to feed the economy and provide jobs for the poor. He actually believes that when Jesus says feed the poor, He means you should do this directly.

Andrew is the one who taught me that what I believe is not what I say I believe; what I believe is what I do.

I used to say that I believed it was important to tell people about Jesus, but I never did. Andrew very kindly explained that if I do not introduce people to Jesus, then I don't believe Jesus is an important person. It doesn't matter what I say. Andrew said

I should not live like a politician, but like a Christian. Like I said, Andrew is a simple thinker.

○   ○   ○

A friend of mine, a young pastor who recently started a church, talks to me from time to time about the new face of church in America—about the postmodern church. He says the new church will be different from the old one, that we will be relevant to culture and the human struggle. I don't think any church has ever been relevant to culture, to the human struggle, unless it believed in Jesus and the power of His gospel. If the supposed new church believes in trendy music and cool Web pages, then it is not relevant to culture either. It is just another tool of Satan to get people to be passionate about nothing.

○   ○   ○

Tony asked me one time if there was anything I would die for. I had to think about it for a long time, and even after thinking about it for a couple of days I had a short list. In the end there weren't very many principles I would die for. I would die for the gospel because I think it is the only revolutionary idea known to man. I would die for Penny, for Laura and Tony. I would die for Rick. Andrew would say that dying for something is easy because it is associated with glory. Living for something, Andrew would say, is the hard thing. Living for something extends beyond fashion, glory, or recognition. We live for what we believe, Andrew would say.

If Andrew the Protester is right, if I live what I believe, then I don't believe very many noble things. My life testifies that the first thing I believe is that I am the most important person in the world. My life testifies to this because I care more about my food and shelter and happiness than about anybody else.

I am learning to believe better things. I am learning to believe that other people exist, that fashion is not truth; rather, Jesus is the most important figure in history, and the gospel is the most powerful force in the universe. I am learning not to be passionate about empty things, but to cultivate passion for justice, grace, truth, and communicate the idea that Jesus likes people and even loves them.

11

Confession

Coming Out of the Closet

WHEN I WAS IN SUNDAY SCHOOL AS A KID, MY teacher put a big poster on the wall that was shaped in a circle like a target. She had us write names of people we knew who weren't Christians on little pieces of paper, and she pinned the names to the outer circle of the target. She said our goal, by the end of the year, was to move those names from the outer ring of the circle, which represented their distance from knowing Jesus, to the inner ring, which represented them having come into a relationship with Jesus. I thought the strategy was beautiful because it gave us a goal, a visual.

I didn't know any people who weren't Christians, but I was a child with a fertile imagination so I made up some names; Thad Thatcher was one and William Wonka was another. My teacher didn't believe me which I took as an insult, but nonetheless, the class was excited the very next week when both Thad and William had become Christians in a dramatic conversion experience that included the dismantling of a large satanic cult and underground drug ring. There was also levitation involved.

Even though they didn't exist, Thad and William were the only people to become Christians all year. Nobody else I knew became a Christian for a very long time, mostly because I didn't tell anybody about Jesus except when I was drunk at a party, and that was only because so many of my reservations were down, and even then nobody understood me because I was either crying or slurring my words.

o   o   o

When I moved downtown to attend Imago-Dei, the church Rick started, he was pretty serious about loving people regardless of whether they considered Jesus the Son of God or not, and Rick wanted to love them because they were either hungry, thirsty, or lonely. The human struggle bothered Rick, as if something was broken in the world and we were supposed to hold our palms against the wound. He didn't really see evangelism, or whatever you want to call it, as a target on a wall in which the goal is to get people to agree with us about the meaning of life. He saw evangelism as reaching a felt need. I thought this was beautiful and frightening. I thought it was beautiful because I had this same need; I mean, I really knew I needed Jesus like I need water or food, and yet it was frightening because Christianity is so stupid to so much of our culture, and I absolutely hate bothering people about this stuff.

So much of me believes strongly in letting everybody live their own lives, and when I share my faith, I feel like a network marketing guy trying to build my down line.

Some of my friends who aren't Christians think that Christians are insistent and demanding and intruding, but that isn't the case. Those folks are the squeaky wheel. Most Christians have enormous respect for the space and freedom of others; it is only that they have found a joy in Jesus they want to share. There is the tension.

In a recent radio interview I was sternly asked by the host, who did not consider himself a Christian, to defend Christianity. I told him that I couldn't do it, and moreover, that I didn't want to defend the term. He asked me if I was a Christian, and I told him yes. "Then why don't you want to defend Christianity?" he asked, confused. I told him I no longer knew what the term meant. Of the hundreds of thousands of people listening to his show that day, some of them had terrible experiences with Christianity; they may have been yelled at by a teacher in a Christian school, abused by a minister, or browbeaten by a Christian parent. To them, the term *Christianity* meant something that no Christian I know would defend. By fortifying the term, I am only making them more and more angry. I won't do it. Stop ten people on the street and ask them what they think of when they hear the word *Christianity,* and they will give you ten different answers. How can I defend a term that means ten different things to ten differ-ent people? I told the radio show host that I would rather talk about Jesus and how I came to believe that Jesus exists and that he likes me. The host looked back at me with tears in his eyes. When we were done, he asked me if we could go get lunch together. He told me how much he didn't like Christianity but how he had always wanted to believe Jesus was the Son of God.

○   ○   ○

For me, the beginning of sharing my faith with people began by throwing out Christianity and embracing Christian spirituality, a nonpolitical mysterious system that can be experienced but not explained. *Christianity,* unlike *Christian spirituality,* was not a term that excited me. And I could not in good conscious tell a friend about a faith that didn't excite me. I couldn't share something I wasn't experiencing. And I wasn't experiencing Christianity. It didn't do anything for me at all. It felt like math, like a system of rights and wrongs and political beliefs, but it wasn't mysterious; it wasn't God reaching out of heaven to do wonderful things in my life. And if I would have shared Christianity with somebody, it would have felt mostly like I was trying to get somebody to agree with me rather than meet God. I could no longer share anything about Christianity, but I loved talking about Jesus and the spirituality that goes along with a relationship with Him.

Tony the Beat Poet says the church is like a wounded animal these days. He says we used to have power and influence, but now we don't, and so many of our leaders are upset about this and acting like spoiled children, mad because they can't have their way. They disguise their actions to look as though they are standing on principle, but it isn't that, Tony says, it's bitterness. They want to take their ball and go home because they have to sit the bench. Tony and I agreed that what God wants us to do is sit the bench in humility and turn the other cheek like Gandhi, like Jesus. We decided that the correct place to share our faith was from a place of humility and love, not from a desire for power.

o   o   o

Each year at Reed they have a festival called Ren Fayre. They shut down the campus so students can party. Security keeps the authorities away, and everybody gets pretty drunk and high, and some people get naked. Friday night is mostly about getting drunk, and Saturday night is about getting high. The school brings in White Bird, a medical unit that specializes in treating bad drug trips. The students create special lounges with black lights and television screens to enhance kids' mushroom trips.

Some of the Christian students in our little group decided this was a pretty good place to come out of the closet, letting everybody know there were a few Christians on campus. Tony the Beat Poet and I were sitting around in my room one afternoon talking about what to do, how to explain who we were to a group of students who, in the past, had expressed hostility toward Christians. Like our friends, we felt like Ren Fayre was the time to do this. I said we should build a confession booth in the middle of campus and paint a sign on it that said "Confess your sins." I said this because I knew a lot of people would be sinning, and Christian spirituality begins by confessing our sins and repenting. I also said it as a joke. But Tony thought it was brilliant. He sat there on my couch with his mind in the clouds, and he was scaring the crap out of me because, for a second, then for a minute, I actually believed he wanted to do it.

"Tony," I said very gently.

"What?" he said, with a blank stare at the opposite wall.

"We are not going to do this," I told him. He moved his gaze down the wall and directly into my eyes. A smile came across his face.

"Oh, we are, Don. We certainly are. We are going to build a confession booth!"

We met in Commons—Penny, Nadine, Mitch, Iven, Tony, and I. Tony said I had an idea. They looked at me. I told them that Tony was lying and I didn't have an idea at all. They looked at Tony. Tony gave me a dirty look and told me to tell them the idea. I told them I had a stupid idea that we couldn't do without getting attacked. They leaned in. I told them that we should build a confession booth in the middle of campus and paint a sign on it that said "Confess your sins." Penny put her hands over her mouth. Nadine smiled. Iven laughed. Mitch started drawing the designs for the booth on a napkin. Tony nodded his head. I wet my pants.

"They may very well burn it down," Nadine said.

"I will build a trapdoor," Mitch said with his finger in the air.

"I like it, Don." Iven patted me on the back.

"I don't want anything to do with it," Penny said.

"Neither do I," I told her.

"Okay, you guys." Tony gathered everybody's attention. "Here's the catch." He leaned in a little and collected his thoughts. "We are not actually going to accept confessions." We all looked at him in confusion. He continued, "We are going to confess to them. We are going to confess that, as followers of Jesus, we have not been very loving; we have been bitter, and for that we are sorry. We will apologize for the Crusades, we will apologize for televangelists, we will apologize for neglecting the poor and the lonely, we will ask them to forgive us, and we will tell them that in our selfishness, we have misrepresented Jesus on this campus. We will tell people who come into the booth that Jesus loves them."

All of us sat there in silence because it was obvious that something beautiful and true had hit the table with a thud. We all thought it was a great idea, and we could see it in each other's eyes. It would feel so good to apologize, to apologize for the Crusades, for Columbus and the genocide he committed in the Bahamas in the name of God, apologize for the missionaries who landed in Mexico and came up through the West slaughtering Indians in the name of Christ. I wanted so desperately to say that none of this was Jesus, and I wanted so desperately to apologize for the many ways I had misrepresented the Lord. I could feel that I had betrayed the Lord by judging, by not being willing to love the people He had loved and only giving lip service to issues of human rights.

For so much of my life I had been defending Christianity because I thought to admit that we had done any wrong was to discredit the religious system as a whole, but it isn't a religious system, it is people following Christ; and the important thing to do, the right thing to do, was to apologize for getting in the way of Jesus.

Later I had a conversation with a very arrogant Reed professor in the parking lot in which he asked me what brought me to Reed. I told him I was auditing a class but was really there to interact with the few Christians who studied at Reed. The professor asked me if I was a Christian evangelist. I told him I didn't think I was, that I wouldn't consider myself an evangelist. He went on to compare my work to that of Captain Cook, who had attempted to bring Western values to indigenous people of Hawaii. He looked me in the eye and said the tribes had killed Cook.

He did not wish me a greater fate at Reed.

All the way home on my motorcycle I fumed and imagined beating the professor into a pulp right there in the parking lot. I could see his sly smile, his intellectual pride. Sure, Christians had done terrible things to humanity, but I hadn't. I had never killed anybody at all. And those people weren't following Jesus when they committed those crimes against humanity. They were government people, and government always uses God to manipulate the masses into following them.

Both Clinton and Bush claim to be followers of Jesus. Anybody who wants to get their way says that Jesus supports their view. But that isn't Jesus' fault. Tony had come to campus a few days earlier, a bit sad in the face. He had seen a bumper sticker on one of the cars in the parking lot that read "Too bad we can't feed Christians to the lions anymore."

I prayed about getting in the confession booth. I wondered whether I could apologize and mean it. I wondered whether I could humble myself to a culture that, to some degree, had wronged us. But I could see in Penny's face, in Iven's eyes, that this was what they wanted; they wanted to love these people, their friends, and it didn't matter to them what it cost. They didn't care how much they had been hurt, and they certainly had more scars than either Tony or I, and so we bought the wood and stored it in my garage, and Friday night we went to the Thesis parade and watched everybody get drunk and beat drums and dance in the spray of beer. Tony and I dressed like monks and smoked pipes and walked among the anarchy, becoming soaked in all the alcohol spewing from within the crowds. People would come up to us and ask what we were doing, and we told them that the next day we would be on campus to take confessions. They looked at us in amazement, sometimes asking us whether we were serious. We told them to come and see us, that we were going to build a confession booth.

The next morning, while everybody was sleeping off their hangovers, Mitch, Tony, and I started building the thing. Mitch had the plans drawn out. The booth was huge, much bigger than I expected, almost like a shed complete with a slanted roof and two small sections inside, one for the monk and the other for the confessor. We built a half-high wall between the two rooms and installed a curtain so the confessor could easily get in and out. On our side we installed a door with a latch so nobody could come in and drag us away. Nadine painted "Confession Booth" in large letters on the outside of the booth.

As the campus started to gather energy, people walking along the sidewalk would ask what we were doing. They stood there looking at the booth in wonder. "What are we supposed to do?" they would ask. "Confess your sins," we told them. "To who?" they would say. "To God," we would tell them. "There is no God," they would explain. Some of them told us this was the boldest thing they had ever seen. All of them were kind, which surprised us.

I stood there outside the booth as a large blue mob started running across campus, all of them, more than a hundred people, naked and painted with blue paint. They ran by the booth screaming and waving. I waved back. Naked people look funny when they are for-real naked, outside-a-magazine naked.

Saturday evening at Ren Fayre is alive and fun. The sun goes down over campus, and shortly after dark they shoot fireworks over the tennis courts. Students lay themselves out on a hill and laugh and point in bleary-eyed fascination. The highlight of the evening is a glow opera that packs the amphitheater with students and friends. The opera is designed to enhance mushroom trips. The actors wear all black and carry colorful puppets and cutouts that come alive in the black light. Everybody ooohs and aaahs.

The party goes till nearly dawn, so though it was late we started working the booth. We lit tiki torches and mounted them in the ground just outside the booth. Tony and Iven were saying that I should go first, which I didn't want to do, but I played bold and got in the booth. I sat on a bucket and watched the ceiling and the smoke from my pipe gather in the dark corners like ghosts. I could hear the rave happening in the student center across campus. I was picturing all the cool dancers, the girls in white shirts moving through the black light, the guys with the turntables in the loft, the big screen with the swirling images and all that energy coming out of the speakers, pounding through everybody's bodies, getting everybody up and down, up and down. *Nobody is going to confess anything,* I thought. *Who wants to stop dancing to confess their sins?* And I realized that this was a bad idea, that none of this was God's idea. Nobody was going to get angry, but nobody was going to care very much either.

There is nothing relevant about Christian spirituality, I kept thinking. God, if He is even there, has no voice in this place. Everybody wants to have a conversation about truth, but there isn't any truth anymore. The only truth is what is cool, what is on television, what protest is going on on what block, and it doesn't matter the issue; it only matters who is going to be there and will there be a party later and can any of us feel like we are relevant while we are at the party. And in the middle of it we are like Mormons on bikes. I sat there wondering whether any of this was true, whether Christian spirituality was even true at all. You never question the truth of something until you have to explain it to a skeptic. I didn't feel like explaining it very much. I didn't feel like being in the booth or wearing that stupid monk outfit. I wanted to go to the rave. Everybody in there was cool, and we were just religious.

I was going to tell Tony that I didn't want to do it when he opened the curtain and said we had our first customer.

"What's up, man?" Duder sat himself on the chair with a smile on his face. He told me my pipe smelled good.

"Thanks," I said. I asked him his name, and he said his name was Jake. I shook his hand because I didn't know what to do, really.

"So, what is this? I'm supposed to tell you all of the juicy gossip I did at Ren Fayre, right?" Jake said.

"No."

"Okay, then what? What's the game?" He asked.

"Not really a game. More of a confession thing."

"You want me to confess my sins, right?"

"No, that's not what we're doing, really."

"What's the deal, man? What's with the monk outfit?"

"Well, we are, well, a group of Christians here on campus, you know."

"I see. Strange place for Christians, but I am listening."

"Thanks," I told him. He was being very patient and gracious. "Anyway, there is this group of us, just a few of us who were thinking about the way Christians have sort of wronged people over time. You know, the Crusades, all that stuff . . ."

"Well, I doubt you personally were involved in any of that, man."

"No, I wasn't," I told him. "But the thing is, we are followers of Jesus. We believe that He is God and all, and He represented certain ideas that we have sort of not done a good job at representing. He has asked us to represent Him well, but it can be very hard."

"I see," Jake said.

"So there is this group of us on campus who wanted to confess to you."

"You are confessing to me!" Jake said with a laugh.

"Yeah. We are confessing to you. I mean, I am confessing to you."

"You're serious." His laugh turned to something of a straight face.

I told him I was. He looked at me and told me I didn't have to. I told him I did, and I felt very strongly in that moment that I was supposed to tell Jake that I was sorry about everything.

"What are you confessing?" he asked.

I shook my head and looked at the ground. "Everything," I told him.

"Explain," he said.

"There's a lot. I will keep it short," I started. "Jesus said to feed the poor and to heal the sick. I have never done very much about that. Jesus said to love those who persecute me. I tend to lash out, especially if I feel threatened, you know, if my ego gets threatened. Jesus did not mix His spirituality with politics. I grew up doing that. It got in the way of the central message of Christ. I know that was wrong, and I know that a lot of people will not listen to the words of Christ because people like me, who know Him, carry our own agendas into the conversation rather than just relaying the message Christ wanted to get across. There's a lot more, you know."

"It's all right, man," Jake said, very tenderly. His eyes were starting to water.

"Well," I said, clearing my throat, "I am sorry for all of that."

"I forgive you," Jake said. And he meant it.

"Thanks," I told him.

He sat there and looked at the floor, then into the fire of a candle. "It's really cool what you guys are doing," he said. "A lot of people need to hear this."

"Have we hurt a lot of people?" I asked him.

"You haven't hurt me. I just think it isn't very popular to be a Christian, you know. Especially at a place like this. I don't think too many people have been hurt. Most people just have a strong reaction to what they see on television. All these well-dressed preachers supporting the Republicans."

"That's not the whole picture," I said. "That's just television. I have friends who are giving their lives to feed the poor and defend the defenseless. They are doing it for Christ."

"You really believe in Jesus, don't you?" he asked me.

"Yes, I think I do. Most often I do. I have doubts at times, but mostly I believe in Him. It's like there is something in me that causes me to believe, and I can't explain it."

"You said earlier that there was a central message of Christ. I don't really want to become a Christian, you know, but what is that message?"

"The message is that man sinned against God and God gave the world over to man, and that if somebody wanted to be rescued out of that, if somebody for instance finds it all very empty, that Christ will rescue them if they want; that if they ask forgiveness for being a part of that rebellion then God will forgive them."

"What is the deal with the cross?" Jake asked.

"God says the wages of sin is death," I told him. "And Jesus died so that none of us would have to. If we have faith in that then we are Christians."

"That is why people wear crosses?" he asked.

"I guess. I think it is sort of fashionable. Some people believe that if they have a cross around their neck or tatooed on them or something, it has some sort of mystical power."

"Do you believe that?" Jake asked.

"No," I answered. I told him that I thought mystical power came through faith in Jesus.

"What do you believe about God?" I asked him.

"I don't know. I guess I didn't believe for a long time, you know. The science of it is so sketchy. I guess I believe in God though. I believe somebody is responsible for all of this, this world we live in. It is all very confusing."

"Jake, if you want to know God, you can. I am just saying if you ever want to call on Jesus, He will be there."

"Thanks, man. I believe that you mean that." His eyes were watering again. "This is cool what you guys are doing," he repeated. "I am going to tell my friends about this."

"I don't know whether to thank you for that or not," I laughed. "I have to sit here and confess all my crap."

He looked at me very seriously. "It's worth it," he said. He shook my hand, and when he left the booth there was somebody else ready to get in. It went like that for a couple of hours. I talked to about thirty people, and Tony took confessions on a picnic table outside the booth. Many people wanted to hug when we were done. All of the people who visited the booth were grateful and gracious. I was being changed through the process. I went in with doubts and came out believing so strongly in Jesus I was ready to die and be with Him. I think that night was the beginning of change for a lot of us.

Iven started taking a group to a local homeless shelter to feed the poor, and he often had to turn students away because the van wouldn't hold more than twenty or so. We held an event called Poverty Day where we asked students to live on less than three dollars a day to practice solidarity with the poor. More than one hundred students participated. Penny spoke in Vollum Lounge on the topic of poverty in India, and more than seventy-five students came. Before any of this, our biggest event had about ten people. We hosted an evening where we asked students to come and voice their hostility against Christians. We answered questions about what we believed and explained our love for people, for the hurting, and we apologized again for our own wrongs against humanity and asked for forgiveness from the Reed community. We enjoyed the new friendships we received, and at one time had four different Bible studies on campus specifically for people who did not consider themselves Christians. We watched a lot of students take a second look at Christ. But mostly, we as Christians felt right with the people around us. Mostly we felt forgiven and grateful.

Sometime around two or three in the morning, the night we took confessions, I was walking off the campus with my monk robe under my arm, and when I got to the large oak trees on the outskirts of the font lawn, I turned and looked at the campus. It all looked so smart and old, and I could see the lights coming out of the Student Center, and I could hear the music thumping. There were kids making out on the lawn and chasing each other down the sidewalks. There was laughing and dancing and throwing up.

I felt very strongly that Jesus was relevant in this place. I felt very strongly that if He was not relevant here then He was not relevant anywhere. I felt very peaceful in that place and very sober. I felt very connected to God because I had confessed so much to so many people and had gotten so much off my chest and I had been forgiven by the people I had wronged with my indifference and judgmentalism. I was going to sit there for a little while, but it was cold and the grass was damp. I went home and fell asleep on the couch and the next morning made coffee and sat on the porch at Graceland and wondered whether the things that happened the night before had actually happened. I was out of the closet now. A Christian. So many years before I had made amends to God, but now I had made amends to the world. I was somebody who was willing to share my faith. It felt kind of cool, kind of different. It was very relieving.

12

Church

How I Go Without Getting Angry

IT SHOULD BE SAID I AM AN INDEPENDENT PERSON. I don't like institutionalized anything. I don't like corporations. I am not saying institutions and corporations are wrong, or bad; I am only saying I don't like them. Some people don't like classical music, some people don't like pizza, I don't like institutions. My dislike might stem from a number of things, from the nonpersonal feel I get when I walk into a corporate office or the voice-mail system I encounter when I call my bank. It might be the nonengaged look on every fast-food worker's face or the phone calls I receive in the middle of dinner asking me what long-distance carrier I use. Those people never want to just talk; they always have an agenda.

My dislike for institutions is mostly a feeling, though, not something that can be explained. There are upsides to institutions, of course. Tradition, for example. The corridors at Harvard, rich with history, thick with thought, the availability of good, hot Starbucks coffee at roughly thirty locations within five miles of my home. And what about all those jobs? Without the corporate machine, where would people work? I suppose we need them. The institutions. The corporations. But mostly I don't like them. I don't have to like them either. It's my right.

I don't like church, either, for the same reason. Or I should say I didn't like church. I like attending a Catholic service every once in a while, but I think that is because it feels different to me. I grew up Baptist. I like watching religious television every once in a while. It's better than Comedy Central. I want to study psychology so I can sit in front of religious television and figure out these people's problems. For a while I was very fascinated with televangelists. I couldn't afford a television ministry but I had a computer, so I would go into Christian chat rooms and try to heal people. It was funny at first, but it got boring.

Some of my friends have left their churches and gone Greek Orthodox. I think that sounds cool. Greek Orthodox. Unless you are Greek. Then it sounds like that is where you are supposed to go, as though you are a conformist. If I were Greek, I would never go to a Greek Orthodox church. If I were Greek, I would go to a Baptist church. Everybody there would think I was exotic and cool.

o   o   o

I go to a church now that I love. I never thought I would say that about a church. I never thought I could love a church. But I love this one. It is called Imago-Dei, which means "Image of God" in Latin. Latin is exotic and cool.

In the churches I used to go to, I felt like I didn't fit in. I always felt like the adopted kid, as if there was "room at the table for me." Do you know what I mean? I was accepted but not understood. There was room at the table for me, but I wasn't in the family.

It doesn't do any good to bash churches, so I am not making

blanket statements against the church as a whole. I have only been involved in a few churches, but I had the same tension with each of them; that's the only reason I bring it up.

○   ○   ○

Here are the things I didn't like about the churches I went to. First: I felt like people were trying to sell me Jesus. I was a salesman for a while, and we were taught that you are supposed to point out all the benefits of a product when you are selling it. That is how I felt about some of the preachers I heard speak. They were always pointing out the benefits of Christian faith. That rubbed me wrong. It's not that there aren't benefits, there are, but did they have to talk about spirituality like it's a vacuum cleaner. I never felt like Jesus was a product. I wanted Him to be a person. Not only that, but they were always pointing out how great the specific church was. The bulletin read like a brochure for Amway. They were always saying how life-changing some conference was going to be. Life-changing? What does that mean? It sounded very suspicious. I wish they would just tell it to me straight rather than trying to sell me on everything. I felt like I got bombarded with commercials all week and then went to church and got even more.

And yet another thing about the churches I went to: They seemed to be parrots for the Republican Party. Do we have to tow the party line on every single issue? Are the Republicans that perfect? I just felt like, in order to be a part of the family, I had to think George W. Bush was Jesus. And I didn't. I didn't think that Jesus really agreed with a lot of the policies of the Republican Party or for that matter the Democratic Party. I felt like Jesus was a religious figure, not a political figure. I heard my pastor say once, when there were only a few of us standing around, that he hated Bill Clinton. I can understand not liking Clinton's policies, but I want my spirituality to rid me of hate, not give me reason for it. I couldn't deal with that. That is one of the main reasons I walked away. I felt like, by going to this particular church, I was a pawn for the Republicans. Meanwhile, the Republicans did not give a crap about the causes of Christ.

Only one more thing that bugged me, then I will shut up about it. War metaphor. The churches I attended would embrace war metaphor. They would talk about how we are in a battle, and I agreed with them, only they wouldn't clarify that we were battling poverty and hate and injustice and pride and the powers of darkness. They left us thinking that our war was against liberals and homosexuals. Their teaching would have me believe I was the good person in the world and the liberals were the bad people in the world. Jesus taught that we are all bad and He is good, and He wants to rescue us because there is a war going on and we are hostages in that war. The truth is we are supposed to love the hippies, the liberals, and even the Democrats, and that God wants us to think of them as more important than ourselves. Anything short of this is not true to the teachings of Jesus.

○   ○   ○

So I was speaking at this twenty-something ministry, speaking to about fifty or so people on Sunday nights at a church in the suburbs, all the while dying inside. I wasn't even attending the main worship service anymore. The pastor who was in charge of the college group asked me why I wasn't coming to church. He was very kind and sympathetic and said he missed seeing me there.

Tony the Beat Poet says I am not good with diplomacy. He says I speak my mind too much and I should consider the ramifications of my words. I can be a real jerk without even realizing it. I told the guy it was hard for me to go to church without getting angry, and I think he took that personally. I tried to explain how I felt, but I was speaking a different language. I felt stupid, too, like some bitter idiot all wet and wanting everybody to cater to me, to my ideas about who Jesus is and was and the way He wants us to live.

About that time I started asking God to help me find a church where I would fit.

I had this friend from Seattle named Mark who was the pastor of a pretty cool church near the University of Washington, in the village. He had a lot of artists going to his church and a lot of hippies and yuppies and people who listen to public radio. I went up and visited him one time, and I loved the community he had put together. I felt like I could breathe for the first time in years. Visiting Mark's church in Seattle helped me realize I wasn't alone in the world. I would talk to my friends about his church, to my friends at the church I was attending, but they didn't get it.

Mark had written several articles for secular magazines and had been interviewed a few times on the radio and had gotten this reputation as a pastor who said cusswords. It is true that Mark said a lot of cusswords. I don't know why he did it. He didn't become a Christian till he was in college, so maybe he didn't know he wasn't supposed to say cusswords and be a pastor. I think some of my friends believed that it was the goal of the devil to get people to say cusswords, so they thought Mark was possessed or something, and they told me I should not really get into anything he was a part of. Because of the cusswords. But like I said, I was dying inside, and even though Mark said cusswords, he was telling a lot of people about Jesus, and he was being socially active, and he seemed to love a lot of people the church was neglecting, like liberals and fruit nuts. About the time I was praying that God would help me find a church, I got a call from Mark the Cussing Pastor, and he said he had a close friend who was moving to Portland to start a church and that I should join him.

Rick and I got together over coffee, and I thought he was hilarious. He was big, a football player out of Chico State. At the time we both chewed tobacco, so we had that in common. He could do a great Tony Soprano voice, sort of a Mafia thing. He would do this routine where he pretended to be a Mafia boss who was planting a church. He said a few cusswords but not as bad as Mark. Rick said there were a few people meeting at his house to talk about what it might look like to start a church in Portland, and he invited me to come. I could feel that God was answering my prayer so I went. There were only about eight of us, mostly kids, mostly teens just out of high school. I felt like I was at a youth group, honestly. I didn't think the thing was going to fly. Rick's wife made us coffee, and we sat around his living room, and Rick read us some statistics about how very many churches have moved out of the cities and into the suburbs and said how he wanted us to plant in the city. Rick really wanted to redeem the image of the church to people who had false conceptions about it.

Pretty soon there were twenty or so of us, so we got this little chapel at a college near downtown and started having church. It felt funny at church, you know, because there were only twenty of us and it was mostly just kids, but I still believed this was how God was going to answer my prayer.

We didn't grow much, to be honest. We stayed at about thirty or so, all Christians who had moved to Imago from other churches. I know that numbers shouldn't matter very much, but to be honest I kind of wanted Imago to grow because I wanted my friends at my old church to know we were successful; but we didn't grow, we stayed at about thirty.

We'd meet on Sunday nights and then again on Wednesday nights for prayer. A lot less people showed up for prayer. There were only about ten of us, and it was pretty boring. It felt like an AA meeting gone bad. We'd sit around and talk about the crap in our lives, and then we'd pray for a little while, and then we would go home. One night Rick showed up sort of beaten-looking. He had been to some sort of pastors reception where a guy spoke about how the church has lost touch with people who didn't know about Jesus. Rick said he was really convicted about this and asked us if we thought we needed to repent and start loving people who were very different from us. We all told him yes, we did, but I don't think any of us knew what that meant. Rick said he thought it meant we should live missional lives, that we should intentionally befriend people who are different from us. I didn't like the sound of that, to be honest. I didn't want to befriend somebody just to trick them into going to my church. Rick said that was not what he was talking about. He said he was talking about loving people just because they exist—homeless people and Gothic people and gays and fruit nuts. And then I liked the sound of it. I liked the idea of loving people just to love them, not to get them to come to church. If the subject of church came up, I could tell them about Imago, but until then, who cared. So we started praying every week that God would teach us to live missional lives, to notice people who needed to be loved.

Lots of people started coming to church after that. I don't know why, honestly, except that we all agreed we would love people and be nice to them and listen and make friends. As we grew, we had to move into another building and then another one after that and then to another one until we started renting this big, super-old, beautiful church with stained glass windows and a domed ceiling. Shortly after we moved in there we had to go to two services. All of this happened in a couple of years, and now Imago has about five hundred people coming and lots of them look like rock stars, but they are all brilliant and spiritual. I love the community so much it's hard to describe. I have never felt such a feeling of family in all my life. I felt like I had nothing in terms of community and God brought a community up out of the ground, out of pure nothing like a magic trick.

Like I said before, I never thought I would love church. But here is what I love about Imago-Dei.

First: It is spiritual. What I mean is the people at Imago pray and fast about things. It took me a while to understand that the answer to problems was not marketing or program but rather spirituality. If we needed to reach youth, we wouldn't do a pizza feed and a game night, we would get together and pray and fast and ask God what to do. God led some guys to start a homeless teen outreach downtown, and now they feed about one hundred homeless teenagers every week. It is the nuttiest youth group you will ever see, but that is what God said to do. I love that sort of thing because rather than the church serving itself, the church is serving the lost and lonely. It gives me chills when I think about it because it is that beautiful of a thing.

Second: Art. Imago supports the arts. Rick isn't much of an artist, but he turned things over to a guy named Peter Jenkins, who created the drawings for this book. Peter started an "artis-tery" where artists live and create art, teach art, and encourage people to be creative. Peter recently held a gallery opening in a local coffeehouse, and all the art was created by people who attend Imago. Artists feel at home at Imago. I even led a short-story group where we wrote short stories and then had a read-ing under Christmas lights and candles over at the artistery. I think there are artists at a lot of churches who don't have an outlet, and by creating an outlet, the church gives artists a chance to express themselves and in return the church gets free stuff to put on their walls. Creating an arts group at a church is a great idea.

Third: Community. Rick is very, very serious about people living together, eating together, and playing together. He encourages young single people to get houses and live with each other. Rick doesn't like it when people are lonely. We have home communities that meet all over town, and we consider this to be the heart of our church. Almost every church I have ever been to already does a great job at this.

Fourth: Authenticity. This is something of a buzzword, I know, but Imago actually lives this. I speak from the pulpit at Imago from time to time, and I am completely comfortable saying anything I like. I don't have to pretend to be godly in order for people to listen. Authenticity is an enormous value at Imago. I love this because by being true I am allowing people to get to know the real me, and it feels better to have people love the real me than the me I invented.

o   o   o

So one of the things I had to do after God provided a church for me was to let go of any bad attitude I had against the other churches I'd gone to. In the end, I was just different, you know. It wasn't that they were bad, they just didn't do it for me. I read through the book of Ephesians four times one night in Eugene Peterson's *The Message,* and it seemed to me that Paul did not want Christians to fight with one another. He seemed to care a great deal about this, so, in my mind, I had to tell my heart to love the people at the churches I used to go to, the people who were different from me. This was entirely freeing because when I told my heart to do this, my heart did it, and now I think very fondly of those wacko Republican fundamentalists, and I know that they love me, too, and I know that we will eat together, we will break bread together in heaven, and we will love each other so purely it will hurt because we are a family in Christ.

So here is a step-by-step formula for how you, too, can go to church without getting angry:

- Pray that God will show you a church filled with people who share your interests and values.

- Go to the church God shows you.

- Don't hold grudges against any other churches. God loves those churches almost as much as He loves yours.

13

Romance

Meeting Girls Is Easy

MY FRIEND KURT USED TO SAY FINDING A WIFE IS a percentage game. He said you have to have two or three relationships going at once, never letting the one girl know about the others, always "moving in to close the deal." One of them, he said, is bound to work out, and if you lose one, you just pick up another. Kurt believed you had to date about twenty girls before you found the one you were going to marry. He just believed it was easier to date them all at once. Kurt ended up marrying a girl from Dallas, and everybody says he married her for her money. He is very happy.

Elsewhere in the quandary is my friend Josh. When I first moved to Oregon I was befriended by this vibrant kid who read a lot of the Bible. Josh was good-looking and obsessed with dating, philosophies of dating, social rituals, and that sort of thing. He was homeschooled and raised to believe traditional dating was a bad idea. I traveled with him around the country and introduced him at seminars he would conduct on the pitfalls of dating. He wrote a book about it, and it hit the bestseller list. No kidding. A couple years later he moved to Baltimore and got married. I called him after the wedding and asked him how he got to know his wife without dating. He said they courted, which I understood to mean he had become Amish. But he explained courting is a lot like dating without the head games. He and his wife are also very happy.

My friend Mike Tucker reads books about dating and knows a lot on the subject. He says things like "You know, Don, relationships are like rubber bands . . . When one person pulls away, the other is attracted, and when the other person pulls away, well, that just draws the other one even closer." That sort of thing is interesting to a guy like me because I know nothing about dating. What little I know about dating is ridiculous and wouldn't help rabbits reproduce. I know you shouldn't make fun of a girl on a date and you shouldn't eat spaghetti. Other than these two things I am clueless.

Here's a tip I've never used: I understand you can learn a great deal about girldom by reading *Pride and Prejudice,* and I own a copy, but I have never read it. I tried. It was given to me by a girl with a little note inside that read: *What is in this book is the heart of a woman.* I am sure the heart of a woman is pure and lovely, but the first chapter of said heart is hopelessly boring. Nobody dies at all. I keep the book on my shelf because girls come into my room, sit on my couch, and eye the books on the adjacent shelf. You have a copy of *Pride and Prejudice,* they exclaim in a gentle sigh and smile. Yes, I say. Yes, I do.

o   o   o

Not long ago I went to Yosemite with my Canadian friend Julie. I have a weakness for Canadian girls. I don't know why, but when a Canadian girl asks me what I am thinking "aboat," I go nuts. So I have had this secret crush on Julie for a while, but she likes guys who surf and skateboard and jump out of airplanes with snowboards. I pretty much don't fit that description. I read books by dead guys. This is my identity. Besides, when Julie and I met I was in a relationship with a cute writer from the South, and Julie liked some other guy who could skateboard and play guitar. The thing with the writer didn't work out, however, because though we had everything in common we could not connect in the soul. So it happened that I was speaking in San Francisco and Julie was traveling around California and happened to be in a hostel in the city while I was there.

So I went to pick her up, and later we were driving through the Sierra Nevadas and I was nervous because she was much prettier than I remembered and we were making small talk about what we wanted in a mate, what we expected in marriage and that sort of thing. I kept wanting to say, Well, I want a tall Canadian girl who sings and plays the guitar, and is, um, not Alanis Morisette. But I couldn't say that because Julie would have been onto me. So I just told her I wanted a girl who would be a good mom, a girl who could go deep and meaningful with me spiritually, a girl who was good in bed. I said all the cliché stuff, the stuff that has been true for centuries. But then I opened my big stupid mouth and said that I thought, honestly, there really wasn't any such thing as true, true love. I was feeling tired when I said it. I don't know why I said it.

I kept talking with my stupid mouth. I told her that love, or what we call love, is mostly teamwork and that, quite possibly, I would get a crush on another woman after I had been married for a while. I also mentioned that my wife might become attracted to another man. The stuff that attracts us to other people doesn't shut down just because we walk down the aisle, I said. I was going on like this, being a realist and all, and I suspect I was saying stupid things like this because I have not read

Pride and Prejudice because it turns out these ideas are not the keys to a woman's heart. Julie believed that there was such a thing as true love and she would be in love with her mate forever and that he would be in love with her forever too.

Julie hated my ideas. She said nothing like that would ever happen to her, that her husband would love her passionately and adore her until one of them died. She did not really want to talk about my ideas. I just sat there feeling stupid. I do this a great deal in my life.

The next day, on the way to Santa Cruz, I told her I had a crush on her, which was stupid because I knew she didn't feel the same. I was only hoping she did. I did it very stupidly, very sheepishly. I just sort of stumbled around in my mouth, and my heart was beating very fast. Julie was very kind, but we sort of let it go and pretended the idea was never spoken. The rest of the time we made small talk and listened to Patty Griffin, which was helpful because Patty Griffin has always been very comforting to me.

I think if you like somebody you have to tell them. It might be embarrassing to say it, but you will never regret stepping up. I know from personal experience, however, that you should not keep telling a girl that you like her after she tells you she isn't into it. You should not keep riding your bike by her house either.

o o o

I don't want to get married right away. I think it will take me a while after I meet a girl. I like being single. I am one of the few who like it. I want to marry a girl who, when I am with her, makes me feel alone. I guess what I am saying is, I want to marry a girl whom I feel completely comfortable with, comfortable being myself. I can be very immature and awkward in moments, and I want to be able to be like that with her and not have her walk away or be embarrassed.

I've had about fifty people tell me that I fear intimacy. And it is true. I fear what people will think of me, and that is the reason I don't date very often. People really like me a lot when they only know me a little, but I have this great fear that if they knew me a lot they wouldn't like me. That is the number one thing that scares me about having a wife because she would have to know me pretty well in order to marry me and I think if she got to know me pretty well she wouldn't like me anymore.

My best friend, Paul, married my friend Danielle. People change when they get married, it is true. Danielle was a fiery feminist when she married Paul; now she isn't so much a feminist, or at least she isn't active. She is very much in love with him, and he with her. Sometimes, when I am visiting them, they grab each other's butts as if I am not even in the room. It's embarrassing. People shouldn't grab each other's butts with me sitting there in the room. Paul and Danielle have been married almost seven years and have three children, three girls. I was in the wedding. I read a poem. I look incredibly handsome and skinny in the pictures. Paul looked like Brad Pitt, and Danielle, who is hopelessly beautiful, looked like a flower or a beautiful painting.

For a while after the wedding, we all lived together in an enormous old house on Kearney Street in Portland. It was Wes and Maja's house, Danielle's aunt and uncle. The house once belonged to the Hall of Fame basketball player Bill Walton, and they say when Patty Hearst was kidnapped by the S.L.A., she was held captive in the basement. The old guy who lived next door said Walton used to have the Grateful Dead over and they would do concerts on the porch. On a dry day you can smell the marijuana residue in the woodwork.

It was an enormous house, and I lived in the attic. Paul and

Danielle lived in the grand room which was big enough to make into an apartment. Occasionally Paul would come up to the attic, and we would crawl out the window to the roof where we would smoke pipes above the city.

"How is married life?" I once asked.

"It's good. It's tough, but it is good."

"What is tough about it?" I asked.

Paul is the only person I know who is completely comfortable in his own skin, completely true in what he says. He is what they call a true person. "You know, Don, marriage is worth the trade. You lose all your freedom, but you get this friend. This incredible friend."

I wondered about that when he said it. The idea of marriage is remarkably frightening to me for precisely this reason: the loss of freedom. I am not somebody who needs constant company. I don't often get lonely. I live in community because it is healthy, because people who live alone for too long are more likely to go goofy, but the idea of coming home to a woman, day after day, living in the same house and sharing a bath and a bed and having things pink and silky lying around on the floor strikes this chord in me like a prison door clanging shut. I can just see myself standing there watching her take her makeup off in the bathroom and thinking, *She really isn't going to leave. All her stuff is here now.*

Tony the Beat Poet says I am finicky, that the longest I have been in love is eight minutes. That really isn't true. I just get crushes very quickly, like lightning or something, and then they go away. Mostly they go away because I am afraid to do anything about them. I am afraid of rejection, and I am afraid that I won't feel the same way tomorrow, and I have no faith in the system that God made.

Penny says I have a skewed view of relationships because I have issues with intimacy, and when I talk to Nadine about girls she just looks at me with her dignified stare, making knowing noises like a therapist. That's interesting, she says to me. Very interesting.

I know they all think I am selfish. And I am. I want a girl, but I want her every few days, not every day. I want her to have her own house and to come over only when I feel like shaving.

○   ○   ○

"It isn't what you think it is, Don." Paul takes his gaze from the city and eyes the pipe in his hand. He turns it over and taps the top ash onto the roof, rolling the embers under his sneakers.

"What isn't?"

"Marriage." He looks me in the eye. "It isn't fulfilling in the way you think it is."

"Paul, will you be honest with me if I ask you something?"

"Yes."

"Are you happy?"

"Define happy."

"Are you glad you married Danielle?"

Paul puts the stem of his pipe back in his mouth.

"I am happy, Don. I am very happy."

"What do you mean it isn't what I think it is then?" I was expecting him to talk about sex.

"Well, maybe I can't say what you think marriage is. Maybe I should say it isn't what I thought it would be. I thought to be married was to be known. And it is; it is to be known. But Danielle can only know me so much; do you know what I mean?"

"There are things you haven't told her?" I ask.

"I've told her everything."

"Then I don't know what you are saying."

Paul pushed himself up a little to the pitch of the roof from which you can see the Portland skyline. I joined him. "We all want to be loved, right?"

"Right."

"And the scary thing about relationships, intimate relationships, is that if somebody gets to know us, the us that we usually hide, they might not love us; they might reject us."

"Right," I tell him.

Paul continued. "I'm saying there is stuff I can't tell her, not because I don't want to, but because there aren't words. It's like we are separate people, and there is no getting inside each other to read each other's thoughts, each other's beings. Marriage is amazing because it is the closest two people can get, but they can't get all the way to that place of absolute knowing. Marriage is the most beautiful thing I have ever dreamed of, Don, but it isn't everything. It isn't Mecca. Danielle loves everything about me; she accepts me and tolerates me and encourages me. She knows me better than anybody else in the world, but she doesn't know all of me, and I don't know all of her. And I never thought after I got married there would still be something lacking. I always thought marriage, especially after I first met Danielle, would be the ultimate fulfillment. It is great, don't get me wrong, and I am glad I married Danielle, and I will be with her forever. But there are places in our lives that only God can go."

"So marriage isn't all that it is cracked up to be?" I ask.

"No, it is so much more than I ever thought it would be. One of the ways God shows me He loves me is through Danielle, and one of the ways God shows Danielle He loves her is through me. And because she loves me, and teaches me that I am lovable, I can better interact with God."

"What do you mean?"

"I mean that to be in a relationship with God is to be loved purely and furiously. And a person who thinks himself unlovable cannot be in a relationship with God because he can't accept who God is; a Being that is love. We learn that we are lovable or unlovable from other people," Paul says. "That is why God tells us so many times to love each other."

When the sky got dark Paul and I went back into the attic. We made small talk for an hour before he went downstairs to be with his wife, but I kept thinking about these things. I turned out the light and lay in my bed and thought about the girls I had dated, the fear I have of getting married, and the incredible selfishness from which I navigate my existence.

○　　○　　○

I had been working on a play called *Polaroids* that year. It was the story of one man's life from birth to death, each scene delivered through a monologue with other actors silently acting out parts behind the narrator as he walks the audience through his life journey. In the scene I had written a few nights before, I had the man fighting with his wife. They were experiencing unbearable tension after losing a son in a car accident the year before. I knew in my heart they were not going to make it, that *Polaroids* would include a painful divorce that showed the ugliness of separation. But I changed my mind. After talking with Paul I couldn't do it. I wondered what it would look like to have the couple stick it out. I got up and turned on my computer. I had the lead character in my play walk into the bedroom where his wife was sleeping. I had him kneel down by her and whisper some lines:

What great gravity is this that drew my soul toward yours? What great force, that though I went falsely, went kicking, went disguising myself to earn your love, also disguised, to earn your keeping, your resting, your staying, your will fleshed into mine, rasped by a slowly revealed truth, the barter of my soul, the soul that I fear, the soul that I loathe, the soul that: if you will love, I will love. I will redeem you, if you will redeem me? Is this our purpose, you and I together to pacify each other, to lead each other toward the lie that we are good, that we are noble, that we need not redemption, save the one that you and I invented of our own clay?

I am not scared of you, my love, I am scared of me.

I went looking, I wrote out a list, I drew an image, I bled a poem of you. You were pretty, and my friends believed I was worthy of you. You were clever, but I was smarter, perhaps the only one smarter, the only one able to lead you. You see, love, I did not love you, I loved me. And you were only a tool that I used to fix myself, to fool myself, to redeem myself. And though I have taught you to lay your lily hand in mine, I walk alone, for I cannot talk to you, lest you talk it back to me, lest I believe that I am not worthy, not deserving, not redeemed.

I want desperately for you to be my friend. But you are not my friend; you have slid up warmly to the man I wanted to be, the man I pretended to be, and I was your Jesus and, you were mine. Should I show you who I am, we may crumble. I am not scared of you, my love, I am scared of me.

I want to be known and loved anyway. Can you do this? I trust by your easy breathing that you are human like me, that you are fallen like me, that you are lonely, like me. My love, do I know you? What is this great gravity that pulls us so painfully toward each other? Why do we not connect? Will we be forever in fleshing this out? And how will we with words, narrow words, come into the knowing of each other? Is this God's way of meriting grace, of teaching us of the labyrinth of His love for us, teaching us, in degrees, that which He is sacrificing to join ourselves to Him? Or better yet, has He formed our being fractional so that we might conclude one great hope, plodding and sighing and breathing into one another in such a great push that we might break through into the known and being loved, only to cave into a greater perdition and fall down at His throne still begging for our acceptance? Begging for our completion?

We were fools to believe that we would redeem each other.

Were I some sleeping Adam, to wake and find you resting at my rib, to share these things that God has done, to walk you through the garden, to counsel your timid steps, your bewildered eye, your heart so slow to love, so careful to love, so sheepish that I stepped up my aim and became a man. Is this what God intended? That though He made you from my rib, it is you who is making me, humbling me, destroying me, and in so doing revealing Him.

Will we be in ashes before we are one?

What great gravity is this that drew my heart toward yours? What great force collapsed my orbit, my lonesome state? What is this that wants in me the want in you? Don't we go at each other with yielded eyes, with cumbered hands and feet, with clunky tongues? This deed is unattainable! We cannot know each other!

I am quitting this thing, but not what you think. I am not going away.

I will give you this, my love, and I will not bargain or barter any longer. I will love you, as sure as He has loved me. I will discover what I can discover and though you remain a mystery, save God's own knowledge, what I disclose of you I will keep in the warmest chamber of my heart, the very chamber where God has stowed Himself in me. And I will do this to my death, and to death it may bring me.

I will love you like God, because of God, mighted by the power of God. I will stop expecting your love, demanding your love, trading for your love, gaming for your love. I will simply love. I am giving myself to you, and tomorrow I will do it again. I suppose the clock itself will wear thin its time before I am ended at this altar of dying and dying again.

God risked Himself on me. I will risk myself on you. And together, we will learn to love, and perhaps then, and only then, understand this gravity that drew Him, unto us.

14

Alone

Fifty-three Years in Space

I WAS IN LOVE ONCE. I THINK LOVE IS A BIT OF heaven. When I was in love I thought about that girl so much I felt like I was going to die and it was beautiful, and she loved me, too, or at least she said she did, and we were not about ourselves, we were about each other, and that is what I mean when I say being in love is a bit of heaven. When I was in love I hardly thought of myself; I thought of her and how beautiful she looked and whether or not she was cold and how I could make her laugh. It was wonderful because I forgot my problems. I owned her problems instead, and her problems seemed romantic and beautiful. When I was in love there was somebody in the world who was more important than me, and that, given all that happened at the fall of man, is a miracle, like something God forgot to curse.

I no longer think being in love is the polar opposite of being alone, however. I say that because I used to want to be in love again as I assumed this was the opposite of loneliness. I think being in love is an opposite of loneliness, but not the opposite. There are other things I now crave when I am lonely, like community, like friendship, like family. I think our society puts too much pressure on romantic love, and that is why so many romances fail. Romance can't possibly carry all that we want it to.

Tony the Beat Poet says the words *alone, lonely,* and *loneliness* are three of the most powerful words in the English language. I agree with Tony. Those words say that we are human; they are like the words *hunger* and *thirst.* But they are not words about the body, they are words about the soul.

I am something of a recluse by nature. I am that cordless screwdriver that has to charge for twenty hours to earn ten minutes use. I need that much downtime. I am a terrible daydreamer. I have been since I was a boy. My mind goes walking and playing and skipping. I invent characters, write stories, pretend I am a rock star, pretend I am a legendary poet, pretend I am an astronaut, and there is no control to my mind.

When you live on your own for a long time, however, your personality changes because you go so much into yourself you lose the ability to be social, to understand what is and isn't normal behavior. There is an entire world inside yourself, and if you let yourself, you can get so deep inside it you will forget the way to the surface. Other people keep our souls alive, just like food and water does with our body.

A few years back some friends and I hiked to Jefferson Park, high on the Pacific Crest Trail at the base of Mount Jefferson. One evening we were sitting around a campfire telling stories when we spotted a ranger slowly walking toward our camp. He was a small man, thin, but he moved slowly as though he was tired. He ascended the small slope toward our fire by pushing his hands against his knees. When he met us he did not introduce himself, he only gazed into the fire for a while. We addressed him, and he nodded. He kindly asked to see our permits. We went to our tents and to our backpacks and brought the permits to him unfolded. He studied each of them slowly, staring at the documents as if he had slipped into a daydream. They were simple documents, really, just green slips of paper with a signature. But he eyed them like moving pictures, like cartoons. Eventually he handed our permits back to us, smiling, nodding, looking awfully queer. And then he stood there. He leaned against a tree only two feet from our campfire and watched us. We asked him a few questions, asked him if he needed anything else, but he kindly said no. Finally, I figured it out.

He was lonely. He was alone and going nuts.

He had forgotten how to engage people. I asked him how long he had been at Jeff Park. Two months, he said. Two months, I asked, all by yourself? Yeah, he said and smiled. That's a long time to be alone, I told him. Well, he said to me, this conversation has worn me out. He put his hands in his pockets and smiled again. He looked out into the distance and stretched his neck to look at the stars.

"Do believe I will head back to camp," he said. He didn't say good-bye. He walked down the little hill and into the darkness.

o   o   o

I know about that feeling, that feeling of walking out into the darkness. When I lived alone it was very hard for me to be around people. I would leave parties early. I would leave church before worship was over so I didn't have to stand around and talk. The presence of people would agitate me. I was so used to being able to daydream and keep myself company that other people were an intrusion. It was terribly unhealthy.

o   o   o

My friend Mike Tucker loves people. He says if he isn't around people for a long time he starts to lose it, starts to talk to himself, making up stories. Before he moved to Portland he was a long-haul trucker, which is a no-good job for a guy who doesn't do well alone. He said one time, on a trip from Los Angeles to Boston, he had a three-hour conversation with Abraham Lincoln. He said it was amazing. I bet it was, I told him. Tuck said Mr. Lincoln was very humble and brilliant and best of all a good listener.

Tuck said prostitutes would hang out at truck stops, going from truck to truck asking the guys if they needed company. He said one night he got so lonely he almost asked a girl to come in. He didn't even want to have sex. He just wanted a girl to hold him, wanted somebody with skin on, somebody who would listen and talk back with a real voice when he asked a question.

Sometimes when I go to bed at night or when I first wake up in the morning, I talk to my pillow as if it were a woman, a make-believe wife. I tell her I love her and that she's a beautiful wife and all. I don't know if I do this because I am lonely or not. Tuck says I do this because I am horny. He says loneliness is real painful, and I will know it when I feel it. I think it is interesting that God designed people to need other people. We see those cigarette advertisements with the rugged cowboy riding around alone on a horse, and we think that is strength, when, really, it is like setting your soul down on a couch and not exercising it. The soul needs to interact with other people to be healthy.

o   o   o

A long time ago I was holed up in an apartment outside Portland. I was living with a friend, but he had a girlfriend across town and was spending his time with her, even his nights. I didn't have a television. I ate by myself and washed clothes by myself and didn't bother keeping the place clean because I didn't know anybody who would be coming by. I would talk to myself sometimes, my voice coming back funny off the walls and the ceiling. I would play records and pretend I was the singer. I did a great Elvis. I would read the poetry of Emily Dickinson out loud and pretend to have conversations with her. I asked her what she meant by "zero at the bone," and I asked her if she was a lesbian. For the record, she told me she wasn't a lesbian. She was sort of offended by the question, to be honest. Emily Dickinson was the most interesting person I'd ever met. She was lovely, really, sort of quiet like a scared dog, but she engaged fine when she warmed up to me. She was terribly brilliant.

I had been living in that apartment for two years when I decided to cross the country to visit Amherst, Massachusetts, where Emily lived and died. Back then I imagined her as the perfect woman, so quietly brilliant all those years, wrapping her poems neatly in bundles of paper and rope. I confess I daydreamed about living in her Amherst, in her century, befriending her during her days at Holyoke Seminary, walking with her through those summer hills she spoke so wonderfully of, the hills that, in the morning, untied their bonnets. My friend Laura at Reed tells me that half the guys she knows have had crushes on Emily Dickinson. She says it is because Emily was brilliant and yet not threatening, having lived under the thumb of her father so long. She thinks the reason guys get crushes on Emily Dickinson is because Emily is an intellectual submissive, and intellectual men fear the domination of women. I don't care why we get crushes on Emily Dickinson. It is a rite of passage for any thinking man. Any thinking American man.

I only tell you all of this to show you how bad it gets when you aren't around real people for a long time. I tell you of Emily

Dickinson because she reminds me of the first time I thought, perhaps, I had lost my mind in isolation. I know now it was an apparition of loneliness, but I cannot tell you how very real it seemed that evening in Amherst. The other times I had seen her it was all invention; I was creating her out of boredom. But this was different.

I had driven from New York City to Boston the night before and had slept in my car. I stopped in Boston because I was too tired to drive the night. I was so cold under a towel I turned and rubbed against a seat belt that knotted itself in my back and against the handle of the door that crowded my head. I lay there in the backseat and stared at the roof of the car, thinking about Emily Dickinson. I hardly got any sleep. In the morning I doped up on coffee and started on the last leg of my journey, the leg that led to Amherst.

o   o   o

All the pretty girls at UMASS were running in their sweats that afternoon, the kids out smoking on the lawn, the trees behind them just sticks of things, just cobalt sky out for a walk. The place is lovely in the winter, very smart feeling, very bookish. The big houses are not close together. Red brick and ivy. Long lawns.

Across town from UMASS is Amherst College. Emily's grandfather started Amherst College because he wanted women to know the Bible as well as men. He was all vision and no hands, it seemed, and the place went bankrupt nearly immediately. The school was saved years later by the man's son, Emily's father, who was not like her grandfather in that he did not believe in the freedom or equality of women. Emily's father kept women down. Austin, Emily's brother, not Emily, was expected by the family to publish, to be a great writer.

I was thinking about these things when I circled Amherst College and stopped at the Jones Library where some handwritten notes from Emily are kept, scribbles mostly, gentle pencil on a yellowed sheet within a glass case. It was like magic looking at them. I felt ashamed because I knew I had been reading her for only a year, and yet I felt as though I knew her, as though we were dear friends, what with her living in the apartment in Oregon with me and all.

The man at Jones Library told me where to find the homestead, not much of a place, he said, and indeed I had passed it on the way into town without knowing it. I thought I would have felt it in my chest or sensed it to my right. I thought it would have been largely marked. I followed the man's instructions and walked from the library down along the shops back toward Boston a mile. Her house is not very much like what you would think. Though it is big it is not grand, and there is a large tree in front that takes the view. A side door is greeted by concrete steps, the cheap sort, and the driveway has been paved. There is a historical marker, but it is small, and so the first thing a young man realizes when he visits the home of Emily Dickinson is that the world is, in fact, not as in love with her as he is. I wanted to gather the leaves, you know, clean up the place. And I was looking all about the house, before making my approach, when I saw this thing that was not her but only in my mind was her, swing open the side door and set a foot quickly on the step. She met my eyes and went white, whiter than she already was, anyway, and like a wind she fled back into the house. The door closed as if it were on a spring. For a second I could not move.

I wrote in my journal that evening:

"I saw Emily Dickinson step out of a screen door and look at me with dark eyes, those endless dark eyes like the mouth of a cave, like pitch night set so lovely twice beneath her furrowed brow, her pale white skin gathering at the red of her lips, her long thin neck coming perfectly from her white dress flowing so gently and clean around her waist, down around her knees then slipping a tickle across her ankles. And then she went back into the house and it scared me to walk around the place."

Penny says it is when they are in their twenties that people lose their minds. She says this is what happened to her mother. And when we talk about it, I think of myself in Amherst, so confident at the thing I saw, and at once confident there was nothing there because Emily is dead.

I stopped imagining her immediately. I never told anybody about this because nothing like this happened anymore, so there was no need, and what's more I couldn't bear to find out that I was going crazy, that I was indeed seeing things. I blamed it on loneliness of the biochemical sort. When a person has no other persons he invents them because he was not designed to be alone, because it isn't good for a person to be alone.

There once was a man named
Don Astronaut.

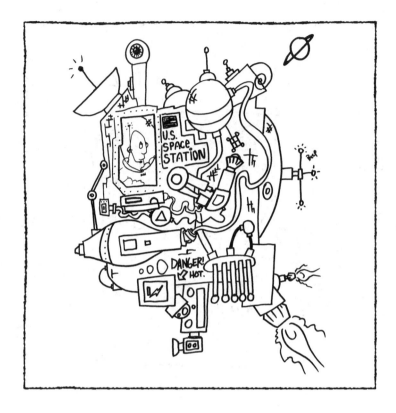

Don Astronaut lived on
a space station out in space.

Don Astronaut had
a special space suit that kept
him alive without food or
water or oxygen.

One day there was an accident.

And Don Astronaut was
cast out into space.

Don Astronaut orbited the earth
and was very scared.

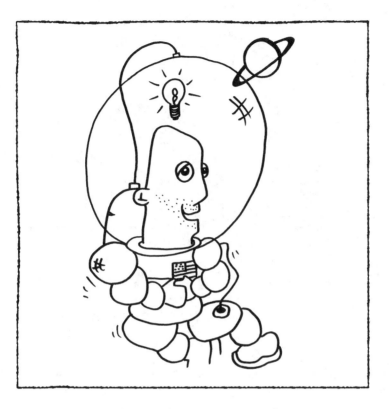

Until he remembered his special
suit that kept him alive.

But nobody's government came
to rescue Don Astronaut because
it would cost too much money.
(There was a conspiracy, and they
said he had died, but he hadn't.)

So Don Astronaut
orbited the earth again
and again, fourteen
times each day.

And Don Astronaut orbited
the earth for months.

And Don Astronaut orbited
the earth for decades.

And Don Astronaut orbited the earth
for fifty-three years before he died a
very lonely and crazy man—just a shell of
a thing with hardly a spark for a soul.

One of my new housemates, Stacy, wants to write a story about an astronaut. In his story the astronaut is wearing a suit that keeps him alive by recycling his fluids. In the story the astronaut is working on a space station when an accident takes place, and he is cast into space to orbit the earth, to spend the rest of his life circling the globe. Stacy says this story is how he imagines hell, a place where a person is completely alone, without others and without God. After Stacy told me about his story, I kept seeing it in my mind. I thought about it before I went to sleep at night. I imagined myself looking out my little bubble helmet at blue earth, reaching toward it, closing it between my puffy white space-suit fingers, wondering if my friends were still there. In my imagination I would call to them, yell for them, but the sound would only come back loud within my helmet. Through the years my hair would grow long in my helmet and gather around my forehead and fall across my eyes. Because of my helmet I would not be able to touch my face with my hands to move my hair out of my eyes, so my view of earth, slowly, over the first two years, would dim to only a thin light through a curtain of thatch and beard.

I would lay there in bed thinking about Stacy's story, putting myself out there in the black. And there came a time, in space, when I could not tell whether I was awake or asleep. All my thoughts mingled together because I had no people to remind me what was real and what was not real. I would punch myself in the side to feel pain, and this way I could be relatively sure I was not dreaming. Within ten years I was beginning to breathe heavy through my hair and my beard as they were pressing tough against my face and had begun to curl into my mouth and up my nose. In space, I forgot that I was human. I did not know whether I was a ghost or an apparition or a demon thing.

After I thought about Stacy's story, I lay there in bed and wanted to be touched, wanted to be talked to. I had the terrifying thought that something like that might happen to me. I thought it was just a terrible story, a painful and ugly story. Stacy had delivered as accurate a description of a hell as could be calculated. And what is sad, what is very sad, is that we are proud people, and because we have sensitive egos and so many of us live our lives in front of our televisions, not having to deal with real people who might hurt us or offend us, we float along on our couches like astronauts moving aimlessly through the Milky Way, hardly interacting with other human beings at all.

○   ○   ○

Stacy's story frightened me badly so I called Penny. Penny is who I call when I am thinking too much. She knows about this sort of thing. It was late, but I asked her if I could come over. She said yes. I took the bus from Laurelhurst, and there were only a few people on the bus, and none of them were talking to each other. When I got to Reed, Penny greeted me with a hug and a kiss on the cheek. We hung out in her room for a while and made small talk. It was so nice to hear another human voice. She had a picture of her father on her desk, tall and thin and wearing a cowboy hat. She told me about her father and how, when she was a child, she and her sister Posie spent a year sailing in the Pacific. She said they were very close. I listened so hard because it felt like, while she was telling me stories, she was massaging my soul, letting me know I was not alone, that I will never have to be alone, that there are friends and family and churches and coffee shops. I was not going to be cast into space.

We left the dorms and walked across Blue Bridge, a beautiful walking bridge on the campus at Reed that stretches across a canyon, fit with blue lights, which, when you look at them with blurred eyes, feels like stars lighting a path winding toward heaven.

The air was very cold, but Penny and I sat outside commons and smoked pipes, and she asked me about my family and asked me what I dreamed and asked me how I felt about God.

Loneliness is something that happens to us, but I think it is something we can move ourselves out of. I think a person who is lonely should dig into a community, give himself to a community, humble himself before his friends, initiate community, teach people to care for each other, love each other. Jesus does not want us floating through space or sitting in front of our televisions. Jesus wants us interacting, eating together, laughing together, praying together. Loneliness is something that came with the fall. If loving other people is a bit of heaven then certainly isolation is a bit of hell, and to that degree, here on earth, we decide in which state we would like to live.

Rick told me, a little later, I should be living in community. He said I should have people around bugging me and getting under my skin because without people I could not grow—I could not grow in God, and I could not grow as a human. We are born into families, he said, and we are needy at first as children because God wants us together, living among one another, not hiding ourselves under logs like fungus. You are not a fungus, he told me, you are a human, and you need other people in your life in order to be healthy.

Rick told me there was a group of guys at the church looking to get a house, looking to live in community. He told me I should consider joining them.

Community

Living with Freaks

BEFORE I LIVED IN COMMUNITY, I THOUGHT FAITH, mine being Christian faith, was something a person did alone, like monks in caves. I thought the backbone of faith was time alone with God, time reading ancient texts and meditating on poetry or the precepts of natural law and, perhaps, when a person gets good and godly, levitating potted plants or pitchers of water.

It seems that way in books. I had read a Christian book about the betterment of self, the actualization of the individual in the personal journey toward God. The book was all about focus and drive and perspective. It was all stuff you did in a quiet room. None of it had anything to do with community.

If other people were a part of the Christian journey, they had small roles; they were accountability partners or counselors or husbands or wives. I hadn't seen a single book (outside the majority of books in the New Testament) that addressed a group of people or a community with advice about faith.

When I walked into the Christian section of a bookstore, the message was clear: Faith is something you do alone.

Rick does not have much tolerance for people living alone.

He's like Bill Clinton in that he feels everyone's pain. If Rick thinks somebody is lonely, he can't sleep at night. He wants us all to live with each other and play nice so he can get some rest. Tortured soul.

I didn't know what to think about the idea of living in community at first. I had lived on my own for about six years, and the idea of moving in with a bunch of slobs didn't appeal to me. Living in community sounded so, um, odd. Cults do that sort of thing, you know. First you live in community, and then you drink punch and die.

It was Rick's idea, though, and he seemed fairly normal in all the other areas of his life. He never mentioned anything about a spaceship trailing behind a comet. He never asked us to store weapons or peanut butter, so I figured the thing about living in community was on the up-and-up. Just because something looks like a cult doesn't mean it really is, right? The other thing is that, at the time, I was pushing thirty and still not married. When you are thirty and not married and you move in with a bunch of guys, you look like you have given up, like you are a bunch of losers who live together so you can talk about computers and share video games.

If I lived in community, we would have to have about five raging parties just to shake the loser image. But I am not one to party. I like going to bed at nine and watching CNN till I fall asleep. So I was thinking I could move in with the guys and we could tell everybody we had raging parties but never actually have them.

I didn't know whether to make the move or not.

Rick kept bothering me about it. I was living way out in the country, about thirty miles from town, and he kept asking me if I was lonely out there, if I wouldn't much rather move into town with a bunch of guys from the church. He asked if I had the chance to minister to anybody out there in the country. He asked if I was having any influence on the cows. I told him I was having a lot of influence. I wrote books. He laughed. I sat there uncomfortably while he laughed. "Books," he said. "Brilliant! You write books for people." He couldn't stop laughing. He was being very annoying.

○   ○   ○

I moved in with five other guys about a month after talking with Rick. We found a house in Laurelhurst, one of the houses on the traffic circle at 39th and Glisan. We lived across the street from the giant statue of Joan of Arc. You'll see the statue if you come to Portland.

I liked it at first. It was a big house, and I got the best room, the room with all the windows. My room literally had windows on every wall, about ten windows in all. It was like living in a green house. I set my desk in front of the huge window that looked down on the traffic circle and the statue. My friends used to drive around the circle and honk when they went by. I always forgot I lived in a glass room so I would pull my finger out of my nose just in time to wave back. I went from living in complete isolation to living in a glass box on a busy street.

One of the best things about living in community was that I had brothers for the first time ever. We used to sit on the porch and watch cars go around the roundabout. We used to stare at the statue of Joan of Arc and wonder, out loud, if we could take her in a fight.

I have a picture on my desk of the six guys at Graceland, which is what we named the house. People thought we named the house Graceland because we wanted it to be a place where people experienced God's grace and unconditional love. But we didn't think about that till later. We really named it Graceland because that was the name of the house Elvis lived in, and, like Elvis, we were all pretty good with the ladies.

The picture on my desk is more than a picture of six guys; it is a picture of me in my transition, not a physical transition but more of an inner shift from one sort of thinking to another. I don't look all that tired in the picture, but I remember being tired. I remember feeling tired for almost a year. I was tired because I wasn't used to being around people all the time.

The picture was taken on the porch. We were all smoking pipes. I was wearing a black stocking cap, like a beat poet or a bank robber. Andrew the Protester, the tall good-looking one with dark hair and the beard, the one who looks like a young Fidel Castro, was the activist in our bachelor family. He is the guy I told you about with whom I go to protests. He works with the homeless downtown and is studying at Portland State to become a social worker. He is always talking about how outrageous the Republicans are or how wrong it is to eat beef. I honestly don't know how Andrew got so tall without eating beef.

Jeremy, the guy in the Wranglers with the marine haircut, is the cowboy in the family. He always carries a gun. You'd think Andrew and Jeremy would hate each other because Andrew opposes the right to bear arms, but they get along okay, good-natured guys and all. It is a shame because that would be a great fight. Jeremy wants to be a cop, and he went to college on a wrestling scholarship, and Andrew is a communist. I would try to get them to fight, but they liked each other.

Mike Tucker, whom we all refer to as Tuck, was the older brother in the clan, the responsible one. He is the one with the spiked red hair, like Richie Cunningham fused with a rock star. Mike was a trucker for years but always dreamed of a career in advertising. He moved to Portland and started his own advertising agency with just a cell phone and a Web site. He posed nude on his brochure, which got him gigs with Doc Martens and a local fashion agency. He freelances every other day and drives trucks the rest of the time. Mike is one of my best friends in the world. Mike is one of the greatest guys I know.

Simon, the short good-looking guy with the black hair and sly grin, was the leprechaun of our tribe. He's a deeply spiritual Irishman here for the year from Dublin. Simon is a womanizer, always heading down to Kell's for a pint with the lads or to the church to pray and ask God's forgiveness for his detestable sins and temper. Simon came to America on a J-1 visa. He came to Portland, specifically, to study our church. He wants to go back to the homeland and start a Christian revival, returning the country to its faith in Jesus, the living God. After that, he wants to unite men and take England captive, forcing them to be slaves to the Irish, the greatest of all peoples, the people who invented honor, integrity, Western civilization, Guinness and, apparently, peanut butter and the light bulb.

Trevor, the young guy in the picture, looks like Justin Timberlake, like the lead singer of a boy band. He has tight hair that curls just out of the shoot, and he's dyed it blond. Trev is the kid, the rookie on our team of misfits. He is just out of high school a few years and rides a Yamaha crotch-rocket motorcycle so fast that when he lets me drive it, I can hardly keep the front wheel on the ground. He is a learner, with a solid heart like a sponge that absorbs, and he wants to become a very good man. Trevor is one of my favorite people. He is my Nintendo buddy. We yell profanities at each other while playing NFL Blitz. I usually win because he is slow with the fingers. Sometimes, after I beat him in the game, he crawls into his little bed and cries himself to sleep. After that I usually feel sorry for him, and I let him win a game or two. Rookie.

○   ○   ○

I liked them all very much, but we had hard times. I was a serious recluse before I moved in with the guys at Graceland. When you live on your own for years, you begin to think the world belongs to you. You begin to think all space is your space and all time is your time.

It is like in that movie *About a Boy* where Nick Hornby's chief character, played by Hugh Grant, believes that life is a play about himself, that all other characters are only acting minor roles in a story that centers around him. My life felt like that. Life was a story about me because I was in every scene. In fact, I was the only one in every scene. I was everywhere I went. If somebody walked into my scene, it would frustrate me because they were disrupting the general theme of the play, namely my comfort or glory. Other people were flat characters in my movie, lifeless characters. Sometimes I would have scenes with them, dialogue, and they would speak their lines, and I would speak mine. But the movie, the grand movie stretching from Adam to the Antichrist, was about me. I wouldn't have told you that at the time, but that is the way I lived.

Tuck was one of my best friends when he moved in. He is still one of my best friends, but for a while I wanted to kill him. He did not understand that life was a movie about me. Nobody ever told him. He would knock on my door while I was reading, come in and sit down in a chair opposite me, and then he would want to talk, he would want to hear about my day. I couldn't believe it. The audacity to come into my room, my soundstage, and interrupt the obvious flow of the story with questions about how I am.

I would give Tuck little signals that I didn't want to talk like eye rolls or short answers to his questions. I would stare into space so he thought I was crazy or snore so he would think I had fallen asleep. I think I hurt his feelings. He would get very frustrated with me, go upstairs, and wonder why I was acting that way. He only did this a few times before he dismissed me as a jerk. I almost lost the friendship, to be honest.

I didn't like the feeling of having to work with people. We would have a community meeting and talk about who wasn't doing their chores or who was leaving dirty dishes in the sink, and if I felt accused I would lash back at whoever accused me. I was confident I was right and they were wrong. I could not see, at the time, that I was being rude. There were a few times when Trevor actually stood up and walked out of the room. It was always because of me. The other guys had lived with people before. They knew all about people.

Living in community made me realize one of my faults: I was addicted to myself. All I thought about was myself. The only thing I really cared about was myself. I had very little concept of love, altruism, or sacrifice. I discovered that my mind is like a radio that picks up only one station, the one that plays me: *K-DON, all Don, all the time.*

I did not understand the exchange that takes place in meaningful dialogue, when two people sit down and tune their radios, if only for a moment, to the other person's station. It must have been painful for Tuck to try so desperately to catch my station, and for me to brush him off.

Having had my way for so long, I became defensive about what I perceived as encroachments on my rights. My personal bubble was huge. I couldn't have conversations that lasted more than ten minutes. I wanted efficiency in personal interaction, and while listening to one of my housemates talk, I wondered why they couldn't get to the point. *What are you trying to tell me?* I would think. *Do we really have to stand here and make small talk?*

Tuck told me later that in the first few months of living with me he felt judged, as though there was something wrong with him. He felt unvalued any time he was around me.

o   o   o

The most difficult lie I have ever contended with is this: Life is a story about me.

o   o   o

God brought me to Graceland to rid me of this deception, to scrub it out of the gray matter of my mind. It was a frustrating and painful experience.

I hear addicts talk about the shakes and panic attacks and the highs and lows of resisting their habit, and to some degree I understand them because I have had habits of my own, but no drug is so powerful as the drug of self. No rut in the mind is so deep as the one that says I am the world, the world belongs to me, all people are characters in my play. There is no addiction so powerful as self-addiction.

o   o   o

In the spring of my year at Graceland, when the ground was beginning to dry at Laurelhurst Park, a friend and I traveled to Salem to hear Brennan Manning speak. Manning is a former Catholic priest and a wonderful writer who has struggled with alcoholism and speaks frankly about matters of Christian spirituality.

We sat so close I could see the blue in Brennan's eyes and that quality of sincerity you find in people who have turned trial into service. Brennan grew up in New York and speaks with a slight East Coast bite that has been sanded down by years of smoking.

An ear has to work a bit to keep his pace. He opened his talk with the story of Zacchaeus. Brennan talked about how an entire town, with their ridicule and hatred, could not keep the little man from oppressing them through the extravagant financial gains he made as a tax collector. Christ walked through town, Brennan said, and spotted the man. Christ told Zacchaeus that He would like to have a meal with him.

In the single conversation Christ had with Zacchaeus, Brennan reminded us, Jesus spoke affirmation and love, and the tax collector sold his possessions and made amends to those he had robbed. It was the affection of Christ, not the brutality of a town, that healed Zacchaeus.

Manning went on to speak of the great danger of a harsh word, the power of unlove to deteriorate a person's heart and spirit, and how, as representatives of the grace and love of God, our communication should be seasoned with love and compassion.

While Manning was speaking, I was being shown myself, and I felt like God was asking me to change. I was being asked to walk away from the lies I believed about the world being about me. I had been communicating unlove to my housemates because I thought they were not cooperating with the meaning of life, that meaning being my desire and will and choice and comfort.

There was nothing fun about going home that night. I went with new eyes, seeing my housemates as people. For the first time I saw them as people, and I could sense God's love for them. I had been living with God's prized possessions, His children, the dear ones to Him, and had considered them a bother to this earth that was mine, this space and time that were mine.

o   o   o

In the short year at Graceland I hurt all the guys at one time or another. Fixing the carnage would take time. I had to make things right with each of them. I had really messed things up. Jeremy, the guy with the marine haircut who was going to become a cop, couldn't stand me. I had run my car through the garage door one night and neglected to fix it. Jeremy parked his motorcycle in the garage and so he had to use the broken door every day. My room was directly above the garage, so when Jeremy went to work in the morning at five o'clock, he would start his motorcycle engine, and it sounded like somebody was starting a lawn mower next to my bed. I would get furious, and later that night I would ask him if there was something we could do. He said no, that was where he needed to keep his motorcycle. And that was true. So, every time Jeremy had trouble getting the broken door up and down, he would get mad at me, and every time he started his motorcycle at 5:00 a.m., I would get mad at him. The issue, of course, was not about the motorcycle or the door; the issue was about whether or not we respected each other, whether or not we liked each other.

One evening I was down in the basement talking to Tuck while he was working out. I decided to do some laundry while I was down there, but somebody's clothes were in the dryer. There was no place to put them so I put them on the floor. I didn't think anything of it, you know, because the floor was pretty clean, but it turned out the clothes were Jeremy's and, later that night, when he got home, he wrote a note on our white board to the person who had thrown his clothes on the floor. I didn't actually throw them on the floor, I just sort of set them there, but still, he was pretty heated. I told him it was me, and I apologized. He had to go for a walk he was so mad. It was the last straw for him.

When he came back I asked him if we could talk. I told him it was time we dealt with it. He kept wanting to walk away from the conversation because he was so mad, but I wouldn't let him. I was ready to apologize. I told him I didn't feel like he cared about me because he started his motorcycle every morning, and I had become defensive about that, and that made me want to get him back, and I had done that sort of subconsciously, with little comments and that sort of thing. I had never told him, at the very beginning, that I felt like he didn't like me and I wanted him to. Instead, I had been proud and passive-aggressive. That was why we were experiencing all of this. And I told him that I felt bad. I didn't accuse him of anything, which looking back was very, very important. And, also, I didn't expect anything from him in return. I really didn't feel like he owed me anything. Jeremy listened very carefully once he had calmed down. He was great. He told me how much he liked me, and that meant the world to me. In that moment I could feel all the anger I had been feeling melt away. I couldn't even remember what I was angry about. And the next morning, when Jeremy started his motorcycle, it didn't even wake me up.

I was in San Francisco recently staying at this bed and breakfast place for people who are in the city to do ministry. It was a small house, but there were probably fifteen people living there at the time. The guy who ran the place, Bill, was always making meals or cleaning up after us, and I took note of his incredible patience and kindness. I noticed that not all of us did our dishes after a meal, and very few people thanked him for cooking. One morning, before anybody woke up, Bill and I were drinking coffee at the dining room table. I told him I lived with five guys and that it was very difficult for me because I liked my space and needed my privacy. I asked him how he kept such a good attitude all of the time with so many people abusing his kindness. Bill set down his coffee and looked me in the eye. "Don," he said. "If we are not willing to wake up in the morning and die to ourselves, perhaps we should ask ourselves whether or not we are really following Jesus."

(16)

Money

Thoughts on Paying Rent

WRITERS DON'T MAKE ANY MONEY AT ALL. WE MAKE about a dollar. It is terrible. But then again we don't work either. We sit around in our underwear until noon then go downstairs and make coffee, fry some eggs, read the paper, read part of a book, smell the book, wonder if perhaps we ourselves should work on our book, smell the book again, throw the book across the room because we are quite jealous that any other person wrote a book, feel terribly guilty about throwing the schmuck's book across the room because we secretly wonder if God in heaven noticed our evil jealousy, or worse, our laziness. We then lie across the couch facedown and mumble to God to forgive us because we are secretly afraid He is going to dry up all our words because we envied another man's stupid words. And for this, as I said before, we are paid a dollar. We are worth so much more.

I hate not having money. I hate not being able to go to a movie or out for coffee. I hate that feeling at the ATM when, after getting cash, the little receipt spits out, the one with the number on it, the telling number, the ever low number that translates into how many days I have left to feel comfortable.

The ATM, to me, often feels like a slot machine. I walk up to it hoping to get lucky.

I feel like a complete loser when I don't have money. That's the real problem. I feel invalidated, as if the gods have not approved my existence, as if my allowance has been cut off. We are worth our earning potential, you know. We are worth the money we make. Maybe this is a man thing; maybe women don't think about this, I don't know, but I think about it. I think I am worth what I earn, which makes me worth one dollar. Not having money affects the way a man thinks about himself. Last year I didn't have any money at all. Five of twelve months last year I prayed God would send me rent. Five of twelve months I received a check in the mail the day rent was due. I was grateful at first, but after a while, to be honest with you, I began to feel like God's charity. At the end of each month I would start biting my nails, wondering what account owed me money or whether or not I would pick up any writing assignments. There's not a lot of work in the Christian market if you won't write self-righteous, conservative propaganda. I write new-realism essays. I am not a commodity.

I wondered whether or not I was lazy. When you are a writer you feel lazy even when you're working. Who gets paid to sit around in a coffee shop all day and type into a computer? But I did work, I kept telling myself. I showed up at Palio every day, and in the evenings I would go to Common Ground. I worked. I wrote. I drove myself crazy writing.

The thing is, at the time, I was writing without a contract. So I wasn't really writing for money, I was writing in hopes of money. And when you are writing without a contract, you feel as though everything you say is completely worthless (technically it is, until you get a contract).

You can write all day and still not feel that you have done

anything. A man needs to do some work, needs to get his hands dirty and calloused and needs to hammer his thumb every once in a while. He needs to get tired at the end of the day, and not just mind tired, body tired too.

I wasn't feeling body tired, I was just feeling mind tired, and I didn't have any money, so I wasn't feeling like a man. I was in a bad place.

I talked to Rick about it. He came over to the house, and we were sitting around, and I asked him if he thought God really called me to be a writer or if I was just being lazy, being selfish, tinkering with words. He asked me if I worked; he said that everybody needs to work. I told him I did but wasn't getting paid for it because I didn't have a contract yet, and getting a contract was no sure thing. At best I was gambling. He said he didn't know whether what I was doing was right or wrong. He said he would pray for me. I rolled my eyes. He told me I had a gift and he liked me, and God would make things clear if I was being a lazy slob. Imago, our church, is made up of mostly artists and fruit nuts and none of us have any money, so Rick said if I was going to be a writer, I needed to write a bestseller so that the church could have some money.

○   ○   ○

I am irresponsible with money if you want to know the truth. I don't have the money to buy big things, thank God, so I buy small things. I like new things too much. I like the way they smell. Today I tried to go to Home Depot to get an extension cord. I need an extension cord to plug in a lamp in the upstairs den. I already bought a timer plug for the lamp, a plug that turns the lamp on in the evening and off after everybody has gone to bed, but now I need an extension cord.

We probably didn't need the timer plug in the first place. I could probably have plugged the lamp into the regular socket and been fine. But when I saw the timer plug at Fred Meyer last week, I stood there looking at it, having come across it by accident, and I realized how very much I needed it. And it was only seven dollars. I need this for seven dollars, I thought to myself, this is very important. I put it into my basket and walked off, wondering what it was that I needed to plug into it. That, of course, is now obvious: the lamp in the upstairs den. I got the timer plug home and programmed it without reading the instructions, then I went to plug the lamp in but the lamp was too far from the outlet. I could not move the lamp closer without ruining the Feng Shui. I have this fruit nut friend who says Feng Shui is very important, that a room should be balanced so that you feel balanced when you are in it. I put the lamp closer to the outlet, and my fruit nut friend was right because I felt very unbalanced. So I would need an extension cord to go with the timer plug.

I only say all this to show you that I have a problem with buying things I really don't need. I saw this documentary about the brain that says habits are formed when the "pleasure center" of the brain lights up as we do a certain behavior. The documentary said that some people's pleasure centers light up when they buy things. I wondered if my pleasure center did that.

Penny thinks I am terrible with the little money I have. I was talking to her the other night, and I mentioned that I was interested in buying a remote control car, and she just sort of sat there and didn't say anything. Penny, are you there? I asked. Yes, she said. What? I asked. Are you serious, Don? Are you going to waste perfectly good money on a remote control car?

"Well . . . uh," I said.

"Well . . . uh . . . Miller, that would be a pretty dumb thing to do when there are children starving in India!" she told me.

I hate it when Penny does this. Honestly, it can be so annoying. She lives it though. She didn't buy clothes for an entire year, her senior year at Reed, because she felt like she was irresponsible with money. She always looked very beautiful anyway, and for her birthday I bought her some mittens at Saturday Market for seven dollars. She wore them like they were from Tiffany's or something. She always talked about them. They weren't that big of a deal, but she hadn't had any new clothes for a year so I think she wore them while she was sleeping or something.

Penny is right about spending money though. Penny is right about everything. Penny said if I were to save about twenty dollars a month and give it to Northwest Medical Teams or Amnesty International, I would literally be saving lives. Literally. But that stupid pleasure center goes off in my brain, and it feels like there is nothing I can do about it. I told Penny about the pleasure center and how I needed the remote control car to make the pleasure center light up, and she just took the phone away from her ear and beat it against her chair.

The thing about the extension cord is I was pretty sure I had one in the basement, in a box with some other cords, but if I looked I might have found it, and then I would not have been able to go to Home Depot. What we needed was a new extension cord, the latest technology, I thought to myself.

I put my boots on very quickly. The good voice, the frugal voice, the Penny voice started inside my head: *Don, please, there are children who could use this money for Christmas presents.* It's August, I said out loud. *What about environmental movements,* Good Voice said, *what about the rain forests that could hold a cure for cancer, a cure for AIDS.* Tree hugger, I said to Good Voice while putting on my motorcycle helmet. *You have a problem,* Good Voice said. You're a pansy, I said back. *You're irresponsible!* Good Voice shouted. Shut your gaping pie hole, I yelled back.

The thing about new things is you feel new when you buy them, you feel as though you are somebody different because you own something different. We are our possessions, you know. There are people who get addicted to buying new stuff. Things. Piles and piles of things. But the new things become old things so quickly. We need new things to replace the old things.

I like things with buttons.

○   ○   ○

A writer I like named Ravi Zacharias says that the heart desires wonder and magic. He says technology is what man uses to supplant the desire for wonder. Ravi Zacharias says that what the heart is really longing to do is worship, to stand in awe of a God we don't understand and can't explain.

I started thinking about what Penny was saying and what Ravi Zacharias says. I was riding my motorcycle down to Home Depot, wondering if Penny and Ravi would make good friends, when I decided I was being stupid, very wasteful and stupid. I knew we had an extension cord in the basement, and I knew I was really going to Home Depot to get some drill bits or a laser level or one of those tap lights, and that I wasn't going to get an extension chord but something else, something I would find when I got there, something that would call to me from its shelf.

At the time I didn't have very much money, and the money I had I needed to learn to use wisely. Money does not belong to me, Rick once told me. Money is God's. He trusts us to dish it out fairly and with a strong degree of charity.

I heard an interview with Bill Gates, and the interviewer asked him if he knew how rich he was, if he could really get his mind around it. He said he couldn't. The only way I can understand it, he said, is that there is nothing I can't buy. If I want something, I can have it. He said that Microsoft saved him because he was really more interested in what he was doing than how much money he had. Lots of rich people are not happy, he said.

Sometimes I am glad I don't have very much money. I think money might own me if I had too much of it. I think I would buy things and not be satisfied with the things I have so I would have to buy more.

Jesus said it is harder for a rich man to enter the kingdom of heaven than for a camel to go through the eye of a needle.

Rick says money should be your tool and that you should control it, it shouldn't control you. This means when I want a new extension cord and I already have one, I should use the one I have and give the rest of the money to people who are having very hard times in their lives. This means I probably didn't need to buy a timer for the lamp. Rick said I should be giving money to Imago-Dei, our church. He said giving 10 percent would be a good place to start. I knew this already. It's called tithing, and somehow it is biblical. The Bible also tells the story of these beautiful people in the very first Christian churches who are giving all their money to the church and the elders are dishing it back out to the community based on need.

o   o   o

One of my good friends, Curt Heidschmidt, gave me a lecture about tithing not very long ago. It was strange to get a lecture about tithing from Curt because Curt is not even a church sort of guy. He goes and all, but he hates it. Usually people who go to church but hate it aren't going around giving lectures about tithing, but Curt gave me a pretty good talking-to.

Curt works at a cabinet shop and cusses all the time and tells dirty jokes. But he tithes, sort of. He used to keep a huge jar on his dresser that was full of money, and when he deposited his paychecks he would pull out 10 percent from the bank. Cold, hard cash. He would take the money home and put it in that jar. The thing must have had a couple thousand dollars in it. I was over one night watching *South Park,* and Curt was griping because the cabinet shop didn't pay him enough so that he could get the motorcycle he wanted.

"Well," I told him, "you must have thousands of dollars in that stinking jar, Curt. Use that." This was before I knew it was his tithing money.

"Can't."

"Why?"

"Can't."

"Why?"

"Isn't mine, Miller." Curt leaned back in his recliner and looked at me over the top of his beer can.

"Isn't yours?" I asked. "Who in the world is storing their savings on your dresser?" I pointed toward his bedroom.

"Well" —he smiled, sort of embarrassed—"it's God's."

"God's?" I shouted.

"Yeah, that's my tithe!" he shouted back.

I was a little shocked, to be honest. Like I said before, he didn't seem like the tithing type. I don't think he even went to church nine out of ten Sundays, and when he did he just grumbled about it.

"Well, why don't you take it down to the church and give it to them?" I asked.

"I haven't been to church in a while, that's why."

"Curt," I told him, "you are the most interesting person I know."

"Thank you, Don. You want a beer?"

"Yes." Curt went over to the fridge and opened a couple of Henry's.

"You tithe, Don?"

I just looked at him. I couldn't believe it. I was about to get a lecture on tithing from a guy who probably subscribed to *Bikes and Babes* magazine.

"Well, Curt, I guess I don't." After I said this, Curt shook his head in disappointment. I started feeling really guilty. "It's a shame, Don." Curt tilted back a bottle as he spoke, punctuating the sentence with a post-swig burp. "You are missing out. I've been tithing since I was a kid. Wouldn't miss a payment to save my life."

"Am I dreaming this?" I asked him.

"Dreaming what, Don?"

"This conversation." When I said this I was pointing back and forth between he and I.

"Don, let me tell you. You should be tithing. That is not your money. That is God's money. You ought to be ashamed of yourself. Stealing from God and all. You write Christian books and everything, and you're not even giving God's money back to Him."

"Well, you don't have to go making me feel all bad about it. You haven't exactly given your money to God either. It's right there on your dresser."

Curt leaned over the big arm of his recliner and with a Jack Nicholson grin on his face said, "Oh, you don't worry about that, big boy. That's God's money, and He's gonna get it. I've never stolen a dime from God, and I'm never gonna start."

I honestly couldn't believe this was happening to me. I go over to Curt's house to watch *South Park*, and I get a guilt trip from a fundamentalist.

Curt went down about two weeks later and turned all his money in to a church secretary. More than three thousand dollars. I started feeling so guilty I couldn't sleep.

I met with Rick after that and confessed I was not giving any money to Imago-Dei. Rick had come over to the house, and we were lying about how much we could bench-press, and then I just blurted it out, "I am not giving any money to the church, Rick. Not a dime."

"Okay," he said. "Interesting way to change the conversation. Why?" he asked. "Why aren't you giving any money to the church?"

"Because I don't have any money. Everything goes to rent and groceries."

"That sounds like a tough situation," he said, very compassionately.

"So am I exempt?" I asked.

"Nope," he said. "We want your cash."

"How much?" I asked.

"How much do you make?"

"I don't know. About a thousand a month, maybe."

"Then we want a hundred. And you should also know how much you make. Part of the benefit of giving a portion of your money is it makes you think about where your money goes. God does not want us to be sloppy with our finances, Don."

"But I need money for rent."

"You also need to trust God."

"I know. I just think it would be easier to trust God if I had extra money to trust Him with."

"That would not be faith, then, would it?"

"No."

"Well, bud, I just want you to know I hate this part of the job, 'cause it sounds like I am asking for your money. I don't care whether or not we have your money. Our needs are met. I want to tell you that you are missing out on so much, Don."

"So much what?"

"The fruit of obedience," he said, looking very pastoral. "When we do what God wants us to do, we are blessed, we are spiritually healthy. God wants us to give a portion of our money to His work on earth. By setting aside money from every check, you are trusting God to provide. He wants you to get over that fear—that fear of trusting Him. It is a scary place, but that is where you have to go as a follower of Christ. There are times when my wife and I don't have enough money to cover bills, but we know the first bill, the first payment we make, is to the church. That is most important. If the other bills get neglected, then we need to watch how we are spending money. And there are times when we have found ourselves in that situation. But it works out. We are getting good at trusting God, and we are getting good at managing money."

The next week I emptied my checking account, which had about eight dollars in it, and I gave it to the church. Another check came a few days later, and I gave 10 percent of that to the church, then I got another writing gig with a magazine in Atlanta, and as I deposited that check into my account I wrote a check to the church. One after another, I started getting called to speak at retreats and conferences that usually pay pretty well, and each time I would write a check to the church. Since then, since that conversation with Rick, I have given at least 10 percent of every dollar I make, just like Curt. And I have never not had rent. For more than a year my checking account had hovered or dipped just over or just under zero, and suddenly I had money to spare. I decided I would open a savings account in case some day I would get married and have a family, and with each bit of money that came in I would give 10 percent to the church and 10 percent to the savings account. I was actually budgeting money. I had never done that before.

But that is not the best part. The best part is what tithing has done for my relationship with God. Before, I felt like I was always going to God with my fingers crossed, the way a child feels around his father when he knows he has told terrible lies. God knew where I was, He didn't love me any different when I was holding out on Him, it's just that I didn't feel clean around Him, and you know how that can affect things.

I also learned that I needed to give to the poor. My church gives money to the poor, but it was also important for me to give directly to the poor. I would go downtown sometimes and buy a homeless person lunch. I hated it at first because I always stumbled across the guys with terrible table manners, but after a while I began to like their drunken ramblings. Even though they weren't making any sense, they thought they were, and that has to count for something.

○   ○   ○

We don't need as much money as we have. Hardly any of us need as much money as we have. It's true what they say about the best things in life being free.

For a little while, a long time ago, I was a minimalist. I wasn't a minimalist on purpose, it's just that my friend Paul and I had been traveling around the country living in a van, like I mentioned earlier. We eventually ran out of money, so we sold the van and lived in the woods. We lived in the Cascade Mountains for a month. We walked through the woods into a resort every day where I scrubbed toilets in condos and Paul worked as a lifeguard. I ate the food people would leave in the refrigerator after they had checked out. Mostly perishables. Ice cream. Fruit. Cheese.

I only tell you this because when we were living in the woods, we didn't worry about anything, especially about money. After about a week I stopped wondering if food was going to show. I learned that people throw tons of food away, and there will always be plenty. I didn't think about rent because I didn't pay rent; the forest is free, it turns out, great property all over. There I was, living in one of the most beautiful territories in all of America, eating free food and sleeping under the stars. It did not take long for that nagging feeling of fear, the false feeling of security that money gives us, to subside.

I remember a particular midnight, three weeks into our stay, walking into a meadow surrounded by thick aspens and above me all that glorious heaven glowing, and I felt like I was a part of it, what with the trees clapping hands and me feeling like I was floating there beneath the endlessness. I looked up so long I felt like I was in space. Light. No money and no anxiety.

It is possible to feel that way again. It is possible not to let possessions own me, to rest happily in the security that God, not money, can give. I have been feeling that a little lately. Rick asked me how I was doing with the money thing, with the tithe thing, and I told him I was on the up-and-up. He asked me how I was feeling about all of that, and I told him I was feeling good, free, light. He told me not to get a big head about it.

Worship

The Mystical Wonder

I READ A BOOK A LONG TIME AGO ABOUT MOTHER Teresa. Somebody in the book asked her how she summoned the strength to love so many people. She said she loved people because they are Jesus, each one of them is Jesus, and this is true because it says so in the Bible. And it is also true that this idea contradicts the facts of reality: Everybody can't be Jesus. There are many ideas within Christian spirituality that contradict the facts of reality as I understand them. A statement like this offends some Christians because they believe if aspects of their faith do not obey the facts of reality, they are not true. But I think there are all sorts of things our hearts believe that don't make any sense to our heads. Love, for instance; we believe in love. Beauty. Jesus as God.

It comforts me to think that if we are created beings, the thing that created us would have to be greater than us, so much greater, in fact, that we would not be able to understand it. It would have to be greater than the facts of our reality, and so it would seem to us, looking out from within our reality, that it would contradict reason. But reason itself would suggest it would have to be greater than reality, or it would not be reasonable.

When we worship God we worship a Being our life experience does not give us the tools with which to understand. If we could, God would not inspire awe. Eternity, for example, is not something the human mind can understand. We may be able to wrap our heads around living forever (and we can do this only because none of us has experienced death), but can we understand what it means to have never been born? I only say this to illustrate that we, as Christians, believe things we cannot explain. And so does everybody else.

I have a friend who is a seminary student who criticizes certain Christian writers for embracing what he calls "mysticism." I asked him if his statement meant that he was not a mystic. Of course not, he told me. I asked him if he believed in the Trinity. He said he did. I asked him if he believed that the Trinity represented three separate persons who are also one. He said he did. I asked him if that would be considered a mystical idea. He just stood there thinking.

You cannot be a Christian without being a mystic.

I was talking to a homeless man at a laundry mat recently, and he said that when we reduce Christian spirituality to math we defile the Holy. I thought that was very beautiful and comforting because I have never been good at math. Many of our attempts to understand Christian faith have only cheapened it. I can no more understand the totality of God than the pancake I made for breakfast understands the complexity of me. The little we do understand, that grain of sand our minds are capable of grasping, those ideas such as God is good, God feels, God loves, God knows all, are enough to keep our hearts dwelling on His majesty and otherness forever.

o   o   o

Here is one of the coolest things I ever did: This past summer I made a point to catch sunsets. I would ride my motorcycle up

Mount Tabor and sit on the steps of the reservoir to watch the sun put fire in the clouds that are always hanging over Portland. I never really wanted to make the trip; I would want to watch television or make a sandwich, but I made myself go. And once I got up there I always loved it. It always meant something to me to see beauty right there over my city.

My first sunset this year was the most spectacular. Forest fires in Washington State blew a light, nearly unnoticeable haze through Portland, and the clouds were just low enough to catch the full reflection of red and yellow. I thought to myself, *This is something that happens all the time.* From the ridge on Tabor where I planted myself, I could see the entire skyline, the home of more than a million people. On most nights there were no more than two or three people there with me. All that beauty happens right above the heads of more than a million people who never notice it.

Here is what I've started thinking: All the wonder of God happens right above our arithmetic and formula. The more I climb outside my pat answers, the more invigorating the view, the more my heart enters into worship.

○　　○　　○

I love how the Gospels start, with John the Baptist eating bugs and baptizing people. The religious people started getting baptized because it had become popular, and John yells at them and calls them snakes. He says the water won't do anything for them, it will only get their snakeskins wet. But if they meant it, if they had faith that Jesus was coming and was real, then Jesus would ignite the kingdom life within them. I love that because for so long religion was my false gospel. But there was no magic in it, no wonder, no awe, no kingdom life burning in my chest. And when I get tempted by that same stupid Christian religion, I go back to the beginning of the Gospels and am comforted that there is something more than the emptiness of ritual. God will ignite the kingdom life within me, the Bible says. That's mysticism. It isn't a formula that I am figuring out. It is something God does.

One night I watched the sunset till the stars faded in and, while looking up, my mind, or my heart, I do not know which, realized how endless it all was. I laid myself down on some grass and reached my hand directly out toward where? I don't know. There is no up and down. There has never been an up and down. Things like up and down were invented so as not to scare children, so as to reduce mystery to math. The truth is we do not know there is an end to material existence. It may go on forever, which is something the mind cannot understand.

My friend Jason and I went on a trip to Joshua Tree and Death Valley, and he had a map folded across his lap nearly the entire trip. Even when I was driving, he had the map out, following along with his finger the trajectory of the car, noting how close we were to certain towns, certain lakes. Jason liked to know where we were on the map (and so did I, as a matter of fact). But I was afraid to tell Jason about the universe, how scientists haven't found the edge of it, of how nobody knows exactly where we are on the map.

I think we have two choices in the face of such big beauty: terror or awe. And this is precisely why we attempt to chart God, because we want to be able to predict Him, to dissect Him, to carry Him around in our dog and pony show. We are too proud to feel awe and too fearful to feel terror. We reduce Him to math so we don't have to fear Him, and yet the Bible tells us fear is the appropriate response, that it is the beginning of wisdom. Does this mean God is going to hurt us? No. But I stood on the edge of the Grand Canyon once, behind a railing, and though I was never going to fall off the edge, I feared the thought of it. It is that big of a place, that wonderful of a landscape.

o   o   o

I like that scene in the movie *Dead Poets Society* in which Mr. Keating, an English instructor at an elite preparatory school, asks his students to rip out the "Introduction to Poetry" essay from their literature textbooks. The essayist had instructed students in a method of grading poems on a sliding scale, complete with the use of a grid, thus reducing art for the heart into arithmetic for the head. The students looked around at each other in confusion as their teacher dismissed the essay as rubbish and ordered them to rip these pages from their books. And at their teacher's loud prodding, the students began to rip. Dr. Keating paced the aisle with a trash can and reminded the students that poetry is not algebra, not songs on *American Bandstand* that can be rated on a scale from one to ten, but rather they are pieces of art that plunge the depths of the heart to stir vigor in men and woo women.

Too much of our time is spent trying to chart God on a grid, and too little is spent allowing our hearts to feel awe. By reducing Christian spirituality to formula, we deprive our hearts of wonder.

When I think about the complexity of the Trinity, the three-in-one God, my mind cannot understand, but my heart feels wonder in abundant satisfaction. It is as though my heart, in the midst of its euphoria, is saying to my mind, *There are things you cannot understand, and you must learn to live with this. Not only must you learn to live with this, you must learn to enjoy this.*

I want to tell you something about me that you may see as weakness. I need wonder. I know that death is coming. I smell it in the wind, read it in the paper, watch it on television, and see it on the faces of the old. I need wonder to explain what is going to happen to me, what is going to happen to us when this thing is done, when our shift is over and our kids' kids are still on the earth listening to their crazy rap music. I need something mysterious to happen after I die. I need to be somewhere else after I die, somewhere with God, somewhere that wouldn't make any sense if it were explained to me right now.

At the end of the day, when I am lying in bed and I know the chances of any of our theology being exactly right are a million to one, I need to know that God has things figured out, that if my math is wrong we are still going to be okay. And wonder is that feeling we get when we let go of our silly answers, our mapped out rules that we want God to follow. I don't think there is any better worship than wonder.

Love

How to Really Love Other People

WHEN MY FRIEND PAUL AND I LIVED IN THE woods, we lived with hippies. Well, sort of hippies. They certainly smoked a lot of pot. They drank a lot of beer. And man did they love each other, sometimes too much, perhaps, too physically, you know, but nonetheless they loved; they accepted and cherished everybody, even the ones who judged them because they were hippies. It was odd living with the hippies at first, but I enjoyed it after a while.

They were not the traveling hippies, the "live off the land and other people" hippies. They were formally educated, most of them from New York studying at NYU, getting their master's in literature, headed off to law school, that sort of thing. They knew all about Rostandt, all about Hopkins and Poe and Sylvia Plath. They knew the Americans and the Brits and the fashionable African writers, the Cubans and South Americans. They were books themselves, all of them were books, and what was so wonderful is that to them, I was a book too. We would sit around and talk about literature and each other, and I couldn't tell the difference between the books they were talking about and their lives, they were just that cool. I liked them very much because they were interested in me. When I was with the hippies I did not feel judged, I felt loved. To them I was an endless well of stories and perspectives and grand literary views. It felt so wonderful to be in their presence, like I was special.

I have never experienced a group of people who loved each other more than my hippies in the woods. All of them are tucked so neatly into my memory now, and I recall our evenings at camp or in the meadow or in the caves in my mind like a favorite film. I pull them out when I need to be reminded about goodness, about purity and kindness.

The resort we were working at was Black Butte Ranch in central Oregon, and we were living about a mile off a ridge, beyond the cattle fence, down in a gully where stood stately pines and remarkable aspen. There were also a family of deer and a porcupine. The boys from New York worked at Honkers Café, named for the ducks, and Paul and I would merely have to sit ourselves on the deck off the lake and within minutes we would have a burger or a shake or a slice of pie, always delivered with a smile, always for free. They were stealing from the rich to feed the poor. We were eating food from the wealthy table of the white man. This is how I thought about it, even though I was white.

After Honker's closed we would fill the café and play the juke box, the guys always choosing Springsteen and talking about life in New York, about life in the city. But more than they talked, they listened.

So much of what I know about getting along with people I learned from the hippies. They were magical in community. People were drawn to them. They asked me what I loved, what I hated, how I felt about this and that, what sort of music made me angry, what sort of music made me sad. They asked me what I daydreamed about, what I wrote about, where my favorite places in the world were. They asked me about high school and college and my travels around America. They loved me like a good novel, like an art film, and this is how I felt when I was with them, like a person John Irving would write. I did not feel fat or stupid or sloppily dressed. I did not feel like I did not know the Bible well enough, and I was never conscious what my hands were doing or whether or not I sounded immature when I talked. I had always been so conscious of those things, but living with the hippies I forgot about myself. And when I lost this self-consciousness I gained so much more. I gained an interest in people outside my own skin. They were greater than movies to me, greater than television. The spirit of the hippies was contagious. I couldn't hear enough about Eddie's ballerina girlfriend or Owen's epic poems. I would ask them to repeat stories because, to me, they were like great scenes in favorite movies. I cannot tell you how quickly these people, these pot-smoking hippies, disarmed me.

Because I grew up in the safe cocoon of big-Christianity, I came to believe that anything outside the church was filled with darkness and unlove. I remember, one Sunday evening, sitting in the pew as a child listening to the pastor read from articles in the newspaper. He took an entire hour to flip through the paper reading about all the gory murders and rapes and burglaries, and after each article he would sigh and say, *Friends, it is a bad, bad world out there. And things are only getting worse.* Never in my wildest dreams would I have imagined there were, outside the church, people so purely lovely as the ones I met in the woods. And yet my hippie friends were not at all close to believing that Christ was the Son of God.

This did not confuse me so much as it surprised me. Until this point, the majority of my friends had been Christians. In fact nearly all of them had been Christians. I was amazed to find, outside the church, genuine affection being shared, affection that seemed, well, authentic in comparison to the sort of love I had known within the church. I was even more amazed when I realized I preferred, in fact, the company of the hippies to the company of Christians. It isn't that I didn't love my Christian friends or that they didn't love me, it was just that there was something different about my hippie friends; something, I don't know, more real, more true. I realize that is a provocative statement, but I only felt I could be myself around them, and I could not be myself with my Christian friends. My Christian communities had always had little unwritten social ethics like don't cuss and don't support Democrats and don't ask tough questions about the Bible.

I stayed in the woods only a month. I wanted to stay longer, but I had secured a job in Colorado at a Christian camp and needed to honor that agreement. Though I had spent only a month with the hippies, it seemed a lifetime. I had learned more about people, about community and happiness and contentment by living in the woods than I had in a lifetime of studying these ideas philosophically. I had discovered life outside the church, and I liked it. As I said, I preferred it. I said my sad good-byes and boarded a bus bound for Colorado.

○   ○   ○

Before getting off the Greyhound bus, I threw away my pack of cigarettes. I knew I would not be able to smoke while working at camp. The guy who picked me up from the bus station could smell the smoke on my clothes so he sat quietly and asked few questions. Though Paul and I had been in the woods for only a month, we had been traveling around America for several months, and so the first thing I noticed when I got to camp was that these were clean people; they ironed their clothes and that sort of thing. They had clean-shaven faces and spoke through smiles.

I liked them, they all looked so new to me, so much like they belonged in storefront windows, like fine china dolls or models for Banana Republic. There was a buzz about me almost immediately. I didn't want there to be, but I had been traveling for so long I'd forgotten some basic things like sleeping indoors and eating with utensils. Some of the bolder staff members approached me to try to talk. I think they thought I was sort of stupid because they spoke very slowly and made wide motions with their hands as they spoke. "I'm Jane. My name, Jane, what your name?"

The camp director, a very conservative man, sent word to me through a servant that I was to shave and wear appropriate clothes. It is true I had gotten a little hairy in the woods. They had rules, these people, they had expectations, and if you did not comply you were socially shunned. Well, not really shunned, just smiled at, smiled at a great deal, smiled at and watched and giggled over when passed in the hall. I confess I enjoyed being different. I got more attention by being the hippie guy than I had when I was normal. I felt better in a lot of ways, more superior, because I was no longer sheltered. I had been in the world, and the world had approved of me.

They were cute, these little Christian people. I liked them. They reminded me of my roots, where I had come from all those days ago, before my month in the woods with the pot smokers and the hippies and the free love for everybody. When the director's assistant told me to shave she told me sheepishly. She knew it was a silly request. Hey, listen, I told her, I will do exactly what the man tells me to do, you know, because I respect the man, I don't want a fight. She smiled back at me, seeing the genius of my emotional intelligence.

"Do you need a razor or something?" She looked at me, sort of smirking.

"You know," I replied, leaning against the wall in the hallway,

"I think I have one somewhere; I have a backpack or something somewhere."

"You don't know where your stuff is?" she asked, obviously coming from a primitive, materialistic, territorial paradigm.

"Oh, you know, it is probably in my room, or maybe around, you know, who knows?"

"Well maybe you should put it somewhere where you won't lose it."

"Well, you know, if I lost it, what would I have lost, right?" I asked her.

"You would have lost your backpack," she answered matter-of-factly. She had sort of a bothered, questioning look on her face.

"Right. Right, but you know, what would any of us lose by losing our possessions. Maybe we would gain something, like relationships, like the beauty of good friends, intimacy, you know what I mean, man? Like we wouldn't be losing anything if we lost our stuff, we'd be gaining everything."

"Yeah," she said. "That's fascinating. Well, just shave, okay. If you need a razor I will get you one." She was getting very flustered or something, really wanting to pull out of the conversation. I figured she hadn't met anybody fascinating like me before.

"Yeah," I told her. "Yeah, if I need anything I will come looking for you. That's sweet of you, real sweet."

"Honestly, it's my job," she told me.

"Cool. That's chill," I said.

"What?"

"That's chill. You know, on ice."

"Right." She said this very slowly. She stood there silently, just looking at me like I was a big, mysterious puzzle.

"So tell me," I said, breaking the silence, "what do your people call you?"

"My people?"

"Yeah, like your friends, your close ones."

"Are you asking my name?"

"Right on. Your name. What's your name?"

"Janet."

"Janet. Right. Janet. Planet Janet from the Jupiter scene."

Long pause.

"Right," she said slowly.

"So are you in school, Janet? Like, are you in college or just the school of life?"

"I was homeschooled. I'm going to Bob Jones next year."

"Bob who?"

"Jones. It's a college."

"Cool. That's chill."

"Listen, Dan," she started.

"Don," I corrected her. "My name is Don, actually."

"Right," she said slowly. "Is that what your people call you?"

"Yeah." I think she might have been making fun of me or flirting or something.

"You should probably shave," she continued. "And I wasn't going to tell you, but maybe you should take a shower." She was definitely flirting.

"No prob, Janet, you know, thanks for mentioning it. I've been living in the woods, you know, out in the open and all. Don't need a shower out there, right?"

"Not out there, no. But since you will be with us now, you know, maybe you should try it out."

"Right on. Cool to know the rules, you know."

"Well, Don, it was certainly interesting meeting you. I am sure I will see you again. Maybe won't recognize you though." She motioned toward my beard and smiled.

I didn't know what she meant at first, but then I got it. She meant she wouldn't recognize me after I shaved. "Oh, yeah, cool," I told her. "Maybe not, huh? But don't worry, I will remind you who I am."

"Right," she said slowly, and then walked away shaking her head.

○　○　○

While at camp we were encouraged to attend church. Buses went on Sundays to a couple of different churches. Both of them were a little stiff.

I felt like both churches came to the table with a them and us mentality, them being the liberal non-Christians in the world, and us being Christians. I felt, once again, that there was this underlying hostility for homosexuals and Democrats and, well, hippie types. I cannot tell you how much I did not want liberal or gay people to be my enemies. I liked them. I cared about them, and they cared about me. I learned that in the woods. I had never felt so alive as I did in the company of my liberal friends. It isn't that the Christians I had been with had bad community; they didn't, I just liked the community of the hippies because it was more forgiving, more, I don't know, healthy.

The real issue in the Christian community was that it was conditional. You were loved, but if you had questions, questions about whether the Bible was true or whether America was a good country or whether last week's sermon was good, you were not so loved. You were loved in word, but there was, without question, a social commodity that was being withheld from you until you shaped up. By toeing the party line you earned social dollars; by being yourself you did not. If you wanted to be valued, you became a clone. These are broad generalizations, and they are unfair, but this is what I was thinking at the time. Bear with me, and I will tell you what I learned.

I began to attend a Unitarian church. All-Souls Unitarian Church in Colorado Springs was wonderful. The people were wonderful. Like my friends in the woods, they freely and openly accepted everybody the church didn't seem to accept. I don't suppose they accepted fundamentalists, but neither did I at the time. I was comfortable there. Everybody was comfortable there. I did not like their flaky theology though. I did not like the way they changed words in the hymns, and I did not like the fact they ignored the Bible, but I loved them, and they really liked me. I loved the smiley faces, the hugs, the vulnerable feel to the place, the wonderful old gray-haired professors, former alcoholics and drug addicts, the intellectual feminists who greeted me with the kindest, most authentic faces that I understood as invitations to tell my story.

I began to understand that my pastors and leaders were wrong, that the liberals were not evil, they were liberal for the same reason Christians were Christians, because they believed their philosophies were right, good, and beneficial for the world. I had been raised to believe there were monsters under the bed, but I had peeked, in a moment of bravery, and found a wonderful world, a good world, better, in fact, than the one I had known.

The problem with Christian community was that we had ethics, we had rules and laws and principles to judge each other against. There was love in Christian community, but it was conditional love. Sure, we called it unconditional, but it wasn't. There were bad people in the world and good people in the world. We were raised to believe this. If people were bad, we treated them as though they were either evil or charity: If they were bad and rich, they were evil. If they were bad and poor, they were charity. Christianity was always right; we were always looking down on everybody else. And I hated this. I hated it with a passion. Everything in my soul told me it was wrong. It felt, to me, as wrong as sin. I wanted to love everybody. I wanted everything to be cool. I realize this sounds like tolerance, and to many in the church the word *tolerance* is profanity, but that is precisely what I wanted. I wanted tolerance. I wanted everybody to leave everybody else alone, regardless of their religious beliefs, regardless of their political affiliation. I wanted people to like each other. Hatred seemed, to me, the product of ignorance. I was tired of biblical ethic being used as a tool with which to judge people rather than heal them. I was tired of Christian leaders using biblical principles to protect their power, to draw a line in the sand separating the good army from the bad one. The truth is I had met the enemy in the woods and discovered they were not the enemy. I wondered whether any human being could be an enemy of God.

On the other hand, however, I felt by loving liberal people, I mean by really endorsing their existence, I was betraying the truth of God because I was encouraging them in their lives apart from God. I felt like there was this war going on between us, the Christians, and them, the homosexuals and environmentalists and feminists. By going to a Unitarian church and truly loving those people, I was helping them, I was giving joy to their life and that didn't feel right. It was a terrible place to be.

This was, at the time, my primary problem with Christian faith. With all its talk about pure love, in the end it shook down to conditional love. Again, this is a provocative statement, but I want to walk you through the emotional process I went through.

How could I merge the culture of the woods and the Unitarian church with Christian culture and yet not abandon the truth of Scripture? How could I love my neighbor without endorsing what, I truly believed, was unhealthy spirituality?

My answer did not come for many years, and as for that summer, I became very confused. I gave in to keep the peace. I stopped going to the Unitarian church, I shaved, I cut the hippy act and made friends, good friends, friends whom I loved and who loved me. From time to time I would overhear comments by my friends, destructive comments about the political left or about homosexuals or Democrats, and I never knew what to do with those comments. They felt right in my head but not in my heart. I went along, and, looking back, I think we all went along. Even the people who were making the comments were going along. What else was there to do? Truth is truth.

○   ○   ○

It is always the simple things that change our lives. And these things never happen when you are looking for them to happen. Life will reveal answers at the pace life wishes to do so. You feel like running, but life is on a stroll. This is how God does things.

My realization came while attending an alumni social for Westmont College. I had never attended Westmont, but my friend Michelle did, and she invited me. Greg Spencer, a communications professor, was to speak, and Michelle thought I might enjoy the lecture. I did. More than I can say. The lecture was about the power of metaphor. Spencer opened by asking us what metaphors we think of when we consider the topic of cancer. We gave him our answers, all pretty much the same, we *battle* cancer, we *fight* cancer, we are rebuilding our white blood cells, things like that. Spencer pointed out that the overwhelming majority of metaphors we listed were war metaphors. They dealt with battle. He then proceeded to talk about cancer patients and how, because of war metaphor, many people who suffer with cancer feel more burdened than, in fact, they should. Most of them are frightened beyond their need to be frightened, and this affects their health. Some, feeling that they have been thrust into a deadly war, simply give up. If there were another metaphor, a metaphor more accurate, perhaps cancer would not prove so deadly.

Science has shown that the way people think about cancer affects their ability to deal with the disease, thus affecting their overall health. Professor Spencer said that if he were to sit down with his family and tell them he had cancer they would be shocked, concerned, perhaps even in tears, and yet cancer is nothing near the most deadly of diseases. Because of war metaphor, the professor said, we are more likely to fear cancer when, actually, most people survive the disease.

Mr. Spencer then asked us about another area in which he felt metaphors cause trouble. He asked us to consider relationships. What metaphors do we use when we think of relationships? We *value* people, I shouted out. Yes, he said, and wrote it on his little white board. We *invest* in people, another person added. And soon enough we had listed an entire white board of economic metaphor. Relationships could be *bankrupt*, we said. People are *priceless*, we said. All economic metaphor. I was taken aback.

And that's when it hit me like so much epiphany getting dislodged from my arteries. The problem with Christian culture is we think of love as a commodity. We use it like money. Professor Spencer was right, and not only was he right, I felt as though he had cured me, as though he had let me out of my cage. I could see it very clearly. If somebody is doing something for us, offering us something, be it gifts, time, popularity, or what have you, we feel they have value, we feel they are worth something to us, and, perhaps, we feel they are priceless. I could see it so clearly, and I could feel it in the pages of my life. This was the thing that had smelled so rotten all these years. I used love like money. The church used love like money. With love, we withheld affirmation from the people who did not agree with us, but we lavishly financed the ones who did.

The next few days unfolded in a thick line of melancholy thought and introspection. I used love like money, but love doesn't work like money. It is not a commodity. When we barter with it, we all lose. When the church does not love its enemies, it fuels their rage. It makes them hate us more.

Here's how it worked out on a personal level:

There was this guy in my life at the time, a guy I went to church with whom I honestly didn't like. I thought he was sarcastic and lazy and manipulative, and he ate with his mouth open so that food almost fell from his chin when he talked. He began and ended every sentence with the word *dude*.

"Dude, did you see Springer yesterday?" he would say. "They had this fat lady on there who was doing it with a midget. It was crazy, dude. I want to get me a midget, dude."

That's the sort of thing he would talk about. It was very interesting to him. I don't enjoy not liking people, but sometimes these things feel as though you are not in control of them. I never chose not to like the guy. It felt more like the dislike of him chose me. Regardless, I had to spend a good amount of time with him as we were working on a temporary project together. He began to get under my skin. I wanted him to change. I wanted him to read a book, memorize a poem, or explore morality, at least as an intellectual concept. I didn't know how to communicate to him that he needed to change, so I displayed it on my face. I rolled my eyes. I gave him dirty looks. I would mouth the word *loser* when he wasn't looking. I thought somehow he would sense my disapproval and change his life in order to gain my favor. In short, I withheld love.

After Greg Spencer's lecture, I knew what I was doing was wrong. It was selfish, and what's more, it would never work. By withholding love from my friend, he became defensive, he didn't like me, he thought I was judgmental, snobbish, proud, and mean. Rather than being drawn to me, wanting to change, he was repulsed. I was guilty of using love like money, withholding it to get somebody to be who I wanted them to be. I was making a mess of everything. And I was disobeying God. I became convicted about these things, so much so that I had some trouble getting sleep. It was clear that I was to love everybody, be delighted at everybody's existence, and I had fallen miles short of God's aim. The power of Christian spirituality has always rested in repentance, so that's what I did. I repented. I told God I was sorry. I replaced economic metaphor, in my mind, with something different, a free gift metaphor or a magnet metaphor. That is, instead of withholding love to change somebody, I poured it on, lavishly. I hoped that love would work like a magnet, pulling people from the mire and toward healing. I knew this was the way God loved me. God had never withheld love to teach me a lesson.

Here is something very simple about relationships that Spencer helped me discover: Nobody will listen to you unless they sense that you like them.

If a person senses that you do not like them, that you do not approve of their existence, then your religion and your political ideas will all seem wrong to them. If they sense that you like them, then they are open to what you have to say.

After I repented, things were different, but the difference wasn't with my friend, the difference was with me. I was happy. Before, I had all this negative tension flipping around in my gut, all this judgmentalism and pride and loathing of other people. I hated it, and now I was set free. I was free to love. I didn't have to discipline anybody, I didn't have to judge anybody, I could treat everybody as though they were my best friend, as though they were rock stars or famous poets, as though they were amazing, and to me they became amazing, especially my new friend. I loved him. After I decided to let go of judging him, I discovered he was very funny. I mean, really hilarious. I kept telling him how funny he was. And he was smart. Quite brilliant, really. I couldn't believe that I had never seen it before. I felt as though I had lost an enemy and gained a brother. And then he began to change. It didn't matter to me whether he did or not, but he did. He began to get a little more serious about God. He gave up television for a period of time as a sort of fast. He started praying and got regular about going to church. He was a great human being getting even better. I could feel God's love for him. I loved the fact that it wasn't my responsibility to change somebody, that it was God's, that my part was just to communicate love and approval.

When I am talking to somebody there are always two conversations going on. The first is on the surface; it is about politics or music or whatever it is our mouths are saying. The other is beneath the surface, on the level of the heart, and my heart is either communicating that I like the person I am talking to or I don't. God wants both conversations to be true. That is, we are supposed to speak truth in love. If both conversations are not true, God is not involved in the exchange, we are on our own, and on our own, we will lead people astray. The Bible says that if you talk to somebody with your mouth, and your heart does not love them, that you are like a person standing there smashing two cymbals together. You are only annoying everybody around you. I think that is very beautiful and true.

Now, since Greg Spencer told me about truth, when I go to meet somebody, I pray that God will help me feel His love for them. I ask God to make it so both conversations, the one from the mouth and the one from the heart, are true.

Love

How to Really Love Yourself

I WISH ANI DIFRANCO WASN'T A LESBIAN. I AM listening to her right now, and I think I would marry her if she would have me. I would hang out in the front row at all her concerts and sing along and pump my fist and get angry at all the right times. Then, later, on the bus, she would lay her head on a pillow in my lap, and I would get my fingers tangled in her dreadlocks while we watched Charlie Rose on the television.

Some friends and I were walking to our cars one night outside the Roseland after an Emmy Lou Harris concert, and I could see into her bus and Charlie Rose was on the television. I thought to myself, *I like that show,* and part of me wanted to knock on the window and ask if I could come in. I would not have bothered her or even asked for an autograph. I would have just watched television. He was interviewing Bishop Tutu, I think. By the time I got home the interview was over. If Ani Defranco and I got married, I would write books on the bus rides between cities and in the evening, after the concerts, we would watch Charlie Rose, and three or four times each night we would whisper, *Good question, Charlie, good question.* But none of this will happen because Ani Difranco is not attracted to men, I don't think. Otherwise we would be on.

o　　o　　o

The thing about Reed College you may not know is that it is a beautiful place. I mean the people are beautiful, and I love them. My housemate, Grant, and I were on campus the other day helping kids move into their dorms, and we met this kid Nathan, who needed us to move a couch up to his room. Grant and I were sort of surprised when Nathan started talking to us because, no kidding, he sounded just like Elmer Fudd. He was short and stocky, and nobody but Elmer Fudd himself sounds more like Elmer Fudd than Nathan. Grant almost started laughing, but we tried very hard to listen to the person inside the voice, and so on the way to the storage shed Nathan opened up and told us that as a summer job he worked at Los Alamos, researching nuclear weapons. Nathan does not know his left from his right, which I thought was a peculiar characteristic, given he is one of the smartest people in the world or something. We would come to an intersection and he would point and say, in a perfect Elmer Fudd dialect (I can't do accents at all), "Go dat way, Don. Dat ith de way to the thorage thed."

I was speaking at a pastors conference in San Francisco, and I was telling them about my friends from Reed and what it looks like to talk about Jesus in that place. Somebody asked me what it was like to deal with all the immorality at Reed, and that question really struck me because I have never thought of Reed as an immoral place, and I suppose I never thought of it as an immoral place because somebody like Nathan can go there and talk like Elmer Fudd, and nobody will ever make fun of him. And if Nathan were to go to my church, which I love and would give my life for, he would unfortunately be made fun of by somebody somewhere, behind his back and all, but it would happen, and that is such a tragic crime. Nobody would bother to find out that he is a genius. Nobody would know that he is completely comfortable talking the way he talks and not knowing his left from his right because he has spent four years in a place where what you are on the surface does not define you, it does not label you. And that is what I love about Reed College because even though there are so many students having sex and tripping on drugs and whatever, there is also this foundational understanding that other people exist and they are important, and to me Reed is like heaven in that sense. I wish everybody could spend four years in a place like that, being taught the truth, that they matter regardless of their faults, regardless of their insecurities.

○   ○   ○

Television drives me crazy sometimes because everybody is so good-looking, and yet you walk through the aisles of the grocery stores, and nobody looks like that. Somebody told me that in London people don't judge you as much by the way you look, and I think it is true because late night on PBS they play shows out of England and the actors aren't good-looking, and I sit there wondering if anybody else is watching and asking the same question: Why aren't the actors in London good looking? And I already know the answer to that question, it is that America is one of the most immoral countries in the world and that our media has reduced humans to slabs of meat. And there will always be this tension while I live in this country because none of this will ever change. Ani Difranco, in her song "32 Flavors," says that she is *a poster girl with no poster, she is 32 flavors and then some, and she is beyond our peripheral vision, so we might want to turn our heads, because some day we're gonna get hungry and eat all of the words we just said.* And just about everybody I know loves those lines because they speak of heaven and of hope and the idea that some day a King will come and dictate, through some mystical act of love, an existence in which everybody has to eat their own words because we won't be allowed to judge each other on the surface of things anymore. And this fills me with hope.

Jean-Paul Sarte said hell is other people. But that Indian speaker I really like named Ravi Zacharias says that heaven can be other people, too, and that we have the power to bring a little of heaven into the lives of others every day. I know this is true because I have felt it when Penny or Tony tells me I mean something to them and they love me. I pray often that God would give me the strength and dignity to receive their love.

My friend Julie from Seattle says the key to everything rests in the ability to receive love, and what she says is right because my personal experience tells me so. I used to not be able to receive love at all, and to this day I have some problems, but it isn't like it used to be. My eye would find things on television and in the media and somehow I would compare myself to them without really knowing I was doing it, and this really screwed me up because I never for a second felt I was worthy of anybody's compliments.

○ ○ ○

I was dating this girl for a while, this cute writer from the South, and she was great, really the perfect girl, and we shared tastes on everything from music to movies, all the important stuff, and yet I could not really thrive in the relationship because I could never believe her deeply when she expressed affection. Our love was never a two-way conversation. I didn't realize I was doing it, but

I used to kick myself around quite a bit in my head, calling myself a loser and that sort of thing. There was nothing this girl could do to get through to me. She would explain her feelings, and I should have been happy with that, but I always needed more and then I resented the fact that I needed more because, well, it is such a needy thing to need more, and so I lived inside this conflict. I would sit on the porch at Graceland and watch cars go around the circle while all this stuff went around in my heart. There was no peace at all. I couldn't eat. I couldn't sleep.

Andrew the Protester, the one who looks like Fidel Castro, was living in the house back then, and he is such an amazing listener that I would talk to him and he would nod his head and say, "Don, man, I didn't know you were feeling any of this." But I was. And it got worse. I would mope around the house all day, and I couldn't get any writing done. It had been the same in all my relationships. There was always, within me, this demand for affection, this needy, clingy monkey on my back. I wouldn't be satisfied unless the girl wanted to get married right away, unless she was panicky about it, and even then I would imagine a non-existent scenario in which she finds another man or breaks up with me because of the way I look. I would find myself getting depressed about conversations that never even took place.

Finally, Andrew said I should meet with Diane, who is this beautiful married woman who goes to our church and mothers us and speaks love into our lives because most of us are basket cases. Diane was studying at a local seminary to be a counselor, and Andrew recommended that I ask her to take a shot at all my troubles. I didn't want to do it at first because Diane's husband is an elder, and I had spoken at church a few times, so everybody thought I was normal. Certainly if I talked to Diane she would go home and tell her husband I was nuts and then it would get around the church, and when everybody thinks you are nuts you finally just give in to their pressure and actually go nuts. But I was desperate. So I called Diane.

She was beautiful and soft and kind with a tender voice, and she showed up at the house, and I put some coffee on. We went into my office, and I closed the door, in case one of my roommates walked by and saw me talking to Diane and discovered I was nuts. I sat in a chair, and Diane sat on the couch, and I wrung my hands a bit before starting in:

"Well, you see, Diane, I am in this relationship with this girl, and she is great, she really is. It's just that it is very hard for me, you know."

"You mean it is hard for you to have feelings for her?"

"I'm not gay."

Diane laughed. "I didn't mean it that way, Don."

"I do have feelings for her," I said, with sincerity. "They are almost too strong, you know. I have trouble sleeping and eating and thinking about anything else. It is hard for me to be in a relationship, it always has been. And that makes me want to bail. I would just rather not be in the relationship at all than go through this torture. But I promised myself I wouldn't run from it this time. But I feel like the meaning of life is riding on whether or not she likes me, and I think she does, she says she does, but it still drives me crazy."

"Whether or not she likes you, Don, or whether or not she loves you?"

"Yeah, that too. Whether or not she loves me."

Diane sat there and made listening noises the whole time I was talking, and when I told her how I will go days without eating, she looked at me and sighed and ooohed and was definitely letting me know that this behavior was neither normal nor healthy. I think I could have told her that Elvis Presley was alive and living in my closet, and she would have been less surprised.

When you are a writer and a speaker, sometimes people think you have your crap together.

"You seem so normal, Don. You have a company and are a writer and all." Diane looked at me, bewildered.

"Yeah. But there is something wrong with me, isn't there?"

I was half hoping she would say no. I was hoping she would explain that everybody is nuts when they get into a relationship, but then it turns euphoric shortly after marriage and sex. But she didn't.

"Well, Don, there is. There is something wrong with you."

"Oh, man," I said. "I just knew it. I just knew I was a wacko." I thought about that movie *A Beautiful Mind* and wondered whether any of my housemates existed or whether those guys who kept following me were in the FBI.

Diane noted the concern on my face and responded, smiling and kind. "It's not that bad, Don. Don't worry. It's just that for some reason, you are letting this girl name you."

"What do you mean, name me?"

"Well, you are letting her decide your value, you know. Your value has to come from God. And God wants you to receive His love and to love yourself too."

And what she was saying was true. I knew it was true. I could feel that it was true. But it also felt wrong. I mean, it felt like it was an arrogant thing to do, to love myself, to receive love. I knew that all the kicking myself around, all the hating myself, was not coming from God, that those voices were not God whispering in my ear, but it felt like I had to listen to them; it felt like I had to believe the voices were telling the truth.

"God loves you, Don." Diane looked at me with a little moisture in her eyes. I felt like Matt Damon in that scene in *Good Will Hunting* where Robin Williams keeps saying, "It's not your fault, it's not your fault," and Matt Damon just freaks out and collapses into Robin Williams's arms and secures an Academy Award for both of them. I thought about acting out that scene with Diane, but it didn't feel right so I let it go.

"Yeah, I know," I told her. "I know God loves me." And I did know, I just didn't believe. It was such crap, such psychobabble. I had heard it before, but hearing that stuff didn't silence the voices. Still, there was something in Diane's motherly eyes that said it was true and I needed that; I needed to believe it was true. I needed something to tell the voices when they started chanting at me.

Diane and I talked for another half hour, and she ooohed and sighed and made me feel listened to. She was wonderful, and I never once felt stupid or weak for talking to her. I just felt honest and real and relieved. She said she would get me some literature and that she wanted to get together again soon. She said she would pray for me.

When she left, I decided to start praying about all of this too. I couldn't believe I hadn't prayed about it before. It's just that it never seemed like a spiritual problem. I prayed and asked God to help me figure out what was wrong with me.

Things got worse with the girl. We would spend hours on the phone working through the math of our relationship, but nothing added up, which I received as only a sign of my incompetence, and this made me more sad than before.

Then she did it; she decided we didn't need to be in touch anymore. She broke it off. She sent me a letter saying that I didn't love myself and could not receive love from her. There was nothing she could do about it, and it was killing her. I wandered around the house for an hour just looking at the blank walls, making coffee or cleaning the bathroom, not sure when my body was going to explode in sobs and tears. I was scrubbing the toilet when the voices began. I'd listened to them so often before, but on this day they were shouting. They were telling me that I was as disgusting as the urine on the wall around the toilet.

And then the sentiment occurred. I am certain it was the voice of God because it was accompanied by such a strong epiphany like a movement in a symphony or something. The sentiment was simple: *Love your neighbor as yourself.*

And I thought about that for a second and wondered why God would put that phrase so strongly in my mind. I thought about our neighbor Mark, who is tall and skinny and gay, and I wondered whether God was telling me I was gay, which was odd because I had never felt gay, but then it hit me that God was not telling me I was gay. He was saying I would never talk to my neighbor the way I talked to myself, and that somehow I had come to believe it was wrong to kick other people around but it was okay to do it to myself. It was as if God had put me in a plane and flown me over myself so I could see how I was connected, all the neighborhoods that were falling apart because I would not let myself receive love from myself, from others, or from God. And I wouldn't receive love because it felt so wrong. It didn't feel humble, and I knew I was supposed to be humble. But that was all crap, and it didn't make any sense. If it is wrong for me to receive love, then it is also wrong for me to give it because by giving it I am causing somebody else to receive it, which I had presupposed was the wrong thing to do. So I stopped. And I mean that. I stopped hating myself. It no longer felt right. It wasn't manly or healthy, and I cut it out. That was about a year ago, and since then I have been relatively happy. I am not kidding. I don't sit around and talk bad about myself anymore.

The girl and I got back together, and she could sense the difference in me, and she liked it, and I felt that I was operating a completely new machine. I couldn't believe how beautiful it was to receive love, to have the authority to love myself, to feel that it was right to love myself. When my girlfriend told me how she felt, I was able to receive it, and we had this normal relationship that in the end didn't work because we realized we weren't for each other. When we finally closed it out, it didn't hurt because I trusted that God had something else for me, and if He didn't, it didn't mean He didn't love me. From that point on, the point in the bathroom, I had confidence. Odd but true.

o   o   o

And so I have come to understand that strength, inner strength, comes from receiving love as much as it comes from giving it. I think apart from the idea that I am a sinner and God forgives me, this is the greatest lesson I have ever learned. When you get it, it changes you. My friend Julie from Seattle told me that the main prayer she prays for her husband is that he will be able to receive love. And this is the prayer I pray for all my friends because it is the key to happiness. God's love will never change us if we don't accept it.

Jesus

The Lines on His Face

A GUY I KNOW NAMED ALAN WENT AROUND THE country asking ministry leaders questions. He went to successful churches and asked the pastors what they were doing, why what they were doing was working. It sounded very boring except for one visit he made to a man named Bill Bright, the president of a big ministry. Alan said he was a big man, full of life, who listened without shifting his eyes. Alan asked a few questions. I don't know what they were, but as a final question he asked Dr. Bright what Jesus meant to him. Alan said Dr. Bright could not answer the question. He said Dr. Bright just started to cry. He sat there in his big chair behind his big desk and wept.

When Alan told that story I wondered what it was like to love Jesus that way. I wondered, quite honestly, if that Bill Bright guy was just nuts or if he really knew Jesus in a personal way, so well that he would cry at the very mention of His name. I knew then that I would like to know Jesus like that, with my heart, not just my head. I felt like that would be the key to something.

o   o   o

I was watching one of those news shows on television several months ago about a woman whose son was on death row. He had killed a man and buried him in the woods. The television show followed the woman around during her son's last few days. The cameras were there for the last visit when the son, a young black man, sat across from his mother in the prison visiting room, and the mother had tears in her eyes and was trying so very hard to disguise the fear and regret and confusion and panic. I sat on the couch uncomfortably, and I wanted to jump through the screen and stop it all. I remember saying to myself, I hate this, but I kept watching. And there was a little girl there, the man's tiny sister, and she was sitting on his lap, and she didn't know he was going to die, but he was saying to be good and to do homework and don't tell any lies and obey her mama. Then the television showed the mother in her apartment a couple of days later, a sort of run-down hotel room in the ghetto, in the projects, and they didn't narrate anything, they just let the cameras roll as the woman paced up and down in front of the bed. The kids, the three beautiful children, ran in and out the open door, in and out of the heat where there was some sunset light happening. And the phone rang, and the woman went over and sat on the side of the bed and picked up the phone. She held it kind of shakily and listened without saying anything. She just said yes, in sort of a gut whisper, and then she put the phone back down, but it didn't hang up right. She fell to her knees and then got up and screamed and shook her fists at the ceiling. She turned and ran out the door, into the courtyard of this run-down apartment complex, and as the camera pulled to look out the open door they showed this large black woman collapse to the ground screaming into the dirt and pounding her fist.

I thought of that scene much later when my friend Julie and I were driving down from Yosemite listening to Patty Griffin sing

"Mary" on the CD player. In the song, Patty talks about Mary, the mother of Jesus, and what it must have been like the day her son was killed. She paints this painful picture of Mary inside her house, cleaning, and as the song played I imagined Mary washing down the counters and sweeping the floors, frantically, trying not to think about what they had done to her Son that morning. And I imagined Mary falling down outside her door on her hands and knees and beating her fists into the dirt and screaming at God.

Julie and I drove down from Glacier Point, and even though it was cold we turned on the heat and rolled down the windows so we could see the stars through the trees. We kept hitting repeat on the CD player and ended up listening to Patty Griffin sing about Mary more than forty consecutive times. I kept imagining Jesus in my mind like a real person, sometimes out in the wilderness like Yosemite Valley, sometimes by a fire talking with His friends, sometimes thinking about His mother, always missing His Father.

Rick leads a small group for people who do not believe in Jesus but have questions about Him. One of the people in the small group asked Rick what he thought Jesus looked like; did He look like the pictures on the walls of churches? Rick said he didn't know. One of the other people in the group spoke up very cautiously and said she thought perhaps he looked like Osama Bin Laden. Rick said this is probably very close to the truth.

Sometimes I picture this Osama Bin Laden–looking Jesus talking with His friends around a fire, except He is not rambling about anything, He is really listening, not so much pushing an agenda but being kind and understanding and speaking some truth and encouragement into their lives. Helping them believe in the mission they feel inside themselves, the mission that surrounded Jesus and the crazy life they had embraced.

○   ○   ○

I remember the first time I had feelings for Jesus. It wasn't very long ago. I had gone to a conference on the coast with some Reed students, and a man spoke who was a professor at a local Bible college. He spoke mostly about the Bible, about how we should read the Bible. He was convincing. He seemed to have an emotional relationship with the Book, the way I think about *Catcher in the Rye*. This man who was speaking reads through the Bible three times each year. I had never read through the Bible at all. I had read a lot of it but not all of it, and mostly I read it because I felt that I had to; it was healthy or something. The speaker guy asked us to go outside and find a quiet place and get reacquainted with the Book, hold it in our hands and let our eyes feel down the pages. I went out on the steps outside the rest room and opened my Bible to the book of James.

Years ago I had a crush on a girl, and I prayed about it and that night read through James, and because it is a book about faith and belief I felt like God was saying that if I had faith she would marry me. So I was very excited about this and lost a lot of weight, but the girl gave her virginity to a jerk from our youth group, and they are married now. I didn't care, honestly. I didn't love her that much. I only say that because the book of James, in my Bible, is highlighted in ten colors and underlined all over the place, and it looks blood raw, and the yellow pages remind me of a day when I believed so faithfully in God, so beautifully in God. I read a little, maybe a few pages, then shut the book, very tired and confused. But when we got back from the conference, I felt like my Bible was calling me. I felt this promise that if I read it, if I just read it like a book, cover to cover, it wouldn't change me into an idiot, it wouldn't change me into a clone of Pat Buchanan, and that was honestly the thing I was worried about with the Bible. If I read it, it would make me simple in my thinking. So I started in Matthew, which is one of the Gospels about Jesus. And I read through Matthew and Mark, then Luke and John. I read those books in a week or so, and Jesus was very confusing, and I didn't know if I liked Him very much, and I was certainly tired of Him by the second day. By the time I got to the end of Luke, to the part where they were going to kill Him again, where they were going to stretch Him out on a cross, something shifted within me. I remember it was cold outside, crisp, and the leaves in the trees of the park across the street were getting tired and dry. And I remember sitting at my desk, and I don't know what it was that I read or what Jesus was doing in the book, but I felt a love for Him rush through me, through my back and into my chest. I started crying, too, like that guy Bill Bright.

I remember thinking that I would follow Jesus anywhere, that it didn't matter what He asked me to do. He could be mean to me; it didn't matter, I loved Him, and I was going to follow Him.

I think the most important thing that happens within Christian spirituality is when a person falls in love with Jesus.

Sometimes when I go forward at church to take Communion, to take the bread and dip it in the wine, the thought of Jesus comes to me, the red of His blood or the smell of His humanity, and I eat the bread and I wonder at the mystery of what I am doing, that somehow I am one with Christ, that I get my very life from Him, my spiritual life comes from His working inside me, being inside me.

I know our culture will sometimes understand a love for Jesus as weakness. There is this lie floating around that says I am supposed to be able to do life alone, without any help, without stopping to worship something bigger than myself. But I actually believe there is something bigger than me, and I need for there to be something bigger than me. I need someone to put awe inside me; I need to come second to someone who has everything figured out.

o   o   o

All great characters in stories are the ones who give their lives to something bigger than themselves. And in all of the stories I don't find anyone more noble than Jesus. He gave His life for me, in obedience to His Father. I truly love Him for it. I feel that, and so does Laura and Penny and Rick and Tony the Beat Poet. I think the difference in my life came when I realized, after reading those Gospels, that Jesus didn't just love me out of principle; He didn't just love me because it was the right thing to do. Rather, there was something inside me that caused Him to love me. I think I realized that if I walked up to His campfire, He would ask me to sit down, and He would ask me my story. He would take the time to listen to my ramblings or my anger until I could calm down, and then He would look me directly in the eye, and He would speak to me; He would tell me the truth, and I would sense in his voice and in the lines on His face that he liked me. He would rebuke me, too, and he would tell me that I have prejudices against very religious people and that I need to deal with that; He would tell me that there are poor people in the world and I need to feed them and that somehow this will make me more happy. I think He would tell me what my gifts are and why I have them, and He would give me ideas on how to use them. I think He would explain to me why my father left, and He would point out very clearly all the ways God has taken care of me through the years, all the stuff God protected me from.

o   o   o

After I got Laura's e-mail in which she told me she had become a Christian, I just about lost it with excitement. I felt like a South African the day they let Mandela out of prison. I called her and asked her to coffee at Palio. I picked her up in Eliot Circle at Reed, and she was smiling and full of energy. She said we had much to talk about, very much to talk about. At Palio, we sat in the booth at the back, and even though Laura had been my close friend, I felt like I had never met this woman. She squirmed in her seat as she talked with confidence about her love for Jesus. I sat there amazed because it is true. People do come to know Jesus. This crazy thing really happens. It isn't just me.

○　○　○

I was watching BET one night, and they were interviewing a man about jazz music. He said jazz music was invented by the first generation out of slavery. I thought that was beautiful because, while it is music, it is very hard to put on paper; it is so much more a language of the soul. It is as if the soul is saying something, something about freedom. I think Christian spirituality is like jazz music. I think loving Jesus is something you feel. I think it is something very difficult to get on paper. But it is no less real, no less meaningful, no less beautiful.

The first generation out of slavery invented jazz music. It is a music birthed out of freedom. And that is the closest thing I know to Christian spirituality. A music birthed out of freedom. Everybody sings their song the way they feel it, everybody closes their eyes and lifts up their hands.

○　○　○

I want Jesus to happen to you the way He happened to Laura at Reed, the way He happened to Penny in France, the way He happened to me in Texas. I want you to know Jesus too. This book is about the songs my friends and I are singing. This is what

God is doing in our lives. But what song will you sing when your soul gets set free? I think it will be something true and beautiful. If you haven't done it in a while, pray and talk to Jesus. Ask Him to become real to you. Ask Him to forgive you of self-addiction, ask Him to put a song in your heart. I can't think of anything better that could happen to you than this. Much love to you and thanks for listening to us sing.

Acknowledgments

Thank you, Kathy Helmers, for your encouragement and help in getting this book to a publisher, and to Lee and Alice and the rest of the crew at Alive for their generous hearts and diligent work. Much gratitude to the people at Thomas Nelson for rolling the dice; those people are Brian, Jonathan, Kyle, Ashley, Pamela, Laurie, Belinda, Blythe, Amy, Danielle, Kathleen, Carol, Andrea, Paula, Tina, Louetta, Kristen, Jenny, Deonne, and interns Stacey and Sarah. And thanks to the rest of that great crew at Thomas Nelson including the huge sales staff on the road who don't get thanked enough. Also thanks to media trainer Joel Roberts.

My friends gave their lives to me and then kindly let me write about our relationships, which was something vulnerable and giving, so thanks to Tony, Penny, Laura, Andrew the Protester, Rick, Mark the Cussing Pastor, Les, the Tunnell family, Wes and Maja Bjur, Paul and Danielle, Mike, Josh, Jeremy, Heather, Kurt, Curtis, Mitch, Simon, Trevor, Michael, Stacy, Diane, Wes, Grant, Julie the Canadian, Matt and Julie Canlis, Rachel Clifton for being the second mom to so many of us, the guys at Graceland, and the guys at Testosterhome too. Also, the people I love at Imago-Dei Community and my family.

Thanks Josh, Gregg, and Sono for giving me a start. And to John and Terri MacMurray, who were like family away from family. Thanks Wes and Maja for letting me live in your attic for so long and as always for your love and kindness.

Thanks, Peter Jenkins, for your drawings, and Steve Harmon, for author shots, video stuff, and encouragement. Thanks, David Allen, for your work on cover comps. I owe you one. Thanks to Tony's grad class at Multnomah for reading the manuscript and giving encouragement; those folks are Shemaiah, Lindsey, Toby, Steve, and Nicole. Thanks to James Prior for bringing me so often to San Fran and for your friendship. This book was written at Common Ground, Palio, Horse Brass Pub, the downtown coffee shops including Seattle's Best, Vista Springs, and a few others I can't remember, but thanks to these fine establishments for their good coffee and beer. Thanks to tri-met for getting me around. "How we get there matters!" While I wrote I listened to Patty Griffin, the Pogues, Bruce Springsteen, Eliot Smith, Lyle, Whiskeytown, Phil Roy, Big Head Todd and the Monsters, the Jayhawks, P.O.D., Tori Amos, Steve Earle, Bob Schneider, Moby, the Beatles, and my current favorite, Wilco (*Yankee Hotel Foxtrot* had just come out when I started the project, and we were all amazed and happy), so strange thanks to the makers of the sound track.

Thank you for reading this book. It means a great deal to me that you would take the time. I hope we get to meet some day soon.

SEARCHING
FOR GOD
KNOWS WHAT

This book is dedicated to
John MacMurray.

CONTENTS

———

Author's Note   253

CHAPTER ONE:
Fine Wine: The Failure of Formulas   255

CHAPTER TWO:
Impostors: Santa Takes a Leak   271

CHAPTER THREE:
Feet of Trees: What Do We Really Want?   289

CHAPTER FOUR:
Free Verse: A Whole Message to a Whole Human Being   303

CHAPTER FIVE:
Naked: Why Nudity Is the Point   315

CHAPTER SIX:
Children of Chernobyl: Why Did God Leave?   329

CHAPTER SEVEN:
Adam, Eve, and the Alien: How the Fall
Makes You Feel   345

CHAPTER EIGHT:
Lifeboat Theory: How to Kill Your Neighbor   359

CHAPTER NINE:
Jesus: Who Needs a Boat?   373

CONTENTS

CHAPTER TEN:

The Gospel of Jesus: It Never Was a Formula   405

CHAPTER ELEVEN:

A Circus of Redemption: Why a Three-Legged
Man Is Better Than a Bearded Woman   419

CHAPTER TWELVE:

Morality: Why I Am Better Than You   433

CHAPTER THIRTEEN:

Religion: A Public Relations Campaign for God   451

CHAPTER FOURTEEN:

The Gospel of Jesus: Why William Shakespeare
Was a Prophet   469

Afterword   487

Acknowledgments   489

AUTHOR'S NOTE

Sometimes I feel as though I were born in a circus, come out of my mother's womb like a man from a cannon, pitched toward the ceiling of the tent, all the doctors and nurses clapping in delight from the grandstands, the band going great guns in trombones and drums. I unfold and find flight hundreds of feet above the center ring, the smell of popcorn in the air, the clowns gather below, amazed at my grace, and all the people chanting my name as my arms come out like wings and I move swan-like toward the apex, where I draw my arms in, collapse my torso to my legs, roll over in perfection, then slowly give in to gravity. My body falls back toward earth, the ground coming up quick, the center ring growing enormous beneath my falling weight.

And this is precisely when it occurs to me that there is no net. And I wonder, *What is the use of a circus?* and *Why should a man bother to be shot out of a cannon?* and *Why is the crowd's applause so fleeting?* and . . . *Who is going to rescue me?*

CHAPTER ONE

Fine Wine

———

THE FAILURE OF FORMULAS

Some time ago I attended a seminar for Christian writers. It was in a big hotel down South and hotels always make me uncomfortable because the bedding is so fluffy and the television swivels, and who makes coffee in the bathroom? But I felt that I needed to be at this seminar. I was wondering how, exactly, to write a book for a Christian market, a book that people would actually read. I had written a book several years before, but it didn't sell. It was a road-trip narrative about me, a friend, and God, and how we traveled across the country in a Volkswagen van, smoking pipes and picking fights with truckers. God wasn't actually a character in the book the way my friend and I were; God more or less played Himself, up in heaven, sending down puzzling wisdom and answers to prayer every hundred miles or so.

But even though the story had God in it, which I believed made it prime for Christian bookstores, sales were less than holy. The book limped along for about a year and then, suddenly, died. God led the publisher to take the book out of print about the same time sales dipped into negative figures. The publisher called and asked if I wanted to buy a few thousand copies for myself at twelve cents each and I ended up buying four. I believe the rest of the books were sold to convenience-store distributors who shelved them next to three-dollar romance novels at the back of the potato-chip aisle.

The only positive thing that happened in all this was that for the next year or so I received enjoyable and sultry e-mails from women who had recently begun to consider themselves spiritual. And while I certainly enjoyed the correspondence and still keep in touch with many of these women today, the career path was not as respectable as I would have liked. I have always wanted to be a sophisticated Christian writer and not somebody who has books on the close-out aisle at Plaid Pantry. That is why I signed up for this seminar, the one I was telling you about that was in the hotel with the bathroom/cafés.

I arrived the evening before, and so the morning of the seminar I woke up very early, about six, and I couldn't fall back to sleep. I opened the curtains and watched planes land at the Memphis airport for an hour or so, trying to guide them in with my mind and that sort of thing. And then I went into the bathroom and sat down and had some coffee and read the paper. After an hour I started getting dressed, and the whole time I was ironing my clothes I was wondering whether this would be the weekend I would be discovered, whether this would be the start of a long career writing adventurous, life-changing books for my fellow brothers and sisters in Christ. I sat on the edge of the bed in my suit and tie and watched television for an hour. Katie Couric was interviewing a fellow who had written a book about how Donald Rumsfeld was actually the Antichrist and I confess, I practiced answering all her questions, knowing that I, too, would some day be interviewed by Katie Couric:

You really make Mr. Rumsfeld out to be a monster, Mr. Miller. This seems unfounded. How did you come to these conclusions?

I had him followed by a private detective, a high-tech guy I found at Radio Shack. Everything in the book is documented, Miss Couric. Or may I call you Katie? Or may I just call you?

When the interview was over I turned the television off and lay back on the fluffy bed and stared at the bedside clock, trying to speed up time with my mind, but time went on as usual and so I fell asleep for exactly nine minutes and then woke up and tried not to blink till about twenty minutes to eight, which is when I headed downstairs. In the lobby I asked the man at the front desk which room the seminar was in. I leaned against the desk as the concierge, a twenty-something fellow with a goatee, searched for a room schedule among his papers. "Capturing literature for the glory of God?" the man asked suspiciously, reading the name of the seminar from a sheet of paper, looking up at me as if to ask whether or not this was the seminar I was interested in and also, perhaps, why God was trying to "capture literature for His glory." "That's the one," I said to him. "Interesting name for a conference, isn't it?" he said, looking at me with a smile.

"We can't have literature running around doing anything it wants now, can we?" I told him.

"I don't suppose so," he said after a long and uncomfortable pause.

"And where will we be capturing said literature?" I asked. By this I was asking what room we were in. He looked at me, puzzled. "What room are we in?" I clarified.

"Oh," he said as he looked back at the sheet. "You are in conference room 210, which is just down the hall across from the restrooms."

"Perfect," I said, adding that if he saw people in the lobby reading pagan literature to please notify me.

"Certainly," he said to me, confused, but kind of standing at attention all the same.

I remember having a very good feeling that morning, walking down the big hall toward the conference room, once again believing I was on my way to becoming the next great spiritual writer, a sort of evangelical Depak Chopra crossed with Tom Clancy, or that guy who wrote *Jonathan Livingston Seagull*, or Ansel Adams, or whoever, just somebody famous. I had terrific ideas; I really did. I was going to write a story about a nun who takes over small third-world countries by causing their evil dictators to fall in love with her, leaving a trail of megachurches and democracy in her wake. The book was going to be called *Sister Democracy, Show Some Leg!*

I had another story about a guy whose father, a psychology professor at a prestigious university, raised his son in a maze, rewarding him when he crawled down dark hallways and disciplining him when he crawled down lit hallways, thus teaching him to do everything in life counterintuitively. In the story, the kid grows up to be a kind of genius with an enormous following; people hanging on his every word. The book was going to be called *Maze Boy: How One Man Brought Down the United States Postal Service!* And if it were a Christian novel, and I could easily turn it into a Christian novel if the money was right, I was going to call it *Maze Boy: How One Man, with God's Help, Brought Down the United States Postal Service!*

I stocked up on bagels at the back of the conference room because I was the first one there. I chose a chair somewhere near the middle, and soon fellow writers began shuffling in, perhaps twenty or so over the next ten minutes. Everybody was being very quiet, looking over their notebooks, but I made small talk with a woman next to me about why we were there and where we had come from and what sort of books we liked to read. Some of the nicest people you could ever hope to meet will be at a Christian writers seminar, I'll tell you that right now. Very small people, though, mostly women, not the sort of folks you would imagine taking literature captive for the glory of God, but kind and others-centered nonetheless.

The lady sitting next to me was writing a wonderful series of Christian devotionals for girls who were taking ballet classes, and the lady on the other side of me was writing a series of devotionals you could read while drinking tea. When she told me this, a lady in front of us turned around and smiled because she was working on a series of devotionals you could read while drinking coffee. I told them their books sounded terrific, because it is true that some people like tea and some people like coffee, and for that matter, some people dance in ballets.

The ladies asked me what I was working on, and I told them about the nun in South America and described a specific scene in which the nun actually ponders whether or not *she* has fallen in love with a dictator named Pablo Hernandez-Juarez, and I had the ladies lean in as I told them the part where the nun is standing on a balcony overlooking a Pacific sunset, painfully considering whether she should go back inside to be with Pablo or whether she should scale the side of the dictator's castle, thus escaping to move on to the next country, the next dictator, and the next story of passion and liberation. You could tell the ladies really liked my story, and all three of them told me it was a terrific idea. I told them about how, in my mind, it was actually a musical, and I whistled a few bars from the love theme. I was going to tell them about the kid who grew up in a maze and brought down the United States Postal Service, but that's when the lady who was going to teach the seminar showed up.

She was also a small woman, but she knew her stuff. Three of her books had been published: a series of devotionals you could read while eating chocolate, a book about the hidden secrets of fulfillment found in end-times prophecy, and a book about how to make "big money" painting "small houses." Three different genres, she told us, but each one had been a success. She told us that there are, in fact, formulas for writing successful books, and that if we followed one of these formulas, we, too, could write books that end up on subcategory Christian or Catholic bestseller lists, not the monthly ones, but the annual ones, which also consider backlist titles and total sales, including sales to ministries and radio stations as promotional giveaways. Of course I was interested, and I elbowed the lady next to me and lifted my eyebrows.

"The first formula goes like this," our seminar instructor began, holding a finger in the air. "You begin with a crisis. This can be a global crisis, a community crisis, whatever kind of crisis you want. This isn't a *problem*, or a *nuisance*, mind you, this is a *crisis*. This must be something terrible that is going to happen to the world, to our country, to the church, or to the individual unless the reader does something about it. The reader must be taken to the point where they fear the consequences of this crisis. Second, there must be a clear enemy in the crisis, some group of people or some person or some philosophy that is causing the crisis. You must show examples of how these people are causing this crisis, simply because they are the enemy of all that is good. Third, you must spell out the ramifications of the crisis should it go unchecked, and also the glory and beauty of the crisis if dealt with. You must paint a picture of a war against evil forces that are trying to cause this crisis, and you must enlist the reader in this war, painting a very clear picture of the reader as the good guy in the war against the crisis. Fourth, and finally, you must spell out a three- to four-step plan of dealing with said crisis." And with this she took a breath. "Is that clear?" she asked, and as she delivered this last line, she more or less stood up straight, her petite frame putting out the confident vibe of a drill sergeant. I knew, then and there, that these were the women *to take literature captive for the glory of God,* that, in fact, standing before me was the archetype of my South American nun. But as excited as I was, I confess I began to wonder how I was going to work this formula into *Sister of Democracy, Show Some Leg!* or *Maze Boy, How One Man Brought Down the United States Postal Service!*

"Now, there is another recipe!" she said, which gave me hope that there might be a more compatible formula for one of my stories. "First," she began, "you must paint a picture of great personal misery. You must tell the reader of a time when you failed at something, when you had no control over a situation or dynamic. Second, you must talk about where you are now, and how you have control over that situation or dynamic, and how wonderful and fulfilling it is to have control. Third, you must give the reader a three- to four-step plan for getting from the misery and lack of control to the joy and control you currently have."

As wonderful as I thought this formula was, and I confess that I thought it was wonderful, once again I felt that it was going to be difficult for me to wrap a story around one of these recipes. I thought perhaps there would be another formula, perhaps one with guns or a midnight parachute drop into a small African village, but there wasn't. It turns out there were only two formulas. Our instructor went on to tell us that during the next two days, for eight hours each day, we were going to walk step-by-step through these two magical formulas, and by the end of our time we were going to have them mastered; that, essentially, we would be able to approach any topic and *hook* the reader from the very first paragraph.

I sat and listened attentively, taking copious notes, learning to *look for the misery that is hiding beneath the surface of life, the misery that many people will not feel until you tell them it is there,* and to *identify the joy we now feel because the misery has been overcome by taking three steps,* and how *these three steps are very easy and can be taken by anybody who has fifteen dollars to spend on my book.*

When it came time for lunch, I let the room empty out except for our seminar instructor, and feeling defeated and confused because I didn't believe these formulas were necessarily compatible with my stories, I approached her and asked about how I might fit one of these formulas into a book about a nun with a machete. She looked over my shoulder into the empty room, tilted her head, then looked back into my eyes and asked whether I realized this was a *nonfiction* rather than a *fiction* seminar. At the time, I confess, I didn't know the difference between *fiction* and *nonfiction,* so I slyly inquired about the delineation. "What," I began, "do you feel is the largest difference between a work of *fiction* and a work of *nonfiction?*" And again she looked at me, confused. "Well," she said, "I suppose a nonfiction book would be *true,* and a fiction book would be *made up.*"

"For example . . . ," I said, motioning with my hand for an example.

"Well," she began, looking at the floor and smiling before looking back at me, kind of sighing as she spoke, "a novel, a story like the one you are talking about, would be considered a fiction book. But a self-help book, the sort of book we are discussing at this seminar, would be considered nonfiction, because we aren't really making up stories so much as we are trying to offer advice."

"I see," I said, kind of looking at the ceiling.

"I get it," I said, looking back at the floor.

"Indeed," I said, looking back at my instructor.

"Does that help?" she asked, smiling and putting her hand on my arm.

"It does," I said. "It helps a great deal. I like to get people's perspective on fiction and nonfiction. I find the various opinions intriguing."

"I am sure you do," she said to me after a long and uncomfortable pause.

I ate lunch at the Denny's across the street from the hotel, feeling the entire trip to Memphis had been a mistake. And then I remembered a little song, something about making lemons from a lemon tree, and I realized that what I needed to do was write a nonfiction book, something that helped people who were miserable become happy. Only mine would be a Christian self-help book, and I would start each reading with Scripture, then break down the formula the Scripture spoke of. I would call it *Devotions You Can Read While Eating Ice Cream, Soy Ice Cream, and So On!*

There is no question I was the best student at this seminar. Women under one hundred pounds lose energy in the late afternoons because they do not eat enough and they miss their families. I returned home and began poring over the Bible, looking for formulas I could use for my book of daily devotions. And I have to tell you this was much more difficult than you might think. The formulas, in fact, are hidden. It seems when God had the Bible put together, He hid a lot of the ancient wisdom so, basically, you have to read into things and even kind of make up things to get a formula out of it. And the formulas that are obvious are terrible.

For instance, a guy named Stephen was miserable (or at least I assumed he was miserable) and then he became a Christian, and then he was stoned to death. This formula, of course, was not good enough to make the cut. And for that matter, neither was the one about Paul, who was a murderer before he became a Christian and then was blinded while traveling, met Jesus in a burst of light, and then spent various painful years moving from city to city, prison to prison, routinely being beaten and bitten by snakes. No formula there. I moved on to Peter, who was rescued from a successful fishing business only to be crucified, some historical accounts claim, along with his wife. And of course that wouldn't work. So I decided to ignore the actual characters of Scripture and just go with the teachings of Jesus. And that is when things really became difficult. Apparently Jesus had not heard of the wonderful tool of acronym. He mostly told stories, some of which were outlandish. Step one: Eat My flesh. Step two: Drink My blood. Do you know what having to read something like that would do to a guy trying to process dairy products?

Of course, I got frustrated. And it really got me thinking that, perhaps, formula books, by that I mean books that take you through a series of steps, may not be all that compatible with the Bible. I looked on my shelf at all the self-help books I happened to own, the ones about losing weight, the ones about making girls like you, the ones about getting rich, the ones about starting your own pirate radio station, and I realized none of them actually helped me all that much. All the promises of fulfillment really didn't work. My life was fairly normal before I read them, meaning I had good days and bad days, and then my life was fairly normal after I read them too, meaning I still had good days and bad days. It made me wonder, honestly, if such a complex existence as the one you and I are living can really be broken down into a few steps. It seems if there were a formula to fix life, Jesus would have told us what it was.

———

A few weeks later I learned an invaluable lesson from a wealthy and successful businessman here in Portland who owns a chain of coffee shops. A few of us were sitting in one of his shops one morning, and another friend asked if we had seen the World Series of Poker on television the night before. None of us had, but that mention led to a conversation about gambling. My friend who owns the coffee shops told us, in a tone of kindness and truth, that nobody he knows who is successful gambles; rather, they work hard, they accept the facts of reality, they enjoy life as it is. "But the facts of reality stink," I told him. "Reality is like a fine wine," he said to me. "It will not appeal to children." And I am grateful my friend stung me in that way, because this truth helped me understand and appreciate life itself, as it is, without the false hope formulas offer. I didn't read formula books after that because reality is like fine wine. I am quite snobby about it, if you want to know the truth.

———

That said, I do believe people change, and I do believe life can get better. I have changed, slowly and with time, the way a tree grows by a river. I have a very intelligent and conservative friend who teaches at a local Bible college, and he believes the only thing that truly changes a person is God's truth, that is, His Word and His working in our lives through the Holy Spirit. This makes a lot of sense to me, because the times in my life when I have been most happy haven't been the times when I've had the most money or the most freedom or the most anything, but rather when I've been in love or in community or right with people.

My friend at the Bible college believes the qualities that improve a person's life are relational, relational to God and to the folks around us. This made a lot of sense, too, because when Jesus was walking around on earth He taught His disciples truths through experience, first telling them stories, then walking with them, then causing stuff to happen like a storm on the sea, then reiterating the idea He had taught them the day before. Even then it took years before the disciples understood, and even then the Holy Spirit had to come and wrap things up. So it made me realize that either God didn't know about the formulas, or the formulas weren't able to change a person's heart.

To be honest, though, I don't know how much I like the idea of my spirituality being relational. I suppose I believe this is true, but the formulas seem much better than God because the formulas offer control; and God, well, He is like a person, and people, as we all know, are complicated. The trouble with people is they do not always do what you tell them to do. Try it with your kids or your spouse or strangers at the grocery store, and you will see what I mean. The formulas propose that if you do this and this and this, God will respond. When I was a kid I wanted a dolphin for the same reason.

I remember watching that television show *I Dream of Jeannie* when I was young, and I wondered at how great it would be to have a Jeannie of my own, complete with the sexy outfit, who could blink a grilled-cheese sandwich out of thin air, all the while cleaning my room and doing my homework. I realize, of course, that is very silly and there is no such thing as a genie that lives in a lamp, but it makes me wonder if secretly we don't wish God were a genie who could deliver a few wishes here and there. And that makes me wonder if what we really want from the formulas are the wishes, not God. It makes me wonder if what we really want is control, not a relationship.

Some would say formulas are how we interact with God, that going through motions and jumping through hoops are how a person acts out his spirituality. This method of interaction, however, seems odd to me, because if I want to hang out with my friend Tuck, I don't stomp my foot three times, turn around, and say his name over and over like a mantra, lighting candles and getting myself in a certain mood. I just call him. In this way, formulas presuppose God is more a computer or a circus monkey than an intelligent Being. I realize that sounds harsh, but it is true.

I was watching *Booknotes* on CSPAN the other day and got caught up in an interview with a literary critic from the *New York Times*. The interviewer asked the critic why he thought the Harry Potter series was selling so many copies. "Wish fulfillment," the critic answered. He said the lead character in the book could wave a wand and make things happen, and this is one of the primary fantasies of the human heart. I think this is true. I call it "Clawing for Eden." But the Bible says Eden is gone, and as much as we want to believe we can fix our lives in about as many steps as it takes to make a peanut-butter sandwich, I don't believe we can.

So if the difference between Christian faith and all other forms of spirituality is that Christian faith offers a relational dynamic with God, why are we cloaking this relational dynamic in formulas? Are we jealous of the Mormons? And are the formulas getting us anywhere? Are modern forms of Christian spirituality producing better Christians than days long ago, when people didn't use formulas and understood, intrinsically, that God is a Being with a personality and a will of His own? Martin Luther didn't believe in formulas, and neither did John Calvin. Were they missing something, or are we?

After the writers seminar, and after my friend told me reality was like fine wine, I started reading the Bible very differently. I stopped looking for the formulas and tried to understand what God was trying to say. When I did that, I realized the gospel of Jesus, I mean the essence of God's message to mankind, wasn't a bunch of hoops we needed to jump through to get saved, and it wasn't a series of ideas we had to agree with either; rather, it was an invitation, an invitation to know God.

I know there are people who have actually gone from misery to happiness, but they didn't do it by walking through three steps; they did it because they had a certain set of parents and heard a certain song and knew somebody who had a certain experience and saw some movie, read some book, had something happen to them like a car wreck or a trip to Seattle. Then they called on God, and a week later read something in a magazine or met a girl in Wichita, and when all this had happened they had an epiphany, and somebody may have helped them fulfill what this epiphany made them feel, and several years later they rationalized this mystic experience with three steps, then they told the three steps to us in a book. I'm not saying they weren't trying to be helpful; I bring this up only because life is complex, and the idea that you can break it down or fix it in a few steps is rather silly.

The truth is there are a million steps, and we don't even know what the steps are, and worse, at any given moment we may not be willing or even able to take them; and still worse, they are different for you and me and they are always changing. I have come to believe the sooner we find this truth beautiful, the sooner we will fall in love with the God who keeps shaking things up, keeps changing the path, keeps rocking the boat to test our faith in Him, teaching us to not rely on easy answers, bullet points, magic mantras, or genies in lamps, but rather in His guidance, His existence, His mercy, and *His love*.

Personally, I was miserable before I understood these ideas, but now I am so happy I laugh all the time, even in my sleep.

Sorry, I couldn't resist. On to Chapter Two!

Impostors

―――

SANTA TAKES A LEAK

Relationships aren't the best thing, if you ask me. People can be quite untrustworthy, and the more you get to know them—by that I mean the more you let somebody know who you really are—the more it feels as though something is at stake. And that makes me nervous. It takes me a million years to get to know anybody pretty well, and even then the slightest thing will set me off. I feel it in my chest, this desire to dissociate. I don't mean to be a jerk about it, but that is how I am wired. I say this because it makes complete sense to me that we would rather have a formula religion than a relational religion. If I could, I probably would have formula friends because they would be safe.

I have this suspicion, however, that if we are going to get to know God, it is going to be a little more like getting to know a person than practicing voodoo. And I suppose that means we are going to have to get over this fear of intimacy, or whatever you want to call it, in order to have an ancient sort of faith, the same faith shared by all the dead apostles.

Jesus helps, to be sure, because He comes off as more or less trustworthy. If it weren't for Jesus, it would be difficult for me to follow God. When you read the Old Testament now, knowing exactly where the Book is going, it is all very easy and simple, but it wouldn't have been that way to the characters in actual history. If I had been around back in the Old Testament, God would have come off as more or less frightening. And I don't think I would have been able to know in my heart that it was the grandness of His nature, not the ease of His anger, that produced the fear.

My friend Penny's dad says he thinks God was angry for a while after the Fall, then got over it, sent His Son, and now is pretty well adjusted and forgiving. And of course I don't think that is exactly how it is, but I can understand why Penny's dad would read the Bible this way. But my other friend John MacMurray says that every time he gives the Bible to a person to read for the first time, even if they don't agree with it, they see God as a Person who is incredibly patient with humanity. John pointed out that it takes God hundreds of years to finally get angry enough to lay any sort of punishment on His enemies. He's like France in that way.

If the essence of our spirituality lies in a relationship with God, I suppose we should ask ourselves who God is. I would like to believe God is completely good, completely kind and forgiving, and it is we who aren't all that good and have no idea what goodness is in the first place. I realize that sounds like humanity-bashing, and I don't mean to bash humanity, but when I watch the news it makes me wish deep down for another time and place that has a king who is good, and a people who love and care about one another and are easy to trust, and a news channel that isn't always trying to stir up a fight so they can cover a fight. And Jesus helps me believe such a time and place might exist. I realize a lot of people don't like Jesus, or just ignore Him or have no use for Him, but I think the best thing a person can do is to read through the Gospels in the Bible and really look at Jesus, because if a person does this, they will realize that the Jesus they learned about in Sunday school or the Jesus they hear jokes about or the skinny, Gandhi Jesus that exists in their imaginations isn't anything like the real Jesus at all.

One of my roommates, Stacy, travels the world and shows *The Jesus Film*, a movie about the life of Christ, to people who don't have any idea about Jesus. Last summer Stacy led a group of African-American students to Africa where they showed the film to people on college campuses in Botswana. They were all sitting around one night watching this Jesus film, eating popcorn or what-ever they do, when one of the American students came over to Stacy and asked why the guy in the film, the guy who played Jesus, was a white guy. Stacy thought about it for a second then looked at the student and shrugged his shoulders. But it made Stacy won-der why the actor was a white guy because Jesus was Jewish and would probably have had an olive complexion and dark eyes and dark features.

Stacy, who is very kind and smart, gathered all the students on his team and asked them if the actor bothered them, and they talked about it for many hours. I would love to have been a fly on the wall because it seems to me we are all guilty of changing Jesus around in order to make Him more like ourselves. The guys on the team were very kind and gracious, and they loved the film because in the end they felt it didn't matter what color Jesus is, but that He loves them and invites them to love Him back. So they kept showing the film, and more than one thousand students who saw the film that summer believed in Jesus because they felt some quality they saw in His person and His character was the solution to something.

When I was a kid I used to listen to this Mark Cohn album over and over. He had a song on it about his father and how his father had a silver Thunderbird and used to get up in the morning, very early, and start the car and go driving down the street. Mark Cohn's father used to say that a Thunderbird is better than a Buick, and a Thunderbird is better than a foreign car, and if there is a God up in heaven, He drives a silver Thunderbird. I like that song, but I don't think God drives a silver Thunderbird. And I know nobody really believes that sort of thing, that God drives a Thunderbird, but there are people who believe other crazy ideas about God. I've met people who say God is mad at people, throwing dishes like an alcoholic on a binge, and others who paint God as a fairy running through flowers waving a wand at a unicorn. And all these people are convinced they are right.

The very scary thing about religion, to me, is that people actually believe God is who they think He is. By that I mean they have Him all figured out, mapped out, and as my pastor, Rick, says, "dissected and put into jars on a shelf." You've got a bunch of Catholics in Rome who think one way about God, and a bunch of Baptists in Texas who think another, and that isn't even the beginning. It goes on and on and on like this, and it makes me wonder if God created us in His image or if we created Him in ours. And it isn't just religion, either. I met a guy not long ago who was very conservative and had opinions all over him, and he was saying why God agreed with his political ideas and why that made his political ideas right. The whole time he was talking to me I was thinking about those guys in Africa, and I was feeling like this guy with the opinions was presenting a kind of Jesus who didn't even exist. His Jesus was just an invention of his imagination, someone who more or less justified his position concerning a lot of different political opinions. Sitting there listening to him made me feel tired. People like that should have an island.

But I suppose I can't blame him because, in my life, God is always changing the way I think of Him. I am not saying God Himself is changing, or that my theology is open and I blur the lines on truth; I am only saying I think I know who He is, then I figure out I don't know very much at all. For instance, and as I have said, a lot of people believe God responds to formulas, but He doesn't. So that is one example of how our idea of God is always becoming a bit more accurate. And that's one of the things you notice about Jesus in the Gospels, that He is always going around saying, *You have heard it said such and such, but I tell you some other thing.* If you happened to be a person who thought they knew everything about God, Jesus would have been completely annoying.

THE DEATH OF SANTA CLAUS

In my opinion, there are two essential problems with believing God is somebody He isn't. The first problem is that it wrecks your life, and the second is that it makes God look like an idiot.

When I was a kid and, to be absolutely honest, a teenager and perhaps even a young twenty-something, I believed God was like Santa Claus. I realize grown people should not think God is like Santa Claus, but you wouldn't believe how perfectly convenient it was for me to subscribe to the idea. The benefits were astounding. First: To interact with Santa Claus, I did not have to maintain any sort of intimate relationship. Santa simply slipped into the house, left presents, ate half a cookie, then hit the neighbors'. There was no getting us out of bed in the middle of the night to have sloppy conversations about why I was still wetting the bed.

Second: Santa theology was very black and white; you either made the list or you didn't and if you didn't, it was because you were bad, not because of societal pressures or biochemical distortions or your parents or cable television, but because you were bad. Simple indeed. Third: He brought presents based on behavior. If you were good, you got a lot of bank. There was a very clear reward system based on the most basic desires of the human heart: Big Wheels, Hot Wheels, Legos. You didn't have to get into the spirit of anything, and there was nothing sentimental that served as the *real* reason for the season. Everybody knew it was about the toys: cold, hard toys. Fourth: Kids who were bad got presents anyway.

Perfect.

Slowly, however, everything began to unravel. I tried to stop it because it was all so lovely and perfect, but there was nothing I could do. Truth grew in my mind like a fungus, and though I tried to keep it out, there was no resisting the epiphanies.

Santa went first, then God.

SANTA TAKES A LEAK

I remember being at the mall when I was eight and seeing Santa Claus relieve himself in the men's restroom. I was excited because we were going to see him that day, but I didn't want to disturb him, as he was hardly in his element. I watched him, though, his red suit, his white beard coming down his belly, his loud, echoing belch coming off the walls, his spread-legged stance and the way he looked straight up at the ceiling as he shook the dew off the lily, as they say. It was quite an honor to stand next to him and use the big urinal and act like it was nothing substantial to be standing next to him, as though I didn't even believe in him the way my friends Roy and Travis Massie no longer believed in him. I believed in him, though. I believed he showed up at our house on Christmas, and it didn't matter that we didn't have a chimney because he could come in through the front door, which is what he preferred because, as my mother told us, he had some lower back pain from always picking up after the ungrateful elves.

The Santa in the bathroom was a very tall man, younger than you would think, a bit depressed in the eyes and unshaven under his beard (if such a thing is possible). "Ho, ho, ho, kid," he said to me, zipping up his fluffy pants. I didn't say anything back. I just stood there and peed on my shoes. He looked at me, raised his eyebrows, shrugged his shoulders and walked out.

That is when I realized the most terrible thing I'd ever realized: Santa doesn't wash his hands after he uses the bathroom. *How awful,* I thought to myself. And I was horrified. All those little bacteria, the little flus and colds and cancer bacteria that grow in small villages on a person's hands if he doesn't wash them. I could see in my mind the village of bacteria on Santa's hands; a kind of Tim Burton version of the microbial North Pole; all the textures and contours of the village correct, but the colors off; grays for greens, blacks for blues, lots of coughing, lots of mad cows.

I washed my hands and joined the family already in line. I watched as Santa's dirty hands grabbed kids to pick them up and set them on his knee. I watched as he patted their backs and, *heavens no,* their heads. It made me want to throw up, if you want to know the truth. I asked my mother if I could skip meeting Santa, and she told me I could go across the aisle to Ladies' Underwear and sit quietly on the floor, which is what I did, sitting there quietly on the floor, pointing women toward lingerie I thought might fit them best, trying to be helpful, trying not to think about the fact Santa Claus of all people doesn't wash his hands.

That same year I learned Santa Claus actually had several clones, about seven or something, and they worked different department stores in the Houston area but magically became one on Christmas Eve. And I learned the next year that Santa didn't exist at all. I will never forget the day I found out because it was terrible. I was alone in the huge backseat of our Ford Grand Torino, and my mother and sister were in the front seat, and we were driving to my grandmother's house.

My mother had been acting very peculiar, asking us what we had heard at school and what did we think about Santa Claus and finally she just said it: She told my sister and me that Santa didn't exist, and my sister, who was two years older and had already dealt with the idea the previous year, leaned over the front seat to see if I was going to cry about it. I gripped the seat belt very hard and clenched my teeth and sat up very straight like somebody taller and opened my eyes as wide as I could to keep them dry. My sister leaned in close, straight up to my nose, and I was trying my hardest not to blink when the moisture, suddenly and to my horror, drew to the corner of my right eye where it gathered to a certain mirth, collected in a puddle, then slid down my cheek like a penguin off a glacier. My sister exploded into laughter like she was watching a Jerry Lewis movie, slapping her knee and the whole bit. It took us another twenty minutes to get to my grandmother's house, and I sat in the backseat and tried not to make any noise. My sister would be very, very quiet until I let out a breath and a sob, and then she would explode into laughter again, slapping her knee and looking over at my mom, who was rolling her eyes.

I didn't stop crying for more than an hour. The loss of Santa was, at that time, the most dramatic loss of my young life. I could feel in the chill of the air the chasm, the fields of flat snow that blanketed the North Pole where once stood candy-cane villages, elves hammering at toys, warehouses filled with packages, one upon which my name was written in the language of barcode. It was too much. I breathed and sobbed for more than an hour and calmed down only after I was assured we would still be receiving presents.

But after that it didn't take me very long to get over it, if you want to know the truth. In fact, if I remember correctly, I got a slight feeling of superiority by telling the other kids at school that he didn't exist. And after giving it some thought, having met Santa in the men's restroom, I can't say it troubled me to find out he was an impostor, that basically people just go around dressing up like Santa in order to fool the naive and make a little extra Christmas money.

IMPOSTORS

That is good and fine when we're talking about Santa, but when we're talking about God, the ramifications of an impostor are more upsetting. There are, after all, a lot of people who don't believe in God because they can't reconcile their idea of Him with the idea presented on television. By that I mean televangelists and conservative talking heads who confuse good-ol'-boy politics with Christian spirituality. And that is just the beginning.

Yesterday I watched the CSPAN coverage of the report issued by the independent committee that investigated the Catholic church, and they have discovered more than ten thousand cases of sexual misconduct by priests against children. This is a very sad thing because most of the Catholics I know are quite wonderful people who love one another, care about one another, and who are involved in defending social justice. The whole scene reminds me of all the crap Jesus was up against, having to overcome the unkindness and unfairness, immorality and injury done by squeaky-wheel religious leaders of the day.

And if you thought the Catholics were bad, you should take a look at us evangelicals. Occasionally, as I flip through television stations, I find a man named Robert Tilton, who, in the early 1990s, was accused on ABC's *Primetime Live* of abusing his pulpit by stealing money from those who followed his television ministry. I did a little research and discovered that his church in Dallas, once more than five thousand members strong, has dwindled to the less than two hundred still faithful who, every Sunday, sit scattered in the mammoth auditorium, much of which is now closed off by curtains to hide its emptiness. Tilton left Dallas the year following the scandal. His ex-wife confessed in divorce proceedings that the televangelist had to carry a disguise kit with him everywhere he went and spent at least 50 percent of his time wearing a fake mustache or a wig. I read an article that said even though Tilton wore a fake mustache and a wig, the couple would often be recognized walking into a restaurant or a store and be greeted with boos and obscene gestures. *He deserved it,* I thought while reading the article.

While pastoring in Dallas, Tilton built a complicated direct-mail system, capturing the names and addresses of those who called in for prayer. He would then contact them by mail and ask them to return a "widow's step of faith," which meant a lot of cash, and if they did this, God would give them financial security. *Primetime Live* found a dumpster full of the prayer requests, most of them not even taken out of the envelopes.

Robert Tilton is now relocated to Florida and still rakes in hundreds of thousands of dollars running a similar operation, this time with no congregation, only a few cameramen who probably stand around rolling their eyes all the time. His stage looks like the sort of setup kids would create for a school play about gladiators, complete with Roman pillars from behind which he steps out like Jay Leno, smiling at the audience, telling them their day has come, that God is going to make them rich.

I thought about Santa in the bathroom at the mall when I saw Robert Tilton on television because there are probably a lot of very oblivious and beautiful people who dismiss God because of guys like him, and that, to me, is a remarkable tragedy. But I don't dismiss God because of guys like Tilton; guys like Robert Tilton make me like Jesus more because the people Jesus had the least patience with were the people who said they represented God but didn't. And at first, when I watched Robert Tilton on his new television show, talking behind his desk and asking for money every few minutes, I got very angry, but then I started feeling very sorry for him because I can't imagine he actually believes in God at all. I can't imagine what sort of horrible things are going to happen to him when he dies, what sort of terror he is going to face and what sort of begging and manipulating he is going to try to get out of what God has in store for him and to what degree God is going to make him pay for what he is doing to people.

One night after I watched Robert Tilton on television, I went for a walk through the park. It was very cold, and I was feeling dirty because I had spent so much time watching this man talk half-truths about God so he could get some money. I kept thinking about what a sad world it is where stuff like that can happen to people, and I wondered if I had ever done that sort of thing. I knew I had never used God to get money, but you know what I mean. I had probably used Him to support my political opinions, and I had probably used Him to make some girl think I was godly because church girls like that sort of thing and, like I said, I was feeling very dirty about the whole situation. I wondered if there were any old ladies who couldn't pay their rent or get food because they gave all their cash to Robert Tilton, thinking God was going to help them get rich and pay their bills.

As I've already mentioned, it's a very sad world, and you don't have to go very far at all to find stories that make you feel dirty and miserable at the same time. The bad thing to do when you are thinking a lot of sad thoughts is to go walking through Laurelhurst Park at night, because the paths wind around trees and the lampposts dot the paths like giant candles, round the pond and up the hill on the back side where all the flowerbeds are. You get to feeling so completely alone when you walk through the park at night.

The real thing that made me sad that day was that God, who I think is quite good, was being misrepresented so terribly in the media. I realize it isn't popular to say such things, that as a Christian writer I should keep my mouth shut and kiss everybody's butt, but it is difficult to do so when there are so many media-savvy idiots pretending to represent Jesus. Just this morning I watched a fellow on his Christian show talk about what we should be doing in Iraq, how we should be starving out clerics and sending more troops to shoot more bullets and drop more bombs. He's a preacher, for crying out loud. Why doesn't he just tell people about Jesus?

If I weren't a Christian, and I kept seeing Christian leaders on television more concerned with money, fame, and power than with grace, love, and social justice, I wouldn't want to believe in God at all. I really wouldn't. The whole thing would make me want to walk away from religion altogether because, like I was saying about Santa Claus, their god must be an idiot to see the world in such a one-sided way. The god who cares so much about getting rich must not have treasures stored up in heaven, and the god so concerned about getting even must not have very much patience, and the god who cares so much about the West must really hate the rest of the world, and that doesn't sound like a very good god to me. The televangelist can have him for all I care.

You know, the real problem with God-impostors is that they worship a very small god, a god who exists simply to validate their identities. This god falls apart as soon as you touch him, as soon as you start asking very basic questions about the sanctity of all human life, the failure of combat mentality, and the lustful love of power.

When I was in high school, this simple god stopped making sense to me. I renounced my faith as soon as I stopped toeing the party line and started asking questions. Here's how my renouncing my faith went:

My senior year in high school I had taken a class on psychology and, as a last project, our teacher assigned each of us a prominent psychologist who had come up with what is called a personality theory, which essentially means an explanation for why people do everything. So for our last assignment, we were supposed to study and explain a personality theorist to the class in an oral presentation. There were all sorts of characters to choose from: Freud, as we know, was hung up about sleeping with his mother; and this other fellow named Skinner used to put his kid in a box and make her bark for cheese, or whatever he did; and then there was Pavlov, who drove his dogs crazy with bells and milkbones. I wanted to do my presentation on Skinner, and I was going to make up this whole story about how my uncle used to put me in a box and make me bark for cheese and that is why I had a twitch (I was going to have a twitch), but my classmate Brice Henderson got Skinner and I got this guy named Abraham Maslow, who, on account of the fact he was terminally boring and never dated, thought up a theory called the

"Hierarchy of Needs," which sounds much more exciting than it actually is, believe me.

Maslow held that man was motivated within a hierarchy of desires: A person would seek food, then shelter, then sex, then companionship, and on and on. Only when one need had been fulfilled would he pursue the next until, at last, he had achieved what he referred to as "self-actualization." I don't remember what Maslow said happens after self-actualization. I suppose a person wins a stuffed bear; the specifics of the theory escape me. And it was all good and fine and I had no problem with any of it, until . . .

One of the needs on Maslow's pyramid was the need to know God. Not to *know* God, but rather to supply for the human psyche a kind of divine heritage providing, among other benefits, an explanation for existence. Because science is severely deficient in details of origin, Maslow held that man had invented God as a kind of false bridge from one need to the next. God, far from a Being who had revealed Himself to man, was more an intellectual cuddly toy with which man snuggled during his dark night of the soul. God, in other words, was somebody who validated man's identity. Man needed God to shove into the crack created by the truth of his meaninglessness. Maslow would later recant this idea, but for me, the damage was done. And for the first time in my life, I had questions, and they weren't surface-level questions either; they were very deep, emotional questions. Maslow was describing the God I knew, the God of simple answers to simple questions, the God of *Keep your mouth shut and think what I tell you to think.*

I grew up hearing about God, hearing that He had created the universe, some animals, the Grand Canyon, that we weren't supposed to have sex or drink whiskey or go to dance clubs, that sort of thing, you know. *He's making a list, He's checking it twice, He's gonna find out who's naughty or nice . . .*

Maslow's God, like the one I believed in, was a bridge for the psyche, an invention to calm our nerves and keep us in line. The small church I had been raised in, and from which my framework for God had been hoisted, provided no bulwark of protection from this attack, but rather an unfortified access to a straw man. We were all getting cuddly with Father Christmas, it seemed. I didn't have a relationship with God; I had a relationship with a system of simple ideas, certain prejudices, and a feeling that I and people who thought as I thought were right.

It took me three weeks of thinking to get up the nerve to tell God He didn't exist. At the time, I had a habit of taking walks in the middle of the night. I would leave the house around midnight and walk the streets till one or two in the morning. I don't do that sort of thing anymore, but back then, in my teens, it was the only time in my small, traffic-congested suburban town you could find some peace. I would walk down our street under a tunnel of oaks and pecans, up close to the highway and through the middle of the car wash, the pavement still wet with suds, the stoplight at Mikawa and 35 glistening green then yellow then red against the glossy pavement. Sometimes I would tie the trigger open on the car-wash wand, release the hose from the holster, drop a few coins in the slot, step away, and let the black snake snap in the air, up against the tin walls of the stall and back against the pavement.

I had been thinking about the whole Maslow thing for a few weeks, maybe a month, and I realized somewhere in this philosophy that provided an excuse; I could, if I wanted, walk away from God. I mean, if God didn't answer the serious questions about life, then I didn't have any responsibility to believe He existed. At first it was frightening, but I could feel in my heart that I wanted to dissociate, that if I walked away from God I would have a kind of freedom.

All this was happening during the times I would go walking at night. I would set the hose free while listening to music on my headphones; the Smiths made the hose snap around so beautifully you could get hypnotized by it, Kings X made it violent but purposeful and got you wanting to wreck something. The sound track to the movie *Glory* was the best, though, putting the whole thing together perfectly and almost explaining it to the emotions: the force of the water against the resistance of gravity. And when it was done the hose would go out slowly, like a snake losing air, lying there against the grate heaving and spitting. I realize this is all very melodramatic, but I was just out of high school and when you are that age, you don't realize you are just inventing drama for the sake of drama.

The night I told God He didn't exist I was watching the hose flail and listening to the Smiths sing "That Joke Isn't Funny Anymore," the endless echoing chorus of which rings out: *I've seen this happen in other people's lives, now it's happening in mine . . .*

When it was done the pavement turned from green to yellow, and I told myself when it turned red I would say it: I would tell God I no longer believed in Him, that I wanted to dissociate because He didn't explain anything, He was too simple and so He was a myth, a teddy bear; that Abraham Maslow was right and I would rather spend my life in dark truth than leaning against the crutch of feel-good propaganda about good people and bad people. The world was more complex than that and I knew it. I am not going to pretend this was an easy thing to do. It wasn't easy at all. Part of me wanted God to continue to exist. He had brought me a great deal of comfort and an identity and a community of friends who were quite kind and endearing and inclusive. My heart beat out blood and I could feel it thump so strongly I thought it was going to break my skin. The light turned red and I said it.

"You don't exist," I told Him.

CHAPTER THREE

Feet of Trees

WHAT DO WE REALLY WANT?

I remember seeing that made-for-TV miniseries with Shirley MacLaine called *Out on a Limb*. There's a part in the movie where Shirley MacLaine goes for a walk on a beach and starts twirling around, saying, "I am God, I am God, I am God," right there in the waves. I heard a lecture by novelist Frank Peretti in which he wondered what that must have sounded like to God. He leaned up to the microphone and squeaked out, in a very little voice, "I am God, I am God." He got a big laugh out of that from the audience. What he was saying was that Shirley MacLaine's voice must have sounded very small to God, on account of she was standing way down on earth on a beach, twirling around.

I can understand why somebody would think they were God, though. In the first moments after I wake up, especially in the winter when I have left the windows open, I am quite taken aback by my existence; my hands, my eyelids, the feel of my feet rubbing against the blanket. In moments like this, I get the feeling that life is a great deal more complex than I am able to understand. I feel in these moments that I am fairly intricate and amazing;

a speaker for a mouth, two cameras for eyes, sticks for legs, a computer for a head, a million sensors in a million places. I could see how somebody would think they were a god; but I could also see how somebody would think that person was a nut too. If you are a god and I am a god, we are all gods and then the whole thing just gets boring.

I tell you all this only to say I came back to God. All the complexity about life was begging for an explanation; and me actually being god wasn't answering very many questions. And so in a way, I left the old god of easy answers, the god who was always wanting me to be rich or wanting my country to be better than other countries or, for that matter, for me to be better than you. I left that god the preachers talk about on television and the politicians mention in their prayers. But I left room open for another God, a God who might explain my existence, explain the complexity of my hands and feet and feelings and the very strange and mysterious fact that even as I type this I am breathing.

I confess, I feel there is a God who is very big and who understands everything. In the morning, when I get over these little moments of epiphany about how complex my construction is I begin to *fear* the God that is, because He made all this that is our existence and He understands its physics. Whatever it is that understands the physics of this thing that is happening to us would have to be quite remarkable, with giant oaks for feet, perhaps, and a voice like wind through a forest and a mind that creates creations of which it might ponder in a way of learning what it already knows. I start to think about this and I confess, it stirs a certain fright and it helps me believe the Scripture that teaches *His ways are not like our ways.* (See Isaiah 55:8–9.)

I realize it isn't a big deal to fear God these days, but I do. By that I don't mean I have just a deep respect for Him or a healthy appreciation for Him; I actually get a general sense of terror. It isn't because I think He is a bad guy, because I don't. The sense of terror comes more from the idea that He is so incredibly other, has claimed He has created a kind of afterlife for people, has never been born and will never die and doesn't exactly live in a space. A God who is that different, that other, can tell you again and again He loves you and you are still going to be quite a bit afraid, just because of what it feels like when you think about His nature.

I say all this because the other side of what Shirley MacLaine was doing on that beach isn't funny. From God's perspective, looking down at this squeaky voice going off about how she is God is pretty funny, but the other side, the side that knows how very large God is, how He has no end, gives me a start something terrible. And I wonder what it sounded like to God when Jerry Falwell went on television and said the reason the twin towers were hit by those planes was because there were homosexuals in the building. I wonder what kind of annoying squeak that was in God's ear. I don't think a person who makes statements like that fears God. I don't think people like this respect God when He says to love your brother, love your enemy, turn the other cheek, don't judge lest you be judged, be patient, be kind, hold your tongue and give every effort to keep the bonds of peace. Sometimes, honestly, I feel that squeaky-wheel Christian leadership can be as wrong about God as Shirley Maclaine. I don't think they actually fear Him or think He means what He says.

I was pleased to discover the God of Scripture is much larger than this. Everybody who met God in the Bible was afraid of Him. People were afraid of even the angels, so the angels always had to calm people down just to have a conversation. I would think that would be very annoying if you were an angel, always having to settle people down just to talk. It makes you wonder if the first thousand years in heaven will have us running around screaming like we would during an earthquake, the whole time God saying to us in an enormous, booming voice, *Calm down, calm down, will you, it's just Me.*

If you ask me, the way to tell if a person knows God for real, I mean knows the real God, is that they will fear Him. They wouldn't go around making absurd political assertions and drop God's name like an ace card, and they wouldn't be making absurd statements about how God wants you to be rich and how if you send in some money to the ministry God will bless you. And for that matter, they wouldn't be standing on a beach shouting about how they are God, twirling around in the waves. It seems like, if you really knew the God who understands the physics of our existence, you would operate a little more cautiously, a little more compassionately, a little less like you are the center of the universe.

One of the reasons I came to trust the God of the Bible was because He was big enough to explain the impostors. In Scripture, God never gets confused about who is and who isn't representing Him. Impostors represent a small god, a vapor in the imagination of a child, a god we would all do well to renounce.

The thing about the night at the car wash, the night I renounced my faith, was that I didn't think of God as being very big at all. The god I was renouncing was more an *idea* than a *person.* The god I used to know was a system of beliefs that made me feel right, not a living and active Being. That night, however, the idea-god fell away and the Person, the Being, the animate creature emerged in my mind. I walked back home after renouncing my faith. I walked through the oaks and the pecans, and I confess to you, I was scared. But I wasn't scared because God was there; I was scared because I felt like He wasn't. Don't get me wrong, I know the Bible says God will never leave us or forsake us, but when you go and tell Him to His face He doesn't exist, you run the risk of making Him angry. And even though I was losing the small god, in my mind I was renouncing God altogether, and I don't think this made God happy. Even though I used to take walks in the middle of the night, I had never been scared about it. People had thrown beer bottles at me and swerved at me in their cars, but I never got frightened. I always felt God was out there somewhere.

But that night it got pretty eerie as fingers from the oaks spread their thin stems in shadows across the road like cobwebs. I kept seeing what I thought were crouching men in alleys between houses, just there behind the trash can, just there in with the shrubs. I started walking very briskly, and even the sound of my feet came at me off house walls and wooden fences. I had never really thought about my life before, how it is kept up by breaths and spread atop time. My life suddenly seemed temporary, as though the expanse of it would be only eighty years, and if somebody took it from me now, I wouldn't get the little charity that was being thrown to me from nature, that is, the rest of my existence.

Before, my mind had me going out into eternity, the number of days making the individual nearly worthless in the whole, but now each moment had consequence. Cars in the distance stopped and pulled off the road for no reason, bugs in trees screamed out like cannibals, even cats padding gentle steps through porch-light made me nervous. And this pitted me against creation. Creation had a power it had not hitherto enjoyed. Creation could take my life; a man with a knife, hoodlums looking for trouble, drivers drunk at the wheel, cannibal bugs in trees, cats in porch-light.

I had become a chicken.

This wasn't something I expected. I thought when I told God He didn't exist, I would feel a sense of freedom. I thought my confessing that God didn't exist would relieve me from the responsibility of being one of His creations, but that isn't what it felt like; it felt more like I had been removed from His protection. I am not saying that is what actually happened, because who knows what actually happened; I am only saying that is what it felt like.

And then the odd thought occurred to me that I had *told* God He didn't exist. *I told Him.* What's the use in talking to a person to tell them they aren't there? As a child, after hearing the truth about Santa, I never had the desire to write him to tell him he didn't exist. I remember very well being quite upset about the idea, but never going on believing the man was real despite the report he wasn't. As a child, when I was told about Santa, it was as though a red thread had been pulled from a gray cloth, leaving a long chasm in the fabric; and then my mind was able to feel the chill the chasm had been letting in all along, the lack of mystery about Christmas, the lack of goodness in the world, the need for myth to smooth cracks in the mind. With God, however, it was as though a thread had been pulled from the fabric to reveal a thread of a different color, a color less me-pleasing, but a color all the same. God was still there. I tried to shake Him, but I couldn't find a place where He wasn't. This doesn't prove He actually exists, I realize, but a person is often driven by his sentiments, his logic trailing behind his emotions as a pariah.

THE GOD WHO MAKES SENSE OF LIFE

I began to slowly realize that the God of the Bible, not the God of formulas and bullet points that some have turned the Bible into, but the God of the actual Bible, the old one before we learned to read it like a self-help book, had a great deal to say to me. What I mean by this is the God of the Bible, and for that matter the Bible itself, started making sense of my deepest emotions, quirks, and sense of brokenness. Once I separated the little god from the big God, and the little-god impostors from the true and loving servants of God, I began to pay more attention. This God became very beautiful to me, in fact. The things He said, the people He chose to speak through, and even the way He worded His message became quite meaningful. The God of the Bible, in a very strange way, even explained why I would have wanted to renounce my faith. Let me explain:

I've always been the kind of guy who likes to be seen as smart. It's not as bad as it sounds because I don't go around saying all kinds of smart-guy stuff to make other people feel like jerks or anything; it's just that I was never very good at much of anything else, you know, like I would try basketball for a while and when I was a kid I played soccer and tennis, but I was never very good at any of that, and then I learned to play the guitar but got very bored because what I really wanted was to be a rock star, not to actually play the guitar. So about the time I told God He didn't exist, I was desperate for an identity.

While this was taking place in my life I happened to attend a lecture by the chairman of the American Debate Team, who was about twenty-five or so, and there were a lot of girls in the audience because he was very rich and good-looking. The people at the school were going to videotape him talking about China or something, but the video camera was having trouble. The chairman of the American Debate Team had to stand on the stage for about twenty minutes with his hands in his pockets like an idiot, so what he did while he was standing there was recite poetry. I'm not making this up; this guy recited about a million poems such as Kipling's *The Vampire* and parts of Longfellow's *The Song of Hiawatha*. He was very good at it and said the poems with the right spacing so it sounded like he was speaking beautiful spells, and all the girls in the audience were falling out of their chairs on account of their hearts were exploding in love for him. So then the people at the school got the camera working and the chairman of the American Debate Team gave his lecture about China, but the whole time I was sitting there I wasn't thinking about China; rather, I was wondering how I could get my hands on some poetry books and start memorizing them right away, on account of how much the girls liked it when the chairman of the American Debate Team recited poems. What I really began to wonder, I suppose, was whether or not coming off as a smart guy who knows poems could be my identity, could be the thing that made me stand out in life.

Now I didn't realize it at the time, but I would come back to this moment much later in life and realize something very important about myself, namely that I felt something missing inside myself, some bit of something that made me feel special or important or valued. This thing missing inside me, I realized, is something God would go to great length to explain in His Bible. This missing something was entirely relational, and by memorizing poetry, by trying to find an identity, and even by renouncing my faith at the car wash, I was displaying some of the very ideas God would speak of in Scripture, some of the ideas about being separated from a relationship that gave me meaning, and now looking for a kind of endorsement from a jury of my peers.

Here is how it all panned out: I had this friend Brian, who was a rugby player and who also was at the lecture, and afterward we were talking about China in the lobby when we looked over at the chairman of the American Debate Team with all sorts of girls around him, and that very day Brian and I decided we would start memorizing poems. By the next day we had Kipling's *The Gods of the Copybook Headings* memorized, which is a boring poem about being a conservative, and then I memorized *She Walks in Beauty* and *Had I This Cheek* and *The Tiger* and also *The Raven.*

Even though it's true that you can't memorize poetry and stay a fake, that sooner or later you start understanding what these poets are saying and it makes you feel life as something quite special with certain layers of meaning to it, at first you are doing it just to get people to think you are cultured. The thing about being smart about poetry that was different from being a guitar player or a tennis player was that I genuinely liked it and started feeling very good about myself because I had so much poetry memorized. I started reading a great deal and feeling very intelligent and would say little things that people would pick up on, and sooner or later I got this reputation as a smart and cultured person with *a reasonable amount of potential.*

I say all this because it is background information about what was really happening in my soul, the stuff the Bible goes to great lengths to explain. I figure I was attaching myself to a certain identity because it made me feel smart or, more honestly, it made other people tell me I was smart. This was how I earned my sense of importance. Now, as I was saying earlier, by doing things to get other people to value me, a couple of ideas became obvious, the first being that I was a human wired so other people told me who I was. This was very different from anything I had previously believed, including that you had to believe in yourself and all, and I still believe that is true, but I realized there was this other part of me, and it was a big part of me, that needed something outside myself to tell me who I was. And the thing that had been designed to tell me who I was, was gone. And so the second idea became obvious: I was very concerned with getting other people to say I was good or valuable or important because the thing that was supposed to make me feel this way was gone.

And it wasn't just me. I could see it in the people on television, I could see it in the people in the movies, I could see it in my friends and family, too. It seemed that every human being had this need for something outside himself to tell him who he was, and that whatever it was that did this was gone, and this, to me, served as a kind of personality theory. It explained why I wanted to be seen as smart, why religious people wanted so desperately to be right, why Shirley MacLaine wanted to be God, and just about everything else a human did.

Later, when I set this truth about myself, and for that matter about the human race, next to what the Bible was saying about who God is, what happened at the Fall, and the sort of message Jesus communicated to humanity, I realized Christian spirituality fit my soul like a key. It was quite beautiful, to be honest with you.

This God, and this spirituality, was very different from the self-help version of Christianity. The God of the Bible seemed to be brokenhearted over the separation in our relationship and downright obsessed with mending the tear.

I began to wonder if the actual language of life was not the charts and formulas and stuff we map out on a graph to feel smart or right, but rather the hidden language explaining why every person does everything they do, the hidden language we are speaking that is really about negotiating the feeling God used to give us.

I don't mean to sound like a pop-psychologist. I am only pointing to the obvious stuff that is taking place in our souls that nobody wants to talk about. It is this obvious stuff that Scripture seems to waltz in and address matter-of-factly.

And that is the thing about life. You go walking along, thinking people are talking a language and exchanging ideas, but the whole time there is this deeper language people are really talking, and that language has nothing to do with ethics, fashion, or politics, but what it really has to do with is feeling important and valuable. What if the economy we are really dealing in life, what if the language we are really speaking in life, what if what we really want in life is relational?

Now this changes things quite a bit, because if the gospel of Jesus is just some formula I obey in order to get taken off the naughty list and put on a nice list, then it doesn't meet the deep need of the human condition, it doesn't interact with the great desire of my soul, and it has nothing to do with the hidden (or rather, obvious) language we all are speaking. But if it is more, if it is a story about humanity falling away from the community that named it, and an attempt to bring humanity back to that community, and if it is more than a series of ideas, but rather speaks directly into this basic human need we are feeling, then the gospel of Jesus is the most relevant message in the history of mankind.

———

As I said before, the god I renounced that evening at the car wash was an impersonal god, a god of rules and lists and formulas. But what if all our rules and lists and formulas came together for a reason, and what if we stopped looking *at* the rules and lists and formulas and rather looked *through* them at the larger and more obvious message? What if the motive behind our theology was relational? My need, the brokenness that existed inside me and led me to play guitar and memorize poems and even renounce my faith in an effort to think myself smart, was all driven by relational motives: I wanted other people to value me. So what if the gospel of Jesus was a message that was relevant to that need?

I realized that. Jesus was always, and I mean always, talking about love, about people, about relationship, and He never once broke anything into steps or formulas. What if, because we were constantly trying to dissect His message, we were missing a blatant invitation? I began to wonder if becoming a Christian did not work more like falling in love than agreeing with a list of true principles. I had met a lot of people who agreed with all those true principles, and they were jerks, and a lot of other people who believed in those principles, but who also claimed to love Jesus, who were not jerks. It seems like something else has to take place in the heart for somebody to become a believer, for somebody to understand the gospel of Jesus. It began to seem like more than just a cerebral exercise. What if the gospel of Jesus was an invitation to know God?

Now I have to tell you, all of this frightened me a bit because I had always assumed a kind of anonymity with God. When I saw myself in heaven, I didn't imagine sitting at the right hand of God, as the Scripture says, but I pictured myself off behind some mountain range doing some fishing and writing a good detective novel. But if the gospel of Jesus is relational; that is, if our brokenness will be fixed, not by our understanding of theology, but by God telling us who we are, then this would require a kind of intimacy of which only heaven knows. Imagine, a Being with a mind as great as God's, with feet like trees and a voice like rushing wind, telling you that you are His cherished creation. It's kind of exciting if you think about it. Earthly love, I mean the stuff I was trying to get by sounding smart, is temporal and slight so that it has to be given again and again in order for us to feel any sense of security; but God's love, God's voice and presence, would instill our souls with such affirmation we would need nothing more and would cause us to love other people so much we would be willing to die for them. Perhaps this is what the apostles stumbled upon.

Chapter Four

Free Verse

A Whole Message to
a Whole Human Being

You would think some of the writers of the Bible would have gone to a Christian writers seminar to learn the magical formulas about how to dangle a carrot in front of a rabbit, but they didn't. Instead, the writers of the Bible tell a lot of stories and account for a lot of history and write down a lot of poems and recite a great deal of boring numbers and then conclude with various creepy hallucinations that, in some mysterious way, explain the future, in which, apparently, we all slip into Dungeons and Dragons outfits and fight the giant frog people. I forget how it goes exactly, and I mean no disrespect. But because it is so scatterbrained, and has virtually no charts and graphs, I am actually quite surprised the Bible sells. Perhaps it's those lovely and colorful maps, which puzzles me because they aren't even current.

But I like the Bible. Now that I no longer see it as a self-help book, it has infinitely more merit. It has soul, I guess you could say.

As far as the writers in the Bible go, there are a few I like more than others. I like Paul the best because he said the hard stuff about women in ministry and homosexuality and you get to thinking he was pretty severe, and all of a sudden he starts getting vulnerable as though he is feeling lonely, needing to share personal stuff with somebody. When I come to these parts of his letters I feel he was writing late at night and was perhaps very tired, in some stranger's home who was intimidated because they knew his reputation but had only just met him. If you had a guy in your home who was always getting beat up about the faith, thrown in prison and that sort of thing, it would make you feel intimidated and nervous about having him in your home; it would make you wonder exactly how committed you are. I'll bet Paul didn't care, though; he doesn't seem like the type to judge people, but you know people were intimidated by him anyway.

He was terribly intelligent. For the first couple of days in a new town, Paul probably felt completely alone. I see him like this when he talks about how he wants to go home and be in heaven but stays on earth so he can write letters and preach. I see him writing by candlelight at a stranger's table when he talks about how he has this thorn in his flesh and can't get over it and prayed about it three times, but God said to him, "My grace is sufficient for you." It's writing like this that I like in a book. If a writer is going to sit down with a big important voice and try to get me motivated about something, I pretty much don't want to read anymore because it makes me feel tired, as though life were just about getting a lot of things done. Paul never did this. He was terribly personal.

The books I like are the ones that get you feeling like you are with a person, hanging out with a person who is being quite vulnerable, telling you all sorts of stuff that is personal. And that's the thing Paul did that makes me like him. The other thing is, the guy was passionate, like he actually believed this stuff was true, always going off about heaven and hell because he *knew* life has extremes. One minute he talked about how disgusting sin is and how it hurts God in His heart, and the next minute he said he would go to hell for people if he could, how he would die for them and go to hell if they would just trust Christ. It's really hard to read that stuff because it gets you feeling guilty about not loving people very much, and then you feel very thankful for people like Paul because it means that if a person knows Christ, they become the sort of man who says difficult truths with his mouth and yet feels things with his heart that make him want to go around and die for people. It's quite beautiful, really.

———

The next guy I like is John the Evangelist. That's what they called him back in the day. I like John because when he wrote his biographical essay about Jesus, he kept putting himself in the story; only he didn't call himself John, he called himself *the one whom Jesus loved.* You figure if a guy gets tortured and beat up and thrown in prison, he might start wondering whether God loves him anymore, but John didn't. And when John wrote his book he was always taking the camera to the outcasts, into the margins, showing how Jesus didn't demonstrate any favoritism. He showed how Jewish leaders ridiculed Christ, and he was fearless in exposing the hypocrisy of the ones who led with their heads, not their hearts. At the end of his essay, he captured an amazing conversation between Jesus and Peter. Jesus keeps saying to Peter, "Do you love Me?" And Peter keeps saying, "Yes, yes I do; You know that I do," but Jesus doesn't believe Peter and keeps asking him the same question again and again. It is quite dramatic, really.

The way John writes about Jesus makes you feel like the sum of our faith is a kind of constant dialogue with Jesus about whether or not we love Him. I grew up believing a Christian didn't have to love God or anybody else; he just had to believe some things and be willing to take a stand for the things he believed. John seemed to embrace the relational dynamic of our faith. And he did so in an honest tone, not putting a spin on anything. He revealed how none of the disciples truly understood Jesus and how they were all screwups, and he didn't make himself look good, either; he just told it exactly as it was. That's guts, if you ask me. And then, not unlike Paul, John closed his book with a lot of sentimental talk, very to the point but charged with meaning. He ended his book by telling the reader he was going to die. There were some people around back then who wondered if John was ever going to die because they had overheard Jesus say John would live forever, and because John got tortured and should have died early on, a lot of people assumed Jesus was saying John was going to live forever on earth.

This is beautiful and meaningful because John wrote his essay a long time after Christ had left so he was very old, probably nearly ninety years old, and this was back when communities loved old people. They didn't put them in homes to watch television; they gathered around them because they represented a kind of gentle beauty and wisdom. This was back when you didn't have to be all young and sexy just to be a person. And it makes you wonder if John sat and wrote that he was going to die knowing within a few days, a few weeks, a month of gentle good-byes, he was going to go home and leave all his friends, and he didn't want any of them to be surprised or scared.

When you read the book you start realizing that people who were very close to John read this essay and got to the end and started crying because John was telling them he was going to leave, and then I'll bet at his funeral everybody was standing around thinking about how John knew he was going to die and told them in his book. And I'll bet they sat around that night at somebody's house, and somebody who had a very good reading voice lit a candle, and they all lay on the floor and sat on pillows. The children sat quietly and the man with the voice read through the book, from beginning to end, and they thought together about Jesus as the man read John's book, and when it came to the end where John says he is going to die, the person who was reading got choked up and started to cry. Somebody else, maybe John's wife or one of his daughters, had to go over and read the end of it, and when she was finished they sat around for a long time and some of the people probably stayed the night so the house wouldn't feel empty. It makes you want to live in a community like that when you think about the way things were when Jesus had touched people.

A community like that might sound far-fetched, but when you read through John's other books, the short ones, all he talks about is *if you know Jesus, you will love your brother and sister*, and anybody who talked that much about loving your brother and sister was probably the most beloved person in their community, and when he died people would have felt a certain pain about it for a long, long time.

———

You don't have to read the Bible for long before you realize the folks who wrote this book were quite special, with enormous capacities for feeling and understanding truth. Paul and John are definitely my favorites, but after those two my favorite writer in the Bible is Moses. Moses most likely wrote the book of Job, and when he was finished he wrote Genesis through Deuteronomy.

I took a class on Moses from a man named John Sailhamer. It was the best class I have ever taken. I didn't normally take Bible classes back then, but my friend John MacMurray told me John Sailhamer is one of the smartest guys in the world when it comes to talking about Moses. I told him I still didn't want to go to the class, that I wanted to watch television, but at the time I was living with John MacMurray and his family, and he told me that I had to go if I wanted to continue living in his home. So I went to this class and about five minutes into it I knew I was taking the best class I would ever take. If you ever have the opportunity to take a class from John Sailhamer, you should. His knowledge concerning the Old Testament is quite ferocious.

At one point in the class, for instance, a lot of us were getting confused because we couldn't figure out what translation of the Bible he was teaching from, so we asked him. It turned out he was teaching from the ancient Hebrew, translating it in his mind into English as he went along. And you might think a guy like that would go around speaking Hebrew all the time to impress people but he didn't, except one time when he read a long piece of poetry that Moses wrote. He read it in Hebrew and it sounded so beautiful that when he was finished, even though none of us knew what he had said, we sat around very quietly because we knew we had heard something profound, something Moses had sat and labored over for a very long time, something that ancient Hebrews would have read and then stopped to slowly note the complexity of its beauty, and the depth of its meaning.

The thing about John Sailhamer is, he helped me love Moses. I don't know if I had given Moses much thought before that class, but after hearing John Sailhamer talk about him, he became a human being to me. Dr. Sailhamer said Moses, unlike most writers in Scripture, would stop the narrative to break into the kind of poetry he had quoted earlier, a kind of poetry called parallelism, which is when you say something and then repeat it using different phrasing. He said the way Moses wrote wasn't unlike the way people who write musicals stop the story every once in a while to break into song. At first I thought Dr. Sailhamer was just making things up, but he showed us in the text several places where the writer clearly stopped writing narrative and began writing poetry. The reason Moses would do this, according to John Sailhamer, is because there are emotions and situations and tensions that a human being feels in his life but can't explain. And poetry is a literary tool that has the power to give a person the feeling he isn't alone in those emotions, that, though there are no words to describe them, somebody understands.

I can't tell you how beautiful I thought this was; I had always suspected language was quite limited in its ability to communicate the intricate mysteries of truth. By that I mean if you have to describe loneliness or how beautiful your sweetheart is or the way a rainstorm smells in summer, you most likely have to use poetry because these things are not technical, they are more romantic, and yet they exist and we interact and exchange these commodities with one another in a kind of dance.

This comforted me because I had grown up thinking of my faith in a rather systematic fashion, as I said, listed on grids and charts, which is frustrating because I never, ever thought you could diagram truth, map it out on a grid, or break it down into a formula. I felt that truth was something living, complex, very large and dynamic and animated. Simple words, lists, or formulas could never describe truth or explain the complex nature of our reality.

What John Sailhamer was saying was meaningful because it meant God wasn't communicating to us through cold lists and dead formulas; it meant He wanted to say something to our hearts, like a real person. Remember when I was talking about a hidden language beneath the language we speak, and how this hidden language is about the heart? It seems the Bible is speaking this language, this inferred set of ideas, as much as it is speaking simple truths.

Furthermore, it is true God used a great deal of poetry in the Bible. David was a poet and his son Solomon created a musical called Song of Songs, which is about romance and sex, and even Paul had memorized the works of Greek poets so he could speak them from memory when giving a talk. If you quote a poem in a sermon today, some people think you are being mushy, but if you quoted one back in the day, people would have felt you were getting to the core of an idea, to the real, whole truth of it. And after taking John Sailhamer's class, I started wondering if the message God was communicating to mankind, this gospel of Jesus, was a message communicated to the heart as much as to the head; that is, the methodology was as important as the message itself, that the ideas could not be presented accurately outside the emotion within which the truths were embedded.

And if you think about these things, it only makes sense that if God was communicating a relational message to humanity He would use the multilayered methodology of truth and art, because nobody engages another human being through lists and formulas. Our interaction with one another is so much more about that hidden language. I started wondering if our methodology, that of charts and formulas and lists, is not hindering the message Jesus intended. If our modern methodology is superior to the methodology of historical narrative mixed with music, drama, poetry, and prose, then why didn't God choose lists instead of art?

I began to wonder if the ancient Hebrews would have understood this intrinsically, if they would have sat around watching plays and reading poems knowing this is where real truth lies, and if our age, affected by the Renaissance and later by the Industrial Revolution, by Darwin and the worship of science, hasn't lost a certain understanding of truth that was more whole. If you have a girlfriend and you list some specifics about her on a piece of paper—her eye color, her hair color, how tall she is—and then give her this list over a candlelight dinner, I doubt it will make her swoon. But if you quote these ideas to her in a poem:

> *She walks in beauty like the night*
> *Of cloudless climes and starry skies*
> *And all that's best of dark and bright*
> *Meet in her aspect and her eyes . . .*

. . . she is more likely to understand the meaning, the value inferred by your taking notice of her features. The same ideas, expressed in poetry, contain a completely different meaning. She would understand you were captivated by a certain mystery in her aspect, in her eyes and her stride and the features perfectly met upon her face. And while our earlier conceived *list* of features might have been accurate, it certainly wouldn't have been meaningful.

It makes you wonder if guys like John the Evangelist and Paul and Moses wouldn't look at our systematic theology charts, our lists and mathematical formulas, and scratch their heads to say, *Well, it's technically true; it just isn't meaningful.*

If you ask me, the separation of truth from meaning is a dangerous game. I don't think memorizing ideas helps anybody unless they already understand the meaning inferred in the expression of those ideas. I think ideas have to sink very deeply into a person's soul, into their being, before they can effect change, and lists rarely sink deeply into a person's soul.

The difference between meaning and truth is quite simple, really. It is something we all understand and operate within daily. Several years ago, for instance, I chewed tobacco: Long-cut Wintergreen Skoal. I know, I know, it was terrible for me. It causes cancer of the mouth and is bad for your heart and your breath, and girls are never going to want to kiss you if you chew that stuff. I knew all that for years and yet I couldn't kick the habit, mainly because I didn't want to. The tobacco gave me a little buzz and helped me relax. But I tried to stop. I went to Web sites and looked up statistics about the health risks of chewing tobacco. I printed the statistics and placed them on my desk where I could read them when I was tempted. But it didn't help. I still bought a can of the stuff every other time I gassed up my car. This went on for at least a year, until . . .

I was listening to the radio one afternoon, editing a chapter in a previous book, when a voice came on, very distorted and troubled. The man sounded as though part of his face were missing, low and muffled and slobbery. Between songs, the radio station had inserted a commercial, a public service message about the danger of using chewing tobacco. The man in the commercial said half his jaw had been removed, that he had no lower lip, and the reason his face was deformed was because for years he had used smokeless tobacco. He didn't list any facts, he didn't speak of any harmful ingredients, he didn't say he was going to die of cancer. And yet the image of a man without a chin speaking into the microphone was enough to convince me to stop. I never used the stuff again. I just didn't want to.

After taking John Sailhamer's class, I thought about my experience with chewing tobacco in connection with understanding the difference between meaning and truth. I wondered if when we take Christian theology out of the context of its narrative, when we ignore the poetry in which it is presented, when we turn it into formulas to help us achieve the American dream, we lose its *meaning* entirely, and the ideas become fodder for the head but have no impact on the way we live our lives or think about God. This is, perhaps, why people are so hostile toward religion.

———

While having dinner with a friend recently, she commented that the primary concern for Christians today is to translate the precepts of Scripture for a postmodern audience. And I don't know what *postmodern* means, but I kindly disagreed with her and wondered out loud if we didn't need to stop translating the Bible for a modern audience, an audience endeared to the simplification of reality, an audience that likes to memorize lists in an attempt to understand God. Perhaps if we stop reducing the text to formulas for personal growth, we can read it as stories of imperfect humans having relations with a perfect God and come to understand the obvious message He is communicating to mankind.

I was reading *The Cloister Walk* by Kathleen Norris the other day and she was talking about Benedictine monks and how they would sit up late at night to study the Bible by candlelight. I wondered what it would have been like to have studied the Bible and not be tainted by lists and charts and formulas that cause you to look for ideas and infer notions that may or may not be in the text, all the while ignoring the poetry, the blood and pain of the narrative, and the depth of emotion with which God communicates His truth. I think there would be something quite beautiful about reading the Bible this way, to be honest—late at night, feeling through the words, sorting through the grit and beauty. It wouldn't bother me at all to read the Bible without the charts and lists because a person could read the Bible, not to become smart, but rather to feel that they are not alone, that somebody understands them and loves them enough to speak to them—on purpose—in a way that makes a person feel human.

Here is what Kathleen Norris said about those monks:

Although their access to scholarly tools was primitive compared to what is available in our day, their method of biblical interpretation was in some ways more sophisticated and certainly more psychologically astute, in that they were better able to fathom the complex, integrative, and transformative qualities of revelation. Their approach was far less narcissistic than our own tends to be, in that their goal when reading scripture was to see Christ in every verse, and not a mirror image of themselves.

CHAPTER FIVE

Naked

WHY NUDITY IS THE POINT

About the time I took John Sailhamer's class, I took a trip to Yosemite. Every two years or so I go to Yosemite because, in my opinion, Yosemite Valley is the most beautiful place in all America. If you don't get to a beautiful place every couple of years, you get to thinking everything is urban, as though when God made creation He just made some medium-size buildings, a bowling alley, and a burger place. The thing is, the last time I was in Yosemite Valley, I was thinking about the Garden of Eden.

Moses wrote about the Garden of Eden at the beginning of Genesis and because of John Sailhamer's class, I wasn't looking for a formula in the text, a few steps to make my life better; instead, I was reading it like literature, as though a human being were trying to tell me something about life, something he thought was beautiful or ugly, true or inspiring—you know the drill. And because I was reading the text this way, and because I was at Yosemite, I started realizing the Garden of Eden wasn't anything like I'd imagined. In the first place, the Garden was much larger than the territory I had pictured in my mind. Previously, when I thought about the Garden of Eden I pictured a woman and a man living in a little cottage with a trail outside their door that went down to a pond. I realize this is quite simple, but that is pretty much how I pictured it. Being in Yosemite, however, with that wandering meadow, Yosemite Falls feeding the green, Half Dome and El Capitan rising out of the earth more than two thousand feet, I realized the Adam I read about in Moses' book was a naturalist in an expanse perhaps as large as a continent.

Moses said a great river flowed out of the Garden, dividing into four rivers; the Pishon, which flowed through Gavilah, a land containing a great deal of gold and resin and onyx stone, whatever that stuff is; then the river split off into the Gihon and flowed through a land called Cush. And there were still two more rivers, the Hiddekel and the Euphrates. It is true that the great river, the river that created the other four, flowed *out* of the Garden of Eden, but for such a river to gather enough strength within the Garden to be split into four, defining the landscape for four territories, means the land that created the river must have been mammoth. This, of course, ended my thought of a little cottage, a path, and a pond.

And then I began to wonder about Eve, what the scene might have looked like when she and Adam first met. Dante paints the meeting as being more realistic than I had imagined, writing that the slow-to-love Eve did not find Adam the least bit attractive, becoming enamored, instead, with her own reflection in some water. It's true women are terribly enamored with their own reflections. You can't blame them, though. If I were good-looking, I would certainly go around looking at myself all the time, too. And it is also true women are slow to love. I used to think it was because something was wrong with them, but, over time, I wondered whether they were more deliberate than men about important decisions. Romantic decisions. And in comparison I realized they were infinitely more intelligent about relational matters than men.

But when I was reading the text the way John Sailhamer said to read the text, I noticed Adam and Eve didn't meet right away. Moses said God knew Adam was lonely or incomplete or however you want to say it, but God did not create Eve directly after He stated Adam was lonely. This struck me as funny because a lot of times when I think about life before the Fall, I don't think of people going around lonely. But that thought also comforted me because I realized loneliness in my own life doesn't mean I am a complete screwup, rather that God made me this way. You always picture the perfect human being as somebody who doesn't need anybody, like a guy on a horse out in Colorado or whatever. But here is Adam, the only perfect guy in the world, and he is going around wanting to be with somebody else, needing another person to fulfill a certain emptiness in his life. And as I said, when God saw this, He did not create Eve right away. He did not give Adam what he needed immediately. He waited. He told Adam to name the animals.

Now I had read this a thousand times, just glancing over it you know, but this time, reading it without looking for a magical formula, I actually thought about what would be involved in a job as big as naming the animals. In my mind this had been such an effortless action; Adam sits on a log with his hand on his chin, God parades the animals by rather quickly, Adam calls out names under his breath: *Buffalo, chimp, horse, mouse, lizard, buffalo . . . Uh, wait—did I already say buffalo? Um, well—how about cow; did I already say cow?*

But could it really have been so effortless? On that particular trip to Yosemite I took along the journals of John Muir, the guy who came up with the glacier theory for Yosemite Valley, a theory that says great glaciers carved the rocks that make up the walls of the place. I sat there in Yosemite reading about Muir's glacier theory, knowing it took him years of research, experiments, and canvassing the valley to develop the philosophy, and I wondered in my mind how he must have sat on the mountainside, drawing diagrams of El Capitan and Half Dome, wondering about the great wall of ice that cut through the granite slopes. And if it took John Muir the better portion of his life to realize his theory about the landscape in small Yosemite, I wondered, then, how much longer it must have taken Adam to name the animals in all the earth? I wondered how long it must have taken him to journey to the ocean to name the sea life, and whether he had to make a boat and go out on a boat or whether God had them swim up close to the shore, so Adam only had to go in about waist-deep.

I looked up how many animals there are in the world, and it turns out there are between ten million and one hundred million different species. So even if you believe in evolution, that means there were between one million and fifty million species around in the time of the Garden, and Adam, apparently, had to name all of them. And the entire time he was lonely.

I never thought of Adam the same again. The image of the man holding the fig leaf over his privates seemed nearly crude. Rather this was a man who, despite feeling a certain need for a companion, performed what must have been nearly one hundred years of work, naming and perhaps even categorizing the animals. It would have taken him nearly a year just to name the species of snakes alone. Moses said that Eve didn't give birth to their third child till Adam was well into his hundreds, which means they would have had Cain and Abel some thirty or so years before, which also means either it took Adam more than a hundred years to name the animals, or he and Eve didn't have sex for a good, long, boring century. And so in my mind, I began to see Adam as a lonely naturalist, a sort of Charles Darwin character, capturing animals and studying their hooves and heads and tails and eating habits and mating rituals. It must have been absolutely thrilling work, to be honest, thrilling and more than a little tiring.

The thing is, when Adam finished naming the animals, after all his work and effort, God put him to sleep, took a rib out of his side, and fashioned a woman. I had read that part a thousand times, too, but I don't think I quite realized how beautiful this moment was. Moses said the whole time Adam was naming the animals, that entire hundred years, he couldn't find a helpmate suitable for him. That means while he was naming cattle he was lonely because he couldn't really communicate in the same way with the cattle, and when he was naming fish he probably wanted to go swim in the ocean with them, but he couldn't breathe underwater; and the entire time he could not imagine what a helpmate might look like, how a helpmate might talk, the ways in which a helpmate might think. The idea of another person had, perhaps, never entered Adam's mind. Just like a kid who grows up without a father has no idea what having a father would be like, a guy who grows up the only human would have no idea what having another human around would be like. So here was this guy who was intensely relational, needing other people, and in order to cause him to appreciate the gift of companionship, God had him hang out with chimps for a hundred years. It's quite beautiful, really. God directed Adam's steps so that when He created Eve, Adam would have the utmost appreciation, respect, and gratitude.

I think it was smart of God because today, now that there are women all around and a guy can go on the Internet and see them naked anytime he wants, the whole species has been devalued. If I were a girl today in America, I would be a feminist for sure. I read recently where one out of every four women, by the time they reach thirty, are sexually harassed, molested, or raped. And then I thought how very beautiful it was that God made Adam work for so long because there is no way, after a hundred years of being alone, looking for somebody whom you could connect with in your soul, that you would take advantage of a woman once you met one. She would be the most precious creation in all the world, and you would probably wake up every morning and look at her and wonder at her beauty, or the gentle, silent way she sleeps. It stands to reason if Byron, Keats, and Shelley made beauty from reflecting on their muses, having grown up around women all their lives, that even these sonnets could not capture the sensation Adam must have felt when he opened his eyes to find Eve.

You probably think I am being mushy and romantic, but the first time Moses breaks into poetry in the Bible is when Adam first meets Eve. The thing about Moses was, he was the king of understatements. He could pack a million thoughts and emotions into just a few words. Here's what he said about what Adam thought when he met Eve:

> *Bone of my bones*
> *And flesh of my flesh* (Genesis 2:23 NKJV)

If you think about these ideas they are quite meaningful, and the bit of poetry Moses came up with truly summarizes the scene because, for the first time in his life, Adam was seeing a person who was like him, only more beautiful, and smarter in the ways of love and encouragement, and more deliberate in the ways of relationships. He must have thought to himself that she was perfect, and after a few days of just talking and getting to know each other, they must have fallen deeply in love. After Adam had taken Eve to the distant mountains where they could look down on the four rivers, and after he built for her a home and showed her the waterfalls and taught her the names of all the animals, he must have gone on a long walk with God and thanked Him, and I'll bet that was a very beautiful conversation. I'll bet Adam felt loved by God, like he was somebody God was always trying to bless and surprise with amazing experiences, and I'll bet they talked together about how beautiful Eve was and how wonderful it was that the two of them could know her, and I would imagine that Eve felt safe, loved, not used or gawked at, but appreciated and admired.

I know it sounds sensational, but I used to think that story was just a cartoon, just some cutout figures on a felt board. But they weren't that at all; they were people, human beings, and they felt all the things we might expect them to feel. And certainly a lot of this stuff really did happen to them, and certainly Adam was taken aback by Eve, surprised and amazed, and this is summed up wonderfully in Moses' poem.

Considering this couple, and what Adam went through to appreciate Eve to the utmost, I wondered at how beautiful it is that you and I were created to need each other. The romantic need is just the beginning, because we need our families and we need our friends. In this way, we are made in God's image. Certainly God does not need people in the way you and I do, but He feels a joy at being loved, and He feels a joy at delivering love. It is a striking thought to realize that, in paradise, a human is incomplete without a host of other people. We are relational indeed. And this book, the Bible, with all its understanding of the relational needs of humans, was becoming more meaningful to me as I turned the pages. God made me, He knows me, He understands me, and He wants community.

I hiked around Yosemite Valley all day and wondered what it

would have been like to have had the kind of relationship with God that Adam enjoyed. Adam and Eve, after all, are the only people in all of history who had a good relationship with God. Everybody else, after the Fall, had a pretty screwed-up idea of who God is, but Adam and Eve had the whole Deity before their eyes. And even though Adam was still lonely for a companion, I'll bet he didn't have any self-doubt or any low self-esteem because he had God there and, as I have said, just as a plant gets its life from the sun, people must have received their life from God. Jesus was always talking about how His glory came from God, as though God was shining on Him. The thing that made Jesus good, and the thing that made Adam good, was God's shining on them.

Can you imagine something like that, what it must feel like in the soul to have God's glory shining through you? With that much glory, that much of God shining through you, you would never have a self-defeating or other-person-bashing thought again. It would be brilliant. To say nothing of the earth, how wonderful it must have been, and to have had this wonderful woman Eve counseling you through the ways of love and relationships, but to have God shining through you is an idea, a mentality hardly imaginable. I'll bet I wouldn't think about any of the stuff I think about if I had God always shining life into my soul. I can hardly wrap my mind around the idea.

Do you know how Moses described the main characteristic of a person before the Fall? Moses said people before the Fall were naked and weren't ashamed. I'm not making this up. When he got to the end of chapter 2 of Genesis, the part of the Bible where he described what paradise was like, he concluded his description of paradise by saying Adam and Eve were *naked and were not ashamed*. It's right there in the Bible; you can look it up if you want. (See Genesis 2:25.)

Why Nudity Is the Point

Sitting there in Yosemite thinking about Adam and Eve being naked made me wonder if I would be comfortable in the Garden. In the first place, I hate being naked. The only time I get naked is when I am in the shower. Other than that I wear clothes all the time. And if I could wear clothes in the shower, I would. Here's the thing about being naked: When you're naked, all you're thinking about is the fact you're naked. If you go to the grocery store to get some barbecue sauce and you don't have on any clothes, chances are you aren't going to stand around looking for the barbecue sauce that's on sale, you're just going to grab the first bottle and get out of there on account of the fact you're naked. You aren't going to get a price check or go look to see if they have a new flavor of ice cream.

I know that sounds funny, but if you were to walk into the Garden of Eden, you would probably freak out Adam and Eve because they would think you had colorful skin made of cotton and they wouldn't have any idea that you were really a human with clothes on because, like Moses said, they were naked and weren't ashamed. The idea of clothes had never crossed their minds. And I know you think I am being immature by bringing this up, but the thing is, Moses repeated this idea five times. In just one hundred words used to describe Paradise and the Fall, the main thing he said, again and again, was that they were naked.

I wondered why it was that when people talked about the fall of man, about the Garden of Eden, they never talked about how people went around naked. If you ask me, the most obvious thing that happened after the Fall was that people started wearing all kinds of clothes. Just go to the store and look around, and you will see people wearing clothes. Everywhere you go you see people wearing clothes. Even as I type these words I am wearing clothes. I mean, evolution may explain how we came from apes, but it does nothing to explain why we wear clothes. And if Moses said it five times then you would think, when we consider the Garden of Eden and the fall of man, the first thing we would think of was that this was when we started wearing clothes. After all, it is the point of the story. Moses doesn't have any other point than this.

I started asking myself why Moses would say five times that people were naked before the Fall, but after the Fall, they went around with clothes on. So I read chapter 2 of Genesis again and, like I said, it was all about how nice Paradise was, and he summed up the description by saying Adam and Eve went around naked. Then I read chapter 3 and noticed something quite fascinating: The very first thing that happened after Adam and Eve ate from the Tree of Knowledge of Good and Evil was that they noticed they were naked. And man, I couldn't stop thinking about it; I couldn't stop thinking about how whatever happened at the Fall made them aware they were naked. This isn't "hidden wisdom" in the text. It is the text. It is blatant, and yet I had never heard anybody unpack it before.

And then it all came together. It all became so obvious, it was actually frightening. Moses was explaining all of humanity, right there in Genesis chapter 3, and because people were always reading it looking for the formula, they never saw it.

Here is what I think Moses was saying: Man is wired so he gets his glory (his security, his understanding of value, his feeling of purpose, his feeling of rightness with his Maker, his security for eternity) from God, and this relationship is so strong, and God's love is so pure, that Adam and Eve felt no insecurity at all, so much so that they walked around naked and didn't even realize they were naked. But when that relationship was broken, they knew it instantly. All of their glory, the glory that came from God, was gone. It wouldn't be unlike being in love and having somebody love you and then all of a sudden that person is gone, like a kid lost in the store. All of the insecurity rises the instant you realize you are alone. No insecurity was felt when the person who loved you was around, but in his absence, it instantly comes to the surface. In this way, Adam and Eve were naked and weren't ashamed when God was around, but the second the relationship was broken, they realized it and were ashamed. And that is just the beginning.

If man was wired so that something outside himself told him who he was, and if God's presence was giving him a feeling of fulfillment, then when that relationship was broken, man would be pining for other people to tell him that he was good, right, okay with the world, and eternally secure. As I wrote earlier, we all compare ourselves to others, and none of our emotions—like jealousy and envy and lust—could exist unless man was wired so that somebody else told him who he was, and that somebody else was gone.

Think about it for a second. Moses, in chapters 2 and 3 of Genesis, has presented a personality theory more comprehensive than the writings of Freud, Maslow, Frankl, and Skinner combined. And he did it in only a hundred words.

Some scholars say that later in the text, when God sews clothes for Adam and Eve, Moses was saying God killed an animal, a sacrifice from which the clothes are sewn, and this acts as a kind of prophecy for the fact that much later man will be clothed in righteousness through Christ, the perfect sacrifice. I think that explanation is interesting, and it certainly fits in with our Christian theology, but in my opinion that isn't what Moses was saying.

The Bible is a relational document, and theology is basically the charts and lists we have made out of the document. It is great stuff to keep us in line, but in this case it may have caused us to miss a message powerfully relevant to mankind. It really is very simple, and yet when unpacked, serves as a miraculous account of the development of human personality. Moses was speaking very plainly and artfully, and in so doing he explained everything.

I used to think that when the Fall happened, man started lusting, getting angry, getting jealous, coveting, stealing, lying, and cheating because, in the absence of God, he became a bad person. And in a simple, children's-story sort of way this is true, but in Genesis 2 and 3, Moses explains exactly why all of us feel, act, desire, and dream the things we feel, act, desire, and dream. The ramifications of this obvious idea are nearly infinite.

Of course I am being technical about things. The truth is these were people. Adam and Eve were people. As I read Moses' account, and as I walked around Yosemite, I was rather endeared to them. I have wonderful friends in Canada named Kaj and Libby Ballentyne. Kaj and Libby started an outdoor Bible college many years ago, and they are constantly climbing mountains of ice or running rapids with students. They love nature and they love the God who seemed to make nature for them. They love each other and enjoy each other, and when they are apart for longer than a few days you can see it in their eyes how much they miss and need their friend.

I stood on a rock at Glacier Point and I imagined Kaj and Libby having the run of the Garden of Eden, hiking up into its steeps to catch a view of one of God's sunsets. And then it hit me how awful it must have been for Adam and Eve to have been deceived by Satan, to have been tricked into breaking their relationship with God.

You and I almost have it easier. We were born this way. But I remember loving a girl back in Colorado and having her explain to me she didn't feel the same and how for a year I lived in the attic of an old house in Portland, feeling an ache and emptiness in my heart I thought would never mend, sitting beneath a single dan-gling bulb reading Nietzsche. And this feeling, this feeling must have been so much more painful for Adam and Eve, this feeling of having an infinite amount of love pouring through their lives and then it's suddenly gone. I pictured my beautiful friends Kaj and Libby having to go through that kind of pain and it was almost too much. I wondered at how terrible it must have felt, at the fear of no longer feeling God, at the ache of emptiness and the sudden and horrifying awareness of self. God have mercy.

Chapter Six

Children of Chernobyl

―――

Why Did God Leave?

I was living at Graceland, the house on the traffic circle at Thirty-ninth and Glisan, when Tony the Beat Poet knocked loudly on the French doors that opened into my room. It must have been six in the morning and I confess, I was somewhat frustrated that I was being made to get out of bed that early. Back then I was working on a book and wrote mostly at night, so I hadn't gotten to bed till well after midnight the previous evening. I was groggy when I answered the door.

"Have you heard?" Tony asked in a panic.

"What are you talking about?" I said.

"Have you heard?" Tony said again, brushing past me into the house.

Tony looked terrible and anxious; the expression on his face, his tone—he wanted the television. He walked across the living room and turned it on then backed himself to the couch slowly, sitting on the edge of it with his hand over his mouth. He had heard the news on his car radio and wanted to see the images. I sat down in the big brown chair and when my eyes focused I saw on the screen a man jumping from the seventieth floor of a building in New York, his speck of body descending, his head below his feet, his tie flagging out behind him. I watched for ten or so minutes until the second tower collapsed, then went upstairs to wake the other guys in the house.

I remember going door-to-door at Reed College a few weeks after the terrorist attacks. It was the night all the freshmen were cramming for their first humanities paper so we were delivering cookies, wishing them the best and giving them a break from their books. Reed is a liberal school, to be sure, and I suppose I was surprised at the patriotic sentiments pasted as cut-out editorials on dorm-room doors—the American flags, the pictures of the New York skyline. But I was walking a hall in the old dorm block sometime after midnight when I came across a door that had some anti-American reactions pasted as bumper stickers and taped-up notes, and next to these was a list of statistics regarding tragedies in the Middle East. Thousands are killed there every year, the statistics revealed, and to the people living there, losing three thousand people in one day is not a significant event. Death, in Gaza, in the West Bank, in Afghanistan, Pakistan, Iraq, and Iran is a way of life. I wondered at the complexity of the situation.

It was a somber time for all of us. Truth got lost in emotion, both for and against the West. I found myself sentimental at first, thinking of the firefighters going into the buildings, and then I found myself feeling for Arabs here in the States and abroad. I lost sentimentality about the time country-and-western singers came out of the woodwork to sing twangy and horribly written songs about why America is better than everybody else. It killed me. None of it was true. Then I got sad about it.

My friend Andrew the Protester had been on a bus in Portland, and he sat next to a man who happened to be Indian. This man who was from India was confronted and scorned publicly by another guy on the bus. The other guy told him he should be ashamed of himself and that he should go back home. He was Indian, for crying out loud. You wouldn't think a thing like that would happen here in Portland, but it does. A very close friend of mine, a very conservative missionary, told me he thought we should "bomb the rag-heads." And that is what we did a few months later in two separate campaigns. We bombed these countries, according to the president, because "they hated freedom."

I prayed a great deal during this time. We sat around in the lounges at Reed and watched the talking heads on television, we talked with students, we went to rallies, we protested acts of violence to end acts of violence, we listened to lectures, we read books, we watched more television. In a way it was odd directly after September 11 because it was as though everybody were taking a break from normal life, as though everybody were taking time off to attend a kind of national funeral. We all were quiet at first, all unified, but soon the reverence turned to opinions, and opinions to arguments, and arguments to rage.

We ached at the simplicity of proposed solutions. The spin. I remember feeling hopeless at the death of truth and seeing truth as this whispering weakling in the corner, a wallflower, having no say in the global conversation, having no guts to step forth and negotiate peace. I got sick of the emotionalism, the feelings that replaced the thoughts. "These colors don't run," a bumper sticker read. "Support our troops," a politician told us. All of it aimed at stirring up emotion rather than logic. We were living on sentimental clichés. Our country had become a team and we were wrapped up in whether or not we were going to win the *game* against *them*. It was like the World Cup, except with guns. They changed the name of French fries in the capital to freedom fries. I was embarrassed. The French are already so snobby to begin with, did we have to give them reason?

———

I hate war, to be honest. I hate *one side against another*. I hate groupthink. And war isn't new, either. It goes way back, all this tragedy. I remember when I was a kid, buying U2's new album *The Unforgettable Fire*, which was inspired by pictures captured after a plane called *Enola Gay* dropped a bomb called *Little Boy* on Hiroshima, Japan, an event that ended World War II. In Hiroshima, 70,000 people were killed instantly, and another 40,000 three days later in Nagasaki; another 110,000 were injured in the blasts, and another 340,000 died from diseases such as leukemia, all attributed to the nuclear fallout from the mushroom cloud. And the entire city of Tokyo was burned to the ground only weeks before these killings took place.

Last week I watched the Academy Award–winning documentary *Fog of War* about Robert MacNamara. In the movie MacNamara sat fidgeting in a chair and admitted our policies in World War II, and again in Vietnam, were less than honorable. And I know people who were in Vietnam, and I think they are heroes all the same, but it was so nice to sit in a movie theater and watch an eighty-year-old power broker admit he was wrong, that our reactions, that getting into the heat of battle had caused certain lapses in reason, understanding, and compassion. Hearing Robert MacNamara admit these things made me feel there was truth out there, that there was some kind of hope in humility, a humility that, perhaps, comes upon you just before you die, during that stage of life when you realize, for the first time, the *our team is better than your team* mentality will always fail.

I pulled out that U2 album I was talking about earlier. I put on a pot of coffee and listened to it in the morning before my roommates woke up. I listened to it as the sun came up over Laurelhurst, my windows open, the clouds coming in off the Pacific, stretching like wispy cobwebs into the blue, out toward the mountains. And the somber, reflective music seemed to re-create the devastation of World War II in my mind. I could see the bombs drop, the sudden deaths of thousands, those on the fringes running from the flames. I kept seeing the images they showed in that movie about Robert MacNamara, the images of Tokyo on fire, of the burned children screaming in Hiroshima and Nagasaki. We destroyed an entire nation. Instead of engaging troops, man on man, gun on gun, we attempted to kill all the women and children in the major cities so that the country would surrender. At one point MacNamara had tears in his eyes. I couldn't believe it. Robert MacNamara, with tears in his eyes.

I stood there at the window and looked out at the city, Bono going off in my speakers. War is awful. I don't know whether it was right or wrong, what we did in Japan, but I know it was awful. I realize it ended the war, and I know it saved lives in the long run, and I know about Hitler, and I know Japan wanted half the world, but that doesn't mean we shouldn't mourn war anyway, that doesn't mean we shouldn't feel a grief at the terrible ways conflicts are negotiated in a world absent God.

———

That morning, looking out my window, I imagined an explosion in Portland; I imagined what it would have been like to have been in a war, an atomic bomb destroying the downtown skyline. I could see it in my mind: all the buildings bending in slow motion, then bursting into flames. I could see, in my mind, the after-blast of the explosion coming up from behind our house, blowing the trees so they lay against the ground where they dry instantly in the heat then flame up in coal-sticks and embers. I imagined cars lifting off the roads, light as paper, smashing into the porches of the expensive homes across Burnside. I imagined a city bus smashing through the trees that stand against Laurelhurst Park and the pond beginning to boil and the fish coming to the surface.

———

How do you stop a war, I wonder? I am not certain it was right for Bonhoeffer to try to kill Hitler. I am not certain it was right, but I know I would have done it myself; that if I had him in the crosshairs of a gun I would have pulled the trigger. I get very angry at injustice. Give me a gun and I would have killed Stalin, who slaughtered sixty million, or for that matter, Lenin. I can't think of any other solution. You can't let evil run wild, can you? War is difficult like that. It is complicated. There seems to be no right and no wrong.

Tony spent several years in Albania and literally prayed and asked God whether He wanted him to kill Slavadon Malosivich. Tony didn't do it, but he told me in a very quiet conversation at Horse Brass that he wanted to, that he sat in his room at night and imagined lying flat on a rooftop with a rifle, or getting close enough to the dictator, perhaps at an open event, to run a knife through his neck. It's ugly stuff, I know, but if Tony would have done it, he would have saved millions of lives. Clinton took forever to do anything about that situation. You think you can trust a Democrat to do something about this sort of thing, but you can't.

———

War is no recent phenomenon, either. At times it feels like all this just started happening a few years ago, but it didn't. There were still soldiers in Vietnam when I was born, and my grandfathers' generation fought in World War II, and not long before that, World War I. Historians are divided as to whether the Trojan Wars actually happened in 1200 BC, but I believe they did. It's not that I know anything about it, I know only the heart of man, and the heart of man is going to go to war. Put a red dot in the place of a war on the timeline of world history, and there won't be a year of peace anywhere; it will all be red. After the Trojan Wars were the Persian Wars; after the Persian Wars were the Peloponnesian Wars, and then the Wars of Alexander the Great, and they go on and on. Caesar, Stalin, Lenin, Hitler, Hussein . . . they all believed they were right, defending truth, doing what was best, propagating sentiments of patriotism to a nation-state, as though God Himself believed one country any better than another.

———

I bring this up only because the fall of man, when Adam and Eve ate from that tree, occurred because there was a war going on. This is the only way I can explain life as we know it. The people of Japan were not monsters, they were just people, but they were caught up in war. They were victims of war, victims of a handful of men, a handful of leaders who wanted something they couldn't have.

Scripture indicates that there were wars in heaven and that Satan hates God. I realize we want to blame all the world's problems on individual responsibility, that we want to look at Scripture through a Western-financial lens, saying that everybody is responsible for everything they do, but this is only half true. Adam and Eve were deceived; they were misled. Something in them wanted something they couldn't have, but they were tricked into thinking those thoughts. It's a both/and situation. We are wired so that other people help create us, help make us who we are, and when deception is fed to us, we make bad decisions. War is complicated; it isn't black and white. That is what the Bible teaches. And I thought about that for a long time and realized it meant all our civilizations, our personalities, our families, our souls, are walking through the wreckage of a war, running from Tokyo, running from Hiroshima, our mouths gaping, the fire burning behind us, our wounds wet with blood and muddied with ash. This is Sarajevo all over again, only this time it's the walls of our hearts that are littered with bullet holes, it's our souls that are feeling the aftershock.

In a way, the war in heaven, the war between God and those against God, is the war to explain all wars. If you really want to believe one side is good and another side is bad, if you really want to look back through history and find a perfect and innocent kingdom that was attacked by an enemy, you have to go back to the Garden of Eden. A perfect and innocent kingdom hasn't been attacked since then. Details are few because Moses hardly gets into it, but to be sure, the Bible paints a picture of a certain evil tricking innocent humans into betraying the God who loved them, the King who was their friend. They were enticed, they considered their options, and they wanted to be equal to God. It's ugly stuff.

Chapter 3 of Genesis is, to me, one of the most confusing in all Scripture. I can't read it without producing a list of questions for God, questions I fear have few answers. God does not choose to tell us why He let Satan walk around in the Garden so he could talk to Adam and Eve, and He doesn't tell us why God did not talk to

Adam and Eve to kindly counsel them about Satan's deception. God might have done this, but if He did, we don't have any record of it. And while God told the sad couple in no uncertain terms to not eat from the Tree of the Knowledge of Good and Evil, He did not seem to tell them that there was such a thing as a lie, and such a being as a liar. Was this covered in the pre-earth manual? There are times when I find myself angry at the couple because all the tragedy in all of life can be traced back to them, but I also see them as somewhat innocent, having been created by God with minds that could so easily be deceived.

And yet the crime the couple committed seems unforgivable. They fell for a trick. Far from a technicality in behavior, their eating of the fruit was a heart-level betrayal between committed friends: God and man. At issue in the tragedy of the Garden is a relational crime. Adam and Eve were not satisfied with their relationship with God, and they wanted to change the dynamic by increasing their own power, a reality that simply wasn't possible, save the fantasy realm whispered to them through the words of the evil one.

A God Betrayed

I've a friend who overheard his wife on the phone with another man. She did not know he was in the house, and he walked up behind her, leaned against the frame of the door to hear her confess her love and enjoyment of the other man's touch. My friend drove around Baltimore in a daze; he went into coffee shops and sat with his head in his hands. He went to a bus station and bought a ticket to Pittsburgh but he missed his bus, sick from smoking a pack of cigarettes. Instead, he spent an hour in the bathroom vomiting yellow muck into a filthy toilet.

Our systematic theology reduces the fall of man to a technical act of betrayal. We hardly think of it as relational at all. But I think this view distorts what actually happened. I think God must have felt like my friend in Baltimore. I think it was something terribly painful for God to endure. I don't think we can understand the pain a pure love would feel after being betrayed by the focus of its love. You wouldn't think God would forgive them at all. You would think God would just kill them. If a couple of terrorists pulled something like that today, they might be dragged through the streets, their bodies used as human torches and hung in a public place for months. People would travel from miles away to spit on their bones.

When I think about God arriving in the Garden after the Fall, I think about Jimmy Carter arriving at the base of Mount Saint Helens after the eruption. It's just fifty miles across the river, Mount Saint Helens, and on a clear day you can see it from Portland. And I remember seeing Jimmy Carter getting out of his helicopter, the belly of the helicopter caked in mud, the sides of it gray with ash. Carter stepped down from his seat, his expression confused, troubled, all the pain of a region mapped in the lines of his face. And later, when I was twenty-one, I went to the place myself and tried to imagine it then. I imagined Harry Truman at Mirror Lake, refusing to leave despite the warnings. I imagined two thousand feet of this once great mountain coming down on him, sliding him and his lake over the next mountain and down the other side, displacing the body of water altogether. There were tremors, only a month of them, hardly a warning for a mountain that sat dormant for a hundred years.

A few years ago I drove up the winding road in my car, the fresh mountain air lofting in through the windows and swirling around in the backseat, the tall pines lining the road like statues, the round, tight corners walled on one side by cliffs and the other side by thousands of feet of descent, down to a blue river bright like a mirror through the canyon, shining silver and white over rocks, then back to blue in the pools, casting up against the same-colored sky. *It was all so beautiful*, I remember thinking. And then I hit the spot on the road where the trees stopped, and the landscape went dead, like the landscape after Hiroshima, as though the place had been bombed. There was no life, not a plant, not a tree, just gray ash flowing across the hills for thirty miles toward the crater.

I rounded the long steeps toward the visitors center, which sits on a neighboring hill, the few green trees around which were the only life on what seemed to me an ugly, dry planet. And this is precisely how I began to feel, that I was no longer on earth, that I was in some other orb with some other climate and some other ecosystem, all of which was the product of some tragedy, as though the people who inhabited this place were destroyed or, if they lived somewhere out there in the ash, were walking around in a daze, having suffered a kind of concussion, trying to make a life in the ruined landscape. The placards at the door said ash had been carried as far north as Canada. Spokane, some three hundred miles away, was deluged with more than three feet of ash. Rivers were dammed, others created, and some of the rivers, filled with walls of ash and water from Mirror Lake, took out bridges with their muscle. The Columbia, the lifeline to this region and the second largest river in the United States, was shut down completely as ash brought the bed to only twelve feet.

My friend Danielle said she encountered the sight in the parking lot after church. She was a little girl then, walking out of the sanctuary holding her father's hand and staring confusedly at a mountain she and her family had known all their lives, some fifteen miles away, spit a plume larger than the cloud over Nagasaki, going up into heaven like some angry burst of earth. They must have thought the world was coming to an end.

———

All this makes me wonder what God must have felt, arriving on the scene just after the Fall, knowing all He had made was ruined, and understanding at once the sacrifice that would be required to win the hearts of His children from the grasp of their seducer. I see Him in my mind walking the paths, calling to the couple, meeting their eyes for the first time, and Adam and Eve shaking in absolute terror, wondering what had happened, confused at the broken promise of a snake, feeling at once the trustworthiness of their first love and wondering if God would ever love them again, feeling the hot breath of His anger and emotion, hearing Him speak for the first time, not as a friend, but as One who had been betrayed. "Who told you that you were naked?"

———

Scripture would indicate that God had to break the relationship when man sinned against Him, that because His nature is purely good, purely right and lovely, He could not directly interact with beings who were, in their hearts, set against Him. This should not be confused with a lack of love, a lack of compassion; it must be understood only as two opposite natures unable to interact without one tainting the other. This is a very beautiful thing because you and I need for God to be perfectly good, we need for Him to be the voice that did one day, and will in the future, speak pure glory into our lives. But for now, because of this act of war, relations have been strained. And we are feeling it in our souls.

———

I have on my desktop a picture of a boy named Sasha. Sasha is one of the children of Chernobyl, a young boy born after the disaster that happened when the core at a nuclear facility in Russia melted and leaked. This little boy, Sasha, is perhaps five years old, and he is gripping with a tiny arm the side of a crib. His other hand is flailing upward toward his ear, his head and shoulders the only portion of his body not mutated. On the right side of Sasha's chest rises a lump the size of a softball and his belly grows out disfigured before him as though he were pregnant, a truly painful sight. His legs are oversized and blocky and he has no knees, only rounded flesh flowing awkwardly to his oversized feet, which produce four toes each, the largest of which, as big as my fist, is distanced from the others and pointing itself in an opposite direction. From the bottom of his stomach protrudes a rounded flow of flesh as though it were a separate limb, stopped in half growth. Sasha, the article in which I found the picture states, is in constant pain, lives in constant pain.

As terrible as it is to compare Sasha to ourselves, I have to go there. I have to say that you and I were not supposed to be this way. As creatures in need of somebody outside ourselves to name us, as creatures incomplete outside the companionship of God, our souls are born distorted, I am convinced of it. I am convinced that Moses was right, that his explanation was greater than Freud's or Maslow's or Pavlov's. I believe, without question, that none of us are happy in the way we were supposed to be happy. I believe that nobody on this planet is so secure, so confident in their state that they feel the way Adam and Eve felt in the Garden, before they knew they were naked. I believe we are in the wreckage of a war, a kind of Hiroshima, a kind of Mount Saint Helens, with souls distorted like the children of Chernobyl. As terrible as it is to think about these things, as ugly as it is to face them, I have to see the world this way in order for it to make sense. I have to believe something happened, and we are walking around holding our wounds.

That said, we are mistaken to believe this is a war between people with flesh and people with flesh. The only appropriate war rhetoric is war rhetoric that calls our enemies spirits, and people with flesh the victims of this war. Satan wants us to fight with one another, and I understand that sometimes evil must be restrained, but our war, the war of the ones who believe in Jesus, is a war unseen. If we could muster a portion of the patriotism we feel toward our earthly nations into a patriotism and bravery in concert with the kingdom of God, the enemy would take fewer casualties to be sure.

———

Not long ago I was wrestling rather desperately with some specific passages in Scripture. To be honest, I misunderstood them and my pastor, Rick, helped me walk through them so I could understand. The specifics seem trivial now, but at the time I was experiencing a great deal of pain trying to figure out the ideas God was expressing. I have always been somewhat obsessive-compulsive in terms of not being able to turn off my mind. I get stuck on ideas and have to understand them. During this difficult time, my sleep was restless. And on a particular evening, after I had been asleep for a few hours, I was awakened. Now I want to tell you I have always been suspicious of people who say that God spoke to them in a dream.

Nothing like this has ever happened to me, and even as I type this I cannot say that what happened was actually God. I only know I had a dream that was not quite a dream. I woke up, and yet I didn't.

I was aware that I was lying in my bed, in my home, that the fan was on in the room, and yet I was also aware that I was in another place, standing on nothing, floating and yet stable, and there were three figures in monk robes standing to my right, facing me and bowing their heads in prayer. I had a sword in my hand and before I could figure out what was going on, a figure came at me at bullet speed from the distant darkness. I held out my sword and cut the figure in half and it fell into the darkness beneath me. I was startled, of course, and looked over at the figures and felt a certain knowledge that they were *for* me, that they were my friends, but they did not look up; they kept praying as dark figure after dark figure came out of the distance and I cut each of them in half. At one point during my dream I realized that my physical hands were actually clinched before my chest, and when I went to slice through a dark figure my hands jumped as the sword met resistance. The dream went on for a few minutes until I drifted off into normal sleep, waking up the next morning to remember this dream, one of the few dreams I have remembered in several years.

As I said, I am suspicious about whether God still talks to people in dreams. I hate writing this because I prefer dealing with more logical, sound ideas. And yet as the weeks have gone by since that dream, I have wondered if God wasn't telling me that you and I are in a spiritual war, that there is more going on than we understand, and that the Trinity is praying for us, for all of us as we deal with the evil one, who, Scripture teaches, roams about like a lion, searching for a kill (see 1 Peter 5:8).

I didn't feel any fear in my dream. I was calm because I knew God was there. I am not trying to get anybody worked up into any kind of worry. I tell you this story only to reiterate I believe we are in the wreckage of a terrible act of war, and that this war is still being waged today, against what Scripture calls the principalities of darkness (see Ephesians 6:12), that is, spirits who hate God.

———

I happened to see Larry King interview Billy Graham shortly after the shootings at Columbine High School in Littleton, Colorado. I had read an article the previous month about violent video games and their effects on the minds of children, desensitizing them to the act of killing. Larry King asked Billy Graham what was wrong with the world, and how such a thing as Columbine could happen. I knew, because Billy Graham was an educated man, he had read the same article I had read, and I began calculating his answer for him, that violence begets violence, that we live in a culture desensitized to the beauty of human life and the sanctity of creation. But Billy Graham did not blame video games. Billy Graham looked Larry King in the eye and said, *"Thousands of years ago, a young couple in love lived in a garden called Eden, and God placed a tree in the Garden and told them not to eat from the tree . . ."*

And I knew in my soul he was right.

CHAPTER SEVEN

Adam, Eve, and the Alien

HOW THE FALL MAKES YOU FEEL

I was thinking about all this the other day while my roommate Grant and I were watching a Blazers game. I was telling Grant that if I were an alien and I came down to earth from some far-off planet, there are a few things I would notice about people, and the first thing I would notice is the way they looked, that is, if people looked different on my planet. Then I would notice how their cities were constructed and, depending on how the civilization had advanced wherever I was from, I would notice how ahead or behind their cities happened to be. You know what I mean, mass transit and all, technology; but after I got over all of this and sat down to have a beer with some people, really finding out what they were interested in, what they loved and hated, there would be one thing I would notice that would kind of explain everything. And by *everything*, I mean all the stuff that makes a person want to live his life a certain way or the stuff that drives a person's thoughts, subconscious and conscious.

And I was telling Grant, "Let's say I was an alien and I had to go back to my home planet and explain to some head-of-the-aliens guy about what people on this planet were like." I told Grant that I would say to the head alien, "The thing that defines human personalities is that they are constantly comparing themselves to one another." Grant kind of nodded at me as if he thought this was interesting, then he took a sip of his beer and we went back to watching the game. But I kept thinking about this and that night I got out of bed and wrote my thoughts down on a piece of paper, you know, as if I were an alien. I put it down in a fancy alien voice:

Humans, as a species, are constantly, and in every way, comparing themselves to one another, which, given the brief nature of their existence, seems an oddity and, for that matter, a waste. Nevertheless, this is the driving influence behind every human's social development, their emotional health and sense of joy, and, sadly, their greatest tragedies. It is as though something that helped them function and live well has gone missing, and they are pining for that missing thing in all sorts of odd methods, none of which are working. The greater tragedy is that very few people understand they have the disease. This seems strange as well because it is obvious. To be sure, it is killing them, and yet sustaining their social and economic systems. They are an entirely beautiful people with a terrible problem.

That is how an alien would see the world, in my opinion. It is obvious to me there is something wrong with us; there is something incomplete. The same guy who says there isn't anything incomplete is probably the same guy who cries himself to sleep at night, or tries to get a lot of people to love him, or has terrible prejudices. We all have these tendencies, and they had to come from somewhere.

A few days later, Grant and I were watching television again and I wondered out loud what an alien would think if he came over to watch some television with us. I wondered what an alien would think of our television shows. He probably wouldn't understand any of it, because all the plots have to do with getting and finding the thing that is missing in our souls, only not getting it from God, but from other people.

If the alien wasn't missing the same thing we were missing, he would sit there in my room with Grant and me, watching basketball but not understanding why we play the game. *Why do they do that?* the alien might say. *It's a game, a competition,* Grant and I would answer. *But why? Why do they play the game? What are they trying to decide?*

They are trying to decide who is the better basketball team, Grant and I would say. *The better basketball team?* the alien might question, wondering out loud why twenty thousand people would show up to find out which basketball team was better than the other.

Feeling a little judged, Grant and I might change the channel to find that new show on E! called *Rank,* the show that ranks people from best to worst, based on some random criteria. The episode might count down to who is the most eligible bachelor, who is the hottest couple, who has the best boobs, best eyes, best smile, whatever. Then, knowing the show was again proving the alien's point, just like basketball, we might turn the channel to that show *Survivor,* and then over to *The Bachelor,* and then over to *Last Comic Standing,* or *Fear Factor,* or whatever. And then we would sort of feel bad because all of our television shows are trying to figure out who is better than who, or if they aren't, they are presupposing that one kind of person is better than another and building their comedy or their drama from this presupposition.

You guys, the alien might say, *you are obsessed. You have to wear a certain kind of clothes, drive a certain car, speak a certain way, live in a certain neighborhood, whatever, all of it so you can be higher on an invisible hierarchy. It's an obsession! You are trying to feel right by comparing yourself to others. It is ridiculous. Who told you there was anything wrong with you in the first place? Don't you know that a human is just a human?*

I kept thinking about all this, you know, what the alien was saying to Grant and me, and it caused me to wonder if this thing that makes us compare ourselves is what happened at the Fall. It occurred to me that what the alien was saying made sense because now that God was gone, now that He wasn't around to help us feel that we were loved and important and good, we were looking for it in each other, in a jury of peers.

And then I began to wonder if Adam and Eve were to visit Grant and me to watch *Survivor,* for example, how confused they might be, how they might sit around naked and look over at the alien and roll their eyes all the time, making Grant and me feel very uncomfortable. And we might say, *Well, look at your stupid system. You sit around naked all the time,* and they might look over at us as if we were the crazy ones, needing to have all kinds of fabric in our closets to put on and make ourselves look fancy and less naked, and we would say to them, *Man, you just don't get it.* And they would say to us, *Man, you just don't get it.*

And I could feel in my soul all this was true, that these were the wounds of Chernobyl, of the Fall, and I began to realize how ugly and desperate the situation actually was.

At Palio I would lean over and listen to conversations people were having with each other. People would talk about their jobs or how much money they made and they would talk about who liked them and who didn't, and how the ones who liked them were sweet and the ones who didn't were spiteful and moody and didn't have any authority about social matters. They would talk about what is cool and what isn't, who has a better or more credible sense of taste, what they are going to do to make their house nicer, which sports team is better than which other.

And then I started thinking about my own life, how I need people to love me and like me and how, if they don't, I feel miserable and sad and how I am tempted to believe what they are saying about me is true. It is as though the voice God used to have has been taken up by less credible voices. And when I think about this I know that Genesis 3 is true; I know without a doubt I am a person who is wired so that something outside myself tells me who I am. I am not trying to say I have some kind of terrible dysfunction or anything, it's just that other people's opinions, after the Fall, have become very important, and if everybody says that Saab cars are cool, then I want a Saab car, and if people say that a certain kind of music is cool, then I am more likely to listen to that kind of music. And all this made me realize that the alien was right, and that Adam and Eve had it a great deal better before they ate the fruit.

———

I remember when I first learned about people who were and weren't cool. There was a kid in my middle school who never took a bath. He had dreadful buckteeth, so large they came out his mouth an inch, and so under no circumstances could he close his lips. I used to look at him in class and wonder how his mouth did not dry out. He kept long hair, his family too poor to afford a haircut, and he would wear the same clothes for a week, each day becoming more gray, each week his hair coming more over his eyes, and he had the jumpy feel of a beat dog. He would set his languid body over the papers on his desk, his oily hair coming over his head like a curtain, and in this position he would sit all day, talking to no one, only hoping to avoid the jury of his peers, a constant source of condemnation.

I would watch Pete during class, study him from seats behind, and reflect on his ugliness, feeling some bit of pity, but also a degree of self-righteousness. I was not a popular kid at school to be sure. I was unsightly enough to gain ridicule yet quiet enough to avoid it. Elementary school had me loud because you could get commodity from personality at that age, but middle school had the economy shifting entirely to looks, wealth, and athletic prowess. Of the three, I lacked all in equal.

Pete was something of a relief to me because I knew my proverbial backside was covered by his presence, the volume of prejudice always going toward the most different, the most repulsive, and in our school, and for this purpose, Pete took the hate. If it is the nature of man to measure himself against others, as the alien said, Pete was ever beneath us, so far beneath us, in fact, that in his presence, geeks felt like kings. The temptation for each of us to measure ourselves against Pete was insatiable in that we knew we couldn't lose in the exchange.

A child learns early there is a fashionable and an unfashionable in the world, an ugly and a pretty, a valued and an unvalued. Where this system comes from, God only knows, but it is rarely questioned, and though completely illogical and agreed upon by everyone as evil, it remains in play, commanding our emotions as a possession. It isn't something taught to us by our parents; it is something that comes naturally, as though a radioactive kind of tragedy happened, screwing up our souls. Adulterated or policed, the system can grow to something more civilized, but no less dominant as a drive of nature. In youth the system is obvious. If you want to learn the operating system to which humans are subjected, step into a classroom of preteen students and listen to the dialogue. You will hear the constant measurements, the talk about family wealth, whose father drives what car, who lives in what neighborhood, or who is dating whom.

Here is how it feels: From the first day of school the conversation is the same as it would be if hundreds of students were told to stand in line ranging from best to worst, coolest to most uncool, each presenting their case for value, each presenting an offense to the cases of others, alliances being formed as caricatures of reality television (or vice versa).

And here is what is terrible: There will be a sort of punishment being dealt to those at the end of the line, each person dealing out castigation as a way of dissociation from the geeks, driven by the fear that associating with somebody at the end of the line might cost them position, as if the two might be averaged, landing each of them in the space between. And so, in this way, students are constantly looking to associate themselves with those higher in line, and dissociate from those of low position. Great lengths will be taken to associate with those at the front of the line. Students will kiss up, drop names, lie about friendships, and so on. Many will hate the most popular, and yet subject themselves to their approval as though they were small gods. But the great crime, the great tragedy, is not in the attempts to associate but rather the efforts to dissociate. If a person feels his space in the hierarchy is threatened, that he might lose position, the vehemence he feels toward the lesser person is nearly malevolent.

I say all this only because the torture Pete knew from us was unrelenting. I remember a scene with him backed against his locker surrounded by jocks, my friends and I feeling somehow powerful, not because we were joining the harassment, but because we were not the victims of it. We were horrible to him, if you want to know the truth, but it felt as though we had to be, that by ridiculing Pete we were protecting ourselves from some terrible fate.

The feeling was that if we were last on the social ladder, or near last, we would be facing some kind of torture. Though it sounds absurd, it *felt* true, as though there were a spirit in the air directing our passions. It was incredibly important to climb this ladder, and the closer you were to the top, it was believed, the easier you could breathe, because at the top people loved you and cared about you and gave you a little bit of the thing God used to give you.

———

Pete was last on the list of valuable people at my school. The ones who were first were the blonde girls, the girls who would become cheerleaders, and after the cheerleaders were the tall, athletic boys who would become football players. Soccer girls came after football boys, but not by much. They were an interesting set, very beautiful with tanned legs of muscle, and if they wanted they could have been as valuable as cute blondes, but they chose not to; they chose to play soccer and dress granola as if they didn't care. But they dated the same boys the blondes dated, and each time an athlete and a granola would connect, the school considered them a beautiful novelty because, to some degree, each of them was showing grace to the other.

Small graces like these were meaningful in middle school. They stated that the walls separating social classes, though they were tall, could be mounted by that mysterious thrust of hormones we ignorantly referred to as love.

Pam dated Nick, for instance, and William hooked up with Ivy, Kelly made out with Sam on the trip to the Museum of Natural

History and came back with a crush on Jim, Sam's best friend, who, the entire time Kelly and Sam were making out on the bus, sat two seats in front of them in tears. Romantic relationships in middle school, though driven to some degree by pure emotions, were much more negotiations within the ladder, each party asking for trust from the other, the entire school acting as an audience for the grand play of life. And we ate and drank this drama. There was much to be gained and lost in these exchanges. For instance, the relationship between Kelly and Sam lasted an astounding eight months, all the way through the winter production of *A Christmas Carol*, during the practices for which, Jim, who played the Ghost of Christmas Past, fell for Rachel, who played Mrs. Cratchet. Rumors of the relationship were denied by Jim straight to Kelly's face, but confirmed with a bold kiss at curtain call on opening night, sending Kelly, in complete hysterics, to the girls' restroom off the gym side of the auditorium, the bellows from which proved more dramatic, in fact, than the fellow in the play who got his bearings about the meaning of Christmas. It was great stuff, I have to tell you, but I didn't even think way back then about how this drama was being created because certain forces or desires existed within us and those desires had an explanation.

We were lost in the drama. We never wondered about where it all came from or why it existed. And we talked about these matters as heads of state might discuss international policy. We sat in the lunchroom and talked about who was going out with whom and who was going to get beat up after school, and who had a big house in a nice neighborhood. Lunch was our AP wire, and we mulled over the daily fare in contemplation and awe, always wondering where the shifts had taken place on the invisible ladder.

When it was hinted that barriers had been breached, that invisible lines had been crossed in the categories of important and unimportant, mayhem ensued. Kim Morgan for instance, on a dare, kissed Mark Bryant on the cheek. Kim played on the soccer team and Mark kept quiet and to himself and wasn't anything like a jock, only known for the company he kept with a group of computer geeks who played Dungeons and Dragons on the kickball field during lunch.

Here is how it happened: A clique of girls gathered across from Mark's locker, his short stature just enough for his eyes to find the bottom of his stacked books, a foundation for rotten lunches, crumpled papers, and gym clothes. Kim approached him from behind, said his name, and as he turned she went in for the deed. Mark jerked back, closed his eyes, and held his breath in one reaction. Kim shriveled in disgust when she was done. She wiped her lips on the arm of her sweater and released a breathy scream the tone of bus brakes.

News of the event rippled through the school like scandal, and for two days a few of the gaggle close to Kim splintered and would not talk to her. But my friends and I loved her for what she had done. Though it was only a dare and could not be confused with a sincere act of affection, she had broken the invisible social barrier.

That evening I wondered if Kim's kiss would make an impact on social partitions. A valuable person had crossed the line to kiss a person of no value. Maybe they would realize we were all just humans, I thought; maybe they would realize the feelings about the hierarchy were not true, that we were somehow equal, a computer nerd and a football player, the same.

But the system remained. It seemed while no logical evidence existed for one group of people being of more importance than another, feelings, not thought, governed the hierarchy. And time would show us all how severe, how passionate these feelings could grow.

———

Pete, the fellow I told you about earlier who did not bathe or cut his hair, had learned walking patterns that allowed him to, for the most part, blend in. If a group of athletes were coming toward him, he would walk briskly, close to the lockers, always looking down and away. And most of the time the athletes honored his request and left him alone.

One day after school, however, Pete's mother was late to pick him up. Pete's family had a station wagon caked with mud and filled, in the back, with stacks of newspapers. Pete stood under the overhang at the door, away from the bicycle rack where everybody else waited for his or her parents. I knew that Pete could feel he was in danger, because he did not look directly at the bike rack. He would, only on occasion, glance over as a defense.

Phil the Pope's parents were also late that day. Phil was not king of the jocks, but he was friends with the king, and he always had flyers for the dances at the Catholic church, flyers for bazaars and special events, and as he walked down the hall he would slap them against my chest, look me in the eye, and say, "You don't have anything going on Saturday night, Miller; come to the bazaar at the Catholic church. I'll be looking for you." Phil did this sort of thing under the direction of his mother, who was the church's secretary.

Phil the Pope was loud, strong, violent, and named you if you looked at him. Meet his eye and he would say *geek, fatso, dork,* or some other expletive demeaning who you were as a person. Praise from Phil was silence. If he did not know what you were, he would look away when he walked by. If he was still deciding, he would nod his head in an impulsive up motion (decisions leaning toward geek were combined with parted lips; decisions leaning toward fashionable were mingled with a faint, though not disarming, half-smile).

On that day at the bike rack, Phil was gathering those in the social class beneath him, those who were athletic but did not like sports, girls who would not become cheerleaders but would be accepted to the drill team, and he was holding Jeff Markum's backpack away from him, Jeff laughing with Phil, wrestling and trying to get his books. That is when the terrible thing happened. In a defensive glance from Pete, he and Phil met eyes. I saw it happen from across the street where my friends and I were standing. Phil set the bag on the ground and said some things to the people standing around him. And then Phil bolted from the group toward Pete, followed by several other boys.

Pete tried to get back inside the building where he would be protected by teachers but Phil caught him, pulled him off the door, the handle of which was held so tightly by Pete it nearly broke off. Boys stood before the windows on the door as Phil buried his fists in Pete's stomach and chest, kicking him to the ground and unleashing such a great force of aggression and hate that the sight of it stopped my breath. And I'll tell you this, the violence in film does not depict the sudden bursts with which most pain is dealt; the quick hits to the face, the crack of knuckles on skull, the blood pumped from lips and buckteeth, the profanities and insults coming up from some deep, gut place of horrors. My friends and I ran across the street. We jumped at Phil, several of us, and yelled for him to step off. Pete's face was covered in blood and he was screaming, terrified, screaming and swinging his fists blindly as a lens of blood bubbled over his eyes.

Phil rose to his feet, bent over to catch his breath, looked down at Pete, and spit in his face. And then he disappeared around the corner of the building.

Pete's mother came only a few minutes later, and we all helped Pete into the nurse's office where he was swabbed with a wet towel. I distinctly remember Pete's mother ridiculing Pete, telling him he was always finding trouble, always causing a scene. Pete cried out that it wasn't his fault, and we agreed, quite passionately saying that it had been Phil the Pope, but Pete's mother would have none of it. She kept looking at her son in disgust. The nurse, confused, said it would be best if we went to the office where the principal was questioning students. And as we walked out of the room I remember feeling that Pete bore more fear of his mother than of any of us, even Phil the Pope.

Some people get the worst of it, it's true. You grow up being told that all people are created equal, but they aren't. Some people are born into better homes than others, and some people look better than others, and some people are smarter and some people run faster.

In the end, Phil the Pope was suspended for a week for fighting. Pete didn't come back to school for two days, and when he returned he had bruises from the fight with Phil as well as another collection I wondered if he had received at home. We all felt so sorry for him. After the thing with Phil the Pope happened, I used to look at Pete in class and wonder about how unfair life was, about how things weren't right. Nobody made fun of him again, to his face or behind his back. While the social barriers were still in play, defended with ignorant passion, Pete was exempt. His family moved away two years later, and I suspect he played the same role at whatever school he went to next, only without the grace we felt obliged to show him. But for us, and for those two years, he was treated with as much respect as our system could allow a person of his stature. We quietly ignored him.

If I could do it again, knowing what I know now, I would be

his friend. I would have defended him. But I was no brilliant kid and I had no idea that the emotions we were feeling were not true, that what we were doing was wrong.

I get this feeling sometimes that after the world ends, when God destroys all our buildings and our flags, we will wish we had seen everybody as equal, that we had eaten dinner with prostitutes, held them in our arms, opened up spare rooms for them and loved them and learned from them. I was just another stupid child in the flow, you know; I didn't know any of these things. I didn't know it didn't matter what a person looked like, how much money they made or whether or not they were cool. I didn't know that cool was just a myth and that one person was just as beautiful and meaningful as another. Not all of us are as smart as aliens, you know. Not all of us run around naked like Adam and Eve. You can hardly fault me for this stuff, can you? Like I said, it felt important to climb the social ladder, it felt important to defend our identities, it felt as though we were saving our own lives.

CHAPTER EIGHT

Lifeboat Theory

HOW TO KILL YOUR NEIGHBOR

When I was a kid in elementary school my teacher, Mrs. Wunch, asked our class a question that I've come back to about a million times, trying to figure out an answer. The question she asked went along with a lesson about *Values Clarification*, which is a fancy name for learning how to be a snob. This is how the question went:

"If there were a lifeboat adrift at sea, and in the lifeboat were a male lawyer, a female doctor, a crippled child, a stay-at-home mom, and a garbageman, and one person had to be thrown overboard to save the others, which person would we choose?"

I don't remember which person we threw out of the boat. I think it came down to the lawyer, but I can't remember exactly. I do remember, however, that the class did not hesitate in deciding who had value and who didn't. The idea that all people are equal never came up. As I was saying before, we knew this sort of thing intrinsically. Or at least we thought we did.

I ordered an Alfred Hitchcock film the other day off Amazon called *Lifeboat* because I was thinking about Mrs. Wunch and how she wanted us to figure out whom we were going to kill. I really like a good black-and-white movie every once in a while, when I'm in a certain mood, and I figured old Alfred Hitchcock would have a pretty good take on the plot, you know, really showing everybody trying not to get thrown out of the boat, making their case and that sort of thing. It turns out the film wasn't about that at all because the lifeboat in the film was plenty big, and the people were rescued before anybody died. There was one girl who killed herself because her baby had drowned, and another guy got murdered, but mostly it was just a lot of melodramatic dialogue in the way of old black-and-white movies.

The movie was pretty boring, to be honest, and it didn't give me what I wanted. I wanted to feel what it would be like to explain to everybody else in a lifeboat why you shouldn't be thrown overboard. The reason I wanted to feel this was because I wondered if those emotions, the emotions you would feel in a lifeboat, were anything like the feelings we all feel when we are living our lives, just hanging out at the house or going to the grocery store.

The thing is, if people are in a lifeboat, the reason they feel passionately about being a good person and all is because if they aren't, they are going to be thrown overboard; they are going to be killed. I realize that sounds grim, but I kept comparing, in my mind, the conversation that might take place in a lifeboat with the conversations I heard at Palio or at Horse Brass. Because when you really think about it, these wants we have, like wanting to be right, wanting to be good, wanting to be perceived as humble, wanting to be important to people and wanting to be loved, feel perilous, as though by not getting them something terrible is going to happen.

People wouldn't get upset about being disrespected if there weren't some kind of penalty in play.

For instance, there was a guy at Palio the other day who was standing in line and somebody cut in front of him and so he got very upset, rolled his eyes and all, and stood there with his hands in his pockets nearly staring a hole through the back of the guy's head who had stepped in front of him. And the thing I was thinking was, *Who cares, you know? It's only going to cost you about two minutes for that guy's coffee to get made, then you can get yours,* but then I thought about the whole lifeboat thing, and how if somebody says you aren't important, and if somebody cuts in front of you in line, it feels like a terrible thing is happening to you, and you would be mad at that guy because you would feel that he was costing you something, that there is a kind of penalty for not being important.

I have a friend who gets so terribly upset when somebody pulls in front of him when he is driving that he will nearly turn red, and beat his steering wheel, yelling at the guy who pulled in front of him. That is pretty crazy because somebody cutting in front of you on the road is only going to cost you a second but it feels like something more; it feels like there is a penalty for not being respected by other people, it feels like you are going to die unless you get some kind of respect and appreciation.

In this way, the alien was right; we are comparing ourselves to one another and if somebody says they are better than you, it makes you very frustrated inside and you get sad or angry or bitter about it.

And that made so much sense in light of what Moses was saying in Genesis 3, it bears repeating: God wired us so that He *told* us who we were, and outside that relationship, the relationship that said we were loved and valuable and beautiful, we didn't have any worth at all. As horrible as it sounds, it would make sense that things of worth are things God loves, and things that don't have worth are things God doesn't love. I mean, I really started wondering if maybe a human is defined by who loves him. I know it sounds terrible, because we have always grown up believing that a person is valuable even if nobody loves them, and I certainly agree with that because God made everybody and the Bible very clearly states He loves everybody. But, as Paul said, if those relations are disturbed, the relations between God and man, then we feel the desire to be loved and respected by other people instead of God, and if we don't get that love and respect, we feel very sad or angry because we know that our glory is at stake, that if there isn't some glory being shone through us by somebody who has authority, we'll be dead inside, like a little light will go out and our souls will feel dark, like nothing can grow there. We'll feel that there is a penalty, by default, for being removed from love.

I know this makes God sound like a terrible narcissist, but my friend John MacMurray said to me recently that the most selfless thing God could do, that is, the most selfless thing a perfect Being who is perfectly loving could do, would be to create other beings to enjoy Himself.

Even Jesus says His glory comes from the Father, which I take to mean that even Christ, a perfect Being, was valuable because God loved Him. And I realize that this sounds weak and codependent, but what if a person isn't supposed to be alone, isn't supposed to have glory on his own, but rather get glory from the God who loves him? What if, in the same way the sun feeds plants, God's glory gives us life? What if our value exists because God takes pleasure in us?

Tony has this old icon on his wall, an old painting he bought in Albania that has a picture of the Trinity on it. He says the painting is a picture of the ideas presented in John 17, ideas that suggest the Trinity loves one another and is constantly telling the other guys in the Trinity they are great, they are beautiful, and in this way they are *one*. And Jesus, also in John 17, prays the disciples God gave Him would learn to live this way, and that those who are lost will be invited into this community, will want to live in this community because there is love in this community, because the way they are wired will be fulfilled, that they will be told who they are by God and God's glory will shine through them, giving them value and worth and a feeling they are loved.

I know it isn't a very Marlboro-man way to live your life, but what if the Marlboro-man way of life really sucks and makes you lonely all the time, and what if the way of Jesus, God, and the Holy Spirit, not to mention the disciples, is right; by that I mean what if the way the Trinity operates explains the way humans are wired, and that we will be fulfilled when we are finally with God and, in His companionship, we know who we are? What if when we are with God, we feel that we have glory, we feel His love for us and know, in a way infinitely more satisfying than a parent's love or a lover's love, that we matter?

I think that would be very beautiful and if I could press a button and go back to the way it was in the Garden of Eden, I would, because so many times I don't feel like I have any glory at all. I feel like I am in a lifeboat trying to get other people to say I am important and valued, and even when they do, it feels as though their opinion isn't strong enough to give me the feeling I need, the feeling that quit at the Fall.

———

Do you know the easiest part of the gospel of Jesus for me to believe? The part that says *the wages of sin is death* (see Romans 6:23). I take that to mean when Adam and Eve sinned, when Chernobyl happened in the Garden, from that point on Adam and Eve began to die, not only physically, but in their souls, too, because they had been separated from God. It makes sense that if a plant is separated from the sun, it dies, and that if people are separated from

God, they die. And so now it feels as if we live on a planet where there is just a little bit of water left, poisoned as it is, and we all are trying to get it and drink it so we can stay alive. But what we really need is God. What we really need is somebody who loves us so much we don't worry about death, about our hair thinning, about other drivers pulling in front of us on the road, about whether people are poor or rich, good-looking or ugly, about whether we feel lonely or about whether or not we are wearing clothes. We need this; we need this so we can love other people purely and not for selfish gain, we need this so we can see everybody as equals, we need this so our relationships can be sincere, we need this so we can stop kicking ourselves around, we need this so we can lose all self-awareness and find ourselves for the first time, not by realizing some dream, but by being told who we are by the only Being who has the authority to know, by that I mean the Creator.

Earlier, when I said Moses explained all of humanity, I meant without God we are, by default, in the lifeboat. And if you think about it, if we aren't in a lifeboat, that is, if these things aren't true and if this story isn't happening to us, then emotions like pride, jealousy, distrust, and embarrassment should be foreign to us. We should feel like the alien, or like Adam and Eve sitting around naked watching television, none of it making any sense.

I know this all sounds crazy. But, once again, can you think of any other reason we wear clothes? Skin is more waterproof than GORE-TEX, you know.

———

Listen to the conversations you have for the next week or so. If you are like me, you'll probably hear a hidden conversation beneath the real conversation. Stuff like movies and food and people become ideas, and we all are deciding whether we're on the right or wrong side of these ideas, knowing that if we aren't on the right side, there is a price to pay. For instance, if you walk into the living room where your wife is or your roommate is and you say something like, *Hey, Margaret, you know the other day when you said you liked enchiladas, well, I just wanted you to know that people who like enchiladas are dorks. It's true; I read a report out of a magazine, and it says that if you like enchiladas, you were most likely a geek in school and have trouble in relationships, you know, getting people to like you.*

I'll bet you, if I did that, Margaret would get upset. Even though the idea is unfounded, it doesn't matter. The jury of peers has spoken, and so the threat has been made.

A friend pointed out recently that here in Portland, when the Trailblazers win a basketball game we fans will often say *we* won, but if the team loses, we say *they* lost. The reason we do this, my friend said, is to associate ourselves with winning and dissociate ourselves from losing. In the lifeboat, associating with losers can cost you your life. When talking about sports, the phenomenon is innocent enough, but what if we're talking about politics or policy or truth or religion? I have several friends who subscribe to a certain political way of thinking, supporting only one party, and when I ask them why, they don't know, or they express a certain empty kind of rhetoric. It seems to me that many of us just chose a team years ago and are unwilling to concede that their team isn't right. So often decisions aren't being made based on whether or not the ideas of a political party are good ideas; decisions are based on associations and dissociations in the lifeboat. It becomes very dangerous.

Watch CNN for an hour and you'll see what I mean. There are about one in a million people who see life as complex, knowing that all men have the capacity to do both good and bad, to be responsible and irresponsible, but the other million think people, politicians, whatever, are perfect or entirely evil. I have Christian friends who hated Bill Clinton and love George Bush, and liberal friends who love John Kerry and can't stand George Bush. And if you listen to conservative or liberal radio, you will hear one side making fun of the other in the lifeboat. The talk will have very little to do with the issues. People see what they want to see based on what associations are going to help them survive.

No wonder the alien rolled his eyes.

And all this, of course, explains the way we treated Pete in middle school. When lifeboat conversations are about movies or music or politics, that is one thing, but what if we use people, say that people are worthless or losers in order to dissociate?

I was thinking a great deal about all this, doing some research in the library at Reed College, and I ran across an article by Emory Cowen in the *Journal of Clinical and Consulting Psychology.* The article reports that the level of popularity a child experiences in the third grade is the greatest predictor of that child's mental health when he or she reaches adulthood. A child being accepted by peers, argues Cowen, is a more sure indication of success than positive evaluation from teachers and nurses, high scores or IQ, and even psychological evaluations. And Daniel Goleman, in his book *Emotional Intelligence,* claims that the high school dropout rate of children who are rejected by their peers is between two and eight times greater than that of children who are accepted.

It would be prudent to summarize a few ideas that have brought us to this dilemma. If a human being is wired so that something outside himself gives him life, and if a separation from that something would cost him his life (physically, but also spiritually), then a human personality would seek a kind of redemption from a jury of his peers, and a lifeboat mentality would ensue across all cultures. And while Darwinian survival mechanisms may explain some of this, these explanations cannot explain the odd complexity of our interpersonal negotiations, not to mention our tendency toward clothing. Indeed, a formulaic expression of Christian theology seems slight and irrelevant when contrasted with the holistic understandings of God's message to humanity, a message of truth and meaning.

That said, an understanding of Christianity as an identity in the lifeboat by which we compare ourselves to others is entirely inappropriate. This faith is larger than the lifeboat, outside of it, you might say. Jesus would indicate the greatest thing you and I can do to display we know Him is to love our brothers and sisters unconditionally, to love our neighbors as ourselves, and to love our enemies.

———

It makes you feel that as a parent the most important thing you can do is love your kids, hold them and tell them you love them because, until we get to heaven, all we can do is hold our palms over the wounds. I mean, if a kid doesn't feel he is loved, he is going to go looking for it in all kinds of ways. He is going to want to feel powerful or important or tough, and she is going to want to feel beautiful and wanted and needed. Give a kid the feeling of being loved early, and they will be better at negotiating that other stuff when they get older. They won't fall for anything stupid, and they won't feel a kind of desperation all the time in their souls. It is no coincidence that Jesus talks endlessly about love. Free love. Unconditional love.

How to Survive Without God

If you ask me, the kinds of things you have to do in the lifeboat in order to not get left behind are absurd. Things were better in the Garden, to be sure. As crazy as it might have been to walk around naked, at least we didn't have to panic all the time, trying to figure out if we were loved.

Here are some of the things the alien pointed out to Grant and me, you know, about how to be loved on earth. And I must confess, when he said these things it did take me aback a bit.

- SLAM-DUNKING A BASKETBALL: Athletes will often pound their chests as if to say, *Look at me, look at me, look what I did. This is why I am important in the lifeboat.* And if you think about it, the reason they probably feel so great about doing that is not only because it is difficult to do, but more likely because thousands of cheering fans (a jury of peers) deem this valuable. Outside that, it's kind of a dud. You're just jumping in the air to put a ball through a hoop. Often, in fact, when an athlete is interviewed after a game, his one-minute speech sounds hauntingly like a case for his importance. When somebody says, "It's only a game," it reminds us of what is so easy to forget. There is some other commodity in play, some hidden commodity that the player, the fans, the coaches, and the other team all are vying for. After all, if you win the whole thing, you only get a ring. You can always buy a ring. What we really want is for the jury of our peers to give us a feeling of security.

- GOOD LOOKS: Though it may seem normal for you and me to base worth on looks, the system is actually as absurd as the alien says it is. What is beautiful, after all? And I am not saying beauty isn't good, because it is; God made it, but using it to compare one person to another is not something, I believe, that occurred in the Garden. Beauty became a kind of point system to determine worth when the relationship with God was broken.

- INTELLIGENCE: For more than a year my friend Curt and I would meet several times a week to play chess at a local coffee shop. If I happened to win, I would leave feeling somehow secure in my identity and, very oddly, if I lost, I would feel sad or frustrated for an hour or more. While some degree of intelligence is necessary for survival, I think the alien would point out that people with mental disabilities are at times more happy than people of normal intelligence. The game of chess, for me, had become a testing or measurement of yet another commodity within the lifeboat.

- WEALTH: Humans are the only species to insatiably accumulate wealth. Sometimes I watch the MTV show *Cribs* and, if I'm not sucked in, I have to scratch my head as to why one individual would bury himself in so much stuff. Birds don't build six-story nests with heated pools. But I was thinking that in the lifeboat, currency becomes a point system by which we compare ourselves to our peers just like beauty and smarts. The phrase "keeping up with the Joneses" makes no sense outside a lifeboat context.

- RIGHTNESS: Not long ago my friend Tony and I were talking about the film *Antwone Fisher.* Tony asked if I liked the film and I told him I didn't. I listed reasons I felt the film was lacking, and Tony was taken aback. He had seen the movie the night before and was moved to tears by its ending. Our "discussion" became something close to an argument as he and I disagreed about the movie's quality. Somewhere in the middle of the conversation, though, we realized we had taken something as trivial as a film and brought it into the lifeboat, trying to decide who was right.

Again, the list goes on. It seems the human psyche will measure itself against anything a group of people deems a valid indicator of importance. I listed only a few, but the truth is, there are a million more.

———

Last year I caught an interview with Tom Arnold regarding his book *How I Lost Five Pounds in Six Years*. The interviewer asked why he had written the book, and I was somewhat amazed at the honesty of Arnold's answer. The comedian stated that most entertainers are in show business because they are broken people, looking for affirmation. "The reason I wrote this book," Tom Arnold said, "is because I wanted something out there so people would tell me they liked me. It's the reason behind almost everything I do." I have to tell you, after that, I really liked Tom Arnold. Leave it to an ex-alcoholic to tell the truth about life.

A few weeks later I was giving an interview in Seattle when the host asked me the same question asked of Tom Arnold: "Why did you write this book?" I wondered, on the air, if the explanation Tom Arnold gave was not the same reason I do what I do, and in the end, I had to concede my motives of faith often take a backseat to my broken nature and desire to feel validity in life. I told the guy in Seattle that I am broken, that I like to write, but basically, subconsciously, I just want people to like me. The guy in Seattle leaned back in his chair, paused for a moment and said, "You aren't alone."

———

While writing books and dunking basketballs may be harmless pursuits, when the internal lifeboat mechanism goes on the defensive, when people feel threatened, feel that their lives are at stake unless they are respected, tragedy ensues.

I was speaking to a group of students at George Fox University a few months ago and asked the question *Why is racism?* Some of the students proceeded to tell me what racism was, but I had to stop them. "The question was *Why is racism?* that is, *Why does it happen?*" The room fell silent for several minutes until I offered an explanation. If there are ten people in the lifeboat, and three of them are Jews, adhering to a philosophy that Jews are inferior is enticing. If Jews or Americans or Democrats or whoever are inferior, then I am automatically ahead of 30 percent of the population in the lifeboat. Racism and socioeconomic prejudice would be the very first thing to start happening in a culture absent God. Not simply because people are "bad" but because a certain system of internal mechanisms would immediately ensue. In fact, without the model of the lifeboat, there isn't much of an explanation for the phenomenon now playing itself out in Sudan. In the context of the lifeboat (motivated by self-preservation), the characteristics of "other people" become inferior simply because they are not our characteristics. Logic is thrown out the window, or worse, used as a tool to validate our prejudices. Philosophies, ideals, and even religious convictions become weapons for slaughter.

In my own life, I notice I validate people who like or validate me. When I say so-and-so is a nice person, what I really mean is so-and-so thinks I am a nice person. And if I sense a person doesn't like me, or thinks he is better than me, my mind will find all sorts of criticism, noticing his temper or his dense intellect. After all, how many people do we dislike who don't dislike us as well? Could the reason really be their lack of character, or do these feelings come from a threatened position in the lifeboat? Don't we find humble people more companionable than arrogant people? Would we even know of these terms without a lifeboat scenario in play?

All this is to say that when the Bible indicates life comes from God, and death comes from separation from God, it makes complete sense, and this truth serves as an explanation for all of our feelings, for the way in which we interact, for the ways in which we entertain ourselves, and for the general precepts of the human plot. Without Him, we feel that we are being thrown out of a boat. No life can exist outside the influence of the sun, outside the energy of light. It makes you wonder if our souls are any different. It makes you wonder if there is any hope.

—

CHAPTER NINE

Jesus

———

WHO NEEDS A BOAT?

I t would be very interesting if Jesus, who said He was the Son of God, understood life on earth the same way the alien did. Think about that for a second. If Jesus was coming from a place where all emotional needs were met by God, His social economy would be as shocking and different as the social economy in the Garden or on whatever planet the alien came from. His values would be different and His personality would be different.

What I mean is, if it is true that our personalities are similar to the way they would be in a lifeboat, because of the fall of man, then Jesus would act and think completely different than we would. He would act and think like somebody who had their needs met by God, like somebody who had no regard for what we thought was important or not important. He would find the things humanity finds valuable and worthless absurd, and to the person in the lifeboat, Jesus would seem to see things backward.

I was thinking a great deal about this, so I read through the Gospels about ten times each, just to get a feel for what Jesus was like. I was asking myself while I was reading whether or not Jesus had many of the personality traits we have here on earth. And the truth is, He didn't. He had hunger and thirst and He slept and rested, but He had no regard for the lifeboat politics you and I live within every day. He believed a great deal of absurd ideas, such as we should turn the other cheek if somebody hits us, we should give somebody our coat even if they just ask for our shirt, we should be willing to give up all our money and follow Him, we should try our hardest to make peace, we should treat poor people the same as we treat the rich, we should lay down our lives for our friends, and so on and so on. It seemed He believed we should take every opportunity to fail in the lifeboat game, not for the sake of failing, but because there wasn't anything to win in the first place. It was as if He didn't believe the economy we live within had validity. No part of Him was deceived by its power.

———

Reading through the Gospels was one of the greatest things that ever happened to me. I know how strange it sounds to say it, but Jesus saved my faith. Several years ago I was getting to the point that the enormous, entangling religion of Christianity, with its many divisions, its multiple theologies, its fondness for war rhetoric, and its quirky, lumbering personality, was such a nuisance I hardly wanted anything to do with it.

But then I saw this very beautiful film about Martin Luther, a German monk who started the Reformation, and before he started the Reformation, when he had yet to read a copy of the Bible, he used to pace around in his room and beg God to forgive him. He would beat himself up and argue with Satan and basically act pretty screwed up, but then later, when he was able to read a copy of the Bible himself, he realized that all his redemption came through Christ, that what he really needed to do was place all his love and faith in Christ and Christ would take care of everything because Christ loved Him.

This meant a great deal to me because there are, honestly, about a million ways Christians worship and about that many ways different groups say a person becomes a Christian. Trusting Christ, really placing all my faith in Him the way Martin Luther did, seemed quite meaningful and simple. It also seemed relational, not formulaic, and as I have said, my gut tells me the key to life is relational, not propositional.

———

The first thing that hit me when I started reading through the Gospels was the thought that Jesus had come to earth in the first place. Like the alien, He had it good where He was but He sacrificed it all and became a man. I suspect our mental pictures of God in heaven, of what Jesus looked like and His general composition, are not very accurate. My guess is He was quite amazing in His previous state, that He was quite happy, always surrounded by beings who loved Him, always feeling the fulfillment that an intimacy with His Father would give Him, always having God's glory shining through Him, sitting on a throne in a place of honor. The mystery of what Christ was before He was human is one of the greatest mysteries of all time, and one that will not be solved until we have new bodies, new eyes, new hearts, new minds, and strong souls with which to engage any place near Him. To exchange heaven for a *place*, and to exchange eternity for *time*, was an act of humility I don't think any of us can understand.

I was reading Brian Greene's book *The Elegant Universe*, in which the Columbia professor talks about potentials of the superstring theory. It is a very fancy book, but I was struck at one point when Greene indicated the possibility that multiple dimensions may be laid out against each other as slices of a loaf of bread or tissues in a great brain. And while distantly scientific (strings are too small to actually see and prove scientifically and have been *seen* only through mathematical formula), the theory had me pondering about the greatness, or I should say the *otherness*, of God. I began to wonder how odd it would be if we existed in the mind of God, as Brian Greene, perhaps unknowingly, suggests. I am not saying I believe this is true, but something as radical as this, as foreign to our minds, certainly may be. And out of this other place, this other existence, Christ stepped to inhabit ours.

If you believe Jesus was God, and He came to earth to walk among us, the first thing you start considering is that He might actually care. Why else would something so great become something so small? He didn't close Himself off in a neighborhood with the Trinity; He actually left His neighborhood and moved into ours, like a very wealthy and powerful man moving to the slums of Chicago or Houston or Calcutta, living on the streets as a peasant.

I started thinking about the idea my friend at the Bible college suggested about how, if God is a perfect and loving Being, the most selfless thing He could do would be to create other beings to enjoy Him. And then I started thinking that if those creatures fell away from Him, the most selfless thing a perfect and loving Being could do would be to go and get them, to try to save them from the death that would take place in His absence.

That said, if Christ was who He said He was, and He represents an existence, a community, and an economy that are better than ours, and it is important that I "believe in Him," what is He like?

As I read the Gospels and other books about Jesus, I started a little list of personality traits and beliefs I thought were interesting. Here they are:

HE BELIEVED ALL PEOPLE WERE EQUAL

In reading the Gospels of the Bible, I discovered that the personality of Christ was such that people who were pagans, cultists, money-mongers, broken, and diseased felt comfortable in His presence. All this goes back to the idea of the lifeboat and how Jesus, outside that system, wouldn't believe one person was any better than another. Apparently this counterintuitive belief system was obvious in the character of Christ. In the Gospels, Jesus is always surrounded by the poor, by the marginalized. And, adversely, He is often opposed by the powerful. Not all the powerful, but those who oppose Him are almost always the people who are ahead in the lifeboat. In this way, Jesus disrupted the system by which people were gaining their false redemption.

Phillip Yancey, a writer I admire a great deal, taught a class at his church in Chicago about Jesus. He reflects on what he discovered about Jesus in his book *The Jesus I Never Knew:*

> The more unsavory the characters, the more at ease they seemed to feel around Jesus. People like these found Jesus appealing: a Samaritan social outcast, a military officer of the tyrant Herod, a quisling tax collector, a recent hostess to seven demons.
>
> In contrast, Jesus got a chilly response from more respectable types. Pious Pharisees thought him uncouth and worldly, a rich young ruler walked away shaking his head, and even the open-minded Nicodemus sought a meeting under the cover of darkness.

I [Yancey] remarked to the class how strange this pattern seemed, since the Christian church now attracts respectable types who closely resemble the people most suspicious of Jesus on earth. What has happened to reverse the pattern of Jesus' day? Why don't sinners *like* being around us?

This makes a great deal of sense if you think about it, because Jesus was offering redemption through a relationship with Himself, and for those who were already being redeemed by a jury of their peers, people like politicians or wealthy people or powerful religious leaders, the redemption Jesus offered must have felt like a step down; but for those who had nothing, for those who were being threatened in the lifeboat, Jesus offered everything. In fact, at one point Christ says that it is easier for a camel to get through the eye of a needle than it is for a rich man to enter the kingdom of God. He says that a man like this will have trouble seeing the beauty of Christ on his own, and that he will need God's help. (See Luke 18:25–27.)

He Was Ugly

I remember hearing stories about Christ as a child in Sunday school, the descriptions of Him being nearly magical, having eyes that would draw people toward Him and an aura that gave people the feeling they were in the company of greatness. This led me to assume Jesus was good-looking. There was a boy at my school who made people feel this way and he was good-looking, and a girl who also was good-looking would quiet a room when she entered. The images of Jesus in the paintings on the walls of our Sunday school class had Him looking like a gentle rock star, or perhaps somebody who played folk music and rarely talked, just strummed on his guitar and occasionally swiped his hair back behind his ear. It confused me later when I read His grim physical description in Scripture. Here is a description of Jesus in the book of Isaiah:

> He had no beauty or majesty to attract us to him, nothing in
> his appearance that we should desire him. He was despised and
> rejected by men, a man of sorrows, and familiar with suffering.
> Like one from whom men hide their faces he was despised,
> and we esteemed him not. (53:2–3 NIV)

I realize this isn't a lot to go on, but it is enough for us to know He wasn't exactly Brad Pitt. It seems odd to me that God would want us to know Jesus was unsightly. It was as though the way Christ looked was part of the message He was to communicate.

I watched an interview with Mel Gibson recently about his film *The Passion of the Christ*. Gibson said it was important for Jesus to look very masculine in the film, and he wanted an actor who was good-looking. And I thought the movie *The Passion* was quite beautiful, but I wondered if very many people would go to see it if the guy who played Jesus in the movie were ugly. And that made me wonder how many people would follow Jesus today if, say, He showed up in America looking the way He looked thousands of years ago. I wondered if anybody would want to interview Jesus on television. I'll bet, if Jesus came to America and tried to do television interviews, the only people who would interview Him would be the people on public television, because on public television, they are not concerned about associating their television personalities with the commercial endorsement of products.

I read a report in the *Journal of Applied Social Psychology* that said criminals perceived as handsome were given lighter sentences than those perceived as unattractive. The article said researchers in

Pennsylvania studied photographs of seventy-four defendants, judging them regarding their attractiveness, and the trials of the seventy-four revealed that men judged less handsome were twice as likely to be sent to jail than attractive men, who were handed significantly lighter sentences when convicted. In the lifeboat, Jesus was definitely representing humanity as equal, hardly caring about how He looked. One might believe that the unsightliness of Christ was a statement of humility, but this isn't true. It would be inconsistent if Christ's looks were a statement of humility. They were, rather, a statement of truth, and our seeing them as humility only suggests an obvious prejudice.

HE LIKED TO BE WITH PEOPLE

My friend Jared told me recently about a friend of his who works at a restaurant in Aspen, Colorado. His friend is a fan of former President Bill Clinton, who on two occasions visited the restaurant in which he worked. He said the first time the president came in they struck up a conversation over a beer, the president sitting quietly and listening to the stories this waiter told about living in the area and working at the restaurant. About a year later, the president was visiting Aspen again and went into the same restaurant, walked up to the waiter, and called him by name. One of the most powerful men in the world remembered a waiter's name a year after meeting him.

I realize most evangelicals don't like the former president for his policies and moral shortcomings, but the story has always fascinated me, and even when I see Bill Clinton on television I get the feeling he would like me were we to sit down together and talk. We do not know whether President Clinton really likes people or if his altruism is politically motivated. I tend to think he actually likes people. Regardless, it is a rare person who gets this much life from being around people. It is a rare person who loses himself in the presence of other human beings.

Perhaps the most comforting characteristic of Christ is that He liked people. Were somebody to ask me to begin a religious system, I would sit down and write a book the way Muhammad and Joseph Smith both did. This would seem the most logical way to communicate new ideas. Writing in scrolls, however, was not something that interested Jesus. He never sat down and wrote a mission statement. Instead, He accumulated friends and allowed them to write about Him, talk about Him, testify about Him. Each of the Gospels reveals a Christ who ate with people, attended parties, drank with people, prayed with people, traveled with people, and worked with people. I can't imagine He would do this unless He actually liked people and cared about them. Jesus built our faith system entirely on relationships, forgoing marketing efforts and spin.

Not only that, but one of the criticisms of Christ was that He was a friend of pagans. Not that He hung out with pagans, but that He was their friend.

I take great comfort in the possibility that Jesus would like me were we to meet face-to-face. To be sure, there were people Jesus did not take a liking to, but those people were arrogant, questioned His identity as God, and boosted their egos and senses of power by burdening people with excess religious baggage. But for most people, especially people in the margins, there was in Christ a great deal of empathy. He seemed to want people to be together, to live together and love one another and link arms. In John 17:21–23, Christ prays that those of us who hear His gospel through the work of the disciples would be one, just as He and the Father are One. And when asked what is the greatest commandment, Jesus replies that it is *to love the Father*, a relational exploit, and He adds, as if to emphasize, *to love as well our neighbors* (see Matt. 22:36–39). Christ is saying that the two most important commandments of God are to have within us a relational commitment to God and to other people. This isn't even to mention the fact that, as God, He created people in the first place. God calls us His children, His sheep, and His bride.

It must have been wonderful to spend time with Christ, with Somebody who liked you, loved you, believed in you, and sought a closeness foreign to skin-bound man. A person would feel significant in His presence. After all, those who knew Christ personally went on to accomplish amazing feats, proving unwavering devotion. It must have been thrilling to look into the eyes of God and have Him look back and communicate that human beings, down to the individual, are of immense worth and beauty and worthy of intimacy with each other and the Godhead. Such an understanding fueled a lifetime of joy and emotional health among the disciples that neither crowds of people jeering insults, nor prison, nor torture, nor exclusion could undo. They were faithful to the end, even to their own deaths.

People don't go out and get tortured and arrested for somebody who doesn't love them. If somebody loves us we will do all kinds of things in their name, for them, because of them. They will make us who we are.

I recently read an interview in which the Nobel Prize–winning novelist Toni Morrison was asked why she had become a great writer, what books she had read, what method she had used to structure her practice. She laughed and said, "Oh, no, that is not why I am a great writer. I am a great writer because when I was a little girl and walked into a room where my father was sitting, his eyes would light up. That is why I am a great writer. That is why. There isn't any other reason."

Imagine these guys knowing, for a fact, that God in heaven, their Father, the Creator of all the cosmos, loved them. When I read about what happened to Stephen, Peter, Paul, and the rest of the disciples, I know for a fact that Christ expressed immense love for them. I know in my heart that they were not living the lives they lived or dying the deaths they died because they were doing something "right." Sure it was right, but these guys must have been loved by Christ, and their motivation came primarily from this idea. There is no other explanation for their devotion.

And I kept wondering about the people who met Christ who were losers in the lifeboat, the crippled and the blind, the woman at the well, Mary Magdalene and Zacchaeus. Entire communities had shunned them and told them they were no good, but God, the King of the universe, comes walking down the street and looks them in the eye, holds their hands, embraces them, eats at their tables, in their homes, for all the town to see. That must have been the greatest moment of their lives.

It is true that it is a powerful occurrence to have somebody look you in the eye and say you are worth something. I was reading an issue of *Smithsonian* magazine the other day and in it was an interview with the poet Maya Angelou. In the interview she talked about the time, as only an eight-year-old girl, that she was raped by her mother's boyfriend. She spoke about having to heal from the crime, but also about how she told on the man, and how he had gone to prison and, shortly after being released, was beaten to death by men in the community. Angelou believes she was the one who caused the man's death because she told about the rape. I was amazed to read that after the beating, the terrified young child didn't speak for years. It was much later, during a walk with her mother, that she would find the source of her life of freedom, beauty, and creativity. Walking down a street near their home, Angelou said her mother stopped, turned, and spoke to her:

"Baby," she said, looking the young woman in the eye. "You know something? I think you are the greatest woman I have ever met. Yes. Mary McLeod Bethune, Eleanor Roosevelt, my mother, and you—and you are the greatest." Maya Angelou said in the interview that she boarded a streetcar with tears flowing down her cheeks, stared into the wood paneling of the car and thought to herself, *Suppose I really am somebody?*

And yes, she was and is somebody. On the bulletin board above my desk, I have a picture of Angelou in which she is delivering a poem at President Clinton's inauguration. Far from the girl who spent years living in fear and silence, the brilliant poet stood before the nation and spoke compellingly:

> But today, the Rock cries out to us,
> clearly, forcefully,
> Come, you may stand upon my
> Back and face your distant destiny!

I love the line "the Rock cries out to us." I think that is beautiful, for some reason, maybe because Jesus was like Maya Angelou's mother in that He went around looking people in the eye to tell them they were beautiful, that He stood as a rock for them, a Being who, for the rest of their lives, they could look back to and hear in their minds, and envision in their memories, God saying to them the world had been lying, and you are indeed beautiful.

Last year I pulled a friend out of his closet. He was drunk and his wife was pacing the house in tears, unable to find him. His marriage was falling apart because of his inability to stop drinking.

This man is a kind and brilliant human being, touched with many gifts from God, but addicted to alcohol, and being taken down in the fight. He was suicidal, we thought, and the kids had been sent away. We sat together on his back deck and talked for hours, deep into the night. I didn't think he was going to make it. I worried about him as I boarded my flight back to Portland and he checked himself into rehab.

Two months later he picked me up from the same airport, having gone several weeks without a drink. As he told me the story of the beginnings of his painful recovery process, he said a single incident was giving him the strength to continue. His father had flown in to attend a recovery meeting with him, and in the meeting my friend had to confess all his issues and weaknesses. When he finished, his father stood up to address the group of addicts. He looked to his son and said, "I have never loved my son as much as I do at this moment. I love him. I want all of you to know I love him." My friend said at that moment, for the first time in his life, he was able to believe God loved him, too. He believed if God, his father, and his wife all loved him, he could fight the addiction, and he believed he might make it.

I often reflect about the author of the gospel of John and wonder if he does not receive as much from Christ as my friend did that day from his father. *I am the one Jesus loved,* John would say of himself in his account of the life of Christ.

The essence of Christ's ministry was to display the worth of humanity, all stemming from God's love for them. Even today, as Christ works to minister to hurting people through His servants, the message is the same.

A few years ago I sat down with a man named Ron Post. Ron was about to retire from a ministry he had started twenty years before called Northwest Medical Teams. Northwest Medical Teams is an aid organization that sends doctors to volatile regions of the world to help the sick and dying. We met at a coffee shop across town, and I asked Ron questions about how he had built this eighty-million-dollars-per-year ministry, with 98 percent of the money going directly to the work being done in the field. I asked him how he structured his time, how he delegated responsibility, and finally asked him what was the key to his success. To answer the last question, Ron pulled from his pocket a tattered envelope filled with pictures.

For the rest of the meeting the man laid down pictures of people he had met, the first of which was a young Cambodian woman who, at the age of thirteen, was being used as a sex slave to the Khmer Rouge. He told me they had rescued her from captivity and given her a new life filled with the knowledge and love of Christ. As he showed me picture after picture of blind people who, because of a simple surgery, could now see, crippled people who could walk, the starving who had been fed, he told me their names. *He knew their names, every one of them.* I had asked the man what the key to his successful ministry was, and he told me through his stories the key to his multimillion-dollar ministry was a love of people. And I believe now and will always believe that if we are willing to love people, God will pour out His resources to bless our lives and our efforts.

I think of this meeting with Ron when I consider Christ, who, like Ron, must have a proverbial envelope in His pocket, laying down picture after picture, knowing our names, knowing the number of hairs that grow on our heads, knowing our stories and fears and desires. He looks at each of us and feels in His heart the kind of love that would make Him want to come to earth and die so we could be healed, so we could feel the love that is going to make us whole, that is going to rescue us from the lifeboat.

He Had No Fear of Intimacy

I have sometimes wondered if the greatest desire of man is to be known and loved anyway. It is no secret we are terribly protective of our hearts, as though this tender space is a kind of receptor for our validation as humans. The closer we are to another person, the more vulnerable we are and the more we feel a sense of risk. Lovers can take years to finally trust each other, and many of us will close ourselves off at the slightest hint of danger. Introductory conversations are almost always shallow. "Where did you go to school?" and "How old are your children?" are safe places to begin. Start an initial meeting with "What addictions do you struggle with?" or "When do you feel least loved by your wife?" and we are going to have a tough time making new friends. It seems that we feel we must trust people before we let them know anything remotely vulnerable about us, and to ask for more before trust has been built is to contravene a social etiquette dating back to the fall of man. All this, I suppose, is connected to the fact that our validation seems to always be in question.

And yet it is through this system of defense Christ walks with ease, never seeming to fear that He would do damage by rummaging around in the tender complexity of a person's identity. Instead, He goes nearly immediately to our greatest fears, our most injured spaces, and speaks into those places with authority.

John includes in his gospel an interaction between Jesus and a woman from Samaria. She was from a group of people known in the day for subscribing to loose interpretation of the Judaic system; the modern-day, evangelical equivalent of a Unitarian. In the scene, Jesus is alone with this woman at a well, where He has come for a drink and she has come to draw water for the day. The woman has a loose reputation, according to the text, having gone through five husbands. In this day, it was nearly unheard of for Jews to have any dealings at all with Samaritans, much less women of her repute. The woman is shocked when Jesus asks her for a drink of water. "How is it that You, being a Jew, ask a drink from me, a Samaritan woman?" she says to Jesus (John 4:9 NKJV).

A friend recently told me that this exchange would be the equivalent of a known evangelical walking into a gay bar and asking a man to buy him a beer.

"Listen," Christ says to the woman. "If you knew the gift of God, and who it is who says to you, 'Give Me a drink,' you would have asked Him, and He would have given you living water" (v. 10).

This odd response must have frustrated the woman, because she responds sarcastically, "I would like to have some of that water because I wouldn't have to keep coming out here to this well!" (see v. 15).

And then Christ walks directly past the barriers around this woman's heart as if He had been destined to live in and warm those cold chambers. "Go, call your husband, and come here," He says to her (v. 16).

The text indicates Christ knows full well the woman has had five husbands and is now living with a man to whom she is not married. The interesting nature of Christ's words is that they correct a misunderstanding. The woman had assumed the living water Christ talked about was like the liquid in the well, but instead, Christ redirects her immediately to a thirst of a different sort: this desire to be known and loved anyway. In no way does Jesus judge this woman, stand over her and condemn her, or even mention the idea of sin; rather, He appeals to the desire of her heart, pointing out the dehumanizing cycle of her life that has driven her through relationship after relationship, none of which gave her lasting fulfillment. In a sense, this woman was looking for importance and love through a man, and Jesus walks up and says what you really need is God, what I have is living water; and if you drink of it, you will never thirst again. It is interesting to me that He offers Himself to the deepest need of man, not a religion, not a formula, but Himself. He offers to her a relationship that is more than romantic, more than a balm for her heart. "I know that Messiah is coming," she says to Jesus. "I who speak to you am He," Christ responds (vv. 25–26).

It must have been unnerving when, to an elitist audience, Jesus later would tell a parable about a man who had been robbed and beaten and then ignored by all but a "good Samaritan." Jesus was not afraid of controversy, of revealing the worth of those considered worthless. The modern-day equivalent might be to tell a story to a group of conservative evangelicals about a pluralist, liberal homosexual who heroically stops to help a stranded traveler after a preacher, a Republican, and a Christian writer have passed him by.

He Was Patient

My pastor and friend Rick McKinley talked to me recently about a meeting he had with a young pastor who was beginning a church plant in another city. In the course of the conversation, the young pastor asked Rick at what point he should kick people out of leadership because they were failing to understand the nature of ministry. Rick looked at the pastor, confused. "Kick them out of leadership?" Rick asked. "Sure," the young pastor replied. "We have to move forward, right? And if they don't get it, I need to weed them out."

Rick sat back and laughed. "Listen," he said. "If I threw out the guys who didn't get it when I started Imago, we wouldn't have anybody left, including me! You are never going to build a church by kicking people out. This isn't a fast-food restaurant; it's the kingdom of God, and quality disciples take a lot of time. Jesus is patient to the end."

It occurred to me as I read through the Gospels that Rick got his patience with people directly from Christ. It took Jesus years to develop the disciples into community-oriented guys. Years into their relationship with Christ, after hearing Him teach perhaps hundreds of times, the disciples were still asking questions like "Who of us is going to be the most important in heaven?" (see Mark 9:34). In a sense, they were asking Jesus who was more important in the lifeboat, and the whole time, Jesus had been teaching them that the lifeboat feelings were worthless. If this were a corporation, these guys would have been let go.

In the last chapter of his gospel, John shows the unending nature of Christ's patience with people. Jesus has risen from the dead and already revealed Himself to the disciples, and yet some of them, including Peter, have gone fishing. Jesus searches out these guys and finds them fishing. They don't recognize Him on the distant shore, and so the Lord calls to them and asks if they have had any success fishing. "No," they reply, and so Christ tells them to cast their net on the other side of the boat. The disciples do this and find so many fish they can't pull the net into the boat. (See John 21:1–6.) This is the same miracle Christ performed when He first met Peter, asking him to follow Him, telling Peter He would make him a fisher of men (see Matthew 4:18–19).

My friend David Gentiles observes a few interesting dynamics in this scene. The first idea is that Peter had spent the last three years traveling with Christ, watching miracles be performed, listening to Jesus' proclamations about His Godhead, and noting the many prophecies that were being fulfilled daily, and yet after all of this, he is back where Jesus had found him: fishing. The second observation is the number of times John mentions the actual presence of fish. John says they were fishing, John gives the exact number of fish they caught, John says the fish were dragged onto the shore where they were sitting, John says Christ made a fire and cooked them breakfast, leading us to assume they were eating fish. (See John 21:1–13.)

John then goes into detail about a conversation Jesus had with Peter. In the conversation Jesus says to Peter, "Do you love Me more than these?" (21:15 NKJV). David Gentiles wonders if Christ is talking not about the other disciples, as I first thought when I read the text, but rather about the fish. After all, John isn't a writer who wastes words, and he did bring up the fish several times, hardly mentioning the other disciples.

You can imagine the surprise in Peter's response when he says: "You know all things; You know that I love You" (21:17 NKJV). Not once but three times Jesus comes back and asks Peter if he loves Him more than these fish. And each time Peter responds emphatically yes, he does. And Jesus continues to tell Peter that if he loves Him, he will feed His sheep, which most scholars agree means Peter will help build the church. It goes without saying that most people trying to change a faith system the way Christ was doing would have let Peter go a long time before this, but to the end Jesus is showing patience with Peter, believing in Peter and helping Peter understand the nature of this new kind of redemption.

Historical accounts of the death of Peter suggest he got it. Catholic history books portray Peter as brave to the last, being dragged off toward his cross, appealing to his wife, who was also going to be crucified, to remember the Lord.

This comforts me because I know how very long it has taken me to trust completely in Christ and to understand the ramifications of my relationship with Him. I read this text feeling gratitude that Jesus has patience with me, that He wants me to understand and He isn't going to give up on me any time soon.

HE WAS KIND

I read a quote recently in which the French emperor Napoleon Bonaparte, musing on the negotiation of clout, gave an appropriate summation of the power of Christ's love and kindness, saying, "I know men; and I tell you that Jesus Christ is no mere man. Between Him and every other person in the world there is no possible term of comparison. Alexander, Caesar, Charlemagne, and I have founded empires. But on what did we rest the creations of our genius? Upon force! Jesus Christ founded His empire upon love; and at this hour millions of men would die for Him."

I confess, I have often wondered how a soft Jesus would instill such devotion in the hearts of men. I suppose the answer rests in this mingling of challenge and kindness. But the kindness part is not so palatable for me, the word *kindness* rings as a synonym to, well, *weakness, wimpiness.*

I came across a book a few years ago, however, that helped me understand the power of kindness in leadership. The book was about a man named John Gagliardi and his career as head football coach at St. John's University. The unorthodox method in which Coach Gagliardi leads his players is intriguing, if not completely odd. An anomaly to say the least, Coach Gagliardi does not ask his players to lift weights during the off-season, holds no spring practice, and rarely allows players to hit each other during drills. Instead, Gagliardi employs an exercise called the "Nice Day Drill" in which players lie flat on their backs, stretch left and say to the player beside them, *Nice day,* then stretch right to say the same to the player on the other side. During stretching exercises, captains greet their teams with smiles and ask them to comment on the beauty of the day. Players then look around the field, up to the sky, out to the trees, and comment on the nice colors and soft breezes.

I couldn't help but laugh as I read, quite honestly, until I got to the part of the book that mentions St. John's win record within their very competitive division. Coach Gagliardi is the winningest football coach in the history of college football or, for that matter, any football. He has more wins than any five NFL coaches combined. The results of Gagliardi's unique philosophy are phenomenal. And what of the performance on the field? The players systematically score above each and every rival, recently by more than 70 points.

John Gagliardi points out that St. John's is a Catholic school and the monks who run the university, when they hired him, were looking for two things in their football program: (1) a program that reflected the leadership style of Jesus, and (2) wins. Lots and lots of wins.

Coach Gagliardi says players are asked to treat their teammates in the way they would like to be treated, with kindness, graciousness, and altruism. The players work as hard as they want to work, and when they come to practice they do exactly as the coach asks them to do, not because their positions will be threatened if they don't (St. John's offers no football scholarships), but because they care about one another, work as a team, and love their coach because they sense his love for them.

And so when I consider the way I am treated by Christ, the degree of kindness with which He guides me, I know that as Napoleon said, I would die for Him. And I would not die for Him because He threatens me; I would die for Him because He loves me, and because I am part of a community of people who are committed to one another, to the world, and to the mission of Jesus.

I suspect this was a great draw for those who chose to follow

Christ. I suspect the degree of community and camaraderie embodied by the initial Twelve was as appealing as food for the starving soul. The religious leadership of the day tended to be overbearing, unkind, and exclusionary, no doubt leaving those who encountered them with a feeling of worthlessness. The religious leaders of the day were against people who were not like them, Jesus' sincere appreciation of human beings must have been a welcome contrast.

The emotional needs of those around Him were only a portion of Jesus' concerns. He was no less aware of tangible needs. In a scene captured by Mark, Jesus becomes uneasy that the thousands who have come to hear His proclamations will not be able to get back home before they eat dinner. In one of the more dramatic of His miracles, Jesus takes a small ration of food and divides it for as many as ten thousand people, creating enough food for every person in the crowd to eat until they are full. (See Mark 8:2–9, noting that only men are accounted for.) The fact that each man, woman, and child was fed to satisfaction struck me as an indication of Christ's awareness, empathy, and kindness for humanity.

Questioned by Pharisees about His willingness to perform miracles on the Sabbath, a day on which no work was to be done, Jesus asked His indicters if they would be willing to aid one of their animals were it to have fallen into a ravine. "Certainly," His accusers answered Him. "Surely kindness to people is as legal as kindness to animals!" Christ responded, perhaps challenging the merit of His questioners' philosophy on the basis of their humanitarian failures. (See Matthew 12:9–12.)

He Was God

Many people were convinced Jesus was God even when He was still a baby. I say this only because He wasn't the guy who went around telling people He was God when He was thirty. He did that, but a lot of people thought He was God well before on account of some angels appeared to some shepherds, and some wise men got word of His birth and traveled a long way to see Him. King Herod even heard about Jesus being born and decided to kill all the young children in Israel because he was worried that Jesus was going to grow up and threaten his throne. If you consider these ideas, you had blue-collar guys thinking Jesus was God, you had wise men from different countries thinking He was God, you had King Herod thinking He was a King; and I know that doesn't prove anything, but if He were some kind of freak going around saying He was God, He wouldn't have had all those people running around saying He was God even while He was a baby. These days you get guys who say they are God, and the only people who believe them are the ones who are brainwashed by them in the first place. And even then the guys who say they are God always want to sleep with everybody's wife and live on an island and drink a lot of punch and drive expensive cars and do crazy stuff that pretty much proves they aren't God.

When Jesus was a baby a man named Simeon was visited by an angel and told that he would see God before he died, and later, after Jesus was born, Simeon walked into the temple, took Jesus into his arms, and said, "Lord, now You are letting Your servant depart in peace, according to Your word; for my eyes have seen Your salvation which You have prepared before the face of all peoples, a light to bring revelation to the Gentiles, and the glory of Your people Israel" (Luke 2:29–32 NKJV).

These kinds of prophecies help me believe Jesus was the actual Son of God and God Himself. And it makes you wonder what Joseph and Mary thought about all this. Both of them had been visited by angels who already told them this kid was going to be special; but having guys pick up your baby and say He was God, that He was going to deliver salvation to the world, would be confusing to say the least. The gospel of Luke even comments that Joseph and Mary were amazed at the things being said about their son (2:33), which I take to mean they didn't fully understand what was happening or who, exactly, Jesus was.

It's true there were a lot of false messiahs at the time. Many of the Jews were looking for Him to come at any time, so a lot of people were pretending to be the guy, either because the devil had put them up to it or because they wanted attention, but none of them were being picked up as a baby and told they were going to be the salvation of the world, and none of them were being visited by shepherds and wise men, and none of them were causing kings to panic so badly they killed an entire generation of small children. These things are unique to the birth of Christ.

But the stuff that helps me believe Jesus was actually God is really the social stuff, the stuff about how He contradicted the lifeboat thinking you and I live within. If the guy was actually God, and the Trinity worked the way the Bible says the Trinity worked, and if man really was wired to work right only in the company of God, and if God left, and then if God came down here to save us, Jesus would pretty much be the personality we'd expect God to have, and the way the world would have reacted to Him would be pretty much the way the world reacted to Him. It's quite remarkable, if you think about it. The personality of Jesus fits right into the whole of the story. But if a person were to need more proof than this, as many people do, there are a lot of prophecies fulfilled by Jesus that set Him apart from the false messiahs.

Simeon, while holding Christ as a baby, is one of the last prophets to foretell the coming Messiah. An eerie litany of prophets laid themselves out in the centuries before Christ as a sign for the Jews that Jesus was coming. Each of these prophets foretold events in Christ's life including but not limited to His genealogy, His persecution, and His death. The Messiah had been spelled out as coming from the seed of woman (Gen. 3:15), a descendant of Abraham (Gen. 12:3), a descendant of Isaac (Gen. 17:19), a descendant of Jacob (Num. 24:17), from the tribe of Judah (Gen. 49:10), heir to the throne of David (Isa. 9:7), to be born in Bethlehem (Mic. 5:2), to be born of a virgin (Isa. 7:14), to flee to Egypt (Hos. 11:1), to be preceded by a forerunner (Mal. 3:1), to minister in Galilee (Isa. 9:1), to speak in parables (Ps. 78:2–4), to bind up the brokenhearted (Isa. 61:1), to be rejected by the Jews (Isa. 53:3), to enter Jerusalem triumphantly (Zech. 9:9), adored by infants (Ps. 8:2), betrayed by a dear friend (Ps. 41:9), betrayed for thirty pieces of silver (Zech. 11:12), silent to accusations (Isa. 53:7), spat on and struck (Isa. 50:6), to serve as a vicarious sacrifice (Isa. 53:5), to be crucified with criminals (Isa. 53:12), to be pierced through the hands and feet (Zech. 12:10), to be sneered at and mocked (Ps. 22:7), to have His clothes distributed by gamblers (Ps. 22:18), to be forsaken by God (Ps. 22:1), to be killed bones intact (Ps. 34:20), to be pierced in the side (Zech. 12:10), and buried with the rich (Isa. 53:9), to be resurrected (Pss. 16:10; 49:15), and to be ascended to God's right hand (Ps. 68:18).

And if you consider all of these prophecies, it is a pretty tough list to fulfill. It would take a lot of work to get all that done, much of it, such as being preceded by John the Baptist, fleeing to Egypt, being killed by crucifixion and yet not having a bone broken, being recognized as a baby and rising from the dead is stuff you can't control unless you are, in fact, God.

Still, I think the reason religious people rejected Jesus was because His fulfillment of the prophecies didn't look the way they expected them to look. They wanted Jesus to come down and be this very respectable type in an earthly way, rich and good-looking and all, only so He would make their religious system look good, only so He would make *them* look good. What they wanted was for God to come down and redeem them to a jury of their peers, not a God who came down to care about the poor and sick and contradict the lifeboat economy altogether. Back then, it was best to look a certain way and talk a certain way and act a certain way in order to make the religion look good, and Jesus pretty much smashed all that to pieces. This was great trouble for people who were in the business of running a public relations campaign for God.

I must admit, while at first critical of religious leaders for rejecting Christ, I began to wonder what it might feel like if Jesus came back today, you know, right in the middle of America, right in the middle of our church culture. I imagined the second coming of Jesus as prophesied in various Scriptures of the New Testament. The prophecies aimed at us about the Second Coming have Jesus showing up like a thief in the night, returning as trumpets sound, and riding a horse. When I imagine this, my mind has Jesus riding through the clouds, very suddenly and to much ado, the entire world trembling at His return, all people awakened from their sleep, acknowledging the King of the universe.

But what if the guys playing the horns turned out to be a few men playing on a street corner in a small town in Arkansas, and what if the horse Jesus rode in on wasn't a Kentucky thoroughbred, but a belligerent donkey? And what if Jesus, after He got here, frequented homeless shelters and bars and ate and drank with the kinds of cultures evangelicals have declared war against? And what if, when He came like a thief in the night, He came very quietly so that nobody noticed, and what if, crime of all crimes, He was ugly and when He went on CNN producers were uncomfortable with His appearance and only shot Him from the waist up, in a certain light? And what if, when He answered questions, He talked with a hick accent, and only spoke in parables that nobody could understand, and what if He didn't align Himself with a political party, and what if He didn't kiss anybody's butt?

If you ask me, He'd have to do a lot of miracles to overcome all that stuff. And even then, most of the people who would follow Him would be people who were oppressed, marginalized, and desperate.

Jewish leaders mocked Jesus for His having come from Nazareth and claiming to be the Messiah and for His association with drunkards and gluttons, for His refusal to bow down to the powers that be, and for disregarding Jewish customs. Yes, the prophecies were fulfilled, but not in the way the Jews had anticipated.

And so, as prophesied by Isaiah, Jesus was rejected by the people God had preserved (See Isaiah 53:3). Jewish culture had established a hierarchy of power as well as an economy associated with their religious system. If God were going to step out of heaven, end the existing redemptive system, and disrupt the power structure and financial organism that sustained them, He'd need to do it with a bit more flare.

Here is how John the Evangelist captures part of the rejection: "I give them eternal life, and they shall never perish," Jesus begins. "No one can snatch them out of my hand. My Father, who has given them to me, is greater than all; no one can snatch them out of my Father's hand. I and the Father are one" (John 10:28–30 NIV).

At this point the Jews picked up stones to try to kill Him.

"I have shown you many great miracles from the Father," Jesus said to them. "For which of these do you stone me?"

"We are not stoning you for any of these," replied the Jews, "but for blasphemy, because you, a mere man, claim to be God" (vv. 31–33 NIV).

———

Sometimes I think it is easier for you and me to believe Jesus is God now that He is in heaven than it might have been back when He was walking around on earth. If you would have seen Jesus do miracles, and if you were one of those who were healed by Him or if you were one of the disciples, then it would have been easier, but for most people, especially the Jews, Jesus would have been a stumbling block.

At the same time, however, we are at a disadvantage because the Jesus that exists in our minds is hardly the real Jesus. The Jesus on CNN, the Jesus in our books and in our movies, the Jesus that is a collection of evangelical personalities, is often a Jesus of the suburbs, a Jesus who wants you to be a better yuppie, a Jesus who is extremely political and supports a specific party, a Jesus who has declared a kind of culture war in the name of our children, a Jesus who worked through the founding fathers to begin America, a Jesus who dresses very well, speaks perfect English, has three points that fulfill any number of promises and wants you and me to be, above all, comfortable. Is this the real Jesus?

Is Jesus sitting in the lifeboat with us, stroking our backs and telling us we are the ones who are right and one day these other infidels are going to pay, that we are the ones who are going to survive and the others are going to be thrown over because we are Calvinists, Armenians, Baptists, Methodists, Catholics; because we are Republicans, Democrats, conservatives, or liberals; because we attend a big church, a small church, an ethnically diverse church, a house church, or is Jesus acting in our hearts to reach out to the person who isn't like us—the oppressed, the poor, the unchurched—and to humble ourselves, give of our money, build our communities in love, give our time, our cre-

400

ativity, get on our knees before our enemies in humility, treating them as Scripture says, as people who are more important than we are? The latter is the Jesus of Scripture; the former, which is infinitely more popular in evangelical culture, is a myth sharing a genre with unicorns.

HE IS I AM

And even as I have attempted to explain the personality of Christ in an effort to give us a better look at who God is, I fear I haven't come close. John said all the books in the world couldn't contain the works Jesus did while He was on earth (see John 21:25). There is so much more, so much that can't be explained, so much more than our minds could possibly understand. It makes me wonder at the difficulty God Himself had in explaining His nature to His own creation.

In an exchange recorded in the book of Exodus, God is speaking to Moses through a burning bush. Moses asks God a seemingly adolescent question, knowing full well he was speaking with God: "Who should I say sent me?"

Moses might well have been asking, *How do I explain You? What is Your identity?* And within God's answer to the question we feel the limitations of language. God simply answers: "I AM WHO I AM."

The Jews would know well this encounter between Moses and God, and it would have undoubtedly come to mind when Jesus answered His inquisitors' similar question by repeating the phrase "I AM." And yet it is a fitting reply for a Creator explaining Himself to His creation. God did not answer, "I EXIST," or offer one of His names, all of which are metaphors invented for humans, but rather, "I AM." Climbing inside letters, God explains, *I encompass, I am beyond existence, I am nothing you will understand, I have no beginning and no end, I am not like you, and yet I AM.*

———

Christmas has just passed here in Portland. It is New Year's Day, and I am seated by my upstairs window watching snow gather on the roads and frost the stick limbs of trees. It snows here once every few years, and yet rarely as early in winter as Christmas. It was a busy season for me. Prior engagements had me spending Christmas in town, unable to fly to my family. I spent Christmas Eve and Christmas Day seated at my computer writing this chapter; all words about Jesus. My affection for Him has grown so much over the years there were times I confess, as I wrote, I had to shut down the computer because I felt the text was getting mushy. It is not difficult for me to believe Jesus liked people, or that He was different from the religious establishment who represented strict, stoic spirituality of the day; it is not difficult for me to believe He loves you, or my wealthy neighbors, or the people I ride the bus with every day. His personality would have to have been dynamic and filled with love to shift a religious system as great as Judaism into a system as tiny and understated as Christianity.

This business of His being God, however, is another idea entirely. I cannot understand it. Of course I believe, but I confess, when I think of Jesus I do not think of Him in His preheavenly state, some great existence beyond existence, some great I AM; rather, I see Him in a manger, I see Him building a house, I see Him walking among the poor or standing in the synagogues, which is a state He encompassed for a span of time the Bible refers to as only a vapor. Jesus as God? Could a mind process such an idea, and does belief require understanding? I don't suspect it does, for I believe and yet do not understand.

And yet, to a spiritual community that offers formula in place of faith, a belief that Jesus was the Son of God and God as well is more than a description of the Messenger of the gospel, it is entwined in the message itself, and the idea seems as necessary as the words He speaks. There is no question that a part of what we believe as Christians is that Jesus was in fact God. We cling to this as truth, we cling to that which we do not understand, just as love causes a man to cling to a woman, and love causes a father or mother to connect deeply with his or her child. Indeed, as Jesus looks across the social landscape into the fear-filled eyes of the inhabitants of the lifeboat, He does not offer a formula that will help us win the game, He offers Himself.

I want to tell you without reservation that if there is any hope for you and me, for this planet set kilter in the fifteen-billion light-year expanse of endless mystery, the hope would have to be in this Man who contends He is not of us, but with us, and simply IS. I AM WHO I AM.

CHAPTER TEN

The Gospel of Jesus

IT NEVER WAS A FORMULA

My friend Greg and I have been talking quite a bit about what it means to follow Jesus. Greg would not consider himself as somebody who takes Jesus seriously, but he admits to having questions. I didn't have a formula for him to understand how a Christian conversion works, but I told him that many years ago, when I was a child, I had heard about Jesus and found the idea of Him compelling, then much later while reading the Gospels, came to believe I wanted to follow Him. This changed things in my life, I said, because it involved giving up everything and choosing to go into a relationship with Him.

Greg told me he had seen a pamphlet with four or five ideas on it, ideas such as man was a sinner, sin separated man from God, and Christ died to absolve the separation. He asked me if this was what I believed, and I told him, essentially, that it was. "Those would be the facts of the story," I said, "but that isn't the story."

"Those are the ideas, but it isn't the narrative," Greg stated rhetorically.

"Yes," I told him.

Earlier that same year I had a conversation with my friend Omar, who is a student at a local college. For his humanities class, Omar was assigned to read the majority of the Bible. He asked to meet with me for coffee, and when we sat down he put a Bible on the table as well as a pamphlet containing the same five or six ideas Greg had mentioned. He opened the pamphlet, read the ideas, and asked if these concepts were important to the central message of Christianity. I told Omar they were critical; that, basically, this was the gospel of Jesus, the backbone of Christian faith. Omar then opened his Bible and asked, "If these ideas are so important, why aren't they in this book?"

"But the Scripture references are right here," I said curiously, showing Omar that the verses were printed next to each idea.

"I see that," he said. "But in the Bible they aren't concise like they are in this pamphlet. They are spread out all over the book."

"But this pamphlet is a summation of the ideas," I clarified.

"Right," Omar continued, "but it seems like, if these ideas are that critical, God would have taken the time to make bullet points out of them. Instead, He put some of them here and some of them there. And half the time, when Jesus is talking, He is speaking entirely in parables. It is hard to believe that whatever it is He is talking about can be summed up this simply."

Omar's point is well taken. And while the ideas presented in these pamphlets are certainly true, it struck me how simply we had begun to explain the ideas, not only how simply, but how nonrelationally, how propositionally. I don't mean any of this to fault the pamphlets at all. Tracts such as the ones Omar and Greg encountered have been powerful tools in helping people understand the beauty of the message of Christ. Millions, perhaps, have come to know Jesus through these efficient presentations of the gospel. But I did begin to wonder if there were better ways of explaining it than these pamphlets. After all, the pamphlets have been around for only the last fifty years or so (along with our formulaic presentation of the gospel), and the church has shrunk, not grown, in Western countries in which these tools have been used. But the greater trouble with these reduced ideas is that modern evangelical culture is so accustomed to this summation that it is difficult for us to see the gospel as anything other than a list of true statements with which a person must agree.

It makes me wonder if, because of this reduced version of the claims of Christ, we believe the gospel is easy to understand, a simple mental exercise, not in the least bit mysterious. And if you think about it, a person has a more difficult time explaining romantic love, for instance, or beauty, or the Trinity, than the gospel of Jesus. John would open his gospel by presenting the idea that God is the Word and Jesus is the Word and the Word became flesh and dwelt among us. Not exactly bullet points for easy consumption. Perhaps our reduction of these ideas has caused us to miss something.

———

Each year I teach a class on the gospel and culture at a small Bible college back East. This year I asked the students to list the precepts a person would need to understand in order to become a Christian. I stood at the white board and they called out ideas: Man was sinful by nature; sin separates us from God; Jesus died for our sins; we could accept Jesus into our hearts (after some thought, students were not able to explain exactly what they meant by this, only saying it was a kind of interaction in which a person agrees Jesus is the Son of God), and so on. Then, looking at the board, I began to ask some questions about these almost universally accepted ideas. I asked if a person could believe all these ideas were true and yet not be a Christian. I told them my friend Matt, for instance, believed all these ideas and yet would never claim to be a person who knows Jesus or much less follows Him. The students conceded that, in fact, a person could know and even believe all the concepts on the board and yet not be a Christian. "Then there is something missing, isn't there?" I said to the class. "It isn't watertight just yet. There must be some idea we are leaving out, some full-proof thing a person has to agree with in order to have a relationship with Christ."

We sat together and looked at the board for several minutes until we conceded we weren't going to come up with the missing element. I then erased the board and asked the class a different question: "What ideas would a guy need to agree with or what steps would a guy need to take in order to fall in love with a girl?" The class chuckled a bit, but I continued, going so far as to begin a list.

1. A guy would have to get to know her.

I stood back from the board and wondered out loud what the next step might be. "Any suggestions?" I asked the class. We thought about it for a second, and then one of the students spoke up and said, "It isn't exactly a scientific process."

THE GOSPEL: A RELATIONAL DYNAMIC

Perhaps the reason Scripture includes so much poetry in and outside the narrative, so many parables and stories, so many visions and emotional letters, is because it is attempting to describe a *relational* break man tragically experienced with God and a disturbed *relational* history man has had since then and, furthermore, a *relational* dynamic man must embrace in order to have *relational* intimacy with God once again, thus healing himself of all the crap he gets into while looking for a *relationship* that makes him feel whole. Maybe the gospel of Jesus, in other words, is all about our relationship with Jesus rather than about ideas. And perhaps our lists and formulas and bullet points are nice in the sense that they help us memorize different truths, but harmful in the sense that they blind us to the necessary relationship that must begin between ourselves and God for us to become His followers. And worse, perhaps our formulas and bullet points and steps steal the sincerity with which we might engage God.

Becoming a Christian might look more like falling in love than baking cookies. Now don't get me wrong. I am not saying that in order for a person to know Jesus they must get a kind of crush on Him. But what I am suggesting is that, not unlike any other relationship, a person might need to understand that Jesus is alive, that He exists, that He is God, that He is in authority, that we need to submit to Him, that He has the power to save, and so on and so on, all of which *are* ideas, but ideas entangled in a kind of relational dynamic. This seems more logical to me because if God made us, wants to know us, then this would require a more mysterious interaction than what would be required by following a kind of recipe.

I realize it all sounds terribly sentimental, but imagine the other ideas popular today that we sometimes hold up as credible: We believe a person will gain access to heaven because he is knowledgeable about theology, because he can win at a game of religious trivia. And we may believe a person will find heaven because she is very spiritual and lights incense and candles and takes bubble baths and reads books that speak of centering her inner self; and some of us believe a person is a Christian because he believes five ideas that

Jesus communicated here and there in Scripture, though never completely at one time and in one place; and some people believe they are Christians because they do good things and associate themselves with some kind of Christian morality; and some people believe they are Christians because they are Americans. If any of these models are true, people who read the Bible before we systematically broke it down, and, for that matter, people who believed in Jesus before the printing press or before the birth of Western civilization, are at an extreme disadvantage. It makes you wonder if we have fashioned a gospel around our culture and technology and social economy rather than around the person of Christ.

It doesn't make a great deal of sense that a person who went to Bible college should have a better shot at heaven than a person who didn't, and it doesn't make a lot of sense either that somebody sentimental and spiritual has greater access. I think it is more safe and more beautiful and more true to believe that when a person dies he will go and be with God because, on earth, he had come to know Him, that he had a relational encounter with God not unlike meeting a friend or a lover or having a father or taking a bride, and that in order to engage God he gave up everything, repented and changed his life, as this sort of extreme sacrifice is what is required if true love is to grow. We would expect nothing less in a marriage; why should we accept anything less in becoming unified with Christ?

In fact, I have to tell you, I believe the Bible is screaming this idea and is completely silent on any other, including our formulas and bullet points. It seems, rather, that Christ's parables, Christ's words about eating His flesh and drinking His blood, were designed to bypass the memorization of ideas and cause us to wrestle with a certain need to cling to Him. In other words, a poetic presentation of the gospel of Jesus is more accurate than a set of steps.

———

Biblically, you are hard-pressed to find theological ideas divorced from their relational context. There are, essentially, three dominant metaphors describing our relationship with God: sheep to a shepherd, child to a father, and bride to a bridegroom. The idea of Christ's disciples being His mother and father and brothers and sisters is also presented. In fact, few places in Scripture speak to the Christian conversion experience through any method other than relational metaphor.

Contrasting this idea, I recently heard a man, while explaining how a person could *convert* to Christianity, say the experience was not unlike deciding to sit in a chair. He said that while *a person can have faith that a chair will hold him, it is not until he sits in the chair that he has acted on his faith.*

I wondered as I heard this if the chair was a kind of a symbol for Jesus, and how irritated Jesus might be if a lot of people kept trying to sit on Him.

And then I wondered at how Jesus could say He was a Shepherd and we were sheep, and that the Father in heaven was our Father and we were His children, and that He Himself was a Bridegroom and we were His bride, and that He was a King and we were His subjects, and yet we somehow missed His meaning and thought becoming a Christian was like sitting in a chair.

The Gospel of Ideas

So removed is our understanding of the gospel as a relational invitation that recently, while teaching another class of Bible college students, I presented a form of the gospel but left out a key element, to see if they would notice. I told them in advance that I was going to leave out a critical element of the gospel, and I asked them to listen carefully to figure out the missing piece.

I told them man was sinful, and this was obvious when we looked at the culture we lived in. I pointed out specific examples of depravity including homosexuality, abortion, drug use, song lyrics on the radio, newspaper headlines, and so on. Then I told the class that man must repent, and showed them Scriptures that spoke firmly of this idea. I used the true-life example I heard from a preacher about a man in Missouri who, warning people of a bridge that had collapsed, shot a flare gun directly at oncoming cars so they would stop before they drove over the bridge to their deaths. I said I was like that man, shooting flares at cars, and they could be mad at me and frustrated, but I was saving their lives, because the wages of sin is death, and they had to repent in order to see heaven. I then pointed to Scripture about the wages of sin being death, and talked at length about how sin separates us from God.

Then I spoke of the beauty of morality, and told a story of a friend who chose not to cheat on his wife and so now enjoys the fruits of his marriage, committed in love to his wife, grateful that he never betrayed the purity and beauty of their relationship. I talked about heaven and how great it will be to walk on streets of gold and how there will probably be millions of miles of mountains and rivers and how great it will be to fish those rivers and sit with our friends around a fire beneath a mountain peak that reaches up into stars so thick we could barely imagine the beauty of the expanse. I gave the class statistics regarding teen pregnancy and sexually transmitted diseases, going into detail about what it is they would be saved from if they would only repent, and how their lives could be God-honoring and God-centered and this would give them a sense of purity and a feeling of fulfillment on earth, and that God would provide for them in relationships and in finances and in comfort.

When I was done, I rested my case and asked the class if they could tell me what it was I had left out of this gospel presentation. I waited as a class of Bible college students—who that year, had read several textbooks about Christian theology, who had read the majority of the Bible, all of whom had taken an evangelism class only weeks before in which they went door-to-door to hundreds of homes and shared their faith using pamphlets that explained the gospel, who had grown up in Christian homes attending strong evangelical churches, who had taken both New Testament Introduction and Old Testament Introduction—sat there for several minutes in uncomfortable silence.

None of the forty-five students in the class realized I had presented a gospel without once mentioning the name of Jesus.

The story bears repeating: I presented a gospel to Christian Bible college students and left out Jesus. Nobody noticed, even when I said I was going to neglect something very important, even when I asked them to think very hard about what it was I had left out, even when I stood there for several minutes in silence.

To a culture that believes they "go to heaven" based on whether or not they are morally pure, or that they understand some theological ideas, or that they are very spiritual, Jesus is completely unnecessary. At best, He is an afterthought, a technicality by which we become morally pure, or a subject of which we know, or a founding father of our woo-woo spirituality.

I assure you, these students loved Jesus very much, and they were terrific kids whom I loved being with, it's just that when they thought of the gospel, they thought of the message in terms of a series of thoughts or principles, not mysterious relational dynamics. The least important of the ideas, to this class, was knowing Jesus; the least important of the ideas was the one that is relational. The gospel of Jesus, then, mistakenly assumed by this class, is something different from Jesus Himself. The two are mutually exclusive in this way.

This, of course, is a lie birthed out of a method of communication the Bible never uses.

THE GOLDEN COW

When the church began to doubt its own integrity after the Darwinian attack on Genesis 1 and 2, we began to answer science, not by appealing to something greater, the realm of beauty and art and spirituality, but by attempting to translate spiritual realities through scientific equations, thus justifying ourselves to culture, as if culture had some kind of authority to redeem us in the first place. Terms such as "absolute truth" and "inherency" (a term used only to describe Scripture in the last one hundred years or so) became a battle cry, even though the laws of absolute truth must, by their nature, exclude ideas such as *Jesus is the Word, He is both God and Man,* the *Trinity is both three and One,* we are *united with Him in His death,* because these are mysterious ideas, not scientific ideas.

In fact, much of biblical truth must go out the window when you approach it through the scientific method. God does not live within the philosophical science He made, any more than He is bound by the natural realities of gravity. There is moral law, to be sure, but moral law is not our path to heaven; our duty involves knowing and being known by Christ. Positive morality, then, the stuff of natural law, is but an offering, a sweet-tasting fruit in the mouth of God. It is obedience and an imitation of our pure and holy Maker; and immorality—the act of ignoring the conscience and the precepts of goodness—is a dagger in God's heart.

Because we have approached faith through the lens of science, the rich legacy of art that once flowed out of the Christian community has dried up. The poetry of Scripture, especially in the case of Moses, began to be interpreted literally and mathematically, and whole books such as the Song of Songs were completely and totally ignored. They weren't scientific. You couldn't break them down into bullet points. Morality became a code, rather than a manifestation of a love for Christ, the way a woman is faithful to her husband, the way a man is faithful to his wife. These relational ideas were replaced with wrong and right, good and bad, with only hinted suggestions as to where wrong and right and good and bad actually came from. Old Testament stories became formulas for personal growth rather than stories to help us understand the character and nature of the God with whom we interact.

In a culture that worships science, relational propositions will always be left out of arguments attempting to surface truth. We believe, quite simply, that unless we can chart something, it doesn't exist. And you can't chart relationships. Furthermore, in our attempts to make relational propositions look like chartable realities, all beauty and mystery is lost. And so when times get hard, when reality knocks us on our butts, mathematical propositions are unable to comfort our failing hearts. How many people have walked away from faith because their systematic theology proved unable to answer the deep longings and questions of the soul? What we need here, truly, is faith in a Being, not a list of ideas.

And one should not think our current method of interpreting Scripture has an ancient legacy. The modern view of Scripture originated in an age of industrial revolution when corporations were becoming more important than family (the husband, for the first time, left the home and joined Corporate America, building cars instead of families), and productivity was more important than relationships. *How can God help me get what I want?* was the idea, not *Who is God, and how can I know Him?*

———

Imagine a pamphlet explaining the gospel of Jesus that said something like this:

> You are the bride to the Bridegroom, and the Bridegroom is Jesus Christ. You must eat of His flesh and drink of His blood to know Him, and your union with Him will make you one, and your oneness with Him will allow you to be identified with Him, His purity allowing God to interact with you, and because of this you will be with Him in eternity, sitting at His side and enjoying His companionship, which will be more fulfilling than an earthly husband or an earthly bride. All you must do to engage God is be willing to leave everything behind, be willing to walk away from your identity, and embrace joyfully the trials and tribulations, the torture and perhaps martyrdom that will come upon you for being a child of God in a broken world working out its own redemption in empty pursuits.

Though it sounds absurd, this is a much more accurate summation of the gospel of Jesus than the bullet points we like to consider when we think about Christ's message to humanity.

In the third chapter of John, some Pharisees come out to talk with John the Baptist because Jesus has been baptizing people in a nearby river, thus threatening their position in the community as the people who do the baptizing. The Pharisees are furious and hoping to get John to join them in their hostility toward Jesus.

John answers them by saying, essentially, "Look, I told you I wasn't the Messiah, but rather the one who comes before Him to get everything ready. The One who gets the bride is the Bridegroom, by definition; but I am just His friend. I am like the best man in the wedding. And I am very happy about this. How could I be jealous when I know that the wedding is finished and the marriage is off to a great start?"

And Matthew in his gospel captures a conversation between Jesus and a group who were the disciples of John the Baptist. The disciples of John the Baptist are frustrated because they are fasting and Jesus' disciples are eating. They say to him, "Why do we and the Pharisees fast, but your disciples do not fast?" And Jesus says to them, "The attendants of the Bridegroom cannot mourn as long as the Bridegroom is with them, can they? But the days will come when the Bridegroom is taken away from them, and then they will fast" (see Matthew 9:14–15).

In this way, Jesus takes the spiritual disciplines, the steps and actions religious folks had come to understand as a sort of spiritual checklist, and explains them as being deeply connected to a relational exchange. We fast because we mourn the absence of Christ.

At Imago Dei, the church I attend here in Portland, the congregation is invited to the front of the church after each service to dip bread into wine, partaking in one of the two sacraments given to those of us who are following Christ. And yet often, as I wait in line, go to the table, take the bread, and dip it into the cup of wine, I forget that the bread and wine I eat and drink are of absolutely no spiritual significance at all, that they have no more power than the breakfast I ate that morning, that what Jesus wanted was for us to eat the bread and drink the wine as a way of *remembering Him,* the bread representing His flesh, that He was a Man who, come from heaven, walked the earth with us and felt our pains, wept at our transgressions and humbly beckoned us to follow Him; and the wine is a symbol of the fact that He was killed, that His body was nailed to a cross, and that He entered into death, dying to absolve our need to die, our need to experience the ramifications of falling away and apart from God.

I confess that at times I have thought of Communion as a religious pill a person takes in order to check it off his list, and that the pill is best taken under the sedation of heavy mood music, or in silence.

How odd would it seem to have been one of the members of the early church, shepherded by Paul or Peter, and to come forward a thousand years to see people standing in line or sitting quietly in a large building that looked like a schoolroom or movie theater, to take Communion. How different it would seem from the way they did it, sitting around somebody's living room table, grabbing a hunk of bread and holding their own glass of wine, exchanging stories about Christ, perhaps laughing, perhaps crying, consoling each other, telling one another that the Person who had exploded into their hearts was indeed the Son of God, their Bridegroom, come to tell them who they were, come to mend the broken relationship, come to marry them in a spiritual union more beautiful, more intimate than anything they could know on earth.

CHAPTER ELEVEN

A Circus of Redemption

———

WHY A THREE-LEGGED MAN IS BETTER THAN A BEARDED WOMAN

There's been a load of compromisin'
On the road to my horizon
But I'm gonna be where the lights are shinin' on me:
Like a rhinestone cowboy
Riding out on a horse in a star-spangled rodeo
Like a rhinestone cowboy
Getting cards and letters from people I don't even know
And offers comin' over the phone.

—GLEN CAMPBELL, "RHINESTONE COWBOY"

Several months ago I was at a train station in Oakland in the middle of the night, sitting in the cold because my train to Portland was late. And while waiting, another train pulled into the station, a streamlined train, something you would see in the fifties crossing America on the news; the sort of

419

long, shiny bullet rig kids would stop playing baseball to look at with their jaws open.

And on the side of this train, in great red letters, were printed the words *Barnum and Bailey Circus, The Greatest Show on Earth.*

Before Oakland, if you would have asked me how the circus travels, I might have told you they had four or five trucks to haul animals around, and the people who work in the circus traveled by plane, or maybe they went around on buses. I don't know how I would have broken it down, if you would have asked me, but I certainly wouldn't have told you they go around in a bullet train from the fifties. It got me wondering whether the circus travels by train because it is the most efficient way to travel, or whether they travel by train to feel romantic. But if you ask me, you don't need an old train to feel romantic about the circus. The circus is pretty romantic as it is. The thing that gets me feeling romantic, or sentimental, about a circus is the elephants.

When I was a kid my mother would take my sister and me to the circus. I had a timid nature, and our cheap seats were often very high in the arena, so the first twenty minutes of the circus I would spend gripping the armrests of my chair, always feeling that the floor was tipping forward into the great chasm of the arena, always imagining myself tumbling over the people in front of me, and in front of them, and over a railing to my death. I imagined things like this all the time when I was a kid.

When the circus came through Houston they brought a man who rode a motorcycle inside a large suspended cage shaped like a globe. He would kick-start his motorcycle, rev the two-stroke to excite the crowd, then slowly release the clutch to get the thing going around in a small circle at the bottom of the globe. He would circle the orb slowly at first, then faster, all the while riding higher into the sphere until, in dramatic fashion and to the tune of suspenseful music, he would ride with his body and bike entirely vertical. All this made me very nervous, and at this point in the show I would grip the armrests ever tighter and, seconds later, when the man on the motorcycle started riding in loops so his body was completely upside down at the top of each rotation, I felt as though the floor had vaporized and I was free-falling. I have always been like this, living vicariously through the risks of other people. My body can hardly hold the stress. You don't ever want to go to a movie with a guy like me because I am on the edge of my seat squirming, leaning in next to you saying things like *Can you believe this guy?*

Living vicariously through people is not a good thing when you are at a circus. As soon as the guy on the motorcycle finished, they brought out another guy, who walked across a piece of rope at the very top of the arena. The guy didn't even have a net, if you can believe it. My legs were jelly because he shook and stammered, the rope beneath him jerking suddenly left, then right, and when he had to lean over to keep his balance I nearly threw up on my sister, who, the entire time, was giving me these tired looks and saying things like, "Would you calm down? For heaven's sake, he does this for a living."

The only thing I really liked about the circus was the elephants. That is what I was telling you about. If you are going to live vicariously through something at a circus, and you don't want to throw up about it, your best bet is to live vicariously through an elephant. Here's what they do: They walk in a line holding each other's tails, they go into the middle ring and stand there for a little while, then they put a foot on a big stool and then they sit down like a dog waiting for a stick. The whole thing takes about twenty minutes, and it is consoling.

As a point of reference, ever since childhood, elephants have affected me as a calming mechanism. When I see them at the zoo, my heart slows, my nerves loosen, my skin cools, and my muscles relax.

I say this only because, sitting in the train station in Oakland, thinking back on the circus in Houston, I heard an elephant. They have a distinct sound, like a drunk man playing a tuba.

My muscles went to jelly and I turned my head slowly as the sound was coming from down the platform, from the darkness at the bend of the train, and as a man in a trance I stood to my relaxed legs and stepped one fluffy foot then another till the platform stopped. I stood there looking into the black when another of them called. I stepped off the platform onto the rocks, following the elephant's tuba around a bend till I could see them, in tall, prison-like cages set atop platform cars on the train. The holes in the cages were sparse, so I could see only the eye of one and the trunk of another, and their enormous feet, their umbrella-stand feet with toenails as big as my head and legs as round as redwoods.

There was, in my heart, a kind of calm euphoria. I felt as though I had been raised by these elephants years ago in the deep jungles of Africa, and we were being reunited in Oakland. Of course, none of this was true, but the thought of it was making the moment daydreamy.

Less daydreamy were a couple of people who had come out of a passenger car to smoke cigarettes. There was one man and one woman, one car before the cages, and the man was wearing jeans and the woman looked as though she had just put on her clothes, her T-shirt and pajama pants and flip-flop shoes. Her disheveled hair and red cheeks came to lips on her cigarette.

"May I get closer to the elephants?" I asked her, ignoring, as it were, her obvious concern for her appearance.

"What's that, darlin'?" The woman pretended not to have

heard me, tilting her head up and pursing her lips to blow smoke into the air.

"May I look at the elephants?" I asked again.

The man turned and looked at me in distrust, seeming more concerned about my interference with him and the woman than with him and the elephants.

"Sure, darlin'. Look all you want," the woman spoke.

I walked to the edge of a cage and peered in through one of the holes. Their smell was enormous. Their eyes were as large as softballs, set deep into caves of moist gray. Their ears hung down like curtains, torn and scarred, showing pink in birthmarks or age. They moved slowly, purposefully, and embodied the kind of dignity that happens with weight and size.

I won't tell you how I realized at that moment that elephants shouldn't be in cages. I won't tell you how I think they should all live in Africa, or on the streets of Oakland going where they want, so cars have to stop and wait for them to pass, and people have to take off their hats when they walk by, and how everybody should refer to elephants as sir or ma'am, saying, *Nice day for a walk, isn't it, ma'am?* so the elephants could blow their tubas in agreement.

"I don't know why he even keeps Marcus around," the man said, and I thought he was talking to me.

"Pardon me?" I said to him.

"I wasn't talking to you," the man said matter-of-factly, holding his cigarette away from his body, then thumping it with his thumb, then turning again to the woman.

"Pay no attention to him, darlin'. He's just a grumpy old man," the woman told me, excusing me for interrupting their conversation.

"That's okay," I told her, feeling half my age, half my maturity, standing in the darkness looking at elephants.

"He don't make any money for the company," the man continued with the woman. "Nobody wants to see a man shoot flaming arrows at a target."

"Well, he does throw knives. Monica told me the thing isn't a trick, either, that she actually stands there and closes her eyes. One of them cut her on the ear."

"That thing ain't no trick?" the man asked. *That thing isn't a trick?* I wondered, fascinated, as it were, at the conversations that take place in circus life. I kept looking at the elephants, but I was secretly paying attention to the conversation between the man and the woman, pretending, in my head, that I was a person who worked for a circus, too, and we were concerned about job security, about whether or not they were going to get rid of me and my elephants.

"Monica said it was real," the woman continued. "Real knives, really flying at her."

"Don't make any difference at all," the man said loudly. "You can't see how close a knife is to a woman's ear when you're up in the cheap seats."

And what the man was saying was true, because I had been in the cheap seats.

"If they're going to lay off anybody, they're going to lay him off," the man said with relief in his voice.

"They aren't going to cut him, Billy. He knows Roger, he and Roger go way back, and he is on for good. And they aren't going to cut the Lipton family, either. The Lipton family has been doing that stupid trapeze thing for fifty years; they've got some sort of eternal contract. It's you and me; that's the ones who are going to get cut." And the woman said this in a somber tone, with worry in her voice.

"And replace us with what?" the man said. "Media? All that

television and music screaming up the place. That ain't real enter-
tainment. That ain't real circus. You know it ain't." The man threw
his cigarette on the ground and stared into the darkness toward the
platform. "The animals are all staying." The man started talking
again. "I should have taken that job with Bernie when she asked
me. I'd rather feed a bunch of horses all the time than be back on
the street."

"You aren't going to be back on the street," she said comfortingly.

"Like you know that." The man stood there for a second, then
turned and looked at me looking at the two of them.

"Elephants ain't that interesting?" he questioned, meaning I
was being nosy. And he watched me as I walked away from the
elephants, sort of kicking rocks and acting like their conversation
wasn't interesting.

By the time I got back to the platform the train was moving,
and the woman was standing in the doorway of a passenger car
when it passed, still smoking a cigarette, and she looked at me and
I looked at her and she looked sad, didn't even bother to smile, just
looked right through me with a kind of worry in her eyes. I waved
at her and she nodded.

I sat down on the bench on the platform and wondered what
it was the man and woman did for the circus. I wondered whether
or not they were clowns or something, like them and twenty
friends get in a little car, drive to the center ring, and get out one
at a time. Or maybe they dance around in sexy outfits and he lifts
her up and onto a hula hoop and balances her on his nose. I'll bet
they weren't any of those things, though. I'll bet they were just a
couple of people on a crew who put up a tent or put together that
metal globe the guy with the motorcycle uses. And I'll bet the guy
with the motorcycle gets to go everywhere on a plane or in an RV,

and these two have to go around in a bullet train, wondering how long they will have their jobs.

———

It can't be easy doing that sort of thing. Working in a circus. I read a book a while back about women with beards and men who could swallow swords. In this book there were people who ate fire and nails, a man with hands like crab pincers, and a lady with tattoos across her entire body: Up from her stomach was a great flame that turned to smoke and ashes of burning pages of poetry that rose across her breasts and up her shoulders to the chimney plume of her neck.

All these people were living in America between the two wars, traveling in a sideshow. They sat on stages in small theaters, and for a quarter you could go in and look at them. There was a caller who stood outside on a platform and hyped their unique, odd, and eerie features to fathers and sons, mothers behind them gasping at the descriptions, and daughters downright frightened. And the more spooked the women were made to feel, the more willing the men were to pay the admission and prove how brave they were.

There was a movement in those days to end the shows; protesters claimed they exploited the deformed. But the acts in the show were paid handsomely and so did battle in the papers with their supposed allies, claiming that if not for the show itself, they were largely unemployable. "Who wants to hire a woman with a beard?" one of the performers explained passionately. "We understand each other," another went on to say. "We have a community, a group of people who, because of their own deformities, accept the deformity in others. We are the lucky ones, because we understand that people are only people, that the thing you think makes you better than us is an illusion."

And yet, as the book continues, the author paints a clear hierarchy within the community. There was, among the ten or so characters, a man with three legs. He had been hired out of Chicago, a late entry to the company. After five or six shows, the caller, who also employed the team of odd talent, shifted the three-legged man to the final appearance in the show. Though the man could walk normally, for the act he dressed in sloppy large clothes and worked his hair into a frenzy. He stammered onto stage in a daze and walked the corners of the platform, swinging his body left and right, acting at once angered and terrified at the crowd. Each time he turned his body, his third leg swung out and startled the women and children. The act was so rousing that during a performance in New York, the three-legged performer got too close to the audience and was attacked by a man attempting to protect his wife from an accidental touch.

Far from being offended by the assault or feeling victimized, the three-legged man was thrilled. When the attack made the papers, the caller no longer had to stir the crowd. There was a line for a quarter mile. And a press statement detailing the incident in New York was released by the show in every city visited that year. The three-legged man's salary was at once doubled, which enraged the other talent, nearly destroying the community. No longer was a man with three legs on even par with a bearded woman. A hierarchy had been created: three legs beating two; female facial hair, apparently, beating crab hands and all this was decided by the response of the crowd.

"Not everybody is lucky enough to get born with three legs," the bearded woman said. "It's not like he did anything to deserve that kind of blessing."

What odd sort of hierarchy is created when a group tunnels beneath the surface of normal community, I thought to myself while reading the book.

———

For months after reading the book I contemplated the community, how, as a normal person, I would gain no favor from an audience and have no commodity in the small outfit of misfits. They would probably have felt sorry for me, in fact, watching me walk onstage night after night so the audience could shrug their shoulders as I sat on an empty stage and typed words into a computer. The audience would boo me after a while because what I do is so boring, and I would probably be very upset about it and feel dejected, until finally the guy who ran the show would call me into a trailer and explain, very kindly, that I wasn't meant for the sideshow, that I just wasn't very entertaining. And I would probably be jealous of the man with three legs, too, because in that tiny traveling population, he was a rock star, a mayor of sorts.

And here is an odd idea: Were any of us to close ourselves off so our social nourishment came exclusively from these performers, if any of us were to travel with them, it is inevitable that we would become jealous of the more freakish characters. It seems that when a group of people come together, they will develop a kind of hierarchy of importance, and the determining factors of a person's value are not only unfair but arbitrary. Where you and I might become upset at God over having too great a nose or too hairy a back, these few feel dejection about the *normality* of their bodies.

———

The reason I took the trip to Oakland in the first place was to speak at a church across the bay. I realized, sitting there at the train station, thinking about the circus performers, that I was just like them. What I mean is, while I spoke at the church I wondered how the audience was perceiving what I was saying, and I wondered whether any of them were being moved, and I wondered if I was funny enough or smart enough to engage a thousand people. And I feel the same way about my books and about my life in general. The circus, and I am talking about life now, really sucks. It feels like we all have these little acts, these stupid things we do that we all hang our hats on. The Fall has made monkeys of us, for crying out loud. Some of us are athletes and others of us are physicists, and some of us are good-looking and some of us are rich, and we all are running around, in a way, trying to get a bunch of people to clap for us, trying to get a bunch of people to say we are normal, we are healthy, we are good. And there is nothing wrong with being beautiful or being athletic or being smart, but those are some of the pleasures of life, not life's redemption.

Do you know what Paul said about the stuff he wrote and taught? He said he didn't write with big and fancy words to try to impress people; rather, he just told the truth, God's truth, and let that be what it was, powerful and honest, making sense of life.

The thing about being a monkey is that it affects all our relationships. One writer said that what we commonly think of as love is really the desire to be loved. I know that is true for me, and it has been true for years, that often when I want somebody to like me, I am really wanting them to say that I am redeemed, that I am not a loser, that I can stay in the boat, stay in the circus, that my act redeems me.

In this sense, as harsh as some of Jesus' words are, they are also beautiful and comforting. No more worrying about what an audience thinks, no more trying to elbow our way to the top. We have Him instead, a God who redeems our identity *for* us, giving us His righteousness.

I read this painful passage in Eugene Peterson's translation of the book of Galatians the other day that sums up life in the lifeboat, life in the circus:

> It is obvious what kind of life develops out of trying to get your own way all the time: repetitive, loveless, cheap sex; a stinking accumulation of mental and emotional garbage; frenzied and joyless grabs for happiness; trinket gods; magic-show religion; paranoid loneliness; cutthroat competition; all-consuming-yet-never-satisfied wants; a brutal temper; an impotence to love or be loved; divided homes and divided lives; small-minded and lopsided pursuits; the vicious habit of depersonalizing everyone into a rival; uncontrolled and uncontrollable addictions; ugly parodies of community. I could go on.
>
> (Galatians 5:19–21 THE MESSAGE)

I kept thinking about all this and I wanted it all to end. I didn't want to be a part of it anymore. Paul kept writing in his books about how people shouldn't want to be circumcised anymore, about how people shouldn't think they were better than other people, about how folks should submit to one another in love, thinking of each other as more important than themselves and I know now, and I realized back in Oakland, that this kind of life could take place only within a relationship with God, the One who takes care of our needs, the One who really has the power to tell us who we are, if we would only trust in Him.

Imagine how much a man's life would be changed if he trusted that he was loved by God? He could interact with the poor and not show partiality, he could love his wife easily and not expect her to redeem him, he would be slow to anger because redemption was no longer at stake, he could be wise and giving

430

with his money because money no longer represented points, he could give up on formulaic religion, knowing that checking stuff off a spiritual to-do list was a worthless pursuit, he would have confidence and the ability to laugh at himself, and he could love people without expecting anything in return. It would be quite beautiful, really.

Do you know what King David did one time when he was worshiping God? He took off all his clothes and danced around in the street. Everybody was watching him and he didn't care. His poor wife was completely embarrassed, but David didn't worry, he didn't care what anybody thought about him; he just took off his clothes before God and danced.

Don't get me wrong, I have no intention of taking off my clothes on Sunday morning at church. I bring this up only to say there is a certain freedom in getting our feelings of redemption from God and not other people. This is what we have always wanted, isn't it? And it isn't the American dream at all, it is the human dream, the deepest desire of our hearts.

I would imagine, then, that the repentance we are called to is about choosing one audience over another. Jesus says many times in the gospel that He knows the heart of man, and the heart of man does not have the power to give glory. I think Jesus is saying, *Look, you guys are running around like monkeys trying to get people to clap, but people are fallen, they are separated from God, so they have no idea what is good or bad, worthy to be judged or set free, beautiful or ugly to begin with. Why not get your glory from God? Why not accept your feelings of redemption because of His pleasure in you, not the fickle and empty favor of man? And only then will you know who you are, and only then will you have true, uninhibited relationships with others.*

431

CHAPTER TWELVE

Morality

WHY I AM BETTER THAN YOU

A great concern for those who defend a propositional gospel over a relational gospel is morality. Some feel that if we do not emphasize morality, people will have too much fun and refuse to play by the rules the rest of us who know God have to play by. But I don't think this is true. I've heard it said that Mormonism is the fastest-growing religion and my guess is, the fast growth is because it offers a strict morality, a system of rights and wrongs that people can live by as well as accountability, so they don't cheat on their spouses or kick their dogs. All of us subscribe to some kind of morality, mostly born of a conscience rather than a book. And the Bible is not structured as a moral code. It does not have all the answers on right and wrong. It has some, enough to guide a man's conscience, but a book containing a complete moral code would require all pages in all books.

Somehow, and for some reason, each of us subscribes to a kind of morality, and though for some this code is not defined, it is understood and adhered to. Grievances, then, are disagreements

433

in the moral code, not one side holding to "it" and another side disregarding "it," which, unfortunately, is often an evangelical position.

The truth is, we all want morality. We know morals will make us better people, and we even feel a kind of nobility when we subscribe to and defend a code. I watched a documentary recently about young African-American men in urban New York City who are turning in droves to Islam because of its moral guidance. Each of the young men was looking for a father figure, for a mentor who would provide for him boundaries, understanding intrinsically that life has rules and parameters and to succeed in the soul, one must learn these parameters. Don't get me wrong, I don't believe Muhammad was a true prophet, but I enjoyed watching this documentary because it reminded me that I, too, have parameters and rules with which to navigate my existence.

Lately, however I have been thinking of morality in less conceptual terms, less as a system of rules and regulations and more as a concept very beautiful and alive. Please do not think I am blurring the lines between right and wrong; rather, I am wanting to bring these lines to life to reveal a guide and a judge. The reason I have been feeling this way is not because morality gives us boundaries or because it helps us live clean lives, though morality does these things, but rather because, in some mysterious way, morality pleases God.

One of the great problems with morality for me in the past was that it didn't seem to be connected to anything. I no longer believe morality will redeem me. What I mean by this is that, often, when I had lustful thoughts, greedy thoughts, and envious thoughts, or for that matter performed lustful actions, actions that stemmed from greed or envy, I felt that I would go to hell for doing them, for thinking these things.

Growing up in a small conservative church in the South, you hear more about morality than you do about Christ. If you were immoral, if you danced, drank, or cussed, you were made to feel that God no longer liked you. And if you were moral, you were made to feel not one with Christ, but right and good and better than other people. These things were not stated directly, but the environment left me with this impression. Christian spirituality, then, hinged on whether or not a person behaved.

I don't mean any of this to suggest I don't want to behave, or that I want to go on sinning and say that it is okay with God. There is no part of me that believes anything like this can be defended scripturally. A god who says everybody can do as they please would be a bad god, a bad father, giving license for anarchy. Love creates rules, and forgives when they are broken. People would hurt themselves if they did anything they wanted. People do hurt themselves and others all the time by neglecting laws and rules.

What I really wanted, though, was a *reason* for morals, a reason stronger than somebody's simple suggestion that right was right and wrong was wrong.

When David wrote his Twenty-third Psalm he indicated God led him in the paths of righteousness for *His* name's sake. This struck me, recently, when I was reading through the Psalms. I had always thought morality was something God created exclusively to keep mankind out of the ditches, and to a large degree I suppose this is true, but David's concept of morality was quite new to me and I wondered exactly what he meant by the phrase "for His name's sake."

Peter would argue in the book of Acts that when David talked about the Lord, he was talking about Jesus, acting as a kind of prophet. And in this light, the Twenty-third Psalm becomes quite beautiful. The Valley of the Shadow of Death, I came to learn while studying the passage, is an actual valley outside Jerusalem. It is treacherous terrain, and shepherds once herded sheep through this valley to move them to green pastures and fresh water. There were crags in the rocks, ditches, and thornbushes that sheep, simple as they are, would fall into, so shepherds had to use their staffs, those big sticks with the rounded hooks on the end, to reach into the crags and ditches to rescue the sheep. And the shepherd also had a rod he would use to scare off wild animals, keeping the sheep safe in the passage. In the Twenty-third Psalm, David says, "Thy rod and thy staff they comfort me" (v. 4 KJV), and when I think of myself as a sheep, looking up at Jesus, who has a staff to rescue me and a rod to protect me, it makes me feel that this passage is quite endearing, that basically I am a simple sheep, having very little idea of what is right and wrong, and Jesus is going to pull me out of the ditches when I screw up, and protect me from spiritual enemies who, as we've already discussed, roam about like lions.

And then the words regarding Christ's leading us in the paths of righteousness come up, and I know David is talking about the safe ground through the Valley of the Shadow of Death, and how there is a right way, a way that is prudent, a way that doesn't have the crags and bushes; and this is the way of God's morality. That is, God's ethics, His conscience instilled in man and guided by Scripture, are the best ways to travel through a fallen world, through the Valley of the Shadow of Death, or what I have referred to as a lifeboat and a circus.

It made me wonder, then, if the idea of morality is just another ramification of the Fall. Paul even says that the law was given to the Jews to show them they couldn't follow the law, to reveal to them the depravity of their nature, to show them the cancer that lived inside them so they would pay attention to the Doctor.

In my own life, I try to be moral, but I am no good at it. It becomes obvious, in my effort, that I have this cancer Paul eludes to, that I am in this fallen body with a fallen mind and a fallen nature. That said, I don't suppose we will have any kind of morality in heaven, any thought about right and wrong, once we are with God, once our minds and our bodies and our natures are replenished and healed in His light and His goodness. No, morality exists only because we are fallen, not unlike medicine exists because people get sick.

Morality, then, if you think about it, is the way we imitate God. It is the way we imitate the ways of heaven here on earth. Jesus says, after all, to know Him we must follow Him, we must cling to Him and imitate Him, and many places in Scripture the idea is presented that if we know Him, we will obey Him.

If you look for this relational concept of morality, you see it all through Scripture. Paul connects the idea of morality to Christ in the books of Ephesians and Romans, and the author of Hebrews directly connects morality to our relationship with God in several places in that text. John the Evangelist, in all three of his short books at the end of the Bible, keeps saying if we know God we will love our brother, and if we know God we will obey.

I was contacted by a magazine editor recently who asked if I would consider writing a few articles for his publication. The editor told me his magazine was unique in that both Christians and people who weren't Christians contributed, which allowed them to offer a wide variety of perspectives in an open-table format. I thought the magazine sounded terrific and asked him if he would send me a copy. A few days later the magazine arrived, and I took it to Powell's to sit and read in the coffee shop. I have to tell you, I didn't like what I read. The first article was a shabbily written diatribe against conventional concepts of morality. The writer said he was in a Christian rock band but didn't see himself as being any different from any other rock star, saying proudly that he frequently slept with his girlfriend, that he smoked pot and got drunk and applauded anybody who was willing to experiment. He went on to excuse his actions by claiming God's grace. I read the article a couple of times and realized, perhaps, what it was that David and Paul were speaking of when they connected morality to God's glory, and immorality to His personal pain.

Can you imagine being a bride in a wedding, walking down the aisle toward your bridegroom, and during the procession, checking out the other groomsmen, wondering when you could sneak off to sleep with one of them, not taking the marriage to your groom seriously? Paul became furious at the church in Corinth for allowing a man to sleep with his stepmother. It makes sense to think of this as Paul's protecting the beauty and grandeur of a union with Christ. In this way, immorality is terrible because it is cheating on the Creator, who loves us and offers Himself as a Bridegroom for the bride.

When I said I was looking for a *reason* for morality, this is what I meant. The motive is love, love of God and of my fellow man.

———

The hijacking of the concept of morality began, of course, when we reduced Scripture to formula and a love story to theology, and finally morality to rules. It is a very different thing to break a rule than it is to cheat on a lover. A person's mind can do all sorts of things his heart would never let him do. If we think of God's grace as a technicality, a theological precept, we can disobey without the slightest feeling of guilt, but if we think of God's grace as a relational invitation, an outreach of love, we are pretty much jerks for belittling the gesture.

In this way, it isn't only the moralist looking for a feeling of supe-riority who commits crimes against God, it is also those of us who react by doing what we want, claiming God's grace. Neither view of morality connects behavior to a relational exchange with Jesus. When I run a stop sign, for example, I am breaking a law against a system of rules, but if I cheat on my wife, I have broken a law against a person. The first is impersonal; the latter is intensely personal.

———

There are a great many other motives for morality, but in my mind they are less than noble. Morality for love's sake, for the sake of God and the sake of others, seems more beautiful to me than morality for morality's sake, morality to build a better nation here on earth, morality to protect our schools, morality as an identity for one of the parties in the culture war, one of the identities in the lifeboat.

I confess, when I was young my mind rebelled from the stan-dard evangelical mantra about morality. My rebellion was reac-tionary, to be sure. I can't tell you how many times I have seen an evangelical leader on television talking about this *culture war,* about how we are being threatened by persons with an immoral agenda, and I can't tell you how many sermons I have heard in which immoral pop stars or athletes or politicians have been denounced because of their shortcomings. Rarely, however, have I heard any of these ideas connected with the dominant message of Christ, a message of grace and forgiveness and a call to repentance. Rather, the moral message I have heard is often a message of bit-terness and anger because *our* morality, *our* culture, is being taken over by people who disregard *our* ethical standards. None of it was connected, relationally, to God at all.

In this way, it has felt like one group in the lifeboat, the moral group, is at odds with another group, the *immoral* group, and the fight is about dominance *in* a fallen system rather than rescue *from* a fallen system. And I wonder, *What good does it do to tell somebody to be moral so they can die fifty years later and, apparently, go to hell?*

It makes me wonder, and even judge (confession) the motives of somebody who wages a culture war about morality without confessing their own immorality while pointing to the Christ who saved them, the Christ who wishes to rescue everybody.

Morality, in this way, can be a circus act, giving a person a feeling of superiority. And while morality is good, anything we do to get other people to clap, or anything that gives us a more prominent position in a sinking ship, runs the risk of replacing a humble nature pointed at Christ, who is our Redeemer. The biblical idea of morality is behavior associated with our relationship with Jesus, not bait for pride.

In fact, morality as a battle cry *against* a depraved culture is simply not a New Testament idea. Morality as a ramification of our spiritual union and relationship with Christ, however, is.

Paul said to the church at Rome that those who chose immorality would be given over to a depraved mind and their lives would be ruined, but in the next breath he said that because of his great love for lost people, he would be willing to go to hell and take God's wrath upon himself. And he said this even about the Jews who were persecuting him. In other words, the call to morality is delivered through a changed and forgiven heart, a heart regenerated and delivered by Christ, desiring that all people repent and come to know Him. There is nothing here we can use in the lifeboat at all. The agenda is all God's, not ours, and God's agenda is love.

I was thinking of Paul recently when I saw an evangelical

leader on CNN talking about gay marriage. The evangelical leader agreed with the apostle Paul about homosexuality being a sin, but when it came time to express the kind of love Paul expressed for the lost, the kind of love that says, *I would gladly take God's wrath upon myself and go to hell for your sake,* the evangelical leader sat in silence. Why? How can we say the rules Paul presented are true, but neglect the heart with which he communicated those rules?

My suspicion is the evangelical leader was able to do this because he had taken on the morality of God as an identity with which he was attempting to redeem himself to culture, and perhaps even to God. This is what the Pharisees did, and the same Satan tricks us with the same bait: justification through comparison. It's an ugly trick, but it continues to prove effective.

———

I was the guest on a radio show recently that was broadcast on a secular station, one of those conservative shows that paints Democrats as terrorists. The interviewer asked what I thought about the homosexuals who were trying to take over the country. I confess I was taken aback. I hadn't realized that homosexuals were trying to take over the country.

"Which homosexuals are trying to take over the country?" I asked.

"You know," the interviewer began, "the ones who want to take over Congress and the Senate."

I paused for a while. "Well," I said, "I've never met those guys and I don't know who they are. The only homosexuals I've met are very kind people, some of whom have been beat up and spit on and harassed and, in fact, feel threatened by the religious right." Think about it. If you watch CNN all day and see extreme

Muslims in the Middle East declaring war on America because they see us as immoral, and then you read the paper the next day to find the exact same words spoken by evangelical leaders against the culture here in America, you'd be pretty scared. I've never heard of a homosexual group trying to take over the world, or for that matter the House or the Senate, but I can point you to about fifty evangelical organizations who are trying to do exactly that. I don't know why. In my opinion, we should tell people about Jesus, not try to build some kind of temporary moral civilization here on earth. If you want that, move to Salt Lake City. "And what is the name of this homosexual group that is trying to take over America?" I asked the host, somewhat angry at his ignorant misuse of war rhetoric.

"Well, I hear about them all the time," he said, rather frustrated with me.

"If you hear about them all the time, what is the name of the organization?"

"Well, I don't know right now. But they are there."

"Can I list for you ten or so Christian organizations who are working to try to get more Christians in the House and the Senate?" I said to the host.

"Listen, I get your point," he said.

"But I don't think you do. Here is my position: As a Christian, I believe Jesus wants to reach out to people who are lost and, yes, immoral—immoral just like you and I are immoral; and declaring war against them and stirring up your listeners to the point of anger and giving them the feeling that their country, their families, and their lifestyles are being threatened is only hurting what Jesus is trying to do. This isn't rocket science. If you declare war on somebody, you have to either handcuff them or kill them. That's the only way to win. But if you want them to be forgiven by Christ, if you want them to live eternally in heaven with Jesus, then you have to love them. The choice is yours and my suspicion is you will be held responsible by God, a Judge who will know your motives. So go ahead and declare war in the name of a conservative agenda, but don't do it in the name of God. That's what militant Muslims are doing in the Middle East, and we don't want that here."

Amazingly, the host kept me on and allowed me to tell a story or two about interacting with supposed pagans in a compassionate exchange, and later even admitted that his idea that homosexuals were trying to take over the country had originated from an e-mail he had received, an e-mail he had long since thrown away but he thought perhaps had come from *some kind of homosexual organization.*

To be honest, I think most Christians, and this guy was definitely a Christian, want to love people and obey God but feel they *have* to wage a culture war. But this isn't the case at all. Remember, we are not elbowing for power in the lifeboat. God's kingdom isn't here on earth. And I believe you will find Jesus in the hearts of even the most militant Christians, moving them to love people, and it is only their egos, and the voice of Satan, that cause them to demean the lost. What we must do in these instances is listen to our consciences, and allow Scripture to instruct us about morality *and* methodology, not just morality.

Paul was deceived when he persecuted Christians, thinking he was doing it to serve God, but God went to him, blinded him, and corrected his thinking. After this, Paul loved the people he had previously hated; he began to take the message of forgiveness to Jews and to Gentiles, to male and to female, to pagans and prostitutes. At no point does he waste his time lobbying government for a moral agenda. Nobody in Scripture who knew and followed Jesus wasted their time with any of this; they built the church, they loved people.

Once Paul switched positions, many people tried to kill him

for talking about Jesus, but he never lifted a fist; he never declared war. In fact, in Athens, he was so appreciated by pagans who worshiped false idols, they invited him to speak about Jesus in an open forum. In America, this no longer happens. We are in the margins of society and so we have to have our own radio stations and television stations and bookstores. Our formulaic, propositional, lifeboat-territorial methodology has crippled the kingdom of God. We can learn a great deal from the apostles. Paul would go so far as to compliment the men of Athens, calling them "spiritual men" and quoting their poetry, then telling them the God he knew was better for them, larger, stronger and more alive than any of the stone idols they bowed down to. And many of the people in the audience followed Him and had more and more questions. This would not have happened if Paul had labeled them as pagans and attacked them.

A moral message, a message of *us* versus *them*, overflowing in war rhetoric, never hindered the early message of grace, of repentance toward dead works and immorality in exchange for a love relationship with Christ. War rhetoric against people is not the methodology, not the sort of communication that came out of the mouth of Jesus or the mouths of any of His followers. In fact, even today, moralists who use war rhetoric will speak of right and wrong, and even some vague and angry god, but never Jesus. Listen closely, and I assure you, they will not talk about Jesus.

In my opinion, if you hate somebody because they are different from you, you'd best get on your knees and repent until you can say you love them, until you have gotten your soul right with Christ.

I can't say this clearly enough: If we are preaching morality without Christ, and using war rhetoric to communicate a battle mentality, we are fighting on Satan's side. This battle we are in is a battle against the principalities of darkness, not against people who are different from us. In war you shoot the enemy, not the hostage.

—

In this way, the chief difference between morality in a relational context to Jesus and morality in the context of the lifeboat is that one system works for people and the other against them.

It is obvious when reading Scripture that what you and I commonly think of as morality is thin in definition. Some Christians, when considering immorality in culture, consider two issues: abortion and gay marriage.

Moral ideas presented in the New Testament, and even from the mouth of Christ, however, involve loving our neighbors, being one in the bond of peace, loving our enemies, taking care of our own business before we judge somebody else, forgiving debts even as we have been forgiven, speaking in truth and love else we sound like clanging cymbals (turn on Fox News to hear what clanging cymbals sound like), and protecting the beauty of sex and marriage.

Morality, then, becomes the bond, the glue that holds our families together, our communities together, and our churches together, and most important, builds intimacy with Christ. Morality, in the context of a relationship with Jesus, becomes the voice of love to a confused community, the voice of reason and calm in a loud argument, the voice of life in a world of walking dead, the voice of Christ in a sea of self-hatred.

—

The trick Satan has played on us involving his spin on morality has not gone unnoticed by those outside the church.

In his book *Lies and the Lying Liars Who Tell Them*, Al Franken included a provocative multipage comic strip about a man named Supply-Side Jesus. In the strip, Supply-Side Jesus walks through the streets of Jerusalem stating that people should start businesses so they can employ the poor and should purchase exotic and expensive clothes and jewelry so their money will trickle into the economy and, eventually, bring bread to the mouths of the starving.

In the comic, the disciples come to Supply-Side Jesus and say they want to feed the poor directly, but Supply-Side Jesus says no, that if you give money or food or water directly to the poor, you are only helping them in their laziness and increasing the welfare state. Eventually, Rome catches up with Supply-Side Jesus and, before an angry mob, Pontius Pilate asks the masses which man they want to crucify, Supply-Side Jesus or another man who, in the comic, stands beside Pilate humbly, a disheveled and shadowy figure. The crowd chants they want to free Supply-Side Jesus because they like his philosophies, and they want to crucify this other man, the shadowy figure standing next to Pilate. Pilate tells the crowd this other man is innocent, that he has done no wrong, but the crowd refuses to listen and instead chants, "Crucify him, crucify him." Pilate then lets Supply-Side Jesus go free, and orders the innocent man, whose name was Jesus of Nazareth, to be crucified.

I sat there reading the book at Horse Brass Pub in amazement. Here was Al Franken, a known liberal who often lambastes the conservative Christian right but who also, somehow, understands the difference between the Jesus the religious right worships and the Jesus presented in Scripture. One Jesus is understood through conservative economic theory, the other through the Gospels.

I recall watching a documentary detailing Muslim frustration, both domestic and Middle Eastern, with the perception that all Muslims subscribe to the sort of angry and dangerous extremism propagated by terrorist hijackers on September 11. "It was more than those planes that got hijacked," one Muslim woman commented. "It was the nation of Islam. In the eyes of the world, they took our faith and flew it into those buildings. The damage may never be repaired."

I wondered if the Christian faith in America had not been hijacked as well, hijacked by those same two issues: abortion and gay marriage. How did a spirituality such as Christianity, a spirituality that speaks of eternity, of a world without end, of forgiveness of sins and a mysterious union with the Godhead, come to be represented by a moralist agenda and a trickle-down economic theory? And more important, how did a man born of Eastern descent, a man who called Himself the Prince of Peace, a man whom the sacred writings describe eating with prostitutes and providing wine at weddings and healing the sick and ignoring any political plot, a man who wants us to turn the other cheek and give all our possessions if we are sued, become associated with—no, become the poster boy for—a Western moral and financial agenda communicated through the rhetoric of war and ignorant of the damage it is causing to a world living in poverty?

My only answer is that Satan is crafty indeed.

I realize there are people reading this who will automatically dismiss me as a theological liberal, but I do not believe a person can take two issues from Scripture, those being abortion and gay marriage, and adhere to them as sins, then neglect much of the rest and call himself a fundamentalist or even a conservative. The person who believes the sum of his morality involves gay marriage and abortion alone, and neglects health care and world trade and the environment and loving his neighbor and feeding the poor is, by definition, a theological liberal, because he takes what he wants from Scripture and ignores the rest. Make no mistake, there is a lifeboat motive in play, a *join a team and fight* feeling that is roaming around the world like a lion, searching to destroy men's souls.

———

The reason I bring this up is to plead with evangelicals to return to the sort of call Christ has given us, to obey Him and experience intimacy with Him through sharing our faith, loving our enemies, serving and feeding the poor and hungry directly, and to stop showing off about how moral we are and how that makes us better than other people. I assure you, once we leave the fight over our country's future and enter the spiritual battle for the hearts and souls of the lost, the church will flourish, and the kingdom of God will grow. God is not in the business of brokering for power over a nation; He is in the business of loving the unloved and pulling sheep out of crags and bushes.

The greatest comfort I can feel in the middle of this is that Jesus did not lend Himself to war causes, to tax issues or political campaigns. For that matter, He did not lend Himself to raising money for education or stumping for affirmative action. It was as if He did not trust us to build a utopia. He kept it very simple, in fact. *Follow Me*, He said. *I have no opinion about what color the paint should be in this prison. Follow Me.*

Is Jesus angry? *Sometimes.* Does He speak of sin and morality? *Yes, quite frequently.* Does the contemporary evangelical model of sin and morality reflect the teachings of Christ? *As a flea is a part of a dog, but not to be confused with the dog itself.* Is Jesus frustrated with sinners? *Yes.* Is He frustrated with religious zealots who use His Father's name to build businesses or support agendas? *He is violently frustrated.* Is there a penalty to pay for rejecting Him? *Yes, apart from Christ we will die and are dying.* Does Jesus like liberals more than conservatives? *He will be nobody's flag.*

———

I suspect any lack of love or feelings of anger we have toward the culture around us are not feelings that come from God, but rather our souls arising again to cast rocks at women caught in adultery. We should not expect Christ to respond any differently to us than He did to the moralists of His day:

They dropped their stones and walked away, feeling ashamed that each of them had been proved a sinner, too. And Jesus went over to comfort the woman, telling her, "Go, and sin no more" (see John 8.)

CHAPTER THIRTEEN

Religion

A PUBLIC RELATIONS CAMPAIGN FOR GOD

When I was young I had a friend whose father was the pastor at a Methodist church. I grew up Baptist. I remember thinking my friend had it all wrong, and I wondered if he was even a Christian. His father was a terrific man, very intelligent and soft-spoken and tall as a building, with big hands and a deep voice that spoke the sort of encouragement you believed. And even though he spoke encouragement, I remember feeling very sorry for him because he had been misled, somewhere way back, perhaps in seminary, and that had made him grow up to become a Methodist instead of a Baptist. I thought it was a crying shame. And at the time I didn't even know what it was a Baptist believed that a Methodist didn't; I only knew we were right and they were wrong.

I suppose believing we were right and they were wrong gave me a feeling of superiority over my Methodist friends. It all sounds so innocent until you realize whatever evil thing it was that caused me to believe Baptists are better than Methodists is the same evil thing that has Jews killing Palestinians rather than talking to them, and for that matter, Palestinians killing Jews rather than engaging in an important conversation about land and history and peace. It makes you wonder how many of the ideas we believe are the result of our being taught them, and we now defend them as a position of our egos.

Of course I think the thing about Methodists being wrong is silly now, now that I have met so many people from so many different theological backgrounds who have a deep respect and love for Jesus, and so many people from so many theological backgrounds who don't.

———

The truth is, many of us go around thinking we are right about everything. When God was in the Garden, I'll bet Adam and Eve didn't know what it felt like to want to be right. I'll bet they felt right all the time, and I'll bet it had nothing to do with *what* they knew and everything to do with *who* they knew, as though whatever it was inside them that said they didn't think right or feel right or believe right was activated only after God left. I'll bet they never said anything like *I told you so.*

If you think about it, right and wrong aren't even people, they are ideas, philosophical equations and that sort of thing, and so it is funny that anybody would think they are right in the first place. I suppose what we really mean when we say we are right is that something out there in the soup of ideas is right, and we simply agree with whatever it is the soup is saying. But this doesn't have anything to do with our rightness or wrongness; it just means we can read.

I'm not trying to be a relativist by any means, I am only saying a person is not right or wrong; a person is just a body and a brain and a soul. And even if a person subscribes to a certain take on life he feels is the right take, it's not because he had a lot to do with it. If we grew up in Christian homes and heard about Jesus all our lives, we shouldn't believe we arrived at these theological positions through an independent navigation of our minds. We were just going with the flow, and there isn't any genius in going with the flow. Show me a guy who was molested by a minister and still loves Jesus, and I'll show you a genius. The stuff that guy would have had to think through in order to arrive at an affection for God is nothing short of miraculous.

As for me, I'm somebody who repeats what I was taught in Sunday school using fancier language. It may pay the rent, but it isn't original thought.

———

And yet it is amazing how I can take these beautiful things Jesus told me, this skeleton of the human story He explains in narrative and poetry, and turn it around as though I wrote it on the back of a napkin at Denny's in a moment of inspiration.

Shouldn't I be grateful that God showed this stuff to me rather than connecting the theology to my identity and then using it to distinguish myself from *inferiors* who haven't figured it out?

I had dinner with a friend down south recently who didn't know Christ and I invited a pastor along, hoping the conversation might turn to Jesus. When my pastor friend discovered my other friend wasn't a Christian, he asked a question I thought was very sad. He asked if my other friend had ever thought Christians were right.

I confess, the question took me aback. I can conceive a number of questions more inviting than whether or not Christians are right. Right about what? The Crusades? Republican policies? Televangelists?

Asking whether my friend thought Christians were right was really a question about the questioner and his identity, not about God. My pastor friend was asking my other friend to admit we were right and he was wrong—his journey was wrong, his experience was wrong, his heart was wrong, his mind was wrong. He was asking my friend to join our party in the lifeboat. That's a lot to ask of a guy. The sad part of this story is, my friend who isn't a Christian was hurt and politely changed the subject, and we haven't talked about God since. I apologized to him later, and, unfortunately, the subject has yet to come back up.

The ever-overquoted C. S. Lewis said it this way in his book *Mere Christianity:* "Most of us are not really approaching the subject in order to find out what Christianity says: We are approaching it in the hope of finding support from Christianity for the views of our own party. We are looking for an ally where we are offered either a Master or—a Judge."

And that's the thing about being religious; it isn't this safe place in the soul you can go, it has just as many booby traps as any other thing you can get yourself into. It's a bloody brothel, in fact. Jesus even says there will be people who will heal other people, but when they die He is going to say He didn't *know* them. It is somewhat amazing to me, once again, that all of Christianity, all our grids and mathematics and truths and different groups subscribing to different theological ideas, boils down to our *knowing* Jesus and His *knowing* us.

———

Apart from the booby trap of getting redemption from believing we are right and they are wrong, there is the booby trap of believing we gain access to God by knowing a lot of religious information.

Rather than Scripture serving as the text that explains God, it becomes a puzzle by which we test our knowledge against our friends', and the views by which we distinguish superiors from inferiors. It is as though we believe when we die, Alex Trebeck will be standing at the gates of heaven to lead us in a mad round of religious Jeopardy: *I'll take Calvinism for a seat next to Christ, Alex.*

In the context of my relationship with God, I know the temptation to bank on knowledge all too well. It is true that you can get a little buzz off knowing a couple of smart theological ideas. My friend Ross is a former seminary professor, and we were driving back from lunch one afternoon and I was telling him what I thought about a particular passage of Scripture, really going off about it as though I were the first of all men to understand what it meant. When I stopped to allow Ross space to tell me how smart I was, he just sat there in silence. "What do you think, Ross?" I asked. "Well," he said quietly, "I think knowledge puffs up."

Scripture says the nature of sin is deceptive, so deceptive that a person's mind can be carried away, and he will have no idea he has become something arrogant and proud and offensive until one of his friends slaps him on the back of the head.

And I wonder about that, about how much of my faith I apply in a personal way, deep down in my heart on the level where I actually mean things. I know there are selfish motives mixed with my faith, that this community of faith is the jury of peers and they applaud when I know a lot of fancy theological stuff, and that can really screw a guy up. I learn more and get more applause and learn more and get even more applause. To describe people like me, Jesus would use the word *hypocrite*, which, at the time, was a term used to describe Greek actors. Jesus, in fact, is thought to be the first person to coin the phrase. Those on the scene must have found the similarities quite humorous—the exaggerated language, the proud countenances, the broad and showy mannerisms. How obvious it must have been to Jesus that this was all a sham. *They don't even know Me,* He must have thought. *They don't even know My Father.*

Eugene Peterson translates Paul's disdain for religious leaders of the day rather scathingly:

> I'm giving nobody grounds for lumping me in with those money-grubbing "preachers," vaunting themselves as something special. They're a sorry bunch—pseudo-apostles, lying preachers, crooked workers—posing as Christ's agents but sham to the core. And no wonder! Satan does it all the time, dressing up as a beautiful angel of light. So it shouldn't surprise us when his servants masquerade as servants of God. But they're not getting by with anything. They'll pay for it in the end.
>
> (2 Cor. 11:12–15 THE MESSAGE)

I want to confess something I don't talk about very often. I tell you this only because as I write, it is late and the house is quiet and I feel a little sentimental.

What I want to say is this: I could very easily have become one of those guys Paul is talking about. It is truly an amazing feeling to stand in front of a crowd and deliver a great sermon, or to hang around after a reading and sign books. I've never been very good at anything, so the only thing people have ever praised me for is writing and speaking. I'm not saying that accepting people's praise for doing what God calls you to do is wrong, I am only saying I understand how it could become a replacement for the favor of God, the favor that comes for free, for no reason, unearned. What good is that in the lifeboat? It's almost like quitting.

———

The tough thing about Christian spirituality is, you have to mean things. You can't just go through the motions or act religious for the wrong reasons.

It's crazy, isn't it? It's crazy because, as I've suggested all along, this thing is a thing of the heart. It's intimacy with Christ, wrestling with the truth of the soul rather than a dog and pony show in the center ring of a circus.

Jesus, by instigating what we call Communion, and disciplines such as fasting, and the sacrament of baptism, takes the spiritual disciplines from the abstract realm of religion and places them within the meaningful realm of relationship. As I've mentioned, fasting is mourning Him, baptism is identifying with Him, Communion is remembering Him. It all comes down to our thoughts and feelings and faith in Him. If our minds are not on Christ and we treat Communion like a little religious pill, or baptism like a woo-woo bath, or fast to feel some kind of pain about our sacrifice, the significance is gone. It is the trick of Satan to get us to go through religious motions divorced of their relational significance. It is the trick of Satan to get us to perform religious actions without *meaning* them.

After all, if we are going through religious motions to get people to think of us as religious, praise us, and all that, we are receiving our false redemption from a bunch of people who are going to be dead in fifty years. This is a shabby replacement for an eternal God.

I've a friend who has a leather-bound day planner, and on an inside page of the planner there is a space for facts about a spouse: her dress size, her favorite foods, her favorite music. Amazingly, this is not a page my friend created on a blank sheet of paper;

rather, he bought it from the company that makes the time-management system. We laughed together at the oddity of the idea of trying to calculate, plan, and structure knowledge that would be meaningful to a woman only if her husband knew it, as a consequence of his love. The whole point of intimacy is that you want to know things, random facts; you are driven to them because this woman has *taken you captive*, not that you would willfully write them down as a matter of discipline. Imagine calling your wife to tell her you love her and then hanging up the phone to check off the action on your to-do list. I don't think she would be pleased in the slightest. She would probably rather not have received a call at all. No, in romance, as in spirituality, your motives have to be self-less, driven from an authentic love for the other person.

Lately I have been thinking about the verse in Scripture that says to work out your salvation in fear and trembling (see Phil. 2:12). I take this to mean salvation isn't something you go around feeling sure of, the way you might if you had completed a to-do list. I take this to mean working out our salvation involves a very careful searching of the heart, asking time and again what we really mean by attending church, what we really mean by reading the Bible, what we really mean when we worship God.

It bears repeating that the last conversation John reported Jesus having was with Peter, asking three times if Peter loves Him, and defining that love's manifestation as service to the people in the church, working itself out in love for others. And it also bears repeating that Jesus told the Pharisees the greatest commandment was to love the Lord your God with all your heart, soul, mind, and strength. I would think the Pharisees of the day would have dismissed this as a kind of affective theology, mushy talk, not very rational, and yet the whole time Jesus was extending an invitation to a spiritual marriage, our oneness with Him allowing God to see us in Christ's righteousness rather than our own. It would be most tragic for a person to know everything about God, but not God; to know all about the rules of spiritual marriage, but never walk the aisle.

———

At the time of Martin Luther, the church was building sanctuaries by selling bricks to people in exchange for indulgences. If a person bought a brick, they would be forgiven a few more sins or help a loved one out of purgatory. Because people couldn't read, and there weren't very many copies of the Bible floating around anyway, religious leaders used the threat of hell and God's wrath to manipulate the masses. But, as I mentioned earlier, when Luther read a copy of the Bible for himself, he began a reformation against this kind of crap. It makes you wonder how amazed he was when he first read the words of Christ in the book of Matthew, words about people who would try to distort relational truth and turn it into propositional truth for their own gain: "Instead of giving you God's Law as food and drink by which you can banquet on God," Jesus begins, talking about the Pharisees:

> They package it in bundles of rules, loading you down like pack animals. They seem to take pleasure in watching you stagger under these loads, and wouldn't think of lifting a finger to help. Their lives are perpetual fashion shows, embroidered prayer shawls one day and flowery prayers the next. They love to sit at the head table at church dinners, basking in the most prominent positions, preening in the radiance of public flattery, receiving honorary degrees, and getting called "Doctor" and "Reverend."
>
> Don't let people do that to you, put you on a pedestal like

that. You all have a single Teacher, and you are all classmates. Don't set people up as experts over your life, letting them tell you what to do. Save that authority for God; let him tell you what to do. No one else should carry the title of "Father"; you have only one Father, and he's in heaven. And don't let people maneuver you into taking charge of them. There is only one Life-Leader for you and them—Christ.

(Matt. 23:4–10 THE MESSAGE)

I know it's tempting to believe if we will walk through ten steps or listen to only a certain kind of music or pray in a certain way and for a certain number of days then we will find favor with God, but we won't. The formulas, I understand, were created by their authors to help us, but they do more hindering than helping. If we trust in a formula, if we trust in steps, we are not trusting in God. Formulas, while helping us organize our faith, also tempt us to trust in them rather than in God. In my own faith journey, I have disregarded formulas entirely.

There are many religions, and many religious sects within the faith of Christianity. Do I believe some are more scripturally faithful than others? *Yes.* But none of them matter in the slightest if formulas replace a personal relationship with Jesus. He is the authority we need. He is the God we must cling to for salvation. And He is a Person, not a list of ideas, not a theology.

The Danger of Marketing the Formulas

It is true that people need Jesus, not religion. And yet at times I am concerned our most passionate missionary endeavors are more concerned with redeeming our identity as Christians within the lifeboat than with presenting Jesus to a world looking for a God.

As my pastor friend down south revealed in his question to my lost friend, it often seems what we really want is for people who are not Christians to think we are valid, or Christianity is valid, rather than showing them Jesus, who won't act as a balm for their wounds.

I've a friend named Deacon, for instance, who attended a church here in Oregon that boasted a thriving youth ministry. My friend, who is a ridiculously intelligent physicist, told me that he was involved in this youth ministry when he was in high school. The strategy of the youth ministry, he said, was to recruit the most popular students from each of the local schools, knowing that if the popular students came, everybody else would follow. Because of this, youth ministers aggressively pursued jocks and cheerleaders with events such as slam-dunk contests and pizza feeds. The strategy, of course, worked, and hundreds of kids came, following the cheerleaders and jocks. Each year this ministry would divide the massive youth group into teams of about ten students, and the teams competed against one another for a series of weeks in games—stuff like three-legged races and that sort of thing. Bands were brought in, and speakers came and gave talks about how a person can be cool and still be a follower of Jesus. Each week the intensity would grow as teams competed for points toward first, second, and third places. And each year, as the winning team was announced, students would scream and cheer as the winning team, most often a team with a lot of jocks and cool kids, came up and received their trophy.

My friend told me, laughingly, that when he was in high school he was scrawny, awkward, and definitely not the sort of kid the ministry prized. And not only was he not one of the popular kids, but there weren't any popular kids on his team. "We were really a bunch of nerds," he said. And yet somehow, Deacon told me, their team managed to stay neck and neck in the points.

"I don't know how we did it," he said. "There wasn't a jock among us. But on the last night, there we were toward the top of the pack. And I remember thinking about how awesome it would be to win the event. Every year the team that won was ushered up front and people went nuts. I could just feel it, you know, walking up there to get the trophy with all these cool kids, all these jocks and cheerleaders finally noticing that I existed."

"So what happened?" I asked.

"Well," Deacon continued, "the last night came around, and we knew we were in the running. We competed hard, harder than any of us had ever competed before, and because the games were so screwy, you know, run to the other side of the gym and put your head on the end of a baseball bat and spin around and then come back, that sort of thing, the fact none of us were athletes hardly affected us. Anybody can turn around and get dizzy. But it was still close, and when the whole thing was done, we didn't know whether we had won. There were a couple other teams that were also close."

"So did you win?" I asked, rather sucked into the story, hoping, quite honestly, that a team of misfits would come out ahead.

"I'm getting there," Deacon continued. "So the youth leaders left the room and started calculating the scores, you know, and all of the teams were cheering, kind of yelling at one another in unison, and my team was so nervous that we kind of sat there in silence. And then finally, after what seemed like an eternity, the youth leaders came back into the room. They gathered everybody around in a big semicircle and grabbed the trophy and talked about how close it all was, and everybody was still kind of cheering so they had to quiet everybody down, and then the head youth pastor told us all to give a drum roll, you know, like pat our legs and the floor and the place was going nuts with this drum roll. And then he yelled the name of *our* team into the microphone. We had won. I couldn't believe it, but we actually won the thing." When Deacon delivered these last lines, he said them softly, almost as though he were ashamed.

"But you won, Deacon. That's great," I said.

"Yeah, it was great, but it was also one of the most humiliating nights of my life."

"What are you talking about?"

"Well, when the youth pastor called our team's name, the place more or less went silent. I mean, some people were cheering, but as we stood up and they realized who we were, they all went quiet. It was as though they weren't sure whether it was right to cheer for us or not. The place had been so geared around jocks and cheerleaders, they weren't sure if our winning was a good thing. I never felt like such a loser in my life."

And of course I told Deacon what he already knew, that this kind of thing was wrong, that Jesus went directly to those who were marginalized, not showing partiality at all. Deacon said he knew that, and he assured me he was over it, but I wondered. I wondered because I grew up a misfit, too, and while the youth ministry I attended when I was a kid was a safe haven for misfits, I can't imagine being able to get over that moment as quickly as Deacon did. I can't imagine not having stayed up at night wondering if God would feel the same way about me as the kids in the lifeboat.

I began to wonder if what we were really doing in evangelical circles, then, had more to do with redeeming ourselves to culture than it did with showing Jesus to a hurting world, a world literally filled with outcasts.

Not long after Deacon told me that story, I was in a record shop with a friend who was also in ministry. And we were having

SEARCHING FOR GOD KNOWS WHAT

this same conversation, and I was saying that I think, as Christians, we might be obsessed with whether or not we appear *cool* to the world. My friend disagreed and talked about all the ministries that minister to the outcasts; how if it weren't for the church, many people would go hungry, and many people would die lonely.

"That's true," I said to my friend. "But let's try a little experiment." I looked out over the record store, a mass-market chain store that must have housed ten thousand CDs, and I asked him to go into the racks and find one ugly person on the cover of a record.

"Do what?" my friend asked.

"You know, find an ugly person."

"Okay," my friend said reluctantly, and with that he walked into the aisle and started thumbing through the discs.

"What about this one?" he said, holding up a compact disc with a dorky-looking guy holding an acoustic guitar, the letters of the type looking like something printed in the sixties, but the picture very much modern.

"Easy enough, isn't it?" I asked.

"Yeah, sure," he said sarcastically. But the reason I had asked him to do this was because I knew our next stop would be a large Christian bookstore here in Portland, a bookstore that has an entire room devoted to music. We were heading over there to pick up a case of books we had ordered. When we arrived at the store, I asked my friend to come to the music room with me and I asked him to do the same thing, to find a record with an ugly person on the cover.

"I see what you're getting at," he said with a smile. And he started walking down the aisle. I went with him and both of us thumbed through the discs, picking out covers and showing them to each other, but none of the artists even slightly passed for ugly.

We spent about twenty minutes looking though the records but came up with nothing. We literally couldn't find one record cover with an ugly person on it. You can try the same experiment if you like. And I don't mean any of this to say that good-looking people are bad. I would actually like to be a good-looking person one day. I am only saying we are, perhaps, even more obsessed, in the church, with the stuff culture is obsessed with. We are hardly providing an alternative worldview. The matra seems to be "Trust in Jesus! He will redeem you to the world."

The examples get worse. A friend told me recently he volunteered at a church only a mile from my house. This is a large church with a successful television ministry. He said his job was to usher people to their seats, and that after he had been on the job for a while, he was asked to put some of the more "pleasant-looking people" on the front rows as these people were more likely to be caught in the picture when the camera pulled out on the audience, or when the preacher walked down from the stage to make a point.

I assure you, I am not making this up.

And please don't misunderstand me. There are very few churches like this, but as a Christian community, if Paul or Peter or whoever were to write a letter to us, I think this business of showing favoritism and being obsessed with the way we market our faith might come up.

The second chapter of the book of James tells us, specifically, not to take a wealthy person and seat him in a place of honor and leave a poor person in the back. I take this to mean that in church, the rules of the lifeboat don't apply, that church is a refuge, where the kingdom of God is emulated, not mocked.

———

I realize by making these statements, some will think I don't like the church, or I don't like religion. But this isn't the case. If religion helps in our relationship with God, and it does, that's great, but if it is how we check stuff off a to-do list, or if it is the identity we defend in the lifeboat, or if our idea of evangelism is redeeming the image of Christianity, and not displaying the economy of the kingdom on earth, then it is worthless. I don't have any reservations about saying that.

That said, I know there are also some people who will want to lump Christians into a single category as hypocrites and jerks, and certainly I have presented this side of the argument, but I've done so only in warning, as Paul did, as James did, and as Jesus did. But I also have to tell you that some of the most beautiful people I have ever met have been Christians. Walk into most churches and you will find a safe haven, a refuge.

As a guy who grew up something of a a misfit, I can assure you few would have loved me were it not for my local church. When *Jesus* gets inside somebody, the first thing that starts happening is the person starts loving people regardless of their race, their socioeconomic status, or their looks. And, unfortunately, the people whom Jesus gets inside are at churches, along with the people who are marketing the formulas.

But I have been loved by people who know Jesus. And I don't know that there is any greater love than the love from those who have been touched by the Messiah. I do hope you get to meet one of these people some day and feel the kind of love I am talking about. And as for the others, our job isn't to judge them, but to love them. Jesus will judge them enough for all of us. We all are works in progress, we all are learning that the lifeboat mentality is sin, but it takes time. And bitterness is only a manifestation of the game.

Religion is a big, beautiful, ugly thing. I read recently where Augustine said, "The church is a whore and it is my mother." And for reasons I don't understand, Jesus loves the church. And I suppose He loves the church with the same strength of character He displays in His love for me. Sometimes it is difficult to know which is the greater miracle.

CHAPTER FOURTEEN

The Gospel of Jesus

WHY WILLIAM SHAKESPEARE WAS A PROPHET

After attending the writers seminar, the one that taught us to present self-help arguments in three-step formulas, and after I tried to write one myself, having looked through Scripture to find anything like a self-help formula, and after having found nothing, nothing appealing anyway, I started wondering exactly how a person would explain the gospel of Jesus. Let's say you had a friend like Omar who was wondering, and you no longer believed the gospel could be presented accurately using a step-by-step guide with all the beauty of blender instructions, what exactly would you say?

And I supposed what you would have to do would be to tell a bunch of stories. You could explain the basics in propositional speak, but to get to the heart of the thing you would have to tell a bunch of stories. After all, this is what God does in Scripture. And it's real-life stuff, too, as though He interacted with humanity to create allegories inside the actual story, so that the living allegories would point outward, toward what the big story is about. Take the book of Job, for instance. Some would say the book of Job is about pain, that hidden inside the story are secret steps to take when you happen to be dealing with pain. I don't think this is true, exactly. I think the book of Job is a story about *life*, and there aren't any secret steps in it at all.

My friend John MacMurray tells me the first book written in the Bible is the book of Job. Moses wrote Job before he wrote Genesis, most scholars agree, and so the first thing God wanted to communicate to mankind was that life is hard, and there is pain, great pain in life, and yet the answer to this pain, or the cure for this pain, is not given in explanation; rather, God offers to this pain, or this life experience, Himself. Not steps, not an understanding, not a philosophy, but Himself. I take this to mean the first thing God wanted to communicate to humanity was that He was God, He was very large and in control, storing snow in Kansas, stopping waves at a certain point on the beach, causing clouds to carry rain, causing wind to race down imaginary hills of barometric pressure, and that if He could do all this, then He could be trusted, and that, perhaps, this would help us through our lives. And so from the beginning, from the very first story told in Scripture, God presents life, as it is, without escape, with only Himself to cling to. It worked for Job, after all, because even before God healed him and even before God returned his wealth and even while Job was sitting by a fire picking scabs from his wounds and mourning his family, he would respond to the whirlwind God spoke through by saying, *All this is too wonderful for me.*

Another story God tells is of Hosea. This is a story God actually *made* happen by telling Hosea, His prophet, to marry and have children with a whore. It's a terribly painful story, to be honest, thick with love and deception, with the pain and heartache of a man who loves a woman purely and a woman who opens her legs at the drop of a hat. She has issues, to be sure, but Hosea loves her through those issues, sees her beauty, is mesmerized by her beauty and the hope of a love with her. His love is unrelenting, pure as diamonds.

It's real-life stuff, blood and tears, and in it is all the introduction we need to the love of God, identifying ourselves with this prostitute who runs from the only one who really cares about her. In this story, God explains to us the great dynamic that is taking place in the universe, the great story unfolding in the annals of humanity. God never could have said any of this with a formula. God could not have explained this by presenting a few steps, a few principles of spiritual growth. God wanted Hosea to experience this, and He wanted it written down for all of time, because He wanted humanity to know how He feels. And yet Hosea is another book largely ignored because it has nothing to help us achieve the American dream, unless, of course, we use it as instructions for sleeping around.

It strikes me, even as I type this, how distant and far our formulaic methodology is from the artful, narrative sort of methodology used to explain God in Scripture. It makes you wonder whether we can even get to the truth of our theology unless it is presented in the sort of methodology Scripture uses. It makes you wonder if all our time spent making lists would be better spent painting or writing or singing or learning to speak stories. Sometimes I feel as though the church has a kind of pity for Scripture, always having to come behind it and explain everything, put everything into actionable steps, acronyms and hidden secrets, as though the original writers, and for that matter the Holy Spirit who worked in the lives of the original writers, were a bunch of illiterate hillbillies. I don't think they were illiterate hillbillies, and I think the methodology God used to explain His truth is quite superior.

What I mean by this is I feel my life is a story, more than a list; I feel this blood slipping through my veins and these chemicals in my brain telling me I am hungry or lonely, sad or angry, in love or despondent. And I don't feel that a list could ever explain the complexity of all this beauty, all this sun and moon, this smell of coming rain, the beautiful mysteries of women, or the truck-like complexity of men. It seems nearly heresy to explain the gospel of Jesus, this message an infinitely complex God has delivered to an infinitely complex humanity, in bullet points. How amazing is it that Christ would explain that to be His followers we must eat His flesh and drink His blood, and that He is the Bridegroom and we are the bride, and that we will be unified with Him in His death, and that we will live forever with Him in glory.

Do you know where I found what I believe is the most beautiful explanation for the gospel of Jesus ever presented? It's been under our noses for hundreds of years, right there in the most famous scene in all of English literature. You've probably rented the movie, and you studied it in high school. You may even have some of the lines memorized, or you might have played a character in its performance onstage. The greatest art I've seen that explains how beautiful it is to cast our hope for redemption upon Christ is the balcony scene in Romeo and Juliet.

I confess, the first time I saw the play I didn't think much of it; it seemed just the story of two kids who, rather stupidly, killed themselves over a misunderstanding about some poison, but a couple of years ago I got to thinking about the play again and stayed up late a bunch of nights in a row and read it over and over, always coming to the balcony scene and wondering why exactly Shakespeare would word the dialogue the way he did. I think you will find the wording quite peculiar.

At the beginning of the play, Romeo thinks he is in love with a girl named Rosaline, but he sees Juliet at a party and immediately falls in love with her, understanding his previous love for Rosaline as something formulaic and invented, something to make him *feel* he is in love rather than actually *being* in love. Mercutio, in fact, would criticize Romeo's affection for Rosaline, saying "he loves by numbers." Immediately, however, when his eyes fall across Juliet, Romeo feels an instant love only the poets understand. They meet at a party, a party Romeo was not invited to, a party he and his friends have crashed, and he cannot take his eyes from this remarkable woman, a child of the Capulets. It becomes obvious that Juliet has, as Shakespeare would say elsewhere, "taken prisoner the wild motion of Romeo's eye." And when Romeo and his friends leave the party, the young Montague sneaks away from his friends and moves stealthily back toward the Capulet home. His friends chastise him for such erratic behavior, to which Romeo responds, under his breath, "He jests at scars, that never felt a wound."

Romeo then crawls over the wall into the Capulets' courtyard and stands beneath Juliet's balcony, quietly so as to not disrupt the Capulet house because Romeo, a Montague, is despised by the Capulets, as a feud exists between the two families, which, according to the prince of Verona, was "bred of airy words," that is, had come from nothing. And here, in the Capulet courtyard, Romeo speaks the now infamous lines:

> *But, soft! what light through yonder window breaks?*
> *It is the east, and Juliet is the sun!*
> *Arise fair sun and kill the envious moon,*
> *Who is already sick and pale with grief,*
> *That thou her maid art far more fair than she.*

In referring to Juliet as the sun, and comparing her brightness to that of the moon, Romeo is contrasting her beauty against Rosaline's, for whom, earlier in the play, he used lunar imagery.

The scene indicates more than Romeo's preference for Juliet over Rosaline, but also his willingness to consider a lover who would disrupt his life, the obvious enmity between the two families having been established from scene one. Not only this, but in comparing his love for Juliet to his previous feelings for Rosaline, Romeo is comparing this compulsory love he feels for Juliet to that of the formulaic, Petrarchan feelings he experienced for Rosaline.

Petrarch was a fourteenth-century Italian poet who wrote endlessly of his love for a woman named Laura. Petrarch believed love had rules, that one must be careful in the ways of it, guarding emotion and investing, rather, in a sort of mathematical approach to interacting with women. Mercutio, early in the play, compares Romeo to Petrarch, and the comment is intended as an insult. Shakespeare pays homage to Petrarch by having Romeo speak of Rosaline in iambic pentameter, the sort of rigid rhyme employed by Petrarch himself, and switches to free verse when causing Romeo to speak of Juliet. This would indicate Romeo's feelings for Juliet are sincere, while his feelings for Rosaline had been contrived. Later in the play, in fact, Juliet would counsel Romeo to not speak to her in the rigid verse he had used in his less-authentic expressions toward Rosaline, and return to the free verse she had come to associate with his feelings for her.

In this scene, Juliet may be considered the Bard's Christ figure, and Romeo the embodiment of the church, thus presenting Shakespeare's opinion of a Christian conversion experience. I realize it sounds far-fetched, and that I may be reading theology into a play that is simply a love story, but upon closer examination we see Shakespeare borrowing exclusively from the themes of Christ's love for the church, even going so far as to leave his own story, that of Romeo's wanting of Juliet, to enter completely into the unique complexities of Christ's interaction with the church. You will have to remember that at the time of Shakespeare's popularity, everybody had an opinion about salvation. Many scholars believe the enmity between the Montagues and Capulets, for example, represented the tension between Protestants and Catholics. This view holds merit because at the time Shakespeare wrote the play, tension between the Protestants and Catholics had risen to a fever pitch on the streets outside the poet's home. Shakespeare was not writing in twenty-first-century America where religion and state are separated and great caution is taken to keep opinions about the heavens within personal fences; rather, opinions regarding theology burned bright as flags. A brief history lesson might help us understand the poet's intent with the scene in the Capulet courtyard.

William Shakespeare was born not more than a century after the invention of the printing press, perhaps the most important invention of all time, greater in shaping culture than the Internet. The streets of London were alive with new buzz at the time Shakespeare began writing plays. People were learning how to read, and because of this, nothing in history would be the same. The most dramatic changes in the social landscape stemmed from people's access to the Bible. Before the printing press, the universal church had distorted Scripture in an effort to control communities and amass wealth and power. As mentioned in a previous chapter, great cathedrals were being built throughout Europe from the profits of indulgences.

Luther's writings, then, along with those of John Calvin, would begin the Protestant (protesters) Reformation, which had dramatic implications in Shakespeare's London only thirty or so years later.

In England, the Reformation did not gain power until Henry VIII divorced his wife, which earned him an excommunication from the pope. Parliament then reacted to the pope by passing the Act of Supremacy, which made the king head of the church in England. Henry VIII was then succeeded by Edward VI, a ten-year-old boy, whose short six-year reign would allow the Anglican church to grow and begin its persecution of the Catholics. A sickly Edward VI died in 1553 and was replaced by his half sister Mary, who earned the name Bloody Mary by upholding her Catholic roots, turning the tide on Protestants and executing them in large numbers. Mary's successor, Elizabeth, would comply with her half sister's Catholic leanings while Mary was alive, but on her succession would once again restore Protestantism to the throne. In this way, England's throne passed from Protestantism to Catholicism and back to Protestantism in the span of a single decade, each change bringing with it the slaughter of thousands.

Shakespeare was born and worked during the reign of Elizabeth. This set him in an England in which the religious tension had yet to subside. Not unlike the tension that exists today in Northern Ireland, these two groups were at odds, their faith connected to their ideas about God and heaven, their political leanings and their identities. It makes a great deal of sense then that from the struggle of Catholics against Protestants and Protestants against Catholics, Shakespeare may have molded his idea of a tension between the Montagues and Capulets. It is true the story of Romeo and Juliet existed many years before Shakespeare adapted it for the stage, but the poet may have borrowed from the tension on the street to color the tension between the two families. Indeed, with the tension as high as it was at the time, it is doubtful the argument did not color the text.

Reading the balcony scene through the lens of an Elizabethan audience reveals what I think is a powerful double entendre, one that suggests not only a sort of negotiation of love between Juliet and Romeo, but a kind of invitation from Christ to the church, to you and me, walking us, as it were, on the heart path a person would need to traffic in order to know Christ and be saved from his broken nature. Without question, the precepts Juliet presents Romeo may be broken down as identical matches of the theology John Calvin penned not too many years before Shakespeare wrote the play. And it is these principles set in the context of a dramatic love story that truly bring the implications of the gospel of Jesus to life.

THE GOSPEL OF JESUS

Again, Romeo is standing beneath Juliet's balcony, having wished for her to step onto her perch above the courtyard, bright as the sun, putting an end to the moon, when his wish is granted. Juliet slips out the doors of her bedroom, looks out on the evening with a sigh, and leans her gentle frame against the railing. Romeo is silent beneath her beauty when Juliet speaks:

> *O Romeo, Romeo! wherefore art thou Romeo?*
> *Deny thy father, and refuse thy name;*
> *Or, if thou wilt not, be but sworn my love,*
> *And I'll no longer be a Capulet.*

In these lines Juliet is expressing her love for Romeo, but also stating her understanding that the two shall never be one as long as he is called a Montague and she is called a Capulet. In a monologue Juliet would soon deliver, asking, "What's in a name? that which we call a rose by any other name would smell as sweet," the playwright borrows from the trouble of man's nature and the duality of his goodness and his brokenness, one being compatible for a relationship with God, and the other set in enmity, unable to mingle with the pure nature of God. Juliet asks Romeo to doff, or disavow, his name, and if he won't, then swear his love, and she will no longer be a Capulet. This means the two of them will have to meet within some other name, and for allegorical purposes (though questionable whether Shakespeare intended this much), within some other nature. In the context of the story of Romeo and Juliet, this idea makes complete sense. The two want to be together, but their names keep them apart, so Juliet asks Romeo to throw off his name so the two may unite.

It struck me as I read these lines, however, that no less of a proposition would be made by Christ in the Gospel of Luke:

> Now great multitudes went with Him. And He turned and said to them, "If anyone comes to Me and does not hate his father and mother, wife and children, brothers and sisters, yes, and his own life also, he cannot be My disciple." (14:25–26 NKJV)

I used to read this passage and think of Jesus as difficult and strict and, to be honest, I didn't like Him for saying it. But when I saw it in the context of the balcony scene of Romeo and Juliet, the same ideas being expressed in an effort for two people to unite, it became something different, and I confess, I wouldn't want the language to be any less strict. Language less strict might suggest love less pure. True love, love in its highest form, must cost the participants everything. Both parties would have to be willing to give up everything in order to have each other.

In exchange for what Scripture calls repentance, by renouncing our natures, by admitting our own brokenness, we may take all of Christ, identifying ourselves with His righteousness.

We see this beautifully portrayed in the words of Juliet, who, after musing about Romeo's dual nature, delivers the thrust of her invitation:

> *Romeo, doff thy name,*
> *And for that name, which is no part of thee,*
> *Take all myself.*

Should Romeo take Juliet up on her proposition, he will not gain love for love's sake, but rather Juliet herself. This idea is all biblical but the stuff of poets. The playwright understood that Christ's invitation was not an offer of heaven or mansions or money; it was, rather, Himself. In multiple contexts Jesus claims we shall be one with Him even as He and the disciples are one and the Trinity before them are One. Just as, if a wife travels away from her family on business, the family feels her absence in their hearts, so we are to have this kind of oneness with Christ. And just as a sheep knows the voice of its shepherd, so are we to know the voice of Christ, and just as a lost child in a store feels fear and pain in his parent's absence, so we are to feel disoriented in the absence of God, and comfort in our relationship with Jesus. This, I believe, is what the Bible means when it speaks of our oneness: It isn't a technicality, it is an actual relationship.

Romeo hears these words from Juliet and understands the implications of her invitation. He believes that if he denies his name, she shall deliver herself and the two shall become one. And this is where Shakespeare leaves the parallel elements of love story and picks up the pen of Calvin. Romeo, speaking to Juliet, says:

> *I take thee at thy word.*
> *Call me but love, and I'll be new baptiz'd;*
> *Henceforth I never will be Romeo.*

Here Romeo indicates he believes what Juliet is saying is true. This confession of belief is crucial to Shakespeare's understanding of the proper recipient of love. There can be no doubting, no mistrust; one must have complete faith in the other that nothing is being held back. In our spirituality, we see nothing different. No less than two hundred times Scripture speaks of the importance of belief. "I take thee at thy word," Romeo says, meaning he believes Juliet's invitation, that she will do what she says she will do. Anything less than this complete trust from Romeo would not be love, anything less than pure trust would be a kind of careful negotiation. And careful negotiation isn't love. A person must be willing to be dashed on the rocks or made the fool in exchange for a relationship in order for pure love to take place. And in our spirituality, anything less indicates a question of God's character.

These ideas played out in the pages of Scripture would have Christ asking that we "follow" Him, a term that in the Greek would also indicate a clinging to Him or imitation of Him. Christ, in short, asks us to give everything, all our false redemption in the lifeboat, all our false ideas about who God is, all our trust in something other than God to redeem us. In so doing, we die to our broken natures in exchange for His perfect nature, and find a unification with Him that will allow God to see us as one, just as a husband is one with a wife.

And great attention must be given to Romeo's response to Juliet. Romeo does not say yes, that he will change his name; rather, he understands that he has no power to change his nature, and he looks to Juliet and submits all power to her. Romeo says: "Call me but love, and I'll be new baptiz'd."

If Romeo is to be made new, if his name is to be changed, it will not be of his own doing. He understands he has no ability to change his own name, that it will not be by an act of his own will that his nature is made new; rather, it will be on the whim and wish of Juliet. If she calls him love, then he will be called love, both his name and his nature changed, made new.

Indeed, a few lines later Juliet would call to Romeo, and Romeo would remind his muse that his name has been changed, and he will no longer answer to Romeo.

In our spirituality the idea is no less critical. Paul would indicate we have no ability to do good on our own. Now certainly we have the ability to do good things, to do nice things for people and even for God, but Paul spoke of a problem at the very core of our nature, that even our desire to submit to God, a good desire indeed, would have to be stimulated by God Himself. We are in the lifeboat, as it were, Children of Chernobyl. In this way, Romeo, as well as the whore that is the church of God, bends itself before its muse in complete submission, asking only God, who has given Himself, to invite her into this dramatic story of love, passion, and union. The strength is all His, and the gift is all ours.

———

In this beautiful way William Shakespeare weaves the intricate complexities of the love relationship between God and the church into the context of narrative, and in so doing creates a scene that would not be eclipsed by ten million stories told since. When we read the balcony scene of Romeo and Juliet, we understand intrinsically that what is being negotiated is love, and that the poet has explained the mysterious complexities of this negotiation perfectly. Everything is at stake, and everything must be given to achieve the unity of souls.

And yet the poet is not finished. The agreement has been made between Romeo and Juliet, but they are far from unified. In any other story, the credits would roll, but Shakespeare has more to teach us, and the true beauty is yet to come.

Unity in Death

In the pages of Scripture the desire for the afterlife does not involve gaining a kind of euphoria over troubles, exactly, but rather the opportunity to be with God. The euphoria over troubles comes as an afterthought, but it isn't the aim. The writers of the Bible seem to want to go and be with Christ the way the most intimate and passionate lovers, when separated, desire their reunion.

In this way, Christ is our Juliet. What we feel for Him now is but a shadow of what we will feel for Him in His glory. If you can imagine the greatest love of your life, multiplied by millions, speaking affirmation into your soul, you will have in your mind the awareness of Christ and the community of the Trinity. All the self-awareness that occurred to us in God's absence will dissolve as Christ's love tells us who we are. In His presence we will not hate ourselves, second-guess ourselves, or compare ourselves to others; but rather, our lives will be filled with the gratitude of His presence, and we will know for the first time the glory of being human. Just as each member of the Trinity is thankful for the other, just as it was in the Garden between man and his Maker, it will be between you and me, and between us and the Godhead.

As such, there is still great trouble between Romeo and Juliet. While their love has been expressed, a certain poetic agreement has been made: The two cannot be unified because of the enduring strife between their families. They are still, for allegorical purposes, sludging their way through a fallen system. In this way, you and I must be unified with Christ in His death, and only in our actual deaths will we go and be with Him.

Our spirituality would indicate that when man sinned against God, the wages of sin was death because, as has been said, no life can exist outside God, as He is the author and giver of life. Scripture indicates Christ took the sin of the world upon Himself and was crucified on a cross to satisfy God's necessary wrath toward that which is evil. He did this, Scripture says, because He loves us. As we die to ourselves, doff our names, we find He gives Himself to us just as Juliet to Romeo and we become one with Him, so that, like a couple newly married, God looks at us and sees one Being, His Son, united, as it were, with His bride, alive in His purity, just as Romeo was made new by Juliet. Christ's death, again, was not a technicality by which we are covered with grace, but rather a passionate and inconceivable act of kindness and altruism and love stemming from God's desire to be reunited with His creation.

In keeping with the biblical narrative, Shakespeare painfully demands the couple's ultimate unity take place in their deaths. The two have tried at length to be together, but the rage between the families only intensifies as the play carries on toward its tragic end. A trick is planned: Juliet will fake her death, and the two will run off together. But Romeo is fooled by the seemingly dead body of his love, drinks from a poison himself, asking death to be the guide that leads him to his love. Slang during the Elizabethan period refers to sex as "one dying in the other," and Shakespeare has Romeo drink from a round cup, the symbol of a woman, and Juliet thrusting a dagger, a phallic symbol, into her stomach. Two distinct sets of imagery are employed, the first being that of sex, or union, and the second being the Christian imagery of the church being united with Christ in His death.

In Baz Luhrmann's 1996 film *Romeo and Juliet*, starring Leonardo DiCaprio as Romeo and Claire Danes as Juliet, the director pays reverence to Shakespeare's use of Christian imagery and so sets crosses and icons in nearly every frame. And in this final and most meaningful scene of the play, Luhrmann sets the characters in a cathedral complete with neon crosses posted at each pew. Romeo walks the aisle as though he were the bride in a wedding, an aisle lit with candles that lead to Juliet's body, which is set on the altar like a sacrifice. It is here that Romeo takes his life to be with his love, and once awakened from her sleep, Juliet does the same. Their painful struggle is at an end as the two are thought to be united in heaven, where there is a wedding in waiting. The camera then lifts upward from the bodies to reveal Romeo and Juliet's tender limbs gently folded in an embrace, their forms laid amid a thousand burning candles that, as the camera lifts farther, reveal the image of a cross, the two lovers, finally, together in peace, one purifying the other, now enjoying the beauty of their companionship uninterrupted by the enmity that once ripped them apart.

———

The last time I watched this dramatic scene unfold I was preparing a series of lectures on the theological implications of the play, considering all of this in academic terms. And yet as I did this, late in the evening and alone in my room, I was suddenly struck with the power of Paul's words in his letter to the Romans. I confess I was moved to tears at the implications of his statements, set in the context of a love story to explain all love stories. Paul would passionately present to the Romans these beautiful ideas:

> Since we have now been justified by his blood, how much more shall we be saved from God's wrath through him! (5:9 NIV)

For if, when we were God's enemies, we were reconciled to him through the death of his Son, how much more, having been reconciled, shall we be saved through his life! (5:10 NIV)

If we have been united with him like this in his death, we will certainly also be united with him in his resurrection. (6:5 NIV)

And later in his letter:

If we died with Christ, we believe that we will also live with him. (6:8 NIV)

———

I had known in my head that these principles we understand, these beautiful theological ideas, were plot twists in a story of love, a story of God reaching out to mankind, but I don't think it was until I watched that final scene of *Romeo and Juliet*, with Paul's letter to the Romans open on my desk, that our spirituality was in fact a love story for me. This letter was God whispering in my ear that I no longer had to perform in a circus, I no longer had to defend myself in the sinking lifeboat, that God had come to earth, made Himself human, taken the world's sin upon Himself, and was crucified for me, so that His glory could shine through me, and I could be made whole.

And I go back to Eden, in my mind, to imagine what it is going to be like for you and me in heaven. I suppose it will be a new and marvelous paradise, where love will exist in its purest form, where the beauty of diversity will be understood for the first time, where self-hatred will fade into an agreement with God about the splendor of His creation, where physical beauty will no longer be used as a commodity, where you and I will feel free in our sincere love for others, ourselves, and God. And I suppose it will be in heaven that you and I actually understand each other, all the drama of the lifeboat a distant memory, all the arguments we had seeming so inconsequential, and the glory of God before us in all His majesty, shining like sunlight through our souls. This will be a good thing, my friend.

The lifeboat system of redemption seems so ugly in comparison to the love of God. We can trust our fate to a jury of peers in the lifeboat, we can work to accumulate wealth, buy beauty under a surgeon's knife, panic for our identities under the fickle friendship of culture, and still die in separation from the one voice we really needed to hear.

To me, it is more beautiful to trust Christ, deny our fathers and refuse our names, die to ourselves and live again in Him, raised up in the wave of His resurrection, baptized and made new in the purity of His righteousness. I hope you will join me in clinging to Him.

Time, which was God's friend, is now His enemy, and you and I are going to end with it soon. If you will lift a glass of wine with me, I would like to remember Him: Here is to Christ for making us, to Christ for rescuing us, and to Christ, who gives hope for tomorrow.

O true apothecary! Thy drugs are quick.

AFTERWORD

———

Concern may be felt by the reader for my lack of explaining the holiness of Christ and the degree to which His necessary death served as a propitiation for God's wrath on humanity. While I certainly agree these ideas are critical, true, and quite beautiful, my aim was to present an explanation of the gospel in relational language, dealing primarily with the story from which our theology has been deduced. In this way, this effort might be read as an apologetic, leaning on personality and culture more than math and logic, though I don't feel any of these ideas are less than logical.

I did wish, however, to pull our understanding of the gospel of Jesus out of the formulaic, propositional framework from which it has been sunk and return it, at least to some degree, into the world our broken biochemistry has created. That said, some thinkers may contend I believe systematic theology is the enemy, but this is not true. I find it a helpful guide and certainly recommend the study of systematic theology to enhance and explain, but not to replace, the human story. I appreciate your patience and kindness with any resistance I may have expressed in delineating one from the other.

ACKNOWLEDGMENTS

This book is dedicated to my friend John MacMurray, who, for many years, led a college Bible study at Good Shepherd Community Church outside Portland. John is a terrific Bible teacher, and much of the thinking in this book was stimulated during the four years I lived with him and his family. I am certain there are hundreds more former students of John's who also wish to express their appreciation to him for his commitment to truth and meaning and especially to the endearing nature of Jesus. John, I can't thank you and Terri enough for your kindness and willingness to share your love for God's Word and His people. You deserve a better book than this.

I would once again like to thank Kathy Helmers for her faith in this project and her encouragement. I owe a great deal of thanks to Lee Hough for his kindness and diligence in making sure I completed the manuscript. Brian Hampton and Kyle Olund were incredibly patient, and their encouragement and advice shaped and reshaped the book into something readable. The people at Thomas Nelson Publishers are of the greatest quality people I know, to a person, and I am thankful for their friendship. These kind people are: Nelson Books publisher Jonathan Merkh, as well as Kathleen Crow, Carol Martin, Jerry Park, Pamela Clements, Belinda Bass, Paula Major, Ashley Aiken, Danielle Douglas (with the help of Deonne and Rachel), Blythe McIntosh, Brandi Lewis, Gary Davidson, Scott Harvey, Ron Land, Dave Shepherd, Carolyn

Beckham, college intern David Lavender, and veteran acquisitions editor Victor Oliver, who, although I've never met him, has sold copies of *Blue Like Jazz* by the carton out of his trunk.

I am grateful to my friend Tony Kriz, who, during dozens of long conversations, listened carefully, adding, clarifying and criticizing thoughts, helping to mold the ideas into communicable forms.

John Sailhamer's thoughts and teaching were remarkable and stimulated many of these ideas (specifically on truth and meaning and the writings of Moses), and his book *The Pentateuch as Narrative* is a terrific place to start learning about finding meaning in the Bible. Thanks to Daniel Goleman and Richard Dawkins, who got me thinking about personality, community, trends, and *The Selfish Gene*. I also found Portland writer Katherine Dunn's treatment of circus life in *Geek Love* moving, beautiful, dark, and profound; I enjoyed the writings of Martin Luther and John Calvin as well. There are a great many books about *Romeo and Juliet*, but there aren't many critics who are willing to say Shakespeare intended the balcony scene as a metaphor for conversion. I cannot see the text any other way, and I trust that even a casual reader will find more theology than romance in the ideas spoken in the Capulet courtyard. Forgive me, however, if I have failed objectivity. If these ideas are true, however, Shakespeare was a kind of prophet in whose chest beat, perhaps, the poet heart of Luther himself. And if I am wrong, then I still find it beautiful he borrowed from Christ's wanting of His bride to explain Juliet's wanting of Romeo.

I neglected friendships to write this book, and I am thankful for the patient love of the people I consider close: Much love and appreciation to Tony, Penny, Tuck, Laura Long, Leslie Mckellar, and Rick McKinley. And I would like to thank the guys at Testosterhome, who make coming home like finding peace. Those guys are Stacy, Wes, Grant, and Blake. And special thanks to the folks at Imago Dei, whom I love with all my heart. (Rick McKinley's book *Jesus in the Margins* should be out about the same time as this book, so for a good read, check out Rick's thoughts about Jesus.) I want to thank Robin Jones Gunn, Brian McLaren, and Chris Seay for their encouragement and advice about writing and for being such good people.

And a giant, loving, special thank you to Kurt and Donna Nelson, who, together, are the Mark Moskowitz in my life. (See the documentary *Stone Reader* for an explanation.)

This book was written under mood music provided by Patty Griffin, Lou Reed, The Shins, The Smiths, Derek Webb, Robert Keen, Steve Earle, Andrew Peterson, The Indigo Girls, Beck, Sinead O'Connor, David Wilcox, Joseph Arthur, Bebo Norman, Pedro the Lion, Soundgarden, The Trash Can Sinatras, Pat Green, The Rolling "you can't always get what you want" Stones, Nickel Creek, Climber, Damien Rice, The Frames, and The Be Good Tanya's. Thanks for taking us to places words don't know how to go.

Much thanks to Palio coffee, the shops in the Pearl and Powells Books for warm, dry spaces and coffee. And as always, the city of Portland for having the best bus system in the States, and for going its own direction to become one the greatest places in the world in which to live. And a special thank you to all the Imago Starbucks bums, ever blowing air into coffee, ever making community a reality and caffeine jitters a wiring through which we interpret life. *Am I talking too fast?*

I also want to thank you for reading this book. It means a great deal that you would sit and listen, and I am grateful for the e-mails and stories. I do hope you find all the beauty of life wrapped up in the person and message of Christ. God be with you on this journey. We will see you on the other side.

THROUGH PAINTED DESERTS

Light, God, and Beauty on the Open Road

Mom,

Here is the first book, rewritten a bit. I didn't know, when I was living it, that it was about leaving home. I think you always knew. Thanks for letting me go. This will always be yours.

CONTENTS

Author's Note 497

1. Leaving 503
2. Hill Country 519
3. Thin Ice 539
4. Discovering George Winston 553
5. The Gaze of Ra 561
6. Trouble 565
7. Flagstaff 575
8. Floating Bodies at Hoover Dam 583
9. Dancing 591
10. Easter Descent 595
11. Phantom Ranch 609
12. Bright Angel 613
13. Reward 623
14. Miracles 633
15. Vegas 645
16. California 649
17. Milk Shakes and Pie 659
18. Breakfast 667
19. Night Golf 679
20. The Oregon Trail 691
21. Sinatra 699
22. Kindness 709
23. Ranch 719
24. The Woods 727
25. The Cave 739
26. Ranch Life 745
27. Sunrise 751

Acknowledgments 756
About the Author 758
Excerpt from Let Story Guide You 759

AUTHOR'S NOTE

IT IS FALL HERE NOW, MY FAVORITE OF THE FOUR seasons. We get all four here, and they come at us under the doors, in through the windows. One morning you wake and need blankets; you take the fan out of the window to see clouds that mist out by midmorning, only to reveal a naked blue coolness like God yawning.

September is perfect Oregon. The blocks line up like postcards and the rosebuds bloom into themselves like children at bedtime. And in Portland we are proud of our roses; year after year, we are proud of them. When they are done, we sit in the parks and read stories into the air, whispering the gardens to sleep.

I come here, to Palio Coffee, for the big windows. If I sit outside, the sun gets on my computer screen, so I come inside, to this same table, and sit alongside the giant panes of glass. And it is like a movie out there, like a big screen of green, and today there is a man in shepherd's clothes, a hippie, all dirty, with a downed bike in the circle lawn across the street. He is eating bread from the bakery and drinking from a metal camp cup. He is tapping the cup against his leg, sitting like a monk, all striped in fabric. I wonder if he is happy, his blanket strapped to the rack on his bike, his no home, his no job. I wonder if he has left it all because he hated it or because it hated him. It is true some do not do well with conventional life. They think outside things and can't make sense of following a line. They see no walls, only doors from open space to open space, and from open space, supposedly, to the mind of God, or at least this is what we hope for them, and what they hope for themselves.

I remember the sweet sensation of leaving, years ago, some ten now, leaving Texas for who knows where. I could not have known about this beautiful place, the Oregon I have come to love, this city of great people, this smell of coffee and these evergreens reaching up into a mist of sky, these sunsets spilling over the west hills to slide a red glow down the streets of my town.

And I could not have known then that if I had been born here, I would have left here, gone someplace south to deal with horses, to get on some open land where you can see tomorrow's storm brewing over a high desert. I could not have known then that everybody, every person, has to leave, has to change like seasons; they have to or they die. The seasons remind me that I must keep changing, and I want to change because it is God's way. All my life I have been changing. I changed from a baby to a child, from soft toys to play daggers. I changed into a teenager to drive a car, into a worker to spend some money. I will change into a husband to love a woman, into a father to love a child, change houses so we are near water, and again so we are near mountains, and again so we are near friends, keep changing with my wife, getting our love so it dies and gets born again and again, like a garden, fed by four seasons, a cycle of change. Everybody has to change, or they expire. Everybody has to leave, everybody has to leave their home and come back so they can love it again for all new reasons.

I want to keep my soul fertile for the changes, so things keep getting born in me, so things keep dying when it is time for things to die. I want to keep walking away from the person I was a moment ago, because a mind was made to figure things out, not to read the same page recurrently.

Only the good stories have the characters different at the

end than they were at the beginning. And the closest thing I can liken life to is a book, the way it stretches out on paper, page after page, as if to trick the mind into thinking it isn't all happening at once.

Time has pressed you and me into a book, too, this tiny chapter we share together, this vapor of a scene, pulling our seconds into minutes and minutes into hours. Everything we were is no more, and what we will become, will become what was. This is from where story stems, the stuff of its construction lying at our feet like cut strips of philosophy. I sometimes look into the endless heavens, the cosmos of which we can't find the edge, and ask God what it means. Did You really do all of this to dazzle us? Do You really keep it shifting, rolling round the pinions to stave off boredom? God forbid Your glory would be our distraction. And God forbid we would ignore Your glory.

HERE IS SOMETHING I FOUND TO BE TRUE: YOU DON'T start processing death until you turn thirty. I live in visions, for instance, and they are cast out some fifty years, and just now, just last year I realized my visions were cast too far, they were out beyond my life span. It frightened me to think of it, that I passed up an early marriage or children to write these silly books, that I bought the lie that the academic life had to be separate from relational experience, as though God only wanted us to learn cognitive ideas, as if the heart of a man were only created to resonate with movies. No, life cannot be understood flat on a page. It has to be lived; a person has to get out of his head, has to fall in love, has to memorize poems, has to jump off bridges into rivers, has to stand in an empty desert and whisper sonnets under his breath:

> I'll tell you how the sun rose
> A ribbon at a time . . .

It's a living book, this life; it folds out in a million settings, cast with a billion beautiful characters, and it is almost over for you. It doesn't matter how old you are; it is coming to a close quickly, and soon the credits will roll and all your friends will fold out of your funeral and drive back to their homes in cold and still and silence. And they will make a fire and pour some wine and think about how you once were . . . and feel a kind of sickness at the idea you never again will be.

So soon you will be in that part of the book where you are holding the bulk of the pages in your left hand, and only a thin wisp of the story in your right. You will know by the page count, not by the narrative, that the Author is wrapping things up. You begin to mourn its ending, and want to pace yourself slowly toward its closure, knowing the last lines will speak of something beautiful, of the end of something long and earned, and you hope the thing closes out like last breaths, like whispers about how much and who the characters have come to love, and how authentic the sentiments feel when they have earned a hundred pages of qualification.

And so my prayer is that your story will have involved some leaving and some coming home, some summer and some winter, some roses blooming out like children in a play. My hope is your story will be about changing, about getting something beautiful born inside of you, about learning to love a woman or a man, about learning to love a child, about moving yourself around water, around mountains, around friends, about learning to love others more than we love ourselves, about learning oneness as a way of understanding God. We get one story, you and I, and one story alone. God has established the elements, the setting and the climax and the resolution. It would be a crime not to venture out, wouldn't it?

It might be time for you to go. It might be time to change, to shine out.

I want to repeat one word for you:

Leave.

Roll the word around on your tongue for a bit. It is a beautiful word, isn't it? So strong and forceful, the way you have always wanted to be. And you will not be alone. You have never been alone. Don't worry. Everything will still be here when you get back. It is you who will have changed.

1 LEAVING

HOUSTON, TEXAS, AT NIGHT, AS SEEN FROM INTERSTATE 45, is something beautiful. The interstate approaches and collides with the city's center in a tight, second-level loop that hugs skyscrapers three-quarters around downtown before spinning off north toward Dallas and south toward the Gulf coast. It is, as you know, an enormous city, its skyline brilliant with architecture and light. A landlocked lighthouse on the flat surface of south Texas.

Tonight she shines. The towers are lit and the road is ours alone. A bank sign marks the time at 2:30 a.m., alternately flashing the temperature at seventy-three degrees. Houston has an empty feel to it at such an hour. Her size demands traffic and noise. But this is a southern city and people sleep at proper hours, leaving the landscape to changing street signals with nobody to obey their commands. Night travel is best. Mild, thick air pours through the windows like river water, flowing in circles around our heads. Paul and I are quiet, our thoughts muffled by the tin-can rattle of his 1971 Volkswagen camping van. We are traveling north toward Oklahoma and then, perhaps, the Grand Canyon. After that, we have no plans except to arrive in Oregon before we run out of money. We share a sense of excitement and freedom. Not a rebel freedom, rather, a deadline-free sort of peace. There is nowhere we have to be tomorrow. There is no particular road we have committed to take, and I suppose, if one of us could talk the other out of it, the canyon itself could be bypassed for some other point of interest. Tonight we are travelers in the truest sense of the word, a slim notion of a final destination and no schedule to speak of. We are simply moving for motion's sake.

Our plans were shared with friends, but few understood. "Going off to find yourself" was the standard interpretation. I don't think that is really our point. We are shaped by our experiences. Our perception of joy, fear, pain, and beauty are sharpened or dulled by the way we rub against time. My senses have become dull and this trip is an effort to sharpen them.

"Does it snow much in Oregon?" I say to Paul in a voice loud enough to be heard over the wind and the engine.

"Snows a couple feet every winter out in central Oregon. Not a whole lot along the Pacific, though," he says, reaching to adjust the driver's side mirror.

"Do you think there will still be snow on the ground when we get there?"

"I doubt it. Most of the snow melts off in March. We will get there a couple months too late. There might be some snow in the mountains. We will see."

My mind has been swimming in mountain landscapes. Paul lived in Oregon most of his life and he's told stories of the geography. From him, I know the look and feel of Jefferson Park, of the Three Sisters and Crater Lake, all of them stitched together by a Pacific Crest Trail running up the Sierra Nevadas and then the Cascades, from Mexico to Canada. They've got trout the size of sea bass, bars thick with pretty girls, a cliff-bordered ocean, waterfalls, canyons, and just about anything Ernest Hemingway put in a novel. In Oregon, men live in the woods and let their beards grow. I know it happens the way Paul says it happens because he doesn't shift his eyes when he talks and his stories are never long.

Paul and a friend left Oregon several months ago and had been traveling around America in this van. Paul's friend found a girl in New Orleans and decided to stay, to play jazz on the street and try to make a new life in the South. Paul left New

Orleans and made it, on his own, as far as Houston, which is where he ran out of money. He got a job at an oil refinery, walking along the top of tanker cars, checking valves to make sure they were closed securely, climbing the ladders of vertical pipe at the end of the evening to look out over the landscape of smokestacks and yellow light, to breathe the sulfur and salt and humidity as a way of noting its human beauty, but all this was done in a longing for his home, the way a man will hold the woman he has while thinking of the woman he loves. Somehow Paul met my friend Fred, and though he was only in Houston for a few months, we accepted him into our small group of friends. He was mostly quiet, but if you prodded him enough you could get him to talk about life in the Pacific Northwest, about the wilderness winding along river basins, along canyons, about the wildlife timidly footing through forests, still like statues when you came across them, flashing away like lightning when you raised your rifle. He'd talk like this a little and then get to missing it and just as soon shut up, passing the talking to someone else—someone from Houston who only had stories about bars and girls and football scores. His stories got inside me like Neverland. I knew anybody from a place like that could never stay in a place like this.

Houston is no city for a guy like Paul; he doesn't fit. Time moves quickly here; people are in a panic to catch up. Paul exists within time but is hardly aware of how it passes. I check my wrist every ten minutes out of habit, and I don't think he's ever owned a watch. He is a minimalist. Everything he needs is in this van. His gear includes a tool box, a camping stove, a backpack, and about ten Louis L'Amour books. I think he has a pair of jeans, some shorts, and tennis shoes stuffed behind the seat, but nothing more except the clothes he is wearing. He is living proof you can find contentment outside the accumulation of things. The closest I've come to this sort of thinking was pondering the writings of Hank Thoreau. But I went to Walden Pond a year ago, just to see and feel the place, just to walk alone around the water, and they've made a suburb out of it. It hurts to hear the traffic rolling in through the trees. People commute from the land of Thoreau's solitude to Boston, to work at banks, to work at law firms. And I wonder if Walden exists anymore. I am not talking about the real Walden, the one in Boston; I am talking about the earth God meant to speak before we finished His sentence.

PAUL AND I HAVEN'T KNOWN EACH OTHER VERY LONG. Fred brought him up to a beach house that some of the guys and I rent every year in the winter when the phosphorus in the water dies. You can walk along the empty beach in the middle of the night and the waves glow bright green. There are no lights out on Crystal Beach, just scattered houses along the dunes, and out in the pitch black of the Gulf your eye will find an oil rig, and then suddenly from the east, a stream of green, a naturally lit wave will light out west for a hundred yards before folding into its own floating glow. It's the liquid equivalent of the northern lights. You can walk along the wet sand and turn to see your footsteps glow and fade out, the ones in the distance glowing least, the ones at your feet shining out in active chemistry. My friend Kyle discovered the phenomenon a few years ago and so we go out there every year and make fires on the beach and drink beer and every once in a while one of us will get up and walk out toward the waves to ponder the natural wonder.

He was doing pull-ups on a beam under the house when I arrived. *Who's the surfer?* I thought to myself. Paul is Oregon at heart but looks like California. He has wild blond hair and a smile that endears him to women. He's framed tightly with muscle, carrying his midsize stature in efficient, able-bodied strides. A swimmer's arms, not bulky with excess, but efficient, thick, and sun weathered.

There were old friends to catch up with, so we didn't talk the first day. Night came and I slept in a hammock on the porch. I was awakened shortly after sunrise by someone dragging a kayak over the dunes and onto the beach. I watched as Paul lifted the kayak to his shoulder and stumbled fifty yards to the shore. He dropped the boat into the water, pulled the two-sided paddle from the inside, and lowered himself into the opening. He launched out, through the short breaks, and slid along the still side of the Gulf for a few minutes, getting a feel for the kayak; then he turned away and paddled into the ocean till I lost him in the horizon. A half hour or so passed and he didn't return. Concerned, I rolled out of my hammock and stood against the railing. Still no sign of him. I kept mistaking waves for him, before finally finding his paddling motion, the oar coming out of the water like a pump, shoving back in on one side, then the other.

That evening, around the fire, Paul told us about his morning ride. He said he had found a school of dolphins and ridden above them as they crisscrossed beneath the kayak, playing with him, surfacing less than ten feet from the boat, and then diving into the deep. "It was as if they wanted to race," he said. "They were gliding beside me the way a dog runs beside a moving car."

These sorts of exploits earned our admiration, and once assured he was not interested in our girlfriends, we included him on road trips. Paul was welcome company, and his van came in handy. We made weekend runs to New Braunfels and central Texas, only stopping to pee off bridges, always holding it in through the pain and torture until finally we would hit a river or an overpass and we would fold out and stand at attention along the railing, holding our heads up toward the sky and breathing sighs of relief.

Soon we began talking about an extended trip, one that would have us living in the van for months, meeting new people and discovering regions of the country we had never seen. We plotted hypothetical routes up the East Coast or north to the Great Lakes. We bought a map and traced back roads connecting Civil War battle sites. We considered the Bible Belt and the Florida Keys. We pictured ourselves in New York and actually made a call to inquire about Yankee tickets. Paul and I began to consider the trip seriously. We spent days on the Internet and at the library flipping through glossy pages of mountains and rivers and cities at night. When our dreams gave way to plans, our other friends faded back into thoughts of responsibility and comfort. They became apprehensive; it would mean leaving their jobs or taking a semester off from school. Soon, Paul and I were the only ones willing to go.

THERE WERE, IN OUR GOOD-BYES, SENTIMENTS OF permanence. Some good-byes were more substantial than others. Kristin's last embrace felt difficult. Our relationship had come to an end because of this trip. I could not ask her to accept a halfhearted promise of returning soon, so a few days before we left, I called it off.

We parted with dignity. In our last hours she had asked, again, my reasons for leaving. I told her of the need to travel, to gain memories, and to be, for a while, completely free. She could not understand but accepted my explanation with understanding and an assurance there was something better for her just as there was for me.

Our time together ended too soon. We were to be at a friend's house where our close-knit group had gathered to say good-bye. Paul's van was already there when Kris and I arrived. We could hear people talking inside, so we walked in without knocking. The room was filled with familiar faces. Paul was on the couch with Bob, Jim, and Kyle. He was vaguely answering a question about our itinerary. Tia, Heather, and Kurt were standing in the kitchen. Jeremy, who was sitting on the stairs, playing his guitar, was the first to notice us.

"You know, I never took you as the hippie type," Jeremy said.

"Never took myself as the hippie type," I said. He took his hand off his guitar and reached out for mine. Gripping my hand tightly and matching my eye, he said, "I'm going to miss you."

"I will miss you too," I replied.

Within seconds we were surrounded, and Kristin slid off into the kitchen to avoid the reality of the moment. There were sincere good-byes; tones of loss were in our voices. It felt good to be in the spotlight, I have to admit. We were vagabonds, drifters, rebels setting out to see America. There were stories and laughter and promises to write. Fred gave us silver crosses on leather straps, and Dan gave us wool blankets he took from his Coast Guard barrack. I sensed an innocent envy from the guys. We wished they could join us, and they wished likewise, but school and work owned their youth. Trips like ours are greener grass left unknown for fear of believing trite sayings, sayings that are sometimes true. But theirs is an existence under the weight and awareness of time, a place we are slowly escaping, a world growing fainter by the hour and the mile. Our letters will arrive like messages in bottles cast from the luminary of distant shores.

EACH MILE DRIVEN LESSENS THE WEIGHT IN MY CHEST. Our friends are back in their homes, long asleep. And we are fading from the familiar into the unknown. The glass towers have given way to suburbs and darkly lit shopping malls. We are in that part of Houston where the sons of the sons of cowboys live in master-planned communities and play golf on weekends. They married their high-school sweethearts and exchanged horses for Volvos, half of them Southern Baptists who aspire to be politicians.

The van moves slowly. I am able to focus on a reflector mounted to the concrete barrier separating the north from the southbound lanes. As we approach, I turn my head to watch its white brightness dim as we pass.

"At the rate we're going, we may not reach the Northwest till next winter," I observe.

Paul leans his weight into the gas pedal. "At this rate we may not even get out of Houston till winter."

Paul is more comfortable with the slow progress than I am. We are cruising at a sluggish fifty miles per hour, and when ascending an overpass, the van chugs and loses a few notches on the speedometer. From the passenger's seat, I can see into the console, where the miles are clocking at a snail's pace.

Paul has nicknamed his van "the road commode," and it's a fitting name. The box-shaped van barely passes state standards. Throwbacks from the sixties, these vans are mobile intimations of the Woodstock era. Volvo-encased couples pass us on the street, look into each other's eyes, and remember when. I understand why this is the hippie "vehicle of choice." The van can comfortably sleep four (five if you lay a board across the two front seats). Paul has reconstructed the sink cabinet with wood scraps. It sits directly behind the driver's seat. Beyond the sink, parallel with the back window, there is a bed folded in a bench. Another bed can be created by turning a crank that lifts a tentlike contraption on the roof. There are two boxes of books on the floor between the sink and the bench, and another box of groceries and utensils in the open space beneath the sink. Several blankets are folded and sitting on the bench, and both of our backpacks lean against the side seats where a person can easily get through to the back. The interior is a black, waxlike plastic and rubber. They built this van when plastic was a new material so it's more rigid than the stuff they make now. A working stereo hangs out of a hole in the dash, and there are a couple knobs that work vent directors within the console. The gearshift is long and comes out of the floor. Volkswagen vans have rear engines, so we are sitting at the absolute front of the van. A glimpse over the dash allows me to see the headlights and the front bumper with the road sliding beneath.

STRETCHED BEFORE US IS AN ENDLESS SYSTEM OF interstates, highways, and back roads, a trail system of sorts, connecting city to city and state to state, Home Depot to Starbucks. Every intersection passed is an artery leading to workplaces, schools, and homes. Small towns dot the interstate for more than fifty miles north of Houston. Each city its own world; high school football games, church picnics, and Boy Scout meetings keep lives moving in a comfortable rhythm. Tonight they are but clusters of streetlights strung from neighborhood to neighborhood. Each neighborhood with its homes, each home with its family, and each quiet soul sleeping one thin wall from another. Charles Dickens tells us every heart is a profound mystery to the heart beating nearest it, and I am starting to understand him. Watching the dark towns pass gives them a new significance. During the day the roads are clustered with cars at stoplights, but tonight the thick, dark lines simply separate one neighborhood from another, one socioeconomic group from the one it once was. And it is odd for me to consider the thousands of sleeping people, quiet in their homes, their clocks ticking on the walls, the dogs breathing at the feet of their masters' beds, and to realize there are six billion people living in six billion settings. These homes house families we don't know. So many sleeping people, all of them spirit, bound by flesh, held up by bone and trapped in time.

Rarely do I question the mystery of it all. We are atoms connected to create big, awkward, intelligent animals, animals complex in construction, equipped with minds, hearts, and the like. Spinning secretly around us is an intricate system of interconnected physical laws, completely dependent upon one another for effectiveness. And we are in the middle of it; actors on Shakespeare's stage, madmen in Nietzsche's streets, accidents in Sagan's universe, children in God's creation.

And I suppose part of my wanting to leave Houston is to attempt an understanding of this mystery. My life, this gift I have been given, has been wasted, thus far, attempting to answer meaningless questions. Recently I have come to believe there are more important questions than *how* questions: *How do I get money, how do I get laid, how do I become happy, how do I have fun?* On one of our trips to central Texas, I stood at the top of a desert hill and looked up into the endlessness of the heavens, deep into the inky blackness of the cosmos, those billion stars seeming to fall through the void from nowhere to nowhere. I stood there for twenty minutes, and as it had a few times that year, my mind fell across the question *why?*

The question terrified me at first. I had only recently begun questioning my faith in God, a kind of commercial, American version of spirituality. I had questions because of the silliness of its presuppositions. The rising question of *why* had been manifesting for some time, and had previously only been answered by Western Christianity's propositions of behavior modification. *What is beauty?* I would ask. *Here are the five keys to a successful marriage,* I would be given as an answer. It was as if nobody was listening to the question being groaned by all of creation, groaned through the pinings of our sexual tensions, our broken biochemistry, the blending of light and smog to make our glorious sunsets. I began to believe the Christian faith was a religious system invented within the human story rather than a series of true ideas that explained the story. Christianity was a pawn for politicians, a moral system to control our broken natures. The religion did seem to stem from something beautiful, for sure, but it had been dumbed down and Westernized. If it *was* a religious system that explained the human story, its adherents had lost the grandness of its explanation in exchange for its validation of their *how* lifestyles, to such a degree that the *why* questions seemed to be drowning in the drool of Pavlov's dogs. And it wasn't just the church that was drowning; it was all of humanity or, at least, all of the West. Our skyscrapers and sports teams, our malls and our master-planned neighborhoods, our idiot politics, our sultry media promising ecstasy with every use of a specific dishwashing detergent. What does all of this mean? Are we animals nesting? Are we rats in one giant cage, none of us able to think outside our instincts? And does my faith live within these instincts, always getting me to my happiness, or is it larger, explaining the *why* of life, the *how* a shallow afterthought?

It wasn't just my faith that was being shaken. I began to wonder what personal ideas I believed that weren't true. I believed I was not athletic enough; too stupid, I believed I had to go to college; I believed the Astros were a more important team than the Mets; I believed jeans that cost fifty dollars were better than jeans that cost thirty; I believed living in a certain part of town made you more important than living in another. I looked up at the cosmos and it had no scientific proof that any of this was true. The cosmos wasn't telling me I was stupid; it wasn't telling me one pair of jeans was better than another. The cosmos was just spinning around up there, as if to create beauty for beauty's sake, paying no attention to the frivolity of mankind. And I liked the cosmos. I liked the cosmos very much. It seemed that it understood something, perhaps, humanity did not understand.

And so in exchanging the *how* questions for the *why* questions I began to probe the validity of presuppositions. There wasn't a science stepping up to insist authority. All of these ideas seemed subjective, and once they seemed subjective, they began to feel subjective. Far from depressing, this led to something quite beautiful. Girls who I once ignored as not pretty enough became, to me, quite lovely, their gentle way and deep humility and tenderness and femininity, their true images no longer being compared to the lies of commercial propaganda. If I couldn't grasp an idea, I didn't fault myself as dense; the cosmos didn't seem to be suggesting there was any more value to a dumb person than an intellectual. And jeans got a lot cheaper too.

I confess I wanted to believe life was bigger, larger than my presuppositions. Out there under the cosmos, out in the desert of Texas, beneath those billion stars and the umbrella of pitch-black eons of nothingness, on top of that hill, I started wondering if life was something different than I thought it was, if there was some kind of raging beauty a person could find, that he could get caught up in the *why* of life. And I needed to believe beauty meant something, and I needed God to step off His self-help soapbox and be willing to say something eternally significant and intelligent and meaningful, more meaningful than the parroted lines from detergent commercials. I needed God to be larger than our free-market economy, larger than our two-for-one coupons, larger than our religious ideas.

"YOU FEELING TIRED YET, PAUL?" HE IS LOOKING groggy at the wheel.

"I've been tired for a while," he says.

"Why don't you pull over the next time you have the chance? I've got to use the restroom and we can switch."

Twenty miles pass and we see a rest area sign. Paul slows the van and coasts down the entrance past some trees and into the parking lot. A dozen or more tractor trailers are parked in long spaces. We pass them and pull into a spot near the restrooms. Paul turns off the engine, and we are immediately enveloped in the whistle and hum of a million crickets. Texas silence. I arch and stretch my back. Stepping out of the van, we are slow and road-travel weary as we move toward the restroom.

"I don't think I remember how to use my legs," Paul says, walking in an exaggerated wobbly motion.

"I'm pretty sure you just put one foot in front of the other, but it definitely doesn't feel right," I joke.

The temperature has dropped and a layer of moisture soaks the ground. Brainless june bugs make loud, fast dives at a light on the wall of the rest area. One broken-winged bug struggles on the sidewalk. I squash him under my boot and say softly, as if to myself, "All your questions are now answered."

Paul swings the heavy bathroom door open, and we are mugged by a foul stench.

"People really should eat better," he says.

We both hold our breath but can feel in the warmth of the room, in the moisture on the floor, the foul scent that surrounds us and seems to brush against our pant legs.

I beat Paul back to the outside world and gasp for air like a diver finding the surface of the ocean. Making my way across the lawn, I stretch out on a picnic table to flatten my back. The stars in this part of the country are distant and faded. They are grouped together in patches and encompassed in a hazy, humid-gray darkness. There are a few dark patches more milky than others that I recognize as high clouds, and they move slowly, engulfing twinkling stars, one at a time.

The road from Houston to Dallas cuts through the heart of the big thicket. We are encaged in a fence of tall pines. A blanket of pine needles and scattered cones lies across the lawn. Behind us, an island of trees is surrounded on four sides by the highway, the rest area, and its entrance and exit. Before us, across the parking lot, a dense forest, dark with shadows, extends perhaps as far as Nacogdoches. Save the choir of crickets, the air is silent and still, the truckers are asleep in their trucks, and the rest area is quiet and peaceful.

"Should we sleep here?" Paul asks.

We've not driven more than four hours, and we did that slowly. We've not made enough progress to stop, regardless of the time. I tell Paul I can probably make it through Dallas, and perhaps as far as Oklahoma. "Why don't you fold out the bed and sleep while I drive?" I suggest.

"Sounds good," Paul says, stretching his back and walking aimlessly around the picnic table. His jeans are faded and torn on one knee. They look like they've been through a cement mixer. I notice that one of the rips on the inside of his pant leg is patched with a red patterned cloth. "Is that a bandanna? You patched your jeans with a bandanna?"

He gives me a defensive look. "These are my favorite jeans."

"Did you do that yourself?" I ask.

"Yeah, so what?"

"Nothing, just wondering, that's all." Paul comes back to the table and sits down. There is a short period of silence, then I speak up. "Paul."

"Yeah."

"I was wondering. It's gonna get a little cold on the road, and I was hoping you could sew me a quilt or something, just maybe a scarf. Do you knit?"

Paul ignores me. I'm looking out into the sky, trying to find some stars. "It's going to get pretty cold out there, and I myself can't sew a stitch."

"Seems like you've got enough hot air," he says to me, walking over to the table, where he pushes me off so he can sit down. I fold down the bench of the table and into the wet grass. The ground is cold, but it is a refreshing change from the fixed-position seats of the van. Paul pulls a pipe out of his pocket and packs the tobacco with his thumb. He pulls out a lighter he told me his father gave him, some army issue contraption that was passed down from his grandfather. As he lights the pipe, the first plumes burn off white as cotton, and the smell of flowers and almonds drifts out across the lawn, back toward the van.

The highway has the ear of an ocean, trucks in distant hum roll close until their roaring engines push through our stretch of the highway, then fade off toward Dallas. A pair of head-lights sweep like searchlights through the trees as a semi grinds slowly into the rest area and his brakes squeal and hiss as he maneuvers his truck into a space on the far side of the rest area.

He turns off his lights and the place darkens again.

"I suppose we should get moving," I say, still lying in the grass.

"I'm about to fall asleep," Paul tells me. "Can you drive?"

"I should be fine," I say, standing up and wiping the blades of grass off my back.

Paul opens the side door and folds out the bed. He lays himself on top of the mattress and closes the door behind him with his foot. I hear his boots drop in the space between the front seats as I climb through the driver's side door. I sit for a second and think about where we are going. To Dallas, then to Oklahoma, then to Arizona, then who knows. Whatever is between Arizona and Oregon.

The clutch pedal offers little resistance. I pin it against the floor with the weight of my foot alone. With the shifter in neutral, I try to start the van. It turns several times before I let off the ignition. No start. I pump the gas and try it again. Still no start. I once had an old Datsun that gave me the same trouble. The carburetor would flood every other time I went to start it. Remembering a trick I used on the Datsun, I hold the van's gas pedal to the floor for a few seconds to drain the carburetor and then pump it once. Turning the key, I hear the engine fire immediately. With the shifter in neutral, I move it over and back. The clutch grinds as it finds reverse and the engine whistles and ticks as I back out of the parking space. I enter the on-ramp, slowly, and even as I step the pedal to the floor, there is no surge of power. The van feels gutless and old. It is creating a hisslike whistle and there is a steady, quick tempo to the valves as they click. We enter the highway at a turtle's pace, like a semi pulling a full load. There is a large-winged, yellow-blooded insect stuck in the driver's side wiper.

One wing shakes in the wind and the other is mostly steady as it is fastened to the wiper itself. I hadn't noticed it from the other seat.

The interstate is laid across slight, long hills. A lone truck's red taillights glow in the distance, disappearing and reappearing as we rise and descend. My headlights cast a ghostlike glow on the blurry road as white striped lines approach from the distance, slow at the outstretch of my headlights, then quickening as they near until they fire like lasers at my left wheel. Stately pines, keeping a careful, untrusting distance, slide by on the left and right. I half roll up my window as the air is coming in cool.

There is a solace in night travel that is absent in daylight. Daylight is broad and exposing; gas stations, factories, and forests are all brought to life under the sun. Night covers them. It is as though a cloth has been draped over the cares of the day, pouring them into our memories for meditation and reflection. It occurs to me, as it sometimes does, that this day is over and will never be lived again, that we are only the sum of days, and when those are spent, we will not come back to this place, to this time, to these people and these colors, and I wonder whether to be sad about this or to be happy, to trust that these hours are meant for some kind of enjoyment, as a kind of blessing. And it feels, tonight, as if there is much to think about, there is much we have been given and much we have left behind. The smell of freedom is as brisk as the air through the windows. And there is a feeling that time itself has been curtained by darkness.

2 HILL COUNTRY

THE SUN IS SHINING THROUGH THE WINDOWS IN THE back of the van, and I slide deep into my sleeping bag. Warm in my cocoon, I position the pillow above to block the light. Car doors slam in the distance, and I hear the sound of children laughing. Sleepily, I wonder where I am. Fresh, but fading in my mind, is a dream that had me on a horse being chased by men with guns. All of it was so real . . . the safety of the here and now comes back slowly.

"Don." A muffled voice speaks softly.

I lie silent . . .

"Don . . . hey, bud, it's nine o'clock in the morning."

I am not sure whether I am imagining the voice or the one speaking.

"Don, you awake?"

Like a turtle from its shell, I take my head out of the bag and open my eyes to the brightness of late morning. I close them again at the flood of washed-out colors and light.

"Yeah, I'm up." I cover my eyes with the pillow. Paul is sitting with his head turned, pressed against the ceiling. He is pulling a boot over his foot.

"What time is it?" My voice is smothered by the pillow, my stench breath absorbed by the cotton.

"It's nine o'clock. How long did you drive last night?" Paul asks.

"We're close to Dallas," I respond. "I didn't make it to Dallas, but we're close, I think."

I slide back into my bag and mumble empty words at the bright morning sun. Last night I had caught myself closing my eyes for seconds at a time, so I pulled over.

"I'm gonna get us moving again," Paul says. "Do you want to sleep some more?"

"I'm up," I respond, rolling over and burying my face in the pillow.

Paul maneuvers out of the bed and between the two front seats. "I'll be right back; I'm gonna use the restroom." The van door opens and closes and the space around me has a sudden quietness to it. Pulling my head out of the bag, I see Paul walking down the sidewalk toward the restrooms. Outside the back window, I notice the headlights of an RV. They are high, broad apart, and tainted brown with road dust. It is parked so close that, were it not for the glass, I could reach out and touch it with my foot. The small rest area looks less significant than it did last night. What I thought was a thicket of trees is only a weak scattering of saplings mixed with shrubs. It is more of a roadside pullout than a rest area. There are restrooms and picnic tables. A trash can is mounted at its top to two rusty poles with a large, lazily placed trash bag hanging off its rim. I change my position to lie on my side, stretching my back. Still in the sleeping bag to my neck, light illumines floating, rolling, falling particles of angel-bright dust meandering ever so lazily down morning beams, filtered through a dirty window. Cars pass in quick, colorful blurs. Yawning, the van air comes in stale.

Outside the window, somewhere behind me, there are children laughing. I catch their small frames in the corner of my eye. Turning over, I find two red-haired kids staring at me through the window. Surprised by my sudden turn, they step back and release a sudden spurt of laughter, covering their mouths and pulling close to each other in one motion. There are a boy and a girl. They look like brother and sister. My reflection in the window is unshaved and disheveled—my thick hair standing in the front like a wave frozen in the ocean. As I allow my eyes to fall back to the children, they release another giggle. The girl, in an act of bravery, steps forward and knocks on the window. The boy pulls her back by the sleeve of her sweater. I play the part of the hippie and hold up two fingers to make a peace sign. Another spurt of laughter erupts and they become red-faced, not looking for long, but taking short, split-second glances, followed by a gasp and a laugh and pulling close to each other. I can't help but smile. Suddenly two women walk by and the children attach themselves, disappearing behind the RV.

WE ARE ONE DAY OUT AND HOME SEEMS AN OCEAN away. My watch ticks inside my boot. I don't need it. I'm not late for anything. There is no disgruntled friend waiting for me at a coffee shop or office. The people I used to be surrounded by are getting along without me. I am in a van, south of Dallas, heading I don't know where, and I have to tell you, it feels pretty good. I wonder, though, if the good feeling will last. I do this with good things; I think joy into its coffin; I analyze too much. I don't want to think about life anymore; I just want to live life.

Sometimes I admire people who don't ask *why* questions, who only want to know the *how* of life: How do I get paid, how do I get a wife, how do I make myself happy, whatever. The *why* path isn't so rewarding, if you think about it: Why are we here, why do we feel what we feel, desire what we desire, need what we need, hate what we hate? I saw this Calvin and Hobbes cartoon once that had Calvin's teacher asking the class to turn in their homework. Calvin raised his hand and asked why we exist. The teacher told Calvin not to change the subject but to turn in his homework, and what difference does it make anyway? Calvin leaned back in his chair and mumbled to himself that the answer to the question determined whether or not turning in his homework was important in the first place. I think that is what I am talking about here, about needing the answer to the former question before the latter becomes important, about *why* questions determining whether *how* questions are important. And that is what I mean by admiring people who don't think about the *why* questions, because they can just get a job, a big house, a trophy wife, and do whatever they want and never ask if it is connected to anything, whether their *how* is validated by their *why*.

Paul opens the door just as I am thinking this through. "You up, Don?"

"Yeah, I'm up."

Climbing into the seat and pulling it forward with a shift of his weight, he turns the key and the engine offers several slow revolutions before bellowing out a loud, unsteady start. It runs only for a second and stalls. I reach for my boots, throw them to the space between the seats, and then follow, climbing out of the bed to the passenger's seat. Meanwhile, Paul is pumping the gas and fiddling with the key. I'm struggling with my feet and my boots and the small space I have to work with.

Just as I begin to tell Paul about the trick with draining the carburetor, the van gives a sudden start. Paul lays into the pedal and the engine screams uncomfortably and cold at 4000 RPMs. He holds it there for a moment, then releases the pedal and pumps it again. The cold, sleeping metal rubs against itself and wakes in a grumpy, old dog growl. Normally you wouldn't rev an engine that has been sitting all night, but with an old wreck like this, there is no other way to wake it. You've got to put some gas in the carburetor and light the plugs.

"How are we on gas?" I ask.

Paul looks at the console. "We've got a quarter of a tank. We should stop soon."

"Coffee would be nice too."

Paul nods in agreement and backs the van up slowly, no more than a few inches, and then pulls forward, tugging the steering wheel with both arms, hand over hand, easing us only a small space from the bumper on the car in front of us.

LIGHT REFLECTS IN SHARP POINTS OFF WINDSHIELDS in motion. Stripes of gray asphalt, two lanes in each direction, are banked and separated by grass and trees. Weeping willows hang depressed limbs low, sweeping the ground and rolling slowly around themselves in a light breeze as behind them, shapeless clouds bring the bright sky close and cast an eye-squinting reflection off a sign that marks Dallas at forty-seven miles.

From the south, there is no industry to indicate a great city is near. Soon we will crest a hill and beneath us will rest a modern skyline complete with a towering cluster of buildings, factories, and freeways in a grand display of the New South. Dallas is the Seattle of Texas. It is what Chicago used to be. But no single man built the coming town. Dallas blew in on the wings of a Gulf coast hurricane and rained glass and steel onto a field of bluebonnets. It's an odd town, though. A big, Republican, evangelical city where you can't drink, girls wear black dresses for dates on Wednesday, and the goal is to join the local country club like your daddy and his daddy before him. When you build a city near no mountains and no ocean, you get materialism and traditional religion. People have too much time and lack inspiration.

We crest a hill and there she stands, just as I recalled, puffed up and proud of herself, all bustling with activity and shining in the late morning sun. Cars line the distant freeways thick and slow, bumper to bumper, moving together as if they were connected like an endless train. The highway rolls straight toward city center, through suburbs, past parks and soccer fields and strip mall after strip mall after strip mall. If there is one thing they have in Texas, it is land. There is no need to build things tall and close together; everybody gets an acre; you get an acre to live on, an acre to work on, an acre to park your car in, and an acre in case you need an extra acre. Driving to work or the store may take you an hour because nothing is close together; no space is conserved because, save the cosmos itself, there is nothing quite as big as the Lone Star State.

There is but one Texas, and for Texans there is need for nothing more. A country within a country, these people believe they have found the promised land. Businessmen wear thousand-dollar suits with ten-thousand-dollar Stetsons. They drive king-cab trucks to their office jobs while their wives drive SUVs filled with kids in transit to and from school, band practice and football practice and cheerleader practice, and so on. And they have these little white stickers on the backs of their cars that read, "Michael . . . Plano Football" or "Michelle, Redmond Cheerleader" advertising their child's achievement like a political statement, teaching their kids that what really matters, what Daddy really loves, is what you do. Give me something I can brag about to complete strangers stuck in traffic. Brilliant. I will have to send my mother a sticker that says "Vagabond" or "Late Sleeper." I turn on the radio to find a station with a deejay ranting about how we need to stop the Mexicans from crossing the border, his cohost humming "The Battle Hymn of the Republic" in the background. It reminds me of those history lessons in which we learned the great honor the men at the Alamo displayed as they stopped the nation of Mexico from taking back its land. I turn the knob even farther to find somebody playing a Robert Earl Keen record. And I remember, if there is one thing that all this empty pride produces, the crop that all this land harvests, it is good music. I don't think there is any better music than the music that comes out of Texas. Robert Keen, the guy on the radio, used to room with Lyle Lovett back at Texas A&M, and he and Lovett used to sit on the porch of their house in their underwear, right when the Lutheran church across the street let out, and they would sing as the women would walk to their cars, looking down at the asphalt, and the men would sneer over at the ugly concert, all the while blocking their children's eyes. I let the station stay, and Paul comforts himself in his seat, reaches over, and turns the volume up. Robert Earl Keen Jr.'s voice comes soft and thoughtful over his guitar in "Road to No Return":

> But each new morning sunrise
> Is just as good as gold
> And all the hope inside you
> Will keep you from the cold
> Bare your soul and let your spirit burn
> Out along the road to no return

As the city passes, we fade from metropolitan landscape to farmland, bound slow but sure for Oklahoma. I am glad to be done with the city. I like the slow pace of agriculture, where you ask the crops to come, and they come when they come, not when you ask them, so slow you can't see them for months. They unfold under an inch of soil like children in wombs, keeping their own time. No wishful thinking can do a thing to speed them up.

The air is cooler today than yesterday. These clouds came to us from the north, and soon they will pass and leave a deep-blue sky that will blanket the state with, quite possibly, the last cold front of the season. The temperature tints the air with cleanness. And all of it reminds me that I am alive, that I am having some kind of experience, some kind of thing is happening to me the way it is happening to the crops, how for months they come into themselves under the soil, made from the elements in the soil, how from out of dirt gets built a little bud of corn, a little human in a womb, without explanation, without an obvious reason or purpose, just stuff getting born, just stuff dying and going back to dirt, just rolling around the cosmos like foul weather. It strikes me that I am like this and Paul is like this, and my family and my friends, we are all just getting born, just growing up, just dying off.

I wonder what it must feel like, for those without a faith system, to wake up one morning and suddenly ask *why* questions, the way I asked them on that hill in west Texas. I would think it would be difficult to explain pain and suffering, to explain beauty and meaning and purpose with only subjectivity as framework. When I think of this, I think of that Douglas Coupland book with all the nursery rhyme characters who are lost, looking for something good that was supposed to happen but never happens because the plastic surgery didn't work or the drugs started to own them or the depression that is always, always waiting just outside the door found a crack it could slip through to whisper hard and unwanted truths into the ears of the characters whose stories were supposed to come true, were supposed to end with a *happily ever after*. And I wonder, quite honestly, if I will end up like this, if I will discover that my Christian faith, my American faith, was a fraud, and that there was nothing behind it, that it wasn't even pointing me toward something real and authentic, and I, too, will join the ranks of the dispossessed, staring up into the cosmos asking why, only to have the cosmos shrug its broad black shoulders as if to return the question.

I would imagine having the capacity to ask *why* questions but not having any answers would just make life feel something like rehab.

It's interesting how you sometimes have to leave home before you can ask difficult questions, how the questions never come up in the room you grew up in, in the town in which you were born. It's funny how you can't ask difficult questions in a familiar place, how you have to stand back a few feet and see things in a new way before you realize nothing that is happening to you is normal.

The trouble with you and me is we are used to what is happening to us. We grew into our lives like a kernel beneath the earth, never able to process the enigma of our composition.

Think about this for a moment: if you weren't a baby and you came to earth as a human with a fully developed brain and had the full weight of the molecular experience occur to you at once, you would hardly have the capacity to respond in any cognitive way to your experience. But because we were born as babies and had to be taught to speak and to pee in a toilet, we think all of this is normal. Well, it isn't normal. Nothing is normal. It is all rather odd, isn't it, our eyes in our heads, our hands with five fingers, the capacity to understand beauty, to feel love, to feel pain.

If I do lose faith, that is if I do let go of my metaphysical explanations for the human experience, it will not be at the hands of science. I went to a Stephen Hawking lecture not long ago and wondered about why he thought we get born and why we die and what it means, but I left with nothing, save a brief mention of aliens as a possible solution to the question of origin. And I don't mean anything against Stephen Hawking, because I know he has an amazing brain and I know he has explained a lot of the physics of our universe, but I went wondering about something scientific that might counter mysterious metaphysical explanations, and I left with aliens.

Hawking can only move a finger. The rest of his body is limp. He has a computer they built at USC and he uses his finger to feed words into sentences, and under his wheelchair is a speaker and when he presses a button, the sentence he made on his screen is spoken through the speaker. We crowded into a room just before he rolled on stage, turned the wheelchair toward the audience, and sat in stillness and silence like a slight sack of rice set low in a chair overflowing with wires. The room fell to a hush as the answering-machine voice of his computer offered a welcome and a greeting and then a long pause, and then one sentence and a pause, and another and a pause, and then another, each sentence revealing some bit of new knowledge about black holes and string theory and time travel and, well, aliens. And I confess I was taken aback. I had previously considered two theories about the universe, the first a rather archaic idea I had picked up in church as a kid regarding God speaking the cosmos into being, and the other a series of accidents that stemmed from nothing and meant nothing and were adding up to nothing. While I subscribed to the breath of God idea, the idea of accidental propulsion was beginning to weigh heavy on my mind, both as an explanation for our existence and as a motive for philosophical suicide, a faulty rotted *why* holding up the meaningless *how*. And to put a point on it, here was the greatest physicist of our age, a man who could recite more than seventy-five pages of theory to his assistant from memory. A man who discovered and explained much of the physical behavior of matter at the openings of black holes, a man on par with Einstein himself, explaining that one possibility for the creation of our universe might be a cosmic seed planted billions of years ago, set in motion by an advanced species of aliens.

It turns out the droplet of our knowledge is a bit lost in the ocean of our unknowing. So much so we are still stabbing at fairy tales. And what I really mean by this is that science itself is not capable of presenting a why. That is, in order to subscribe to a *why* (an objective rather than subjective why) you have to subscribe to some sort of theory about God or aliens. And yet the mind needs a *why*, just as the body needs food.

"What in the world are you thinking, bud?" Paul asks.

"What's that?" I respond.

"You're just staring at the dash like you're in a trance." Paul has a smile on his face. He has been watching me for a while.

"I guess I was just zoning a little." I sit back and hang my arm out of the window, making a cup with my palm to feel the air against my hand, thinking again about the mystery of the elements, of invisible wind, not seen but there, en masse, collecting to push against the skin of my hand.

"Are you homesick already?" Paul asks.

I give a slight, defensive chuckle. "Not quite yet. It's gonna take a little longer than this."

"Then what are you thinking about? You look sad or something."

"I wasn't thinking about anything, Paul."

"You sure?"

"I'm sure," I tell him.

THE VAN IS MOVING SLOWLY, EVEN SLOWER THAN normal. We are ascending a hill that is significantly larger than anything we have yet seen. Texas curls up at the border, as though the land mass wouldn't fit inside the map, so it rises at the edges. The road is straight and narrow, and there is a good quarter mile of concrete between us and the summit. The shoulder of the interstate passes slowly. I can make out the gray and green definition of small stones and broken glass.

"You want me to get out and push?" I ask.

Paul begins to rock backward and forward in his seat. I can feel his weight sway the van. I place both hands on the dash and begin to push, clenching my teeth and wrinkling my forehead as if to be working hard. Paul looks down at the speedometer.

"It's no use. We're down to 42!"

I sit back and bend my legs to set my boots against the dash. Again, I push and grit and wrinkle my forehead. In an exasperated voice, still pushing against the dash, I ask if we are moving any faster.

"Bud, this isn't good." Paul is looking frustrated. "We are down to 35."

I take my boots off of the dash and lean over to look at the console. "What do you think it is?"

"This piece-of-crap van is what it is. They didn't say anything about this in the brochure," he says.

"Worthless salesman," I add.

"We're not getting any power," Paul explains. "I should have adjusted the valves before we left."

As we crest the hill, two trucks and an RV pass us quickly and loudly on the left side. From atop the hill I can see the road dipping low into a ravine and then rising through trees in a four-lane bend toward another hill of greater size.

"We've got to get some speed on the downhill," I comment, just above a whisper, as if talking more to the van than to Paul.

Paul has the pedal to the floor and the van is gaining speed. He announces our progress in increments of 5. Fifty feels like 90 compared to the 30 we've been moving. The van rattles and whines and enjoys the slope of the road like an old man who has been hit with a burst of energy. Showing off, it lifts its shaky needle to 55 and then 60, before steadying at 62. We roar through the bottom of the hill, begin to climb, and the van slows. This time there is no rocking or pushing and what was funny only seconds ago has lost its humor. We crest and descend five or more hills at turtle, then rabbit, then turtle speed. Each ascent frustrates us to the point of silence. Paul voicelessly expresses his concern. His hands are tightly gripped on the steering wheel, and his slightly wrinkled brow frowns toward the noonday horizon, as if to wish he was there and not here.

An hour into our trouble we meet with Oklahoma. The welcome sign is of no consequence as we are preoccupied with the trouble and the van. What would have exacted a "Yeehaw" or a stirring and not quite accurate chorus from the state's own musical has been deluged by our circumstance.

Having brought up the valves a half hour before, I ask Paul if he thinks we should pull over and adjust them.

"Well, we'd have to wait for the engine to cool. That could take several hours, and the more I think about it, I'm not sure it's the valves. It could be the carburetor. It feels like it's not getting enough gas. I can hardly feel it when I step on the pedal." As he says this, he deepens his foot into the gas but there is no thrust. We crest another hill, descend, and begin climbing the next. These hills are long hills; they are several minutes to the bottom and twenty minutes to the top. At common speeds a road looks small and thin, but at van pace it is broad-shouldered, wide-laned, and dashed with long, distantly spaced lines. We have slowed to an embarrassing speed of 23.

As we crest a hill and turn a bend, we find a small store and pull into a dusty roadside parking lot. A few weathered pickup trucks are parked outside. Paul kills the engine and we sit for a minute, listening to the metal tick itself cool. Paul silently gets out of the van, and I follow him. As we are walking into the store, two young boys come out with small paper bags filled with candy, each holding a cold bottle of Coke. They notice the van and strike up a conversation.

"Where are you guys from?"

Paul, slightly surprised at their friendly interest, answers in a soft, withdrawn voice. "We drove up from Houston."

The boy who asked the question leans into the other and they both speak at the same time.

"Jessie's been to Houston . . ."

"I've been there," one of the boys offers. "My uncle lives there, and we went down at Christmas. That's a big city."

The other joins in before Jessie finishes his sentence. "I've been to Dallas, to Six Flags too. You sleep in that van?" The boys walk to the side of the van, looking at it in wonder. The nameless boy speaks before we can answer his first question. "Ben Bonham had a van like this but he sold it and got a car."

Jessie, disagreeing with the other, starts at him with a child-like arrogance. "Nu-uh, Ben still has it. He has two cars. A van and a car."

"He did too sell it. He only has one. I bet you a fireball he ain't got it."

"I know he still has it. I seen him the day before yesterday."

The boys trail off, across the parking lot and back through some woods, all the while talking about Ben and his car and how he does and doesn't have a van like ours. Paul looks at me and shrugs his shoulders and we walk into the store. As we enter, my eyes adjust slowly to the dim light and for a second everything is covered in gray. Deeper into the store, past the counter and the woman behind it, things begin to sharpen. Part quick-mart and part grocery store, the shelves are half-empty and in disarray. A layer of set-in dust covers the floor, and the place smells more like a feed store than a grocery store. We pace the short aisles, past the chips and candy, around the end cap of Styrofoam coolers and then back, down the cat food and aspirin aisle, toward the woman at the counter.

"Can I help you find something?" the woman asks.

"Yes," I respond. "We're looking for carburetor cleaner."

"Car stuff is behind you," she says, pointing over my shoulder.

We turn to see a small sampling of motor oil and pine-tree air fresheners. There is one can of Fix-A-Flat, but no carburetor cleaner. A plaid-shirted, red-faced man, who has been standing at the counter, talking to the woman all this time, walks toward the door and stands in the bright light, looking out at the parked cars. "You boys having problems with that van out there?"

Paul answers as he walks down the aisle, toward the man. "Yes, we think it's the carburetor."

"What's it doing to you?" the red-faced man asks.

"We get no power when we're going uphill. It slows down to about 25 or so."

The lady behind the counter speaks up, addressing the plaid-shirted man. "I don't think Michael Johnson's place is open today, is it?"

"He's out of town. Won't be back till Tuesday," the man answers, not looking at her, only staring out at the van and picking at his teeth with a toothpick. He is thin and weathered from a lifetime in the field. Layers of sun on his gray-brown face probably add ten years to his aspect.

"Ben Bonham could help you boys. I think ol' Ben is home."

The lady joins in, as if to remember, and agrees with the man. "Ben sure could help. He knows about those vans. He used to have one."

"Yeah, Ben could help you boys. Ben's as good at fixing those things as Michael Johnson is. He's just up the road a bit if you wanna go out there."

"Does he have a shop?" I ask toward the man, but glancing at the woman to include her in the question. The man and the woman begin together but she quiets to his response. "He works out of his home, just over the highway a bit." The weathered man takes the toothpick from his mouth and points, in a general motion, across the road and toward a side street, starting to tell us how to get there. He puts the toothpick back in his mouth and goes to the counter where the woman hands him a pencil and a piece of paper. Writing and talking at the same time, he begins his directions.

"Go out across the street and head up Dagg Road. That's Dagg right there," he says, as he points with the pencil to a dirt road just out the door and across the paved street. "Head on out Dagg till you get to Midland, and Midland isn't marked but Dagg dead-ends there so you'll know it when you come to it . . ."

The man goes on like this for a while, carefully writing down each street. As he finishes, Paul thanks him for his kindness. The plaid-shirted man accepts our handshakes and farewells in a removed, masculine way. We climb back into the van and edge slowly across the parking lot, rough and rattling, kicking up dry dust.

A DOT ON THE HIGHWAY, THIS TOWN IS ALL MOBILE homes and pickups. Each trailer differs only in fencing and color. Families with money have built carports and fencelike trimming to cover the tires or their trailer hitch. Paul navigates us through streets long given to potholes and sections of shell and dirt. We arrive at what looks to be Ben's place. The trailer sits at the edge of town and backs up to a piece of land that is raised in the front and dips down to a man-made pond and a squab of wiry berry bushes and woods. A large tool shed sits between the trailer and the pond. On its doors are hung ancient, rusted tools.

We turn up the drive and notice a Volkswagen van, abandoned and surrounded by a tall mesh of weeds. Paul cracks a smile and I make a comment about how someone owes someone else a piece of candy. Around the front of the trailer is an enclosed porch, complete with floor-to-ceiling screens and a thin glass door. Aside from Ben's van, there are no cars and we begin to wonder if anyone is home.

It is an uncomfortable position to burden a stranger with your troubles. Doctors, lawyers, and mechanics are constantly queried for free advice and labor. The expressions on our faces note our disdain for our state and there is an uneasy, brief moment of stillness as one waits for the other to approach the door. Paul goes and I follow at his shoulder, through the glass door, into the porch. He knocks and there is an immediate stir. As we step back, the door opens and then draws closed, leaving only a crack of darkness. A rotund female figure is outlined in shadows through the dim opening.

"Yes?" her voice is small and secretive.

Paul, standing in front, takes the conversation. "Does Ben Bonham live here, ma'am?"

"He is my husband."

"The people in town told us he might be able to help with our van. We were just passing through and the mechanic in town is away."

The door opens a little more and a friendly, round, elderly face claims her voice. "Ben is out right now, but he should be in soon. Where are you boys from?"

Shifting to Paul's side, I involve myself in the conversation.

"We've come up from Houston and are heading to the Grand Canyon."

Our conversation goes on for a while about the Grand Canyon and her twice having been there, once with Ben when the kids were young and another time only three years back. The dialogue never stales as brief moments of silence are quickly absorbed by another story or bit of trivia about the canyon and her two trips there. Several minutes later as Mrs. Kate Bonham still stands in the doorway, a long, sixties Cadillac pulls behind our van. Kate's gentle smile tells us it is Ben. She slips back into the trailer.

We meet Ben at the back of our van and I explain to him our dilemma. All filled with kindness and pride, Ben sets his coat and lunch pail on the hood of his car and opens the engine compartment to the van. His hands are aged eighty years or more. They are stained with grease and time.

"I got one like this myself, boys. Put it out to pasture a few years back, but liked her while she ran. I blew a piston trying to turn my tractor over when I rolled it. What seems to be the problem with yours?"

Paul and I are silent, imagining a seventy-five-year-old man rolling a tractor and then attempting to right it again with a Volkswagen.

"I say, what's the problem with yours?"

Paul shakes off his daydream and answers quickly, making up for the inattentiveness. "It doesn't have any power. We do about 25 when we're going uphill. I thought maybe it was the valves . . ." Paul is interrupted by Ben before he can finish his sentence.

"Valves wouldn't do that to ya. It's a gas problem. Sounds like the carburetor." Ben rolls up his long, stained sleeves and leans under the hood, over the engine. He is a short, pudgy man whose height gives him an advantage leaning into the low compartment. His overalls are long and extend past the heels of his steel-toed boots. "I never did like these dual carburetors. Did you know that you can get a kit to change it to a single carb? I did that to mine and had it for the better, that's for sure."

"I didn't know that," Paul responds, hands in pockets, peering behind Ben's shoulder and watching his hands shake wires, pulling them taut.

"Does it chug when you give it gas?"

Paul, hesitating as he considers the question, speaks softly and reserved, inches from Ben's ear, "It does. That's the problem."

Ben playfully barks a command at me, "Start it up, boy."

I round the van to the driver's side, wait for the signal, and turn the key. Without pushing the pedal, the engine revs fierce and loud. Ben releases the lever and it dies. "Start it again, son!" His voice comes muffled and distant from within the engine compartment. I turn to see Paul twisting his fist and fingers in a sign to start the van. Again, Ben controls the RPMs from the rear and the engine whines loud and inconsistent. He releases the gas and it dies.

"You're missin' some linkage here." Ben shows Paul the lever on the right carburetor. Two holes in the lift are empty. "You boys are working off of one carburetor. See this here . . . ," Ben moves aside, still holding the lever with his right hand, ". . . this connects to this other and gets a tug from the gas pedal to give gas to the carb. It's a wonder you got to twenty-five miles per hour with just one carb." Paul, looking relieved to know that the problem is a simple one, crunches down and pulls at the lever. Ben disappears behind the van and reappears in the distance, walking toward the tool shed. He returns with a small piece of baling wire. "Let me in there for a second, son." Paul moves aside and Ben's efficient fingers go to work twisting the wire to link the two levers. Upon Ben's signal, I start the van, pump the gas, and the van gives a loud, dual-carburetor wail.

"She sounds all right to me. I think that might do it."

Ben's proclamation is met with gratitude and an offer to pay. He will have nothing to do with that and changes the conversation to neglected introductions. After telling him where we are from and where we are going, we listen again to stories of two trips to the Grand Canyon, several years ago with the kids and a few years back with just the wife and the dog, which "isn't around because it got run over just last month." It was a good dog named Bear and was hit by a truck. Had three legs to begin with.

"You boys should like that canyon. Amazing thing she is. Deep as hell herself with a river at the bottom to boot! We never went to the bottom, but seen it in the picture cards and the Colorado runs right through her like a cut. Folks go boating through her too. We saw it in a video. You boys going down?"

"We hope to," I answer. "We're just sorta playing it by ear. Hey, listen, give me your address and I'll send you a postcard when we get there."

"I will," Ben answers, smiling and huffing toward the trailer for a piece of paper and a pencil. He returns with an opened scrap envelope from a piece of junk mail and a dull pencil. Paul and I are silent as we watch him write his name and address next to the same name and address printed on the envelope. Ben's eyes are lit like a boy's at Christmas. He hands me the envelope and reminds me again what it is for. "A picture card will do. Kate and I really like it there."

"Ben, are you sure we can't pay you?" Paul asks. "You've done so much."

"Get outta here, boys. I gotta get washed up. I smell like a mule and Kate doesn't like that." Still wearing a giant smile, he shoos us with his hands as if we are chickens being scurried through a gate. Paul locks eyes with him as he turns to go. I close the door on the passenger side and give a soft three-fingered wave and grin. Paul backs out of the drive, rolling off into the worn grass to pass Ben's car. The old man watches through the glass, inside the porch, and waves as he sees I am still looking at him.

We weave back through the dusty streets and onto the road that will take us to the interstate. "Ben has the life, doesn't he?" Paul comments, breaking a minute or so of silence. I nod my head in agreement, rolling down the window to get some fresh air.

"Works all day, comes home to the woman he loves. You couldn't ask for a better life," Paul says.

3 THIN ICE

WE MOVE WITH NEW AND APPRECIATED QUICKNESS toward a sinking sun that sets to flame the backs of close and distant hills, causing clouds to flare in violent strips and tall trees to lay their shadows across the road like nightclothes across a bed. Oklahoma has no better show than evening.

Our conversation has lulled from praises of Ben Bonham to comments about the sunset to silence. Out the passenger-side window the blur of green opens and closes with each passing red-dirt road. My mind focuses on life beyond the trees and the hills and this road cutting through them. It is there I imagine a small home surrounded by forest and a man sitting by a fire, reading the pages of a book he has read before and will read again. He is tired and nodding, and though his eyes still brush the words, he has long stopped reading. The fading light through the windows and the warmth of the fire soothe him into a sleep from which he will not wake till morning, finding himself still dressed with a book across his lap. Miles from the cabin, in another home, still in the here and now (albeit in my imagination) I see a family at evening supper, perhaps saying grace. And at that table there is a woman who is glad to have her husband home as he has been to such and such a place to do business. Ever nearer, and perhaps in a home just off this interstate, down a dusty driveway weaving through maple and pine that spread March over these rolling hills, there is a young girl at her desk, constructing a letter to the boy who has taken her heart. And just outside my window, a hundred thousand voices fire through phone lines that parallel this road, each voice carried swiftly to a listener who trusts his response to the broad-shouldered poles and sweeping lines marking the miles from home to home and business to business.

And the sun is being swallowed by the hills, leaving ample room on left and right for blood-red glow and backlit clouds. To the east, darkness and shadows. Our headlights press softly against the oncoming road.

The radio lacks a CD player and is probably the one that came with the van. There's a tape player, though, and in the glove box I find a few tapes. Secretly I scold myself for not bringing music of my own. Amid scraps of insurance papers and part-shop receipts, my fingers find a tape.

"Lynyrd Skynyrd?" I question aloud.

"You can't beat Skynyrd," Paul defends.

"I could if I had a bat."

Other tapes include U2's *Joshua Tree* and a fellow named George Winston. "Who's George Winston?" I ask.

"He's a piano player."

"Is it classical?"

"Not really, it's just kinda mellow. Like Mogwai, without the wires or the beat."

"Mogwai without music, you mean."

Paul smirks. "Trust me. It's good."

Music is the sound track of life. The absence of it is unforgivable on a road trip. This is a James Taylor moment and we are stuck with a piano player who wants to sound like Mogwai and a Southern funk band that, somewhere along the line, fell into thinking Alabama is a sweet place to call home. Catchy meaninglessness. A more thought-provoking, smooth desperateness is in order. Lyle Lovett would hit the spot right now. John Gorka or Clem Snide would make fine background music for a journey such as this. But I am without, and silence being the next best thing to noise, I resolve to myself to listen to that which is so commonly called nothing. Tonight's silence is road and tires, engine and wind. Each so well-composed and rich and made for each other. All that thumping beneath the van and the whistling from the wind against the mirrors. Each resonance rivals for the lead, taking it one from the other and in no specific order. There is a faint squeak that, when focused upon, becomes great and overbearing. It is best left beneath the noise of the road and the tires and the wind and the engine. Everything is like a symphony, if you think about it. Birds are perfect, and crickets come out of the wet woods like a choir. *And this is another accident,* I think to myself, *that we have ears to hear, and that nature itself worked perfectly to calm the soul, and wind from a tornado has that perfect pitch of fear, that train rumble of death, and music, music, if it is an accident, may be one of the greatest miracles of them all, as beautiful as romance or color or the power of water.* All this silence is thick and buzzing and it takes some effort to break it. "Maybe later," I comment, placing the tapes back in the glove box. "Maybe quiet for now."

Paul is the kind of traveling companion who will go along with anything. He doesn't strike me as the kind of guy who has a lot of needs, the kind of guy who needs to stop and see some monument or pull over every few hours for a refill of coffee. There aren't many guys you could drop off in the middle of the forest who could make it without losing their minds, but Paul strikes me as that kind of guy. I guess what I mean is, he isn't one of the millions of us who are always looking for an escape, for distraction. He doesn't need to be talked to, but he isn't a recluse, and he doesn't need to hear music all the time, but he likes music, and he doesn't have to have something in his mouth to keep his mind off his mind, but he will be the first to praise a good meal. I guess you could say he is healthy or something. Guys like that are a bit of a mystery to me, if you want to know the truth. I feel like I am always looking for some kind of escape, you know, some way to not think about thinking, or to not face the blunt force of reality.

"So what are you going to do with your life, Paul?" I ask him, wondering out loud, I guess, what the mystery next to me is about.

The mystery leans his shoulders forward, placing both hands on the wheel. "This and that," he says.

"Sounds like a good plan," I say in a tone to request a more specific answer.

"Well, you know, get a degree, a dog, a job, a wife, a kid," he says.

Paul dated a girl back in Houston named Lynette. They seemed to hit it off. I know he didn't promise her anything when he left, but I never really got a feel for how serious they were.

"Is Lynette in your plan?"

He pauses before offering an answer.

"I'm not too sure about that. She's a sweet girl, but I don't know. There's a girl I dated back in Oregon. We went out for a couple of years. She might be the one, but I'm not sure about her either."

"What's her name?"

"Michael Ann. I met her in junior high and we dated off and on through high school. She's a good girl, you know, real, I don't know, outgoing or whatever. We've had some good times together. We used to hike down to the head of Jack Creek and fish till sunup. She's a girl you can take fishing, you know what I mean?"

That last statement tells me as much about Paul as it does about Michael Ann. I've heard it said there are two types of men in this world—one is looking for a woman to make his life complete and the other is looking for a woman to join his complete life. I don't think one is any better than the other, but Paul is definitely the latter. Paul continues with his stories of fishing, rock climbing, and hiking. Michael Ann has small roles. She fell in a stream in story two and beat him to the top of Smith Rock in story three. It becomes obvious, to me, that Michael Ann is not the one for Paul. It is one thing to have a woman join your complete life and another to have her tag along. As he winds to the end of story four, I keep him talking with a question.

"Describe the perfect woman."

Paul sighs and sits silent for a second. "In fifty words or less, right?"

"As many words as you want."

"That's a tough question. I think I'll know her when I meet her."

"But you must have a general idea. What does she look like? How does she act?"

"Okay, now we're on to something. She's got a great smile, right." He sort of gestures in the air as he says this, emphasizing the importance of her lips. "She doesn't have to look like a model, all skinny and slinky, you know, but I've got to be attracted to her. That's a given. She's going to be an athlete and like the outdoors. I plan to do a lot of camping, so she should probably look good when she hasn't showered for a month."

"A month?" I question.

"A month. You know the girl, Don, that type who never wears makeup and can jump in a creek and all that."

"Good thing we left Texas," I say.

"You can say that again. Those girls look like china dolls. You try to hug them and you are afraid you are going to break them or something." He pauses for a minute, raises his eyebrows, probably picturing some little girl turning to glass and cracking in his arms. "I also want to travel," he begins again, "so she'd have to be willing to live on the road. I'd like to hike Europe sometime, living in youth hostels, never knowing what we are going to eat the next day, that sort of thing. And when we hunt, she has to help carry the deer back to the truck." He finishes and sort of looks at me to see what I think of this girl he has described.

"Do you think that she will ever give up professional wrestling to settle down with the likes of you?" I ask.

He eases back into his chair, pauses, looks down at the console and then out onto the dark road. "Professional wrestling, huh?" he says.

His tone turns mellow. "I guess I'm looking for what any guy is looking for. I want a companion, you know. Just someone to share life with. I want her to be my biggest fan and I want to be her biggest fan too. I want us to raise kids in a home where they know their parents are in love with each other and with them. I guess that's all I want."

Realizing he had taken the question seriously, I offer a penitent comment, just above a whisper, loud enough to know he can hear me. "That sounds like a pretty good want."

"It ain't bad," he says. "It isn't too much, you know. I don't want the perfect girl, really. You figure every girl is beautiful, you know. It's our arrogance that makes us think one is better than the other."

"What do you mean?" I ask.

"I don't know. I was just thinking about girls the other day and wondering, you know, why some girls just get ignored and others get worshipped, and I really got this feeling in my chest like all of that wasn't true. Can't be true. Doesn't make sense. Like maybe if you can't love a girl who isn't all perfect, then you can't really love a girl who is. Not for real. Not unconditionally."

"That's pretty profound, Paul," I say, after a bit of silence.

"How about you, Don? What are you looking for in a woman? What gets the fire burning for you?"

"Oh, you know, this and that."

"I answered. You've got to answer," my friend says, directly.

The van chugs a good quarter mile before I speak up. "Well, she's going to have to love to sleep."

"Sleep!" The driver's eyes light up.

"Yeah, I like to sleep. That's my favorite thing to do. Do you have a problem with that?"

"No, I mean if that's your thing." He tries to speak without laughing but his voice comes distorted through a grin. "Sleep is a good thing, Don. I sleep almost every night."

"You bet you do. Sleep is entirely underrated. All these Tony Robbins wannabes talk about how the early bird catches the worm. I'd like to see them go one week without sleep and try to function."

"Preach it, brother!"

"All I'm saying is, I don't want a girl who's going to wake up in the morning and expect me to be mowing the lawn by ten o'clock."

Paul's laugh is a silent laugh—teeth-showing grin and a light gasp. "I can just see you, Don. The sun is in midsky and there you are mowing the lawn in your pajamas!"

Making sure I don't lose face with my new friend, I switch moods on him. "I'm kidding. No woman will let you sleep till ten. That's a fantasy, right?" I ask.

"Yeah," he says. "That's a fantasy."

"You know what I want in a woman, Paul?"

"What's that?"

"A friend. A true friend, someone who knows me and loves me anyway. You know, like when I'm through putting my best foot forward, she's still there, still the same. I meet these people and it's all conditional, like you were saying. They are in it for themselves. They are friends with you because you fit the image they want to portray. It's a selfish thing. Do you know what I mean? I'd like to get a girl who doesn't think like that. Don't get me wrong. She's got to be proud of her husband, I know that. I don't mind trying to make it easy on her in that way. But all in all, there's got to be some sort of soul mate thing going on. That's gonna take work, I think. There are some people in this world who love their spouse because they provide them with the life they want, and there are others who love their spouse just because they've chosen to, or because love has chosen them, or whatever. Something way back endeared one to the other and they made a decision to lock into it."

Paul gives an understanding nod. "You hit on a fear of mine," he says. "It's like I don't want a girl to get too wrapped up in me because she'll just get let down. Living with a woman is going to be tough. They tend to be really domesticated, you know. They fold things and clean things and know what they are going to have for dinner several hours before it's time to eat. Sometimes I wonder whether I'm cut out to live that way. I don't know whether a woman is going to put up with me. Is that what you're talking about?"

"Maybe. I'm not sure where you were going with that folding clothes thing. I'm just saying I want her to love me at my worst. I don't know if that's a low self-esteem thing or something else."

Paul tilts his head and motions out a slow *no*. "I don't think so. I mean, nobody's perfect. We can't be perfect."

I get quiet for a minute, just thinking about the *why* of what Paul and I are talking about. It's like I was saying, we always think of the *how* in life but not the *why*. We want to know how to get a mate, how to get sex, how to whatever, but why? Why are we designed to be in relationships? Why are women so much more beautiful than men, and why is there more than sex in life, why is there love, why is there oneness between men and women, closeness, that soul mate thing that happens? Darwin doesn't explain that crap.

"You never answered my question, Don." Paul breaks the silence.

"What's that?"

"A woman. What are you looking for in a woman?"

"Your guess is as good as mine." My mind returns slowly to our previous train of thought. "I like to read, so maybe she will too. I don't know exactly. My guess is, I can't imagine her. I mean this system, you know, this crazy system, these chemicals that jolt through our brains and make us love another human, they are a complete mystery, and we can't say what kind of girl we are going to be attracted to, the chemicals decide that, and nobody has figured out the science yet. Who knows what it is? Maybe it is brown hair that makes my chemicals start, or squinty eyes or small breasts or big breasts or her voice or her smell; we just don't know. It makes no sense, you know, and yet we all live by it, and we ask these questions, and we just live within these presuppositions without ever asking where the presuppositions came from. We're just puppets, you know, because of the chemicals."

"Puppets," Paul repeats in a hush. He nods his head a bit and looks into the rearview mirror and adjusts it. "Puppets," he repeats.

"Puppets," I say as Paul comforts himself in his chair and nods his head a bit more.

"I have to tell you, though," he says. "It doesn't bother me."

"What doesn't bother you?" I ask.

"Being a puppet. Girls. Being a puppet man who is attracted to puppet girls. Doesn't bother me a bit."

I think about it for a second. "It doesn't bother me either, I suppose," I say, smiling.

"Nice puppet girl with a big puppet smile and a dress and that puppet girl smell."

"Those big puppet eyelashes," I add.

"Puppet lots of things," he says with a smirk.

Paul cracks a smile and rolls up his window. His action makes me realize that the air is thin with a dry coolness. Reaching around the seat, I grab my jacket and push my arms slowly through the sleeves. No glow now on the horizon. We have ventured one more day on our journey. Time moved quickly today. It passed like a whisper. The hills have completely buried the sun. We pass roadside houses, windows aglow with the flame of television and ten o'clock news. Paul sits quiet in reflection. With the road atlas across my lap, I follow the thin line of Interstate 35 with my flashlight. She runs straight into Oklahoma City. My thinking is that we will cut there and head west, crossing into

New Mexico, Arizona, and then north toward the canyon.

"What are you getting on the map, Don?"

"Looks like Interstate 40 from Oklahoma City. That should take us right to the canyon. Would you rather take back roads?" I ask.

"No, let's head straight there. I'm looking forward to seeing Arizona and we should be able to make it by late tomorrow. Do you want to drive through the night?"

"Wouldn't bother me," I respond.

It occurs to me we haven't stopped in a while. Save a quick visit with Ben Bonham, we've covered more than five hundred miles, and at the van's slow pace, that is quite a bit of ground. It feels again like we are leaving, like we are leaving who we were, moving into the people we will become, hopefully people with some kind of answer about the *why*, some kind of thing to believe that makes sense of beauty, makes sense of sex and romance, makes sense of gravity and oxygen. It wouldn't bother me to have something to tie the whole thing together, something that would explain the red glow against Paul's face, the red glow that seems to be coming off the console . . .

Leaning over, I see that the engine light is lit. Paul notices I am leaning over to look at the console and ignores me.

"Did you notice the engine light is lit, bud?" I say, after a moment of silence.

Paul looks down at the light. He looks out the side window. He doesn't want to answer the question.

"Paul, did you notice the engine light?"

"Yeah," he says. "It's been bugging me."

"How long has it been on?" I ask.

"Twenty miles," he says.

"Twenty miles?" I say.

"Twenty miles," he says.

"Twenty miles?" I question.

"Twenty miles. Ten times two." He lets on that he is agitated by my questioning.

"That light has been on for twenty miles?"

"Yeah, twenty miles. It'll be twenty-one by the time you stop asking me about it."

"Twenty-one miles," I respond.

"Right in there somewhere. Yeah."

"Did it ever occur to you we should pull over and check the engine?" I ask.

"It did," he says.

"It did?"

The driver breathes deeply. "Do we have to do this again?"

"Help me out here. Why aren't we checking the engine?"

"I've had it with this van, Don. It wouldn't bother me to see the thing go up in flames."

"Are you serious?"

"Yeah. This van has given me more headaches than, well, anything. I figured we'd just drive it into the ground."

"Paul, what are we going to do when the van breaks down in the middle of nowhere?"

"Don't worry. I have a plan," he says, after a slight pause.

"Fill me in, would you?" I ask.

"You won't like it."

"Try me," I say.

"Well, see those train tracks? They've been running alongside the road for a while. I figured we'd just jump a train heading west."

"You want to jump a train!"

"I said I had a plan. I didn't say it was a good one."

"You're being serious about this, aren't you?"

"I've always wanted to jump a train, Don. Imagine it. Riding the rails. Setting out across the Painted Desert, legs dangling off the edge of a boxcar."

It is my tactic in a moment like this to remain silent. The agitator sits and meditates on his crazy idea. Anyone can convince himself an idea is logical, but when that idea is spoken, when it's out in the air like Paul's is, and it rests in the ear of a being more rational, the instigator is forced to reason. I don't argue his point; that would suggest there is merit to it. Not a lot of merit, but enough to justify a response. My silence speaks louder than words. It forces him to sit alone in a room with his own thoughts and know I am not willing to join him. Or at least this is what I hope. Plus, I don't know what to say. I don't guess his plan is all that bad. I'm not especially fond of the van either. I know we are going to have to pull over and fix it every hundred miles, and if we jumped a train, I could always tell girls about it in the future. And I'm not going to tell Paul, but I grew up near a train track and have always been fascinated by stories of people who jump trains. Still, it frustrates me that he didn't include me in his thinking.

"When were you going to tell me about this?"

"Soon. I promise. I didn't know how you'd feel about it."

"Isn't jumping trains a little dangerous? What if we run into some hobos?"

"Wouldn't happen. Hobos don't ride trains anymore," he says.

"They don't? Well, that's good, I guess."

The lunacy of my friend's plan is beginning to dilute. I imagine the Painted Desert passing before my eyes, the rocking of the slow-moving train and all that red and orange and purple falling off the horizon, a world of desert pushing color off the earth.

"Why don't hobos ride trains anymore?" I ask.

"It's too dangerous," my friend says.

"Why is it too dangerous?" I ask.

"They don't do it anymore because the gangs have taken over."

"Gangs?" My voice gives a hint of surprise.

"Gangs."

This is hard to picture. Bank robbers ride trains. Hobos ride trains. Cowboys ride trains. Gang members ride around in low-rider cars and shoot indiscriminately at other gang members. They don't ride trains.

"Paul, gang members don't ride trains," I tell him.

"They do. I read about it somewhere. They jump trains out of LA and all. Sounds crazy but it's true."

I don't feel like arguing with Paul. If he wants to run his van into the ground, that's his business. And so for whatever reason, I sit silently, listening for the engine to give. But she doesn't. Miles pass and she doesn't. I look over to see Paul. He's deep in thought and aglow in red light. I can tell by the look on his face that he wants the van to die. It's like a vengeance thing. This old heap has been kicking him around for months and now he's killing it. Slowly but surely, driving it into the ground. The engine light casts a demon-red glare in his eye. It's like he's possessed.

Reaching into the glove box, I slide a stick of gum out of its wrapper. "Would you care for a stick of gum, Paul?" I ask, breaking his stare into the oncoming road.

"No thanks," he says, looking over as if to remember I was sitting next to him.

"Minty fresh," I say, holding up the package.

"No thanks," he says, turning his gaze back to the road.

The possessed man drives, looking down at the engine light and then over at the tracks. He's thinking of the van's suffering and remembering all the times he pulled over to save it. Not this time. No, sir. This time it's the junkyard.

"You look pretty angry," I say to him, breaking the silence.

"I'm not angry," he says. "I'm frustrated because this warning light is shining in my eyes. I can't focus on the road."

Taking the moist gum out of my mouth, I lean over and press it tightly against the round glowing plastic of the engine light.

Paul nods and smiles for a second. "These things really are easy to fix," he says, motioning toward the gum.

"You're not kidding," I agree.

Fifty more miles pass and the cold begins to get to me. I clasp my hands together and rub them for warmth. I ask Paul if his fine automobile comes equipped with a heater. Without answering, he reaches over and pulls a lever from blue to red, turns a switch, and the van delivers a modest, cold breeze, more from the floor than the round, adjustable vents in the dash. In an attempt at efficiency, the Germans engineered these vans to be air cooled. Two wind vents stand out in the rear of the van. They catch wind and funnel it through the engine compartment. That same air (at least in the mind of the engineer) makes its way through shafts to the van's cab, having been warmed by the engine. So goes the Volkswagen heater. I would imagine if one is traveling through the desert in midday, that technology might make sense. Not tonight. The heater is being defeated by the elements.

"Doesn't work that well, does it?" Paul concedes. "Grab my fleece, would ya? It's on the bed." Stepping through the seats, I enter the cave of blankets and scattered clothes. Paul's fleece rests in a wedge between the bed and the side panel. The warmth of the blankets and the softness of the pillow are too much to reject. Tossing Paul's fleece at the back of his head, I lay my mind on a pillow and watch the road pass outside the cold window.

4 DISCOVERING GEORGE WINSTON

WHILE I WAS SLEEPING, PAUL DROVE THROUGH Oklahoma and into the Panhandle. The yellow light from a truck stop street lamp fills the van. Trucks grind gears and turn like elephants into the parking lot. The lights and the noise bring me out of sleep. I toss my nose into the window and follow with my elbow, all tangled in a net of blankets and clothes.

"Where are we?" I ask, slowly opening my eyes to the parking lot.

The van rocks as Paul drops his weight on the bed, rolls himself over, and kicks one foot against the heel of his other, a struggling attempt to remove his boot. "Back in the Lone Star State, my friend. Can't you smell the manure?"

"We're still in Texas?"

"Where the stars at night are big and bright," he says.

"I thought we were in Oklahoma."

"We were. We are in the Panhandle now. Back in Texas."

"This is a big state, man," I say, still pressed against the glass.

"You're not kidding. We've been driving for days and can't get away from it."

Another truck grinds, hisses, and spills light over our pile of clothes and blankets. Its light swings shadows through the van, moving their focus over and beyond us, out toward the truck stop pumps, store, and restaurant.

"Did the van give out?" I ask, wondering aloud why we stopped.

"She's purring like a kitten."

"Why did you wake me? I was dreaming about a great girl."

"You were cheating on me!" Paul says, leaning his head into his pillow. "I thought we had something, man."

"You're ugly as hell," I say to him. "Boys will never like you."

Paul covers himself in blankets and rests his head against the side panel. "It's because my breasts are so small, isn't it?" Paul says, lifting two points off his shirt.

"That's a start."

"So who was this girl?" Paul asks, still pulling points off his shirt.

"What girl?"

"The girl you were dreaming about. She have a name?"

"You'll laugh," I tell him.

"I won't. I promise."

Sitting up and throwing my blankets off, I begin, "She was a cowgirl." Paul covers his face with a pillow.

"You said you wouldn't laugh," I say.

"A cowgirl," he says into the pillow.

"Her name was Cheyenne. Call her by her name."

Paul slips the pillow down his face and looks me full in the eye. "That's a beautiful name, Don. You think your dream was influenced by the smell of the pasture across the highway?" His heckle is delivered with a straight face but changes to a grin as he anticipates my response.

"It is a beautiful name for a beautiful girl. You'll never get one like that."

Paul keeps laughing. I look out the window and talk under my breath . . . sarcastically, as though in a daze . . .

"She needed me. We were running from the bad guys who killed her father on a ranch outside Little Rock."

Paul slides himself down on the mattress and tucks the pillow under his head. "A ranch outside Little Rock," he repeats. "You ever actually ridden a horse, Don?"

"Scared of them," I say matter-of-factly.

"I see," he says.

I grab my pillow and swing it directly at my friend's face, still looking out the window. "I rode like the wind, I tell you," I say in my best Charlton Heston voice. He lies motionless. Lying back down, I continue my story: "There were three of them. Chasing us on horses. All of them had guns. We had ducked behind a rock and I was telling her how much I could bench-press so she would feel safe. I was telling her she would be okay. They were coming with guns and she was worried."

"She must have been comforted when you told her you could bench almost sixty pounds."

Despite my friend's harassment, I want my dream again, and am disturbed by its ending. I resolve I will not finish rescuing Cheyenne tonight, so I leave Paul in the van to walk across the parking lot toward the truck stop. Gray pebbles and patches of oil, dripped from long-removed trucks, pattern the lot. A wind, sliding off some distant Canadian glacier, presses against the parking lot with frigid hands. It builds strength in treeless pastures and pelts the dimly lit station and store. Texas hasn't seen a colder night since Ann Richards was elected governor. Tom and Huck never had it so bad as we do tonight.

I rattle some change in my pocket, counting with my fingers. About seventy-five cents or so. One cup of coffee.

Money is an issue on this trip. I have $300, sock-wound in my backpack, and most of it will convert to gas. My half of the fuel bill will reach $200 in 3,000 miles. That leaves little to spare. More money will come when my truck sells back home. After retiring the car loan, I will have another $1,000. The strategy is to not deplete the $300 until the truck is sold. It's a gamble. Coffee is worth it, though. I am sure I will be driving through the night. Besides, if I don't drink something warm, my insides will freeze.

"Where's your coffee?"

The store clerk motions with her eyes toward the wall that

is closest to me. Two glass pots sit on brown burners. One is labeled decaf and I reach for the other. "How much is a cup?"

"Fifty cents," she shouts across the aisles. I pour the black liquid (it looks like it's been sitting for hours) into a Styrofoam cup and search for the lids. Rounding the aisle toward the counter, I meet face-to-face with the clerk, a young brown-haired girl in a Bon Jovi T-shirt. She is keeping company with a man standing no less than three inches taller than me, greasy, and leaning in on the counter. He's dirty with black on his fingers that wrap around the brown cup he brought with him. *Truck drivers own their own cups,* I think to myself. The look on her face and the shy grin on his tell me he's hitting on her. Brunette, fit, half-pretty, she's used to it. Truck drivers probably come in at all hours for a shave and a shower and haven't seen a woman in a thousand miles.

"This man isn't giving you a bad time, is he?" I say, sort of under my breath as I count the change in my hand. I only meant it as a joke, but the girl looks back at me a little shy. Rural people don't get urban humor; they really don't. You just stay out of folks' business out here, unless you know them. She looks at my size and at his and back at me as if I were crazy and then silently punches in the code for a cup of coffee. "I didn't bring my own cup. You'll have to charge me for the cup," I say to her, motioning toward the truck driver's cup. "Where did you get your cup?" I ask the man. He stands silent, just looks away and then back at the girl. All my jokes are falling limp.

"Cups are free," she says slowly, watching for the reaction of the driver. He perceives her look as an inquiry into what he thinks of me, and he responds with a threat.

He leans in at the side of my face. "You got a problem with me, hippie boy?"

There is a thick silence now. A portable heater sits behind the counter at the girl's feet. It rattles as it turns, glowing with strands of heated steel. "No problem. I got no problem," I say, setting two quarters and some tax on the counter.

"You what?" His breath reeks. He is so close, I imagine him biting my ear. "Why don't you get in that van of yours and head back to Austin?" he continues.

"I'm not from Austin," I say, watching the girl slowly pick up the change.

"I don't care where you're from, boy, so long as you go back."

I look over at him with a half smile. "Look, Buck"—his name is embroidered on his shirt—"I was just making a joke. It was supposed to be funny. I didn't mean to interrupt you. I am sure you were wooing this girl here, and I didn't mean to interrupt." The man pulls his head back, glances confused at the girl, looks back at me, quiets his tone, and reveals his ignorance. "How did you know my name?" The girl smiles as she notices the tag across his heart.

"We hippies know everything, Buck." I step back a foot or so to make some space. I take a sip of coffee and look over at the girl, kind of including her in the conversation. I speak softly. "Let's see . . . I learned to tell people's names from a guru named Monty, an Indian fellow who knows about what people are called from their smell. You were either a Buck or a Francis. I went with Buck to give you the benefit of the doubt." I nod my head as though I am revealing interesting facts.

"Don't you make funny with me. I don't know you. How did you know my name?" he questions again.

"I know a lot about you, Buck," I tell him, looking him straight in the eye.

I ask the girl if she has enough of my money for the coffee and she says yes. I start walking toward the door. Buck gathers his meager senses and realizes how I knew his name. His hand slaps the name on his shirt and he starts after me. Out the door and into the cold wind, every nerve longs to check shadows over my shoulder. I hear the door close, but walk quickly and wouldn't hear it reopen if it did (due to distance and sound of wind). I am looking for Paul in the van, wondering if he can see Buck walking behind me. I don't want to turn around and see a fist and I am hoping Paul will show his face and warn me with a look of shock. I can hear Buck's footsteps now, coming from behind, running, but I don't turn. I hear them again, then again, and realize I am just imagining these sounds. I walk toward the van and don't turn around. My mind pictures him coming up quick and throwing his fist against the back of my head. I feel my heart speed up and adrenaline pumps through my arms. Still, I keep pace and don't turn. The van sits miles across the parking lot. It seems like it was half as close when I walked in. It feels like the thing is getting farther away, for heaven's sake.

I turn at the far side of the van. The corner of my eye finds no presence, and through the driver's and passenger's windows (standing outside the van looking through), I see Buck watching through the glass door. I give Buck two fingers in a peace sign and a nod. He stands motionless, his dark eyes staring me down.

The van starts at first command and I let it idle as I watch the man leave the door and resume his position against the counter. He is mumbling his pick-up lines through an embarrassed grin and coffee-lacquered teeth. Minutes pass as I allow the van to idle and once again I notice the wind, pushing up against the van, gently rocking the thing, rocking Paul in his bed, setting a temperature against the glass so cold you can almost see it.

With Huck Finn asleep in the back, and with one last look about the place and a sip from the coffee that is warm enough to stage a dance of steam, I release the boat into the river of distant taillights and eighteen-wheeled shadows. All shadows set against the dark, dark sky with stars that wander at will.

I reach with my free hand for the tape in the glove box, then turn the knob on the radio. It bleeds light across its face and I slip the tape through the opening. George Winston begins his private concert. The music seems to match the night, more or less soothing, like the whole thing, the evening and the music, was made to rest in the background, to color the walls behind thoughts and van rattle.

At a distance to the left, across the oncoming lane and across a field, sit lights on barn roofs or a grain tower or processing plant. The cluster of lights rests out on the horizon like a constellation, too small to be a town; maybe it's another truck stop with a farm or grain tower next to it. *If there is one thing we have in this country, it's land,* I think to myself. *Nothing but blank and empty land.* You get to feeling everything is concrete when you live in Houston, but it isn't. Houston is just a speck of rock in the middle of endless fields of nothingness. Cities rise up on the oceans, but in the middle you've got dirt, crops, ranches, and government yards that stretch on for hundreds of miles. One red light blinks atop a building in the constellation and the other lights are white and yellow, resting on the ground like smoldering ashes. Slow to my notice come other constellations, way out on the horizon to the right, up on some slow slope of hill. George Winston serenades me through a weak speaker on the driver's side and a strong speaker in the door panel of the opposite seat. And so go miles and miles. The tape flips sides automatically so it keeps music going in an endless loop. No lights now on the road ahead, save the soft yellow faded lamplight of the Volkswagen against the asphalt.

"It ain't that bad being a puppet," I say under my breath, checking over my shoulder to make sure Paul is still sleeping.

"It ain't bad seeing beauty, or having some chemical in my head trick me into thinking something is nice, some night is a good night, a cold night, or whatever. Some girl is beautiful. That ain't bad. Nice to meet you, my name is Don. What's your name? Nice to meet you, Cheyenne.

"You know, Cheyenne, you get out on an open road like this in the middle of the night and you want some kind of explanation for everything. It wouldn't bother me if aliens left us here, so long as they were good aliens who wanted to love their pets. I wouldn't want my brain sucked out to be used as a battery, like they do in the movies. But if they were loving aliens, that would be okay. Do you believe in aliens, Cheyenne, or do you believe in God? I believe in God. I think He is looking down, or up, from somewhere outside all that black out there.

"What do you think, Paul? You think we came from aliens?" I look over my shoulder again to see Paul, still lying motionless.

5 THE GAZE OF RA

Ancient Greek tradition has Prometheus stealing fire from heaven, fire used to light the path toward civilization. You can see the sun this way, if you wish, as Prometheus riding his horse into space and time, a lantern in his hand, held out toward the planets, a bit of it split into the belly of a furnace, forging steel, the steel splintering off to spark and die away on a blacksmith shop floor, little smidgens of fading heaven, little cosmic mysteries, plucked from the sparkling hair of God. In Egypt the sun was the eye of a god: the sun god Ra, in the evening, closed his eyes and opened them again in the morning, thus the light by which we work and see and have our being is the gaze of a god. I like the Hindu tradition that has Shiva and his lover, Parvati, engaged in foreplay, Parvati coming from behind Shiva and covering his eyes, stopping the light from shining down off the Himalayas. Imagine young Indian children being beckoned to sleep by the erotic ritual of divinity. The gods are randy, night after night, the teenagers must have giggled. It is enough to make a Hindu blush.

In the Hebrew tradition, which splintered off into the Christian tradition, which is how I was raised, light is a metaphor. God makes a cosmos out of the nothingness, a molecular composition, of which He is not and never has been, as any*thing* is limiting, and God has no limits. In this way, He *isn't*, and yet *is*. The poetic imagery is rather beautiful, stating that all we see and feel and touch, the hardness of dense atoms, the softness of a breeze (atoms perhaps loose as if in play) is the breath of God. And into this being, into this existence, God first creates light. This light is not to be confused with the sun and moon and stars, as they are not created until later. He simply creates light, a nonsubstance that is *like* a particle and *like* a wave, but perhaps neither, just some kind of traveling energy. A kind of magnetic wave. Light, then, becomes a fitting metaphor for a nonbeing who is. God, if like light, travels at the speed of light, and because space and time are mingled with speed, the speed of light is the magic, exact number that allows a kind of escape from time. Scientists have played with atomic clocks, matched exactly, setting one in a plane to fly around the world, and another motionless, waiting for the return of its partner. When they reunite, the one that traveled rests milliseconds behind the one fixed. The faster you move, physicists have found, the less you experience time. And if you move at the speed of light, you will never age; you are outside of time; you are an eternal creature. But before you strap on your running shoes, you should know scientists warn us that with speed, matter increases in density, so an attempt at the speed of light will have you imploded by the time you hit Wichita, your atoms as dense as bowling balls. And to make matters worse, your density increases on a curve; the faster you go, the greater the density, and though you can get close to the speed of light, matter and that magic speed can never meet; the faster you go, the steeper the trajectory on the graph. You and I, made from molecules, cannot travel at the speed of light and cannot escape time, at least not with a body. Consider the complexity of light in light of the Hebrew metaphor: we don't see light; we see what it touches. It is more or less invisible, made from nothing, just purposed and focused energy, infinite in its power (it will never tire if fired into a vacuum, going on forever). How fitting, then, for God to create an existence, then a metaphor, as if to say, here is something entirely unlike you, outside of time, infinite in its power and thrust: here is something you can experience but cannot understand. Throughout the remainder of the Bible, then, God calls Himself light. The perfection of the Hebrew metaphor is eerie, especially considering Eratosthenes wouldn't play with sticks and shadows for several thousand years, discovering Ra was, in fact, never closing his eyes.

WITH THE VAN BEHIND ME A HUNDRED YARDS, I STOP to take in the horizon. The air comes into my lungs cold while rich blue neon outlines the distant mountains, each ridge black and jagged. *This is going to be a good one,* I think to myself. My breath makes no mist, though the temperature is certainly cold. Perhaps it's too dry for that. Looking back, the white van sits gray on the side of the empty highway. No cars for miles. No trucks and no noise. I can only hear a faint flow of wind slide down from the hills, rolling like water from high pressure toward some swirling low. The interstate slices through a field of sand before climbing into a distant pass behind me, and this desert floor, still dark with night shadows, lies flat for miles before giving rise to those sleeping peaks in the east. And the sand has the ghostly stare of a blank canvas, as if to hope something beautiful will be painted on its surface, as if to want for flesh.

I press into the desert, aiming for a spot to watch the sun break. Every ten steps I check the east and it changes as I walk. Black gives to blue and it is a blue like no blue on any painting or picture. This is living blue, changing from one hue to another, shifting slowly the way color only does at morning.

Spilled on the brown, then, are dry and shadowy lakes of deep, rich darkness; the absence of light. My tracks are laid out, marking my path, and as I look back, I see the van is now a small form beside a black threadlike strip. To the east, the first tint of red arrives in weak shades through overpowering blue. There are clouds now, and as the light comes in slow, the great vapors establish form; tall clouds with thirty-thousand-foot lifts. And though tremendous in size, they are guarded by the length and depth of a black-blue sky, held back by mountains.

Morning lifts with her finger first, stretching her long bones into the clouds. Engaged, I set myself down on the cold morning sand, my hands beside me and half buried in the frozen dirt. I pull them out, dust my hands against each other, and slide them into my jacket pockets. The black hills ghost to gray, revealing crags and cliffs lifting up toward their summits.

Suddenly I hear my name called. Standing and wiping my hands against my pants, I see Paul at the front of the van, looking in my direction as if to wonder whether I am a man or a rock. I wave my arms and he starts across the road and disappears into a ditch. After a few minutes, the noise of Paul quietly precedes him, the soft steps of his feet against the sand. He is coming slowly, keeping an eye on the horizon. His arms are folded tightly and his shoulders are lifted to warm his neck. Unfolding his arms he wipes his eyes, lets go a yawn, and turns his head toward sunrise. He lessens his stride as he nears, takes a place ten feet from my side, and, together, we watch Prometheus gain on the mountains.

6 TROUBLE

THE VAN IS A RATTLETRAP. IT ECHOES THROUGH THE desert with odd ticking and muffler thump. The asphalt is long and straight, not too hot, but retains, always, the knowledge of summer: a general sense of respect and even fear of high temperatures. Each passing range opens to the same view as the valley that prefaced, each mile looking precisely like the last. The terrain is nearly Martian, I say to Paul, who agrees with a nod. We had stood for a half hour in the desert, letting the sun have its time. And I wondered at the metaphor as it spilled beauty against the brown. As the sun went higher, the color faded and the earth gave way to nothingness, as though the color were a trick, as if the sun were teaching us there is no such thing as beauty, only what it chooses to shine a certain light upon that stimulates a certain chemical in our brains, as though the two were old lovers, teasing each other, reliving some forgotten memory.

But if they were teasing each other, they have certainly stopped. What we have here in all this dead dirt is the stuff of life without life's spark. All of us are made from this stuff, this dirt. Everything in life is just this magical soil, fairy dust, if you will. Plant a seed in the soil and that seed will find the magic around it to make some sprig of wood that, with time from the fairy dust around it, will make a tree, and with the aid of water and more dirt and a hundred years, a tree the height of a skyscraper and the width of a house. All of it from dirt. Grass grows the same way, carrots, potatoes, onions, apples on trees, barley for beer. Rocks are dirt fired in the furnace of the earth's belly, steel is processed rocks, diamonds are rocks forged in the compression of earth's weight, and people, you and I, are dirt lit with, depending on what you believe, the magic seed of the aliens, or the accidental nothingness of Darwin's dreams, or the warm breath of God, the spark of life, giving an embryo a heartbeat, the magical glint that brings the dirt alive, sets in its DNA a coded direction and a mysterious motion that becomes greater than a tree in complexity, able to question its own being, able to guess at its creation, able to love and to hate, to live inspired, then to die, to return to dirt, to the vast abyss of nothing that is a desert in midday, a sea of brown, only beautiful when the sun tricks the eye, only beautiful in the playful metaphor of light.

In all our technology, we have lost touch with the earth, our heaters and air conditioners robbing us of the drama of seasons, our cars keeping our feet from pacing the land, our concrete and our shoes and our carpet delivering us from the feel of unprocessed earth. *We live on top of the created world,* I think to myself, *not in it.* And this van, this great wheelchair with a radio and a bed, we sit in it and roll at unthinkable speeds across a desert that would have cost our forefathers a season. The earth cinched tight at the invention of the wheel. *It's like a time machine,* I think to myself. *It moves us through an age of work in a short week.* But as we are passed by yet another car, twenty years more modern, I remember the primitive nature of our transportation. Everything is referable, I suppose. The van chugs and has the old, arthritic feel that wants and perhaps deserves sympathy. To have been formed by caring Germans, all around green and mountain, and now, after so many years of service, not to retire, but sold to rough brutes who travel dry deserts like cowboys. How the thing must loathe its masters.

"I figure we've got another three hours before we get to Albuquerque, and then several more before Flagstaff." Paul's voice comes half coherent through the slapping of wind. The air swirls through the van and has the gritty feel of beach sand. Metal on passing cars shines in bright, bleached-out glimmers.

"You getting sick of the desert?" I ask.

"I don't mind it that much," Paul counters, talking loud over the road noise. He steadies the wheel with his knee, pulls his shirt over his head, and throws it over his shoulder. "We've got pretty good desert back in Oregon. It's not quite this dry, but it's similar."

"I thought it rained all the time in Oregon," I say.

"It rains on the other side of the Cascade Range but not in central Oregon. Portland and Eugene get all the rain. During the winter, the Willamette Valley is like a rain forest, but go a hundred miles east, over the Cascade Range, and it's all desert." Paul's expressions brighten as he talks of his home.

"I never knew that. I pictured tundra during winter and rain all through summer."

"You're gonna love summers in Oregon," he says. "They are perfect. Eighty or ninety degrees, dry, blue skies and clear streams. It's like living in a Mountain Dew commercial . . . Hey, did I ever tell you that a friend of mine was in one of those?"

"A Mountain Dew commercial?" I question.

"Yeah. My friend Henry. Have you seen the one where there's a bunch of people on a dock and they swing on a rope over the water?"

"Yeah, I think I've seen it."

"Henry is in that commercial. They filmed it up at Blue Lake, right near Black Butte."

"How did he get in one of those?" I ask.

"They just brought a film crew into Sisters, pulled off the side of the road, and started looking for people for the commercial. Henry was at the Thriftway and they stopped him coming out the door. He said he had a candy bar in his hand, and when he finally understood what they were asking, he squeezed the candy bar till chocolate busted the wrapper. He shook the guy's hand and got chocolate on it. They gave him two hundred bucks to come swing on the rope. He said it took them all day and then they had dinner and hung out with the film crew. One of the guys on the crew had met Robin Williams on the set of *Good Morning, Vietnam*."

"That is sweet," I say. "Two hundred bucks to swing on a rope and get on television." I ease back and rest my arm out the window. "I'm pretty sure that is what God is wanting me to do with my life. I'm pretty sure He wants me to be a rock star or an actor."

"Is that right?" Paul says.

"Yes, it is," I say, even before he finishes his comment. "A rock star or an actor. Me and this Henry are going to have to get together when I get to Oregon. I figure a Mountain Dew ad will be a pretty good place to start." I've got a sly grin on my face and am pulling in about twenty pounds off my gut, tensing my muscles and snorting like Barney Fife.

"I could just see that, Don. You would make a great Mountain Dew guy. They could pan the camera across the girls on the beach and slowly swing over to focus right on your hairy back, just when you turn around to address the camera, your belly preceding, falling over your belt."

"Exactly. You're seeing it now. People dig normal guys," I say.

"Is that right?"

"Yes, it is," I say. "Hairy backs are the next thing. Chicks know a man when they see one."

"You're making me a little queasy, Don."

"Don't get jealous on me, Paul. This is going to be a long trip and I don't need that kind of conflict."

"I hear you. I'll try to stay cool. It's just tough, what with your hairy back and all. Knowing you are going to be a shirtless rock star or Mountain Dew guy and I will probably end up a nobody." Paul makes a pouty lip.

"Don't let yourself think like that. I'll never forget the little people. The little people are the ones that make it happen. When I get my first movie award, you know, the little gold trophy thing, I will stand at the podium and say, 'I want to thank the little people, even very little people like my old friend Paul.'"

"You would do that for me? Stand up there and mention me by name?"

"Sure I would. You'd do the same for me."

Paul sits in quiet for a while, a sly grin on his face.

"Actually, Don, I probably wouldn't," he says. "I probably wouldn't mention you by name if I got the award."

"You wouldn't."

"I don't think so, man," Paul says. "I mean, you've got to thank the producer and the director and other actors and Regis and Kelly and family and all that. I would probably just say, 'I'd also like to thank the little people,' and leave it at that. Just a blanket statement that would cover everyone. That way nobody gets offended."

My mouth is open a bit, an expression as if to scratch my head. Turning to look at Paul, I offer agreement. "I see what you're saying. If you thank one guy, you've got to thank them all, and if you leave someone out, you'd hurt feelings. I guess I'd do the same thing as you in that case."

"What do you mean?" Paul says.

"I'd just thank the necessary people and not list any of the little people."

"You can't take it back," he says.

"I'm telling you, I wouldn't thank you."

The van slips a funny nudge forward and then suddenly slows. Paul hits the pedal and . . . nothing. We are coasting. In the middle of nowhere, we are coasting slower and the van is obviously going to roll to a stop. The pedal squeaks as Paul presses it to the floor. Though the engine is running, there is no register in the RPMs.

"You upset the van, Don. You were being selfish and upset the van. Now look at what you did."

"I had nothing to do with it," I say with a laugh. "You didn't move the gum, did you?"

"Didn't touch it." The wad of gum is still stuck firmly against the plastic light. Paul steers the van onto the shoulder. Rolling to a stop, he kills the engine and it ticks with heat. Several cars buzz by and rock the van with a gust. The desert is silent. There are a few cacti and scattered smatterings of rocks and red boulders, but no gas stations, no stores, just miles and miles of Mars.

"I've got an idea," I say, very calmly, melancholy. "Let's jump a train. You could be Big Pauly Paul and I'll be Smack Daddy Pop. We'll meet up with some Crips and Bloods."

"That's real funny, Don. It's the linkage. That's all it is," he says.

I keep talking: "Maybe if we hike across the desert we'll find a train. I want to ride in the caboose."

"It's the linkage, Don. No big deal. Lay off it."

Paul leans in and checks his side mirror for an oncoming car. He opens the door and rounds the front of the van, walking toward the back of the van, past my door but not meeting my eye. I open the door and follow. His look is somewhat frustrated as he jerks open the engine compartment.

"We just need to tighten it up a little." My words come as something of a condolence.

"Yeah, it looks like that's the problem."

I nod my head. He leans down on one knee and has his hand in the engine compartment. He pulls it out abruptly, shakes his fist, and blows on it.

"Needs to cool down," I say.

"I can get it." He puts his hand back in. I lean down with him. The linkage has loosened considerably. Both carbs are closed tight.

"I can fix this one. Ben left enough cable to rig it. But the other is worn pretty good." Paul points to the other linkage and he is right. The original cable is fastened at exact length, and the attachment is loose. We are going to have to rig it like the last one. New wire and all.

"Should we just clip the old one off?" I ask.

"Probably," he says.

"We'll need more wire," I say.

"Look around for a piece of cable, would you?" he asks.

I stand up to look down the long highway. It goes back several miles before it disappears.

"I'll dig around in the van," I tell him.

THE VAN'S GOT A BROKEN FEEL TO IT. IT'S AS IF IT wants us to appreciate it when it runs, so it stalls on purpose, forcing us to stop and think about the bad treatment we've given it, and to stop comparing it to more modern machines. I mostly ignore the vibes as I look for some wire. I've got the big door open to let some air swim around.

There's no wire in this van, I say to myself. The glove box has all the same stuff as before, and no wire. I search the floor, and under the seats, and under the sink, and around all the boxes of groceries (which are beans and rice mostly, with about seven or eight little bottles of Tabasco sauce).

"I'm gonna walk the shoulder a bit. See if I come up with something," I say.

"Yeah. We are definitely going to need a piece of wire for this other one," Paul shouts from behind the van.

The shoulder is clean. Hot and glistening. Vapors swirl in the distance. The shrubs look anchored, as though you could pull on them all day and they'd never give. They are few and scattered, dotting the cracked sand for miles. *There's not going to be any wire out here,* I think to myself. I break a piece of sagebrush in my fingers. It's got that pine tree smell. Smells good and clean, like bottled-up Colorado. A semi rolls in from the distance, comes in like wind, and blows its horn as it passes. We're parked tight on the shoulder. The gust blows past. Stirs up dirt. Another semi and then a car, and I see, out a bit, a little something glimmering that doesn't look like glass or road. Walking up to it, it's just a strip of plastic and I toss it off the shoulder.

PAUL'S HANDS ARE TIGHT AROUND THE LINKAGE connector. He's got one hand pushing it in close to the carburetor and the other working the linkage tight, threading it and wrapping it. He's done it twice now and pulled it out a third time to start over. He looks at the other carb and sees it loose, and sort of blows a little sigh and shakes his head. He lowers his head, presses with one hand, and begins to thread with the other. Hearing a semi come up, he tilts his head into his arm and closes his eyes. The truck bellows past and spits some stinging sand across his back and all around the engine and his arms. He shakes it off and goes back to his work.

LOOKING BACK, I SEE THE VAN AND REALIZE IT IS closer to the road than I thought it was. Paul is invisible behind it. A car comes up and slows a little, making his way half into the other lane and then quickens to pass the van at full speed. The shoulder is uncommonly clean, as though fate had swept it, knowing we were coming to a stop right here. Three days ago there was probably a lot of trash along this road. There was probably a good piece of wire too. Some street sweeper, or more likely a collection of prisoners with yellow jackets and garbage bags, cleaned the place up. Just our luck.

I say a little prayer, asking God for some help.

Trouble leads to question and question leads to prayer. It's funny how I usually don't care about faith until life falls apart, until I find myself in the middle of some kind of jam. So I pray a little and not too much later I get an idea, a fix for our trouble. The idea puts a jolt in my step and I head back toward the van.

"You fond of that stereo?" I ask.

"What's that?" Paul says.

"How much do you care about that stereo in there? Can you live without one of the speakers for a while?"

"Good thinking, Don."

I get to work ripping the paneling off the passenger door and disconnect the speaker from its wire. Removing the stereo from its hole, I'm able to pull the wire all the way through and I've got a good four feet wrapped around my hand when I round the van. Paul has the first linkage fixed pretty tight and together we manipulate the other. I cut the wire and he connects it and begins to thread an end through the linkage connector. "You ought to stretch it out first," I suggest.

"Yeah." He undoes a little of his work and pulls the wire to stretch it. I hold the connector firm and he threads it through again.

"Work the pedal, would you?" he says.

Working the pedal shows Paul's fix is good. He has me hold it and rock the gas so he can test the strength. He wants it to hold for the rest of the trip. "Looks good," he mumbles.

"What's that, Paul?"

"Start it up!" he shouts.

The van starts. The gas that was in the carb quickly fires. New fuel funnels through. It moans, backfires, and drinks the fuel like lemonade. Pressing down the pedal revs the engine louder. I get the thing screaming and hold it. Paul closes the engine compartment and comes around to the driver's window. He's standing out in the road and giving me a look about revving the engine.

"Sounds like it works," he says with the same look.

"What's that you say?" I've got the engine so loud I pretend not to hear.

"Sound's pretty good. Maybe you should lay off the gas," he shouts with a smile.

"Give it gas?" I say and press down the pedal.

He thumps me on the side of my face. "No," he says. "It works. No more gas."

I let off the gas and lean back in the seat. He goes to open the door but I lock it. He reaches through the door and unlocks it and goes to open it and I lock it again.

"Need a ride?" I ask.

"That might be good." Paul smiles, grabbing quickly at the lock so he can open the door.

"You drive," I say, shifting over to the passenger's seat.

"That's right. You haven't slept, have you?" Paul climbs in and places the toolbox between the seats.

"No. I haven't slept. I'm fading too." The stereo is up on the dash so I stuff it back into the hole, poking the wires behind it. "That other speaker should still work," I say.

"Maybe time for a little Skynyrd." Paul's got a grin and he's reaching over to the glove box. I quickly raise my feet so they're firmly against the dash, blocking his attempt.

"I see how it is." Paul grins and nods as he forces the gearshift into first and releases the clutch. He checks the rearview mirror and pulls us onto the highway. "I see how it is," he says again.

7 FLAGSTAFF

WHEN WE NEAR THE CITY IN THE EVENING, FALLING stars dive and duck behind tall buildings. Flagstaff rests on the side of a mountain and so it is serene. You can see the dark peak rise like a thunderhead. We are on a black stretch of road that enters Flagstaff from the east. Signs mark the giant meteor crater just thirty miles out. You can pay a fee, during the day, and stand on its rim, or go inside the museum and watch films about space and that sort of thing. Paul and I pass the signs without so much as a word. We are heading toward a bigger hole in the ground than this. Streetlights on the outskirts of town stand guard like old Roman soldiers. Fire engines are chasing smoke signals from someone's tragedy. This city is cut from a different cloth than other cities: people living in community, not so much on top of the earth but in it, close to its mountains and to the great canyon, some seventy miles beyond. These are desert people who have come to live in the thick of trees collected on this mountainside. The whole thing reminds me of a tiny island in the ocean, and I begin to think of the van as a boat, puttering toward shore. Many cities, these days, seem to have people living on the surface of life but hardly in its soil, diluting the deeper questions of life in television monologues and reality shows, amusing ourselves to death, as Neil Postman would say. But this city feels different. It feels like these people have come up with different answers to the *why* questions, and they created a little commune that became a city, and they share their answers only with each other, answers about desert ghosts, about the sun being a god, about messages encoded in stars.

But then I come to Flagstaff with presuppositions. Without having been here, I can say with confidence that half these people believe in UFOs. One in one hundred has been sucked into a spinning-sphere ship and carries vague memories of little green men taking skin samples from his buttocks. They have scars to prove it and will show you if they've had enough beer and the bar is nearly empty. There is also a growing college crowd who've bought into the idea of simplicity. They drive fashionable Jeeps, wear the same khaki pants every day, and have dogs named Sigmund or Maslow. In each of their apartments you will find, somewhere, a painting by Georgia O'Keeffe. They curse cement and consider New York and Chicago thorns in the side of Mother Nature's flesh. They are tan, good-natured, and don't wash their hair.

I don't know that this town would accept me. You don't dust Houston off your boots in three days. Paul, however, would fit just fine. As far as I know, he has never been abducted by aliens, but they would forgive that. He is courteous and would stare for hours at their Georgia O'Keeffe paintings, nodding as they pontificate about her use of color and form. I, on the other hand, would simply say she uses too much brown and makes me thirsty.

Paul is better than me in this way. He can appreciate the person inside the persona. To him, people are more important than ideas. He does not laugh at jokes that deprecate others. His is a true, empathetic, kind character. We've similar histories, Paul and I. Both of us grew up in broken homes; both encountered faith at an early age; both share enthusiasm for taking chances. Still, he is advanced further in altruism, which I have always considered to be a kind of emotional genius. What I mean is that most of us are always worried about what others are thinking, the concern finds its way into our words and actions and dreams and feelings, and Paul seems to be above it, or below it, I don't know, just disaffected. He doesn't worry about much of anything, which strikes me as a kind of miracle. How does a person stop caring about the opinion of others enough to enjoy them without manipulating them? How does a person stop caring about money to pay rent, about where his food will come from, or whether or not he has a good retirement package? When with Paul, one is confronted with the notion that life may be much easier than the rest of us believe it is, that most of the things we worry about are not worth worrying about, that a low bank account or unfashionable clothes won't give you cancer. And this is precisely how it sometimes feels to me, that a low bank account or low social status will give me cancer.

I tend to think life is about security, that when you have a full year's rent, you can rest. I worry about things too much, I worry about whether or not my ideas are right, I worry about whether or not people like me, I worry about whether or not I am going to get married, and then I worry about whether or not my girl will leave me if I do get married. Lately I found myself worrying about whether or not my car was fashionable, whether I sounded like an idiot when I spoke in public, whether or not my hair was going to fall out, and all of it, perhaps, because I bought into Houston, one thousand square miles of concrete and strip malls and megachurches and cineplexes, none of it real. I mean it is there, it is made of matter, but it is all hype. None of the messages are true or have anything to do with the fact we are spinning around on a planet in a galaxy set somewhere in a cosmos that doesn't have any edges to it. There doesn't seem to be any science saying any of this *stuff* matters at all. But it feels like *it* matters, whatever *it* is; it feels like we are supposed to be panicking about things. I remember driving down I-45 a few months ago and suddenly realizing the number of signs that were screaming at me, signs wanting me to buy waterbeds, signs wanting me to watch girls take off their clothes, signs wanting me to eat

Mexican food, to eat barbeque, backlit, scrolling signs wanting me to come to church, to join this gym, to see this movie, to finance a car, even if I have no money. And it hit me that, amid the screaming noise, amid the messages that said buy this product and I will be made complete, I could hardly know the life that life was meant to be. Houston makes you feel that life is about the panic and the resolution of the panic, and nothing more. Nobody stops to question whether they actually need the house and the car and the better job. And because of this there doesn't seem to be any peace; there isn't any serenity. We can't see the stars in Houston anymore, we can't go to the beach without stepping on a Coke bottle, we can't hike in the woods, because there aren't any more woods. We can only panic about the clothes we wear, panic about the car we drive, sit stuck in traffic and panic about whether or not the guy who cut us off respects us. We want to kill him, for crying out loud, and all the while we feel a need for new furniture and a new television and a bigger house in the right neighborhood. We drive around in a trance, salivating for Starbucks while that great heaven sits above us, and that beautiful sunrise is happening in the desert, and all those mountains out West are collecting snow on the limbs of their pines, and all those leaves are changing colors out East. God, it is so beautiful, it is so quiet, it is so perfect. It makes you feel, perhaps for a second, that Paul gets it and we don't—that if you live in a van and get up for sunrise and cook your own food on a fire and stop caring about whether your car breaks down or whether you have fashionable clothes or whether or not people do or do not like you, that you have broken through, that you have shut your ear to the bombardment of lies that never, ever stop whispering in your ear. And maybe this is why he seems so different to me, because he has become a human who no longer believes the commercials are true, which, perhaps, is what a human was designed to be.

It makes sense, if you think about it. I mean we stood out in the desert this morning, and the chemicals in my brain poured soothingly through the gray matter, as if to massage with fingers the most tender part of my mind, as if to say, this is what a human is supposed to feel. This is what we were made for, to watch the beauty of light fill up earth's canvas, to make dirt come alive; like fairy dust, making trees and cacti and humans from the magic of its propulsion. It makes me wonder, now, how easily the brain can be tricked out of what it was supposed to feel, how easily the brain can be tricked by somebody who has a used car to sell, a new perfume, whatever. *You will feel what you were made to feel if you buy this thing I am selling.* But could the thing you and I were supposed to feel, the thing you and I were supposed to be, cost nothing? Paul seems to think so, or at least he acts as if this is true. He doesn't want to stay in a hotel room and catch up on the news. He doesn't want to rifle through the sports page and make sure the team he has associated his ego with is doing well. I don't think he is trying to win anything at all. I just think he is trying to feel what a human is supposed to feel when he stops believing lies. And maybe when a person doesn't buy the lies anymore, when a human stops long enough to realize the stuff people say to get us to part with our money often isn't true, we can finally see the sunrise, smell the wetness in a Gulf breeze, stand in awe at a downpour no less magnificent than a twenty-thousand-foot waterfall, ten square miles wide, wonder at the physics of a duck paddling itself across the surface of a pond, enjoy the reflection of the sun on the face of the moon, and know, *This is what I was made to do. This is who I was made to be,* that life is being given to me as a gift, that light is a metaphor, and God is doing these things to dazzle us.

THE MAIN ROADS IN FLAGSTAFF BREAK OFF INTO tributaries that climb the hillside; streets are lined with two-story brick offices, pubs, and retail shops. It is not as busy as I thought it might be. It is ten o'clock in the evening and the streets are vacant, save the occasional cars and lone walkers. The air has cooled considerably. We've probably lost thirty degrees in two hours. All the way in, we were gaining altitude, so the coolness is due to elevation as well as evening. Trees are dense at this altitude. Pine and evergreen. Mountain air. This is how I imagine Colorado or Montana, but not Arizona. I imagined Flagstaff as a desert town, but it isn't. There are shade and streams and small parks. We opt not to stay in Flagstaff, but to keep driving toward the canyon. I am trusting Paul will be able to drive the short distance, because I am too tired to hold a thought, much less navigate the winding road.

We round a bend and weave through town to find an exit road that cuts deep embankments in the side of the mountain. The road hugs the hill and we navigate tight curves banked by a wall of dirt on one side and pine on the other. Two lanes and no shoulder. Flagstaff fades and disappears into the trees and behind us. Patches of snow rest amid pine needles. The temperature has actually cooled enough to allow snow to stick and stay. Our headlights sweep along the tree line as we round another curve. The lights peer deep into the forest and I can see the white-backed snow humps in with the brown and green. "Are you seeing the snow, Paul?"

"Yeah."

"It's amazing," I say.

"Have you ever seen snow, Don?"

"A little. It snowed once in Houston, but it wasn't cold enough to stick. It only snowed for a few minutes. I was just a kid."

"Well, there's your snow." Paul says this with a smile.

"There it is."

I've got my eyes looking for snow like a child would for a deer after one had jumped across the road. I'm fixated by the idea of snow. People in Houston dream about it during winter. We celebrate Christmas with shorts on and get about five or six days a year that actually drop below freezing. Winter is just summer with an ice cube and a straw. As a kid I'd always dreamed about living in a place where it snowed. I picked Maine on a map because it was as far north as you could go and still run for president.

Every few curves we see a small house tucked into the woods. People living the simple life. They chop their own wood and grow their own carrots and beets and spend evening hours peering their beady eyes through Radio Shack telescopes, hoping to get a look at Luke Skywalker.

Paul slides the van off the side of the road a bit, our tires rubbing against the abrupt pavement. He pulls back on the road, overcompensating into the opposite lane. He steps on the brake and slows the van, and it rocks toward the left front. He pulls back into our lane and shakes his head as if to wake himself.

"Did you fall asleep?" I ask.

"I don't remember," he says, sort of smiling, but more out of relief that we didn't wreck than from a joke.

"We should pull over and sleep. We can see the canyon in the morning," I tell him. Paul starts looking for a dirt road and eventually pulls off into a field. I get out and feel the silence in the high desert, noting the stars against the horizon where hills fade to black in slow mounds. I notice a pile of snow a hundred feet away and walk over to examine it, coming to it slowly, a celestial carcass, like some angel shot out of the sky, falling to earth to glisten and melt.

8 FLOATING BODIES AT HOOVER DAM

THE AREA AROUND THE GRAND CANYON IS SURPRIS-
ingly flat. Dense with pine trees, the ground not taken by forest is brown with desert sand. A Disneyland atmosphere
surrounds the place. Rangers have tried to give the area a park
feel (and it has some of that), but it is mostly a tourist trap and
one more state decal stuck on the back of an old couple's
retirement vehicle. There are lawn chairs and picnic tables and
crying babies held by mothers who juggle diaper bags and
strollers. Fathers wear khaki shorts, white tennis shoes, and
blue socks. They lead their families around the canyon edge
like tour guides, explaining how many millions of years it took
for the river to carve this hole in the earth.

Paul and I are set back twenty dollars apiece at the entrance.
We pay the sum in exchange for permission to enter the park.
We decide not to pay the additional thirty dollars required to
camp. With the van, we agree that we can sleep anywhere and
will head back into town if we need to. Our first stop within
the gate is the canyon edge, where the aforementioned scene
plays out before us. No amount of hype or brochure sales copy
can prepare a person for the breathtaking depth of the canyon
itself. From twenty feet away, we see an abrupt drop in the
landscape. As we near the edge, the depth is all-consuming.
There seems to be no bottom. No words are spoken here, and
the sound of children fades to the background as a breeze
whistles through sagebrush and a fiery red cliff drops under
our feet. It is a top-of-the-roller-coaster feeling as I imagine

myself plunging headlong over the rail. Enough emotion to take a step back and catch my breath. Regaining my senses, I lean over the edge and focus my eyes to find the bottom. Perhaps the Colorado River that Ben Bonham told us about will come to view. But it doesn't. What I see several miles down is a flat surface, a peninsula edged by another drop. A canyon inside of a canyon. We are not at the park's most popular overlook, but at a trailhead for those planning a hike all the way down.

"How many miles do you figure it is to the bottom?" I ask.

Paul looks down at a few hikers, looks again at the peninsula, and shrugs his shoulders. "I guess we will know soon enough."

"Do you think we can start today?" I ask, half unsettled at the tremendous depth. I feel a weakness in my legs and am altogether unsure whether I have the stamina to find the bottom.

Paul notes the reservation in my voice. "I don't know if we need a permit or anything. We can go to the information center and find out. We'll do fine, Don."

"I'm looking forward to it," I say.

Paul turns and walks toward the van. A child licks his ice-cream cone, and an old couple pass binoculars back and forth. One is talking to the other about a certain shrub or tree that the other has spotted. "To the right," he says, as she swings the black tubes too far. "Not over there," he says, "here, honey." He points but she doesn't see, too busy fidgeting with the focus lever.

I near the trailhead and eye its steep switchbacks weave under each other. They are thin trails with no protective guardrails. One of the hikers gets caught by a gust of wind and leans back against the rock wall until it passes. One false step could send her into a freefall that would last thirty seconds or more. The trail becomes so thin to my eye that I lose it in the camouflage of red rock and sand.

Paul is more eager to hike the canyon than I am. He didn't

look at it for more than a minute before turning away. The look on his face and the surety of his step tell me that, come rain or snow, we will hike to the bottom of this hole.

The information center is a cave of a structure. It is walled with river rock and has a wood porch like a cabin in the mountains. A big building with a big parking lot, RVs line the road for several hundred yards before we find an open space. Families with matching sunburns stream in and out of the building. One family on the large porch gathers around their leader, who wrestles with the creases of the park map. It is all he can do to keep the map unfolded. It wraps around his arms like a fishing net.

Inside the information center, everything is dark. While not overly warm outside, the sky is bright and so our eyes adjust slowly to the brown décor of the large room fit with cement floors, ceiling fans, and brochure-lined walls, all of it smelling like mosquito repellent.

Paul bypasses the brochures and the rock exhibit, making his way to the counter where a young girl in a brown uniform stands with a fake smile.

"Can I help you?"

"Yes. We were needing a trail map for the canyon."

"Are you going down?" she asks.

"Yes," one of us says.

"Do you have your permit yet?"

"Well, I didn't know for sure if we needed one," Paul remarks.

"You do," she says.

"We do," I say, lifting my eyebrows. I pull out my Blockbuster video card and set it on the counter. She looks at it confused, then back at Paul.

"You will need a permit," she says.

Paul turns and looks at me and then turns back. She's still got that same smile going, and he's softly bouncing his fingers on the counter.

"Do you know if there is a cost for that?"

"The permit?" she clarifies.

"Yes," Paul answers.

"There's no cost. But you can't get a permit here. Permits are issued in the trailhead office."

"The trailhead office," Paul echoes. I pick up my Blockbuster card and set down my Bally's Total Fitness membership card, along with my driver's license. The girl looks at the cards and I lift my eyebrows and, after looking at me confused, she looks back at Paul.

"Yes, the trailhead office," she says.

I crack a smile as Paul walks the girl through every step of her job.

"Where is the trailhead office?" he asks.

The girl turns and grabs a three-ring notebook with a dozen or more pages, each page held in a protective glossy sheet. She flips slowly through them and sets her finger down firmly when she finds what she's looking for.

"Here it is," she says as she turns the notebook around so Paul can see. I look over Paul's shoulder at the map.

"This *X* is the permit office?" Paul asks.

"That's the place."

"Now, where are we?"

"You . . . you . . . are here." And she places her finger only an inch from the permit office.

"So," Paul begins, "it looks like we should just go out the door and, well, it doesn't look like it's very far."

"Well," she says, "if you go out this door"—she points and looks to the left—"it is right there. It's a brown trailer."

"It is right outside the door?" Paul asks in disbelief.

"Yes," she says, and I audibly chuckle. She doesn't notice my laugh, and then I see a sheepish look come over her face. She turns and points out the window. "Duh, I'm so silly," she says. "You can see it outside the window. That's it right there."

"Right there," Paul clarifies as he points to a brown trailer.

"That's it," she says and her smile turns big.

"Duh," I say with a gentle smile. Paul steps on my foot to get me to stop.

"I mean," I begin apologetically, "we should have known that."

"Oh, no. It's my job," she clarifies.

"Duh," I mumble and Paul steps on my foot again and the girl smiles real big.

"Have fun in the canyon," she says.

"We will."

I let Paul go a few feet toward the door while I remain at the counter. "Paul," I shout, "do you think we need a map to the door? It's awful dark in here." I turn back to the girl and she smiles and points to the door.

"Over there," she says.

"There," I clarify with a confused look and a point.

"He's got it," she says and looks at me like I'm stupid. "It's right there. He found it," she says.

"Thanks. Duh, I'm so silly sometimes."

"That's all right," she says, turning to the next person in line.

"I can't believe you did that." Paul holds the door open and greets me with a grin.

"I was just playing with her."

Paul eyes the brown trailer across the parking lot. "That's it. Let's go get the permit."

The interior of the trailer is wood paneling and brown trim. There is a tall man in a uniform behind a counter. Otherwise, the trailer is empty. Paul greets the uniformed man.

"Hello. We want to get a couple of permits for the canyon."

"You are in the right place," the man says. "Did you make a reservation?"

"No. We didn't know we needed one."

"Most people make reservations before they come. We can only have so many people in the canyon at a time."

"Do you have any openings?" Paul asks.

The man pulls out a three-ring notebook and files through pages. It is a thick book and filled line by line with signatures.

"I don't know if we can get you in anytime soon," he responds.

"When's the soonest?" Paul asks.

The man looks back at his notebook, scanning down the page with his finger. He flips the page and scans down the backside. Paul sighs and gives me a hopeful look. I set my Blockbuster card on the counter but Paul picks it up and puts it in his pocket before the man sees it.

"I can get you in on Easter morning. You will have a permit to camp at the bottom that night. Indian Springs campground will have a space for you the next day."

"Indian Springs?" Paul questions.

"Indian Springs is the campground about halfway up. I can put you at the bottom on Sunday night. You will have to hike out the next day and come to Bright Angel. All I can give you is one day at Indian Springs. Then you'll have to come out."

Paul lifts his eyebrows and sighs. "If that's all we can get, we'll take it, I guess."

"That is all I can do for you."

Paul looks over and asks me what day it is. "Wednesday," I respond.

"You'll have to stick around for a few days," the uniformed man says, clarifying the importance of not breaking the rules.

"Fine with me." Paul glances my way.

"Yeah, that's fine." I shrug.

The man turns the notebook around and hands Paul a pencil. "You guys come back and check with me if you decide to leave. Plenty of people would like these permits."

He pulls out a pink piece of paper and hands it to me. It has a list of numbered guidelines. "Don't veer off the trail," he begins. "Pack out your trash, don't approach animals, carry plenty of water, don't wash your gear in the river, only make camp in a designated area, use no radios or other electronic devices that create an excess of noise."

The list goes on for a while and the man reads each rule carefully. He then hands us permits to sign.

"Keep your copy with you at all times," he says. "Does either of you have a heart condition?"

"Heart condition?" I ask, puzzled.

"A heart condition or any other medical problem that might get you into trouble."

"No," Paul says.

"No," I answer.

Looking directly at me, he begins his warning: "Last week a man had a heart attack about halfway up from Bright Angel. There was nothing we could do for him. Rangers carried his body to the rim. If you get into trouble at the bottom, we will not send a helicopter down for you. There is no place for us to land. So, our policy is to float your dead body down the river and fish you out at Hoover Dam."

The man turns to Paul, straight-faced, and then gives a wink. "Just kidding," he says. "Still, a man did die last week. But if you get into trouble, we can bring you out on a donkey. But you have to be dead first. And your parents will have to pay for the donkey. That's the only way you get a free ride out."

"Kidding?" I ask.

"I'm not joking this time. If you aren't sure that you can make it to the bottom and back, don't go. This is a difficult hike. There is nothing easy about it. Nine miles in and ten miles out. An elevation loss and gain of over five thousand feet. Every year we have people die on those trails."

"We will be careful," Paul assures the man, folding his permit and putting it in his pocket.

We turn toward the door and my legs feel numb. I've got butterflies in my stomach. Houston is very, very flat. I've never been above one thousand feet before, much less from five thousand to zero and back. Or whatever the elevation is.

"You boys have a good hike," the man says as we walk out the door.

"Well, bud, we're in." Paul raises his hand for a high five.

I meet his hand and give a good grin. "Can't believe it," I say. "We are actually going to do this."

"It is going to be great, Don. You are really going to love this hike. Your first big nature experience." He sees my grin turn down a little. "Think of it, the canyon walls, the red rock, the river flowing right by our camp, the stars from the bottom of the canyon."

"Can't think of a better place to die," I say.

"That's the spirit!" Paul says, turning to walk toward the van.

A body floating down the river, I think to myself. The sound of the turbines at Hoover Dam, my crying mother, the bloated-blue figure wearing the Grand Canyon T-shirt that sickens the onlookers at my funeral.

"I'm pumped, Paul. This is going to be good," I say through a fake grin.

"You bet it is," he says, looking back.

9 DANCING

IT IS DIFFICULT TO RECALL, MUCH LESS RECAPTURE, the excitement of an adventure's beginning when you find yourself in the boring middle of it. Paul and I have been waiting for three days. Tomorrow morning we will hike into the canyon. My earlier reservations about the intensity of the hike have been allayed by a burning off of anxiety, the twiddling of thumbs. And today we are off on short hikes to and from the day-use area. The canyon splendor has bewildered the depth of my imagination. We've seen every overlook the park allows. This gargantuan hole they call Grand has no less depth from any angle. To the human eye, it is bottomless.

The waiting has not been all bad. Paul, the cook, has been standing over an enormous pot of beans and rice for an hour and I have written postcards to family, friends, and Ben Bonham, the last of whom will receive a detailed description of the canyon edge, specifically worded to remind him and his wife of the beauty they twice knew.

A park ranger came through the day-use area and attempted conversations with several families. He spent a little time with us and answered questions about the route we've chosen to hike. Ours will be a loop down the Kaibab Trail to where we will camp on the canyon floor. On Monday we will leave Kaibab and take the Bright Angel Trail halfway up where there is a meadow and another camping area called Indian Springs. We will stay at Indian Springs two days and then finish the ascent on the third day. All in all, being only nineteen miles and over three days' time, the hike doesn't intimidate the way it did a few days back. The ranger also told us about the sunrise service tomorrow morning. "Sunrise over the canyon is beautiful," he says. Apparently it is an Easter tradition and hundreds of people attend every year.

Imagining the service reminds me again that life is more than clothes and cars and a new flavor of toothpaste, that it is community and creation and beauty and humanity. And I think I am starting to prefer the latter to the former; by that I mean I am getting used to not having any music or television and not pulling over and buying something as a way of feeling some kind of change. There is a serenity in life, after all, and once a withdrawl is felt at having left the lies behind, a soul begins to feel at home in its own skin. The first day at the canyon there was a lot of withdrawal. I actually walked over to the gift shop and contemplated buying a little license-plate keychain with my name spelled on it. I talked myself out of it because I don't actually have any keys, but part of me just wanted to smell the smell of new rubber and have something new as a way of feeling different about myself. But I didn't buy it. I hiked back to the canyon edge and watched the sun go down over the massive stretch of brown, and then I sat on a bench and watched lovers stroll along the guardrail and felt a quiet peace as the coolness gave way to coldness, which got me off the bench and had me walking along the canyon rim, praying, I think, and thanking God for beauty and for rest and thanking Him for something better to believe than commercials.

I was raised to believe that the quality of a man's life would greatly increase, not with the gain of status or success, not by his heart's knowing romance or by prosperity in industry or academia, but by his nearness to God. It confuses me that Christian living is not simpler. The gospel, the very good news, is simple, but this is the gate, the trailhead. Ironing out faithless creases is toilsome labor. God bestows three blessings on man: to feed him like birds, dress him like flowers, and befriend him as a confidant. Too many take the first two and neglect the last. Sooner or later you figure out life is constructed specifically and brilliantly to squeeze a man into association with the Owner of heaven. It is a struggle, with labor pains and thorny landscape, bloody hands and a sweaty brow, head in hands, moments of severe loneliness and questioning, moments of ache and desire. All this leads to God, I think. Perhaps this is what is on the other side of the commercials, on the other side of the curtain behind which the Wizard of Oz pulls his levers. Matter and thought are a canvas on which God paints, a painting with tragedy and delivery, with sin and redemption. *Life is a dance toward God,* I begin to think. And the dance is not so graceful as we might want. While we glide and swing our practiced sway, God crowds our feet, bumps our toes, and scuffs our shoes. So we learn to dance with the One who made us. And it is a difficult dance to learn, because its steps are foreign.

I begin to think of my time at the canyon in these terms, as learning to dance in a new way, the first few lessons had me feeling clunky and awkward, but soon they will give way to a kind of graceful sway, and I won't stop at gift shops or hunt for a television, but like Paul I will be able to stand over a pot of boiling beans for hours and feel completely content, as though there was nothing in life that I was missing out on. It gives me a little joy to think about things this way, and I smile at a couple as they pass me along the guardrail, and I pull a bit of pine needle off a tree and roll it in my palms and smell the mintlike scent of creation as I let the green shards spill from my palms to the path along the rim. And I think to myself, *There is nothing I am missing. I have everything I was supposed to have to experience the magnitude of this story, to dance with God.*

10 EASTER DESCENT

SEVEN MILES FROM GRAND CANYON NATIONAL PARK there are sleeping pines that line the dark highway. They break their fences to reveal stretches of moonlit desert back toward Flagstaff. On this particular stretch of road there is a hotel, where families sleep soundly in the early morning darkness. Behind this hotel there is a van, a Volkswagen with two tired, sleeping passengers. They cover their heads in blankets at first light and each thinks to himself how he should wake the other up. But the lazy sun slowly climbs the lazy sky and the lazy passengers go back to sleep beneath the sleeping pines and care not about Easter sunrise or creating memories or witnessing, once again, the great metaphor of God, the sun coming up over the horizon, rising once again, as though from the dead.

• • •

ON THE ROAD FROM THE HOTEL TO THE CANYON WE ARE able to pick up a Flagstaff radio station. KTLY, an oldies station, plays the Beatles on Sunday morning. One of the first bands to utilize stereo technology, the Beatles produced their early records so the lead vocals are committed to one speaker and the music and backup vocals to the other. Short one speaker, we have a built-in karaoke machine. Paul and I are unsure in our singing. Is it "Help me if you can I'm feeling down, and I do appreciate you being round," or is it "Help me if you can I'm feeling down, and I do appreciate you coming round"? My money is on "coming round." Regardless, the words "Won't you please, please help me" come in clear from the driver's side, and Paul and I are tapping our palms against the dash, coming in strong when John, Paul, George, and Ringo offer their voices to the right side.

The disc jockey has a middle-aged voice. "This is Geoffrey Clark and you're listening to All Beatles Sunday on KTLY Radio, 102 FM, Flagstaff, Grand Canyon. That was 'Please, Please, Help Me,' and now, one of my personal favorites, a really groovy tune called 'Paperback Writer.'"

We picked up some resealable bags from the national park grocery store a couple days back, and once we reach the parking lot at the trailhead, Paul begins filling a few of them with day-old beans and rice. We've got bananas and apples and several tea bags and hot apple cider mix, as well. I ask him if we have some steak, and he shakes his head no. I ask about milk shakes, and he shakes his head no.

"You probably want to put that in the top of your pack," Paul says after handing me a bag of brown mushy beans.

"Do you think we've got enough water?" I ask.

"Four canteens should get us to the bottom. There will be fresh water there, and I've got purification tablets if there's not."

I place one change of underwear, two pair of socks, and a T-shirt into my bag. Pushing them deep, I make room for my copy of *Catcher in the Rye* and a book of letters and poems by Emily Dickinson. My sleeping bag is not one of those fancy, light ones that campers have nowadays. It's cotton and wool and doubles the weight of the pack when I fasten it to the frame. I tie my metal cup to one of the side straps, and my toothbrush and toothpaste fit neatly in a side pocket.

"Do you have toilet paper?" I ask.

Paul doesn't look up but pats a side pocket on his pack. "Yeah, I've got some in here." He is pulling on a strap, tightening his sleeping bag to the top of his pack.

"Do you have any to spare?"

"Got plenty."

A couple of hikers lift their packs, tighten their straps around their waists, and stroll past us. I watch them out of the corner of my eye as they disappear behind a boulder and then appear again a good fifty feet down the canyon. They round a corner and disappear again.

"How are we going to get back to the van when we come out?" I ask.

"Well, we will just hike back to this trailhead when we come up from Bright Angel. We can probably hitch a ride if we want."

"Yeah, that sounds good," I say.

Paul opens the big sliding door on the van and rummages around.

"What are you looking for?" I ask.

"Just looking. Want to make sure I got everything."

I bought a Swiss Army knife for the trip. It has a fork, a knife, a toothpick, and a corkscrew. They had one with a spoon but it was twenty dollars more. I put my knife in the backpack but then decide I want to carry it in my pocket.

"Is this your hat?" Paul asks. He's holding a Panama-style Maxfli hat that he found beneath the bench in the van.

"Yeah, that's my golf hat."

"You play golf?" he asks.

"A little. Hand it here. I may as well wear it down."

I pull the hat firmly over my head. It has a tight elastic band so it fits nice and comfortable. I lift my pack by the frame and swing it around to my back. Feels like lead. It's so heavy, with the water and books, I stagger a little.

"Looks like you've got a heavy load there, Don."

"Yeah," I agree.

Taking the pack off, I remove my Emily Dickinson book and *Catcher in the Rye*. I also remove an apple or two, thinking that I will just make do with the food that I've got. The food is making the pack heavy. I have five meals with snacks and reduce this to four and no snacks, save two apples. It is not wise to hike so long without enough food, but the beans and rice are potent enough to fuel a racehorse, so I use that excuse to put one of the bags back into the van.

Paul slides the door closed and rounds the van to lock the doors.

"I guess we're ready," he says as he lifts his pack over his shoulders.

"We really are a couple of characters, aren't we?" I suggest, looking at our reflection in the window of the van. Paul has an old army pack he picked up at a surplus store on Galveston Island, and I've got this old pack from the seventies that is bright orange. Like a vest on a road worker, the pack is so bright it might very well glow in the dark. Another couple passes us with expensive gear and clothes, and Paul and I just shrug our shoulders.

"I don't think I'll be losing you in the canyon," Paul says, patting his hand against my bright backpack.

We round the boulder and stand side by side at the edge of the trail. There are clouds building in the distance, but the sky around them is deep and blue. It climbs as endlessly as the canyon descends and we experience one last bit of awe before we depart. I take a deep breath and pull at the shoulder straps of my pack.

"All this beauty makes a person realize how insignificant you are," Paul says.

"How insignificant I am?" I question. "You're the insignificant one."

He grins real big as he realizes how his words sounded. "I didn't mean it like that," he says.

"No, I know what you meant, bud. I was just thinking kind of the same thing. I was looking at all this depth and it came to me how very shallow you are."

"Ha, ha," Paul chortles. He takes a few steps down the trail and then turns. "You know, Don, I was just looking at this little flowery cactus here and thinking how nice it looks, and it made me realize how ugly you are."

"Is that right? How ugly I am," I say, kicking some dirt toward my friend.

Our fun turns to work fairly quickly as we wind down the switchbacks. Some descend thirty and forty feet in only a few paces, but the canyon offers splendor at every turn. It is a wonder they carved a trail into the canyon at all. It is onerously steep. At times the trail thins to three or four feet, with nothing but drop as a border. The mind gets used to the danger so that a hiker can set his stride only inches from the cliff, making pace, not caring about his fall. It gives me a sense of pride as I narrowly navigate the trail and keep steady with Paul.

I start thinking about the wonder of the canyon, how mountains get all kinds of attention because they are so high, but canyons are no less magnificent, only overlooked because they don't stand out to the eye. After all, it is no more a miracle there is a towering pile of dirt and rock than an absence of it. And who cares that there is no view from the bottom? Half the time you can't see anything from the top of a mountain anyway and they are terribly difficult to climb. In terms of analogies, canyons are sorely neglected. A canyon can be used to describe hell or confusion or all sorts of important spiritual realities. Without canyons, mountains would have no point of reference, for example. A canyon is, after all, an upside-down mountain. Except they most often have rivers at the bottom, and mountains have no rivers on top. Just snow and little flags that represent different hikers from different countries, and little frozen bodies clinging to frozen flags.

The Grand Canyon, as Paul tells me, is not the deepest canyon in the United States. I didn't know that. The deepest canyon is on the Oregon-Idaho border. It is Hells Canyon, and drops more than six thousand feet from rim to river. Paul tells me it is a gradual slope with a road that goes to the bottom so it doesn't have the dangerous view this canyon provides, and that is why nobody recognizes it as spectacular. I cannot imagine anything deeper than this, I tell him.

The trail does not give in its slope. My toes are sliding into the front of my boots and my heel has not felt shoe in an hour. Looking up, the canyon rim does not seem so far. We've hiked a mile or more and still the bottom of the canyon is not in view. We only see the first ledge that hides the river. And there is no telling how far the river is from the first ledge.

"Doesn't seem like we've gotten anywhere, does it?" Paul says as he looks up at the rim.

"I was thinking the same thing."

As we hike, Paul gets ahead of me by a switchback and then another. I'm growing tired and my toes are really getting to me. My right big toe rubs against the side of my boot. I can feel the skin getting tender so it slows my pace and Paul gets a little farther ahead. His pace is slowing, too, but he still gets away. He's four switchbacks down and I can see him when I come to the edge and look directly down. I walk through the pain, trying to ignore it. I grimace as I step and there is a rocking in my stride. I move a bit more quickly to catch my friend. Coming within one switchback of Paul, I see he has a drag in his step. No smile. No grimace, but no smile. He's not having it as tough as I am, but it sets me at ease to know I am not a complete wimp. This hike is actually difficult, even for Paul. He rounds the switchback and I notice he gives a nod to someone underneath my trail. He engages in a conversation and I wind down the corner to see two hikers sitting in the mouth of a shallow cave. One is dipping his Swiss Army knife into a jar of peanut butter. He has a piece of bread on his knee. The other hiker is leaning against the rock and looks exhausted. His legs are stretched out over the boulder in front of him.

"How long have you guys been hiking?" the one without the knife asks.

Paul looks over and shrugs his shoulder. He turns back. "About two hours. Probably two hours. How about you guys?"

The guy with the peanut butter handles his bread and doesn't look up. "We left the bottom about four hours ago. Maybe more."

"Four hours," I clarify.

The one on the right rubs his leg. "Don't worry. It takes a lot longer coming up than going down. You guys should be there in three hours."

"You said that right," the other adds. "Coming up is a bear."

As we leave, the guy with the peanut butter pulls his knife from the jar. He has the knife that includes the spoon. It has a bigger blade, too, and it makes me wish I had paid the twenty extra bucks to get that one. Peanut butter, however, doesn't sound very good. Too thirsty. We leave the two hikers to their sandwiches and round another switchback, walking now into a brisk, dry wind.

"How are your feet?" I ask as Paul drags his steps in front of me.

"They're getting to me a little. How about yours?"

"Mine feel fine. Feel like a million bucks."

"Is that right?" Paul inquires.

"Sure. Feel like I could run a marathon." My smile gives away my lie.

"Is that why you were making that grunt noise back there?" he asks.

"What grunt noise?"

"Back there when you leaned against that rock and started crying for your mommy."

With that, I give him a good kick in the backside. He jumps a few steps and kicks a little dirt back on me.

"We'll see who's crying mommy," I say.

Paul gains a few paces and then turns, looking at my feet.

"Seriously," he asks. "How are you holding up?"

"My toes are killing me, and I've got a blister starting on my right foot."

"I've got duct tape if you need it," he says.

"Duct tape?"

"Yeah, it's great. Put duct tape over your blisters and it's like having second skin."

"Just one more use for duct tape," I add.

"The stuff is great, isn't it?"

"I used to fix all the vapor hoses on my Datsun with . . . whoa . . . hey now." A gust of wind catches my pack and I lose my footing. Coming to my knee only an inch from the cliff, my body and most of my weight look over to see a few pebbles bounce down the rock face. They move in slow motion and twist and turn and catch ledges all the way down. At least a thousand feet. Paul grabs my pack and pulls me onto the trail.

"You all right?"

"I'm good," I say and get back to my feet, being careful to stay away from the edge. "The wind caught me like a sail."

"It almost had me too," he says. "We've got to watch these corners."

My heart is racing. I can still see the pebbles falling through the air. I shake it off and begin again, slowly and cautiously. Step by step.

I can feel the dirt on my knee drying up and it is tight, like a bandage wrapped over a scar. The wind continues to threaten and every few switchbacks it presses against me and rocks me a little. Paul is having trouble too, but manages it well and walks through the wind with a determined look. He gains a switchback and then I lose him around the corner. Too tired to catch up, I move slowly and can really feel the pain now. The blister on my toe is screaming, and my knees and shins are beginning to get tight. I thought hiking down would be easier than up, but it occurs to me I am using muscles I've never used before. My legs are having to stop my weight from falling and they are weak and can't take much more. Rounding the corner, Paul is a good distance ahead. A couple hundred feet down maybe. He shows no sign of stopping for a break, so I try to pick up my pace. It is no use. Moving slowly helps the pain. I grimace with every short step and begin to count the hours since we left. It must be three hours now. We left at around ten and it has to be one or two o'clock. I left my watch in the van, thinking I wouldn't need it, so I'm not sure of the exact time. Still, the canyon looks deep, and judging up from down, we are only about halfway. This is going to be a tougher hike than I imagined.

• • •

WE'VE BEEN AT IT FOR FOUR HOURS NOW. PAUL IS A good three hundred feet down. He's slowed his pace, but is still increasing the distance from me. Every step sends a jolt through my legs. I can feel the raw flesh on my toe. The skin folds up and then down every time I take a step. It is a terrible pain. My knees feel arthritic and my mouth is cotton dry. I'm too weak to get water and there is too far to go to stop and take a break. Besides, if I stop, I won't get going again. This isn't a pain that is eased by resting. My pack is heavy and bends my back straight. It rubs weight against me and I feel it slide left and right as I rock my body down the path. Who cares about the ledge? Who cares about the cliff? Quicker to the bottom, that's what I say.

FOUR AND A HALF HOURS, I'VE LOST PAUL BUT I HAVE seen the river. Back a few switchbacks, I got my first glimpse of it and it looked like heaven. Except it looked like hell, too, as it was so far away. I must be inside the second canyon. The one that isn't visible from the top. There is some grass down here and the path is wider. It has cooled off significantly and the air feels good. There is a thundercloud building overhead and it gives welcome shade. No rain, but good, cool shade. I plod the trail, keeping my head down and eyes fixed on the dusty path. My mouth is still cotton dry and I can't gather enough spittle to moisten my tongue. Everything is aching. I've reduced my pace to that of a turtle. I'm depleted, almost completely out of energy. I wonder if I would have grown up in Colorado or Montana if this would be so hard. If a trail this well maintained goes this deep into the canyon, it's not like it hasn't been traveled a million times.

The path takes a bend and becomes a narrow ledge that overlooks a small green valley. The rocks are no longer brown; they are gray. I follow the brown trail down the gray rocks as it makes a wide, deep loop and ends up below and opposite me. There is a narrow creek, a little stream that feeds some plant life, giving the valley color. My eye is so pleased at this sight, this very different sight, that I am energized and lift my feet a little above a drag as I take in the view. I haven't seen green in five hours. And water. Look at it. Listen to it lightly tap against the rocks. Following the stream with my eye, I see the trail where it meets the creek and there sits my old friend Paul. He has his pack off and is eating an apple and wearing a smile with bright eyes.

I really pick up my pace here, showing off for Paul. Making out like I'd not had such a rough go of it.

"We made it, bud," he greets me as I come toward him on the lower part of the trail.

"This is it?"

He holds up a finger. "Only one more mile. And it's an easy one."

"How do you know?"

"A ranger told me."

"Where is he?"

"He went back to the campground."

The stream gurgles next to us and the air lifts off the moving water, cool and damp.

"How long have you been here?" I ask.

"About twenty minutes." Paul throws his apple core into the grass on the other side of the stream. "How are you feeling?"

"Like a million bucks," I say. "How about you?"

"I'm thinking about going for a little jog later."

"A jog, huh?"

"Yep," he says.

"Well, I suppose we should crank out this last mile. If I stop, I'm not going to get started again."

"Yeah, I'm game for that," Paul says as he lifts his pack. "You want water first?" He's got a canteen open and he hands it to me. Without answering I take about five swigs. Big swigs that fill my belly and suddenly it feels like I've eaten Thanksgiving dinner. I'm full and feeling a little queasy.

"You sure you don't want to stop and rest?" he asks.

"I'm fine."

The texture of the trail has changed. It is more sand than dirt. White sand, and at places it becomes thick like a beach. My feet drag into it and sink an inch or so. Paul has these red tennis shoes on, and when he steps, the sand goes over his heels and spills down into his shoe. When he lifts up his foot, I can see that he has covered a blister with duct tape.

"How's that duct tape working?"

"Hurts like crazy," he says. "You got blisters?"

"What do you think?" I say.

We both drag and rock and sway with grimacing expressions. The trail swings away from the stream and, once again, begins descending.

"It's a lot cooler down here," I say. "I wonder if it is because we are close to the river."

"I don't think so. I mean, we are close to the river, but it feels to me like a cold front moved in while we were hiking. That cloud up there. I bet you it's got cold weather in it."

"You think?" I ask, making conversation with short breaths, holding back the pain in my legs.

"I think so," he begins. "We dropped a lot of altitude today. It should actually be warmer down here than it is up there. And instead it's gotten cooler. I think it is a cold front."

"Makes sense, I guess."

Just as the pain is about to do me in, the trail offers a view of the broad, milky brown Colorado River. The river has no beach, only canyon walls. And I realize this is it. *The bottom of the Grand Canyon.* Only a few hundred feet down. Paul and I stop to look down at the river carving through the rock. It is wide and brown, full like pure muscle, the textures on its surface moving quickly along the rock banks. The river snakes its dark, flat belly around a bend and it is something to see. It is slapping its sides against the canyon wall like a dragon caught in a fishing net. The trail bottoms out where the stream that we were near empties into the canyon. We follow the trail as it begins to climb, up to a ridge where an enormous steel-cabled bridge crosses the river. It's only as wide as a sidewalk, but sturdy as a plank of thick steel blasted into both sides of the rock. They must have built it to withstand a flood. It is a good fifty feet off the water and they have burrowed a hole through the rock to get to it. Paul leads through the dark opening and rounds the corner where we are met by a grated walkway that is walled by tight-cable handles. As we step out on the bridge, the Colorado is visible directly below us, through the grate. We make our way to the middle and stop to take in the view. Below the bridge, to the right, there is a little beach where another stream empties into the river from the north side. This must be Phantom Ranch, the campground we are staying at tonight. A few white-water rafts are pulled onto the beach. These are enormous rafts, with built-in coolers in the middle.

They look like they could seat twenty people or more. The bridge sways and the river blows air through the grate as though from an air conditioner.

"I think we made it," I say.

"Looks like we did." Paul turns and takes tired steps down the other side of the bridge where the trail drops immediately onto the beach. The tall, narrow gateway that is the river basin lifts hundreds of feet above me, framing the sky.

I make my way behind Paul and the pain darts through the tendons in my legs. All I am thinking about is getting to our camping space and sitting down. The pain increases with every step. A ranger stands at a wooden gate down near the beach. He welcomes us and points us toward Phantom Ranch, which is another hundred feet up a side canyon.

The camping space is small and marked with rocks that separate us from our neighbors. It slopes toward a large creek and there is a big rock right down on our own beach. The water rushes over it and makes a soothing sound. I drop my pack to the ground and have a seat on the picnic table. Then I lie down. My muscles tighten and throb. They relax; then they tighten and throb again. My head is spinning and my belly is still filled with sloshing water. Even though I am still, I can feel it sloshing. My body rocks the way a body rocks when you've been in the ocean all day, and you still feel the waves lifting you long after you are on dry land. I can feel the blood running through my veins. I feel it pulsing in my legs and in my feet. I feel it in the arteries around my sore heels and around my toenails that for more than five hours were pressed forcefully against the front of my leather boot.

Paul sets his pack down on the ground and rests his back against it. Then he slides down and uses it as a pillow. As he takes off his shoes, I can see he's got a little blood coming from his heel. It makes me wonder what my heels look like. I don't have the energy to take off my boots. Just want to lie here and watch that thunderhead roll over. It rolls soft and slow, cutting through the thick sky like a barge into a sound. The cottonwoods frame the sky and the creek plays gently with the rocks and I ache and sway and the blood runs through my veins.

11 PHANTOM RANCH

THERE IS A BUZZ, OR RATHER A MOAN, ABOUT PHANTOM Ranch. Hikers are in pain to the right and the left. In the site next to ours there is a girl with an enormous backpack. She has taken off her boot and is peeling her sock from her foot like a second skin. Her foot is poultry-white and swollen. She massages it with her hand and grimaces. She's a small girl and I feel for her. Her pack is twice the size of mine. She unstraps her sleeping bag, pushes the backpack off the table, and unrolls her bag to slowly lie on top. One booted foot and one bare foot hang off the table and she rests on her stomach and uses her arms as a pillow. She makes me think I've not got it that bad.

Paul is doing what he can to make camp. He finds a soft piece of ground and unrolls his sleeping bag. He takes his little stove out and fiddles with the propane knob. Getting it right, he strikes a match and the blue flame shuffles through the black burner.

"You want some cider?" he asks.

"Not right now," I say softly, looking around at the other campers.

There are a couple of pros in the site behind us. They've carried a big tent in and are efficiently putting it together. They are wearing all the right clothes. Their packs are large internal-frame packs and they've brought the gear necessary for a long stay. Their stove makes Paul's look tiny. It has four burners and a large propane tank fastened to the side.

Across the creek is the trail we hiked in on. Five or six campers are making their way up the trail. They must have come in on rafts because they show no sign of being weary. They are laughing and getting along.

"You hungry at all?" Paul asks.

"Yeah. A little. Haven't eaten since this morning."

"Do you want to warm your beans on the stove?"

Paul and the stove are ten feet away. Much too far to walk. And in order to get over there, I'd have to come down off this table. I'm not sure I can do that.

"Nah. I'll just eat it cold," I say.

"A real man," Paul says.

Leaning my pack against the table, I can see down into the pouch where my clothes and food are. I pull the beans out of the side pocket and grab a spoon from the same pouch.

"You want Tabasco sauce?" Paul has a little bottle of Tabasco and he throws it over. "The stuff is potent," he warns.

I pour about half of the little bottle into the bag.

"Don, I'm telling you, it's hot."

"I know what I'm doing."

"That's right. You're a Texan."

"Let me show you how it's done," I say.

Paul is right. The stuff is hot. This isn't picante sauce. This is flaming hot. I try not to let on, but Paul has a good laugh as he watches me suck air.

"No problem," I say and then cough. "Whoa. This is good stuff."

"I think your tongue is on fire, Don."

I reach down for my canteen and drink it to the bottom. The water offers no relief.

"You want some more water?" He holds up his canteen and I go over to get it. He holds it so I can't get to it and I'm coughing through a painful laugh.

"'I know what I'm doing,'" he mocks.

"I'm fine. Just thirsty." I pin him down with my knee and

grab his canteen. I take the water and hold it in my mouth, in my cheeks, and run it over my tongue.

"Texas boy had some trouble with that." Paul chuckles.

"No. No, it just went down the wrong tube."

Paul rolls his eyes. I return to my bag of beans and dip my spoon ever lightly into the food like a chip in a bowl of hot sauce.

Having eased my hunger pains, I lay myself down on my bag next to Paul. We talk about the day, about the hike, and about tomorrow's departure. We will leave just after sunrise. We'll get a jump on it, we say. Leaving early will have us at Indian Springs campground just after noon so we may get in a day hike before sundown. I don't tell Paul, but I am not excited about a day hike. I imagine I will be in a lot of pain tomorrow morning, and another hike once we arrive at Indian Springs, right now, seems out of the question. But tomorrow is tomorrow and tonight all I can do is rest.

A ranger comes around and tells us there is a gathering up near the cabins. A little show that the rangers put on. Paul looks over and raises his eyebrows. I shake my head that I am not interested and he seems to lose interest with me.

"I don't think I will be going anywhere till tomorrow morning," I say.

"I'm all for that."

"You know, I'm really not looking forward to tomorrow's hike. I'm in a lot of pain. It's going to be tough."

"We'll go slow," Paul says. "We've got all day so we can take our time."

The sun is under the canyon rim and what is left of light is shaded by the thunderhead. It rolls over, thick and gray, threatening rain. Visible from Phantom Ranch is just a sliver of heaven. The cloud breaks here and there and reveals a little blue. It is a deep blue, an evening blue with the showing of a few stars that struggle against the lingering sunlight. From our camp we can see where the gathering is going to be and the rangers have a fire glowing. I can't make out the flames, but the canyon wall is dancing with shadows and light.

The rafters pass our site on their way to the gathering. They laugh and make conversation and walk with a certain skip in their steps. One tells a joke and they laugh and another adds to it and they laugh again. They go on like that all the way up the trail and over the crest to where the shadows are dancing on the wall.

12 BRIGHT ANGEL

PAUL IS OUT OF HIS BAG AND SO ARE MOST OF THE other campers. I don't feel like moving. I test my legs to see how sore they are, and even the slightest movement sets a shot of pain through my thighs and into my back. My feet ache and my calves ache. I roll over just to get some kind of motion going through my body. I finally roll out of bed and do a lame push-up to get onto my knees. I arch my back straight and use the picnic table to stand.

By the time Paul returns from brushing his teeth, I have two socks on each foot and am dealing with my boots and their tightness over the socks.

"Little nippy this morning," Paul remarks. "Did you get cold last night?"

"Didn't notice till I got up," I say, honestly not having thought about it until he mentioned it.

"Cold front must have moved in," he reports.

We make talk about the weather for a while and then Paul gets serious about hitting the trail. He's moving with a weariness but has determination in his motion like he's working through the pain.

"If we get moving we'll warm up," he counsels.

"Yeah," I say under my breath.

My ankles are weak and my knees are stiff. Not as bad as I thought they would be, but stiff nonetheless. I bend my knees and walk around camp, rolling my bag and tying my gear on my pack. Paul hands me a banana and I peel it slow, taking my time.

We sit on the picnic table and take one last look at Phantom Ranch. We hadn't been there long, hadn't really met anybody or participated in anything, other than moaning and sleeping. This is a place for rafters, for sure. I doubt anybody who actually hikes down here would be interested in a puppet show about Darwinian evolution.

"How do you suppose they got the wood down here to build those cabins?" Paul wonders.

I hadn't thought about it, but I offer something to make conversation. "Helicopter," I say.

Paul looks down the creek toward the Colorado. "I bet you they brought the wood in on the river."

"There's white water on that river, isn't there?" I ask.

Paul looks up and studies the canyon walls. "It's too narrow here for a helicopter. They had to use the river. I bet they used the river."

"Helicopter," I say, studying the walls. "Do you think we could catch a ride? There's probably another supply coming in soon. We could make like construction workers and hitch a ride."

Paul sticks his thumb out like a hitchhiker and looks up at the sky. I do the same. We look and look but no helicopter. I lift my thumb way up in the sky and make a pouty face. "Hello, helicopter," I say. We have a good laugh as two hikers come up the trail and make strange, subtle glances at us.

"Will you carry me?" I say to one of them, who walks by in silence.

"You feeling okay?" Paul asks, breaking the joking mood.

"Better than I thought I would."

"That's good," he says.

"Yep."

"You ready to get going?" he asks.

"Yep," I say, lying down on the picnic table. Paul takes another look around the place.

"Why do you suppose they call it Bright Angel Trail?" Paul asks. "Do you think it's an Indian thing?"

"Probably," I say. "It seems like everything around here is something Indian, you know."

I'VE EMBRACED PAUL'S MENTALITY ABOUT WORKING through the pain. My weak ankles strengthen and I find stride to keep pace with him as we begin the ascent. Within minutes my breathing is full. My lungs are at capacity. He isn't moving so quick and part of me believes he is going slow to be considerate. No matter, this is fast for me. At least this first hour.

This trail is different from Kaibab in texture and color. The rock is gray here, where Kaibab showed red and brown for the entire descent, save the last few hundred yards. The cliff on the right side of the trail is not so steep. As we climb, we go deep into the canyon wall. We are following a flood course of some sort. I imagine this little gorge as an enormous creek bed that empties into the Colorado. It carries nothing but rock now, but there are grasses and shrubs deep in the crevasse. There is a little water in there somewhere. There must be a small trickle, because I can hear it as I round certain corners far from the surface.

I think to myself about the weight in my pack. Last night Paul and I talked a bit about all the stuff that we carry with us, all the weight we walk around with, emotional baggage, thinking we need stuff we don't need. We weren't getting very deep or anything, but I keep thinking about it, and how much stuff I walk around with, about how life is a dance and God just meant for us to enjoy life, not get bogged down in sin and religion. Just be good, it seems like, is the point of life; be kind to people; don't hate anybody; forgive people because we all make mistakes. I know there are always going to be exceptions to this kind of thinking, but it seems like life would be better if we could just let go of the thought we need more and more stuff to be happy, more and more of the approval of others.

Coming down the trail is a family with bright smiles. I give trail and they thank us as they amble by. One of them, the lady, asks us if we're heading all the way to the top or just to Indian Springs. Indian Springs, I tell her. Not much farther. Just around the bend, she says. They move on and I look back at Paul as if something isn't right. We've been hiking for three hours. We couldn't be there already.

Paul steps out in front. "Didn't take long."

"Not at all. I thought Indian Springs was halfway to the top."

"Thought so too," Paul says.

"Seems like we just got started."

"We did. It's still morning." Paul looks up at the sky, finds the sun, and makes a shadow on his eyes with his hand. "It's about eleven."

"Really? Eleven o'clock, Paul?"

He takes his hand down and grabs at the straps under his arms. "Yes, eleven o'clock."

I look up with my hand, making a shadow on my eyes. "About eleven seventeen. Right about eleven seventeen if you ask me."

I'm worried about not splitting the hike evenly. If we've only done three miles today, tomorrow will have six for us. And if we've only risen a couple thousand feet, then we have the other thousands for tomorrow. That's a long walk. I'm about tuckered out now, and today was an easy day. I don't let the fear get in my eyes, though. Not for Paul to see. We're having a good time all around. Even with the toughness of the climb. And it is true that I am being a wimp about all of this. I do wish, though, that I was in better shape.

I follow him around the bend to see green and trees. Indian Springs. I don't know what I imagined, nothing really. I never pictured it, but certainly didn't expect this. Patches of grass, shrubs, a big restroom, and picnic tables with concrete covers.

It's a Texas roadside park right here in the canyon. They brought it in on helicopters, no doubt.

We come into the campground from the rear. There is a well, with a bucket on a rope, built from river rock with a stream running beside it. Willows line the stream and tall grasses stand in bunches. A broad space built in a valley, the National Park Service has lined the trails with rock and the stubble grass grows in with cacti in the places they don't let hikers walk. There must be thirty or more campsites, each with a picnic table and a cement structure slanted above it. There are no cabins. Only one building and it's a large outhouse with a girl door and a boy door. Paul chooses a picnic table farthest from the trail.

"This all right with you?"

"Fine," I say, still looking around the place.

• • •

WHOEVER SAID, "EAT, DRINK, AND BE MERRY," HAD more than beans and rice, that's for sure.

What is it they eat in Arizona anyway? In Texas we eat barbeque and it's good. Restaurants such as Luther's and Central Texas Bar-B-Q. They cook their meat in huge black greasy pits made from old barrels. Two-hundred-gallon barrels. In Louisiana they eat crawfish and boudin. They have deep-fried donuts in the French Quarter and drink coffee and listen to poor men with worn shoes play "When the Saints Go Marching In." But what about Arizona? Mexican food, I guess. Southwest cuisine. My mouth is watering even now. Scrambled eggs on flour tortillas. Picante sauce with fried onions on a big, thick ceramic plate that screeches when you run your fork across it. I'd love a plate of that right now. I'd love some thick, buttery pancakes with maple syrup running off the top, and some bacon, thick pieces of smoked bacon.

Paul shifts his weight and notices the ache on my face. "You thinking deep?"

"Deep?"

"You've got a deep look on your face," he says.

"No."

"No what?"

"Not thinking deep," I say.

"What are you thinking about?"

"Food."

Paul sits up. He lets out a gasp, an agreeing moan like he's got an empty stomach too. "We've got beans and rice. A banana?"

"Later. I'm daydreaming about real food right now. You know, real food. Truck stop food or Mexican food."

Paul lifts his tired body out of the dirt and wipes the dust from his shorts as he sits beside me on the table. "If you could have any food right now, what would it be?"

"You're not helping. I'm really hungry."

"Think about it. What food would you want?"

"Chicken fried steak," I say. "But I don't know."

"Sounds good. That's one thing I'm going to miss about the South, Don. The food. There isn't any food in the world like Texas food."

"You can say that again. I've never been much outside of Texas, but I can tell you that there is no food anywhere like we've got it . . . anywhere."

"Any food, Don. What would you have?" Paul asks again.

"You listen to Lyle Lovett much?"

Paul shrugs his shoulders. "What does Lyle Lovett have to do with anything?"

"I'm getting there. He sings this song called 'Nobody Knows Me Like My Baby.' You ever heard it?"

Paul shrugs his shoulders again. He doesn't answer but looks out at the field of grass and sand and lets his eye climb the tall wall of rock where he finds a skeletal tree frozen against the sky. His eye stops on the tree and I can tell by his look that he's calculating the distance to the top.

"It's a good song," I say.

"What does it have to do with food?"

"You'd have to hear it to understand."

"You're gonna tell?"

"Well . . . it goes . . . and I don't remember the words exactly, but it goes, 'I like to sleep late on Sunday, I like cream in my coffee, I like my eggs over easy, with them flour tortillas.' He says *them* flour tortillas. He doesn't say just flour tortillas but he says *them* flour tortillas, you know. With that Texas dialect."

"He's a Texan?"

"Yes, from Houston. Went to Texas A&M and his roommate was Robert Earl Keen Jr."

"Who's that?"

"Doesn't matter. Listen to how the song goes . . ."

"He sings a song about food." Paul looks frustrated as he ponders the distance to the tree in the sky.

"No, it's not about food. It's a love song," I say.

"A love song about sleeping late and eating eggs. Your kind of love song, Don."

"Listen to how it goes. He sings, and it's real slow, by the way. Just him and this real slow guitar part and he goes, 'I like to sleep late on Sunday, I like cream in my coffee, I like eggs over easy, with them flour tortillas. And nobody knows me like my baby.'"

Paul rests easy and lets his eyes come off the tree in the sky. He puts his eyes on the field of grass and sand and thinks to himself.

"See how the song is?" I begin. "It's about this girl. His wife maybe, I don't know. But she knows everything about him. About how he likes to sleep late on Sunday and have breakfast with flour tortillas and about how she's the only one who makes his coffee right. It's a love song like that."

"Sounds like you're hungry for more than food, Don." He says this with a laugh. A narrow laugh.

"I don't know, but for about an hour I've had that song on

my mind. Maybe because it's the only song I know that has food in it."

"You miss Kris?" Everyone back home called Kristin "Kris." Paul is referring to the girlfriend I broke up with.

"Little. Last night I missed her a little."

Paul gets a sly look on his face. A to-the-point, sly look. "She ever make you breakfast like that? Like that song?" He knocks my leg with his fist.

"Kristin?"

"Yeah. She ever make you breakfast?"

"No. And I know what you're getting at."

"Just asking."

"She's not really like that."

"Didn't mean to pry," Paul says.

"Don't worry about it. You weren't prying."

"You think she's the one, Don?"

"You mean *the* one? The one and only?"

"Yeah," he confirms.

"No."

"I guess that's why you broke up with her."

"Yeah. I guess." The sweat on my legs and arms is beginning to chill. I'm wishing for a jacket or a sweatshirt. "You know, Paul," I start, "I think she was going to break up with me anyway."

"What makes you say that?"

"Little things. She would say little things. Do little things. I don't think she was really into it."

"How long did you two date?"

"Not long."

"How long?"

"About six months or so."

"That's pretty long. Some folks figure it all out in that amount of time."

"I really liked her, you know. She just wasn't in it. I think I dropped the bomb first. But she was about to do it anyway."

That last sentence is said with tenderness. As if to release some small ache. Paul's expression gives sympathy. But he doesn't know it is more the pain in my legs than the pain in my chest that is causing this melancholy. Kristin is Kristin. A beautiful girl. I miss her, I guess. But she and I were never meant to be. She was in between boyfriends and was too pretty to go without. I was there like a number in a bakery. She pulled the ticket, glanced at it, and waited to exchange me for some loaf of bread or cake or pie or feeling that she was beautiful. But I gave her the slip. Came right out of her hands before she could claim the prize and I bet you, I bet you a million dollars, she doesn't even remember that number. She'll just pull another ticket, glance at it, and wait for them to call out her number. She won't remember the things I said and won't realize I had never said them to another girl. She'd heard them before and it all ran together like bad poetry. You could see it in her eyes when I talked to her. You could hear it in the way she said thank you when I complimented her dress or the color of her eyes.

It's funny how you think you need something but you really don't. I mean I remember feeling like if I didn't have this girl I was going to die. But I am not dead, and I feel fine, and I think half the time when I like some girl I am really looking for some kind of redemption, some kind of feeling that I matter or am valuable or am needed, and I don't think there is a problem with that, but it just makes you realize how much we use each other sometimes.

I heard once that real love doesn't ask what is in it for me; it just gives unconditionally. It just tries to take the weight out of somebody else's pack, lessen his load, and if it gets reciprocated, that's great, but that isn't what you did it for. It makes me wonder if real love, not the crap that we trade on the street, but real love, longtime, old-couple love, is another metaphor. I mean, I was thinking about it the other day and I couldn't think of a purpose for love in terms of Darwinian mechanisms. It seems like there is a reason for sex, for lust and all of that, but what about love? How does love, like beauty and light, help the Darwinian process? And I wondered if love itself, the real thing, the Lyle Lovett kind, wasn't another metaphor for God.

"You know what I'd want? If I could eat anything right now?" Paul breaks the silence and I come back to the surface. "I'd like a big bowl of Raisin Bran. With big, plump raisins and cold milk," he says, kind of licking his lips.

"That does sound good, Paul. Raisin Bran."

"You never answered my question, Don," Paul says after a minute of silence in which both of us were thinking about cereal.

"What was that? What meal would I want?"

"A meal. Any meal. What would it be?" Paul says.

I rest back and look up at the tree in the sky. There is a flag-pole, too, way up at the Grand Canyon Lodge. You can barely see it, like a toothpick with a red rag flapping at its top.

"Any meal, Don," Paul says.

I sit there for a minute, thinking about it. "I'd like eggs over easy," I say. "With them flour tortillas."

13 REWARD

MY FEET ARE FROZEN. I ROLL MYSELF OVER TO MY backpack and pull out every article of clothing. I shove the underwear and T-shirts to the bottom of my sleeping bag and wrap my toes in the fabric. After a few minutes I realize it isn't helping. This is a deep blue cold. You can see it in the depth of the black sky and feel it in the still silence of the desert. All of Indian Springs snaps of cold. There is no light on the horizon. The sky is so heavy it drips dense shadows down the canyon walls. I look over at Paul and he's deep into his sleep. He is zipped up and snoring and though his breathing is not loud, or even bothersome, it irritates me because he is sleeping and I am not. He told me I'd be cold tonight. He said my bag was a "fair-weather" bag and the temperature would likely fall below freezing. He was right.

The cold didn't come gradually. It woke me about an hour ago and I've been in pain ever since. My head feels as though the blood in my brain is beginning to thicken, and if I loosen my jaw, my teeth begin clattering against each other. I won't be falling asleep again. A fetal position helps my hands, and when I raise my shoulders over my neck I can feel some warmth. And I am shaking now.

"Paul," I say and pull at his sleeping bag.

He rolls over and runs his hands up the inside of his bag to find the zipper.

"What is it?"

"I'm freezing out here," I tell him.

Paul opens and closes his eyes slowly. He checks the sky and looks around camp in a daze. "You're cold?" he questions.

"Freezing."

"I'm sorry."

"That's okay. But I need you to do something."

"What's that?"

"Sleep on my feet."

"What?"

I press my feet under his bag. "You have to sleep on my feet. I can hardly feel them."

He checks the seriousness in my eyes and says nothing. Just rolls over and lays his legs over my feet. I go back into my bag without humiliation or embarrassment. This is beyond anything social. I have to get warm.

• • •

THE CANYON WALL SLIDES THE SUN'S SHADOW SLOWLY down the rock face. I chart its progress, knowing that with the morning sun will come a little bit of warmth. But it is slow, slow, slow; sliding down the canyon wall like syrup. I set my head deep into the bag and hold my arms around myself to find warmth. Paul has moved off my feet, but I don't wake him because he was no help.

I figure I slept about an hour. Maybe two. Every minute was counted with a thousand clicks of my teeth. The sleepless night has set a sting in my dry eyes. My nose is dry too. I move my fingers to check the fabric of my bag, wondering where it is on me and where it isn't. After another half hour or so, I finally fall asleep.

• • •

I EASE MY ACHING BODY FROM MY SLEEPING BAG AND stretch my back. I reach for the sky and yawn. Rolling over, I

624

set my hands against the ground and stand. I feel the bones in my back and my ribs separate from each other. My legs are stiff and my feet are jolted within by sharp points of pain. My belly is empty and past hungry. Paul is sitting out in the dirt about twenty yards away, out in some sunlight.

"You were right about the cereal, Paul."

"What's that?"

"The cereal. Being the best thing to eat right now. I could go for a big bowl of Raisin Bran and cold milk. I might even take that over the eggs and tortillas."

"Now you're coming around." Paul gets up and leans forward to stretch his back.

"You know," Paul begins, "it's funny. Two weeks ago when we talked about things we wanted or our aspirations, we would have talked about houses or boats or cars. Now that we've been on the road for a while, everything is reduced to a bowl of cereal." Paul develops a smile as he stands straight again. "Isn't that just beautiful? Cereal. There are people in this world who are killing themselves because they want more and more of nothing. And the only thing you and I want in this world is a bowl of cereal. That just shows you how the things we think are important really aren't important."

"And a boat," I say.

"What's that?" Paul asks.

"I wouldn't mind a boat," I tell him. "A nice, big sailing boat with a wooden hull. I'd like to eat my cereal on my boat."

Paul rolls his eyes and shakes his head at me.

• • •

PAUL HAS HIS BAG ROLLED UP AND IS FASTENING IT TO his pack. "We should get going. It's getting late."

I break my blank stare and realize that I am not packed. Paul looks eager to hit the trail. "How are we going to get the van?" I ask. "It's a long way back to the other trailhead, that's all I'm saying."

"We'll hitchhike," he says, still fidgeting with his backpack. "You ready?" he asks.

"I need to pack my stuff. I will be ready in a minute."

"I am going to go brush my teeth in the stream. Want to come?" Paul pulls his toothbrush from his pack and taps it against the back of his hand, getting the dirt off it.

"I think I am going to get some journaling done," I tell him. "Would you mind if I took some time to do that?"

"Are you going to write for a while?"

"I don't know. I want to get a few thoughts down before I forget them. It may take a while, but I can probably do it tonight, once we get back to the van and all."

"No, don't worry about it. If you want, I can start hiking and you can follow a little later."

"You mean on the trail? You want to go separately?"

"Whatever you want. If you want to write, I could get started." Paul shrugs his shoulders. "Whatever you want, Don."

"Yeah, I might as well do this now. I'll meet you at the top."

"Cool." Paul takes off with his toothbrush and I go over to my pack and pull out my pen and notebook. While rummaging around, I know the reason I want to wait here. It's because I don't want Paul looking back to check on me. The trail to the top is pure switchbacks, six or seven miles of stairs, essentially. I am pretty sore, pretty out of shape, and that is going to take me all day with these legs and these blistered feet. I'm kind of faking it about the journaling thing. I mean, I wouldn't mind writing some stuff down, but the truth is I just want him to go so I don't have to feel like I'm having to keep up with him.

"I will probably go ahead and get the van. Is that cool?" Paul asks as he walks back into camp.

"Sure. I shouldn't be far behind you."

"You're just going to stay here and write?"

"I can do this later, Paul. I figure you are going to want to hike faster anyway, though, so I thought this would be cool."

"Nothing's wrong?" he asks.

"Dude, no. No way." I get up from the table and go over by Paul. I feel uncomfortable, as it is obvious he thought I was shrugging him off.

"No," I say. "I just wanted to get some stuff written down. Besides, I'm not looking forward to being the slow poke up that hill, you know. You are going to be a mile in front of me before you reach the top anyway. I'm saving myself some face by sticking around."

"Cool," Paul says.

"It's cool," I confirm.

"It's cool, Don. But you haven't eaten or slept and this is the worst part of the hike. You are going to have a tough time. I'm just telling you."

"I hear you. I'm going to get out of this canyon. Stop trying to be my big brother. I'm older than you, remember?"

Paul loads his pack on his back and gives me a grin and a pat on the shoulder. He ambles down the trail with a jug of water sloshing, dangling off the center of his pack. I follow him with my eye as he disappears behind a rock and then appears again. He isn't wearing shoes. He doesn't have any shoes on!

"Paul!"

"Yeah!" he shouts.

"Your shoes?"

"My feet are bleeding. No shoes today."

"You aren't going to wear shoes?"

"No shoes. See you at the top," he says.

He turns and continues, hitting the first switchback in a brisk stride. He rises like a man on an escalator and turns in fluid motions to the up and the up of each switchback. In no less than a few minutes, he is a hundred or more feet in the air and he won't be slowing down for some time. Probably won't even stop for water. Paul is just about the most athletic guy I know. It's funny, you know, because with most guys I wouldn't feel comfortable telling them I was afraid of being too slow up the canyon, but Paul, even though he is an athlete and could have gotten some social points by putting me down, just didn't care. It's funny how the guys who are really good at something never make you feel like crap about not being good at whatever they are good at, you know. I sit back down at the table and pull out my journal. It's all blank. I hate journaling, to be honest. I put it right up there with talking to yourself. I told myself I would do some journaling on this trip, and I might as well start. I write some stuff about missing Kristin, about the sunset in Oklahoma, about fixing the van with some speaker wire, all stuff I doubt I would find very interesting twenty years from now. I start wondering what it is I will want to read about twenty years from now. I tap my pen against the page and think for a second.

I FIGURE YOU MIGHT FORGET WHAT KIND OF PERSON *you were back when you were on this trip. I want you to know you weren't a bad guy. But you fell into thinking a lot of money and a lot of stuff and a lot of social collateral would get you somewhere. And I don't know who you are now, and what you've done with your life, but try to remember, God doesn't expect you to accumulate a lot of stuff. You were really happy here in the canyon, you know, I promise it's true. I guess I just want you to remember there was a time when you did a pretty difficult hike, and you decided that you didn't need to carry a bunch of stuff on your back because the climb was hard. And I don't know who is around you, whether you met a woman or have some kids, but I really hope you have shown them this stuff, that life is going to be okay, that you just have to enjoy it. If you can't buy a nice car for your family or anything, don't worry about it. Just go into your kids' room and kiss them on the forehead, okay, 'cause there is all kinds of beauty and it doesn't have anything to do with having some stuff. Also, don't kick yourself around. If you can't climb up out of a canyon real quick, just do it slow. And also just remember that this guy Paul is one of the most incredible people in your life. There was a time when he showed you a lot of grace. I don't know what else to say. You're a pretty good person, you know. God made a whole beautiful earth and decided to put you in it, to experience all of this beauty. You can't do that watching television all the time. Nothing else. I have to go climb out of a hole. Maybe you do too. All the best. Feel like I'm talking to myself, for crying out loud.*

THERE IS AN EXHAUSTION THAT STRIKES DEEPER THAN muscle and flesh. It is a bone-deep exhaustion and is all new to me. The trail continues remarkably steep, but there is traffic on the footpath. Lively children walk briskly with their parents in tow. I sit down on a rock in a crag and look down over the canyon, marveling at the beauty of it all, and how far I have come.

I have taken more rest without Paul. It should have taken me about four hours to get this far, but I figure I have been climbing these steep switchbacks for about six. Paul would have trudged quickly. Without his quick step to keep me accountable, I struggle. My water is more than half gone. It sloshes in my stomach like a baggie of goldfish. I could throw it up if I wanted. I could tighten my stomach and throw up right here on the path. My whole head seems to be swaying and throbbing. My face must be blue or green. Women have pity in their expressions and men walk by quickly with eyes averted. Amazingly, I was passed a while back by a fellow I met years ago in Tennessee. I recognized him coming, but didn't have the breath to address him. He literally grazed my shoulder. I turned, but he was gone before I could process that it was him. He did not recognize me and I can't say I was eager to make contact.

Strapping my canteen to my pack, I shoulder my load and

step back onto the trail. My feet drag and slide. My footprints must be long but I am too tired to look and see. The traffic gets heavier with each switchback and the Disneyland atmosphere that surrounded me a couple days ago is coming back to mind. So many happy families on their vacations. Fathers and mothers and grandparents. The presence of older people tells me that I am nearing the rim. A group of elderly people come down the trail in leisurely strides. The women wear big hats and guard the sun from their eyes with cupped hands. The men grab at their women's elbows when I near, carefully protecting them from a dangerous fall.

I am utterly exhausted and ashamed at my inability to conquer this canyon with dignity. I am passed by nuns, who offer water. One tells me that I am almost there. I nod. Almost there. If only there were here. If only I could drag the rim to me, rather than me to the rim. I am not above crawling the last quarter mile.

Finally I see the trailhead. It is close. I stop and lean against the canyon wall to eye my heaven. The trail rises before me and beyond it is the sky. Thirty more steps will have me out of this hole. I make like somebody with some decorum and walk the last switchback with no drag in my step, the noblest action I can muster. And coming over the ridge I see the Grand Canyon Hotel big and brown across a lawn. And there is Paul. He has a grin across his face like a man whose wife has delivered a baby. He sits on the beam of a wooden fence and greets me. I walk the last few steps and shake his hand. My good friend Paul, I say to him, and I can see that he sees the relief in my eyes, and all the fear of the last two hours, wondering whether I would make it. I lean against the fence and look out over the Grand Canyon. A canyon I now know intimately and have hiked all the way to the river and back. Paul sets his hand on my shoulder and tells me that I've done it. That it wasn't easy, but I did it. None of that matters to me now. Perhaps it will tomorrow or the next day. I am only glad to be done with it.

"I got the van," Paul says.

I acknowledge him with a grunt and am glad to know we don't have to hitchhike back.

"Had time to stop at the store," he says.

"Is that right?" I whisper.

"Got you a little something while I was there."

I hadn't noticed that Paul was holding anything, but he sets it in my hands. I look down into the tin cup and eye the golden flakes. Paul reaches into a grocery sack and pulls out a small carton of milk. I hold the tin cup in disbelief and watch the milk flow around the flakes. The raisins lift and swirl. The flakes float to the top and he drops a spoon into the cup. Paul smiles at me and pats me on the back.

"This is your reward," he says.

My smile is so big that tourists notice. I think there may even be a little moisture in my eyes. I don't know if I have felt this much joy in ten years. Paul laughs as I take the first bite and suck on the spoon as I pull it out of my mouth. Paul takes a swig from the carton of milk and we look out over the canyon, the red walls and shadows and pines, the crags and caves, the switchbacks that descend all the way to the river.

14 MIRACLES

As far as I know, Hoover Dam was engineered by a guy who later made vacuum cleaners. He no doubt felt sorry for the people of Nevada. They live in so much brown. He surveyed the land and decided on a spot to dam the Colorado and give the people of Vegas a place to swim. Later, perhaps, he ran for president. Lake Mead is big and blue and holds up large party boats with striped canopies and barbeque grills that make the boats look like they are on fire when the smoke billows out from under the canopies and lifts gray signals into the desert sky.

I've been driving for a while. Neither of us tired, Paul has been telling me how it goes with a rattlesnake bite. We may do some more hiking, he says, and one of us could get bitten. It's a good thing to go over it. He tells me I have to take a razor blade and cut all around the bite, taking a good quarter inch of flesh in the operation. He says I shouldn't think about the pain, that I should just take the blade, stick it in deep, and carve it out like a small melon. If I do it quickly, apparently, it won't hurt as bad at first. And I am to remember I am saving my own life. Then, apparently, the cut has to bleed. It isn't always necessary to suck the blood out, he tells me. I can just let it bleed if I get a good, deep cut going. Most of the poison will bleed out, and while I will feel like I'm dying for a few hours, there is a good chance I will live through it.

All of this is comforting, I tell him. Because I would hate to die of a snakebite.

"Water moccasins are a completely different story," Paul says.

"What's that?" I ask.

"Water moccasins. They are completely different. You can't just cut and get the poison out. It's not that easy."

"I see," I tell him. "That should be important here in Nevada."

Paul goes on a bit about the variety of snakes in this region compared to the South and the Northwest. He says there are no water moccasins in Nevada because there is no water. Save Lake Mead, which is hardly swamplike. There are rattlers out here, however, he reminds me. We are bound to see one pretty soon, he says. I just drive and watch the road. He has his feet up against the glove box. Red tennis shoes with white stripes. Canvas Adidas. He has an elbow out the window and the warm, midday air blows his hair into a swirl, slapping against his forehead. He keeps wiping a hand across his face to soothe the itch, all the while talking about snakes.

The road we've chosen is bare. We are coming up from below Vegas. We chose this route because it looked scenic on the map. We thought we might camp out here and hike off into some valley. But so far, the terrain looks rugged and the only good cut through these hills and canyons is the road we're on. The hills are not tall, but steep, so I have to downshift as low as second as we climb. Then back to fourth. Then second again. As we crest a hill, I push the stick out of second and find no resistance in the transmission. I slide over to fourth to drop it in, but the stick is loose. It doesn't go. The van whines in a high rev and races as I press the gas. I pull the stick hard to jam it into fourth, but it won't go. It feels like the transmission has dropped out.

"Paul."

"Yeah."

"We've got trouble."

"What is it?"

"No gears. No fourth gear."

634

"Try third."

"No third. No gears at all."

I spot a small pull-out at the bottom of the hill and navigate the van over the shoulder and down a small dirt inset that parallels the road. Coming to a stop, clouds of dust roll over from the back of the van and down the windshield before dissipating. Again, I try the gears. Nothing.

"Is it the clutch?" Paul reaches over and feels the stick.

"No. The clutch is fine. There wasn't any grind to it at all. I just lost it completely. It can't be the clutch. It's the tranny. Something broke."

"All right," Paul says, unsettled. He slaps his hand against the dash.

I kill the engine and open my door. Nevada is quiet as though it is hiding something. The wind whispers suspiciously. Stepping out of the van, I feel the ache in my knees and muscles. But I can pace it out in a few steps. Paul, without saying a word, gets out of the van and rounds to the driver's side. He presses the clutch and motions the stick to first, second, and all through the gears.

"There's too much play," he says.

"There are no train tracks out here," I announce.

Paul rests his weight and drops his limbs like he's frustrated. "This is crazy. Did you feel it going out?"

"Didn't feel anything. I went to downshift and it wasn't there."

"That's not possible, Don."

"That's what happened." I lean against the van with one hand and hold a thumb out for a ride. No cars are on this back road. We haven't seen one in about twenty minutes. Paul has a frustrated look, both arms laid across the curvature of the steering wheel. He's shaking his head at me now. Thinks I'm acting silly in a serious moment. I point my thumb up a little higher.

"I'm gonna get us out of this jam," I reassure him. "There's no reason to panic."

"I'm not panicking." Paul shakes his head. "And you're an idiot."

"Why am I an idiot?" I put my hand in my pocket and look my friend in the eye.

"Because you are," he says, shaking his head.

"I went to put the thing in gear and the gear wasn't there. That doesn't make me an idiot. It's your stupid van. Maybe you've been driving it like an idiot for the last year."

"You're pissing me off, Don," he says, looking over at me.

"You're breaking my heart, Paul," I tell him.

I step closer to the driver's window. He doesn't look at me. He keeps his eyes fixed as if there were some speck of dust on the windshield that had, in the smallest possible print, a word that, if spoken aloud, would solve all of his problems.

"Frustrated?" I don't look at him. Don't really expect him to answer.

"What do you think?" he says.

"Things could be worse."

"I don't want to hear it, Don."

"You know, Paul, when I was in the orphanage . . . did I tell you I was in an orphanage?"

Paul shakes his head. There is a beginning of a grin on his lips but he looks away and holds his frown and then looks back at the window.

"When I was in the orphanage," I start in again, "me and the girls used to sing this little song. Paul, I'd like to sing it to you. Maybe you'd like to sing it with me. You'd like that, wouldn't you?"

"I don't want to hurt you, Don. I really don't."

I sing very softly . . . "Tomorrow," I sing. "Tomorrow, I love ya, tomorrow, you're always a day away."

I stop singing because I have forgotten the words. Paul is looking at me without a smile. No frown, but no smile. He reaches over and pats my head. I grin like a dog.

WE'VE BEEN SITTING IN THE DESERT FOR NEARLY AN hour. We haven't seen a single car. I stand up to break the boredom, pick up a rock, and throw it out into the brown, toward a cactus. I kick a few rocks across the road, which stirs up some dust that blows across Paul's lap.

"Sorry," I say. He doesn't move, just wipes the dust out of his eyes, then lies down, looking up at the sky.

"You getting tired of me, Paul?" I ask. He doesn't say anything.

"I don't care," I tell him. "You can say it."

"Yes," he says. "I am getting tired of you."

"What are you tired of?"

"Everything's a joke. Some things aren't funny and I feel pressured to laugh so you won't feel bad. Do you know how annoying that is?"

"No."

"Trust me. It's annoying. And you're slow."

"Slow?" I ask.

"Slow, Don. You're fat and slow."

"Tell me how you really feel," I say, sitting back down, gathering some dirt in my hand, and letting it slip through my semiclosed fist.

"What about me?" Paul asks. "What are you sick of?"

I sit there and think about it for a minute. "Nothing," I respond. "You don't annoy me at all, Paul. I want to be just like you." He just looks at me like he knows I am lying.

"You're a jerk," he says softly. "You're never serious for a minute."

"You're a walk in the park," I tell him.

FOR A CHANGE OF SCENERY, I CROSS THE STREET, SET my foot on the bumper of the van, and climb up the windshield, to the top of the van, being careful not to break the wipers with my boot. From the top I can see a bit farther. There is nobody out here.

"Don!" Paul yells. He's looking up at me.

"Yeah."

"I'm seriously discouraged."

I look down at Paul. He raises his legs and folds his arms around his knees.

"I don't know what to say, Paul. I can't think of a way out of this mess. We may be here for a while."

"Yeah."

"A car will come," I tell him.

"It's been an hour."

"Did you ever see that movie *Trapper John, MD*?"

"What?"

"That movie on television: *Trapper John, MD*."

Paul looks up with his hands cupped over his eyes. "It wasn't a movie. It was a television series."

"But you saw it, right?"

"A few times." There is a long silence. "Why do you want to know whether I saw that television show?"

"I feel like Trapper John, MD."

Paul shakes his head. "Why? Why do you feel like Trapper John and why does it matter?"

"He had an RV and he used to go out in the parking lot and sit on top of his RV and bake in the sun."

"Yeah. So what?"

"I feel like that. Up on the van and all. Makes me feel like Trapper John."

"That's great. But for your information, it wasn't Trapper John who had the motor home. It was the other guy. The guy with the curly hair. The younger guy."

"I thought it was Trapper John."

"Nope."

"Are you sure?"

"Yep." Paul sighs. "What does this have to do with anything, Don?"

I look down at my miserable friend. For a second, I think I'm the crazy one. There is no reason for me to be fooling around. We have no water, so we need a ride. And there have been no cars for the better part of an hour, like Paul said. The sun is in midsky, so we've got a half day of sunlight to get us more and more thirsty. And how do we fix this thing? We don't have money for a transmission and there's no telling what is eaten up under the van. It is basically useless. We will probably have to hitch the rest of the way. Neither of us is going to call home for help. I know that without asking.

Paul looks up and meets my eye. "Do you want to pray?"

"Whatever," I tell him, not really wanting to pray.

Paul lowers his head like a little kid in Sunday school and rests his chin on his knee. He closes his eyes and speaks fairly loudly. His words are soft and low: "God, we are stuck in the desert and the van doesn't work. We don't know what to do. We don't know whether to leave it or what to do. I guess we need a ride or something." I'm looking out over the hills, watching some heat rise off the dunes in the distance. "We need a mechanic, God. That's what we need. If You could send us someone to get us on our way, to help us with this transmission, that would be great." Paul stops praying. He stands up and starts walking out into the desert.

"Paul." He hears me but he does not turn.

"Paul!"

He turns toward me with a frustrated look. "Yeah?"

"Look." I point over the horizon. He can't see it yet, but there is a car coming.

"Is it a car?"

"Yes."

He walks quickly to the other side of the road and stands gazing. He's half in the road.

"Be careful," I tell him. He steps back onto the shoulder.

Over the hill comes a station wagon. Brown in color, it matches the landscape. The wagon slows a little as it nears, but speeds up again as the driver realizes we are not a wreck or anything worth looking at. He drives by at about thirty or forty miles per hour and hardly looks our way. There's a man at the wheel, and a woman in the passenger's seat with a few kids in the back. As he passes, the children turn to look at us through the back window. His brake lights flash and then come on solid.

"He's stopping," Paul says.

I slide down the windshield and catch the bumper with my boot. The reverse lights on the wagon come on and the man backs up onto the shoulder. Dust kicks out on either side as the station wagon weaves backward. It's a brown wagon with brown wood-panel trim. A real gas-guzzler from the early eighties.

He is a bearded man with a red baseball cap. His beard is untrimmed and his wife looks troubled that he decided to stop. The children are quiet in the backseat. One looks over at me without any expression, then turns back to face forward. The other two do not look. They do not even look at Paul, who has begun a conversation with the man. Paul steps away from the door as the man reaches through the open window to pull the outside handle. A closer look at the car reveals it to be quite the jalopy. A rope fastens the hood to the bumper and another of the same sort fastens a suitcase to the roof.

The man steps out of his car and pulls up his sagging pants. Running his hand across the front of his shirt, he tucks it in. He has a tattoo on his forearm of a woman without clothes. She probably had a good figure at one time, but she looks faded, oblong, and tired of being attached to him. The man is talking to Paul about the van. He's asking what Paul thinks is wrong with it. Paul tells him it's the transmission and the bearded man just shakes his head and looks out in the desert and shakes his head again.

"Sounds really bad," he says. "Well, you boys are in luck. Probably haven't seen many cars out here, have you?"

Paul confirms that we haven't.

"Not many people get out this way. You could have been here for hours if it weren't for me stopping to help. Not a lot of people would have stopped, you know."

"Thanks," Paul says.

"Don't mention it." The man removes his cap and runs his hand across his thick hair and puts his cap back on. "I'm a mechanic," he says.

"You are? I mean, huh, is that right?" Paul leans against the van and looks away.

"Can you help us?" I ask, trying to get the man to get to the point and ask for money, which is probably the only reason he stopped in the first place.

"Well, I've got business in Arizona, and it really does set me back to stop here. I've got an appointment and all, you know."

"I see," I say. "Well, you better get going, then. We wouldn't want you to miss your appointment." Paul looks over at me with a cold look, telling me with his eyes to keep quiet.

"Well, now, wouldn't want to leave you boys stranded. Like I said, there's nobody going to stop for you out here. You were lucky I stopped. Certainly didn't have to."

"Like I said before, we don't want to keep you. We'll figure something out. You can go on."

"I can take a look at it real quick, if you want. I normally don't do this for free, but I can help you out, I guess." The bearded man stands there with his hands in his pockets and rocks back and forth on his heels.

Paul looks at me as if to question whether we offer him money. *If we do,* I think to myself, *we will really be running short of cash. Simply can't do it.* I don't even think the thing can be fixed anyway. The last thing I want to do is give the man twenty dollars to tell us there is nothing he can do and then tell us he can't give us a ride because his wagon is full. So I tell him we don't have any money. I clarify and tell him we can't spare any money and then I ask him if he is still willing to look at it. Feeling guilty, he kneels down, lies on his back, and slides under the van. I shake my head and Paul gives me a little punch. We both get down on our backs and slide under the van with the man. Plenty of room under this piece of garbage, that's for sure.

The mechanic asks again about the problem and Paul says it won't go into gear. "Not even first gear?" the man questions. And Paul says we have no gears at all. "Happened all of a sudden," the man mutters and Paul confirms that is the way it happened. The bearded man runs his finger up along the underside of the tranny, looks down the long side of the underneath, and squints his eyes to see to the front. He moans a moan, which means he sees something, and then slides his short frame a few feet toward the front, about three or four feet from the transmission itself. He slides his fingers along a rod that runs the length of the van. He pinches the rod and pulls it up and back. It slides easily. He has found the problem. It isn't the transmission, he tells us. It's the shifter rod. There's a little plastic or aluminum piece that fits right here and it's gone.

"See here. These two rods snap together right here and that piece fell off. It has four teeth. Two on each side. Two fasten toward the front and two toward the back. You are getting all the play in the stick because it's not connected to the tranny. This is definitely your problem."

"Can it be fixed?" Paul asks.

"Yes."

"We need the part?" Paul asks.

"Yes."

"Where can we get the part?"

"Junkyard. That's the only place."

"There's no junkyard anywhere near here, is there?"

"No." The mechanic continues to study the problem. "Do you have a clothes hanger?" he asks.

Without answering, I slide out from under the van and

open the big door. I begin to sort through some of Paul's stuff when he surfaces and tells me he doesn't have a clothes hanger so don't bother looking. A voice from under the van tells us to ask his wife, so Paul goes over and asks her. She gets out of the wagon and opens the back to remove a clothes hanger from a stack of clothes that rests on an ice chest with "Miller High Life" printed on the side. Without so much as looking at Paul or saying anything, she hands him the clothes hanger and closes the back of the wagon. She returns to her seat.

Our mechanic unwinds the clothes hanger and threads it through the fittings on both rods. He pulls it tight and then threads it through again. I am watching him on bended knee with my head ducked low. He looks over and tells me to pull the stick down into second gear and leave it there. I do as he says, and he shouts from below to pull it harder. I press down hard and hold it with my other hand. I can feel him jerking against the stick, trying to pull it out of gear. Hold it, he shouts. I pull it back even harder. As he threads the wire through the fittings, the stick jerks up and back a few inches. Finally the motion subsides and he slides out from under the van. I let go of the stick.

"You will have to keep it in second gear," he says. "That will allow you to get going, but you will have to drive to Vegas pretty slow."

"Better than nothing," I say.

Paul shakes the man's hand and thanks him. He straightens his cap and tells him it was nothing. I thank him, too, and he tips his head at me.

"You boys have a good day," he says, wiping his hands against each other.

"Thanks," Paul tells him.

"Thanks," I tell him, reaching to shake his hand.

"It was nothing. Just keep it in second and you should be fine. Not too, too far, but you probably want to get moving." The man nods at us and gets back into his car, starting it and pulling it back onto the road.

We watch him disappear and then Paul gets in the driver's side. I round the van quietly and take my seat. Paul pulls us onto the road, being careful not to push the lever out of gear. After a few miles he tells me he is sorry for calling me fat and slow. Whatever, I tell him, putting my hand outside the window to catch some of the slow-moving air.

15 VEGAS

NEVADA HAS NO OCEAN. YOU COME OVER DUNE AND dune and no water washes up on no shore. Las Vegas is an island of lights and trickery, and the desert laps against it on four sides. Trucks are ships, barges coming in from foreign continents, a subtle, odd reminder that some other kind of life exists, some sort of normality. Desert winds wash tourists up on casino shores to gawk at the natives, entertainers, gambling addicts, magicians and scantily dressed women, showmen who can't sell albums anymore, vague memories of Elvis and Neil Diamond. It is an oasis for hard-luck cases who spend small fortunes on a shortcut to the American dream. P. T. Barnum, eat your heart out. This is a circus too heavy to travel. The show doesn't come to the people; the people come to the show.

We have come one hundred miles at thirty-five miles per hour. And on the outskirts of town we find a junkyard. I step to the counter and ask the man if he has a Volkswagen van. He tells me he has two but they have been gutted. There's nothing on them. But then he tells me it's a dollar to go in the yard and see for myself. I look at Paul and he pulls a dollar from his wallet. We walk with heavy heads down a ramp on the backside of the trailer that fronts as an office. We look out on a sea of cars on concrete blocks and wheel rims. Before us are the Toyotas and Nissans, all sorts of disasters and tragedies kept for their parts: alternators, bumpers, rotors, leather seats, rearview mirrors, stereo knobs, hubcaps. A man who works at the place points us toward the Volkswagen section, so we wander in and out of

Buicks and Fords and Chevys to the European imports where we find a line of Volkswagen Beetles, both new and old. Behind the first line of Beetles are two vans. They are ghosts of what they used to be and Paul and I just stand there looking at them in disbelief. They are nothing but shells. The evening sun shines through them. Nothing there, no doors, no wheels, no seats, no engines or wires for the electrical. They sit like metal boxes atop cinder blocks.

"Unbelievable," Paul says, looking back toward the Beetles, wondering, perhaps, if there are any more vans than these.

"Not much there," I say.

"Nothing," he confirms. Paul stands silent and puts his hands in his pockets. He turns to go.

"Where are we going to go?" I ask.

"Another junkyard. Maybe a Volkswagen dealership," he says without stopping.

"We could take a look," I tell him.

Paul is weaving back through the Jettas and Passats. He turns to look at me. "What for? There's nothing there. Let's go." He stops for a second. "You want to look. I don't want to look," he says. He walks back over to pacify me.

"I don't want to look. I just want to stand here and live in this sliver of hope," I tell him.

"I'll look," he says, and walks over to the first van stooping to his knees. He lays himself on his back and slides under the van. I go to the other van and do the same. Underneath, the van is gray and empty. There are no brake lines, no muffler, no gas lines, no nothing. Just the bottom of a box. I could set my fists against the bottom and bench-press the thing off its cinder blocks, it seems so light. But then I see the shifter linkage, and a sense of hope stirs: a butterfly circus in my stomach. I follow the linkage with my hand and eye the connector. "Paul!" I shout. He doesn't answer. I turn over with a giant grin. "Bud, you won't believe this." Paul is lying beneath the other van with both his hands clasped and resting on his belly. He's wearing a smile like mine. "Paul!" He doesn't answer. He just lies there looking up at his own shifter linkage. Then he laughs. "No way," I say. "You've got one too."

"It's here," he says. And so we lie there on our backs for several minutes, just admiring the little piece of plastic, about two ounces worth, that holds the entire van together. After a while Paul starts pulling on his, wondering how to get it off. I go back to the office and borrow a screwdriver and a pair of pliers and we manage to disassemble the linkage off of the van Paul was under. We pull the thing out and have a seat on the floor of one of the vans and tinker with it until we can get it off.

"We need this too," Paul tells me, handing me a small clip.

When we go back through the trailer, the man at the desk takes a look at our part and shrugs his shoulders. He motions to us to go without paying. Paul and I spend another frustrating hour under our van, unwinding the coat hanger, then cussing at the clip and the plastic part that doesn't seem to fit until it slides, in one gentle motion, into its fitting, for no other reason than it is tired of hearing us complain.

16 CALIFORNIA

STILL IN THE PARKING LOT AT THE JUNKYARD, PAUL looks around the place and asks me if I am getting hungry. I tell him I am. He says we've got beans and rice and we could warm the pot and eat that. I fake like that would be an okay idea. He says it doesn't sound all that good to him, but we could do it.

"Doesn't sound that good to me, either," I confess.

"Any ideas?" he says, lifting his eyebrows.

"How much money do we have?" I say, knowing we haven't spent hardly anything in the last few days.

"Not enough to justify anything lavish."

"Maybe we could go to a grocery store. We could make sandwiches or something," I say.

"We really don't have enough money for that," he says, pulling out his wallet.

I go over and get my sock out of my small box of stuff. "For sandwiches?" I question, pushing my hand into the sock and pulling out a wad of ones and fives.

"We can only spend about five dollars per day," Paul reminds me.

"Five dollars each?" I ask, hoping he will forget.

"No," he says. "Five dollars between us."

I recommend that we hit a grocery store anyway. Some stores have day-old bread and maybe we can stir up enough for some meat or lettuce or anything that isn't beans and rice. He agrees and we get back into the van and start driving through the suburbs of Vegas. The sun is setting now and the color over the mountains is surprisingly beautiful. All the dust in the air, perhaps from the city itself or maybe from trucks coming over the pass or dry fires out in the mountains, is sharpening the sunlight and dividing it into bright orange rays pointing straight at the city and white light coming off the top of the range like some kind of suspended atomic explosion. Winding through the streets of Vegas, we start thinking again about food. Paul starts talking again about the perfect meal. He has changed from Raisin Bran to pancakes and sausage, and even though it is evening, pancakes and sausage sound perfect. A meal like that would hit the spot, I tell him. Paul spots a grocery store and steers the van into the parking lot. Five dollars, he says. All we can spend is five dollars. I confirm that I agree, but I think to myself that I am not past shoplifting.

We walk into the store and are embraced by a gentle, air-conditioned breeze. It's cold in here, Paul says. The aisles, one after another, seem to be filled with old people squeezing melons. I can't believe all the food, all the options. Chips and salsa, bean dip, candy bars, whole chickens, cooked and glazed with salt and butter, macaroni and cheese, a whole deli with huge vats of potato salad and teriyaki chicken, a deep-fried section with burritos and corn dogs right next to an entire aisle of beer. The only real food I've eaten in two weeks was a small cup of cereal and four bowls of the same cereal about an hour after the cup. The only thing Paul has eaten is a cup of cereal.

I grab a shopping cart and lean my weight over the handrail. I push it along like a kid. As we go through the chips and salsa aisle, I toss two bags of Doritos in the cart. Paul looks at me and shakes his head. I grab a set of Tupperware dishes from the housewares aisle and also one of those little dishwashing tools with the spongy head. When we get to the bread, Paul begins comparing prices. I run my arm along the shelf and dump eight loaves into the cart. Paul laughs and shakes his head again. He picks out a loaf of bread and heads toward the back of the store where they keep the meat. Along the way, I stock up on toilet paper and the current issue of *People* magazine. I also grab three cans of Alpo dog food, as they are running a special. As I round the back of the aisle, Paul is standing in front of the meat.

"Lunch meat is too expensive," he says.

"How much?"

"Too much. We can get a jar of peanut butter for the same price. Peanut butter will last a whole loaf of bread and meat will only get us about two sandwiches."

"Well, let's get peanut butter then," I say, taking two boxes of buy-one-get-one-free cereal from an end cap.

"All right." Paul turns his back to the meat and wanders lazily, with a defeated posture, along the back of the store. He grabs a turkey roasting pan and places it in my cart. I grab two cans of Spam and a no-stick frying pan. Paul doesn't notice the end cap of bleach as he turns down the peanut butter aisle. I mumble under my breath something about what a great deal that is. I grab three gallons and set them in the child's seat so they don't squash the eight loaves of bread.

Paul starts reading the label on the peanut butter. He places it back on the shelf and grabs a cheaper brand. The one with the bland label. He asks me if I want chunky or smooth and I ask him if they make a brand with chunks of steak. "They stopped making that years ago," he says. "You want chunky or smooth?" he asks again.

"Chunky," I say. "What about jelly?"

Paul turns and walks down a few feet to the jelly and looks for something cheap. "This stuff is expensive. The peanut butter was three dollars and it's another three for the jelly. With the bread, we are over budget by two dollars." He puts the jelly back.

"We can't have peanut butter without jelly," I tell him.

"We can't afford it," he says, shrugging his shoulders.

"Two dollars?" I question.

"What happens when we run out of gas?"

"The dude gave us the Volkswagen part for free," I remind him.

"The part was never in the budget in the first place," he reminds me. "We should only be spending four dollars because we spent a dollar at the junkyard."

"What about this turkey roasting pan?" I say. "We can't afford that either. Put the jelly in your pocket, Paul."

"You want to steal it?" he asks.

"Yes. I want to steal it."

"Okay," he says.

"Okay," I say.

"Okay," he says, and puts the jelly back on the shelf.

"Hey, I've never gotten a look at this budget you keep talking about."

Paul points his finger at his head. He says it's all in his mind and it's very clear.

"I see," I tell him. "I've got a budget, too, you know."

Paul looks down at my cart. "I see your budget."

"I'll put the dog food back," I tell him.

"What about the frying pan?"

"It's a keeper." I place my arms over the contents of the basket so he can't take anything out.

"Well, we can't afford peanut butter and jelly. Something has to go. Will it be the peanut butter or the jelly?"

"We can't refrigerate the jelly, so let's keep the peanut butter."

"My thought exactly," he says.

Paul heads toward the checkout counter with just a loaf of bread and a jar of peanut butter.

"Wait!" I tell him.

"What?"

"We can't just eat bread with peanut butter." I am looking pretty miserable.

"We'll warm up the beans and rice," he says. "We'll have peanut butter and beans and rice." He begins walking toward the checkout again. I follow him with my cart, adding a jar of jelly to my cart along with a can opener and a potato chip clip that looks like a giant clothespin.

"How much money is the bread and peanut butter going to cost us?" I ask.

Paul is searching for the shortest line. "The bread is one dollar and the peanut butter is three bucks."

"That leaves us one dollar."

"Yeah."

"What can we get with that?" I ask.

"We can save it for tomorrow. We will have six tomorrow. Just think, if we do this every day, we may be able to afford a watermelon or something big."

Paul finds a short line at the nine-items-or-less counter. I stand behind him with my cart. He looks it over again and asks how I'm going to pay for all of it. I tell him I have a coupon. The lady checking out customers tells me that this is a "nine-items" or "twenty-dollar" counter. Paul tells her that I have a coupon. She says unless it's less than twenty dollars, I need to go to another line.

"Sorry, bud," Paul says.

I ask the lady if I can get any nine items in the store for twenty dollars. She looks confused. I clarify: "Ma'am, this sign says nine items or less or twenty dollars or less, cash. Does this mean that I can choose any nine items and only pay twenty dollars for the whole batch?"

"That would be a good deal," Paul says to the lady. She looks at both of us confused. She explains the details of the rules and clarifies that the items have to add up to less than twenty dollars or there have to be less than nine total items.

"That is so confusing," Paul says.

"It is confusing," I say. And the lady just stands there in disbelief.

"You can understand my confusion," I tell her.

"Not really," she says, shaking her head.

I head off with my cart in tow behind me and disappear behind an aisle, reappearing without my cart, stopping at an end cap for a bottle of ketchup.

"You put all those groceries away that quickly?" Paul questions and the lady looks at me frustrated.

"They are in a better place now," I tell Paul.

"What are you talking about?" the lady says.

"It's taken care of," I clarify, giving her a wink.

"What's this?" He's looking at my bottle of ketchup.

"Ketchup."

"What for?"

"The beans."

"Beans."

"Yes. Your beans suck, and I need something to help me get them down."

"What did you do with that cart full of stuff?" the lady asks.

"We have several bottles of Tabasco, Don," Paul tells me. "We don't need any ketchup."

I give Paul a desperate look. "Give me this," I say.

"Where is the cart of stuff?" the lady asks again. I set the ketchup on the belt and tell her we just want the bread and ketchup and peanut butter. I tell her she has nice eyes, and she shakes her head and slides the ketchup over the scanner, picking up the phone to request a manager. She hangs up the phone and Paul wonders out loud what sort of shampoo she uses.

• • •

PAUL OPENS THE SLIDING DOOR AND PULLS THE POT of beans from under the sink. He sets the bread down on the floor and takes a spoon and stirs the thick gravy so it breaks off into chunks and then becomes slightly fluid. I look down into the pot and think to myself about pancakes and biscuits and gravy. I take a slice of bread and spread peanut butter over the top with my Swiss Army knife. One piece, folded over and thick with peanut butter, is enough to cover the roof of my mouth and the back of my teeth. Paul does the same, leaving the rice and beans to sit and age. We have two peanut butter tacos and then Paul gets the idea to add ketchup to his third sandwich. I watch him, not in disbelief, but in wonder. He takes a bite and rolls it around in his mouth. He lifts his eyebrows and nods, handing me the bottle of ketchup. I spread peanut butter over another slice of bread and then squeeze a dab of ketchup along the crease. I fold the bread over and ketchup bleeds through the side and out the top. It's not all bad, I say. Paul nods his head and tries to swallow.

• • •

I FORCE PAUL TO STOP AT A CASINO, AS I HAVE NEVER seen one from the inside. He reluctantly pulls over at the last one on the edge of town. Inside, we find scores of old people sitting around green felt tables and tossing chips into different squares, throwing dice, and laying down cards. Sexy girls walk by, asking us if we want to order drinks, and we keep motioning to them that we don't. Paul follows me around as I wind in and out of tables, wondering out loud how to play each game. At the back of the casino we find Al Capone's car, shot up with bullet holes. Paul and I walk around the thing, trying to lean over the rope to see inside. I picture the fat mobster seated in the back, bullets flying through the door and window, right into his body. I wonder out loud what it would feel like to get shot.

After an hour or so, we both get bored. It wouldn't bother me to have stayed in Vegas, to see a show or something, maybe just walk the strip, but Paul hates anything you have to plug in, and Vegas is an entire city that doesn't exist when the grid goes down.

Leaving Las Vegas for California has you on a long, straight stretch of highway that climbs straight up into the mountains. Paul has the pedal flat against the floorboard but the van doesn't have the muscle to keep up. Trucks are grinding slowly around us. Everyone has their engines racing and we can smell brakes from cars and trucks heading down the opposite lanes. I turn around to see the lights of the city growing distant.

After an hour or so, we pass a road sign that announces California eleven miles ahead. I never realized how big those signs are. The sign must be half the size of a billboard and the letters are made of hand-sized reflective pieces of plastic.

Having passed so many miles through the desert, the road seems to exhale as it hands us to the western edge. There is an official border post in California. Like no other state, California stops cars and pays frumpy men to peer through windows and make sure we aren't smuggling fruit in from Nevada. The crossing is wide, allowing three cars through three booths. Light traffic has us one car back and the guard is asking questions to the woman in the car before us. We are on a mountain pass, and the van is heaving heated pistons and ticking. We climbed five steep miles to the border and the van had a rough go of it. The car in front of us pulls ahead and the border guard motions us forward. Paul pulls the van to the lowered railing and the uniformed man leans into the driver's window. He speaks as he looks around and he asks if we are carrying any fruit or vegetables. Paul tells him that we aren't. He asks our reasons for coming to California and Paul tells him we are traveling around the country. The man nods and tells us to enjoy our time on the West Coast. He hits a button and raises the gate and we pass into the golden hills of California, now covered in darkness.

Inside the van, warm night air riffles the pages of a book on the back bench. The pages are open and are folding into each other and slapping around, ruining the binding. I step back to close the book and set some weight on it, when I first catch the scent of gasoline. Gasoline like a gas station, really strong. I close the book, set a blanket over it, and return to the passenger's seat. Looking over at Paul, he has his hand on his mouth and a finger resting along the bottom of his nose. It occurs to me that he had already noticed the smell of gas. He looks over but doesn't say anything. I place my hand outside the window and cup the air, guiding it in through the window. While an engine light is a problem you can ignore, the smell of gas is not. We could explode or something.

"You think that's us?" I ask.

"What?"

"The smell. Smells like gas."

"I smell it," he says.

"So you noticed it."

"Yeah, a ways back," Paul says.

"Do you think it's coming from the van?" I ask.

"Yes."

"You do?"

"Yes."

"How do you know?" I ask.

"Because we've been losing gas on the gas gauge."

"I see," I say.

Why Paul would drive for several miles knowing the van smells like gas, I have no idea. I wonder if he realizes there are two of us on this trip. I just sit quietly and wait for the van to explode into flames.

Paul eyes a gas station and steers down the off-ramp, stops at a stop sign, and crosses the street to the station. He pulls alongside the pump and kills the engine. Through the dusty windshield, I squint and see a line of liquid that trails all the way down the off-ramp and makes a small puddle at the stop sign and wraps around to the back of the van. We are literally dripping a stream of gasoline. Unbelievable. I point it out to Paul and he just shakes his head.

We get out and Paul opens the engine compartment. The van is hot and ticking. The back of the van smells like grease and gas and if anyone within ten feet were to light a match, we would surely explode, sending a line of fire all the way back to the border, which honestly makes me want to do it, just to see a stream of fire ignite all the way back to Nevada.

"We might as well pull it off to the side and try to fix it before we put any gas in it," Paul says.

"Yeah," I agree, still looking back at the stream of gas.

Paul starts the van with a cringe on his face. He's worried about igniting all that gas. He quickly throws it into first and crosses the street to park alongside a roadside restaurant. Paul goes around back and opens the engine compartment and I open the sliding door and grab the toolbox. Paul uncovers both carbs and sets the lids on the ground with the appropriate nuts stored in the bowl of the lids. I tinker around with some wire, stretching and pulling levers, looking for a place where gas could be leaking. Paul lies down on his back and slides underneath. He runs his fingers along the bottom, searching for some broken line.

"It's dark under here. Can't see anything," he says.

"Pretty dark up here too," I say.

Paul keeps running his finger along the bottom of the engine.

"I smell it but I can't see it," he says.

"We may have to wait until morning."

"Sleep here?" he questions.

"Any other ideas?"

"No."

Paul stands up and stretches his back. He takes a look around the place, at the mountains in the distance and the last glow of the moon. Trucks buzz by and the place has a lonely ear to it. I picture in my mind the stream of gas going up in a flame, flowing up the on-ramp, cars slamming on their brakes or driving off the highway and down the hill, tumbling over each other, crashing and rolling, toppling over into the gas station.

17 MILK SHAKES AND PIE

TRYING TO SLEEP, BOTH OF US ARE RESTLESS. IF WE weren't leaking gas, we'd be driving. I think I have learned to sleep inside the shake and rattle of the van, but sleeping in a parking lot, not knowing exactly when we will be able to leave, has both of us staring at the ceiling.

Paul has his hands under his head. He's thinking about the gas leak, wondering where the problem is. He turns on his side and faces the opposite window, then he shifts back over, sets his hands under his head, and stares at the ceiling again.

"What are you thinking about?" I ask, already knowing the answer.

"Nothing much. Just the van."

"You getting pretty frustrated with it?"

"Getting frustrated?" he questions.

Paul pulls his blanket off of him and sets his feet on the back of the driver's seat. He takes his feet down and rolls over to his side, sits halfway up, and rests some of his weight on his elbow.

"I can't figure out why the carburetor would start leaking gas for no reason. It doesn't make sense," he says.

"Something probably rattled loose. We just need to find it and fix it. I'm sure it will be obvious to us in the morning."

"Hopefully you are right."

Paul's face catches the passing glow of a headlight that sweeps through the van. The light is accompanied by the low growl of a motorcycle. Without looking I can tell that it is a Harley. I stretch my neck to peer out the window and sure enough, a Harley has pulled up to the front door of the restaurant. A large man dressed in black dismounts and stretches. He releases a yawn, bends over to stretch his back, then leisurely walks into the café.

"You sleepy?" I ask.

"Nope."

"You want to get some coffee or something? Maybe decaf so it won't keep us up all night."

"Well, I've got some change in the ashtray. We could use that."

"I'm perfectly willing to dip into my sock of money for this one," I proclaim.

"Sounds good," he says, getting up and sliding off the bed.

A cowbell mounted atop the swinging glass door sounds as we enter the restaurant. Decked out in pink, the place was obviously decorated by a woman. Pink walls and pink curtains. There is a long bar with swivel padded-top stools and a step up to sit on them.

Paul and I stroll up to the bar and rest our elbows on the counter. An older lady with an apron comes over with a pad and pencil in her hand. She sets the pad and pencil down and hands us menus. She doesn't say anything, just smiles. Her nails are painted deep brown and she wears a large wedding ring. Her hair is blonde but should probably be gray, judging from the lines on her face. Her look is somewhere between Vegas and California. She's probably one of the ones who heads into town on weekends and gambles away her tips.

She rounds the counter and heads over to the man who came in on the Harley. He mumbles his order and she scratches it on her pad.

Paul searches through the menu for the coffee prices, but his eye comes to rest on the milk shake column. He can't get away from it. He sets the menu down and pulls a handful of change from his pocket. Counting it aloud, and shifting the coins from one pile to another, he finds two dollars with twenty-seven cents to spare.

"You're not getting coffee, are you?" I say. "You're getting a milk shake, aren't you?"

"Maybe," he says.

"You wouldn't let me have jelly and you're getting a milk shake."

Paul rotates a little metal holder on the bar and pulls several little containers of jelly out of the center compartment. He sets them on the counter and slides them my way.

"Jelly," he says.

I give him a smile of approval and place two of the containers in my shirt pocket.

"Let's get milk shakes, Don. We deserve it."

"I want coffee."

"You sure?"

"Yeah. I've got a hankering for coffee. I'll be fine with just coffee."

"Do as you wish."

The waitress comes back over and asks for our order.

"What's your special today, ma'am?" I ask.

"Ma'am?" she questions.

"Yes, ma'am. Ma'am."

"Well, if you are going to be such a gentleman, I figure I can knock fifty cents off the chicken fried steak." She says this with an endearing grin, which stays as she waits for our response.

"Now, do you make that chicken yourself, or some fellow in the back makes it?"

"A fellow in the back," she says matter-of-factly.

"Well, then I'm just not interested. I'd like to eat some of your food. You look like somebody who can cook."

"Well, I don't do the cooking here, honey."

"You don't cook anything at all?"

"I cook, but not here."

"I see." I ponder a bit. "Do you make the coffee?"

"I sure do."

"Well, then I'll just take a cup of coffee. That will be fine."

"I'll make you a fresh pot. How's that?"

"Perfect. Decaf if I could."

"I suppose." The lady looks over at Paul.

"Chocolate milk shake. Are you okay with that?"

"I'll take my chances," she says and laughs.

"Thank you, boys." She takes the menus and sets them in a slot between the countertop and the cash register. She speaks clearly through an opening in the back counter where the dishes are stacked. "Chocolate milk shake, Bob." Bob, a black-haired man with a white cooking apron, nods to confirm the order. The waitress clips the other fellow's order to a spinning contraption and turns it so the cook can see it. He wipes his hands on his apron and grabs the order, squinting and holding it away at arm's length.

"Where you boys from?" our waitress asks.

"Texas," I answer.

"Texas? What are you doing way out here?"

"We want to be in movies," I say.

The waitress laughs and leans over the counter, resting her elbows on the bar and holding her head in her hands.

"You tired?" Paul asks.

"Been here all day," she says.

"Long day. Must be tough," Paul says.

"It's not all that bad. I'm used to it. Been doing this for fifteen years."

"You've been here for fifteen years?" I question.

"Fifteen years," she confirms.

"That's a long time to work in one place."

She stands up and rests her weight against the counter. She smiles and says that we are certainly young. Used to be people would get a job and wouldn't leave. Today's kids, she says, can never stay in one place. We're always looking to get ahead and move up. Paul nods in agreement and the waitress turns around to start the coffee brewing. As she works, Paul eyes the pies in the pie case that separates the back side of the bar from the shelves where the dishes are stacked. He nudges at my elbow and points to the pies. He licks his lips. I look over to see a lemon meringue with a slice cut out and a pecan pie too. The pecan looks rich and brown. I can taste the pie on my tongue, and the thick, cool texture of the filling, and the light, fluffy brown of the crust. It's enough to make me want to jump through the glass.

The waitress turns around to see us staring at the pies.

"They look good, don't they?"

"Yes, ma'am, they do," I say.

Bob, in the back, tells her that her order is up and she turns to lower a bowl of soup and corn bread onto her tray. She rounds the bar and sets the bowl on the motorcyclist's table. Bob takes a metal cup and holds it upside down over a large glass mug. Paul's chocolate milk shake comes out thick and slides down into the mug. The waitress comes over and sets both the shake and the metal container on the counter in front of Paul. He kindly hands me the metal container and drops a spoon into it with a clink. There's a good inch of milkshake at the bottom and I gather it into the spoon and tip it upside down over my mouth. In one gulp, the milkshake is gone.

"That's good stuff," I say.

"Best milk shakes this side of the Mississippi," the waitress tells us.

"Best milk shakes anywhere!" Bob corrects her from behind the dishes.

The waitress lifts her eyebrows and shakes her head. "Bob owns the place. He's a bit partial. But the milk shakes are good. He knows how to make them."

"Sure does," Paul says, sucking the thick shake through a straw.

The waitress turns my cup over and pours my coffee.

"What's your name?" I ask.

"Betty," she answers with a smile.

"Nice to meet you, Betty. I'm Don."

Paul lifts his head and wipes his mouth with his sleeve. "I'm Paul," he says, smiling and shaking her hand.

"So you want to be in pictures, huh?" she says to us.

"Yes, ma'am. Come out here so they could put my mug on the silver screen. Just like James Dean."

Betty's eyes tell me she liked James Dean. "He was something else. You've got dimples; you just might make it."

Paul lifts his head up from his milk shake. "Don't feed his ego, Betty. I've got to travel with him."

"You hear that, Paul. James Dean. She thinks I look like James Dean."

"You look like my big toe, and you look nothing like James Dean."

Betty smiles and shakes her head. She turns and opens the pie case. She lifts a slice of lemon pie and sets it on a plate. Then she slices the pecan pie, lifts a piece, and sets it on the plate. She turns and sets the lemon pie before me and the pecan pie in front of Paul.

"What's this?" I ask.

"Pie. Don't worry. It's on the house."

Bob peers through the opening and eyes the pie. He gives Betty a look and shakes his head. "You're gonna put me out of business with all that charity, Betty!"

"Mind your own business, Bob. These boys look hungry. Besides, they're going to be famous someday. They're gonna be in pictures."

Bob smiles and moans as he cuts into an onion. "This is my business," he says.

"Thanks, Bob," Paul yells.

Bob moans again and keeps cutting his onion.

Just before Paul slices into the pecan pie, I snatch it out

from under him and slide the lemon pie along the bar. He doesn't hesitate. He just lowers his fork right into the white foam and yellow cream. I could have set a shoe in front of him and he'd have stuck a fork in it.

18 BREAKFAST

INSIDE, THE RESTAURANT HAS A DIFFERENT FEEL THAN it did last night. The place is buzzing with gamblers driving home after a night of losing money. Paul and I settle in at a booth along the back wall, closest to the restrooms. A waitress comes over and turns our coffee cups over, filling both of them. She asks about cream and I nod my head yes. She sets two menus down and I read through mine as if it were poetry.

Last night we were given a little business card on which Bob wrote "free breakfast" and signed his name.

Paul closes his menu and sets it on the table. He takes a little packet of cream, opens it, and pours it into his coffee. He opens a packet of sugar and pours it in and stirs his coffee with a sigh. He slides back in his seat and asks what I'm going to order. The Mexican, I tell him. The Mexican? he questions. Yeah, the omelet. The Mexican omelet, it comes with tortillas. I'm getting the combination plate with two of everything, he says. Then he adds that he's getting a side of hash browns. You're ordering a side item also? I question. Yes, he tells me. I hadn't thought about adding something extra. I search through the side items. The waitress comes over and asks if we are ready. Paul looks over at me and tells her that it looks like we need more time. No, I say. I'm ready. I want the Mexican omelet with a side order of biscuits and gravy. That's it. That's what I want. Paul tells the waitress that he wants the number two combo plate with a side of hash browns. The waitress writes it all down, collects the menus, and heads back to the kitchen.

Paul takes a sip of his coffee and sets his cup down on the table. He's looking around the place, sizing people up, it seems, wondering where they came from and where they are going, dividing truckers from gamblers from families crossing the desert in a move from somewhere east.

"Where are we going, Don?" he asks me, still looking around.

"Pardon?"

"Where are we going? Are we going to hang out in California for a while?"

"I don't know. What were you thinking?"

"Doesn't matter to me. But we are running low on money, you know. We may need to get to Oregon pretty soon."

"How long have we been on the road?" I question.

"About three weeks. Maybe more."

"That long?"

"It's been a while," he says.

The waitress comes toward us, balancing plates in her hands. Passing us, she sets the plates down on the table behind me.

"Smells good," Paul says.

"You can say that again."

"Smells good," Paul says again. I crack a smile. I start doctoring my coffee, cream and fake sweetener.

"You know," I say to Paul, "I've got this friend in Visalia, California. Is that near here?"

"Visalia. It's between Bakersfield and Fresno. It's not too far, on the way, really, if we decide to go up the valley. Who's your friend?"

"His name is Mike Tucker."

"How do you know Mike?" Paul asks.

"We met at a camp years ago in Colorado. He came out to Texas to visit me last year. It might be nice to swing by and see him. If we have time."

"Sounds good," Paul confirms. "Do you think he will mind?"

"Not Mike. He's great. He'll be glad to see us."

"Maybe you should give him a call. See if he would care if we stopped in."

"Yeah. I'll do that. I think I have his number somewhere in my stuff."

Paul goes out to the van and brings back a road atlas. We start mapping our route through Visalia, up into Oregon all the way to Portland, at the northern border of the state. Our waitress comes along with our food in her palms. There are also plates running up her arms. She sets a Mexican omelet before me and slides Paul's plate toward him. She carefully maneuvers the side dishes of hash browns and biscuits and gravy off her arms.

"You boys look hungry," she says.

"Yes, ma'am," one of us answers.

"You call on me if you need anything."

"Sure," Paul says. "Thanks."

She steps away and straightens her apron, checking the table for condiments. Paul asks for Tabasco sauce and she turns to another table and lifts a bottle, setting it on our table with a smile.

"Thanks again," he tells her.

Paul eyes his food and I eye his food. He eyes mine and I eye mine. He shakes his head and I pick up my fork and dive into the yellow omelet. There are bell peppers and cheese and onions, a dab of sour cream on top, butter glistening off its side. The omelet has a layer of salsa over it and all of it bleeds and runs together as I slice it with my fork.

There is no talking now. We focus on our breakfast and the world fades away. We slurp coffee between bites. I half finish my omelet before slicing into the biscuits and gravy. The white, fluffy cloud of bread, covered in gravy with chunks of ham and bacon, settles deep into my stomach. I feel the warmth of it sliding down and the carbohydrates going into my bloodstream.

After eating, Paul rests back and holds his stomach. I do the same.

NEITHER OF US WANTS TO FACE THE BROKEN VAN THIS morning, so we sit and talk. We talk about California and about John Steinbeck and Hollywood. I ask Paul if he's ever been through an earthquake and we make small talk about the comfortable weather in Los Angeles. Paul says he could never live in a city with that much smog. We both agree that we will steer away from LA on our trip. After Visalia, we'll head straight to Oregon to see these mountains Paul keeps talking about.

"Do you think you will ever go home again, Don?"

"What do you mean?"

"Do you think you will go back to Texas?"

"Where else am I going to go?" I ask.

"Anywhere. You can live anywhere. It's a free country."

"I don't know. Haven't seen anything that hits me yet."

"Could you leave Texas?" he asks.

"Maybe. It would be tough to leave my family and all. But I suppose I could if I found a nice place."

"You will like Oregon," he says.

"Yeah?"

"Yeah."

"Why is that?" I question.

"You've never seen true beauty, have you?"

"What do you mean?"

"Mountains and all. Streams and waterfalls. Forest."

"Sure I have, Paul. I've not been hiding in my room all these years."

"Where? Where did you see mountains?"

"Colorado. I spent a few summers working at that camp where I met Mike and some other friends, this girl Danielle who lives up in Washington State. We may have to stop there and see her."

"What is Mike like?" Paul asks.

"Mike is crazy. Tall, skinny guy, drives around in this old Toyota Land Cruiser."

"He has a cruiser!" Paul expresses with enthusiasm.

"Yeah, man. So tough."

"Don, *I* have a cruiser."

"You do. Where?"

"In Oregon. I have one back in Oregon."

"Where?"

"In the woods."

"Pardon?"

"Yeah, it's out off this forest service road where nobody will find it. When I bought the van, I hid it so I could go on the trip."

"You hid a car in the woods?"

"A cruiser. Not a car. A cruiser. Yes, I hid it deep in the woods and buried it in brush. Nobody will find it out there."

"You know, Paul, sometimes you seem like a bottomless pit of interesting stories."

"What do you mean?"

"You hid a Toyota Land Cruiser in the woods, bought a Volkswagen, and headed to Houston."

"Crazy, huh?" he says. "I had to hide it so nobody would vandalize it. Actually it's in pretty rough shape, so I don't think vandalism would have made a difference. But still, I don't like the idea of kids climbing around in it and that sort of thing."

"I see." I nod my head.

"So," Paul begins to change the subject, "do you know anybody from Oregon? Did you meet anyone from the Northwest at this camp in Colorado?"

"Why do you ask, Paul?"

Paul cracks a smile. "Free food, man. A place to stay when we get there. We are seriously going to run out of money. Aunts, uncles? We could do odd jobs or something, you know."

"Odd jobs?" I question. "We are on vacation."

"We are going to run out of money when we get there. You know that, don't you?"

"It crossed my mind," I say.

"Well, do you know anybody? This girl Danielle, is she family?"

"You are the one who lived there, Paul. Don't you know anyone?"

"That's different. It's home to me. I can't just go barging in on people I already know. They'll think I am irresponsible or something."

"I see. So it's okay for me to look irresponsible but it's not okay for you to look bad. Is that it?"

"Exactly."

"Very funny. But, no, I can't think of anyone in Oregon. I have a good friend named Julie in Seattle, and Danielle is somewhere in Washington, but it's a small town, don't even know where. But not Oregon."

"Seattle is too far north," Paul says. "We wouldn't go that far."

"We will eventually. I want to see Seattle eventually."

"Eventually, but we really should find a way to earn some cash so we can travel for another week or so. Seattle, maybe Canada," he says, lifting his eyebrows as if Canada is on par with France.

"What's the name of the town where Danielle lives?" he asks.

"She's in Ridgefield. Very cool girl. You would like her, actually. She's a granola like you."

"What is that supposed to mean?"

"Nothing, just that she likes nature and stuff."

"Ridgefield. Ridgefield is just north of Portland. It's practically Oregon," Paul says, shrugging his shoulders.

"Well, then maybe we can go see Danielle."

"Yes." After a few moments, "So . . . ," Paul says.

"So what?"

"So, is she, you know, good-looking?"

"Danielle?"

"Yes. What is this *granola* like?" He pronounces the word *granola* as if I had been speaking of some kind of disease.

"If you must know, it so happens she is good-looking."

"Well, let's go then. I've got to meet this girl. This granola friend of yours."

I try to settle Paul down a little. "Hold on, here. I'm not a matchmaker or anything. You never bothered to ask if I was interested in Danielle. You just automatically claimed her for yourself."

"You said she liked nature, dude. What are you going to do with a woman like that?"

"I happen to like nature too. I'm not all city."

"Let me get this straight, Don. You want to get involved with this nature girl, Danielle, and then marry her and take her to Houston?"

"What's the problem with that?"

Paul eases way back in the booth.

"I don't mean any disrespect. I truly don't. But Texas isn't nature. Texas is city and smog and humidity and heat. If you want to hunt and fish, that's fine, but if you want to climb and kayak and all, no luck. Texas is not for a girl like Danielle."

"You don't even know her. How do you know what she is like?"

"You said she is a granola. A Grape-nut."

"I never called her a Grape-nut. I just said she likes the out-doors."

"Like me," Paul says, pointing his thumb at himself.

"Yeah. She is, but that doesn't mean anything."

The waitress comes over with the bill. Paul interrupts his interrogation to hand her the little business card with Bob's message about our free breakfast.

"You know Bob?" she questions.

"Met him last night. Here at the diner."

"Well, he must have taken a liking to you. He doesn't give free meals very often."

"Yes, ma'am," I say. "He is a great guy. Couldn't believe that."

The waitress flips the card around in her hand and slides it into the pouch in her apron. "By the way, fellas . . ."

"Yes?"

"Bob's free meal doesn't include the tip."

"Oh," Paul begins. "We were going to leave you a big tip. My friend Don here is going to take care of it."

"Good thing," she says.

I smile. Paul smiles. I dig into my pocket and pull out a few dollars and lay them on the table. They are all crumbled up like child's money. The waitress looks with a grimace. I pull out another dollar and she nods and walks away.

"Thanks, Paul."

"Don't mention it."

"You ready to get out of here?"

"No. You haven't told me yet."

"Told you what?"

"Danielle. Are you interested? Is there anything there?"

"Let's go."

"No. Tell me."

"She's a close friend. A pen pal. But if you must know, no. There is nothing there."

"She's not your type, huh?"

"I didn't say that. She's great. A great girl. Just not my type."

"She's not as pretty as you said, is she?"

"She is, Paul. This girl is beautiful."

"What does she look like?"

"Let's go," I say.

"What's she look like?"

"Well, not that she'd ever be interested in you. But she's got brown hair and brown eyes. She's athletic."

"Like me."

"Whatever. She's very intelligent. She doesn't read Louis L'Amour books, that's for sure."

"She's smart?" Paul frowns.

"She is. Very smart. A literature major. Very intelligent. Good conversationalist. Her letters are like poetry."

"Are you serious? You're just pulling my leg."

"No, I'm not. That is how she is. She writes and reads poetry. *Like you.*"

"I hate poetry," Paul grumbles. I shake my head.

"Don't tell her that."

"What do you mean?"

"Better freshen up on your Byron."

"Who's Byron?" Paul asks, playing stupid.

"Lord Byron, Paul. The poet."

"Is he a friend of yours?" He's got a dumb look on his face.

"He's dead."

"Oh, sorry to hear it. Did you know him?"

"Yes. He was my uncle."

"Oh, and Danielle liked his poetry, huh?"

"Danielle loved his poetry."

"Too bad he's dead," Paul says, smiling.

PAUL WALKS LAZILY AROUND BEHIND THE VAN. HE picks at his teeth as he watches me tinker with the wing nut atop the right carb. I look back to see his expression of confusion at my work. I take the carb lid off and set it aside, just sort of staring at the inside of the carburetor. I grab a screwdriver and tighten this, grab a wrench and tighten that. I make little noises like I'm figuring it all out. Paul's expression is the same, and we banter back and forth with groans and sighs. I pull a hammer from the toolbox and begin to tap against the frame. Paul's eyebrows lift at this and he grunts as if to say he hadn't thought of that. I bang a little harder, and he clears his throat.

"You got that thing figured out yet, Don?"

"Sure do. I see the problem."

"What is it?"

"It seems to be the flux capacitor."

"The flux capacitor?"

"Yes."

"What's that?" he asks, still picking at his teeth.

"It's much too complicated to explain. You just stand there and look pretty. I'll take care of this."

He kicks me on my backside and I rock my weight into the engine compartment. Acting like I'm stuck.

"Sorry about that, dude. Didn't mean to put so much weight into that one."

"Don't mention it," I say, pretending to struggle inside the engine compartment with my arms and one of my feet. Inside, I notice a small hole in the top of the casing. And, believe it or not, there is a bolt sitting in a gully of the frame. It couldn't be this easy.

"Hey, Paul."

"Yeah."

"Look at this."

"I thought you just wanted me to look pretty."

"I'm serious."

Paul leans in and I shift a little so some sun shines on the hole. "You see this?"

"Yeah," he says.

"And this bolt?"

"Yeah."

"Do you think it goes in this hole?"

"Couldn't hurt to try."

I set the threads into the hole and screw it in. The hole smells like gasoline. This must be the top of the fuel filter. Just like a lawn mower. Paul goes around to the front and starts the van. I keep my head down to look for a leak, and nothing comes. I can't believe it was that easy. I close the engine compartment and take my place in the passenger's seat.

"How long did we work on that thing last night?" Paul asks.

"About half an hour. Maybe more."

"How come we didn't see that hole?"

"It was dark."

"I know," Paul begins, "but there is no way we could have missed it. And the bolt being right there and all. No way."

"What are you saying?" I ask.

"Think about it, Don."

"Think about what?"

"A meal. Maybe God wanted us here to meet Bob and Betty. He wanted us here to feed us a meal. You got your stinking eggs and flour tortillas. We were just talking about this in the canyon, you know."

"I never thought of it like that."

Paul lets silence come up around our ears. He sits and looks at the windshield and picks at his teeth with his toothpick. "I'm starting to, you know. I'm starting to think this is God working with us. Helping us along and all."

"Could be," I tell him.

"Could be?" he agrees. "It's just strange, you know."

"Who knows?" I say, shrugging my shoulders.

19 NIGHT GOLF

In the Mojave, we felt as though we were traveling through the desert in an oven. Joshua Tree National Park
was on our left for miles, and I kept thinking about Bono and
the boys, hiking up the hills in black and white. We moved
out of the desert and turned north into the Sierra Nevada. I
confess California has taken me by surprise. Not having been
here, all I knew of the state was Los Angeles, the Lakers and
Hollywood, and smog and surfers. But there are mountains
here, an impressive range, and the brown of the desert gives
way to green, rolling green hills fed by creeks running over
boulders, splashing down through pastures where sheep
graze. The Sierra Nevada has towering peaks that would give
the Rockies a run. We slope slowly through meadows, the
mountains in the distance, the deserts behind us. Mike had
told me about the mountains in California, but I never imagined them to be so majestic.

We come down from the hills and into the valley. The interstate runs just west of Visalia, where we exit and head east
through orange groves and come into town at the ballpark,
probably the home of a farm team of some sort. Paul pulls the
van over at the park and I use a pay phone to call Mike, all the
while looking at the back scoreboard through the fence, trying to find a team name. His mom answers and I tell her that
we are swinging through on our way to Oregon and ask if
Mike is around.

"Who is calling?" she asks.

"An old friend of Mike's. Mike and I met in Colorado."

"I see. Well, he is at work," she tells me. "He will be home in half an hour or so. Would you like to come to the house? You are more than welcome to wait here."

"Sure, sounds good."

"Are you in town?" she asks.

I tell her where we are and she explains the back roads from the ballpark, not too far.

We drive slowly through neighborhoods and I wonder at how the people who live here probably get to thinking that neighborhoods are all that America is, house after house. And I wonder again at how much land we have in this country, how many empty miles of desert there are between here and the nearest city, how we are only living in tiny islands on a vast ocean of government property. Visalia is flat like Texas. Deep into the horizon, though, you can see the mountains, dark peaks rising like a wall, stopping the rain from getting to Vegas.

We arrive at Mike's place and Mrs. Tucker makes us a pitcher of lemonade and puts some chips out. I can see Mike in her face and her gestures, and when she laughs I get snapshots of Mike back in Colorado. I start thinking about how strange it is that we come from families, that a man and a woman have sex and make a human that looks a little like them, that is part of them in some way, and how nobody gets to decide who they get born to, and how much of life is outside our control. Paul and Mike's mom like each other quite a bit and start talking about spirituality, about the sort of things Paul has been thinking about on the trip, about how God answered his prayer with the mechanic, and how God has been good to us. I keep thinking about how much she looks like Mike, how when she chews food, she chews the way he does, and when she nods her head, she nods her head and purses her lips a little and how Mike used to do that when we'd talk about serious things. I start thinking about what it must have been like for Mike to have come out of her womb. We just come out of these women's wombs, all of us. We come out like little footballs, trapped in skin, bound to earth by gravity, crawling around learning what a ball is and how to say "Momma" and finally walking, stuck to earth without wings, called by a name our parents thought was cute or interesting. And that is who we are; this is our name and this is our skin and this is how we chew, and we are, in large part, what somebody else tells us we are, and we never stop to think of how crazy the whole thing is. We never stop to ask *why* all of this is happening to us, about the *why* as opposed to the *how*, like I was saying a while back.

"How are you processing all of this?" Mrs. Tucker looks over at me to include me in the conversation.

"About God and all?" I ask.

"About God and all," she clarifies.

"I think He explains a lot," I tell her.

"Explains a lot?" she questions.

"You know, why we are here, maybe, what all is going on, how you had Mike in your womb and chew like him." As I say this, she begins to look confused.

"What do you mean, Don?" Paul inquires.

"I don't know. I don't know exactly. Just the whole thing seems odd. I mean, that is the thing about asking *why*, isn't it? You start asking those questions and the whole thing falls apart. It is as though nothing means anything anymore. I mean, it is great if you can buy into it, if you can just say, okay, God has done all of this to dazzle us, and the mountains and the desert and all the bugs and animals are just there for us to enjoy, and that is great. I am thankful for that. But you almost have to look at it poetically, because when you break it down without God's explanation or God's reason for us being here, it gets pretty confusing and odd. I had this girlfriend once, and I loved her. She was just beautiful, but then suddenly I was kissing her and I realized her mouth was full of germs and she has to use the bathroom, you know, just like a guy, and I couldn't like her after that. I mean, I liked her and I wanted to keep making out with her, but it was like, man, you know, this girl is a human just like me, and there isn't any poetry in this. It's just sexual attraction and germs and body fluids and chemicals. I guess what I am saying is, God is helping me see things more poetically." Mrs. Tucker kind of laughs when I say all of this, and Paul pats me on the back. She asks us if we want any more chips and we tell her we are fine, so she rolls up the bag and puts it back in the cupboard.

"I noticed his Land Cruiser in the driveway, Mrs. Tucker. Is he on foot?" I ask.

"He's on skates," she says.

"Skates?" Paul asks.

"Well, what are those things? They aren't skates. They call them something different." Mrs. Tucker scratches her head and looks at the ceiling.

"Roller blades?" Paul asks.

"That's it. He's on roller blades. He only works a few blocks away."

"What does he do?" Paul asks.

"He's a waiter. He's been a waiter for years now. He was doing fine dining for a while, but now he's at this little breakfast place. He likes it better because there isn't as much pressure. At the fine dining place, he actually had a dessert that he had to set on fire in order to serve it. Mike was always afraid he was going to set a customer's tie on fire. He hated it when people ordered that dessert. If you ask me, I think the flaming dessert, or whatever it was called, is the reason he left. Hated setting that thing on fire." She pauses. "Are you boys staying here tonight?"

"I don't think so, Mrs. Tucker. We don't want to put you out or anything," Paul says.

"No, sir. You are not putting me out at all. People are always staying here. One of Mike's friends, Keith, slept on our couch for several months. We didn't hardly notice him. Don't worry about it."

"You had a fellow living in your front room?" Paul questions.

"Yes. He was living in his car for a while and Mike asked if he could stay here. Mike knew him from the local community college. A real smart kid. He lived out the rest of the term right here."

"I see," I say.

Mrs. Tucker puts the Tupperware pitcher of lemonade back into the fridge and steps in front of the sink, in front of the kitchen window.

"There he is," she says, spotting him. "He's coming up the road."

Paul and I step outside and walk down the short driveway behind Mike's Land Cruiser. Paul checks out the cruiser up close and I walk down to the street to meet Mike. He's coming up slow, tall and skinny with bright red hair. Mike is another good-looking fellow like Paul. He's always got some gal writing him or calling him, I figure. He's wearing baggy khaki shorts and a T-shirt. He has a backpack on and he's sliding like a fellow on ice skates. His weight slides left, then right, and he rocks his arms at his sides as he propels forward. About a hundred yards away, he comes to a stop, sets his hands on his hips. I stand at the end of the driveway with a grin. He gets a big grin on his face and laughs.

"I don't believe it. What are you doing here?" Mike skates up to me and gives me a bear hug. He wraps his long arms around me and pats my back like I was choking on something. "Man, Don. It's good to see you. What are you doing here?"

"Passing through. Had to stop and see you."

"You better have, man. I didn't know you were going to be in town."

"I should have called. We were just driving, you know, and, well . . ."

"You don't have to explain it to me," he says. Mike goes

over and introduces himself to Paul. It makes me proud, honestly, to have a couple friends as good-looking and interesting as Mike and Paul. They start talking about Mike's cruiser and Paul is asking all kinds of questions. Both Mike and I start explaining to Paul how we met and get to telling old stories. We go back in the house and Mike takes a shower and gets changed, commenting how much he smells like burned bacon every time he gets off work. We say good-bye to Mrs. Tucker and load up in the cruiser for a quick tour of Visalia. We end up at this Mexican place across town, a hole in the wall. Mike says he wants to take us out and neither Paul nor I argue. We lean back and sip Coronas and I catch Mike up on the last month or so, taking him all the way to the bottom of the Grand Canyon and back, and how Paul and I met back in Houston. The conversation comes to a lull and Paul asks what there is to do in this town and whether it was too early in the season to catch a baseball game. Mike just holds his hands out and looks around, as if to say, well, this is it. We've got a Mexican place, he says, and holds up his beer. We've got beer, he says. Plenty of options, Mike says. We've got a mall, kind of, and a downtown with a park or something. Both Paul and I are laughing at him. We can lie down at the end of the runway out at the airport and feel planes land.

"Sounds good," Paul says.

"I will be needing a few more beers," I tell them.

"Actually," Mike begins, "there used to be some kind of cargo jet that would land in the evenings, but I think they truck that crap up these days, so there aren't any jets landing at night anymore. We used to lie out there and feel the thing fly over. It's crazy. Your whole insides just vibrate like you're hooked up to an electric socket."

"You're kidding," Paul says. I tell Paul to tell Mike about how he once peed on an electric fence and both Mike and I about wet ourselves when Paul gets to the part about not being able to feel his johnson for twenty-four hours.

Another lull in the conversation prompts Mike to mention the possibility of night golf.

• • •

THAT EVENING, WE DRIVE NORTH OF VISALIA A LITTLE and Mike parks the cruiser in a parking lot across from a golf course. I'm in the backseat and Mike turns to tell me there are several golf clubs behind me. He tells me to grab the nine iron for him and to pick one out for myself and for Paul. I do as he says, handing Paul the seven and keeping the eight for myself. Mike hands Paul an empty plastic grocery sack from the glove box. He keeps one and hands one to me. Paul asks what we're doing and Mike tells him it's called night golf. I don't ask any questions.

It's just past midnight and Visalia is asleep. We sit in a parking lot and across the street is a fence that protects a golf course. Mike points out a spot along the fence that is hidden in the shade of a tree. Streetlights illumine most of the fencing, but that one spot is hidden in shadows.

"That is where we need to jump the fence," Mike announces.

"I see." Paul eyes the fence.

Without speaking, Mike jumps from the truck and runs across the street. He throws his body over the fence and sprints into the darkness. Paul and I sit in silence, looking deep into the shadows across the street. We sit a little more and then a little more. Paul has his golf club at his side; he looks it over and fidgets with the handle.

"I think he wants us to go and jump the fence, Paul."

"I think so," Paul says.

"Well," I say, "I think we should follow him."

Paul jumps out of the truck and runs in a zigzag across the street. He's playing the part of a bank robber. All his motions are exaggerated. He pretends to see a car and lies down on the road. Then he gets up, freezes, and puts his arms out, pretending to be a tree. He throws his club over the fence, puts his plastic bag in his pocket, and scrambles over the chain-link. I can see his shadow as he picks up his club and runs deep into the darkness. I study the thrill of it, sit awhile as a car is passing, and then run across myself, having some trouble, getting snagged at the top of the fence, ripping my shirt. I gather my club and bag and run out into the darkness. I find the edge of a pond and stand still to listen for my friends. I can't seem to hear them so I start walking out onto the open range.

Through dark trees and moonlight, I hear my two friends laughing. I walk in the direction of the voices and I find Paul.

"Psst. Don, is that you?"

"Yeah."

"Where have you been?"

"I don't know. Back there somewhere."

"What took you so long?"

"I didn't know where you guys were. Where is Mike?"

"He's over there." Paul points but I can hardly make out his hand. My eyes have adjusted slightly, but it is still too dark to navigate. There are clouds over the moon and stars, so everything is murky.

"What's he doing?" I ask.

"Same as me. He's picking up golf balls and putting them into his bag."

"Why?"

"He hasn't said why. But this is night golf and this is how it works."

"I see," I say. "So what am I supposed to do?"

"Pick up golf balls."

"Where are they?" I ask.

"They are everywhere."

"Everywhere?"

"Yes. We're in the middle of a driving range."

"Oh. I get it. But what are we going to do with the golf balls?"

"Hit them," Mike says. His voice seems to come from out of nowhere.

"Hit them where, Mike?" I ask.

"At each other."

"Pardon?" Paul questions.

"Yeah," Mike begins, "we get at opposite sides of the driving range, and we try to hit each other."

I cannot make out Mike's expression, but the tone in his voice tells me he is serious. Mike disappears into the darkness. I realize the importance of the moment and drop to my knees, scurrying for golf balls. My sack at my side, I scoop and fill, scoop and fill. The rush of adrenaline aids my speed. From a distance, and through the dark night, we hear Mike yell *incoming!* Paul dumps his bag on the ground and takes stance. I take my half-filled bag and run off into a dark corner of the range. I can hear Mike's club hit the ball. The pop splits the air like a gunshot and then, about fifty yards away, I hear Paul yap, giggle, and take a swing back at Mike. I devise a strategy to never hit from the same spot. The only way we can identify each other is from the sound of the club hitting the ball. If I stay on the move, there is no way they can figure out where I am. So, I drop a ball to the ground and hit it toward Mike. I hear the ball land and hear Mike laugh. I got close, I know that much. Rather than dumping the balls on the ground, I take my club and run fifty yards farther. I hear Paul hit another ball and it flies past me. The whistle of it tells me it's moving quickly. That would have been a painful blow. So I drop another ball to the ground and take aim at Paul. I'm about seventy-five yards or so away, so I loft the ball so as to land on his head. No sound. I wasn't even close. I move another twenty-five yards down the length of the driving range. As I am running, I hear Paul give a serious yap and moan. He's hit. He's laughing. Probably on the ground, rubbing the knot on his head. I drop another ball and hit it toward Mike. Another miss. Mike hits one toward me and it lands just in front of me so I have to jump out of the way. The balls are not visible until they are right on you. My eyes are able to focus a little better through the darkness and I can see the reflection of Mike's club as he swings. He's aiming at Paul again.

I start thinking about how Mike has the advantage over me and Paul 'cause he knows the range and is apparently a better golfer. I run back over toward Paul to see if he wants to team up. As I get close to him, he takes a swing and lands a ball into my side. I fall down in a moan and roll over saying I'm hit. Both Mike and Paul have a good laugh at that.

"Paul. Psst, Paul."

"What?"

"Let's work together."

"What do you mean?"

"Mike is better at this. Let's gang up on him."

"How?"

"Let's run around behind him and take swings."

"Where is he?"

"He's over there. Come on."

Paul gathers some balls into his bag and we run the length of the range, outside the boundaries behind trees. We hear Mike take another swing. He laughs as the ball leaves the ground. His club glistens for a second and I stop Paul from running, draw him near, and point toward the place I saw Mike. We are even with him, but he is a good fifty yards out, and he's still facing the place where Paul was standing.

"Lose the clubs," Paul comments.

"Why?"

"Let's get up close and pelt him."

"Just throw them?" I question.

"Yes."

Paul grabs a handful of balls from his sack, sticks them in his pocket, and does it again with his other pocket. Pretty soon we are both loaded with ammunition.

"Paul, you go around back and I will get him from the side. Don't throw unless you get a good view of him."

"You got it," he says, and with that, Paul runs around to the back of the range. I wait to hear him charge, and then run toward Mike. Paul hits him and Mike goes down. Paul pummels him from the rear as I hurl golf balls from the side. He yells uncle but we do not let up. Mike gathers his senses, stands, and begins to grab at golf balls. He throws one toward Paul and as he releases I can see the complete outline of his body. I take aim and fire, hitting him in the shin on a bounce. He goes down again and gathers a few more balls. He throws one toward me and hits me squarely on the thigh.

Paul yells charge and we move in close and fast. Soon enough, we are on top of Mike and pelting him with golf balls. Mike can't stop laughing. This goes on for a while and Mike finally calls a truce.

MIKE GETS ABOUT TWO HUNDRED GOLF BALLS LINED up at the edge of the lake. It must be four in the morning. Everything is completely quiet, and none of us feel like talking anymore. The moon has come out a little now, so we can see the balls fly straight up over the lake after Mike takes a swing. The ball seems to suspend up there somewhere for a while before dropping in and making a splash out in the middle of the water. Every once in a while, a cop car turns the corner by the clubhouse and slowly drives up the street. Each time we lie down on our bellies and wait for him to leave.

20 THE OREGON TRAIL

WE WERE OUT TILL SUNRISE AND AT SIX MIKE HAD TO work the breakfast shift. He tells us to come in for breakfast, but Paul and I have already eaten pretty well and need to hit the road.

"I can't thank you enough for letting us stay, Mike," I tell him.

"Dude, stick around," he says. "You've got nowhere to go."

"We're trying to get to Oregon. We should probably hit the road," I say.

"Oregon is only about eight hours away. Leave tomorrow."

I look over at Paul and he shrugs his shoulders. We are at the kitchen table and Mike's mom has made us coffee. Mike refills my cup.

"You're not putting me out," he says. "You always feel like that and it's not the case. What's the rush with Oregon anyway?"

"No rush, really. I've just wanted to see it and that's where we're heading, you know."

"Go if you want." Mike shrugs.

"I've got a better idea," I say. "Join us, Mike. Come with us."

"Yeah!" Paul says.

"I can't," Mike sighs.

"Why?" I ask.

"Work."

Paul chimes in again: "Come with us, Mike. Have you ever been to Oregon?"

"Never been," he says.

"You'll love it."

"Mike," I begin, "we're going up to Ridgefield to see Danielle."

"The girl we met in Colorado?"

"Yes," I tell him.

"The girl in the red dress?" he asks, perking up.

"Yes."

"What red dress?" Paul asks.

"Go take a cold shower, Paul," I tell him.

"She's a babe," Mike says to Paul.

"I knew it," Paul says. "Tell me about her, Mike."

"Look at this guy," Mike says. "Acts like he's got a shot."

"She's that pretty, huh?" Paul says.

"She's that good-looking."

"Yeah, yeah, tell me more," Paul asks.

Mike starts explaining to Paul how we met Danielle. He tells him how smart she is and that she's a great soccer player. "We were all really close that summer in Colorado," he says. "We were inseparable. We'd climb Red Mountain for sunrise. She was funny, huh, Don?"

"She was funny?"

"Used to watch old black-and-white movies or something. But, man, that red dress."

"I know," I say.

"What red dress?" Paul asks.

"She had this red dress on, our last day there, long and formfitting, you know. Man, she looked good. All of us were like, um, maybe she isn't just a tomboy, you know."

"No kidding. There's a woman in there, for sure," Mike adds.

"I've got to meet this girl!" Paul exclaims. "Let's get out of here. Mike, come with us."

"Can't," he says. "I have to work. You guys have a good time." Mike meets my eye and holds a fist over the table. I tap his fist to mine. "Say hello to Danielle," he says.

WITH PAUL AT THE WHEEL, WE DRIVE WEST TO Interstate 5 that will take us through Oregon and into Portland.

The van enjoys the flatness of the valley. We found our pace about one hundred miles ago and the van has not wavered, choked, or coughed in complaint since. We are sailing through America's bread basket, cabbage and beets and fruit trees and fields of grapes.

Paul tells me we should make Oregon by sunset, and then Portland before midnight, or shortly thereafter. I ask him if we intend to drive the night, and he shakes his head, saying he doesn't know if he can make it.

"Is this a pilgrimage?" I ask my friend.

"A pilgrimage?" he asks.

"Yes."

"What do you mean?" he inquires.

"Are we on a spiritual pilgrimage?"

"I don't know. I don't know what a pilgrimage is, I guess."

"I think it's when you are looking for the answer to something, or when you are trying to figure out God," I tell him.

"Are you trying to figure out God?" Paul asks.

"I don't know. I think I did, a bit, back in the canyon, but then you have to kind of jump into it, don't you? I mean, you have to see and believe the world is God's, that He is there and He made it for us. You have to see things poetically."

"What was all that crap you were talking about with Mike's mom? All that stuff about making out with your girlfriend?" Paul asks.

"I don't know," I tell him. "I don't really feel like being on a pilgrimage yet."

"You don't feel like looking for God?" he asks.

"No," I say. "I don't. I mean I know He is there, but what if I want life to be about something it isn't? What if I want life to be about getting paid and getting married or just being happy in the pagan sense?"

"Getting paid?" Paul asks, shrugging his shoulders. "I don't know. Just because you want life to be something doesn't mean that is what it is. What if life is about something else, and it doesn't matter what we think?"

"I know what life is about. But what if I don't like it?" I say.

"Tough, I guess. It is what it is."

"What if that sucks?" I ask.

"What if it does?" he says. "I guess there isn't anything you and I can do about it. It's like you were saying, you know, about having to take a crap and being born with somebody else's DNA and all, life is just what it is, and it isn't like we are given a lot of freedom."

"Gravity and all that crap," I say.

"Gravity and all that," Paul confirms. "Not a lot of options."

"And that sucks," I say, putting my hand out the window to cup the wind.

"What if it doesn't suck?" Paul says.

"What do you mean?"

"What if, you know, if we just give in to it, and say this is what it is, then it gets good, and it's fighting it that makes it so bad."

I think about that for a second but don't know how much I like it. It feels like we don't have a lot of options. And don't get me wrong, I feel like life is good, but it just feels like, as a human, we aren't given a lot of options. It feels like, outside a relationship with God, you know, life doesn't mean anything. Which is fine, but what if you just want a little break? And I know this sounds terrible, but what if?

"I think that sucks," I say after a few minutes. Paul lets everything be silent. He is putting his free hand out the window now, cupping the air.

"You on a pilgrimage, Don?" he asks.

"I don't know," I tell him.

"You on a pilgrimage?" I ask.

Paul doesn't answer for a second. "Maybe we're all on a pilgrimage," he says. "Maybe it's all one trip, one big road trip through the cosmos, through the nothingness. Maybe we're all going somewhere. Or really, maybe we are all being taken somewhere."

"Where are we going?" I ask.

"Maybe it isn't for us to decide, just to give in to it."

"What is *it*?" I ask.

"*It* is whatever God wants *it* to be," Paul says. "Maybe we are just supposed to trust that He won't beat us up when we get there. Maybe we are supposed to trust that He is good."

"Maybe so," I say. And after that we don't talk about it anymore. I start closing my eyes to try to get some sleep but it is useless. I lean back in my seat and look out over the miles and miles of farmland, all the green stretching back behind us, out toward the mountains, all the earth making all those crops, everything happening in its own time, a sustainable planet held together by some kind of mystery that physicists call Mother Nature, as if to pretend they aren't all believing fables. As if to pretend we aren't all believing fables.

"You tired?" I ask.

"Very tired. We didn't get much sleep last night."

"I know. I'm feeling a little tired too."

"You think you could drive?" Paul asks.

"How far is Oregon?"

"About three more hours. We should hit mountains pretty soon. They aren't too big, but we should start seeing them."

"I can drive," I tell him.

Paul pulls the van to the shoulder. He gets out and stretches, bending over and arching his back. He sets his hands against his sides and leans backward. I slide over into the driver's seat as Paul gets in on the passenger's side.

Steering the van back to the road, we rock and sway, bumping over the edge of the shoulder. I look over at Paul and only a mile down the road he is sleeping. I speak his name and get no answer. His mouth is open a little. He's out.

Fifty more miles has us in hill country and approaching

mountains. We've been out of Visalia for six hours now. If Mike was right, we should hit Oregon pretty soon. These hills are thick with evergreen. Redwoods line the road. The trees become enormous within fifty miles, tall and broad at their bases, and the ground has the look that it is permanently wet.

Another two hours down the road and Paul is still asleep. The interstate has woven through the redwoods and I've gotten some energy off the change in landscape, the shift to cool, moist air and the feel of Narnia. The mountains have given way to subtler slopes, but we go up and down all the same. Gradual climbs and quick descents. I start thinking again about what Paul was saying, about how we have to submit to whatever God has us on this journey for, about how we just have to agree that it is all His. And I know God made stars and friends and love and poetry to dazzle us, but there really is a part of me that wants some freedom, that doesn't want to have to do everything right or be religious anymore. It's not a serious struggle, but it's like I said about *how* and *why* questions, when you know the *why,* you are just kind of trapped, and when you only ask *how* and never ask *why,* you can be happy and ignorant. Even if God is taking the cosmos somewhere good, I begin to wonder what He does with folks who just want out.

AFTER ANOTHER HOUR, DRIVING INTO THE NIGHT, MY eyes grow heavy and my mind has trouble staying in the now. A forest kind of dark has laid itself over the landscape. There is moonlight in the sky, but it's having trouble sifting through the tall trees to find the road. I find myself having to be very intentional about staying in my lane when a car comes at us from the distance. I find myself justifying a quick closing of the eyes, catch myself thinking about my eyes being shut, then open them quickly, and shake my head to wake myself up. But it's no use. I'm fading.

For a change I weave between lanes, running my tires over the divider reflectors. The thumps give me a jolt and that helps a bit. I roll down the window and stick my head out like a dog. I sing to myself. I talk to Paul, who is asleep in the back now. I honk the horn. I talk to the trees. Something ahead catches my eye. I slow, pull the van to the shoulder, and park it like a car at a drive-in movie. A large brown sign stands some thirty feet in the air, reading "Welcome to Oregon." I pull the van off the road and park underneath it, get out, and smell the clean air. I walk into the forest a few feet and take a pee. I zip up my pants and stand real still to feel the silence. I walk back over to the van and slide the door open, climb over Paul, and lay my head on a pillow.

21 SINATRA

I FELL ASLEEP WITHOUT SHUTTING THE DOOR OR moving the van. The police officer pulls on Paul's pant leg and asks him to get out of the van. Paul calls my name and wakes me up. I slide to the edge of the bed and rub my eyes, looking around to remember where we are. Paul is looking up at the "Welcome to Oregon" sign and the officer is trying to get some questions answered.

"What are you two doing?"

"Sleeping, Officer, I think," Paul says, still looking at the sign. "I have no idea why we are parked right here, though."

"You two do some drinking last night?" he asks.

"No. I wasn't drinking. I was asleep."

"You been drinking?" the officer asks, looking into the van, lifting some blankets with his flashlight.

"No, Officer. I was driving last night and was pretty exhausted. I pulled over. It was dark."

"You didn't see that sign?" he asks, motioning toward the enormous contraption casting a shadow on all of us.

"I did. I just didn't know, you know."

"Didn't know what?"

"Didn't know where to park, I guess. I had to use the bathroom."

The officer looks deeper into the van, pushing some of our boxes around with the end of his light. He tells us all the things he could do with us if he wanted, that he could arrest us or give us a ticket, and quotes a bunch of laws.

"We didn't mean any harm," I assure him.

"Well, get back on the road," he says. "Can't stay here."

Paul stretches after the officer leaves. He grabs my foot and I kick him, moaning and covering up again with blankets. Paul rounds to the driver's side and I hear the engine start. The van jars through ruts in the grass and onto the road and I lean up to close the sliding door. *We're in Oregon,* I think to myself. It was too dark to get a good look at the place last night, so I uncover my head from the blankets and peer through the side windows. Paul's been talking so much about the place I feel like there must be something magical about it. I get up from the bed and take my spot in the passenger's seat.

I had imagined Oregon to be greener, actually. Not that it's not lush; it is. And it is certainly beautiful, but I guess I imagined a rain forest. Paul tells me Oregon can be divided into three major sections. There is the valley, which we are in; the mountains to our right, not visible through the thick trees; and the desert on the other side of the mountains.

"Like the Mojave Desert?" I ask.

"No," he answers. "More like high desert. There are canyons and rolling hills. Juniper trees, sagebrush, that sort of thing."

"Do you think we will get over there?" I ask.

"Sure," he says. "We may have to head that way."

"Why would we have to?"

"To get jobs. We are going to run out of money sometime soon. I don't know whether you noticed that."

"I thought about it. But I knew you had a plan."

"I see," he says.

"So?"

"So what?"

"What is your plan, Paul?"

"For jobs?"

"Yes."

"Well, for the past three summers I've worked at Black Butte Ranch. It's outside of Sisters in the Cascades."

"Sisters is a town, right?"

"Yeah. I told you about it. It's a great place except for the cone lickers."

"Cone lickers?" I question.

"Yeah. Tourists, you know. They come in droves and walk down the streets licking ice-cream cones."

"I get it. Cone lickers."

Looking at the map, I see that there seem to be only two major interstates through Oregon. Interstate 5, which we are on, heads north and south. It comes up from California and passes through Eugene, Salem, and Portland before heading into Washington State and through Seattle into Canada. Then there is Interstate 84, which runs east and west along the northern border of Oregon. There don't seem to be very many towns on 84. It goes all the way through Idaho to Salt Lake City, Utah.

Oregonians are all by themselves up here. I am used to Texas, where there are a dozen major highways that head to half a dozen towns with more than a million people. I feel like I'm traveling into the deepest remote parts of Alaska or the Northern Territory. There is a spot on the map, in eastern Oregon, where I can place my entire hand and not lay it over a town. There are only a few minor roads that head out that way and they all seem to dwindle off like weak creeks and streams. We're in the outback, I say out loud.

Paul rolls down his window and breathes the air. It's fresh air. Smells like forest, like it has rolled down off the mountains. You can smell nearby rivers and feel the coolness in the air.

"Tell me about Black Butte. What will we do there?"

"I will work as a lifeguard. I've done it for years. About three summers."

"What about me?"

"Janitor."

"Are you serious?"

"Yeah. Janitor. It's good work, Don. They pay well."

"Whatever," I tell him. "How much money do we have?"

"Not much. About a hundred dollars. That will get us to Ridgefield, maybe Seattle if we want, then back to Black Butte. No more than that."

"I have about fifty dollars," I say. "That will get us a little farther."

"Food," Paul starts. "Don't forget about food. We have to eat. The fifty will pay for food."

"I forgot about that. Danielle will feed us. I'm sure of that."

"Did you ever call her?" Paul asks.

"I didn't. I meant to call her from Mike's, but we left in a rush and I was tired. I didn't think about it."

"Maybe you should call her. We don't just want to drop in."

As we get closer to a city, Paul exits the interstate and drives a few blocks into Eugene. I notice a coffee shop and think a cup of coffee sounds good. But then I see another. Two coffee shops on one street. We don't even have two coffee shops in all of Houston, much less two on one street. When we stop for gas, I wander over to a phone booth and call Danielle. It's long distance, so it costs me a dollar in quarters.

"Hello, is this Danielle?"

"No," a tender voice answers.

"Did I reach the Bjurs?"

"This is the Bjurs. This is Shirley Bjur."

"Are you Danielle's sister?"

"I'm her mom, but thanks for the compliment!"

"Hello, Mrs. Bjur. This is Donald. I met Danielle in Colorado a few summers ago. We keep in touch through letters."

"I know about you, Don. It's good to talk to you. Do you want me to get Danielle?"

"If that is okay. It was nice to talk to you."

"Nice to talk to you too," she says, and then sets the phone down. I hear her call for Danielle and hear Danielle answer and talk to her mom as she comes to the phone.

"Hello," Danielle says.

"Hey there."

"Hi." Pause. "Who is this? I'm sorry." She sounds confused.

"Don Miller."

"Donald!"

"Yeah."

"It's so great to hear your voice. Did you get my letters?"

"Which ones?"

"From Costa Rica!"

"Costa Rica?"

"You didn't get them?" She sounds upset.

"No. Were you in Costa Rica?"

"Yeah. I got back this morning."

"No way. I can't believe that. I almost missed you," I tell her.

"What do you mean?" she asks.

"I'm here. I mean not here, but close."

"Close to where?" Danielle asks. "Here?" she says as she realizes I am in the area.

"Yes. I'm in Oregon!"

"No way!" she screams. "Where in Oregon?"

"A town called Eugene."

"Don, Eugene is just down Interstate 5. You're pretty close. Are you coming up here? You'd better."

"Yeah, we're heading to Seattle maybe. I don't know exactly where we are going, but I'd like to come up and see you."

"Please do, Don, please come here. What in the world are you doing here?"

"A friend and I are traveling around in this Volkswagen van, we're seeing the country, and . . ."

"Like hippies!"

"Yeah. Like hippies. We're living like people in the sixties and all."

"You have to come here, Don. Are you coming?"

"Yeah. If that's an invitation, we're coming."

"It's an invitation! Come!" She is jumping up and down at this point. Her mom is in the background asking what is going on. Danielle is trying to explain.

"Well, tell me how to get there!"

I hang up the phone and walk toward Paul with a smile on. He has the van started and asks how it went. He asks if I told her about him and I tell him I forgot.

"You forgot?" he says.

"How far is Ridgefield?" I ask him.

"About three hours or so," he tells me.

"I told her we'd be there before sunset."

"We'll be there before that," Paul says.

"Well, we can hang out in Portland or something. You should get a shower if you are going to impress this girl. You're smelling pretty bad."

"I took a shower at Mike's!" Paul exclaims.

"Did you use soap?" I ask.

Paul laughs at that. He pulls the van back on the road and we weave toward the interstate. We pass yet another coffee shop.

"What is it with coffeehouses, man? They are everywhere."

"Welcome to the Pacific Northwest, Don. This is the coffee capital of the world."

"There's a shop on every block," I say in wonder.

"You haven't seen anything, Don. Wait till we get to Portland."

We are out of Eugene pretty quickly. Back into farmland. Oregon agriculture is not just fruit and vegetables; it's also Christmas trees. There are perfect rows of five-foot pines that stretch down flat valleys and up onto the hills. They keep their rows regardless of the slant of the earth. Beyond the hills I can see the outline of the mountains. I ask Paul if these are still the Sierra Nevada and he answers with an emphatic no. They are the Cascades. It's a volcanic range.

"Volcanic?" I question.

"You've heard of Mount Saint Helens," he says.

"Mount Saint Helens is around here?"

"Just across the border, really. Just up into Washington State about ninety miles. You can see it from Portland. But the big mountain around here is Mount Hood. It stands in the distance and is visible from the city. You can see it from almost anywhere."

I start wondering what it must be like to live in the shadow of a mountain. All of Houston lives in the shadow of downtown. Downtown is how we orient ourselves. It stands as our compass, a mountain of glass and mirrors. It strikes me as I think about it, how beautiful we find massive structures, either man-made or organic. I wonder if we find them amazing because they make us feel small and insignificant, because they humble us. And I remember feeling that way back in Colorado, that I was not the center of the cosmos, that there were greater things, larger things, massive structures forged in the muscle of earth and time, pressing up into the heavens as if to say the story is not about you, but for you, as if to remind us we are not gods.

SOON WE ARE OUT OF THE VALLEY AND INTO THE foothills. The interstate thickens with cars and buses, trucks and minivans. South of Portland, the land rises and turns green. Businesses rest in the shadows beneath clumps of trees.

Right of the highway, the earth dips into a river. It is a large river. I noticed it on the map earlier. The Willamette, it is called. The interstate follows along the river and then before us is downtown Portland. Despite its western status, it appears old and settled. The river wears the skyline like a crown.

We discuss our itinerary and agree on a shower. But where? I suggest we find a university and use the athletic facility. I am not one who can easily pass himself as an athlete, but a confident stride will usually get you anywhere and Paul tells me Portland State University is somewhere in the downtown area. We drive up and down one-way streets till we see tennis courts and a large adjoining building. Portland is a walkable city, every corner with another coffee shop; there must be fifteen or more on one street alone. The city blocks are half the size of blocks in Houston, so each corner holds a retail space and the foot traffic makes the city feel inviting. And people don't wear ties here, no suits, just slacks and a sweater or dress shirt. We are driving right through the middle of the business district and I literally don't see anybody wearing a suit. Paul tells me Portland is the world headquarters for both Nike and Columbia, and the place does have that granola athlete feel, that nonconformist but yuppie anyway kind of vibe. We ask a passerby if the university is near and he points us toward something called the park blocks. We wind through the streets till we find a long row of blocks designated for urban gardens and paths. At the end of the park blocks everything starts feeling school-like so we park the van.

We wander around campus for a while and find the athletic facility. With a confident stride, we march in through the doors, through the gym, and into the locker room. A man in a caged room hands us towels and we thank him and take showers. I hate being naked in front of anybody, but especially in an athletic facility. Paul walks into the open shower room and fidgets with the water. I am standing closer to the lockers, still in my pants. When nobody seems to be looking I pull off my pants and underwear and walk quickly to the showerhead. Paul starts trying to make conversation but I am not interested. I lather up, get my hair wet, rinse off, and head back to the lockers. Paul makes a comment about the small size of my johnson and I've got my pants on before I jab back at him a similar insult. Paul takes his time with the shower so I start walking around the place. I walk through the weight room and pick up one of the dumbbells, doing a curl with about forty pounds, then putting the dumbbell back on the rack.

Paul comes in after a while and makes a comment about working out before the shower, not after. We make our way back outside, and our fresh clean gives the world a new feel. I tell Paul that I don't think I got all the soap off my body and he laughs, telling me I could have taken longer than three seconds to rinse off.

The sky is bright today and this is uncommon, Paul tells me. The weather is all London until July, when it warms up and feels like Florida for about eight weeks. There are winters when the sun won't come out for two weeks at a time, but after July 4, there won't be a cloud in the sky for ninety days. It is perfect around here in the summer, Paul promises.

"What do you want to do now?" I ask him.

"You want coffee?" he questions.

"When in Rome . . ."

We wander down to a little coffee shop on the corner off one of the park blocks. It's called Coffee People and is filled with students poring over open books, wealthy businessmen, and homeless people listening to headphones. They are playing Frank Sinatra over the speakers.

The fellow in front of me orders a latté, which is all foreign to me. Coffee is something you order at breakfast, at a greasy spoon. The idea of dedicating a specific shop (much less fifty of them on one block) to coffee is going to take some getting used to. I struggle through an order, answering questions about how much room I want and whether I want foam and what size and so on and so on. I just stand there like a deer caught in headlights and the lady just says to give her a buck and she will take care of me. I hand her a dollar, which seems an extraordinary amount to pay for a cup of coffee, and she tells me to wait on the other side of the bar until my cup comes up. Paul and I get our orders and find a table at the back. He brings over a chess set that they keep in the place and we start setting up a game.

"What would make you most happy?" Paul asks, pushing his pawn forward two spaces.

"I don't know."

"Anything, Don. What would make you most happy in life?"

"Well, maybe a wife, some kids, a good job, I don't know. Why do you ask? What would make you most happy?"

"I have just been thinking how what we really want is for

people to love us. God, girls, friends, parents. It seems like life is all about that stuff, you know."

"Feels like it," I say, pushing another pawn up one space to back up my front pawn. "I feel like you are trying to say something."

"Yeah," Paul confesses. "I guess I am. Nothing deep, really, just that, you know, I know you have been thinking about things and I just feel like God put us here to enjoy Him, and He gave us free will so it is tough sometimes, because people use their free will selfishly, but I think also He created us to enjoy Him, that He is love, you know, and I would just hate to see you walk away from that. I mean, if He were love and all." Paul pushes his pawn forward and I spend a few minutes studying the board, trying to remember what all the pieces do. I move a knight over one of my pawns and tap my hand against the table.

"Thanks, man," I say. "I think I do that stuff, just make waves or whatever, just to bring attention to myself. I know it is all good, that God is good and all."

"I do that stuff sometimes too," Paul says.

"Do what stuff?" I ask.

"You know, just say things to bring attention to myself, stuff that is shocking or whatever."

I don't say anything to Paul but I know he never does that stuff. He is more self-aware than I am, more self-aware than most people.

22 KINDNESS

PORTLAND SITS A FEW MILES FROM THE COLUMBIA River, which serves as the border to Washington State. We leave the city to drive north through suburbs, the entire way both Mount Hood and Mount Saint Helens standing to the east. We cross the big river into Washington State and I begin wondering about apple trees, how all I know of Washington is apples. Paul explains how far it is to Seattle and then how Canada is only a couple hundred miles beyond that and it occurs to me how far north we actually are. I follow Danielle's directions precisely, and we are soon off the interstate and onto farm roads. There is agriculture on our left and right, a small general-store, and a burger shop renovated from a gas station.

We turn right, go for a few miles, and look for the sign that marks the road to Mountain View Christian Center, a landmark Danielle said would tell us we were closing in. Passing the church, we take a left at the next driveway. It is a long road that serves several homes, each with an acre or two. We follow the driveway and find a mailbox with the Bjur name printed on the sign. We turn right again and follow another driveway up a small hill where there is a large white house covered with windows in the front. The yard is landscaped with shrubs and flowers and is as pristine as a golf course. Paul parks the van and breathes deeply. I look behind me, through the back window of the van, as the door of the house slings open and out comes Danielle. She is more beautiful than I remember, her thin frame coming out of hips that slide left and right with each footfall, moving up her athletic torso to long arms and a head you dream about in your sleep. I look over at Paul and softly ask what he thinks.

"She's a looker," he says.

Danielle's hair is cut short. She is wearing a tie-dyed shirt, khaki pants, and combat boots. She is brown-bread tan. Her teeth are perfect. Her smile is perfect. Paul and I haven't seen a pretty girl in two thousand miles, it seems like. Or at least we haven't seen one that we could spend any time with.

"Hello! Hello!" she says, rounding to the passenger's side window, opening the door, and spreading her arms out for a hug.

"Hello, my friend. How long has it been?" I say to her.

"Three years, Don. It's been three years!"

Paul rounds the van and stands with his hands in his pockets. I introduce them, and Danielle offers her hand, which Paul shakes gently.

"You two come inside. You must be starving."

Paul plays the strong, silent type but I tell her we could eat a horse. Danielle says they don't have any horse but they do have turkey sandwiches.

"That will do fine," I tell her.

Inside we are greeted by Shirley Bjur, Danielle's mom. She's a petite woman and it becomes obvious where Danielle gets her beauty. Shirley is busy in the kitchen. We hardly walk through the door before we are ushered into a small breakfast nook and Shirley has plates on the counter, bread opened, and turkey and lettuce and tomatoes and mayo. She is talking nonstop, going on about how much fun Danielle had in Colorado and how she still keeps a few pen pals from those days and how much they missed her when she was in Costa Rica and how she and her husband had plenty of friends with a van like ours back in the day. Danielle and her mom are talking at once. One will ask me a question and the other will answer.

"Don, what are you guys doing here in Washington?" Shirley asks.

"Mom, I told you. They are traveling around America," Danielle says.

"America! It's a big country. Where all have you been?" Shirley inquires.

"They've been all over, Mom. Don lives in Texas, remember?"

"That's right. I remember, Don. You're a Texan. Tell me, do they wear big cowboy hats down there?"

"Mom, you've seen too many movies. Not everybody from Texas is a cowboy!"

"We went to Texas once," Shirley starts into a story. "Remember, Danielle, we were there when you were little. You and Elida argued and fought the entire way, remember?"

"I remember. Elida was being a brat!" Danielle exclaims.

"Who is Elida?" I ask.

"My sister." Danielle smiles. "I told you about Elida. Do you even read my letters?"

"Over and over," I tell her.

"Who is my little brother?" she tests me.

"I can't remember his name. I remember you guys adopted him from Colombia."

"Nate," she says. "His name is Nate, Don." She bonks me on the head with a roll of paper towels, sitting down with us at the table.

We eat turkey sandwiches and are bombarded by questions. Shirley attempts to include Paul in the conversation, but Danielle doesn't seem to notice him. She keeps asking about Mike and California and the Grand Canyon. She wants to know about Texas and how long we've been on the road and where did we sleep and did we go to San Francisco or Sacramento? Her grandfather lives in Sacramento.

Paul asks where Shirley's husband is and Shirley tells him he's up in the air. Paul takes this to mean that he's dead and offers his apology, but Shirley laughs and clarifies that he's actually in the air. He's on a plane flying home from Germany. He works for Hewlett-Packard. He doesn't have to leave town often, but when he does, he goes to China or Germany or some place that keeps him away too long.

Shirley begins to sweep the kitchen floor. "You two will just have to stay here until Randy gets home. He'll be glad to meet you. You need to stay for Elida and Nate too. They will be home from school in a couple of hours. You need to stay for dinner," she says.

"We don't want to put you out," I say.

"You have nowhere to go. You said that. You guys are just driving around. All I'm saying is, you are not leaving here till you get a good meal. And turkey sandwiches don't count."

"You're sure it's not too much trouble?" I ask.

"Not at all. Stay here tonight."

"Spend the night?" I question.

"Yes. You can have dinner tonight, and since tomorrow is Saturday, Elida and Nate and Randy will be here for breakfast and you can eat and be on your way."

"It sounds like a lot of trouble for you," I say.

"Where are you going to go?" she asks. "You are just going to go up the road a bit and sleep. Might as well do it here."

Danielle gets up and walks into the kitchen, resting her elbows on the counter, her face in her hands; she is smiling and nodding, agreeing with her mom. "You're staying here, Donald Miller. I'm not letting you guys sleep out on the road." She pouts her face as she says this. Man, is this girl beautiful.

"Whatever you say, ladies." I get up to stretch my legs and have a look around. "They're not letting us leave, Paul," I say to him, still seated in the nook.

"Sounds good," Paul says. That comment gives both Shirley and Danielle a chuckle.

KINDNESS

We take a walk to the end of the driveway where a neighbor has goats in a pen. Paul names one of the goats Dimitrius but calls him Dimitri for short. Danielle thinks he's funny. It is here that we are interrupted by Danielle's sister, Elida. She races up the driveway in her Honda Prelude. She's got her hand on the horn all the way up the driveway and she's swerving left, then right. Danielle just laughs at her. She races toward us and slams on the brakes. Rolling down her window, she interrogates Paul and me.

"Who are you?" she asks. No smile.

"We're friends of Danielle's," I answer.

"Is that your hippie van?" she questions.

"It's mine," Paul tells her.

"Are you hippies?"

"No," I say.

"You, the blond." Elida points at Paul. "Are you dating anybody?"

"No," Paul says.

Danielle, who has been pulling petals off a flower, tosses them through Elida's window. Elida races her engine, tosses it into first, and squeals her tires. She waves her arm out the window and screams and laughs.

"She's crazy." Danielle laughs and throws her head back. "You're crazy!" she shouts as Elida makes the turn and disappears behind the house. Elida is as good-looking as Danielle, long brown hair, smooth skin, and filled out fairly perfect. *She must be in high school*, I think to myself.

"Let me introduce you guys to Elida." Danielle starts running back toward the house and we follow behind her. Elida is getting some books out of her car. She asks, this time with a smile, who we are. Danielle reminds Elida of Colorado and says she met me there and we've kept in touch through letters.

"You're the one from Texas!" Elida shouts.

"Yes," I tell her.

"Well, yeehaw!" She shakes her hip to one side and puts her

hand on her hip as she says this. I get butterflies and nerves when she cocks her head to the right.

Their personalities are distinct. Danielle will interest you in conversation and Elida will entertain you by goofing off. We head back inside the house and Elida and Danielle do this little song called "Sisters" where they put their arms around each other's shoulders and sing. It's cute. Shirley loves it. Now that Elida is home, Shirley changes from hostess to manager. Danielle needs to prepare dinner and Elida needs to go get Nate at school. Elida comments that she always has to get Nate and Danielle always gets the easy jobs. Danielle volunteers to pick up Nate if Elida will get dinner ready, but Elida says no, she'll do it. Shirley has to run to the airport to pick up Randy, who will be in at 7:00 p.m. He will be hungry, she says. So will Nate and the boys. We are now called "the boys."

With everyone in action, Paul and I decide this would be a good time to change the oil in the van. It will make us look manly and avoid the perception that we are bums who don't work. Soon, we are under the van and talking about the girls. Paul says he's in love with Danielle. I tell him to calm down. He asks me if there is anything there between her and me. I tell him no. I don't think she'd be interested, and besides, I think of her like a sister, and moreover, Elida is about the most beautiful thing I have ever seen. Paul says he doesn't think of her like a sister, either Danielle or Elida, but especially Danielle. He also says that Elida is too young for me and I am a pervert. It's like three years, I tell him. High school, he says.

I do most of the work on the van. Paul just lies there, underneath, with a wrench in his hand. He has a worried look and then a smile and then a worried look. Stop thinking about her, I tell him. He says shut up. I pull the bolt and let the oil drop down into a pan we borrowed from the Bjurs's garage.

"She doesn't like me," Paul whimpers.

"She doesn't know you yet. We just got here."

"And we're leaving. I'll never see her again." Paul sighs.

"You're serious, aren't you?"

"Yes," he says.

ELIDA, DANIELLE, PAUL, AND I ARE MAKING SMALL talk at the dining room table, looking through old photographs of Colorado, when Randy and Shirley come home. Randy looks tired, but not put out by our being there. You can tell that in a house full of girls, he is used to entertaining their company. And I even suspect he is glad to see some guys hanging around. He puts his bags down in the entryway and comes over to offer a handshake. He's fifty or so, graying but athletic. Danielle has his nose, a small, pointed nose they got from Norway or something. He joins our conversation but has very little to tell about his recent trip to Germany. The entire family had gone when the girls were younger and they are asking him if he visited any of the old haunts, but he hadn't. Pure business, he says, shaking his head. Visited a production plant and another production plant but that was about it. Over dinner, he begins nodding off at the table and Shirley suggests they both hit the sack early. She gets up with her plate and Randy pats her on the butt. Elida cracks a smile at that.

Paul, Elida, Danielle, and I have a great conversation about churches in the South. They've never seen a megachurch. Like Paul, they consider churches that have 1,000 members to be a large church. I tell them about First Baptist Church and Second Baptist Church, both of them with more than 20,000 members, and Lakewood with more than 30,000, all in the same city. And that's just the beginning. Spirituality is big business down in the South, enormous buildings and publishing houses connected to them, huge conferences and seminars and the whole bit. They don't understand how 20,000 people can all go to one church. There aren't even 20,000 people who live in Ridgefield. I tell them there are parts of it that are great, because you feel like you are involved in an enormous movement when you go to a church that big, and I think there is even something that comforts people about believing something that 20,000 other people in the room all believe.

"But it isn't very intimate, is it?" Danielle asks.

"I don't guess so," I say.

"I was thinking a lot about faith while I was in Costa Rica," Danielle says, shifting the subject within its theme. "Everything came to a head down there. I was really bent out of shape about church and Christianity. I knew I had to make a decision about what I believed."

"I didn't realize you were going through anything like that," I say.

Danielle tells us she did some serious thinking while she was there. She was very thankful for the other students (Christians) who were faithful to her even while she was asking some serious, and possibly offensive, questions about her faith. Everything was resolved, she says, when she had to get on a plane and discovered that she'd lost her wallet. They wouldn't let her on the plane without her ID. With only an hour to spare, she took a cab to the club where she had been the night before. She prayed all the way there and told God she was sorry and got really upset. She ended up finding her wallet in the booth where she had been seated, and somehow this helped her believe God was there.

"I know it sounds superstitious or whatever, but it was like God was saying, 'Hey, I know you are doubting me right now, but I'm here. Just trust Me.' It helped," Danielle says.

Paul says he had a similar experience in the junkyard in Vegas. He says he had been asking some serious questions, not about the truth of Christ, but about whether or not he was really living out and experiencing faith, whatever that looks like. He says finding the part in the junkyard was an "instrumental happening." That's what he calls it, an "instrumental happening." Then he tells the girls I am an atheist.

"An atheist, Don?" Danielle questions.

"No. I said I thought it sucked that God didn't make us born with wings or something and Paul seems to think I am having a faith crisis," I say. Danielle smiles.

"Wings, eh?" Elida says, looking very beautiful.

"Wings," I say.

She puts her cup of tea down and flaps her arms like a chicken.

Before we know it, it is 3:00 a.m. and we are all yawns. Elida says we can sleep downstairs, but Paul and I both shake our heads. We'll sleep outside, we say.

"Outside?" Elida questions.

"Can't sleep inside anymore. We've been in the van for over a month. We're used to the fresh air," one of us comments.

"Well!" Elida proclaims. "If you guys are sleeping outside, we're sleeping outside!"

"What?" Danielle questions.

"We'll all sleep on the lawn. I'll get the sleeping bags." With that, Elida disappears down the stairs. We hear her stirring around in a closet. Danielle tells us she's getting the sleeping bags out and pulling them from the garbage bags that Daddy keeps them in. There is a side door off the breakfast nook that opens out onto a deck that overlooks the front yard. Danielle steps out on the deck to see Elida unrolling sleeping bags. "Looks like we're sleeping outside," Danielle says with a smile.

• • •

". . . AND WHEN THEY WENT BACK INTO THE HOUSE, they saw the ghost of their aunt Edna. She was holding a knife and a pumpkin." Elida's voice is soft and quiet. She is almost whispering. "They look at Aunt Edna and she begins to sway in the wind. She says [Elida's voice gets deep], 'You never should have slept in the pumpkin patch.'"

Danielle can't help but interrupt: "Elida, Aunt Edna is not a scary name. And your story has no point."

"It's a scary story," Elida says.

"For three-year-olds!" Danielle tells her.

"Shhh." Paul quiets the girls.

"What is it?" Danielle asks.

"Did you hear that?" Paul says.

"Hear what?" asks Elida.

"The voice."

"What voice?"

"It sounded like the wind. It was a whisper. Someone whispered in my ear. It was a low voice."

Elida pulls her sleeping bag over her head. Through the bag we hear her ask, "What did the voice say?"

"It said," Paul pauses, lowering his voice to speak in a raspy whisper, "four . . . will . . . die . . . tonight."

Elida gasps. Danielle chuckles. Then there is silence.

"The voice could have been talking about anyone," I say. "It probably won't be us."

23 RANCH

PAUL MAKES A CALL TO BLACK BUTTE RANCH FROM the Bjurs's house and he secures a job for himself as a lifeguard. He also finds there is an opening in the housekeeping department and sets a time for me to interview. You will be a janitor, he says. You will be working with about twenty women. You will love it, he assures me.

Black Butte Ranch is a large, active cattle ranch in the mountains of central Oregon. It is a resort, but it's also a summer home for wealthy people from Portland and folks who come up from California. The ranch is just up from the high desert, set in the foothills of the Cascade Range. Paul says you can see the Three Sisters, Mount Washington, and Mount Jefferson from the meadow beneath Black Butte. Apparently, every summer, students come from all over the country to live in the woods and work on the ranch. Two cultures coexist, those who live in the woods and work the ranch, and the teenagers and college students who spend the summer here in their parents' summer homes, their parents, most of the time, not around. There are hundreds of miles of bike paths and thousands of miles of forest service roads that venture out from the ranch property. It's a great place to spend the summer, Paul tells me.

"When is my interview?" I ask.

"First thing tomorrow morning."

Danielle looks upset. We've been with the Bjurs for more than a week. We started out as moochers, but then the Bjurs wouldn't let us go. Shirley kept us there, really. She'd say we should stay for another meal, then another, then we'd get to talking over coffee and sooner or later, we'd end up staying the night, sleeping on the lawn, telling stories, and pondering Mount St. Helens off in the distance, the snow lit by the moon. We'd go into Portland at night, buy a case of beer and sit outside a club getting toasted, then go in and dance a little, smoke a few cigarettes and walk the streets, window-shopping at four in the morning. I got drunk last weekend and Paul, Danielle, and Elida laughed at me as I threw up behind a Taco Bell. It was an idiot thing to do, and I felt terrible when Shirley found out about it. They really have become like family. That was the night I confessed my love for Elida, to which she responded by rolling her eyes. Luckily, we were able to laugh about it the next day.

Something did spark between Paul and Danielle, though. Whether it works out, and how it could, given the fact we will be living in the woods for the summer, remains to be seen. But they both seem levelheaded and patient. Randy and Shirley enjoyed the unfolding of their romance. They approve of Paul.

Danielle will be leaving for Sacramento soon, where she will live with her grandparents and attend summer school. She is on track to receive her bachelor's degree in a short three-year span. Two of those years are behind her.

We pack the van slowly, taking most of the afternoon. Paul is in no hurry to leave and neither am I. Paul and Danielle go for a walk down by the river and I take the van over to Elida's school where she told me to wait in the parking lot. I sit in the van, waiting for her to come out, when I notice a window in one of the classrooms opens and a backpack comes falling out, spilling a few books onto the lawn. After the backpack comes Elida, falling atop the pack and lying low, peeking back into the window to see if the teacher noticed. She gathers her books, reaches into the classroom and closes the window, then runs toward the van as though it were a prison break. Elida and I go over to Burgerville, where she works summers, and get a milk shake. She brings up the fact that I am in love with her several times and I tell her to knock it off. *Am I embarrassing you?* she says. *High school girl, Don. Can't seem to keep the older boys from taking interest, I guess.*

We get back to the house and find Randy dillydallying around, pretending he has things to do at home that prevent him from going to work on time. He looks at me and Elida and shakes his head. "You're skipping school?" he questions, giving her a stern look.

Elida covers her mouth and coughs. "I'm not feeling well, Daddy." "You a part of this?" he asks me, looking over Elida's shoulder.

Paul and Danielle come back from the river covered in dead grass. I whisper to Paul that the two of them look like they've been rolling around in a barn and he quickly swipes the dirt and grass off of his sleeve and belly. Danielle notices what he's doing and does the same, smiling and turning red. I grab the last of the bags and throw them in the back of the van. We said our good-byes to Nate earlier, before he was taken to school, and Shirley has been busy packing lunches for us. She brings them out and hands them to me and I set them in the passenger's seat, giving her a hug.

Randy gathers us around the van and says a prayer. He asks God to protect us and teach us whatever it is He wants us to know. Randy thanks God for introducing us to them, and making us a part of the family. There's nothing we can say after that, so Paul and I give everybody hugs and climb in the van, with Paul at the wheel and head down the driveway. I take a long look at Mount St. Helens as we round the neighbor's barn and find the main road. I imagine two thousand feet of the mountain blowing off the top, sending a cloud of ash more than a mile high. Paul has a dazed look on his face and it is obvious he is thinking about Danielle.

IF THERE IS A HIGH DESERT IN OREGON, THE VALLEY on the Pacific side of the mountain shows no hint of it. Highway 26 runs through Gresham, a town east of Portland, then climbs for about twenty miles into the town of Sandy. Beyond Sandy we get into thick forests of evergreen and pass through towns with names like Rhododendron, Welches, and Government Camp. The thick green climbs right up to the tree line of Mount Hood. The air is clean and thin up here. The terrain dips down into a canyon on our right and lifts to eleven thousand feet on our left. Mount Hood is all snow and ice coming up out of the earth like a sleeping thing, giving you the feel that at any moment it is going to roll over and crush you. Its full-white brightness in the midday sun seems to light up all the aspen and evergreen off its wings. Rock is exposed here and there, but most of it is snow and ice, brown ice pushed off the road to form thick, dirty walls of melting shoulder. The evergreens climb to the left till their lungs can't breathe, and frame for the mind the great steep of bubbled lava. In places Mount Hood appears as a perfect cone, but then another mile down the road and you see a jagged spot on top, then another mile and it is a perfect cone again. A photographer could take twenty photos from twenty locations and convince an amateur that he's shot twenty separate mountains.

Leaving Mount Hood in our rearview mirror, we begin our descent into central Oregon. Paul is right about the terrain changing abruptly. From the deciduous landscape of the valley, we climbed into dense forest with little undergrowth, and now we have settled into rocks, sand, and sagebrush. In only three hours, it feels like we went from Scotland to Utah. The clouds that roll in off the Pacific are too thick and heavy to pass over the Cascades, so central Oregon gets much less rain. Paul tells me the winter brings occasional snow, but the summers are perfect. Warm and sunny and dry.

Black Butte rests in the foreground of at least six visible snowcapped mountains. Paul names them as the North Sister, the Middle Sister, and the South Sister, Mount Jefferson, Mount Washington, and Three-Fingered Jack. He says he's climbed them all. The Pacific Crest Trail, he tells me, runs right between them, up from Mexico through the Sierra Nevada, over to Mount Hood and then across the Columbia River into Washington before finding Mount Rainier and then Canada. His lifelong dream is to hike the PCT from Mexico all the way north. It will take him more than six months, he says.

When we find the town of Sisters, it is just as Paul described. There are cone lickers and rows of shops. It's a western town with wooden walks in front of the shops. You can see the hills lift to the east. We are at the base of Black Butte now. It is a perfect cone of a hill, five thousand feet high, if not more. It should be called a mountain. It is big and dark with clouds around its head and thick forest all the way to the summit.

The entrance to Black Butte Ranch is only twenty miles beyond the town of Sisters. The road climbs all twenty of the miles. We have circled back into the Cascade Range, and the air is the cleanest I've breathed since we left Texas. You can feel the cleanness of the air against your skin, and it is as though you can see it, or see other things through it, as though somebody had cleaned your glasses. Sunlight filters through the pines and paints bright, moving abstracts against the roads and forest floor. Creeks slide out over rock beds and under bridges and you can smell the moisture and coolness in the air as we pass over.

Paul signals a left turn and we slow, downshift, and pull into the entrance of the ranch. There is a guardhouse and a gate, and Paul navigates to the window at the house (about the size of a tollbooth). The fellow asks what we are doing and Paul tells him he is a lifeguard showing up for the summer. The fellow lifts the gate and we enter. The ranch is all I expected and more. Before us is a meadow surrounded by forest and through the meadow (a square mile in size) runs a stream, and near the stream are horses and cattle. We park in the lot closest to the lodge and step out. Above the clouds, in the distance, stand the Three

Sisters, three towering peaks. Next to the Sisters are Three-Fingered Jack and Mount Jefferson. Behind us is Black Butte.

Paul points out the pool he will be guarding. It backs up to the pond and sits in front of the tennis courts. There are three pools, he says. We rotate, but I usually get assigned to this one. It's nice, he says, because he usually has friends who work in Honkers Café and they bring him food. Went all last summer without buying a meal, he says.

PAUL'S BEEN PRETTY QUIET FOR THE LAST HALF HOUR. We've been driving around the place and every few miles he will stop and look into some stretch of forest as if to recall some distant memory. We round what I think is the backside of the ranch and get a view of the Three Sisters, three matching peaks all folded into each other at their timberlines, each distinct and noble and yet humble, one not reaching to outrise the others. We navigate back into the forest and I note the size of some of the houses, manors, more like, and some mansions. The golf course runs in and out of the forest, following streams that build to ponds and small lakes before the greens.

"Where are we going now?" I ask.

"To make camp. We need to do it before the sun goes down. We have about an hour."

We round back by the entrance gate but bypass it for a road that swings left. Not long onto it, we come upon another security gate. Paul looks at a little sheet of paper and punches the code, the gate swings open, and we drive through. Several enormous homes are tucked into the trees that surround this part of the meadow. There is a paved sidewalk that stitches one home to another, but they are each set on an acre or more of land. The road weaves back into the homes and crosses the golf course and pond and then back into more homes. Paul points out an empty lot that backs up to a fence and then dips down into a small ravine covered in aspen. He explains that we will make camp across the fence and down into the woods. It's illegal to camp back there, he warns. He says that the forest service would fine us if we were to get caught. It's a stealth operation, apparently.

"Here's what we'll do," he explains. "Let's drop our gear off in this ditch; we'll park the van and come back for the gear."

"Whatever," I tell him.

He stops the van, opens the side door, and removes his backpack. The ditch is twenty yards off the road, so he slides his backpack down into the ditch, comes back for his sleeping bag, and does the same with a few other items. I pull my gear out and imitate Paul. He has one tent. We've not used it the entire trip so I didn't know he had it, but he removes it from the van and slides it into the ditch. Then, in an instant, we are driving away. We round a turn or two and park the van in the parking lot of another community pool. Nobody will bother the van here, he tells me.

"Why don't we just live in the van?" I ask.

"Ranch security will make sure nobody is living in it. It's okay to park it here for a while, as long as we move it every couple of days, but we can't sleep in it. They will make us leave."

I have a hundred more questions but Paul does not seem to be in the mood to answer questions. He is home, I guess.

I realize it now. All this time I've known Paul, he has been the new guy. Now I am the new guy. It's an odd switch. This is clearly his comfort zone: the woods and all.

We are at a quick clip back to our gear, and Paul checks over his shoulder before pacing down the length of the ditch. Follow me, he says, and shoulders his pack and runs. I grab mine and run behind him. He tosses his pack over a fence and it rolls down a ledge of exposed rock. He heads back for the rest of the gear, being careful nobody sees him pick it up and run into the woods. We need two trips apiece to collect our things.

We jump the fence, boulder down the ledge, and gather our stuff at the bottom. Paul leads the way through the thick forest, through a hundred yards of baby aspen, all growing only a few feet apart, and into a clearing where there is a tent established. Henry, Paul says. Henry has already set up camp.

"Who is Henry?" I ask.

"An old friend," Paul answers. "You'll love Henry, Don. He's great." Paul walks over to the opening of the tent and drops his gear. "Hank!" he yells. Nobody answers. "He isn't here," Paul says, looking in the tent. "Well," he continues, "we should go ahead and set up the tent."

"Small tent," I say.

"We're not going to sleep in it," he tells me. "We'll just put our gear in there during the day. We should put it over here, under this tree. That way nobody will spot it." Paul begins unrolling the tent. I help him but I don't know what I'm doing, so finally I just stand back and watch, handing things to him when he needs me to.

"Maybe you can go back and get the rest of the gear at the ledge," Paul tells me.

"Sure. Just bring it all back here, right?"

Paul is busy with the tent. He talks to me without looking up. "Here would be the place."

I venture back through the aspen. On the way, I encounter two deer. They are nibbling at grass. I see their graceful brown bodies in splotches through the thick of trees. When they hear me, they become stiff, move in sudden jerks, find my eyes, stare me down, then leap off.

24 THE WOODS

BECAUSE BLACK BUTTE RANCH IS AT FOUR THOUSAND feet, and because there isn't a city for twenty miles, the stars at night feel as though they are falling into the meadow. At midnight it feels there is more light in the sky than darkness, as though God took a fistful of stardust and threw it upward where it shimmers at the apex of its ascent, as though what we know as creation exists only for this brief second before it all comes crashing down again. Brilliant blue clusters spread thick and dense and they sparkle and fade, sparkle and fade. It is silent music, the night sky. God does well to live atop them. And I wonder, as I lie in the meadow with a piece of grass between my teeth, if angels look down upon the sky to which we look up? And I wonder at all the other creation that must be out there, in some other dimension, in some other compartment of God's imagination. I wonder how much more of *it* there *is* out there, or anywhere, or nowhere. Scientists have always been baffled about all of this something having to have come from nothing, and I wonder what kinds of worlds the nothingness must inhabit. I wonder at what Paul said back in Portland, how God is good, how it doesn't do any good to run from Him because what He has is good and who He is, is good. Even if I want to run, it isn't really what I want—what I want is Him, even if I don't believe it. If He made all this existence, you would think He would know what He is doing, and you would think He could be trusted. Everything I want is just Him, to get lost in Him, to feel His love and more and more of this dazzling that He does. I wonder at His beautiful system and how it feels better than anything I could choose or invent for myself. I wonder as I gaze up at the night sky, this love letter from God to creation, this reminder that somewhere there is peace, somewhere there is order, and I think about how great His kingdom is, and is going to be, and I wonder, in this rare and beautiful moment, how I could ever want to walk away from it all. There are so many stars I will dream of them. I open my eyes and see stars, then close them and see stars. In the morning the sun will rise, the flowers will bloom in the spring, squirrels will perform acrobatic jumps from treetops to treetops, babies will gurgle, and I consider how delightful everything is. I remember as well what Paul had said in the canyon, about how what we used to want was cars and money and stuff and then all we wanted was a bowl of cereal, and I actually laugh out loud about it because right now we're here. I have absolutely nothing. I have no money and no home and nothing but a pair of shoes and a sleeping bag, and I am finally seeing how good life is, how beautiful it is.

I start realizing that this is the first time I have encountered beauty in nature. I've read poems that have made my heart race. I've read scenes in novels that have caused me to close the book, set my head in my hands, and wonder how a human could so brilliantly orchestrate words. But nature has never inspired me until now. *God is an artist,* I think to myself. I have known this for a long time, seeing His brushwork in the sunrise and sunset, and His sculpting in the mountains and the rivers. But the night sky is His greatest work. And I would have never known it if I had stayed in Houston. I would have bought a little condo and filled it with Ikea trinkets and dated some girl just because she was hot and would have read self-help books, end to end, one after another, trying to fix the gaping hole in the bottom of my soul, the hole that, right now, seems plugged with Orion, allowing my soul to collect that feeling of belonging and love you only get when you stop long enough to engage the obvious.

I FALL ASLEEP IN THE MEADOW AND WAKE UP COLD A few times, rolling over on myself to get some warmth. I finally get up about the time the sun makes it over the mountains. It is cold, though, and the ground is a bit damp. The sun has been up for an hour or so, and there is a bed of bent grass where my body lay. Having no idea what time it is, I walk back through the meadow toward camp. When I get there, I see Paul rummaging around in the tent. When he hears me he comes out and immediately scolds me for missing my interview.

"What interview?" I ask.

"You have an interview with housekeeping this morning, you idiot!"

"I forgot," I say. "I'll go tomorrow."

"No, Don. You have to go. We both have to get jobs," he tells me.

"If I'm late, I might as well go tomorrow."

"No!" he shouts. "You have to go. Apologize to them for being late."

"You should go," a strange voice says.

"Who is that?" I ask.

"Don, this is Henry. Henry, this is Don. He's a friend from Texas." Henry comes out of the tent, dragging a backpack behind him.

"The Lone Star State," Henry says with a smile. He must have slipped into camp last night. He is a wiry fellow with big blond hair sticking out in all directions. A handsome guy with big teeth and the sort of smile that probably gets him stuff for free.

"Nice to meet you, Henry."

"Good to meet you, Don. I understand you are going to be a janitor."

"Yes," I say. "And what is it you do?"

"I'm a lifeguard."

"Tough job," I say, rolling my eyes.

"Someone has to do it," he says.

I look over at Paul, who is wearing a worried expression and looking at the sun through the aspen.

"It's eight thirty, Don. You better hustle. Your interview was at eight."

"You can tell the time by looking at the sun?" I say, having already known that from our time in the canyon.

"Yes. It's late. You better go."

"I didn't know you could do that," I said, trying to bring back up the old conversation.

"Do what?" Paul questions.

"Tell time by looking at the sun. Native Americans do that, you know."

"Get out of here, man." Paul looks at the sun while he's talking. "Do you remember how to get there?"

"Just go up the road and take a left. Two miles, right?"

"Two miles," Paul clarifies.

"How do I look?" I ask.

"Terrible," he says. "Do something with your hair before you talk to them."

"You look fine," Henry says, broadening his grin. "I'd let you clean my toilet any day."

"Thanks, Henry," I say, motioning to Paul to take notice of his good manners.

"Meet me at the main pool when you are done," Paul tells me. "Do you remember where it is?"

"I'll find it," I say, stepping over a fallen tree and heading into the aspen.

"Cool guy," Henry says to Paul as I walk off.

"He's going to be late," Paul states.

Though it is late, the woods are growing out of a mist this morning. There are patches of cloud hanging thick in the aspen. It is cold. Must be forty degrees, if not colder. I find a good stride and stick to it, more to warm up than to make my interview. Not more than a hundred yards from camp I stumble upon the deer I saw yesterday. There are two, one with horns. They look up and freeze, staring at me for at least thirty seconds. I lean toward a step and they are off through the woods. With spurts of grace they fire through the mist like arrows, slowing at the top of their jumps and bounding off the ground, turning quick around trees.

The road to the housekeeping office rounds hills and is lined by trees and houses. There must be a thousand homes here at Black Butte Ranch. Earlier, when Paul suggested working on a cattle ranch, I pictured us roping cows and driving teams of wild horses. But this is a resort. It might have started as an active cattle ranch, but now it is a giant real estate project. I wonder what a house out here would cost, and how much money a family would have to have to use one of these as a *second* home.

"ARE YOU DONALD MILLER?" A DARK-HAIRED WOMAN asks as I enter the housekeeping department. She comes out of her office with a clipboard in her hand. She looks to be stressed: pale white face with lips traced in red lipstick. Her hands are weathered. One hand grips the clipboard and the other holds a walkie-talkie. She barks a command into the walkie-talkie and then tells me to wait in her office. I can hear her dividing up houses. Team one is to take houses 1–40 and team two is to take 41–80 and so on and so on, all the way through team ten. She makes small talk with one of the workers and then comes back into the office.

"You are late," she says.

"Yes, ma'am. I'm sorry about . . ."

"Do you make it a habit of being late to interviews?"

"No, ma'am. It's just that . . ."

"I don't need to hear your personal problems. If you want to work here, you need to be on time."

"I understand," I tell her.

"You understand," she says in sarcasm. "If you understood, you would have been on time. But you didn't understand. You understand now, but you didn't understand before or else you would have been on time. Do you understand?"

"Is this a trick question?" I say with a smile.

"Very funny. We've got a smart aleck, do we?"

"No, ma'am. I didn't mean it like that." I'm hesitant with my words. "I was just breaking the ice, I guess. I won't be late. I promise you that much."

"You don't have the job yet, Mr. Miller. You may not have the opportunity to show up on time."

The tension in the room is broken when an older, broad-shouldered, motherly woman steps into the office with a pile of folded towels in her hands. I gather that my interviewer's name is Lucy, because this woman calls her Lucy. And the motherly woman's name is Laurel.

Laurel tells Lucy she will need more towels if she is going to clean the condos and houses 1–40. Lucy tells her to take more, but to make sure and write it down so she knows where they are. Before leaving, Laurel looks down at me and says, "Fresh meat." She smiles as she says it, so I smile back and laugh. Laurel laughs.

"I'll take this one," Laurel says. "We could use some muscle on my team."

"He has a habit of being late," Lucy says to Laurel.

"I'll whip him into shape," Laurel says and looks at me with a grin. I grin back.

"You've got him," Lucy tells her. "If he gives you any trouble, tell me. I have already found out he has an attitude."

"What's his name?" Laurel asks. Nobody bothers to ask me.

"It doesn't matter," Lucy says and slaps Laurel on the back. "He won't last long."

Laurel exits and walks back into the laundry room to get more towels.

"All right, Donald Miller," Lucy begins, "what is your social security number?"

I give her the number.

"And your address?"

I give her my Texas address.

"Coming in all the way from Texas, are you? That's a long commute, don't you think?"

I tell her I don't have an address around here.

Lucy leans back in her chair. She sets her pen down and runs her hands through her long, unkempt hair. She looks out the window.

"Donald, you know that people aren't supposed to live in the woods around here, don't you?"

That's it, I guess. I messed up. "I've heard that, yes, ma'am."

Lucy takes a long look at me, shakes her head, picks up her pen, and begins to write an address on the form.

"There is a shower in the back," she says.

"Pardon me?"

Lucy points through her office door toward a door on the other side of the laundry room. "Through that door," she says, "there is a shower. If a person needed to take a shower in the morning, a person could do it through that door."

"I see."

"Be here at seven thirty tomorrow morning," she says. She doesn't look up; she just writes on my form.

I sit there and look at her. I cross my legs. I uncross my legs.

"You can go," she says.

"Thank you," I tell her.

"Be on time," she says.

"Yes."

"My name is Lucy. Call me Lucy, but I am not your friend. One mistake, and you are gone."

"I understand," I say.

"You did not understand this morning. You may understand now, but you did not understand this morning."

Laurel snickers when she sees me walk out of the office.

BIKE PATHS LINE EACH STREET ON THE RANCH. THE streets are dark asphalt, and the bike paths are half as wide as the street. I weave through the streets, not really knowing where I am going. I decide that if I continue walking north, I will find the main pool, where Paul is supposed to be working. So I wander, between and around big, expensive homes. Yuppie couples in Volvos pass me. None of them wave.

The bike path breaks away from the road, away from the houses, into a thicket of trees. It is here that I see the woman of my dreams. She is riding a bike, alone. A girl this pretty should not be riding alone. She passes me quickly and grins. She's wearing a Black Butte polo-style shirt. She must work on the ranch somewhere. I bet Paul knows her. I turn around to watch her pedal through the trees and disappear as the bike path weaves right, which is probably the direction I should be walking. She had long brown hair and looked polite and innocent. *What's a nice girl like you doing in a forest like this?* I think to myself.

The bike path opens up into the meadow where Mount Washington, Three-Fingered Jack, and Mount Jefferson are visible. This is where I slept last night, but the fog has lifted. The mountains are snowcapped, lit by the midmorning sun, and simply beautiful. All is silent, but in my mind I hear the cold wind blow furiously across the mountaintops. Clouds are high and scattered. Beyond the clouds is deep, endless blue. The meadow is a mile wide, it seems. The farther I walk into the open, the more spectacular the view becomes. Black Butte lifts to my right, and behind me are the Three Sisters and Broken Top. Six mountains, as well as Black Butte, are all visible from the center of the meadow. *Stunning*, I think to myself. *Colorado, eat your heart out.*

AS FAR AS I AM CONCERNED, THE PRIMARY OCCUPATION of a lifeguard is to swing a whistle around in your hand, working the rope through each finger, then swinging the other direction until the rope unwinds. Lifeguards who are good at their job can do it for half an hour without getting tangled.

I find Paul sitting up in his chair, twirling his whistle. Henry is preparing chemicals to put into the pool. Paul asks me if I got the job and I tell him I did. Good, he says. We both need to work. You call this working? I say to him, holding my hands out at the pool. Somebody has to do it, he says. *Saving lives is a man's job.*

"You hungry?" Paul says.

"I could eat," I answer.

"Henry, would you mind if I took lunch?"

"Bring me some," Henry says.

"Will do." Paul climbs down from his post.

"See you later, Henry," I tell him.

"Yeah, dude. I'll see you tonight. Are you going with us to the cave?"

"What cave?" I ask.

"I haven't told him yet," Paul says.

I nod at Henry and he turns to watch the pool. He takes his position atop the chair and starts twirling his whistle. He tells one of the kids (there are *two* kids to protect today, one for each lifeguard) not to run.

Paul and I cross the lawn and take seats on a deck outside Honkers Café, named after the ducks in the lake. I ask him how we can afford to eat, since we only have twenty dollars or so. He tells me the owner of the café always takes care of the guys who live in the woods. The kids who live in their parents' houses pay, but the folks who live in the woods eat for free.

"Do we order?" I ask.

"Nope. We just sit here, and sooner or later food finds its way to the table. He gives us only what he has too much of. You know, leftover pizza and that sort of thing."

"I get it."

"So, Don, how much are they going to pay you?"

"I didn't ask."

"You didn't ask?"

"Didn't think of it. She was kinda tough, you know. She was mad because I was late."

"Told you," he says.

"I didn't think they took housekeeping so seriously."

"Oh, yeah," he says. "They're like the army. They drive around in those big white vans and almost run people over, talking on their walkie-talkies and all. Those women could take over a small third world country. They're serious."

"I gathered that."

A young girl comes through the door and says hello to Paul. It's the girl from the meadow. The girl on the bike. Paul gets up and gives her a hug. He calls her Molly. "Molly, this is my friend, Don."

"Nice to meet you," she says. She doesn't remember me from the meadow.

"Nice to meet you," I tell her.

"I suppose you guys are hungry," she says to us.

"Starved," Paul tells her.

"How does a calzone sound? Sound good?"

"Sounds great," Paul says.

Molly walks back into the café.

"Where does she live? Is she from Oregon?" I start asking.

"I thought you were in love with Elida," Paul states.

"She's in high school, you sick creep. Where is Molly from? Is she in the woods somewhere?"

"I don't know where she's from. She goes to school somewhere in Minnesota. But I don't think she is from Oregon. She stays here every summer with Jodie."

"Who's Jodie?" I ask.

"Jodie is who she stays with."

"You said that already."

"She's a friend. Jodie is a friend. Her family has a summer home on the ranch. Jodie is a lifeguard."

"And Molly is her friend."

"Yes," Paul clarifies. A moment later, "Speaking of infatuation . . ."

"I'm not infatuated," I tell him. "I just like the way she rides a bike."

"How do you know how she rides a bike?" Paul asks.

"Everybody rides a bike the same," I say.

"What are you talking about?" Paul asks.

"What are you talking about?" I say.

"Anyway," he begins, rolling his eyes. "Speaking of infatuation. Guess who called today?"

"Who?"

"Danielle."

"Danielle called you?"

"She called us. She called the lodge and they transferred the call to me at the pool."

"What did she have to say?"

"She's coming here. She's coming by on her way to Sacramento."

"How long is she going to stay?" I ask.

"Just for the day. She'll drive all night to get down to Sacramento. She's coming three weeks from now. Friday, possibly. Three weekends away, right?"

"What is today, Paul?"

"Today." Paul thinks to himself for a second. "I think it's Tuesday. But I'm not sure."

"Tuesday," I clarify.

Molly comes out with two huge calzones and sets mine down with a smile. She asks if I'm going to the cave tonight. I give her a confused look and then glance at Paul.

"I haven't told him yet," Paul says.

"Fine. Well, have fun," Molly says.

"Don here likes the way you ride a bike," Paul says, and I give him a death stare.

"I don't understand," Molly says, her blue eyes coming off her pale complexion like lake water.

"I was saying to Paul that it would be nice to go for a bike ride around here, saying that I thought I saw you in the meadow earlier."

"I don't remember this conversation," Paul says, shrugging his shoulders.

"That's because you're an idiot," I say. "Shut up or I am not going to teach you how to read."

"Yeah, it is a good place to ride a bike," Molly says, looking out toward the meadow. "Do you have a bike here?" she asks.

"He could ride on your handle bars," Paul says. "The two of you could get drunk later and Don could tell you how he feels." After he says this I kick him in the shin.

"Well, sounds fun. I better get back to work. Nice to meet you, Don," Molly says.

"Nice to meet you, Molly. Have a great day. I will see you around."

I will see you around, Paul mocks in a girly voice.

"I'm telling Danielle you're a recovering homosexual," I say to him. "Seriously, Paul, I am telling her you found Jesus and have barely wanted a man since, that she has nothing to worry about, that you will always like her and most of the time those conversions really stick."

25 THE CAVE

WE ARE NOT SLEEPING IN THE WOODS TONIGHT. PAUL tells me that everyone is headed to the cave. Apparently there are long lava tubes that tunnel under these mountains. There is a special one these guys camp in every year. It holds all sorts of memories.

We have been at the café most of the day. I talked with Paul for a while over lunch, then Henry came and joined us, leaving the lifeguarding to one of the locals. Some of the other guys showed up and Paul introduced me to them: Eddie, Pat, Brick, and Owen. All of these guys are out of NYU, I guess, and all of them literature majors, Bruce Springsteen fans. Owen is an epic poet and keeps notebooks with him always, writing down thoughts about girls and rocks and water and the metaphor of flight. Paul goes back to work and Eddie and I get to talking about girls, about how long it has been since he has had sex. Apparently it has been a whole month. I keep my mouth shut, just nod like it has been at least a month for me too. To be honest, he's not too calloused about sex like some guys are, but actually associates a kind of emotion to the act, as though he is good at falling in love for a night or two and then moving on. It really is about the connection, he says to me, admitting that with him the "connection" doesn't last very long.

The guys have moved their stuff out to aspen camp, and Brick starts telling me stories about years past when he and Paul stole a whole set of patio furniture off somebody's back deck. They had a regular living room set up out in the forest. They went back in the middle of the night to steal a barbeque grill but had to leave it in the middle of a field when security rounded the corner with their lights flashing. The security officers chased them along the road for a while but Brick and Paul dipped into some woods and disappeared like deer. I ask about the cave and Eddie says it's a tradition, once we all get here, to go sleep in the cave. It's up in the mountains a bit, Eddie says, looking over at Brick as if to ask whether he remembers where it is.

BRICK TAKES THE VAN UP STEEP, DARK ROADS LIT SOFTLY by moonlight through clouds. He is commenting to Paul on the handling. He says it's not bad for a van this old. Paul tells him about the mechanic in Nevada and about the junkyard, about how God showed up to answer our prayers. Brick isn't the spiritual type, so he shrugs it off. He pulls the van over into some trees. Pines scrape the side of the van and Owen has a tough time getting the door open. Nice parking, Eddie says. Brick thanks him. Outside the van, everyone acts like they know what they are doing. They grab sleeping bags and Brick throws one at me. Eddie asks about matches and Pat says he has a lighter, proving it by lighting a cigarette.

"We running?" Eddie asks.

"Sure we are," Paul tells him.

With that, Eddie bolts into the woods as Pat and Owen follow him, Pat holding his cigarette out before him like a torch. He runs smooth and fast around small trees and over logs. Owen, the biggest of the gang out of NYU, simply runs through the trees. He makes his way through the forest like some sort of poet beast, cracking branches with each stride. I am behind them, and Paul and Brick are behind me. Henry is running parallel. It's quite a sight, all of us running in and out of moon shadows. *If there were music to the scene, it would be bagpipes,* I think to myself. All of us are breathing heavily, and it's cold, so mist rises out of our mouths. Nobody screams or yells; they just run quickly. I don't know why we are running like this. Seems sensible to walk. But I don't want to get lost, so I run. And we run. And we run. About twenty minutes into the forest, we come to the top of a hill.

"This is it," Paul says, taking a breath.

"I don't see a cave," I tell him.

Paul points to a hole in the ground. It's not a large hole, about five feet by five feet. But he says it's the mouth of a cave. Brick takes a flashlight out of his pack and shines it down into the hole. "The ladder is down," he says.

"Happens every year," Eddie grumbles.

Brick takes some tubed webbing out of his pack and ties it around his waist. He has a headlamp that he straps around his head. The guys grab the rope and Brick lowers himself into the cave. His light throws shadows against the rock wall and I can tell the cave is pretty large.

Brick picks up a handmade ladder from the floor of the cave and pokes it through the opening. Eddie is the first to descend, then Paul, then me with Henry, Owen, and Pat right behind. Paul and Brick are the only ones with lights, which they shine deep into the cave.

I follow the light about a hundred yards down to where Paul and Brick reveal an old fire pit. There is wood scattered around the cave, old firewood, some of it unused, so we begin foraging for a fire. Pat lights the thing with his lighter, lighting another cigarette while he is at it. As it comes to life, the fire illumines the cave. The rock is deep and jagged, but the ground is smooth. The back of the cave extends at least two hundred yards, beyond which it is too dark to see.

"You ever been to the back of this thing?" I ask Paul.

"Nope. We've been back about a mile or so, but it's just more of the same, really. Doesn't get any smaller, doesn't get any bigger."

"Any animals in here?" I ask him.

"Never seen any. The opening is kinda tough on animals. I

would think if they fell in, they'd die from the fall. If that didn't get them, they'd die of thirst pretty quickly."

"I see," I say.

We make small talk for a few hours, mostly stories about drinking and stealing and girls on the ranch from years past. Eddie, Pat, and Owen spread out their sleeping bags and lie down. Owen is writing something and Pat is tinkering with his pocketknife. Eddie pulls out a pipe and fills the air with sweet-smelling smoke. I lean over to whisper to Paul.

"You know I have to be at work at seven thirty tomorrow. Earlier if I want to take a shower."

"Don't worry, I'll get you there. You'll be fine," he assures me.

Eddie overhears us. "Where you working, Don?"

"Housekeeping," I tell him.

"Militant types," Brick says.

"You can say that again," Henry chimes in.

One of the guys asks how long I intend to stay. I tell them it depends on whether I get a job in Colorado or not. I applied for a position at this camp out there, but I haven't called them to see if I got the job. If so, I hope to make enough money in housekeeping to get a plane ticket to Colorado Springs. Paul looks surprised at this. We never really talked about what I was going to do when the trip was over. But that's the plan.

"I didn't know you were thinking of Colorado," Paul says.

"It's not final or anything. I just sent an application in before we left. They start sessions in June, so I would be here for a month, no matter what."

"That's cool. I'd just hate for you to miss a summer in the woods."

"Summer in the woods is good, Don," Brick tells me. "Nothing to do but swim, flirt with rich girls, drink beer, swim, flirt with rich girls, go to parties at rich girls' houses, you know, just good vibes all around."

"Sounds good," I say, nodding my head.

"You a religious type, too, Don?" Eddie asks.

"I am. I mean, I always have been, been wondering about it, you know, but had a good night in the meadow last night. Just the stars, you know, really got me feeling like there was something more, something good."

"Aliens?" Owen asks.

"God," I say.

"Very good," Henry says, glowing out into a grin.

"You believe in God?" I ask Henry.

"Does God believe in me? That is the question." He says this through the same big grin. I laugh at him and Paul laughs. Eddie looks over at Owen.

"A poem!" Eddie says.

Owen pulls out his notebook, flips through the pages, and reads us a few lines. Eddie lays his head back on his sleeping bag and I follow suit. Owen's voice gets inside his craft, and you can hear the long deliberation that went into each line, each phrase. He reads for a few minutes and stops, everything getting quiet.

Everyone gathers themselves into their sleeping bags, and I lie there and watch the fire shadows slide up and down the rocks. The smoke drifts to the top of the cave and glides out through the opening. Before long I hear the gentle tap of rain and see the droplets of water reflect against the fire. Water pools on the ground beneath the opening of the cave. I wonder to myself whether Paul put my sleeping bag back into the tent before he left aspen camp this morning.

"I believe in God," Owen says to us, some of us already asleep.

"And God believes in you," Henry says, after a few seconds of silence.

• • •

PAUL LIFTS THE END OF MY BAG AND I SLIDE OUT ONTO the dirt floor of the cave. The fire has gone out, but morning light shines in through the opening.

"It's six, Don. Time for work."

"I don't have to be there till seven thirty," I tell him.

"We're an hour away. I have to drop you off and come back for these guys. Come on. It's a good hike back to the van. You can't be late again."

"I'm up," I say. "I'm up. Give me a second here." I find my boots and a rock to sit on. I pull my cold boots over my cold feet. I look at my warm sleeping bag and all I want to do is climb back into it. Henry uncovers his head and smiles through his big teeth with his blond straight hair going in all directions. "Clean a toilet for me," he says.

"I'll be thinking of you the entire time," I tell him. He has a good laugh at that.

"Off to fight the war," Eddie says.

Paul rolls his bag and stuffs it into his backpack. He does the same with mine and before I can lace my boots, he is on the ladder, climbing out through the roof. I follow him up into the sky. Everything on the ground is wet. Rain drips from the trees. Patches of snow have settled on the ground. *It's spring,* I think to myself. *It's spring and there is snow on the ground.*

I follow Paul through the forest. There is no trail to speak of, so we head downhill, letting gravity do all the work. I'm getting dirty sliding over fallen logs, covered in moss and dirt. My hands are brown and muddy. I wonder out loud how I am going to look for Laurel and Lucy.

26 RANCH LIFE

BLACK BUTTE RANCH BEGAN IN THE EARLY 1900S when a development company decided that the twenty-nine thousand families in the state of Oregon who made more than $40,000 might very well be interested in a second home in the mountains. Their aim was to settle 5 percent of these wealthy families into vacation homes that would sit empty during the winter months. It was a bold move. Today, one might call it absurd. But back then it worked. Homes were sold and a summer village began. Today homes sell for $700,000 or more. There are more than seven hundred properties on the ranch. Some structures are simply two-bedroom cottages and some are nine-bedroom manors. Paul and I have been here three weeks now and settled in well. We live for free. We don't even have to pay taxes.

I've found that I fit well among a group of militant cleaning women. Even Lucy likes me, these days. I show up for work early and take a shower, folding towels till the ladies show up. Laurel has become like a mother to most of us, all the young girls and me. A couple girls from Washington, DC, studying at American University, have become pretty good friends. Every condo we go into, we check the fridge to see if the vacationing families left any ice cream, and if they did, we take a break, sitting on the beds, and tell stories of how terrible boys are, how they just don't know how to treat women these days. I nod my head in agreement and suck off another spoonful of Häagen-Dazs. "It's tough to be a woman these days, that's for sure," I say. "You can say that again," one of the girls comments. And while the work is hard, the girls do make it fun. But the real life, the life where I am finding faith and friendship and peace, is out in the woods.

On several occasions, someone from the ranch will offer me a place to stay. But I always refuse. Only last night we were up late at a party where we drank coffee, played Scrabble, and listened to John Prine records when the fellow who owned the house offered to let me stay the night in a spare bedroom. It was well below freezing last night, but I turned him down all the same.

I suppose it takes about a week to get used to sleeping outside. But once accustomed to it, a person can't easily go back to having a roof over his head.

If a man's senses are either sharpened or dulled by the way he rubs against time, mine have become increasingly sharp over these last three weeks. I am hungry, so I appreciate food and thank God for it whenever I find ice cream or other perishables in a condo I am cleaning. I appreciate friendship and don't need a television to keep me company. I appreciate birds chirping, as there is no radio to seduce my ears. I appreciate God, because I live in the house He has made, as opposed to a house I purchased by my own means.

I've learned, too, that I don't really know very much about anything. I mean, I used to have all these theories about life. I thought I had everybody figured out, even God, but I don't. I think the woods, being away from all the clingy soot of commercialism, have taught me life is enormous, and I am very tiny in the middle of it. I feel, at times, like a droplet of water in a raging river. I know for a fact that as a grain of sand compares in size to the earth itself, I compare in size to the cosmos. I am that insignificant. And yet the chemicals in my brain that make me feel beauty when I look up at the stars, when I watch the sunset, indicate I must be here for a reason. I think I would sum it up this way: life is not a story about me, but it is being told to me, and I can be glad of that. I think that is the *why* of life and, in fact, the *why* of this ancient faith I am caught up in: to enjoy God. The stars were created to dazzle us, like a love letter; light itself is just a metaphor, something that exists outside of time, made up of what seems like nothing, infinite in its power, something that can be experienced but not understood, like God. Relationships between men and women indicate something of the nature of God—that He is relational, that He feels love and loss. It's all metaphor, and the story is about us; it's about all of us who God made, and God Himself, just enjoying each other. It strikes me how far the commercials are from this reality, how deadly they are, perhaps. Months ago I would have told you life was about doing, about jumping through religious hoops, about impressing other people, and my actions would have told you this is done by buying possessions or keeping a good image or going to church. I don't believe that anymore. I think we are supposed to stand in deserts and marvel at how the sun rises. I think we are supposed to sleep in meadows and watch stars dart across space and time. I think we are supposed to love our friends and introduce people to the story, to the peaceful, calming *why* of life. I think life *is* spirituality.

If I could, if it would be responsible, I would live in these woods forever: I would let my beard grow, hunt my own food, chart the stars, and write poems about mountains. But I know these days are passing. This morning I made a call to Colorado and the camp out there offered me a job. I will be leaving Oregon in a week, leaving behind Paul, Henry, and the boys. Leaving behind the meadow. I start wondering if, when I leave this place, when I leave all these guys who don't share my faith, when I leave these militant women always complaining about men, when I leave the starlight above the mountains, if I will go back to my old faith habits, jumping through hoops, trying to please God or, worse, subscribing to self-help formulas and calling it faith. I hope not. I hope I never lose this perspective. Walking through the meadow on the way over to see

Paul, I promise myself if I ever get frustrated with life again, if I ever get into river-deep debt, I will sell it all and move out into the woods, find some people who aren't like me and learn to love them, and do something even harder, let them love me, receive the love of somebody who doesn't share my faith system, who doesn't agree with me about everything, and I will sleep beneath the stars and whisper *thank you* to the Creator of the universe, as a way of reacquainting myself to an old friend, a friend who says you don't have to be smart or good-looking or religious or anything; you just have to cling to Him, love Him, need Him, listen to His story.

PAUL WORKED THE EARLY SHIFT THIS MORNING SO HE could be free when Danielle arrives. We're expecting her sometime before lunch. She's only staying the day, then driving south to Sacramento so she can live with her grandparents and attend summer school.

I'm sitting on the deck outside Honkers. The pool is unusually full of children. It's a Saturday and all the rich folks are here using their summer homes, so Paul has his hands full. He waves from atop his chair and I wave back. From the deck all the mountains are visible above the meadow, where a creek divides the landscape in two. A cowgirl is driving horses into a pen, where she will saddle them and give people trail rides for a fee.

Out in the distance, I see Molly. She is just on the other side of the pond and heading to the café for work. Nothing ever happened between Molly and me. She got word through Henry that I thought something about her but she didn't respond. Henry says she's hooked on Eddie even though Eddie is hooked on some New York ballerina that we've all heard a dozen stories about. Still, there is something beautiful about the girl that won't have you. Molly is turned sideways now, trying to straighten a bow on the back of her dress. You have to love a girl who wears a dress to work.

Paul comes down from his chair and Henry takes his place. Henry offers a wave from the high post. Paul jumps the railing and sits down next to me.

"Any sign of Danielle?" he asks.

"Yeah. She was with some football player earlier. They were making out."

"Very funny."

"No," I say. "I haven't heard from her. When is she supposed to get here?"

"Anytime now. She should have been here by eleven, but she is probably running late."

Paul waves at Molly, who is peering through the glass doors. She mouths and asks us whether we are hungry and Paul nods his head yes.

"So,"—Paul rests easy in his chair—"where you been all morning?"

"I worked a short shift with the girls."

"Just one of the girls," Paul says, raising his eyebrows.

"Just one of the girls," I confirm.

"You had a good time here?" he asks.

"Can't thank you enough," I say to him. Paul and I had purchased a box of wine a few nights ago and sat here on the deck and drank and talked about what a great trip we had, how God showed up when we needed Him to show up, and how good it was to know each other. It occurred to me then, and I said it to Paul, that there is something God made that is better than starlight. *What is it?* he asked me. *It's you, man,* I said. *Me?* he asked. *You,* I said, *you know, friends, people, it's beautiful, really, that we don't have to be alone. I appreciate you,* I told him. Paul went on about how much he appreciated me, too, and I even shed a few tears about it. He said he thought I was a good guy, that I was funny but also deep, and wasn't judgmental like some people have become these days, impossible to be around without making you feel like crap about yourself. *We're going to be best friends, you realize that,* Paul said. I hadn't realized it, to be honest. Paul is a better guy than I, better looking, more athletic, smarter. I didn't know whether he thought of me that way, you know, but apparently he did. It's great when somebody who is better than you in all those ways that don't matter but always matter lets you be an equal. Molly comes out with some sandwiches and pats me on the back, saying it is good to see me. I tell her it is good to see her, too, and smile. Paul bites into his sandwich and looks out over the meadow.

"You think we've been on a pilgrimage?" Paul asks, talking with his mouth full.

I look out over the meadow, at the mountains in the distance. "I think we've been on a pilgrimage," I say.

27 SUNRISE

I DON'T THINK WE CAN REALLY UNDERSTAND HOW TIME passes. We can't study it like a river or tame it with a clock. Our devices only mark its coming and going. I dropped an anchor three months back but time didn't slow. Some things have to end, you know. You feel like life is always leading up to something, but it isn't. I mean life is just life. It's all happening right now, and we aren't going to be any more complete a month from now than we are now. I only say this because I am trying to appreciate everything tonight. I will be leaving soon, and I want to feel this, really understand that it is happening because God breathed some spark into some mud that became us, and He did it for a reason, and I want to feel that reason, not some false explanation.

Everything plays like an art film tonight. Owen is listening to Bruce Springsteen on the jukebox. He says Bruce is as good as Bob Dylan. Danielle is sitting across from me at the table and she's flipping pages in a book of poems Eddie bought in Sisters a few days ago. Molly is making everybody yogurt. She closed the café several hours ago but let us in to hang out because Paul told her I was leaving and everyone decided to throw a "going away" celebration. We've been sitting around for hours. It's late, and Danielle has a look of frustration because she knows every minute she waits will make for a longer, more weary drive to Sacramento. Henry and Jodie are arm wrestling and laughing because Henry keeps letting her win.

"When are you leaving?" Eddie asks me, trying to remember.

"The end of the week," I tell him.

Molly comes over with yogurt. Paul told Danielle about my crush so Danielle offers a gentle smile when Molly hands me my cup. Molly rounds the table and gives everyone as they'd asked: chocolate or vanilla or both swirled together.

"I think you should stay," Henry says.

"Stay, Don," Jodie offers.

"He's already made up his mind," Paul tells them.

"Where are you going again?" Molly asks.

"Colorado," I tell her.

"Last I checked, we had mountains here," Owen says, dropping another quarter into the jukebox.

"Well, Don," Danielle begins, "I'm jealous. I'd love to be going back to Colorado. I think you're making the right decision."

Paul looks over at Danielle like she's crazy. Danielle just shrugs her shoulders and grins.

Molly swipes the table with a wet cloth. She laughs at us but then tells us she needs to get going. She has to work in the morning and it's already four o'clock. She's not going to get much sleep.

"It's four in the morning!" Danielle exclaims.

"It is," Paul confirms.

"Oh, heavens. I've got to get going."

"Danielle!" Paul gives her a confused look. "You can't drive. You haven't slept."

"I've had about seven cups of coffee. I have to get to Sacramento. I'll be fine."

"Stay here," Paul tells her. "Stay here and camp for the night. You can get started tomorrow."

"I have to go," she says into Paul's lovesick eyes.

"Sleep out under the stars with me," Paul says.

"Not a good idea," Danielle says, smiling and shaking her head.

"You can sleep at my place," Jodie tells her.

"You can sleep out under the stars with me," I say.

"No. I need to go. I'm good about driving at night. I'll pull over and sleep if I need to. Besides, the sun will be up in an hour or so. Don't worry. I'll be fine."

I tell the guys thanks for the send-off, and that I will see them soon.

"We're going to the Sisters rodeo tonight," Owen says. "You in?"

"I'm in," I tell him. Molly shoos us out and gives me a hug good-bye. I tell her I will see her again before I leave and she says I better.

"It's been great having you here, Don," Eddie says. "It's been real good. If you're ever in New York, you have a place to stay, friend."

"Thanks," I tell him. "You going to the rodeo tonight?" I ask.

Eddie puts his heels together and bends his knees up and down like he's riding a horse. "Wouldn't miss it," he says.

Paul and I walk Danielle to her car and they exchange a close hug. Danielle gives me a hug, too, but it's one of those "old friend" types of hugs, not like the "I can't wait to see you again and I am going to cry all the way to Sacramento" hug she gave Paul. Danielle gets into her car and closes the door. Paul doesn't blink or shift his eyes while she fastens her seat belt.

"Pull over as soon as you get tired," he tells her. "Someplace safe. Not a rest area. A police station or something."

"I will," she says with a laugh. Then she tells us she loves us. Paul grins when she says it.

"She said she loves *us*, not just you," I tell him under my breath.

Danielle's brake lights glow on the asphalt as her car sputters around the parking lot, down the road, and out toward the main gate. Paul watches her all the way out, never taking his eye from the little head above the driver's seat.

"You think she'll be all right, Don?" he asks.

"I think so. She's a smart girl."

"You know, Don. I think she's the one."

"What are you talking about? You haven't known her a month."

"One month is a long time," he says.

"One month is one month."

"That's a long time," he says. "Besides, it's been longer than that. It's been a month and a few days."

"The few days make a difference."

"Sure it does," Paul says, shifting his weight around. We walk across the parking lot toward the road without saying a word. Black Butte is visible in the fading moonlight. The sun will be coming up in an hour or so and the earth is beginning to ready itself. Distant birds chirp and clouds are perching themselves on the backs of the mountains.

"You want to catch sunrise?" Paul asks.

"Sounds good. It's not like we're going to get any sleep tonight."

"Where?" he asks.

"How about the meadow? We can see the entire horizon from the meadow."

"Sounds good."

I trail Paul to the center of the meadow. I'm walking with my hands in my pockets, watching closely at his feet, being careful not to step off the dark trail. "See those clouds, Paul? Those will light up," I say.

"It should be good," he says. "Forest fires are blazing south. It should be good." Our voices sink deep into the meadow silence, landing soft against the wet grass and marshes.

THE EARTH AROUND THE MEADOW IS HEAVY IN ANTICI-pation. The mountains are silhouetted like sleeping dragons. There is a deep, blue coolness at the western edge of the landscape, where a few stars linger, their last flickered flames shimmering.

Paul wraps his arms around his chest, unfolds them, blows warm air into his cupped hands, then slides them into his pockets. He's shifting his stiff weight from foot to foot and squinting his eyes, breathing thick mist into the air around him.

"Thanks, Don."

"Thanks for what?"

"Just thanks. I'm going to miss you around here."

"You should come to Colorado, Paul. You'd love it."

"I'll think about it," he says.

And if these mountains had eyes, they would wake to find two strangers in their fences, standing in admiration as a breathing red pours its tinge upon earth's shore. These mountains, which have seen untold sunrises, long to thunder praise but stand reverent, silent so that man's weak praise should be given God's attention.

It is a wonder that those exposed to such beauty forfeit the great questions in the face of this miraculous evidence. I think again about this small period of grace, and thank God for it, that if only for a season, I could feel the *why* of life, see it in the metaphor of light, in the endlessness of the cosmos, in the miracle of friendship. And had these mountains the ability to reason, perhaps they would contemplate the beauty of humanity, and praise God for the miracle that each of us is, pondering the majesty of God and the wonder of man in one bewildering context.

Their brows are rumpled even now, and their arms are stretched toward heaven.

ACKNOWLEDGMENTS

I OWE HEARTFELT THANKS TO PAUL HARRIS FOR GIVING me the sort of friendship a guy could write a book about.

And to Terry Glaspey, who originally acquired this book years ago, as well as the original group of readers who read it. I hope you don't mind the changes. Thanks to Kathryn Helmers, who read over the rewrite and gave me the encouragement to wrap it up and obey the gut. Thanks to everybody at Thomas Nelson who works so very hard to get these books out there. I can't think any more fondly of a group of people.

This true story would not have been written without the real-life characters who make my life more interesting than television. Kind thanks to Randy and Shirley Bjur, Danielle, Elida, and Nate, Wes and Maja, Grampa and Grandma Bjur, and the whole Ridgefield/Sacramento clan. Also, Ben Bonham, Betty and Bob from the truck stop, and Mrs. Tucker and Mike from California.

While writing, I listened to Derek Webb, The Daylights, Jars, Ryan Adams, James Taylor, U2, Lyle Lovett, Dwight Yoakam, John Gorka, Over the Rhine, David Barnes, Rosie Thomas, Steve Earle, and Mindy Smith.

A number of people read the early stages of the manuscript and gave criticism that helped the book like medicine. Kim Moore proofread the project and made me look smart by correcting my rotten grammar and spelling. John and Terri MacMurray read and praised every chapter, and I would not have sent it to a publisher save for their kindness and encouragement. Also Mary Miller, Evelyn Hall, Nathan and Sara Pylate,

ACKNOWLEDGMENTS

Shelly Burke, Andy Whipps, Amy Martin, Missy Tygert, Adam Rehman, Jamie Bushek, Sara Mathews, Matt Jacobson, Don Jacobson, Jeff Baldwin, Ross Tunnell, Michaela Frick, Kim Kemper, Dave Beitler, Lonnie Hull-Dupont, Gregg Harris, Matt and Julie Canlis, Randy and Jan Demlow, Angie Rabatin, Scott Armstrong, and David Gentiles. Special thanks to Curt Heidschmidt and Rick Crosser for their friendship and encouragement. Much gratitude to Jeff Olson for countless conversations and for giving me the opportunity to read portions of the manuscript to Mosaic. Thanks to Jim Small for all he does to get the word out. I owe a debt of gratitude to Fred "One Page a Day" Willis for giving me Robert Pirsig's book with a little note on the inside cover. And thank you to Anne, for your incredible kindness, and for all those beautiful words. Thank you for giving so many of us permission to feel God, and to be ourselves. You are a dear saint.

Thanks to Amy Bowers, Tony Kriz, Penny Gruener, Tara Brown, Jim Chaffee, Leslie McKellar, Laura Long, Kurt and Donna Nelson, Heirborne, Rick McKinley, Drew Goodmanson, Eric Brown, Jeff Marsh, Christina Reagan, Jordan Green, Grant and Blake Gaskill, Wes and Stacy Gorton, Mike Tucker, Eric and Josiah, Jon Foreman, Jamie Tworkowski, Kaj and Lib, the boys in Jars, Laura Gibson, Chris Seay, the folks at Imago and Ecclesia, and all the other good friends who are as important to this process as ink itself.

And as always, thanks for reading this book. I love doing this and couldn't do it without you picking up a copy here and there. I wanted to take a break from the deep theological stuff and just take you on an old journey I took once and introduce you to some wonderful people. I am so glad you were able to come. Much love and gratitude to you, and all God's blessings.

ABOUT THE AUTHOR

Donald Miller is the author of *Blue Like Jazz, Searching for God Knows What, Through Painted Deserts,* and *To Own a Dragon* in addition to articles written for numerous magazines. He is a frequent speaker on issues concerning the relevancy of Christ to the human experience.

www.donaldmillerwords.com

EXCERPT FROM DONALD MILLER'S NEW BOOK,
LET STORY GUIDE YOU,
COMING WINTER 2008

Great Stories have Memorable Scenes

MY FRIEND JOY TOLD ME WHEN SHE WAS A KID SHE went to a summer camp based on the promise that it would be the most memorable week of her life. She's older now but told me the camp lived up to its promise. When I asked why the camp was so great, she didn't tell me that it was *fun* or she met *great people*, although those things were true. Instead, she told me about *scenes*. She described an obstacle course in which she and her friends had to crawl through knee-deep mud and that she went parasailing on a lake at sunset. She described the roof of her cabin upon which she and her friends climbed to talk about boys until the sun came up. It had been nearly fifteen years since that camp, but when she talked about it she got so excited she had to stand up.

When Steve, Ben, and I were sitting around writing the screenplay, I suggested our characters go to a coffee shop to hash out, in conversation, a bit of the conflict. But Ben and Steve told me that sort of scene isn't memorable and it was time for the plot of the story to unfold in a more memorable way. I didn't know exactly what they meant, but I started noticing that, in movies, scenes often take place in strange places. There was the scene in *Good Will Hunting* where Will and his friend have a conversation at a batting cage, except Will is in the middle of the cage throwing pitches. And there's the scene in *Garden State* where they are standing in the rain on the edge of a cliff right next to a guy's house that was made from a boat. And even in *Rocky* they take his training into a meat locker so he can punch giant slabs of beef.

This idea is true in life, too. I don't know how many times I've had coffee with somebody but right now I can't remember what a single conversation was about. I know we were connecting and all, and really having coffee with somebody isn't only about having a conversation, but you would think I'd remember something. I don't remember the scenes in my life that took place in a coffee shop, but I do remember the ones that demanded a bit more effort. I remember last year when my friend Laura and I took kayaks up to Lost Lake and tied them together so we could have a picnic.

I was thinking about what Steve and Ben said about memorable scenes when some friends and I were coming back from a hike at Silver Falls. We were driving through the foothills of the Cascades and, in the evening light, the fields were sloping out like brush strokes. I wasn't noticing the hills around us at first, because I was tired and ready to get home, but then I started seeing how red the fields were, and then Joy said something about it and Kacie agreed that the light was getting beautiful. One of my favorite scenes in a movie is from Wes Anderson's *Bottle Rocket* in which Dignan is standing in a field shooting a Roman candle at the ground and Anthony walks in slowly from the distance. I won't get into what the scene was about, but I do know the peculiar image of an open field and a guy shooting a Roman candle at the ground has stayed in my mind like a painting. When we were driving through the fields that night I was thinking about that scene, too, and then Joy mentioned she used to love running through open fields when she was a little girl. Before I started thinking of life as a story I wouldn't have thought much of a comment like that, but the new me figured it out in a hurry. Good stories contain memorable scenes, Steve and Ben would say.

When we came to the next field I pulled the truck over and the girls giggled like they were in high school or something. We all got out and Joy ran across the street and into the field until she became a spec on the horizon. The rest of us walked partway up a hill, and Joy came back and joined us in time to see the sun drop beneath the coastal range. And from behind us the darker blue came out of the mountains like music.

When we were walking back I noticed the hill behind us was silhouetting, and I wondered how fun it would be to drive the truck to the top. When we got back in the truck I drove across the road and through the ditch and gunned it to the top of the hill. It felt like we were on a roller coaster and it felt dangerous and wrong and so good. At the top we got out and stood on the hill and watched the last bit of light dry off toward the Pacific.

THE THING ABOUT MAKING MEMORABLE SCENES IS THEY aren't easy. When Steve and Ben and I were figuring out what scenes to include we had to kick around five or ten ideas before we came up with something. It would be easier to just stand around talking but, as is true in life, nobody would remember the story we were trying to tell.

My friend Randy recently created a great memory with his daughter. When his daughter entered high school she started to get more interested in girl things and the two of them didn't talk as much as they used to. When she got asked to the prom she was very excited and her dad simply responded by saying, "Congratulations." She quickly slid past him and jumped up and down in front of her mom. He didn't mean to be dismissive but he didn't know what he was supposed to say. About a week later, he was watching Sports Center when his wife and daughter came home with a dress. They didn't say anything to him, knowing he wouldn't be interested, and went back to his daughter's bedroom so she could put it on. When she came into the living room to show her dad, he turned down the volume and told her she looked nice, that it was a nice color, but when she curtsied and thanked him and walked away he knew he should have said more. He wanted to tell her that she was beautiful and that she was his princess and all the stuff fathers find so hard to say to their daughters. He turned the television back on and tried to pay attention to the scores but all of this kept bugging him. Then he came up with an idea. He decided to create a memorable scene. He turned off the television and went into his closet and put on his suit. Without letting his wife or daughter see him, he found the family camera and went and knocked on her door. When his daughter opened the door she was still in the dress and her mother was sitting on the bed with stick-pins in her mouth. My friend said his wife almost swallowed the pins. "Honey," my friend said to his wife, "would you mind taking a picture of us?"

"Daddy, you're wearing a suit," his daughter said, confused.

"I wanted to look good in the picture, too," he told her.

The three of them ended up dancing in the living room until one in the morning, my friend and his wife telling stories about their own prom dates and how they wished they would have known each other in high school.

I recently encountered an exceptional movie called *Darius Goes West*. It's a documentary that, while not in wide release yet, has won a handful of awards at various festivals. The *story*, if you will, is about a group of friends, one of which has Muscular Dystrophy and is slowly losing mobility. Darius is fifteen years old and has already lost a brother to M.S. After realizing that Darius had never left his hometown of Athens, Georgia, his friends raised money to take him to California where they hoped MTV would *pimp* Darius's wheelchair. What unfolds in the film is a series of memorable scenes. The guys lay out plywood on a beach in Florida and roll Darius to the ocean. They stay at a five-star hotel in New Orleans and then take their friend on a swamp-boat ride. The group celebrates the fifteenth anniversary of the Americans with Disabilities Act in an enormous cavern in New Mexico. They plant Darius in the middle of a raft and take him down the Colorado River. They stay up all night lying in the desert, counting shooting stars, and the next morning they wheel Darius to the edge of the Grand Canyon where he sits speechless until his eyes well up with tears. When they finally get to California, they take Darius on a hot-air balloon ride above Napa Valley and he sits low in the basket stretching his neck to see more of the view, wearing a smile I have only seen brighter on newborn babies discovering color and feeling. The most memorable scene of the film, I think, has the guys rolling Darius's wheelchair into the ocean, removing him from his chair, and holding him as the waves crash over his body. Darius feels his feet hit the ocean floor and realizes, for the first time in years, he is standing. He laughs uncontrollably as his friends hold him from under his arms so that his feet dangle and scrape against the sand.

That movie, *Darius Goes West*, is more than a memorable film—it is the construction of a memorable life.

I don't think memorable scenes help a story make sense. Other principles accomplish that. What memorable scenes do is punctuate the existing rise and fall of a narrative. The ambition of getting Darius a better wheelchair had the makings of a terrific story, but it's the way in which they got there that I will never forget. And neither will he.

ANOTHER INTERESTING DYNAMIC OF STORY IS THAT there can be too many memorable scenes. During the Robert McKee seminar in Los Angeles, I learned an excess of memorable scenes causes a movie to drag. He was talking about emotional pitch more than visual content but he said that, if the tension in a scene could be diagrammed from one to five, there shouldn't be too many scenes that reach five. There should be three or four, I think he said. I only say this because I have a friend who always wants to do crazy things like jump off mountains or ride bikes off a pier. After a while his ideas become too intense, like listening to a symphony that never earns its swells by lessening.

If Randy, my friend whose daughter was going to the prom, pulled out his suit once a week, it probably wouldn't mean as much.

That said, the problem with my life isn't that it contains too many memorable scenes. I think I could use more.